SIPRI Yearbook 1997
Armaments, Disarmament and International Security

SIPRI Yearbook 1997

Armaments, Disarmament and International Security

sipri

Stockholm International Peace Research Institute

OXFORD UNIVERSITY PRESS
1997

Oxford University Press, Great Clarendon Street, Oxford OX2 6DP
Oxford New York
Athens Auckland Bangkok Bagotá Bombay
Buenos Aires Calcutta Cape Town Dar es Salaam
Delhi Florence Hong Kong Istanbul Karachi
Kuala Lumpur Madras Madrid Melbourne
Mexico City Nairobi Paris Singapore
Taipei Tokyo Toronto Warsaw
and associated companies in
Berlin Ibadan

Oxford is a trade mark of Oxford University Press

Published in the United States
by Oxford University Press Inc., New York

© SIPRI 1997

Yearbooks before 1987 published under title
'World Armaments and Disarmament:
SIPRI Yearbook [year of publication]'

British Library Cataloguing in Publication Data
Data available
ISSN 0953–0282
ISBN 0–19–829312–7

Library of Congress Cataloging in Publication Data
Data available
ISSN 0953–0282
ISBN 0–19–829312–7

Typeset and originated by Stockholm International Peace Research Institute
Printed and bound in Great Britain by
Biddles Ltd., Guildford and King's Lynn

Contents

Armed Forces in Europe on the Scope and Parameters of the Process Commissioned
in Paragraph 19 of the Final Document of the First CFE Treaty Review Conference

Part II. Military spending and armaments, 1996

8. Arms production   239
Elisabeth Sköns and Julian Cooper

Appendix 8A. The 100 largest arms-producing companies, 1995   261
Elisabeth Sköns, Renaud Bellais and the SIPRI Arms Industry Network

9. The trade in major conventional weapons   267
Ian Anthony, Pieter D. Wezeman and Siemon T. Wezeman

Part III. Non-proliferation, arms control and disarmament, 1996

Annexes

Preface

The Stockholm International Peace Research Institute presents in this volume the 28th edition of the *SIPRI Yearbook*. In his essay 'How SIPRI began', written for SIPRI's 30th anniversary commemorative volume, Frank Blackaby, the editor of the first editions of the *Yearbook*, noted: 'One of the long-term objectives of the Yearbook was to build up an accurate picture of the world war industry'. Today our goals and tasks are much broader. For many years SIPRI has published in the *Yearbook* the results of research conducted on the arms trade, military expenditure, chemical and biological warfare, arms control and disarmament, producing data, facts and analysis. The findings have been based on 'hard-boiled' research, to use the words of Gunnar Myrdal, who, together with Alva Myrdal, is recognized as the founder of SIPRI. Since the late 1960s, when SIPRI's tasks were laid down in its statutes, the situation in the world, not least in the fields of armaments and security, have undergone a substantial change. This has found its expression in both the structure and content of the *Yearbook*, which now also reports on major armed conflicts and global and regional security.

In a lecture delivered at SIPRI's 30th Anniversary Conference in October 1996, Sir Brian Urquhart, former UN Under Secretary-General, characterized the new situation as follows: 'The sudden and unexpected end of the cold war gave rise to series of fleeting and irrational enthusiasms, but nothing you could really call a security agenda'. In the view of Sir Brian, who served for 10 years as a member and vice-chairman of the SIPRI Governing Board, 'SIPRI, with its respected position in the world, can do a lot to feed and stimulate a responsible debate on the requisite agenda of future international and human security, and the measures and the institutions needed to provide it'.

This *Yearbook* goes a long way towards meeting these expectations. All the chapters and appendices but one reflect the results of research conducted at the Institute. I would like to express our gratitude to Professor Peter Wallensteen and his collaborators at the Department of Peace and Conflict Research, Uppsala University, for their contribution on major armed conflicts. My appreciation also goes to Julian Cooper for his contribution to the arms production chapter and to William M. Arkin and Robert S. Norris for the tables of nuclear forces.

The editorial work was competently led by Connie Wall. Her experience, professionalism and commitment to SIPRI, paralleled by the proficiency and devotion of Billie Bielckus and Jetta Gilligan Borg, editors, and Rebecka Charan, editorial assistant, contributed to making this *Yearbook* not a collection of separate chapters but a comprehensive volume of easily accessible material. I am also indebted to the coordinators—Ian Anthony, Eric Arnett, Trevor Findlay and Zdzislaw Lachowski—for their expert attention to other parts of this volume in addition to their own contributions. Finally, I would like to express my appreciation of the work of Gerd Hagmeyer-Gaverus, information technology manager; Billie Bielckus, cartographer; Peter Rea, indexer; and all other members of the SIPRI staff who provided the necessary support for the production of this *Yearbook*.

Dr Adam Daniel Rotfeld
Director
April 1997

Acronyms

Additional acronyms of UN observer, peacekeeping and electoral operations and weapon systems are given in appendix 2A and appendix 9B, respectively. Acronyms not defined in this list are defined in the chapters of this volume.

ABACC	Brazilian–Argentine Agency for Accounting and Control of Nuclear Materials	BDA	Bilateral Destruction Agreement
ABM	Anti-ballistic missile	BIC	Bilateral Implementation Commission
ACDA	Arms Control and Disarmament Agency	BMD	Ballistic missile defence
ACM	Advanced cruise missile	BMDO	Ballistic Missile Defense Organization
ACRS	Arms control and regional security	BSEC	Black Sea Economic Cooperation
ACV	Armoured combat vehicle	BTWC	Biological and Toxin Weapons Convention
AIFV	Armoured infantry fighting vehicle	BW	Biological weapon/ warfare
ALCM	Air-launched cruise missile	CBM	Confidence-building measure
APC	Armoured personnel carrier	CBO	Congressional Budget Office
ARF	ASEAN Regional Forum	CBSS	Council of Baltic Sea States
ARV	Armoured recovery vehicle	CBW	Chemical and biological weapon/ warfare
ASEAN	Association of South-East Asian Nations	CCW	Certain Conventional Weapons (Convention)
ASLCM	Advanced sea-launched cruise missile	CD	Conference on Disarmament
ASM	Air-to-surface missile	CEE	Central and Eastern Europe
ASW	Anti-submarine warfare		
ATBM	Anti-tactical ballistic missile	CEI	Central European Initiative
ATC	Armoured troop carrier	CFE	Conventional Armed Forces in Europe (Treaty)
ATTU	Atlantic-to-the-Urals (zone)		
AWACS	Airborne warning and control system	CFSP	Common Foreign and Security Policy
BCC	Bilateral Consultative Commission	CGE	Central government expenditure

C^{3}I	Command, control, communications and intelligence	DMZ	Demilitarized Zone
		DOD	Department of Defense
C^{4}I	Command, control, communications, computer and intelligence	DOE	Department of Energy
		DOP	Declaration of Principles
		DPKO	Department of Peacekeeping Operations
CIA	Central Intelligence Agency	DPSS	Designated permanent storage site
CIO	Chairman-in-Office		
CIS	Commonwealth of Independent States	EAPC	Euro-Atlantic Partnership Council
CJTF	Combined Joint Task Forces	ECA	Economic Commission for Africa
CMEA	Council for Mutual Economic Assistance	ECOMOG	ECOWAS Monitoring Group
COCOM	Coordinating Committee (on Multilateral Export Controls)	ECOWAS	Economic Community of West African States
		ECU	European Currency Unit
CPC	Conflict Prevention Centre	EMU	Economic and Monetary Union
CPI	Consumer price index	Enmod	Environmental modification
CSBM	Confidence- and security-building measure	EPU	European Political Union
CSCE	Conference on Security and Co-operation in Europe	ESDI	European Security and Defence Identity
		EU	European Union
CSO	Committee of Senior Officials	EUCLID	European Cooperative Long-term Initiative on Defence
CTB	Comprehensive test ban		
CTBT	Comprehensive Nuclear Test-Ban Treaty	Euratom	European Atomic Energy Community
CTBTO	Comprehensive Test-Ban Treaty Organization	EUROFOR	European Force
		FIG	Financial–industrial group
CTR	Cooperative Threat Reduction		
CW	Chemical weapon/ warfare	FMCT	Fissile Material Cut-Off Treaty
		FOC	Full operational capability
CWC	Chemical Weapons Convention		
DHA	Department of Humanitarian Affairs	FSC	Forum for Security Co-operation
		FY	Fiscal year

FYROM	Former Yugoslav Republic of Macedonia	IMS	International Monitoring System
G7	Group of Seven	INF	Intermediate-range nuclear forces
G-21	Group of 21		
GATT	General Agreement on Tariffs and Trade	IPP	Individual Partnership Programme
GDP	Gross domestic product	IPTF	International Police Task Force
GLCM	Ground-launched cruise missile	IRBM	Intermediate-range ballistic missile
GNP	Gross national product	JACO	Joint Armaments Cooperation Organization
HCNM	High Commissioner on National Minorities		
HDE	Hydrodynamic experiment	JCC	Joint Consultative Commission
HEU	Highly enriched uranium	JCG	Joint Consultative Group
HLTF	High Level Task Force	JCIC	Joint Compliance and Inspection Commission
HNE	Hydronuclear experiment	JDA	Japan Defense Agency
IAEA	International Atomic Energy Agency	KEDO	Korean Peninsula Energy Development Organization
IBRD	International Bank for Reconstruction and Development	LDC	Less developed country
		LDDI	Less developed defence industry
ICBM	Intercontinental ballistic missile	LEU	Low-enriched uranium
ICFY	International Conference on Former Yugoslavia	LWR	Light-water reactor
ICJ	International Court of Justice	MBT	Main battle tank
		MD	Military District
ICRC	International Committee of the Red Cross	MEADS	Medium Extended Air Defense System
IDB	Inter-American Development Bank	Minatom	Ministry for Atomic Energy
IEPG	Independent European Programme Group	MIRV	Multiple independently targetable re-entry vehicle
IFOR	Implementation Force		
IFV	Infantry fighting vehicle	MOU	Memorandum of Understanding
IGC	Intergovernmental Conference	MTCR	Missile Technology Control Regime
IMF	International Monetary Fund	MTM	Multinational technical means (of verification)

NAC	North Atlantic Council	OPANAL	Agency for the Prohibition of Nuclear Weapons in Latin America
NACC	North Atlantic Cooperation Council		
NAM	Non-Aligned Movement	OPCW	Organisation for the Prohibition of Chemical Weapons
NATO	North Atlantic Treaty Organization		
NBC	Nuclear, biological and chemical (weapons)	OSCC	Open Skies Consultative Commission
NGO	Non-governmental organization	OSCE	Organization for Security and Co-operation in Europe
NNWS	Non-nuclear weapon state	PA	Palestinian Authority
NPT	Non-Proliferation Treaty	PFP	Partnership for Peace
NRRC	Nuclear Risk Reduction Centre	PLO	Palestine Liberation Organization
NSG	Nuclear Suppliers Group	PNC	Palestinian National Council
NTM	National technical means (of verification)	PNE(T)	Peaceful Nuclear Explosions (Treaty)
NWFZ	Nuclear weapon-free zone	PrepCom	Preparatory Commission
NWS	Nuclear weapon state	PTB(T)	Partial Test Ban (Treaty)
OAS	Organization of American States	PTS	Provisional Technical Secretariat
OAU	Organization of African Unity	R&D	Research and development
OBDA	Official budget defence allocation	RDT&E	Research, development, testing and evaluation
ODA	Official development assistance	REDWG	Regional Economic Development Working Group
ODIHR	Office for Democratic Institutions and Human Rights	RPV	Remotely piloted vehicle
		RV	Re-entry vehicle
OECD	Organisation for Economic Co-operation and Development	RWG	Refugee Working Group
		SACEUR	Supreme Allied Commander, Europe
OIC	Organization of the Islamic Conference	SADC	Southern Africa Development Community
O&M	Operation and maintenance		
		SAM	Surface-to-air missile
OMB	Office of Management and Budget	SAM	Sanctions Assistance Mission

SCC	Standing Consultative Commission		UNCLOS	United Nations Convention on the Law of the Sea
SFOR	Stabilization Force		UNHCR	UN High Commissioner for Refugees
SLBM	Submarine-launched ballistic missile			
SLCM	Sea-launched cruise missile		UNPA	UN Protected Area
SMTS	Space and Missile Tracking System		UNPREDEP	UN Preventive Deployment Force
SNDV	Strategic nuclear delivery vehicle		UNPROFOR	United Nations Protection Force
SNF	Short-range nuclear forces		UNSCOM	United Nations Special Commission on Iraq
SRAM	Short-range attack missile		VEREX	Verification experiment
SRBM	Short-range ballistic missile		WEAG	Western European Armaments Group
SSBN	Nuclear-powered, ballistic-missile submarine		WEU	Western European Union
SSD	Safe and Secure Dismantlement (Talks)		WMD	Weapon of mass destruction
SSGN	Nuclear-powered, guided-missile submarine		WTO	Warsaw Treaty Organization (Warsaw Pact)
SSN	Nuclear-powered attack submarine			
START	Strategic Arms Reduction Talks/Treaty			
ST&I	Safeguards, Transparency and Irreversibility			
SVC	Special Verification Commission			
THAAD	Theater High-Altitude Area Defense			
TLE	Treaty-limited equipment			
TMD	Theatre missile defence			
TNF	Theatre nuclear forces			
TTB(T)	Threshold Test Ban (Treaty)			

Glossary

RAGNHILD FERM and CONNIE WALL

The main terms discussed in this *Yearbook* are defined in the glossary. For acronyms that appear in the definitions, see page xiv. For the members of global, regional and subregional organizations, see page xxviii. For summaries of and parties to the arms control and disarmament agreements mentioned in the glossary, see annexe A.

Agency for the Prohibition of Nuclear Weapons in Latin America and the Caribbean (OPANAL)	Intergovernmental agency established by the Treaty of Tlatelolco to resolve, together with the IAEA, questions of compliance with the treaty.
Anti-ballistic missile (ABM) system	*See* Ballistic missile defence.
Anti-tactical ballistic missile (ATBM) system	*See* Theatre missile defence.
Arab League	The principal objective of the League of Arab States, or Arab League, established in 1945 and with headquarters in Cairo, is to form closer union among Arab states and foster political and economic cooperation. An agreement for collective defence and economic cooperation was signed in 1950. *See* list of members.
Association of South-East Asian Nations (ASEAN)	Established in the 1967 Bangkok Declaration to promote economic, social and cultural development as well as regional peace and stability in South-East Asia. The ASEAN Regional Forum (ARF) was established in 1993 to address security issues. *See* list of ASEAN and ARF members.
Atlantic-to-the-Urals (ATTU) zone	Zone of the 1990 CFE Treaty and the 1992 CFE-1A Agreement, stretching from the Atlantic Ocean to the Ural Mountains, which comprises the entire land territory of the European NATO states, the Central and East European states and the CIS states (i.e., it does not include the Baltic states).
Australia Group	Group of states, formed in 1985, which meets informally each year to monitor the proliferation of chemical and biological products and to discuss chemicals which should be subject to various national regulatory measures. *See* list of members.
Ballistic missile	Missile which follows a ballistic trajectory (part of which may be outside the earth's atmosphere) when thrust is terminated.
Ballistic missile defence (BMD)	Weapon system designed to defend against a ballistic missile attack by intercepting and destroying ballistic missiles or their warheads in flight.
Baltic Council	Established in 1990 for the promotion of democracy and development of cooperation between the three Baltic states. It comprises a Council of Ministers, Secretariat and Baltic Assembly (its parliamentary organ). *See* list of members.

Bilateral Implementation Commission (BIC)	Forum established by the START II Treaty to resolve questions of compliance with the treaty.
Biological weapon (BW)	Weapon containing living organisms, whatever their nature, or infective material derived from them, which are intended for use to cause disease or death in man, animals or plants, and which for their effect depend on their ability to multiply in the person, animal or plant attacked, as well as the means of their delivery.
Canberra Commission	The Canberra Commission on the Elimination of Nuclear Weapons was set up in 1995 to develop a programme to achieve a world totally free of nuclear weapons. In 1996 it presented its report to the 51st session of the UN General Assembly and to the Conference on Disarmament.
Central European Initiative (CEI)	Regional forum for cooperation and political contacts, initiated in 1989 and established as the CEI in 1992. *See* list of members.
Chemical weapon (CW)	Chemical substances—whether gaseous, liquid or solid—which might be employed as weapons because of their direct toxic effects on man, animals or plants, as well as the means of their delivery.
Combined Joint Task Forces (CJTF)	Concept declared at the June 1996 Berlin meeting of NATO foreign ministers to facilitate NATO contingency operations, including the use of separable but not separate military capabilities in operations led by the WEU, with the participation of states outside the NATO Alliance in such operations as IFOR/SFOR.
Common Foreign and Security Policy (CFSP)	Institutional framework, established by the Maastricht Treaty, for consultation and development of common positions and joint action related to European security questions. It constitutes the second of the three EU 'pillars' which are under consideration for review at the 1996–97 Intergovernmental Conference.
Commonwealth of Independent States (CIS)	Organization of 12 former Soviet republics, established in 1991 to preserve and maintain under united command a common military–strategic space. *See* list of members.
Conference on Disarmament (CD)	Multilateral arms control negotiating body, based in Geneva, composed of states representing all the regions of the world and including the permanent members of the UN Security Council. The CD reports to the UN General Assembly. *See* list of members.
Conference on Security and Co-operation in Europe (CSCE)	*See* Organization for Security and Co-operation in Europe.
Confidence- and security-building measure (CSBM)	Measure to promote confidence and security, undertaken by a state, which is militarily significant, politically binding and verifiable. The CSBMs of the CSCE are embodied in the 1986 Stockholm Document and the Vienna Documents.

Confidence-building measure (CBM)	Measure taken by a state to contribute to reducing the dangers of armed conflict and of misunderstanding or miscalculation of military activities which could give rise to apprehension. The Document on CBMs is included in the 1975 CSCE Helsinki Final Act.
Conventional weapon	Weapon not having mass destruction effects.
Conversion	Term used to denote the shift in resources from military to civilian use, usually the conversion of industry from military to civilian production.
Cooperative Threat Reduction (CTR)	Programme originally established under the auspices of the US Defense Department to facilitate bilateral cooperation between the USA and the former Soviet republics with nuclear weapons on their territories (Belarus, Kazakhstan, Russia and Ukraine), primarily for US assistance in the safe and environmentally responsible storage, transportation, dismantlement and destruction of former Soviet nuclear weapons. The programme also provides assistance for the destruction of chemical weapons in Russia. Often referred to as the Nunn–Lugar programme after the two senators who sponsored the authorizing US legislation in 1991.
Council of Europe	Established in 1949, with its seat in Strasbourg, the Council is open to all European states which accept the principle of the rule of law and guarantee their citizens human rights and fundamental freedoms. Its main aims are defined in the European Convention on Human Rights (1950) and the Convention for the Protection of Human Rights and Fundamental Freedoms (1953). Among its organs is the European Court of Human Rights. *See* list of members.
Council of Baltic Sea States (CBSS)	Organization comprising the states bordering on the Baltic Sea plus Iceland and Norway, established in 1992 to promote common strategies for political and economic cooperation and development. *See* list of members.
Counter-proliferation	Measures or policies to prevent the proliferation or enforce the non-proliferation of weapons of mass destruction.
Cruise missile	Guided weapon-delivery vehicle which sustains flight at subsonic or supersonic speeds through aerodynamic lift, generally flying at very low altitudes to avoid radar detection, sometimes following the contours of the terrain. It can be air-, ground- or sea-launched (ALCM, GLCM and SLCM, respectively) and carry a conventional, nuclear, chemical or biological warhead.
Dual-use technology/ weapon	Dual-use technology is suitable for both civilian and military applications. A dual-use weapon is capable of carrying nuclear or conventional explosives.

Euro-Atlantic Partnership Council (EAPC)	New council to be established in 1997 which will merge the activities of NACC and the PFP, agreed in December 1996 by the NATO foreign ministers (initially called the Atlantic Partnership Council). The EAPC will be a single forum for practical cooperation between NATO and the PFP partners, with an expanded political dimension. NACC will cease to exist when the EAPC has been launched.
European Atomic Energy Community (Euratom)	Based on a treaty signed in Rome in 1957 at the same time as the treaty establishing the EEC, Euratom aims to integrate the programmes of the EU member states for the peaceful uses of atomic energy. Also known as the EAEC.
European Security and Defence Identity (ESDI)	Concept aimed at strengthening the European pillar of NATO while reinforcing the transatlantic link by creating militarily coherent and effective forces capable of conducting operations under the control of the WEU.
European Union (EU)	Organization of 15 West European states established by the Maastricht Treaty, which entered into force in 1993. The highest decision-making body is the European Council. Other EU institutions are the Council of Ministers, the European Commission, the European Parliament and the European Court of Justice. An EU Common Foreign and Security Policy (CFSP) was established by the Maastricht Treaty. An Intergovernmental Conference (IGC) opened in Turin, Italy, in March 1996 to review the treaty. The IGC will present proposals for revision of the treaty at the June 1997 session of the European Council, in Amsterdam. *See* list of members.
Fissile material	Material composed of atoms which fission when irradiated by either fast or slow (thermal) neutrons. Uranium-235 and plutonium-239 are the most common fissile materials.
Forum for Security Co-operation (FSC)	*See* Organization for Security and Co-operation in Europe.
Group of Seven (G7)	Group of seven leading industrialized nations which have met informally, at the level of heads of state or government, since the late 1970s. *See* list of members.
Group of 21 (G-21)	Originally 21, now 30, non-aligned CD member states which act together on proposals of common interest. *See* list of members under Conference on Disarmament.
Hydrodynamic experiment (HDE)	Explosion in which fissile material is compressed but does not reach critical mass and no significant nuclear yield is released. A subcritical experiment for measuring the non-nuclear properties of fissile material.
Hydronuclear experiment (HNE)	Explosion in which fissile material is compressed until it briefly reaches critical mass and a small nuclear yield is released.
Intercontinental ballistic missile (ICBM)	Ground-launched ballistic missile with a range greater than 5500 km.

Intergovernmental Conference (IGC)	*See* European Union.
Intermediate-range nuclear forces (INF)	Theatre nuclear forces with a range of from 1000 km up to and including 5500 km.
International Atomic Energy Agency (IAEA)	Independent, intergovernmental organization within the UN system, with headquarters in Vienna. The IAEA is endowed by its Statute, which entered into force in 1957, to promote the peaceful uses of atomic energy and ensure that nuclear activities are not used to further any military purpose. It is involved in verification of the NPT and the nuclear weapon-free zone treaties and in the activities of the UN Special Commission on Iraq (UNSCOM). *See* list of members.
Joint Consultative Group (JCG)	Established by the CFE Treaty to promote the objectives and implementation of the treaty by reconciling ambiguities of interpretation and implementation.
Joint Compliance and Inspection Commission (JCIC)	Established by the START I Treaty to resolve questions of compliance, clarify ambiguities and discuss ways to improve implementation of the treaty. It convenes at the request of at least one of the parties.
Kiloton (kt)	Measure of the explosive yield of a nuclear device equivalent to 1000 tonnes of trinitrotoluene (TNT) high explosive. (The bomb detonated at Hiroshima in World War II had a yield of about 12–15 kilotons.)
London Guidelines for Nuclear Transfers	*See* Nuclear Suppliers Group.
Maastricht Treaty	The Treaty on European Union.
Megaton (Mt)	Measure of the explosive yield of a nuclear device equivalent to 1 million tonnes of trinitrotoluene (TNT) high explosive.
Minsk Group	Group of states acting together in the OSCE for political settlement of the conflict in the Armenian enclave of Nagorno-Karabakh in Azerbaijan (also known as the Minsk Process or Minsk Conference). *See* list of members under Organization for Security and Co-operation in Europe.
Missile Technology Control Regime (MTCR)	Informal military-related export control regime, established in 1987, which produced the Guidelines for Sensitive Missile-Relevant Transfers. Its goal is to limit the spread of weapons of mass destruction by controlling their delivery systems. The regime consists of the Guidelines, revised in 1992, and an Equipment and Technology Annex, last revised in 1995. *See* list of members.
Multiple independently targetable re-entry vehicles (MIRV)	Re-entry vehicles (RVs), carried by a single ballistic missile, which can be directed to separate targets along separate trajectories. A missile can carry two or more RVs.
National technical means of verification (NTM)	Technical intelligence means, under the national control of a state, which are used to monitor compliance with an arms control treaty to which the state is a party.

Non-Aligned Movement (NAM) — Group of countries established at Belgrade in 1961, sometimes referred to as the Movement of Non-Aligned Countries. NAM is a forum for consultations and coordination of positions on political and economic issues. The Coordinating Bureau of the Non-Aligned Countries (also called the Conference of Non-Aligned Countries) is the forum in which NAM coordinates its actions within the United Nations. *See* list of members.

Non-strategic nuclear forces — *See* Theatre nuclear forces.

Nordic Council — Political advisory organ for cooperation between the parliaments of the Nordic states, founded in 1952. The Plenary Assembly is the highest political organ. The Nordic Council of Ministers, established in 1971, is an organ for cooperation between the governments of the Nordic countries and between these governments and the Nordic Council. *See* list of members.

North Atlantic Council (NAC) — *See* North Atlantic Treaty Organization.

North Atlantic Cooperation Council (NACC) — Created in 1991 as a NATO institution for consultation and cooperation on political and security issues between NATO and the former WTO states and former Soviet republics. *See* list of members.

North Atlantic Treaty Organization (NATO) — Political and military defence alliance of 16 nations established in 1949 by the North Atlantic Treaty, with headquarters in Brussels. The principal organs are the North Atlantic Council, a permanent body which meets in foreign ministerial session twice a year, the Defence Planning Committee, the Military Committee and the Nuclear Planning Group. The North Atlantic Assembly is the NATO interparliamentary organization. At its July 1997 summit meeting in Madrid, NATO will take decisions on the first stage of enlargement of its membership. *See* list of members.

Nuclear Suppliers Group (NSG) — Also known as the London Club, the NSG has been in session since 1975. It coordinates multilateral export controls on nuclear materials and in 1977 agreed the Guidelines for Nuclear Transfers (London Guidelines), revised in 1993. The Guidelines contain a 'trigger list' of materials which should trigger IAEA safeguards when exported for peaceful purposes to any non-nuclear weapon state. In 1992 the NSG agreed the Guidelines for Transfers of Nuclear-Related Dual-Use Equipment, Material and Related Technology (Warsaw Guidelines, subsequently revised). *See* list of members.

Open Skies Consultative Commission (OSCC) — Forum established by the 1992 Open Skies Treaty to resolve questions of compliance with the treaty.

Organisation for Economic Co-operation and Development (OECD) — Established in 1961 with the objective of promoting economic growth and social welfare by coordinating national policies. *See* list of members.

Organisation for the Prohibition of Chemical Weapons (OPCW)	Forum established by the Chemical Weapons Convention to resolve questions of compliance with the convention. Its seat is in The Hague.
Organization for Security and Co-operation in Europe (OSCE)	The 1994 Budapest Summit of the Conference on Security and Co-operation in Europe (CSCE) changed the name of the organization to the OSCE as of 1995. The OSCE comprises the Summit Meetings of Heads of State or Government; the Ministerial Council, the central decision-making and governing body; the Senior Council meetings of high-ranking officials to discuss policy guidelines, which meets at least twice a year in Prague; the Permanent Council (Vienna); the Secretariat (Vienna); the Conflict Prevention Centre (CPC, Vienna); the Office for Democratic Institutions and Human Rights (ODIHR, Warsaw); the Forum for Security Co-operation (FSC, Vienna); the Chairman-in-Office (CIO, Vienna); the High Commissioner on National Minorities (HCNM, The Hague); the Court [on Conciliation and Arbitration] (Geneva); and the Parliamentary Assembly (PA, Copenhagen). *See* list of members.
Organization of African Unity (OAU)	Established in 1963, the OAU is a union of African states with the principal objective of promoting cooperation among the states in the region. Together with the UN, it worked out the 1996 African Nuclear-Weapon-Free Zone Treaty (Treaty of Pelindaba). *See* list of members.
Organization of American States (OAS)	Group of states in the Americas, established in 1890, which also has member states and permanent observers from other continents. Its principal objective is to strengthen peace and security in the western hemisphere. *See* list of members.
Organization of the Islamic Conference (OIC)	Initiated in 1969 and established in 1971 by Islamic states to promote cooperation among the member states and to support peace, security and the struggle of the people of Palestine and all Muslim people. The Secretariat of the organization is in Jedda, Saudi Arabia. *See* list of members.
Pact on Stability in Europe	French proposal presented to the European Union in 1993 for inclusion in the framework of the EU Common Foreign and Security Policy (CFSP). The objective is to contribute to stability by preventing tension and potential conflicts connected with border and minorities issues. The Pact was adopted by over 50 states in Paris in 1995, and the instruments and procedures were handed over to the OSCE. The Pact consists of a declaration and a large number of agreements on and arrangements for good-neighbourliness and cooperation.
Partnership for Peace (PFP)	NATO programme, launched in 1994, for cooperation with NACC and other OSCE states in such areas as military planning, budgeting and training, under the authority of the North Atlantic Council. It provides for enhanced cooperation to prepare for and undertake multilateral crisis-management activities such as peacekeeping. States seeking partnership must sign a Framework Document, provide Presentation Documents to NATO, identifying the steps they will take to achieve the PFP

goals, and develop Individual Partnership Programmes with NATO. A 'PFP Plus' (also known as 'Super PFP' or 'enhanced PFP') programme is being developed to make the PFP more operational, strengthen its political consultation dimension and involve Partners more closely in operational planning and the partnership decision-making process. *See* list of partner states under North Atlantic Treaty Organization.

Peaceful nuclear explosion (PNE)	Application of a nuclear explosion for non-military purposes such as digging canals or harbours or creating underground cavities. The USA terminated its PNE programme in 1973. The USSR conducted its last PNE in 1988.
Re-entry vehicle (RV)	That part of a ballistic missile which carries a nuclear warhead and penetration aids to the target, re-enters the earth's atmosphere and is destroyed in the terminal phase of the missile's trajectory. A missile can have one or several RVs; each RV contains a warhead.
Safeguards agreements	Under the NPT and the nuclear weapon-free zone treaties, non-nuclear weapon states must accept IAEA safeguards to demonstrate the fulfilment of their obligation not to manufacture nuclear weapons.
Short-range nuclear forces (SNF)	Nuclear weapons, including artillery, mines, missiles, etc., with ranges of up to 500 km.
South Pacific Forum	Group of South Pacific states created in 1971 which *inter alia* proposed the South Pacific Nuclear Free Zone, embodied in the 1985 Treaty of Rarotonga. *See* list of members.
Stability Pact	*See* Pact on Stability in Europe.
Standing Consultative Commission (SCC)	Consultative body established by a 1972 US–Soviet Memorandum of Understanding. The USA and Russia refer issues regarding implementation of the ABM Treaty to the SCC.
Strategic nuclear weapons	ICBMs and SLBMs with a range usually of over 5500 km, as well as bombs and missiles carried on aircraft of intercontinental range.
Subcritical experiments	Experiments designed not to reach nuclear criticality, i.e., there is no nuclear explosion and no energy release.
Submarine-launched ballistic missile (SLBM)	Ballistic missile launched from a submarine, usually with a range in excess of 5500 km.
Tactical nuclear weapon	Short-range nuclear weapon which is deployed with general-purpose forces along with conventional weapons.
Theatre missile defence (TMD)	Weapon systems designed to defend against non-strategic nuclear missiles by intercepting and destroying them in flight.
Theatre nuclear forces (TNF)	Nuclear weapons with ranges of up to and including 5500 km. In the 1987 INF Treaty, nuclear missiles are divided into intermediate-range (1000–5500 km) and shorter-range (500–1000 km), also called non-strategic nuclear forces. Nuclear weapons with ranges of up to 500 km are called short-range nuclear forces.

Throw-weight	Sum of the weight of a ballistic missile's re-entry vehicle(s), dispensing mechanisms, penetration aids, and targeting and separation devices.
Toxins	Poisonous substances which are products of organisms but are inanimate and incapable of reproducing themselves as well as chemically induced variants of such substances. Some toxins may also be produced by chemical synthesis.
Treaty-limited equipment (TLE)	Five categories of equipment on which numerical limits are established in the CFE Treaty: battle tanks, armoured combat vehicles, artillery, combat aircraft and attack helicopters.
Visegrad Group	Group of states comprising Czech Republic, Hungary, Poland and Slovakia, formed in 1991 with the aim of intensifying subregional cooperation in political, economic and military areas and coordinating relations with multilateral European institutions.
Warhead	That part of a weapon which contains the explosive or other material intended to inflict damage.
Warsaw Guidelines	*See* Nuclear Suppliers Group.
Warsaw Treaty Organization (WTO)	The WTO, or Warsaw Pact, was established in 1955 by the Treaty of Friendship, Cooperation and Mutual Assistance between eight countries: Albania (withdrew in 1968), Bulgaria, Czechoslovakia, the German Democratic Republic, Hungary, Poland, Romania and the USSR. The WTO was dissolved in 1991.
Wassenaar Arrangement	The Wassenaar Arrangement on Export Controls for Conventional Arms and Dual-Use Goods and Technologies, provisionally established in 1995 in Wassenaar, the Netherlands, and formally established in Vienna in July 1996, aims to prevent the acquisition of armaments and sensitive dual-use goods and technologies for military end-uses by states whose behaviour is a cause for concern to the members. *See* list of members.
Weapon of mass destruction	Nuclear weapon and any other weapon which may produce comparable effects, such as chemical and biological weapons.
Western European Union (WEU)	Established in the 1954 Protocols to the 1948 Brussels Treaty of Economic, Social and Cultural Collaboration and Collective Self-Defence among Western European States. Within the EU Common Foreign and Security Policy (CFSP) and at the request of the EU, the WEU is to elaborate and implement EU decisions and actions which have defence implications. The principal WEU organs are the WEU Council (comprised of the Ministerial Council and the Permanent Council) and the WEU Assembly. The WEU Institute for Security Studies is a research institute. The Western European Armaments Group (WEAG) is the WEU armaments cooperation authority with activities on harmonization of requirements, arms cooperation programmes, and policies on armaments research, development and procurement. *See* list of members.

Yield   Released nuclear explosive energy expressed as the equivalent of the energy produced by a given number of tonnes of trinitro-toluene (TNT) high explosive.

Zangger Committee   The Nuclear Exporters Committee, established in 1971 and called the Zangger Committee after its first chairman, is a group of nuclear supplier countries that meets informally twice a year to coordinate export controls on nuclear materials. It was formed to establish guidelines for implementing the export control provisions of the NPT (Article III(2)). In 1974 it agreed the original 'trigger list' (subsequently revised) of equipment or material which, if exported to a non-nuclear weapon state, would be subject to IAEA safeguards. *See* list of members.

Membership of international organizations, as of 1 January 1997

The UN member states and organizations within the UN system are listed first, followed by all other organizations in alphabetical order. Note that not all the members of organizations are UN member states. Where confirmed information on new members became available in early 1997, this is given in notes.

United Nations (UN) and year of membership

Afghanistan, 1946
Albania, 1955
Algeria, 1962
Andorra, 1993
Angola, 1976
Antigua and Barbuda, 1981
Argentina, 1945
Armenia, 1992
Australia, 1945
Austria, 1955
Azerbaijan, 1992
Bahamas, 1973
Bahrain, 1971
Bangladesh, 1974
Barbados, 1966
Belarus, 1945
Belgium, 1945
Belize, 1981
Benin, 1960
Bhutan, 1971
Bolivia, 1945
Bosnia and Herzegovina, 1992
Botswana, 1966
Brazil, 1945
Brunei Darussalam, 1984
Bulgaria, 1955
Burkina Faso, 1960
Burundi, 1962
Cambodia, 1955
Cameroon, 1960
Canada, 1945
Cape Verde, 1975
Central African Republic, 1960

Chad, 1960
Chile, 1945
China, 1945
Colombia, 1945
Comoros, 1975
Congo, 1960
Costa Rica, 1945
Côte d'Ivoire, 1960
Croatia, 1992
Cuba, 1945
Cyprus, 1960
Czech Republic, 1993
Denmark, 1945
Djibouti, 1977
Dominica, 1978
Dominican Republic, 1945
Ecuador, 1945
Egypt, 1945
El Salvador, 1945
Equatorial Guinea, 1968
Eritrea, 1993
Estonia, 1991
Ethiopia, 1945
Fiji, 1970
Finland, 1955
France, 1945
Gabon, 1960
Gambia, 1965
Georgia, 1992
Germany, 1973
Ghana, 1957
Greece, 1945
Grenada, 1974

Guatemala, 1945
Guinea, 1958
Guinea-Bissau, 1974
Guyana, 1966
Haiti, 1945
Honduras, 1945
Hungary, 1955
Iceland, 1946
India, 1945
Indonesia, 1950
Iran, 1945
Iraq, 1945
Ireland, 1955
Israel, 1949
Italy, 1955
Jamaica, 1962
Japan, 1956
Jordan, 1955
Kazakhstan, 1992
Kenya, 1963
Korea, Democratic People's Republic of (North Korea), 1991
Korea, Republic of (South Korea), 1991
Kuwait, 1963
Kyrgyzstan, 1992
Lao People's Democratic Republic, 1955
Latvia, 1991
Lebanon, 1945
Lesotho, 1966
Liberia, 1945

Libya, 1955
Liechtenstein, 1990
Lithuania, 1991
Luxembourg, 1945
Macedonia, Former Yugoslav
  Republic of (FYROM), 1993
Madagascar, 1960
Malawi, 1964
Malaysia, 1957
Maldives, 1965
Mali, 1960
Malta, 1964
Marshall Islands, 1991
Mauritania, 1961
Mauritius, 1968
Mexico, 1945
Micronesia, 1991
Moldova, 1992
Monaco, 1993
Mongolia, 1961
Morocco, 1956
Mozambique, 1975
Myanmar *(Burma)*, 1948
Namibia, 1990
Nepal, 1955
Netherlands, 1945
New Zealand, 1945
Nicaragua, 1945
Niger, 1960
Nigeria, 1960
Norway, 1945

Oman, 1971
Pakistan, 1947
Palau, 1994
Panama, 1945
Papua New Guinea, 1975
Paraguay, 1945
Peru, 1945
Philippines, 1945
Poland, 1945
Portugal, 1955
Qatar, 1971
Romania, 1955
Russia, 1945[a]
Rwanda, 1962
Saint Kitts (Christopher) and
  Nevis, 1983
Saint Lucia, 1979
Saint Vincent and the
  Grenadines, 1980
Samoa, Western, 1976
San Marino, 1992
Sao Tome and Principe, 1975
Saudi Arabia, 1945
Senegal, 1960
Seychelles, 1976
Sierra Leone, 1961
Singapore, 1965
Slovakia, 1993
Slovenia, 1992
Solomon Islands, 1978
Somalia, 1960

South Africa, 1945
Spain, 1955
Sri Lanka, 1955
Sudan, 1956
Suriname, 1975
Swaziland, 1968
Sweden, 1946
Syria, 1945
Tajikistan, 1992
Tanzania, 1961
Thailand, 1946
Togo, 1960
Trinidad and Tobago, 1962
Tunisia, 1956
Turkey, 1945
Turkmenistan, 1992
Uganda, 1962
UK, 1945
Ukraine, 1945
United Arab Emirates, 1971
Uruguay, 1945
USA, 1945
Uzbekistan, 1992
Vanuatu, 1981
Venezuela, 1945
Viet Nam, 1977
Yemen, 1947
Yugoslavia, 1945[b]
Zaire, 1960
Zambia, 1964
Zimbabwe, 1980

[a] In Dec. 1991 Russia informed the UN Secretary-General that it was continuing the membership of the USSR in the Security Council and all other UN bodies.

[b] A claim by Yugoslavia (Serbia and Montenegro) in 1992 to continue automatically the membership of the former Yugoslavia was not accepted by the UN General Assembly. It was decided that Yugoslavia should apply for membership, which it had not done by 1 Jan. 1997. It may not participate in the work of the General Assembly, its subsidiary organs or the conferences and meetings it convenes.

UN Security Council

Permanent members (the P5): China, France, Russia, UK, USA

Non-permanent members in 1996 (elected by the UN General Assembly for two-year terms. The year in brackets is the year at the end of which the term expires): Botswana (1996), Chile (1997), Egypt (1997), Germany (1996), Guinea-Bissau (1997), Honduras (1996), Indonesia (1996), Italy (1996), Korea (South) (1997), Poland (1997)

Note: Costa Rica, Japan, Kenya, Portugal and Sweden were elected non-permanent members for 1997–98.

Conference on Disarmament (CD)

Members: Algeria, Argentina, Australia, Austria, Bangladesh, Belarus, Belgium, Brazil, Bulgaria, Cameroon, Canada, Chile, China, Colombia, Cuba, Egypt, Ethiopia, Finland, France, Germany, Hungary, India, Indonesia, Iran, Iraq, Israel, Italy, Japan, Kenya, Korea (North), Korea (South), Mexico, Mongolia, Morocco, Myanmar (Burma), Netherlands, New Zealand, Nigeria, Norway, Pakistan, Peru, Poland, Romania, Russia, Senegal, Slovakia, South Africa, Spain, Sri Lanka, Sweden, Switzerland, Syria, Turkey, Ukraine, UK, USA, Venezuela, Viet Nam, Yugoslavia,* Zaire, Zimbabwe

* Yugoslavia (Serbia and Montenegro) has been suspended since 1992.

Members of the 'Group of 21': Algeria, Bangladesh, Brazil, Cameroon, Chile, Colombia, Cuba, Egypt, Ethiopia, India, Indonesia, Iran, Iraq, Kenya, Korea (North), Mexico, Mongolia, Morocco, Myanmar (Burma), Nigeria, Pakistan, Peru, Senegal, South Africa, Sri Lanka, Syria, Venezuela, Viet Nam, Zaire, Zimbabwe

Members of the Eastern Group: Belarus, Bulgaria, Hungary, Poland, Romania, Russia, Slovakia, Ukraine

Members of the Western Group: Argentina, Australia, Austria, Belgium, Canada, Finland, France, Germany, Israel, Italy, Japan, Korea (South), Netherlands, New Zealand, Norway, Spain, Sweden, Switzerland, Turkey, UK, USA

International Atomic Energy Agency (IAEA)

Members: Afghanistan, Albania, Algeria, Argentina, Armenia, Australia, Austria, Bangladesh, Belarus, Belgium, Bolivia, Bosnia and Herzegovina, Brazil, Bulgaria, Cambodia, Cameroon, Canada, Chile, China, Colombia, Costa Rica, Côte d'Ivoire, Croatia, Cuba, Cyprus, Czech Republic, Denmark, Dominican Republic, Ecuador, Egypt, El Salvador, Estonia, Ethiopia, Finland, France, Gabon, Georgia, Germany, Ghana, Greece, Guatemala, Haiti, Holy See, Hungary, Iceland, India, Indonesia, Iran, Iraq, Ireland, Israel, Italy, Jamaica, Japan, Jordan, Kazakhstan, Kenya, Korea (South), Kuwait, Lebanon, Liberia, Libya, Liechtenstein, Lithuania, Luxembourg, Macedonia (Former Yugoslav Republic of), Madagascar, Malaysia, Mali, Marshall Islands, Mauritius, Mexico, Monaco, Mongolia, Morocco, Myanmar (Burma), Namibia, Netherlands, New Zealand, Nicaragua, Niger, Nigeria, Norway, Pakistan, Panama, Paraguay, Peru, Philippines, Poland, Portugal, Qatar, Romania, Russia, Saudi Arabia, Senegal, Sierra Leone, Singapore, Slovakia, Slovenia, South Africa, Spain, Sri Lanka, Sudan, Sweden, Switzerland, Syria, Tanzania, Thailand, Tunisia, Turkey, Uganda, UK, Ukraine, United Arab Emirates, Uruguay, USA, Uzbekistan, Venezuela, Viet Nam, Yemen, Yugoslavia,* Zaire, Zambia, Zimbabwe

* Yugoslavia (Serbia and Montenegro) has been suspended since 1992. It is deprived of the right to participate in the IAEA General Conference and the Board of Governors' meetings but is assessed for its contribution to the budget of the IAEA.

Note: North Korea was a member of the IAEA until Sep. 1994.

Arab League

Members: Algeria, Bahrain, Comoros, Djibouti, Egypt, Iraq, Jordan, Kuwait, Lebanon, Libya, Mauritania, Morocco, Oman, Palestine, Qatar, Saudi Arabia, Somalia, Sudan, Syria, Tunisia, United Arab Emirates, Yemen

Association of South-East Asian Nations (ASEAN)

Members: Brunei, Indonesia, Malaysia, Philippines, Singapore, Thailand, Viet Nam

ASEAN Regional Forum (ARF)

Members: The ASEAN states plus Australia, Cambodia, Canada, China, European Union (EU), India, Japan, Korea (South), Laos, Myanmar (Burma), New Zealand, Papua New Guinea, Russia, USA

Australia Group

Members: Argentina, Australia, Austria, Belgium, Canada, Czech Republic, Denmark, Finland, France, Germany, Greece, Hungary, Iceland, Ireland, Italy, Japan, Korea (South), Luxembourg, Netherlands, New Zealand, Norway, Poland, Portugal, Romania, Slovakia, Spain, Sweden, Switzerland, UK, USA

Observer: European Commission

Baltic Council

Members: Estonia, Latvia, Lithuania

Central European Initiative (CEI)

Members: Austria, Bosnia and Herzegovina, Croatia, Czech Republic, Hungary, Italy, Macedonia (Former Yugoslav Republic of), Poland, Slovakia, Slovenia

Associate members: Albania, Belarus, Bulgaria, Romania, Ukraine

Commonwealth of Independent States (CIS)

Members: Armenia, Azerbaijan, Belarus, Georgia, Kazakhstan, Kyrgyzstan, Moldova, Russia, Tajikistan, Turkmenistan, Ukraine, Uzbekistan

Council of Europe

Members: Albania, Andorra, Austria, Belgium, Bulgaria, Croatia, Cyprus, Czech Republic, Denmark, Estonia, Finland, France, Germany, Greece, Hungary, Iceland, Ireland, Italy, Latvia, Liechtenstein, Lithuania, Luxembourg, Macedonia (Former Yugoslav Republic of), Malta, Moldova, Netherlands, Norway, Poland, Portugal, Romania, Russia, San Marino, Slovakia, Slovenia, Spain, Sweden, Switzerland, Turkey, UK, Ukraine

Council of Baltic Sea States (CBSS)

Members: Denmark, Estonia, European Union (EU), Finland, Germany, Iceland, Latvia, Lithuania, Norway, Poland, Russia, Sweden

European Union (EU)

Members: Austria, Belgium, Denmark, Finland, France, Germany, Greece, Ireland, Italy, Luxembourg, Netherlands, Portugal, Spain, Sweden, UK

Group of Seven (G7)

Members: Canada, France, Germany, Italy, Japan, UK, USA

Missile Technology Control Regime (MTCR)

MTCR partners: Argentina, Australia, Austria, Belgium, Brazil, Canada, Denmark, Finland, France, Germany, Greece, Hungary, Iceland, Ireland, Italy, Japan, Luxembourg, Netherlands, New Zealand, Norway, Portugal, Russia, South Africa, Spain, Sweden, Switzerland, UK, USA

Non-Aligned Movement (NAM)

Members: Afghanistan, Algeria, Angola, Bahamas, Bahrain, Bangladesh, Barbados, Belize, Benin, Bhutan, Bolivia, Botswana, Brunei, Burkina Faso, Burundi, Cambodia, Cameroon, Cape Verde, Central African Republic, Chad, Chile, Colombia, Comoros, Congo, Côte d'Ivoire, Cuba, Cyprus, Djibouti, Ecuador, Egypt, Equatorial Guinea, Eritrea, Ethiopia, Gabon, Gambia, Ghana, Grenada, Guatemala, Guinea, Guinea-Bissau, Guyana, Honduras, India, Indonesia, Iran, Iraq, Jamaica, Jordan, Kenya, Korea (North), Kuwait, Laos, Lebanon, Lesotho, Liberia, Libya, Madagascar, Malawi, Malaysia, Maldives, Mali, Malta, Mauritania, Mauritius, Mongolia, Morocco, Mozambique, Myanmar (Burma), Namibia, Nepal, Nicaragua, Niger, Nigeria, Oman, Pakistan, Palestine, Panama, Papua New Guinea, Peru, Philippines, Qatar, Rwanda, Saint Lucia, Sao Tome and Principe, Saudi Arabia, Senegal, Seychelles, Sierra Leone, Singapore, Somalia, South Africa, Sri Lanka, Sudan, Suriname, Swaziland, Syria, Tanzania, Thailand, Togo, Trinidad and Tobago, Tunisia, Turkmenistan, Uganda, United Arab Emirates, Uzbekistan, Vanuatu, Venezuela, Viet Nam, Yemen, Yugoslavia,* Zaire, Zambia, Zimbabwe

* Yugoslavia (Serbia and Montenegro) has not been permitted to participate in NAM activities since 1992.

Nordic Council

Members: Denmark (including the Faroe Islands and Greenland), Finland (including Åland), Iceland, Norway, Sweden

North Atlantic Treaty Organization (NATO)

Members: Belgium, Canada, Denmark, France,* Germany, Greece, Iceland, Italy, Luxembourg, Netherlands, Norway, Portugal, Spain,* Turkey, UK, USA

* France and Spain are not in the integrated military structures of NATO.

North Atlantic Assembly

Associate Delegations: Albania, Belarus, Bulgaria, Czech Republic, Estonia, Hungary, Latvia, Lithuania, Macedonia (Former Yugoslav Republic of), Moldova, Poland, Romania, Russia, Slovakia, Slovenia, Ukraine

NATO North Atlantic Cooperation Council (NACC)

Members: Albania, Armenia, Azerbaijan, Belarus, Belgium, Bulgaria, Canada, Czech Republic, Denmark, Estonia, France, Georgia, Germany, Greece, Hungary, Iceland, Italy, Kazakhstan, Kyrgyzstan, Latvia, Lithuania, Luxembourg, Macedonia (Former Yugoslav Republic of), Moldova, Netherlands, Norway, Poland, Portugal, Romania, Russia, Slovakia, Slovenia, Spain, Tajikistan, Turkey, Turkmenistan, UK, Ukraine, USA, Uzbekistan

Observers: Austria, Finland, Sweden and Switzerland have observer status, as participants in the Partnership for Peace.

Partnership for Peace (PFP)

Partner states with approved PFP Framework Documents: Albania, Armenia, Austria, Azerbaijan, Belarus, Bulgaria, Czech Republic, Estonia, Finland, Georgia, Hungary, Kazakhstan, Kyrgyzstan, Latvia, Lithuania, Macedonia (Former Yugoslav Republic of), Moldova, Poland, Romania, Russia, Slovakia, Slovenia, Sweden, Switzerland, Turkmenistan, Ukraine, Uzbekistan

Partner states with approved PFP Presentation Documents: Albania, Armenia, Austria, Azerbaijan, Belarus, Bulgaria, Czech Republic, Estonia, Finland, Georgia, Hungary, Kazakhstan, Kyrgyzstan, Latvia, Lithuania, Macedonia (Former Yugoslav Republic of), Moldova, Poland, Romania, Russia, Slovakia, Slovenia, Sweden, Switzerland, Turkmenistan, Ukraine, Uzbekistan

Partner states with approved PFP Individual Partnership Programmes (IPP): Albania, Armenia, Austria, Azerbaijan, Bulgaria, Czech Republic, Estonia, Finland, Georgia, Hungary, Kazakhstan, Kyrgyzstan, Latvia, Lithuania, Macedonia (Former Yugoslav Republic of), Moldova, Poland, Romania, Slovakia, Slovenia, Sweden, Switzerland, Ukraine, Uzbekistan

Nuclear Suppliers Group (NSG)

Members: Argentina, Australia, Austria, Belgium, Brazil, Bulgaria, Canada, Czech Republic, Denmark, Finland, France, Germany, Greece, Hungary, Ireland, Italy, Japan, Korea (South), Luxembourg, Netherlands, New Zealand, Norway, Poland, Portugal, Romania, Russia, Slovakia, South Africa, Spain, Sweden, Switzerland, UK, Ukraine, USA

Organisation for Economic Co-operation and Development (OECD)

Members: Australia, Austria, Belgium, Canada, Czech Republic, Denmark, Finland, France, Germany, Greece, Hungary, Iceland, Ireland, Italy, Japan, Korea (South), Luxembourg, Mexico, Netherlands, New Zealand, Norway, Poland, Portugal, Spain, Sweden, Switzerland, Turkey, UK, USA

The European Commission participates in the work of the OECD.

Organization for Security and Co-operation in Europe (OSCE)

Members: Albania, Andorra, Armenia, Austria, Azerbaijan, Belarus, Belgium, Bosnia and Herzegovina, Bulgaria, Canada, Croatia, Cyprus, Czech Republic, Denmark, Estonia, Finland, France, Georgia, Germany, Greece, Holy See, Hungary, Iceland, Ireland, Italy, Kazakhstan, Kyrgyzstan, Latvia, Liechtenstein, Lithuania, Luxembourg, Macedonia (Former Yugoslav Republic of), Malta, Moldova, Monaco, Netherlands, Norway, Poland, Portugal, Romania, Russia, San Marino, Slovakia, Slovenia, Spain, Sweden, Switzerland, Tajikistan, Turkey, Turkmenistan, UK, Ukraine, USA, Uzbekistan, Yugoslavia*

* Yugoslavia (Serbia and Montenegro) has been suspended since 1992.

Members of the Minsk Group: Belarus, Finland, France, Germany, Hungary, Italy, Russia, Sweden, Switzerland, Turkey and USA, plus Armenia and Azerbaijan

Organization of African Unity (OAU)

Members: Algeria, Angola, Benin, Botswana, Burkina Faso, Burundi, Cameroon, Cape Verde, Central African Republic, Chad, Comoros, Congo, Côte d'Ivoire, Djibouti, Egypt, Equatorial Guinea, Eritrea, Ethiopia, Gabon, Gambia, Ghana, Guinea, Guinea-Bissau, Kenya, Lesotho, Liberia, Libya, Madagascar, Malawi, Mali, Mauritania, Mauritius, Mozambique, Namibia, Niger, Nigeria, Rwanda, Western Sahara (Saharawi Arab Democratic Republic, SADR*), Sao Tome and Principe, Senegal, Seychelles, Sierra Leone, Somalia, South Africa, Sudan, Swaziland, Tanzania, Togo, Tunisia, Uganda, Zaire, Zambia, Zimbabwe

* The Western Sahara was admitted in 1982. Its membership was disputed by Morocco and other states. Morocco withdrew from the OAU in 1985.

Organization of American States (OAS)

Members: Antigua and Barbuda, Argentina, Bahamas, Barbados, Belize, Bolivia, Brazil, Canada, Chile, Colombia, Costa Rica, Cuba,* Dominica, Dominican Republic, Ecuador, El Salvador, Grenada, Guatemala, Guyana, Haiti, Honduras, Jamaica, Mexico, Nicaragua, Panama, Paraguay, Peru, Saint Kitts (Christopher) and Nevis, Saint Lucia, Saint Vincent and the Grenadines, Suriname, Trinidad and Tobago, Uruguay, USA, Venezuela

* Cuba has been excluded from participation since 1962.

Permanent observers: Algeria, Angola, Austria, Belgium, Cyprus, Egypt, Equatorial Guinea, European Union, Finland, France, Germany, Greece, Holy See, Hungary, India, Israel, Italy, Japan, Korea (South), Lebanon, Morocco, Netherlands, Pakistan, Poland, Portugal, Romania, Russia, Saudi Arabia, Spain, Switzerland, Tunisia, Ukraine

Organization of the Islamic Conference

Members: Afghanistan, Albania, Algeria, Azerbaijan, Bahrain, Bangladesh, Benin, Brunei, Burkina Faso, Cameroon, Chad, Comoros, Djibouti, Egypt, Gabon, Gambia, Guinea, Guinea-Bissau, Indonesia, Iran, Iraq, Jordan, Kazakhstan, Kuwait, Kyrgyzstan, Lebanon, Libya, Malaysia, Maldives, Mali, Mauritania, Morocco, Mozambique, Niger, Nigeria, Oman, Pakistan, Palestine, Qatar, Saudi Arabia, Senegal, Sierra Leone, Somalia, Sudan, Syria, Tajikistan, Tunisia, Turkey, Turkmenistan, Uganda, United Arab Emirates, Yemen

South Pacific Forum

Members: Australia, Cook Islands, Fiji, Kiribati, Marshall Islands, Micronesia, Nauru, New Zealand, Niue, Palau, Papua New Guinea, Samoa (Western), Solomon Islands, Tonga, Tuvalu, Vanuatu

Wassenaar Arrangement

Members: Argentina, Australia, Austria, Belgium, Bulgaria, Canada, Czech Republic, Denmark, Finland, France, Germany, Greece, Hungary, Ireland, Italy, Japan, Korea (South), Luxembourg, Netherlands, New Zealand, Norway, Poland, Portugal, Romania, Russia, Slovakia, Spain, Sweden, Switzerland, Turkey, Ukraine, UK, USA

Western European Union (WEU)

Members: Belgium, France, Germany, Greece, Italy, Luxembourg, Netherlands, Portugal, Spain, UK

Associate Members: Iceland, Norway, Turkey

Observers: Austria, Denmark, Finland, Ireland, Sweden

Associate Partners: Bulgaria, Czech Republic, Estonia, Hungary, Latvia, Lithuania, Poland, Romania, Slovakia, Slovenia

Members of WEAG: Belgium, Denmark, France, Germany, Greece, Italy, Luxembourg, Netherlands, Norway, Portugal, Spain, Turkey, UK

Zangger Committee

Members: Australia, Austria, Belgium, Brazil, Bulgaria, Canada, Czech Republic, Denmark, Finland, France, Germany, Greece, Hungary, Ireland, Italy, Japan, Luxembourg, Netherlands, Norway, Poland, Portugal, Romania, Russia, Slovakia, South Africa, Spain, Sweden, Switzerland, UK, USA

Observer: Korea (South)

Conventions in tables

. .	Data not available or not applicable
–	Nil or a negligible figure
( )	Uncertain data
b.	billion (thousand million)
m.	million
th.	thousand
tr.	trillion (million million)
$	US dollars, unless otherwise indicated

Introduction
The emerging international security agenda

ADAM DANIEL ROTFELD

Events in 1996 confirmed that the development of a new international security system is still under way.[1] There is no single organizing principle for global security. Globalization, often referred to and identified with Westernization, neither describes nor explains the problems of the present-day world. The criterion for the effectiveness of international security structures, both global and regional, is whether and to what extent they are adequate to meet new kinds of threat. What should have been done to prevent the large-scale carnage around the Great Lakes of Central Africa and the conflicts in Chechnya (Russia), Tajikistan and Afghanistan, Algeria and Kurdistan, Sri Lanka and East Timor (Indonesia), Sudan and Myanmar (Burma), and many other places the world over? There is no common denominator for all these conflicts. They are different in every aspect but one: all but one of the 27 major armed conflicts worldwide in 1996 were internal in nature.[2] In his opening statement at SIPRI's 30th Anniversary Conference Sir Brian Urquhart, former UN Under Secretary-General, noted that at present any effort to formulate a broad security agenda for the future confronts a basic paradox:

The main elements of normal human activity—trade, communications, culture, finance—not to mention society's scourges—drugs, crime, disease, terrorism—increasingly transcend national boundaries and national sovereignty. There is a steady globalisation of institutions in these fields. In *political* life, however, nationalism, and also ethno-nationalism, has re-emerged as a strong and intransigent force. This constitutes a major challenge to internationalism and multilateralism which seemed to be the most sensible course for the nations to pursue after the second world war.[3]

I. Shaping a new security system

The process of shaping a new security system, initiated in the early 1990s, is taking place on many planes. An important constituent part of this process is the tangible progress in arms control, limitation, reduction and disarmament, on the one hand, and, on the other, the diminishing significance of military factors. The priority has become armed conflict prevention, crisis manage-

---

[1] Boutros-Ghali, B., *UN Secretary-General: The 50th Anniversary: Annual Report on the Work of the Organization* (UN: New York, N.Y., 1996), p. 327.
[2] The sole interstate conflict is that between India and Pakistan over the Kashmir. See chapter 1 in this volume.
[3] Urquhart, B., 'The future security agenda', Keynote speech delivered at SIPRI's 30th Anniversary Conference, Stockholm, 3 Oct. 1996.

ment, peaceful settlement of disputes and conflict resolution. During 1996 the United Nations was involved in 26 peace operations, 19 of which it designated as peacekeeping operations. In addition, different activities in this regard were undertaken by regional and subregional organizations. The year 1996 brought a cease-fire and the end of the war in Chechnya as well as negotiations aimed at a peaceful settlement of conflicts in numerous other countries in practically all regions of the world.[4]

The end of the cold war brought the political marginalization of nuclear weapons. As a result, significant reductions in nuclear potentials became possible, and in 1995 the parties to the 1968 Non-Proliferation Treaty (NPT) reached the decision to extend the nuclear non-proliferation regime indefinitely. The 1996 Comprehensive Nuclear Test-Ban Treaty (CTBT) brings the international community of states closer towards achieving the ultimate goal of a totally denuclearized world. On 10 September 1996 the UN General Assembly adopted the text of the treaty and opened it for signature by all governments. The historical significance of this act cannot be overestimated.[5] In another important development, the African Nuclear-Weapon-Free Zone Treaty (Treaty of Pelindaba) was signed on 11 April 1996.

Considerable progress continued to be made in implementing the 1991 START I Treaty; in June 1996 Ukraine fulfilled its pledge to become a non-nuclear weapon state. In parallel with successes at the multilateral level, some progress in the bilateral reduction of strategic nuclear weapons under the 1993 US–Russian START II Treaty was achieved.[6] The agreements reached among the nuclear powers at the Moscow Summit on Nuclear Safety and Security in April 1996 to better control, manage and secure the stockpiles of nuclear weapons and weapon-grade material are of special significance.[7] This was a concrete step taken exactly 10 years after the Chernobyl disaster with the intention to prevent future nuclear catastrophes, the long-lasting effects of which are unpredictable.

---

[4] See chapter 2 in this volume.

[5] See chapter 12 and for the text of the CTBT see appendix 12A in this volume.

[6] The ratification of START II by the USA in Jan. 1996 and the announcement by Russian President Boris Yeltsin in Mar. 1997 that he would press for the quick ratification of the treaty by the State Duma opened the way for further nuclear arms control. *International Herald Tribune*, 22–23 Mar. 1997. In addition, France declared in Feb. 1996 that it would reduce its nuclear forces, closed a weapon-grade uranium facility and ceased production of fissile material. In the UN Secretary-General's view this demonstrates a downward spiral in the nuclear arms race. See Boutros-Ghali (note 1), pp. 311–16.

[7] In this context, Albright, Berkhout and Walker identify 4 areas in which knowledge of the scale and whereabouts of fissile material inventories has become increasingly important to international security: (a) regional nuclear proliferation—the monitoring and control of fissile materials and the associated technologies have long been central to the nuclear non-proliferation regime; (b) nuclear arms reductions by the nuclear weapon states—the dismantlement of thousands of nuclear warheads has involved the extraction of large amounts of plutonium and highly enriched uranium; (c) civil spent-fuel management—an increase in reprocessing could lead to a substantial growth in the international circulation of plutonium; and (d) theft of fissile materials—unauthorized trade could exacerbate nuclear weapon proliferation and increase the risks of nuclear terrorism. This new SIPRI book points to the need for greater transparency in all these areas and calls for all states to publish regular summaries of inventories of fissile materials held on their territories or held on their behalf by other states. Albright, D., Berkhout, F. and Walker, W., SIPRI, *Plutonium and Highly Enriched Uranium 1996: World Inventories, Capabilities and Policies* (Oxford University Press: Oxford, 1997), pp. 4–7.

Although they constitute part of the new security system which is taking shape, these and other arms control agreements cannot be identified with it.[8] In his address to the Jose Ortega y Gasset Foundation, Johan Jørgen Holst made the following remarks after the end of the cold war: first, a new security system 'is possible only within the framework of multinational communities, of common institutions designed to provide common responses to common changes'; and second, '[i]ncreasingly the politics of nations revolve around the careful management of interdependence'.[9] In other words, in search of a new security system states will increasingly be involved in integration processes and seek to take advantage of multilateral institutions to manage international interdependence. Thus the first item of a future security agenda must be 'to preserve, rationalize and strengthen the international and multilateral framework that has been built up over the last fifty years'.[10]

The point is that institutions, by their very nature, are static, while security processes, particularly in the course of a fundamental restructuring of the international system as a whole, are dynamic. The conclusion to be drawn from this is as follows: the existing security structures which were called into being after World War II, such as the United Nations, or during the cold war, such as NATO and the Western European Union (WEU), call for reforms that are adequate to the changes that have radically altered the security environment. The transformed and adapted multilateral institutions must respond to the new requirements, new policy areas, new competences, and new instruments and decision-making procedures 'for a functional and politically adequate and effective handling of the institutions' list of tasks'.[11]

In 1996 reform of the United Nations was high on the Secretary-General's agenda as well as on the agenda of its intergovernmental machinery and the General Assembly. However, it seems that in the case of both the UN—a global organization—and many regional organizations there is a risk that the management reform measures and budget reductions will postpone or even substitute for the fundamental transformation of their security structures and their adaptation to the new global and regional environment.[12]

In the past, security tasks were, as a rule, reduced to the prevention of a new world war or a surprise attack by a state or a group of states against other states. The aim of the United Nations, as defined in the preamble to its Charter, is 'to save succeeding generations from the scourge of war, which twice in our life-time has brought untold sorrow to mankind'. The mandate of the

---

[8] More than 6 years ago Edward N. Lutwak noted that 'the waning of the Cold War is steadily reducing the importance of military power in world affairs'. 'From geopolitics to geoeconomics', *National Interest*, no. 20 (summer 1990), p. 15.

[9] Holst, J. J., 'The new Europe: a view from the North', ed. O. F. Knudsen, *Strategic Analysis and the Management of Power: Johan Jørgen Holst, the Cold War and the New Europe* (Macmillan: London, 1996), p. 198.

[10] Urquhart (note 3).

[11] Peters, I., 'New security challenges and institutional change', ed. I. Peters, *New Security Challenges: The Adaptation of International Institutions: Reforming the UN, NATO, EU and CSCE since 1989* (St. Martin's Press: New York, N.Y., 1996), pp. 11–17.

[12] See Boutros-Ghali (note 1), pp. 3–4; and the statement by the new UN Secretary-General, Kofi Annan, at the UN Headquarters. Press Release, SG9SM/6183, New York, N.Y., 17 Mar. 1997.

United Nations, based on the experience of the past, retains its relevance. On the other hand, there is at present no threat of a world war or even a major international war. For this reason the UN and other security institutions should be reformed and transformed so that they are able to ward off new threats and meet new requirements. It is worth considering how different states see the main sources of threat today and, consequently, which tasks they would assign to international security structures.

II. Strategic assessments

The situation during the cold war was marked by both high stability and high military threat, while the current state of world affairs is characterized by both low military threat and a low level of stability. The essential characteristics of the present strategic environment are often identified as uncertainty and change. Many observers claim that, in fact, everything has changed but geography. A return to the concept of geopolitics[13] and geo-strategy[14] is an expression of intellectual helplessness in efforts to understand the new realities rather than a promising future-oriented proposition. It is a truism that geographic location is one of the factors in the security of a state; however, physical geography is the one factor that is unchangeable, while political and economic geography have undergone a fundamental change. It is enough to recall that in Europe, after the breakup of the Soviet Union and Yugoslavia, the division of Czechoslovakia and German unification, more than 20 new states appeared. Along with the process of decolonization, the number of states-subjects of international law has tripled in the past half century. Much more important than geographical location is the system of values by which a state is guided—whether it is of a totalitarian, authoritarian or democratic nature. In the past a shift in the world was indicated by a change in the answers to three questions: who are the major players, what can they do to one another, and what do they wish to do to one another?[15] From this perspective, the degree of convergence of basic world security assessments published by US, Chinese and Russian national centres of strategic studies is remarkable.

In the understanding of many US analysts, one of the new order's basic defining characteristics is the relationship between the major powers and the fact that none of them is currently preparing for conflict with another. From the US perspective, a positive assessment of the major trends in the world includes the following elements: the major powers are still cooperating despite increasing tension among them; democracy and the market system are models

[13] Gray, C. S., 'A debate on geopolitics: the continued primacy of geography', *Orbis*, vol. 40, no. 2 (spring 1996), pp. 247–59. Alfred von Staden, Chairman of the Peace and Security Council of the Netherlands, recently wrote: 'Security concerns have become a function of geographic proximity'. von Staden, A., 'Europe's security in the context of economic globalization and political fragmentation', ed. E. Reiter, *Europas Sicherheitspolitik im globalen Rahmen* [Europe's security policy in the global framework] (Peter Lange: Vienna–Frankfurt, 1997), p. 19.

[14] Binnendijk, H. A. (ed.), *Strategic Assessment 1996: Instruments of U.S. Power* (National University–Institute for National Strategic Studies: Washington, DC, 1996), pp. 1–10.

[15] Binnendijk (note 14).

to which nearly all nations aspire; the USA is a world leader in information technology (which is increasingly the source of national power, both economic and military); the US economy has improved its performance relative to that of all other major powers but China;[16] and the USA is the dominant military power in the world. On the pessimistic side are: chaos and massive humanitarian disasters connected with the violent fragmenting of multi-ethnic states; traditional alliances under stress, with differences regarding how to respond to failing states and how to incorporate the former communist states into the new security structures; international organized crime and terrorism; instability that may be generated by nuclear proliferation; and the focus of US policy on domestic issues, resulting in lower expenditures to prepare to respond to international threats.[17]

The Chinese evaluation of the present global strategic situation proceeds from the assumption that 'multipolarization is an irreversible historical trend', on the one hand, but 'the United States became the sole superpower after the end of the cold war', on the other, and 'the US always wants to have the final say over significant global issues'.[18] Chinese analysts, like US experts, formulate a thesis that 'world wars are unlikely to happen' and 'the intensity of local wars and regional conflicts are on the decrease'. They see as a serious threat the fact that, although the cold war is over, a deep-rooted thinking in cold-war terms prevails 'in the US and some Western countries', the manifestation of which is the drive to expand NATO.

The Russian reasoning is similar. The findings of the Moscow-based Military–Political Research Centre identify as the main positive element of the strategic situation the low likelihood of a large-scale war.[19] As in the Chinese assessment, the United States is perceived as the centre of gravity in the global dimension. The authors of this and some other Russian forecasts put particular emphasis on the military dimension of security, especially on the stabilizing effect of nuclear potentials.[20] In Sergei Kapitsa's view, the most significant of all global problems is world population growth.[21] Nevertheless, international security in the world is, as a rule, seen mainly, if not exclusively, through the prism of US military policy. Furthermore, the whole reasoning of the forecast elaborated by experts of the Russian military establishment, particularly its

---

[16] Apart from the USA, the other major powers are considered to be the countries of Western Europe, Russia, China and Japan. Binnendijk (note 14), p. 2.

[17] Binnendijk (note 14), p. 8.

[18] 'New trends in the current strategic situation', *International Strategic Studies* (China Institute for International Strategic Studies, Beijing), no. 1 (1997), pp. 1–2.

[19] Sorokin, Y., 'Voyenno-politicheskaya obstanovka v mire i prognoz yeyo razvitiya v 1997 godu [The military–political situation in the world and a forecast of its development in 1997], *Nezavisimoye voyennoye obozreniye*, no. 1 (11–18 Jan. 1997) and no. 2 (18–24 Jan. 1997) (published as a supplement to the daily *Nezavisimaya Gazeta*).

[20] Krivokhizha, V. (ed.), *Yaderny faktor v sovremennom mire* [The nuclear factor in the contemporary world] (Russian Institute of Strategic Studies: Moscow, 1996).

[21] Kapitsa, S., *World Population Growth and Global Problems* (Euro-Asian Physical Society: Moscow, 1996), p. 57.

assessment of NATO enlargement to the east, is predicated on the belief that the United States and NATO are preparing for war with Russia.[22]

III. Regionalism versus globalism

The evolution of a security system is not linear. Since the threats which the security system was to meet in the past have changed fundamentally, consequently, the driving forces, dimensions, forms, procedures and mechanisms of operation of the process must change as well. In the past, the great powers claimed to be 'international security wardens'. In the bipolar system, the options were limited and non-great powers had to reconcile themselves to the existing state of affairs. In the multipolar world, small and medium-size states are gaining in significance. Similarly, domestic factors play an increasing role in shaping international security. This leads Samuel Huntington to a concept of neo-isolationism, reflected in his proposition on the remaking of the world order based on civilizational *realpolitik*: 'In a multipolar, multicivilizational world, the West's responsibility is to secure its own interests, not to promote those of other peoples when those conflicts are of little or no consequence to the West'.[23] In this extreme form, a concept has been created of immunizing the world of the wealthy—the United States and the West—against the problems that beset the poor countries of Africa, Asia and Latin America. The practical effects of such a construct, were they treated as a point of reference for political action, would lead in the long run to a catastrophe, irrespective of whether it occurred as a 'clash of civilizations', as propounded by Huntington, or a confrontation between the rich North and the poor South, as other political thinkers warn. Security is based both on common values being the product of history, culture, civilization, religion or common institutions and on the community of vital interests—political, economic, military and other. It is these vital interests that largely determine the rules of conduct of states.

Among the factors shaping Russia's political behaviour, nostalgia for the lost empire, the sense of isolation and of being pushed into the periphery of world politics, and so on, play as essential a role as the changed military and economic situation of the country.[24] This is the ground for:

---

[22] As an illustration of the author's language and tenor, one may quote one line: 'The main hypothetical military–strategic threat of NATO expansion eastward consists in the NATO states gaining areal possibility to launch a surprise air-rocket assault against essentially the whole state and military operational system with the aim of radically diminishing the CIS states' capability to fight back the aggression'. Sorokin (note 19), p. 2.

[23] Huntington, S. P., 'The West unique, not universal', *Foreign Affairs*, vol. 75, no. 6 (Nov./Dec. 1996), p. 43. The article is drawn from his book *The Clash of Civilizations and the Remaking of World Order* (Simon and Schuster: New York, N.Y., 1996). For an evaluation of Huntington's book see Barry Buzan's review essay: Buzan, B., 'Civilizational *Realpolitik* as the New World Order?', *Survival*, vol. 39, no. 1 (spring 1997), pp. 180–83.

[24] 'Russia is suffering from something similar to the Versailles Syndrome that hit Germany after World War I. It feels isolated, and it is bitter about the contrast between its post-Cold War situation and its past superpower status. Moscow thinks it is the victim, with others taking advantage of its temporary difficulties. It resents being treated as a loser in the Cold War when it feels that rather than losing it evolved in a way advantageous to all.' Binnendijk (note 14), p. 2.

a substantial inertia which exists both on the level of perceptions, norms and values and in terms of military and political 'hardware': the legacy of the superpower mentality endures, the military–industrial complex looks for self-justification and seeks to reproduce itself, and powerful interest groups profess a clear sympathy for isolationist protectionism or even confrontational assertiveness rather than for openness, adaptation and cooperation.[25]

This assessment facilitates an understanding of Russia's position in the debate on NATO enlargement much better than many other analyses, studies and commentaries.[26] Security-related processes are intertwined. Russia's status and external security will be determined more by its success or failure in implementing domestic reform than in preventing NATO enlargement. This does not mean that Russia's legitimate security interests can be ignored. The meeting of the presidents of Russia and the United States in Helsinki on 20–21 March 1997 demonstrated that it is possible to accommodate different security interests while maintaining opposing assessments with regard to the announced invitation to one or more Central European countries to join the North Atlantic Alliance. In their joint statement on European security of 21 March 1997, Presidents Bill Clinton and Boris Yeltsin agreed that 'the evolution of security structures should be managed in a way that threatens no state and that advances the goal of building a more stable and integrated Europe'.[27] To minimize the potential consequences of disagreement on the issue of NATO enlargement, they announced an elaboration of a document that will establish cooperation between NATO and Russia. Such an arrangement will be an important constituent element of a new comprehensive European security system. In this way, while respecting each other's different perceptions of national and regional security interests, both leaders demonstrated their will to shape the mutual relations of the two powers on the principles of cooperativeness and *inclusiveness* rather than deterrence and *exclusiveness*, the latter pair of principles having been the organizing tenets of their relations in the past.

Cooperative enlargement of NATO constitutes an essential part of, but certainly cannot be substituted for, the whole process of restructuring regional security in Europe. This process covers the enlargement of practically all the existing multilateral organizations in Europe: the European Union (EU), the WEU, the Organization for Security and Co-operation in Europe (OSCE), the Council of Europe, the Organisation for Economic Co-operation and Development (OECD) and many other subregional structures. It is also worth noting the fact that admitting new democratic states to European organizations is not being criticized, with the sole exception of NATO enlargement to the east. The most authoritative and forceful of the criticisms voiced by Western opponents was expressed by George F. Kennan, who warned that 'expanding the North Atlantic Treaty organization would be the most fateful error of

[25] Arbatov, A. *et al.,* ed. V. Baranovsky, SIPRI, *Russia and Europe: The Emerging Security Agenda* (Oxford University Press: Oxford, 1997), p. 3.

[26] See also chapter 5 in this volume.

[27] Joint US–Russian Statement released by the White House at the Helsinki Summit, 21 Mar. 1997.

American policy in the entire post-Cold War era'.[28] This criticism rests on the belief that enlargement will lead to Russia's isolation, inflame the nationalistic, anti-Western and militaristic tendencies in Russia, and be counterproductive for the development of democracy in Russia. Here two general reflections come to mind which, as a rule, are overlooked by the opponents of NATO enlargement: the first concerns the motives by which the aspirants are guided in seeking membership of the Alliance; and the second concerns the principle of equal treatment to be applied to the security interests of the states of the region. The candidates are motivated exactly by the same considerations, concerns and reasons for which the present members of the Alliance do not want to leave it.

Indivisible international security cannot be identified with equal security. Moreover, the often declared principle of equal security does not exist in practice. Great powers, by definition, have a greater ability to independently ensure their own security than do the small and medium-size states, which see their admission to multilateral structures as a *sui generis* 'insurance policy' against worst-case scenarios. The security interests of this group of states should be taken into account to the same degree as those of Russia. This applies in equal measure to those small and medium-size states that aspire to NATO membership and those which want to remain outside the Alliance's structure. Tarja Hallonen and Lena Hjelm-Wallén, the foreign ministers of Finland and Sweden, respectively, emphatically drew attention to the inter-relationship of the subregional, regional and global dimensions of security.[29] One of the conclusions of the 1996 SIPRI Report on *A Future Security Agenda for Europe* is that three basic values should be included in the security agenda: 'each state must still be responsible for its own security, even if it belongs to an alliance; security problems should be addressed according to the principle of subsidiarity, i.e., where feasible, be dealt with on the subregional or regional level; and there must be solidarity between states with regard to security issues'.[30]

Enlargement of the NATO and EU security structures would overcome the historical tendency for Central Europe to be either a region in which armed conflicts erupt and tend to radiate outward or the point of collision between

---

[28] Kennan, G. F., 'NATO expansion would be a fateful blunder', *International Herald Tribune*, 6 Feb. 1997, p. 8.

[29] 'Europe's security is indivisible. Finland and Sweden reject any proposal for regional security arrangements for the Baltic area that is not based on this self-evident principle. We wish to emphasize the value of continued strong US involvement in the area as well as the sense of responsibility for the Baltic region manifested collectively and individually by EU states.' Hallonen, T. and Hjelm-Wallén, L., 'Working for European security outside the NATO structure', *International Herald Tribune*, 15–16 Mar. 1997, p. 8.

[30] *A Future Security Agenda for Europe*, Report of the Independent Working Group established by SIPRI, Stockholm, Oct. 1996, p. 11. The report also drew up some recommendations for the search for comprehensive and cooperative security for the 21st century in Europe: (*a*) to go beyond existing frameworks and to suggest directions in which multilateral efforts towards security should be aimed; (*b*) to adopt a more systematic approach to preventing and resolving conflicts; (*c*) to allow for the enlargement of Western institutions; and (*d*) to rebalance and reapportion security responsibilities in the OSCE area so that each player understands and accepts not only its own role but also the role of the other players. (p. 12).

adversaries from the east and west. The report recommended that more attention should be paid to the content and volume of cooperation between institutions than to their structures. The practical harmonization of globalism and regionalism is reflected in the conclusion that Europe must engage the countries of its adjacent regions (North Africa, the Middle East and Central Asia) which are fraught with tensions and which pose potential security problems.

IV. SIPRI findings

The authors of chapters in this *SIPRI Yearbook* have produced original data, figures and analyses on security and conflicts; on military spending and armaments; and on non-proliferation, arms control and disarmament.

Conflicts. In 1996 there were 27 major armed conflicts worldwide (in 1995 there were 30 armed conflicts while during the last year of the cold war, 1989, 36 conflicts were registered). All but one of the conflicts recorded for 1996 were domestic in nature.[31]

Conflict prevention, management and resolution. The year was notable for peace settlements in Guatemala, the Philippines and Sierra Leone, but progress was frustratingly slow in other better known cases such as the Middle East, Northern Ireland, and Bosnia and Herzegovina. Africa and an arc of instability around Russia's periphery remained the most troubled regions. The UN remained prominent in conflict prevention, management and resolution efforts, even while its budget crisis continued and the Security Council remained shy, to the detriment of its credibility, about launching new initiatives, even in desperate situations like those of Burundi and Zaire. UN peacekeeping consequently continued its dramatic decline, the largest extant peacekeeping mission in 1996 being the non-UN NATO-led Implementation Force (IFOR) and its successor mission, the Stabilization Force (SFOR), in Bosnia and Herzegovina. The kaleidoscopic instabilities of the African Great Lakes region during 1996 were, however, a continuing reminder that the 'end of history' is not nigh for peace operations. With its leadership crisis over, the UN could, at the end of the year, look forward to less uncertainty, more robust reform and, the US Congress willing, improved financial health. With regional organizations worldwide still struggling to create the capacity to deal with potential and actual conflicts in their own bailiwicks, competent subregional organizations only just emerging and the UN overburdened, unreconstructed and under-funded, the clear answer was for cooperative and integrated approaches by all parties willing and able to contribute to a particular peace process.[32]

The Middle East. After four years of active negotiation, the major conflict in this region was still not close to resolution. The new Israeli Government, elected in May 1996, signalled that it wanted to revise what many regard as the basic understandings of the peace process. This caused the process to grind to a halt for several months. Indeed, many regarded 1996 as a year in which

[31] See chapter 1 in this volume.
[32] See chapter 2 in this volume.

the process moved backwards, before tentatively inching forward in the early days of 1997 with the deal on Israeli redeployment in Hebron.[33]

Russia: conflicts and its security environment. In 1996, five years after the dissolution of the USSR, the new post-Soviet states continued to face numerous security-related challenges in domestic developments, in conflict settlement efforts and in organizing the post-Soviet geopolitical space. Among the significant domestic developments, Boris Yeltsin was re-elected President of Russia and Alexander Lukashenko established a de facto authoritarian regime in Belarus. Considerable progress was made in two conflicts: in Chechnya— the most serious armed conflict in terms of casualties and the most dramatic challenge experienced by Russia in the past five years—the war was ended, and in Tajikistan the political dialogue between the conflicting parties received a significant boost. In other conflict areas the situation remained relatively stable, but without successful moves towards political settlement.

The area of the Commonwealth of Independent States (CIS) has become the focus of Russia's attention. In the European part, there was a spectacular *rapprochement* between Russia and Belarus, but in 1996 there was new evidence of an alienation of some CIS states from Russia, with Ukraine the most persistent in pursuing an independent policy.[34]

Europe. By 1996 Europe had achieved its highest degree of institutionalized regional security cooperation and assigned a high priority to the debate on organizational and procedural matters. The internal transformation and enlargement of the originally Western institutions (e.g., the Council of Europe, the OECD, the EU and NATO) are often perceived as contradictory processes of deepening *versus* widening and creating new divisions. Based on democratic rules and common security interests and values, the OSCE states committed themselves at the Lisbon Summit to *act in solidarity* and to consider the undertaking of *joint actions.* This is a stage in the shaping of a new principle for the international community, offering the right to 'cooperative intervention' in domestic conflicts. Another decision was to develop a model of security for Europe for the 21st century.[35]

Conventional arms control. A new period of negotiation and conceptualization was opened in the field of conventional arms control with the aim of adapting the 1991 Treaty on Conventional Armed Forces in Europe (CFE Treaty) to the new security conditions, including the prospective enlargement of NATO. Similarly, the place of arms control in the European security debate has undergone a reappraisal with the aim of elaborating guidelines for security cooperation and an agenda for current and future arms control. The Florence Agreement of June 1996 made progress towards a military balance among the former warring parties in the former Yugoslavia, with the support of the international community. Outside Europe, conventional arms control is for the most part at the stage of a dialogue or is slowly trudging through first-generation confidence-building measure (CBM) arrangements.

---

[33] See chapter 3 in this volume.
[34] See chapter 4 in this volume.
[35] See chapter 5 in this volume.

The land-mines problem has acquired special importance in the light of the growing awareness of their widespread use in local conflicts and the civilian carnage wreaked by them. More than 100 million land-mines have been laid in nearly 70 countries. In 1996, 30 additional states called for a total prohibition on land-mines, bringing the number to 53. The US decision, supported by Britain and France, to side-step the Ottawa Group in favour of negotiations in the Conference on Disarmament (CD), involving all the relevant producers and exporters, has lessened the chances for rapid progress and seems to have shifted the focus towards a phased approach (a ban on exports first).[36]

Military expenditure. Spending by the NATO countries and members of the former Soviet bloc continued to decline in 1996, with expenditure in the United States alone falling by 5 per cent in real terms over the previous year. Overall NATO expenditure fell by almost 3 per cent in 1996, indicating a levelling off from the average reduction of 4.8 per cent for the previous three years. As NATO expenditure is the dominant component of overall world military spending, it is clear that the decline in aggregate global military expenditure noted in recent years was maintained in 1996. However, the lack of reliable information on defence spending for China, Russia and many countries in the developing regions makes it unfeasible to determine a meaningful global figure for military expenditure. Despite the downward trend in overall military spending, two important regions, the Middle East and South-East Asia, continued to increase their military expenditure in 1996, while aggregate military spending in South Asia remained stable.[37]

Military research and development. Global R&D expenditure continues to decline. Most is going to combat aircraft and missile defences. Japan and South Korea continue to increase their military R&D activities steadily. Their build-ups are explicable only if one assumes that these states see the development of an independent arms industry as a desirable end in itself. Among the five declared nuclear weapon states, the USA and the UK are shifting strongly towards research on conventional weapons, China and Russia are retaining a nuclear emphasis, and the position of France is somewhere in between.[38]

Arms production. While during the past five years the dominant development in the global arms industry was the declining levels of arms production, this trend is now becoming weaker. In spite of remaining excess capacity of the order of 25 per cent, reductions in the volume of arms production are levelling out, at least in the leading arms-producing companies in the Western world. Currently, the more important trends are structural changes in the arms industry, its commercialization and the greater importance attached to military exports.

The pace of consolidation in the US arms industry was extremely rapid in 1996. The Russian arms industry is also undergoing fundamental changes towards new corporate structures and a strong concentration in fewer and larger companies. Although the restructuring process in Europe is slower,

[36] See chapter 13 in this volume.
[37] See chapter 6 in this volume.
[38] See chapter 7 in this volume.

there are efforts to create conditions for further change, such as the establishment of the Joint Armaments Cooperation Organization (JACO) and the decisions in France to speed up changes in its defence industrial structure.[39]

The arms trade. In 1996 the volume of international transfers of conventional weapons was broadly constant compared with 1995. The SIPRI global trend-indicator value of international transfers of major conventional weapons in 1996 was $22 980 million. Among supplier countries a small group of countries remained predominant. The United States alone accounted for 44 per cent of deliveries while France, Germany, Russia, the UK and the USA together accounted for 87 per cent of total deliveries.

Among the arms recipients, the most notable trend in recent years has been the growing importance of countries in North-East Asia as centres of demand. In 1996 three recipients in this region—China, South Korea and Taiwan—together accounted for 30 per cent of total deliveries.[40]

Multilateral military-related export control regimes. Through a process of gradual evolution the membership and behaviour of multilateral military-related export control regimes has changed considerably since the end of the cold war. Regime membership no longer reflects the pattern of cold war alliances which dominated earlier export control efforts while the emphasis of the regimes has shifted away from technology denial and towards conditional access to technology. This trend also continued with the admission of Brazil, South Korea and Ukraine to the Nuclear Suppliers Group, the admission of South Korea to the Australia Group and the participation of Brazil in the Missile Technology Control Regime. At the formal launch of the Wassenaar Arrangement on Export Controls for Conventional Arms and Dual-Use Goods and Technologies five new states—Argentina, Bulgaria, South Korea, Romania and Ukraine—participated in the working of the group for the first time.[41]

Nuclear arms control. Encouraging progress was made in advancing the nuclear arms control agenda. In the USA and across the former Soviet Union the large-scale dismantlement of strategic nuclear weapons and associated infrastructure proceeded apace within the framework of the 1991 START I Treaty, with Belarus and Ukraine completing the withdrawal of the nuclear warheads based on their territories. The progress made in eliminating nuclear arms in the former Soviet republics was facilitated by the bilateral assistance provided by the USA under its Cooperative Threat Reduction programme; this assistance also supported a growing range of activities aimed at enhancing the security of fissile materials in the former Soviet nuclear weapon complex. However, in 1996 there were clear signs that the momentum behind further nuclear arms control and confidence-building measures was waning. In Geneva, the CD had yet to form a committee to negotiate a global convention banning the production of fissile material for nuclear explosives. Finally, negotiations between Russia and the USA to clarify the scope of the 1972

---

[39] See chapter 8 in this volume.
[40] See chapter 9 in this volume.
[41] See chapter 10 in this volume.

Anti-Ballistic Missile (ABM) Treaty continued to generate discord, with powerful voices on Capitol Hill in Washington calling for the USA to abandon the ABM Treaty altogether.[42]

The Comprehensive Nuclear Test-Ban Treaty was completed and opened for signature in 1996. China's acceptance of the treaty marked a watershed in its arms-control policy. By the end of the year, the majority of states had signed and only one—India—had declared unconditionally that it would not. India's refusal to sign could prevent the treaty from achieving its full legal force, but the international norm against testing is universally accepted. Although modernization of delivery systems has become more important than modernization of warheads, the CTBT has an important effect on both established arsenals and proliferation.

Chemical and biological arms control. With the 65th ratification deposited, the Chemical Weapons Convention (CWC) will enter into force on 29 April 1997. While the creation of the first global, verifiable disarmament regime is firmly on course, some important issues must be resolved. The domestic political, economic and other factors influencing a decision by Russia and the USA on ratification of the CWC are complex. Restrictions on chemical trade and effective implementation of the CWC may, however, play the key role in convincing both countries to ratify. Verified destruction of chemical stockpiles and production facilities as well as of old and abandoned chemical weapons will become one of the major political and technological challenges in the next few years. Chemical weapon proliferation and the threat of use by terrorist or criminal organizations may be expected to remain a top security issue for many governments.

The Fourth Review Conference of the 1972 Biological and Toxin Weapons Convention (BTWC) endorsed the efforts to establish a Verification Protocol for the BTWC. Although the problems remain formidable, some encouraging signs none the less emerged during 1996 that the BTWC might become a verifiable disarmament treaty early in the next century.[43]

V. Conclusions

The determinants of the emerging international security agenda may be identified with three new factors. There are no clear external threats but, at the same time, there are menacing domestic conflicts around the world. The political significance of the military dimension has diminished while the role of the economic dimension is growing in the search for a new security system on both the global and regional levels. The significance of transnational structures is stronger and in various parts of the world states' control over developments on their territories has become weaker. The paradox is that in parallel with advancing globalization the emerging international security

---

[42] See chapter 11 in this volume.
[43] See chapter 12 in this volume.

agenda is more focused on domestic, local and regional issues[44] than was the case under the bipolar system. This leads to the following concluding remarks:

1. Institutional forms and instruments of cooperation in the sphere of security should be adequate to the new realities of a pluralistic world—multipolar, multicultural and multi-civilizational.

2. The existing security structures were formed to respond to the threats which are the least prevalent today; they are meant to ensure the inviolability of borders that are no longer disputed. The initiated reforms aim at readjusting the security institutions to new tasks: domestic conflict prevention, crisis situation settlement, peacemaking and developing the new concept of post-conflict peace building. In addition, the expectations with regard to security that are addressed to regional and subregional organizations as a rule extend beyond the territories of their member states.

3. Shaping a new security system, both globally and regionally, is part of the broader historical process in which neither the powers nor the security organizations have exclusive rights. If the regime of global and international security that is emerging as a result of trial-and-error processes and new experiences is to adhere to the declared democratic values—the rule of law, pluralistic democracy, respect for human rights and market economy—it cannot be based on the hegemony of one or several powers.[45] Such a system should give expression to the interdependence of states, where mutual relations are governed by generally accepted principles of international law.

---

[44] Buzan, B., 'Rethinking security after the cold war', *Cooperation and Conflict*, vol. 32, no. 1 (Mar. 1997), p. 12.

[45] The concept of a 7-polar world, with 7 hegemons, as envisaged by Johan Galtung ('The United States in the Western Hemisphere and the Middle East—clearly aspiring to be the hegemon's hegemon'), like Samuel Huntington's vision of a 'clash of civilizations' (see note 23), may, the authors' intentions notwithstanding, well become a self-fulfilling prophesy. Galtung, J., 'Geopolitics after the cold war: an essay in agenda theory', eds V. De Lima and C. Karagdag, *Peace, Disarmament and Symbiosis in the Asia–Pacific* (Solidaridad Foundation: Quezon City, Philippines, 1995), p. 55.

Part I. Security and conflicts, 1996

Chapter 1. Major armed conflicts

Chapter 2. Armed conflict prevention, management and resolution

Chapter 3. The Middle East peace process

Chapter 4. Russia: conflicts and its security environment

Chapter 5. Europe: in search of cooperative security

1. Major armed conflicts

MARGARETA SOLLENBERG and PETER WALLENSTEEN

I. Global patterns of major armed conflicts, 1989–96

In 1996 there were 27 major armed conflicts in 24 locations around the world. Both these numbers were lower than the previous year (in 1995 there were 30 major armed conflicts and 25 locations)[1] and significantly lower than the 36 conflicts in 32 locations registered for 1989, the last year of the cold war.

A 'major armed conflict' is defined as prolonged combat between the military forces of two or more governments, or of one government and at least one organized armed group, and incurring the battle-related deaths of at least 1000 people for the duration of the conflict. A conflict 'location' is the territory of at least one state. Since certain countries may be the location of more than one conflict, the number of conflicts reported may be greater than the number of conflict locations.[2] A major armed conflict is removed from the table when the contested incompatibility has been resolved and/or when there is no recorded use of armed force related to the incompatibility between the parties during the year. The same conflict may reappear in a table for subsequent years if there is any renewed use of armed force.

All but one of the conflicts recorded for 1996 were internal, that is, the incompatibility concerned control over the government or the territory of one state. The sole interstate conflict, that between India and Pakistan over the Kashmir issue, last appeared in the table for 1992. Although this was the only interstate conflict registered, regular troops of some states were involved in the internal conflicts of other states, including Tajikistan, where troops of the Russian Federation and other members of the Commonwealth of Independent States (CIS) were used against the opposition. In addition, the USA conducted air strikes against Iraq in connection with the Kurdish conflicts in the north of that country.[3]

Although several conflicts received much publicity during the year this does not necessarily indicate that they fulfilled the criteria for inclusion in the table as major armed conflicts. In the case of eastern Zaire, for example, the conflict did not reach the required level of intensity, as measured in the number of deaths, for inclusion in the table.

---

[1] See appendix 1A in this volume for the table of major armed conflicts in 1996 and for the definitions of the criteria. For comprehensive definitions, see Heldt, B. (ed.), *States in Armed Conflict 1990–91* (Department of Peace and Conflict Research, Uppsala University: Uppsala, 1992), chapter 3.

[2] Some countries may also be the location of minor armed conflicts. The table in appendix 1A presents only the major armed conflicts in the countries listed.

[3] This incident is not included in the table for 1996 as a resumption of the 1991 Persian Gulf War since that war involved a different incompatibility, the territory of Kuwait.

While several conflicts were ended during the year through comprehensive peace treaties, including those in Chechnya,[4] Guatemala and Sierra Leone, they remain in the table because military force was used in these conflicts in 1996, either before or after the conclusion of such agreements.[5]

II. Changes in the table of conflicts

New and resumed conflicts in 1996

Three major armed conflicts were recorded for 1996 that did not appear in 1995. Two of these were old conflicts registered prior to 1995, while one was new. In Northern Ireland, last recorded in the table for 1994, the cease-fire with the Provisional Irish Republican Army (IRA) was broken in February 1996 and a limited number of incidents occurred during the year. The inter-state conflict between India and Pakistan again resulted in armed action. A rocket launched against Pakistan in late January 1996, for which India denied responsibility, sparked artillery duels along the Line of Control dividing the parts of Kashmir controlled by India and Pakistan. These recurred later in the year. The conflict which fulfilled the criteria for inclusion in the table for the first time in 1996 was the internal conflict in northern Uganda between the government and the Lord's Resistance Army (LRA) which began in 1993. The upsurge in fighting during the year was probably related to the continuing armed conflict in southern Sudan, from where the LRA operates with the support of the Sudanese Government.

Conflicts recorded in 1995 that did not reappear in 1996

Four peace treaties concluded in previous years were in the process of implementation in 1996, resulting in an absence of armed conflict during the year and hence the removal of these conflicts from the table. Two of these were the last remaining conflicts in the former Yugoslavia—in Bosnia and Herzegovina and in Croatia. The third was Angola, which was eliminated as the location of a major armed conflict for the first time since the country's independence in 1975. Although the peace process ran into trouble concerning *inter alia* demobilization and power-sharing arrangements, the instances of violence reported were not judged to be related to the incompatibility. The conflict was therefore removed from the table.

The fourth case was Liberia, where implementation of the 1995 peace agreement was severely disrupted by fighting between two new conflicting parties. This involved the Ulimo-J (the Roosevelt Johnson faction) fighting the forces of the government and the Economic Community of West African States Monitoring Group (ECOMOG) following the suspension of Johnson

---

[4] See also chapter 4 in this volume for the conflicts in Russia and its immediate environment.

[5] See also chapter 2 in this volume for a discussion of international efforts to prevent, manage and resolve armed conflict in 1996.

from the cabinet in early March. Since there is no evidence that this resulted in more than 1000 battle-related deaths, the conflict does not appear in the table.

Two conflicts did not reappear in the table owing to what appeared to be a victory by one side—the Indian Government in Punjab and the Myanmar Government over the Mong Tai Army (MTA), which had been fighting for the independence of the Shan State. New incompatibilities may, however, have arisen. In the first case Sikh groups were aligning themselves with Kashmiri factions rather than giving up the armed struggle. In the second case, splinter groups from the MTA vowed to continue the struggle after the surrender in early January 1996 of MTA leader, Khun Sa, which observers considered resulted from a deal with the government connected to the heroin trade.

Changes in intensity of conflicts and peace efforts

Although in six of the locations the major armed conflicts recorded for 1996 resulted in over 1000 battle-related deaths in 1996 alone—Afghanistan, Algeria, Russia (Chechnya), Sri Lanka, Sudan and Turkey—there were no cases of a dramatic escalation compared with previous years. In most conflicts the intensity of the armed conflict, as measured in the number of deaths, decreased or was at a very low level. The conflict in Chechnya was less intense following the August cease-fire agreement. A similar pattern was seen in Sierra Leone following its peace agreement. Low intensity also characterized, for example, the conflicts in Bangladesh, Guatemala, Indonesia (East Timor), Iran, Iraq, Myanmar and the Philippines.

The Middle East peace process was marred by suicide bombings, the assassination of the Prime Minister of Israel and the escalation of the war in southern Lebanon in April.[6] The Israeli–Palestinian conflict therefore remains in the table.

Towards the end of the year significant developments seemed to be unfolding in the Sudan conflict, with military setbacks for the government. The Sudanese People's Liberation Army (SPLA), fighting the Sudanese Government, was reported to have bases in Uganda and to be receiving support from the Ugandan Government. Fighting between Sudanese and Ugandan opposition organizations complicated the situation. The prospects for more neighbouring countries becoming involved was high, with Ethiopia and Eritrea increasingly supporting a more united opposition against the regime in Khartoum.

The character of two other major armed conflicts also changed significantly. In Afghanistan a remarkable realignment took place among the warring parties. While at the beginning of 1996 the government was isolated, by the end of the year all the formerly warring parties had united against the Taleban. The Taleban captured Kabul in August, but government forces and their allies fought back in other areas of the country throughout the year.

---

[6] See chapter 3 in this volume for an account of the peace process and other developments in the Middle East.

The second case was the conflict in Cambodia, although it remained at a much lower level of intensity than that in Afghanistan. In 1996 several factions of the Khmer Rouge switched sides and joined the ruling coalition government. Thus, the Pol Pot faction was weakened. This led, however, to rivalry between the coalition parties, each of which attempted to recruit the break-away factions to its side, and to armed clashes between the remaining Khmer Rouge forces and the defectors.

III. Regional patterns of major armed conflicts 1989–96

The regional distribution of locations with major armed conflicts is shown in table 1.1. In 1996 none of the regions surveyed was entirely spared armed conflict. For the period 1989–96 there was an almost constant decline in the number of major armed conflicts worldwide. However, there were significant regional variations. The decline in the number of conflicts in Africa began only in 1992, in Central and South America in 1991 and in the Middle East in 1995. Asia is the only region which showed no decline, as the number of conflicts rose again in 1996. The number of major armed conflicts in Europe has gradually declined since the peak year of 1993. In fact, after the peace treaty for Chechnya, by the end of 1996 there was only one major active armed conflict in Europe—that in Northern Ireland—and even there violence was sporadic.

Table 1.1. Regional distribution of locations with at least one major armed conflict, 1989–96

	1989	1990	1991	1992	1993	1994	1995	1996
Africa	9	10	10	7	7	6	6	5
Asia	11	10	8	11	9	9	9	10
Central and South America	5	5	4	3	3	3	3	3
Europe	2	1	2	4	5	4	3	2
Middle East	5	5	5	4	4	5	4	4
Total	**32**	**31**	**29**	**29**	**28**	**27**	**25**	**24**

[a] Only those regions of the world in which a conflict was recorded for the period 1989–96 are included here.

Source: Uppsala Conflict Data Project.

The Middle East region has shown very little variation over the years in the number of major armed conflicts. Many of the conflicts were of low intensity in 1996. The exception was the conflict in Turkey between the Turkish Government and the Kurdish Worker's Party (PKK). The conflict in Northern Iraq continued, escalating in 1996 owing to an invasion of the Kurdish autonomous region by Iraqi forces on 31 August. Iraq intervened on behalf of one of the

Table 1.2. Regional distribution, number and types of major armed conflicts, 1989–96

Location	1989 G	1989 T	1990 G	1990 T	1991 G	1991 T	1992 G	1992 T	1993 G	1993 T	1994 G	1994 T	1995 G	1995 T	1996 G	1996 T
Africa	7	3	8	3	8	3	6	1	6	1	5	1	5	1	4	1
Asia	6	8	5	10	3	8	5	9	4	7	4	7	4	8	4	7
Central and South America	5	–	5	–	4	–	3	–	3	–	3	–	3	–	3	–
Europe	1	1	–	1	–	2	–	4	–	6	–	5	–	3	–	2
Middle East	1	4	1	4	2	5	2	3	2	4	2	4	2	4	2	4
Total	**20**	**16**	**19**	**18**	**17**	**18**	**16**	**17**	**15**	**18**	**14**	**17**	**14**	**16**	**13**	**14**
Total	**36**		**37**		**35**		**33**		**33**		**31**		**30**		**27**	

G = Government and T = Territory, the two types of incompatibility.

a The total annual number of conflicts does not necessarily correspond to the number of conflict locations in table 1.1. and in table 1A, appendix 1A, since there may be more than one major armed conflict in each location.

b Only those regions of the world in which a conflict was recorded for the period 1989–96 are included here.

Source: Uppsala Conflict Data Project.

groups, the Kurdistan Democratic Party (KDP), against the other, the Patriotic Union of Kurdistan (PUK), leading to US air strikes against Iraq in September.

Conflicts in Asia were all low-level except for those in Sri Lanka and Afghanistan. In 1996 Asia had the only major interstate conflict—that between India and Pakistan—which is in effect a 'cold war' which periodically becomes 'hot'. In many Asian conflicts governments have become strong enough to force their armed opposition into negotiations. This pattern was seen in Myanmar, where capitulation took place, and the Philippines, where a peace treaty resulted in limited autonomy for parts of Mindanao (rather than the independence or complete autonomy that the rebels sought).

One new conflict was recorded for Africa, that in Uganda, and two were removed from the table, those in Angola and Liberia. The total number of conflicts for Africa was thus lower than in 1995. The conflict in eastern Zaire and the surrounding areas involved Rwanda and Burundi and to a limited extent Tanzania and Uganda, but since none of these involvements resulted in over 1000 deaths by the end of 1996 the conflicts are not listed in the table. Nor is the conflict in Burundi between the Government of Burundi and the Conseil national pour la défense de la démocratie (CNDD) included. Owing to the lack of information on who is responsible for the many deaths in Burundi, it was unclear whether in 1996 the conflict met the criteria for inclusion.

Central and South America shows a pattern of declining numbers of conflicts and of declining intensity in most of the remaining major conflicts. Peace negotiations were successfully concluded in Guatemala in 1996. In Peru, the Movimiento Revolucionario Tupac Amaru (Tupac Amaru Revolutionary Movement, MRTA) occupied the Japanese Embassy in Lima in late December 1996, proving that the claim by the Peruvian Government that the MRTA guerrilla had been defeated was exaggerated.

IV. Conclusions

The pattern of a declining number of major conflicts since 1989 continued in 1996. However, a number of old conflicts remained active or were resumed after a period of inactivity. In fact, of the 27 major armed conflicts recorded for 1996, the origins of 22 can be dated to the period before 1989. This remarkable continuity means that conflicts initiated after 1989 have to a large degree been contained. The dearth of comprehensive peace agreements reached and implemented in relation to the older conflicts suggests that the longer a war or the more intense a war, the more difficult is its peace process (for example, the Israel–Palestine and Sri Lankan conflicts).

Five of the conflicts active in 1996 did not have such a record of continuous activity—Algeria, Chechnya, Sierra Leone, Tajikistan and Uganda. None of these was related to the former cold war dynamics but to issues which were more local in nature, such as religious, ethnic or other identities.

Thus, 1996 may have witnessed the end of the post-cold war period. There has been an at least partly successful termination of those conflicts where cold war superpower involvement was the greatest (in Southern Africa and in Central and South America). In addition, most of the conflicts emanating from the breakup of the Soviet Union and Yugoslavia were at least contained by the end of 1996. Some conflicts persist but today may have a different character: a case is the continuing war in Afghanistan, which is now closely intertwined with that in Tajikistan.

The global total of battle-related deaths in 1996 was lower than in any previous year of the post-cold war era. The total number of armed conflicts was also lower, as was the number of full-scale wars claiming tens of thousands of deaths. Protracted conflicts claimed fewer lives but their longevity tended to validate violence as a means of resolving political conflicts, as exemplified by Central Africa since 1994.

Another phenomenon was that not only were armed conflicts spreading over larger territories and giving rise to new conflicts but so was general social and political instability, pointing to a lack of state legitimacy. The causal links obviously go both ways: armed conflict leads to instability and instability leads to armed conflict. Thus, a region becomes locked into a vicious spiral, in some cases towards complete state failure, as in Somalia and Zaire.

Appendix 1A. Major armed conflicts, 1996

MARGARETA SOLLENBERG, RAMSES AMER, CARL JOHAN
ÅSBERG, BIRGER HELDT and ANN-SOFI JAKOBSSON*

The following notes and sources apply to the locations listed in table 1A:[1]

[a] The stated general incompatible positions. 'Govt' and 'Territory' refer to contested incompatibilities concerning government (type of political system, a change of central government or in its composition) and territory (control of territory [interstate conflict], secession or autonomy), respectively.

[b] 'Year formed' is the year in which the incompatibility was stated. 'Year joined' is the year in which use of armed force began or recommenced.

[c] The non-governmental warring parties are listed by the name of the parties using armed force. Only those parties which were active during 1996 are listed in this column.

[d] The figure for 'No. of troops in 1996' is for total armed forces (rather than for army forces, as in the *SIPRI Yearbooks 1988–1990*) of the government warring party (i.e., the government of the conflict location), and for non-government parties from the conflict location. For government and non-government parties from outside the location, the figure in this column is for total armed forces within the country that is the location of the armed conflict. Deviations from this method are indicated by a note (*) and explained.

[e] The figures for deaths refer to total battle-related deaths during the conflict. 'Mil.' and 'civ.' refer, where figures are available, to *military* and *civilian* deaths, respectively; where there is no such indication, the figure refers to total military and civilian battle-related deaths in the period or year given. Information which covers a calendar year is necessarily more tentative for the last months of the year. Experience has also shown that the reliability of figures improves over time; they are therefore revised each year.

[f] The 'change from 1995' is measured as the increase or decrease in the number of battle-related deaths in 1996 compared with the number of battle-related deaths in 1995. Although based on data that cannot be considered totally reliable, the symbols represent the following changes:

+ +   increase in battle deaths of > 50%
+   increase in battle deaths of > 10 to 50%
0   stable rate of battle deaths (± 10%)
–   decrease in battle deaths of > 10 to 50%
– –   decrease in battle deaths of > 50%

[1] Note that, although some countries are also the location of minor armed conflicts, the table lists only the major armed conflicts in those countries. Reference to the tables of major armed conflicts in previous *SIPRI Yearbooks* is given in the list of sources.

* R. Amer was responsible for the data for the conflict location of Cambodia; C. J. Åsberg for India and India–Pakistan; Birger Heldt for Angola, Liberia, Sierra Leone, Somalia, Sudan and Uganda; and A.-S. Jakobsson for the United Kingdom and Israel. M. Sollenberg was responsible for the remaining conflict locations. Ylva Nordlander and Ulrika Gustin provided assistance in the data collection.

n.a.   not applicable, since the major armed conflict was not recorded for 1995.

Note: In the last three columns ('Total deaths', 'Deaths in 1996' and 'Change from 1995'), '. .' indicates that no reliable figures, or no reliable disaggregated figures, were given in the sources consulted.

Sources: For additional information on these conflicts, see chapters in previous editions of the *SIPRI Yearbook:* Sollenberg, M. and Wallensteen, P., 'Major armed conflicts', *SIPRI Yearbook 1996: Armaments, Disarmament and International Security* (Oxford University Press: Oxford, 1996), chapter 1; Sollenberg, M. and Wallensteen, P., 'Major armed conflicts', *SIPRI Yearbook 1995: Armaments, Disarmament and International Security* (Oxford University Press: Oxford, 1995), chapter 1; Wallensteen, P. and Axell, K. 'Major armed conflicts', *SIPRI Yearbook 1994* (Oxford University Press: Oxford, 1994), chapter 2; Amer, R., Heldt, B., Landgren, S., Magnusson, K., Melander, E., Nordquist, K.-Å., Ohlson, T. and Wallensteen, P., 'Major armed conflicts', *SIPRI Yearbook 1993: World Armaments and Disarmament* (Oxford University Press: Oxford, 1993), chapter 3; Heldt, B., Wallensteen, P. and Nordquist, K.-Å., 'Major armed conflicts in 1991', *SIPRI Yearbook 1992* (Oxford University Press: Oxford, 1992), chapter 11; Lindgren, K., Heldt, B., Nordquist, K-Å. and Wallensteen, P., 'Major armed conflicts in 1990', *SIPRI Yearbook 1991* (Oxford University Press: Oxford, 1991), chapter 10; Lindgren, K., Wilson, G. K., Wallensteen, P. and Nordquist, K.-Å., 'Major armed conflicts in 1989', *SIPRI Yearbook 1990* (Oxford University Press: Oxford, 1990), chapter 10; Lindgren, K., Wilson, G. K. and Wallensteen, P., 'Major armed conflicts in 1988', *SIPRI Yearbook 1989* (Oxford University Press: Oxford, 1989), chapter 9; Wilson, G. K. and Wallensteen, P., 'Major armed conflicts in 1987', *SIPRI Yearbook 1988* (Oxford University Press: Oxford, 1988), chapter 9; and Goose, S., 'Armed conflicts in 1986, and the Iraq–Iran War', *SIPRI Yearbook 1987* (Oxford University Press: Oxford, 1987), chapter 8.

The following journals, newspapers and news agencies were consulted: *Africa Confidential* (London); *Africa Events* (London); *Africa Reporter* (New York); *Africa Research Bulletin* (Oxford); *AIM Newsletter* (London); *Asian Defence Journal* (Kuala Lumpur); *Asian Recorder* (New Delhi); *Balkan War Report* (London); *Burma Focus* (Oslo); *Burma Issues* (Bangkok); *Conflict International* (Edgware); *Dagens Nyheter* (Stockholm); Dialog Information Services Inc. (Palo Alto); *The Economist* (London); *Facts and Reports* (Amsterdam); *Far Eastern Economic Review* (Hong Kong); *Financial Times* (Frankfurt); *Fortnight Magazine* (Belfast); *The Guardian* (London); *Horn of Africa Bulletin* (Uppsala); *Jane's Defence Weekly* (Coulsdon, Surrey); *Jane's Intelligence Review* (Coulsdon, Surrey); *The Independent* (London); *International Herald Tribune* (Paris); *Kayhan International* (Teheran); *Keesing's Contemporary Archives* (Harlow, Essex); *Latin America Weekly Report* (London); *Le Monde Diplomatique* (Paris); *Mexico and Central America Report* (London); *Middle East International* (London); *Monitor* (Washington, DC); *Moscow News* (Moscow); *Newsweek* (New York); *New Times* (Moscow); *New York Times* (New York); *OMRI (Open Media Research Institute) Daily Digest* (Prague); *Pacific Report* (Canberra); *Pacific Research* (Canberra); *Reuter Business Briefing* (London); *Prism* (Washington, DC); *RFE/RL (Radio Free Europe/Radio Liberty) Research Report* (Munich); *S.A. Barometer* (Johannesburg); *Selections from Regional Press* (Institute of Regional Studies: Islamabad); *Southern African Economist* (Harare); *Southern Africa Political & Economic Monthly* (Harare); *SouthScan* (London); *Sri Lanka Monitor* (London); *The Statesman* (Calcutta); *Sudan Update* (London); *Svenska Dagbladet* (Stockholm); *Tehran Times* (Teheran); *The Times* (London); *Transition* (Prague); *World Aerospace & Defense Intelligence* (Newtown, Conn.).

Table 1A. Table of conflict locations with at least one major armed conflict in 1996

Location	Incompat- ibility[a]	Year formed/ year joined[b]	Warring parties[c]	No. of troops in 1996[d]	Total deaths[e] (incl. 1996)	Deaths in 1996	Change from 1995[f]
Europe							
Russia	Territory	1991/1994	Govt of Russia vs. Republic of Chechnya	1 500 000 5 000–10 000	10 000– 40 000	> 3 000	– –
United Kingdom	Territory	1969/1969	Govt of UK vs. Provisional IRA	226 000 ..	1 500*	8	n.a.

Provisional IRA: Provisional Irish Republican Army

*   The total number of deaths in political violence in Northern Ireland is approximately 3200. The figure given here is an estimate of the deaths incurred between the Government of the UK and the Provisional IRA; the remaining deaths were mainly caused by other paramilitary organizations such as the Ulster Volunteer Force (UVF) and the Ulster Freedom Fighters (UFF).

Middle East							
Iran	Govt Territory	1970/1991 1972/1979	Govt of Iran vs. Mujahideen e-Khalq vs. KDPI	513 000* .. 8 000	..	..	..

KDPI: Kurdish Democratic Party of Iran

*   Including the Revolutionary Guard.

Location	Incompatibility[a]	Year formed/ year joined[b]	Warring parties[c]	No. of troops in 1996[d]	Total deaths[e] (incl. 1996)	Deaths in 1996	Change from 1995[f]
Iraq	Govt	1980/1991	Govt of Iraq vs. SAIRI*	350 000–400 000	..	..	..
	Territory	1977/1980	vs. PUK	10 000** ..***			

SAIRI: Supreme Assembly for the Islamic Revolution in Iraq
PUK: Patriotic Union of Kurdistan
*   Most of the Shia rebels belong to this group.
**   Total strength of Shia rebels.
***   PUK troop strength is possibly some 10 000–12 000.

Israel	Territory	1964/1964	Govt of Israel vs. PLO groups* vs. Non-PLO groups**	170 000–180 000	1948–: >13 000	250–400 (civ.) 150 (mil.)	+

PFLP   Popular Front for the Liberation of Palestine

*   The Palestine Liberation Organization (PLO) is an umbrella organization; armed action is carried out by member organizations. Although Al-Fatah, the largest group within the PLO, did not use armed force in 1996, other groups (e.g., PFLP) which reject the 1993 Declaration of Principles on Interim Self-Government Arrangements (Oslo Agreement) did. These groups opposed the PLO leadership but were still part of the PLO in 1996.
** Examples of these groups are Hamas, PFLP–GC (Popular Front for the Liberation of Palestine–General Command), Islamic Jihad and Hizbollah.

Turkey	Territory	1974/1984	Govt of Turkey vs. PKK	500 000 10 000–12 000	>19 000	>2 000	–

PKK: Partiya Karkeren Kurdistan, Kurdish Worker's Party, or Apocus

Asia

Location	Incompatibility	Government and opposing parties	Year formed/ Year joined			
Afghanistan		Govt of Afghanistan*		>20 000**	>1 000	0
		vs. Jumbish-i Milli-ye Islami	1992/1992	..		
		vs. Taleban	1994/1994	..		
Bangladesh	Territory	Govt of Bangladesh		117 500	<25	0
		vs. JSS/SB	1971/1982	2 000–5 000	3 000–3 500	
Cambodia	Govt	Govt of Cambodia		130 000*	>25 500**	..
		vs. PDK	1979/1979	5 000–10 000		
India	Territory	Govt of India		1 145 000	>20 000*	>500*
		vs. Kashmir insurgents**	../1989	..		
	Territory	vs BdSF	../1992	..		
		vs. ULFA	1982/1988	..		

Afghanistan

* It is unclear whether fighting occurred between the Government of Afghanistan and the Hezb-i-Islami in 1996.
** Note that this figure includes deaths in the fighting since 1992, in which other parties than those listed above also participated.

Bangladesh

JSS/SB: Parbatya Chattagram Jana Sanghati Samiti (Chittagong Hill Tracts People's Co-ordination Association/Shanti Bahini [Peace Force])

Cambodia

PDK: Party of Democratic Kampuchea (Khmer Rouge)

* Including all militias.
** For figures for battle-related deaths in this conflict prior to 1979, see *SIPRI Yearbook 1990*, p. 405, and note p, p. 418. Regarding battle-related deaths in 1979–89, that is, not only involving the Govt and PDK, the only figure available is from official Vietnamese sources, indicating that 25 300 Vietnamese soldiers died in Cambodia. An estimated figure for the period 1979–89, based on various sources, is >50 000, and for 1989 >1000. The figures for 1990, 1991 and 1992 were lower.

India

BdSF: Bodo Security Force
ULFA: United Liberation Front of Assam

* Only the Kashmir conflict.
** Several groups are active, some of the most important being the Jammu and Kashmir Liberation Front (JKLF), the Hizb-e-Mujahideen and the Harkat-ul-Ansar.

Location	Incompatibility[a]	Year formed/ year joined[b]	Warring parties[c]	No. of troops in 1996[d]	Total deaths[e] (incl. 1996)	Deaths in 1996	Change from 1995[f]
India–Pakistan	Territory	1947/1996	Govt of India vs. Govt of Pakistan	1 145 000 587 000	..	..	n.a.
Indonesia	Territory	1975/1975	Govt of Indonesia vs. Fretilin	300 000 100–200	15 000– 16 000 (mil.)	< 50	0
Fretilin:	Frente Revolucionára Timorense de Libertação e Independência (Revolutionary Front for an Independent East Timor)						
Myanmar	Territory	1948/1948	Govt of Myanmar vs. KNU	300 000 4 000	1948–50: 8 000 1981–88: 5 000–8 500	< 100	– –
KNU: Karen National Union							
The Philippines	Govt	1968/1968	Govt of the Philippines vs. NPA	107 000 8 000	21 000– 25 000*	< 50	–
NPA: New People's Army							
* Official military sources claim that 6500 civilians were killed during the period 1985–91.							
Sri Lanka	Territory	1976/1983	Govt of Sri Lanka vs. LTTE	120 000 6 000–10 000	> 35 000	> 3 000	–
LTTE: Liberation Tigers of Tamil Eelam							
Tajikistan	Govt	1991/1992	Govt of Tajikistan, CIS Collective Peacekeeping Force in Tajikistan/ CIS Border Troops* vs. United Tajik Opposition**	5 000–7 000 c. 25 000 ..	20 000– 50 000	> 300	–

* The CIS operation includes Russian border guards and peacekeeping troops with minor reinforcements from Kazakhstan, Kyrgystan and Uzbekistan.

** The major groups constituting the United Tajik Opposition (formerly recorded as the Popular Democratic Army) are the Islamic Resistance Movement, the Democratic Party of Tajikistan and the Rastokhez People's Movement.

Africa

Location		Govt/Territory, year	Warring parties	Total deaths	Troops 1996	Deaths in 1996	Change
Algeria	Govt	1992/1992 1993/1993	Govt of Algeria vs. FIS* vs. GIA	150 000	30 000– 50 000	>2 000	..**
Sierra Leone	Govt	1991/1991	Govt of Sierra Leone vs. RUF	12 000–18 000 2 000–4 000	>3 000	200–500	–
Somalia	Govt	1991/1991	Govt of Somalia* vs. USC faction (Aideed)	.. 1 000	..	300–600	+
Sudan	Territory	1980/1983	Govt of Sudan vs. SPLA (Garang faction)	80 000 30 000–50 000	37 000– 40 000 (mil.)*	>2 000	+

FIS: Front Islamique du Salut, *Jibhat al-Inqath* (Islamic Salvation Front)

GIA: Groupe Islamique Armé (Armed Islamic Group)

* The Islamic Salvation Army (Armée Islamique du Salut, AIS) is considered to be the armed wing of the FIS. There are also several other armed Islamic groups under the FIS military command.

** The minimum number of deaths in 1996 is 2000, but it has not been possible to determine the change from 1995.

RUF: Revolutionary United Front

USC: United Somali Congress

* Taken to be the USC faction (Mahdi).

SPLA: Sudanese People's Liberation Army

* Figure for up to 1991.

Location	Incompat- ibility[a]	Year formed/ year joined[b]	Warring parties[c]	No. of troops in 1996[d]	Total deaths[e] (incl. 1996)	Deaths in 1996	Change from 1995[f]
Uganda	Govt	1993/1994	Govt of Uganda vs. LRA	40 000–50 000 2 000	>1 000	200–500	n.a.
LRA:	Lord's Resistance Army						
Central and South America							
Colombia	Govt	1949/1978 1965/1978	Govt of Colombia vs. FARC vs. ELN	146 400 5 700 2 500	.:*	400–1 000	0
FARC:	Fuerzas Armadas Revolucionarias Colombianas (Revolutionary Armed Forces of Colombia)						
ELN:	Ejército de Liberación Nacional (National Liberation Army)						
*	In the past three decades the civil wars of Colombia have claimed a total of some 30 000 lives.						
Guatemala	Govt	1967/1968	Govt of Guatemala vs. URNG	44 200 800–1 100	<2 800 (mil.) <43 500 (civ.)	<25	– –
URNG:	Unidad Revolucionaria Nacional Guatemalteca (Guatemalan National Revolutionary Unity). URNG is a coalition of three main groups: Ejército Guerillero de los Pobres (EGP), Fuerzas Armadas Rebeldes (FAR), and Organización del Pueblo en Armas (ORPA)						
Peru	Govt	1980/1981 1984/1986	Govt of Peru vs. Sendero Luminoso vs. MRTA	115 000 3 000 500	>28 000	50–200	–
Sendero Luminoso:	Shining Path						
MRTA:	Movimiento Revolucionario Tupac Amaru (Tupac Amaru Revolutionary Movement)						

2. Armed conflict prevention, management and resolution

TREVOR FINDLAY*

I. Introduction

Although no armed conflicts were definitively resolved in 1996, historic breakthroughs occurred towards ending decades-old but little known conflicts in the southern Philippines and Guatemala. Sierra Leone also surprised the world with a credible peace agreement, while rejuvenated ones were negotiated for Liberia and Tajikistan after earlier ones had broken down. Armed conflict in Chechnya ended through negotiations and then Russian withdrawal, but a mutually acceptable resolution of the conflict remains distant.[1] Talks continued between the conflicting parties to internal conflicts in Azerbaijan, Georgia and Moldova, where cease-fires were largely adhered to but no agreements reached. Peace talks continued in attempts to resolve numerous inter-state disputes that had produced armed conflict in the past, including those between Eritrea and Yemen, Peru and Ecuador, and Indonesia and Portugal (over East Timor). Despite progress in some areas the high expectations engendered by peace processes initiated in previous years in Angola, Niger, the Middle East,[2] Northern Ireland, and Bosnia and Herzegovina remained unfulfilled in 1996, although in most of these cases armed conflict at least ceased or significantly waned.

Conflict management, in the sense of controlling the level of violence but without an accompanying peace process, was common, including in those cases where long-standing peacekeeping operations were maintained, such as in Cyprus. Even management efforts failed as cease-fires collapsed in Bougainville in Papua New Guinea, in the Kurdish area of Iraq and in Sudan.

Conflict prevention was notably applied to potential maritime conflicts during the year, including those between Greece and Turkey and over the Spratlys in the South China Sea.[3] Elsewhere in East Asia, despite heightened tension, driven by nationalist opinion, over island disputes between Japan on the one hand and China and Taiwan on the other,[4] and between Japan and South Korea, the governments themselves were careful to prevent escalation

---

[1] For details of this and other conflicts in former Soviet republics see chapter 4 in this volume.

[2] For details see chapter 3 in this volume.

[3] Chinese and Association of South-East Asian Nations (ASEAN) officials talked directly in June 1996, *International Herald Tribune*, 11 June 1996, p. 4.

[4] The islets in question are called the Senkakus by Japan and the Diaoyus by China.

* Olga Hardardóttir of the SIPRI Project on Peacekeeping and Regional Security assisted in researching this chapter.

to armed clashes.[5] While all peacekeeping operations have a preventive function, the only explicitly preventive deployment force, UNPREDEP in Macedonia, continued its mission. In the ultimate in armed conflict prevention,
Malaysia and Indonesia and Botswana and Namibia responsibly agreed to
send their respective maritime disputes to the International Court of Justice
(ICJ) before they came anywhere near military action.

Armed conflict in Afghanistan, Algeria, Burundi, Somalia, Sri Lanka,
Turkey and Zaire waxed and waned, seemingly oblivious to any attempts to
prevent, manage or resolve it. New or renewed intra-state conflict flared in
Colombia, Mexico and Peru. There were also several new but minor inter-
state clashes between India and Pakistan; Uganda and Sudan; the USA and
Iraq; Zaire and Burundi; Rwanda and Uganda; and North and South Korea.
Israel and Hezbollah guerrillas again clashed in Lebanon.

Although the United Nations (UN) continued its involvement in relation to
most armed conflicts and crises,[6] its peacekeeping activity again declined in
size, prominence and newsworthiness. The multilateral non-UN operation in
Bosnia and Herzegovina—the Implementation Force (IFOR)—and its accompanying civilian components remained the largest peacekeeping mission in
1996, bringing peace to the country but failing to achieve implementation of
key non-military elements of the 1995 Dayton Agreement.[7] It was replaced by
a smaller but similarly constituted Stabilization Force (SFOR) in December.
Another multilateral force, led by Canada, was to be assembled in November
to assist in repatriating and providing humanitarian relief for millions of
refugees returning from eastern Zaire to Rwanda, but was progressively scaled
back as the crisis receded and eventually cancelled. Peacekeeping reform continued at the UN but the organization's continuing financial crisis and lack of
institution-wide reform placed a fundamental brake on expanded UN activity
in conflict prevention, management and resolution. Conceptual progress was
made in regard to conflict prevention.

Hopes continued to be placed in regional efforts when the UN is forced to
leave off, particularly in Africa. Several new initiatives attempted to
strengthen that continent's capabilities for conflict prevention, management
and resolution but were hampered by political, organizational and financial
barriers. Individual countries, especially the USA and other great powers,
again played prominent, sometimes pre-eminent, roles in preventing, managing and resolving armed conflict. Individuals and non-governmental actors
occasionally supplemented these efforts usefully.

[5] The 2 barren rocky islets disputed by Japan and South Korea are known as Takeshima by Japan and
Tok-to by Korea. *The Economist*, 12 Oct. 1996, pp. 69–70; and *Jane's Defence Weekly*, 2 Oct. 1996,
p. 21.
[6] For a comprehensive overview see United Nations, The 50th Anniversary Report of the Secretary-
General on the work of the Organization (UN Department of Public Information: New York, 1996).
[7] The text of the General Framework Agreement for Peace in Bosnia and Herzegovina is reproduced
in *SIPRI Yearbook 1996: Armaments, Disarmament and International Security* (Oxford University
Press: Oxford, 1996), pp. 232–33.

This chapter surveys efforts undertaken in 1996 to prevent, manage or resolve armed conflict between or within states.[8] Section II focuses on the UN, the key multilateral actor, while section III deals separately with peace-keeping. Section IV surveys the UN role in peace enforcement, while section V analyses the role of regional and other multilateral organizations. Section VI provides an overview of the role of other actors, comprising individual states, ad hoc groups of states, non-governmental organizations (NGOs) and prominent individuals.

II. The United Nations

While the UN retained its pre-eminent role in international conflict prevention, management and resolution, its limitations became more starkly apparent in 1996. Major reform, which many hoped would be stimulated by the 50th anniversary celebrations, was conspicuously absent because of disagreements over the scope, pace and type of reform, vested interests in particular UN activities and inertia. The financial crisis remained acute, impinging on a range of UN activities in the area of peace and security, including ambitious plans for further improving the launching, management and operation of peacekeeping missions. The Security Council, chastened by its Somalian, Rwandan and Bosnian experiences and escalating costs, declined to launch substantial new UN-funded peace operations. The only large-scale operation attempted in 1996, in Zaire/Rwanda, was intended to be financed and managed by the participating states. As the year ended the Secretary-Generalship was itself in crisis, with the USA vetoing a second term for Boutros Boutros-Ghali and his supporters initially refusing to accept an alternative. Eventually consensus was reached on Kofi Annan of Ghana, Under Secretary-General for Peace-keeping Operations, who was scheduled to take office for a five-year term on 1 January 1997.

The General Assembly, Secretary-General and Secretariat

The General Assembly's role in conflict prevention, management and resolution in 1996 continued to be mostly hortatory. It did, however, challenge the Security Council's traditional conceptualization of the Western Sahara dispute by calling for direct talks between the parties, which it treated equally for the first time. A subsequent Council resolution followed this lead.[9] The Assembly also adopted UN Model Rules for the Conciliation of Disputes Between States.[10] The report of the Assembly's High-level Open-ended Working Group on the Strengthening of the United Nations System, unlike the products of similar groups, did contain substantive proposals for reform, such as

---

[8] Institutionalized disarmament and arms control measures, including security- and confidence-building measures, while clearly a form of conflict prevention, are considered elsewhere in this volume.

[9] See Chopra, J., 'Quitting Western Sahara', *Geopolitics and International Boundaries*, vol. 1, no. 1 (summer 1996), pp. 70–74; and UN Security Council resolution 1084 (1996), 27 Nov. 1996.

[10] UN General Assembly Resolution 50/50, 11 Dec. 1995.

enhancing resources available to the President of the General Assembly to permit him or her to play a more active role and making future UN personnel salary increases performance-based.[11]

The Secretary-General continued his hectic pace. His special representatives, special envoys and other emissaries were actively engaged, on a resident or visiting basis, in implementing mandates from the General Assembly or Security Council in regard to Afghanistan, Burundi, Cambodia, Cyprus, East Timor, El Salvador, Georgia, Guatemala, Haiti, Liberia, Macedonia, Myanmar, Nigeria, Papua New Guinea, Rwanda, Sierra Leone, Somalia, Tajikistan and Western Sahara.[12]

With no end to Afghanistan's civil war in sight the UN managed in November to convene for the first time a one-day meeting in New York of all the parties involved (plus the Organization of the Islamic Conference) but with no notable outcome.[13] The Secretary-General's Special Mission to Afghanistan, led by Special Envoy Norbert Holl, continued to work for a cease-fire and had its political, military and civilian police staff boosted.[14] In October, in view of the deteriorating situation along the Zairean border with Rwanda and Burundi, the Secretary-General appointed Canadian Ambassador to the USA, Raymond Chrétien, as his Special Envoy to the Great Lakes Region.[15] The second meeting of the All-Inclusive Intra-East Timor Dialogue was held in March at Burg Schlaining in Austria[16] but Indonesia was likely to be even less enthusiastic about such meetings after two of the key opposition participants, Fretilin leader José Ramos-Horta and Bishop Carlos Felipe Ximenes Belo, were awarded the 1996 Nobel Peace Prize.[17] Boutros-Ghali also convened the seventh, eighth and ninth rounds of inconclusive foreign minister-level talks between Indonesia and Portugal in London, Geneva and New York, respectively.[18] In East Timor itself unrest flared as the year ended.

In the conceptual area the Secretary-General made a major change to the terminology employed in his 1992 *An Agenda for Peace* by sensibly conceding that 'preventive diplomacy', which had previously been taken to include such patently non-diplomatic approaches as the deployment of preventive military forces, should now be known in UN parlance as 'preventive action'.[19] Preventive diplomacy will henceforth be seen as just one kind of preventive

[11] United Nations, Report of the High-level Open-ended Working Group on the Strengthening of the United Nations System, UN document A/50/24, 23 July 1996.

[12] United Nations (note 6), p. 193.

[13] *Daily Highlights* (UN Department of Public Information), 19 Nov. 1996, URL<http://www.un.org/News/dh/>.

[14] *Daily Highlights* (UN Department of Public Information), 2 Dec. 1996.

[15] *Daily Highlights* (UN Department of Public Information), 30 Oct. 1996.

[16] United Nations, Press Release SG/SM/96/70, Geneva, 18 Mar. 1996.

[17] Press release, The Norwegian Nobel Institute, Oslo, 11 Oct. 1996.

[18] United Nations, Question of East Timor: progress report of the Secretary-General, UN document A/51/361, 16 Sep. 1996.

[19] United Nations (note 6), pp. 193–94. Boutros-Ghali, B., An Agenda for Peace: Preventive Diplomacy, Peacemaking and Peace-keeping, Report of the Secretary-General pursuant to the statement adopted by the Summit Meeting of the Security Council on 31 January 1992, UN document A/47/277 (S/2411), 17 June 1992 is reproduced in *SIPRI Yearbook 1993: World Armaments and Disarmament* (Oxford University Press: Oxford, 1993), appendix 2A, pp. 66–80.

action, along with other means such as preventive deployment, preventive disarmament, preventive humanitarian action and preventive peace-building. However, since all UN activities, including social, economic and humanitarian, might be considered preventive of conflict, there is now a need to more narrowly conceptualize the meaning of 'preventive' for it to have analytical and practical utility. Boutros-Ghali also attempted to disperse some of the confusion surrounding the term 'peacemaking' by reserving it for diplomatic means used to persuade parties to cease hostilities and negotiate a peaceful settlement. Peacemaking thus excludes the use of force to end hostilities, an activity known in UN parlance as 'peace enforcement'.

In regard to conflict prevention the Secretariat's Department of Humanitarian Affairs (DHA) significantly augmented its capacity for early-warning of humanitarian disasters and assessment of appropriate responses by assuming management of ReliefWeb, an on-line global information system.[20] Its website on the World Wide Web was inaugurated on 3 June,[21] featuring five continuing complex emergencies: the Great Lakes region of Africa, Angola, Liberia, the Caucasus and Sudan. ReliefWeb will be progressively developed to include: 24-hour access to a central repository of continuously updated information and news; national civil disaster inventories; and a management plan that includes agreements with donors, other agencies and relief NGOs for information exchanges. It was not clear how ReliefWeb would relate to the UN Secretariat's existing internal Humanitarian Early Warning System (HEWS).[22] Norway meanwhile announced a $1 million donation to help establish a UN Fund for Preventive Action.[23]

The particular problems of Africa again attracted considerable attention from the Secretary-General, the Secretariat and, for the first time, the UN system as a whole. On 15 March Boutros-Ghali launched a 10-year, $25 billion UN System-wide Special Initiative on Africa, the UN system's most significant mobilization of support for the development of a single continent and its largest ever coordinated action.[24] To support peace processes in the continent it will help augment the conflict prevention, management and resolution capacity of the Organization of African Unity (OAU) and selected organs of civil society engaged in peace-building; and promote the use of mass media, particularly radio, for peace-building. Three subregional centres are envisaged to promote conflict prevention and resolution, linking public and private organizations within Africa to the UN and to NGOs involved in human rights and social justice issues.

[20] Following information supplied by the UN Department of Humanitarian Affairs, Geneva: 'Relief-Web mandate and objectives', 4 Apr. 1996; Project ReliefWeb, rev. 09/96; and ReliefWeb project description, June 1996, rev. 09/96. ReliefWeb began in 1994 as a combined project of US Government agencies and NGOs involved in international humanitarian relief.

[21] URL <http://www.reliefweb.int>.

[22] For background see Findlay, T., 'Conflict prevention, management and resolution', *SIPRI Yearbook 1996* (note 7), p. 35.

[23] *International Peacekeeping News*, vol. 2, no. 4 (Sep./Oct. 1996), p. 28.

[24] 'The United Nations system-wide special initiative on Africa', *UN Chronicle*, no. 2 (1996), pp. 4–9.

The Secretariat continued its involvement in electoral assistance and observation at roughly the same level of activity as in previous years.[25] In particular it coordinated electoral observers for the presidential and legislative elections in Côte d'Ivoire and Tanzania, assisted Brazil in securing voting equipment and helped organize the successful elections in Sierra Leone. Despite its wealth of experience the UN was not asked to assist in organizing elections in Bosnia and Herzegovina because of disenchantment with its previous record in that country, with the result that the Organization for Security and Co-operation in Europe (OSCE), inexperienced in such matters, struggled with the task. The UN was, however, charged with organizing, assisting with and certifying the results of elections in the neighbouring, less problematic area of Eastern Slavonia in 1997.

The Security Council

While the Council continued to meet intensively, the scale of its activity, at least as measured by the number of resolutions and presidential statements, continued to fall from the all-time highs of 1992–93.[26] The trend towards unanimity in adopting resolutions did, however, largely continue. Only one draft resolution, dealing with the situation in Lebanon, failed to be adopted owing to the lack of required votes in its favour. With the exception of the 'unofficial' veto by the USA of Boutros-Ghali for a second term as Secretary-General in a supposedly secret 'straw poll' in November, no veto was cast in 1996. However, the usual unanimity on extending the life of existing peace operations broke down over Haiti, with China threatening to veto, for extraneous reasons, recommended force levels for that operation.

With the problem of Bosnia now largely out of UN hands, the Council's major preoccupation was with Africa. From 1 January to 5 December it adopted 21 resolutions on African issues out of 51. The situations in Angola, Liberia, Sierra Leone, Somalia and in the Great Lakes region (particularly Burundi, Rwanda and Zaire) were deemed particularly troublesome. The Council's international commission of inquiry into the attempted assassination of the President of Burundi in October 1993 and subsequent massacres reported that acts of genocide had occurred against Tutsis and Hutus but that high-level responsibility could not be determined, nor could individuals be identified to permit prosecution.[27] The report noted that guilt for the massacres was so widespread that no legal system could cope and that any chance of justice must await the restoration of law and order and good governance in the country. Urgent pleas by the Secretary-General and offers of troops by Ethiopia, Tanzania and Uganda failed to move the Council to launch a preventive peacekeeping operation in Burundi.

---

[25] See graph in United Nations (note 6), p. 319.

[26] United Nations (note 6), p. 14.

[27] United Nations, Letter dated 25 July 1996 from the Secretary-General addressed to the President of the Security Council, UN document, S/1996/682, 22 Aug. 1996.

Despite the urgings of the Secretary-General and particular Council members no significant initiatives were taken in regard to any other African conflicts in 1996. In regard to the refugee crisis in eastern Zaire, the tragic press of events eventually induced Canada, France and Spain, belatedly joined by the USA, acting outside the Council, to cobble together plans for an international intervention force. As in the cases of Bosnia and Rwanda in previous years, the Council's disarray over Burundi and Zaire—caused notably by the lack of bold and imaginative leadership by the USA and the UK and the acquiescence of China and Russia—damaged its credibility as the principal protector of international peace and security in 1996.

The Council did, however, manage to respond to continuing concerns of member states about the lack of transparency in its work. As a result of a proposal by France, the Council held a number of open meetings, chaired by the Council President, for consultation and exchange of information with countries contributing troops to peacekeeping operations and on the situations in Afghanistan, Angola, Liberia and Somalia. The Council undertook to hold such meetings prior to new missions being established and old ones altered. It also initiated a series of open 'orientation debates' with the participation of non-members on such subjects as developments in Afghanistan, the Israelis' opening of a tunnel near Muslim holy sites in Jerusalem, Israeli attacks on Lebanon and demining in the context of peacekeeping.[28] However, no overall reform of the Council was in sight despite the close attention given to the issue by the General Assembly's long-winded but hopelessly deadlocked Open-ended Working Group on the subject.[29]

International legal mechanisms

In 1996 the International Court of Justice had 13 cases before it, one fewer than in 1995. Eleven were contentious and two sought advisory opinions. One new contentious case was added, while two were removed from the General List. To manage this heavy case-load the Court deliberated in three cases simultaneously. In his annual report to the General Assembly, ICJ President Judge Mohammed Bedjaoui of Algeria said that despite greatly increased activity in its 50th anniversary year, the Court faced material difficulties including staff cuts and decreased financial support.[30] As a result of such challenges the Rules Committee of the Court began a review of the ICJ's operations.

In July the Court dealt with the two requests for advisory opinions on the use or threat of use of nuclear weapons, dismissing the request by the World Health Organization and rendering an opinion on that sought by the General

[28] Security Council press release SC/6313, 14 Jan. 1997.
[29] United Nations, Report of the Open-ended Working Group on the Question of Equitable Representation on and Increase in Membership of the Security Council and Other Matters Related to the Security Council, UN document A/50/47, 13 Sep. 1996.
[30] *Daily Highlights* (UN Department of Public Information), 16 Oct. 1996.

Table 2.1. Cases before the International Court of Justice, 1996

- Application of the Convention on the Prevention and Punishment of the Crime of Genocide (Bosnia and Herzegovina v. Yugoslavia (Serbia and Montenegro))
- Aerial Incident of 3 July 1988 (Iran v. USA)
- Maritime Delimitation between Guinea-Bissau and Senegal
- Maritime Delimitation and Territorial Questions between Qatar and Bahrain
- Questions of Interpretation and Application of the 1971 Montreal Convention arising from the Aerial Incident at Lockerbie (Libya v. United Kingdom)
- Questions of Interpretation and Application of the 1971 Montreal Convention arising from the Aerial Incident at Lockerbie (Libya v. USA)
- Oil Platforms (Iran v. USA)
- Gabcikovo–Ngymaros Project (Hungary/Slovakia)
- Bakassi Peninsula (Cameroon v. Nigeria)
- Legality of the Use by a State of Nuclear Weapons in Armed Conflict (World Health Organization)*
- Legality of the Threat or Use of Nuclear Weapons (UN General Assembly)*
- Fishing Rights (Spain v. Canada)
- Boundary and legal status of Kasikili/Sedudu Island (Botswana/Namibia)

Note: Cases listed as one party versus another are those in which one party (the first mentioned) has brought to the ICJ a case against another party; the others are cases where both parties jointly seek a Court ruling. Cases marked with an asterisk (*) are those in which an advisory opinion has been sought by one party.

Source: UN, The 50th Anniversary Report of the Secretary-General on the work of the Organization (UN Department of Public Information: New York, 1996), pp. 27–31.

Assembly.[31] The maritime delimitation case between Guinea-Bissau and Senegal and the case between the USA and Iran were removed from the Court's docket after agreement between the parties. In the case of Cameroon versus Nigeria the Court ordered in March that both parties observe their foreign ministers' agreement at Kara, Togo, on 17 February 1996, to cease all hostilities in the Bakassi Peninsula; ensure that the presence of any armed forces on the peninsula did not extend beyond the positions occupied prior to 3 February; take all necessary measures to conserve evidence relevant to the case within the disputed area; and lend every assistance to the fact-finding mission which the UN Secretary-General proposed sending to the peninsula.[32] Also in July the Court decided, against the objections of Yugoslavia (Serbia and Montenegro), that it had jurisdiction in the genocide case brought against Yugoslavia by Bosnia and Herzegovina: the case remains on the ICJ docket. In May a new case was added to the Court's case-load when Botswana and Namibia jointly notified it of their agreement to submit to the Court their dispute over the boundary around Kasikili/Sedudu Island. Future maritime disputes between states parties to the 1982 United Nations Convention on the Law of the Sea may be handled by the convention's Tribunal, based in Hamburg, Germany, which was established during the year.[33]

---

[31] See chapter 11 in this volume for details. See also Moore, M., 'World Court says mostly no to nuclear weapons', *Bulletin of the Atomic Scientists*, vol. 52, no. 5 (Sep./Oct. 1996), pp. 39–42.

[32] United Nations (note 6), pp. 29–30.

[33] *UN Chronicle*, no. 2 (1996), p. 71.

The International Criminal Tribunal for the Former Yugoslavia, established in the Hague in 1993, had by September issued more than 70 indictments and by the end of the year had 7 indictees in custody.[34] One trial was concluded and sentence passed, the first international war crimes case successfully prosecuted since the post-World War II Nuremberg and Tokyo trials.[35] Warrants were issued during the year for the most well-known suspects, former Bosnian Serb leader Radovan Karadzic and Bosnian Serb General Ratko Mladic after public (Rule 61) hearings of evidence against them had confirmed their indictments.[36] IFOR encountered strong criticism, including that from the tribunal itself, for continuing to refuse to arrest these and other suspects. Tribunal officials also complained of a lack of international public and political support and lack of cooperation from Yugoslavia and the Republika Srpska, both of which feared that their current or past leader would be brought to trial.[37]

The International Criminal Tribunal for Rwanda, established in Arusha, Tanzania, in 1994, was in much worse shape. It postponed its first trial until January 1997 for legal reasons and by October had indicted only 25 of 80 000 suspects held.[38] The tribunal also faced serious administrative problems, including lack of funds, poor facilities and corrupt, incompetent support staff, and a scandalous lack of cooperation from Kenya, whose President, Daniel Arap Moi, threatened to arrest court officials if they entered Kenyan territory.[39] The UN and the USA conducted investigations into the tribunal's management difficulties. The USA none the less pledged further funding.[40] Justice Richard Goldstone of South Africa was succeeded by Canadian judge and criminal law expert Louise Arbour as Chief Prosecutor for both the Yugoslav and Rwandan tribunals.

The creation of an international criminal court which would in future obviate the need for such special tribunals inched forward as the Preparatory Committee on the Establishment of an International Criminal Court, mandated by the General Assembly in 1995, undertook a comprehensive analysis of the draft statute elaborated by the International Law Commission.[41] There was general agreement that the cases prosecuted by the court should be limited to 'core crimes' of international concern—genocide, war crimes and crimes against humanity—but differences persisted over whether the so far undefined crime of aggression should be included. The General Assembly in December asked that a new draft be ready for finalization and adoption by a plenipotentiary conference in 1998.

---

[34] *International Peacekeeping News*, vol. 2, no. 4 (Sep./Oct. 1996), p. 17; and *Daily Highlights* (UN Department of Public Information), 20 Nov. 1996.

[35] *Daily Highlights* (UN Department of Public Information), 29 Nov. 1996.

[36] Klarin, M., 'Appointment in the Hague', *Tribunal*, no. 5 (Sep./Oct. 1996), p. 1.

[37] Klarin, M., 'Crisis time in the Hague', *Tribunal*, no. 4 (June/July 1996), p. 1.

[38] *Wireless File* (US Information Service, US Embassy: Stockholm, 28 Oct. 1996).

[39] Chege, M., 'Africa's murderous professors', *National Interest*, winter 1996/1997, p. 37.

[40] *International Herald Tribune*, 1 Nov. 1996, p. 10; and *Wireless File* (US Information Service, US Embassy: Stockholm, 28 Oct. 1996).

[41] *UN Chronicle*, no. 2 (1996), p. 70.

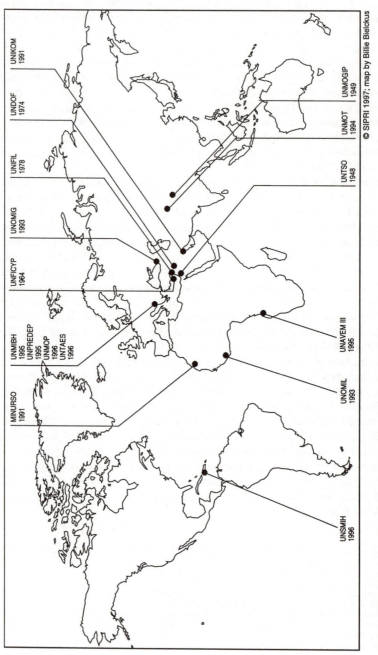

Figure 2.1. UN peacekeeping operations in the field as of 31 December 1996

Note: Dates refer to the start of operations.

III. UN peacekeeping operations

The year was one of further contraction and consolidation for UN peace-keeping owing to financial difficulties, streamlining of existing missions and the reluctance of the Security Council to launch new missions. Significant reform efforts continued.

Having relinquished its predominant role in Bosnia and Herzegovina and with the end of several large-scale African missions, UN peacekeeping had a lower profile and was less controversial than for many years. Although the number of missions, 16, remained the same at the end of 1996 as at the end of 1995, this disguised the fact that two substantial operations, the UN Confidence Restoration Operation in Croatia (UNCRO, which had begun life as the UN Protection Force, UNPROFOR) and the UN Assistance Mission for Rwanda (UNAMIR) were replaced by only one substantial mission, the UN Transitional Administration for Eastern Slavonia, Baranja and Western Sirmium (UNTAES), and one of the tiniest observer missions ever authorized, the 28-person strong UN Mission of Observers in Prevlaka (UNMOP) on Croatia's Prevlaka peninsula. UNAMIR was withdrawn by April at Rwanda's request despite UN efforts to convince the government of its value. There was a proposal that it be replaced with an all-civilian non-peacekeeping UN Office for Rwanda (UNOR), headed by a Special Representative of the Secretary-General, to assist with national reconciliation, strengthening of the judicial system, the return of refugees and rehabilitation of infrastructure.[42] Other long-standing missions were scaled back after efficiency audits and under pressure of the UN's financial crisis. These changes left the UN Angola Verification Mission (UNAVEM III) as the UN's largest peacekeeping operation. There was also a trend in the Security Council towards mandating shorter and conditional mandates for peacekeeping operations, including those in Angola and Liberia.

The number of troops under the UN flag also dropped again, from roughly 31 000 at the end of 1995 to roughly 25 000 at the end of 1996, the lowest in five years.[43] Costs fell correspondingly. The projected peacekeeping budget for July 1996 to June 1997 was $1.3 billion, a drop of well over 50 per cent on the $3 billion of the previous 12 months.[44] Fewer countries participated in peacekeeping: 71 compared to 76 at the end of 1995.[45] While funding was cut for the Department of Peace-keeping Operations (DPKO) as part of budgetary stringencies at UN headquarters, Kofi Annan reported that it would be able to 'preserve its structural integrity in order to maintain the Organization's capacity to manage existing operations effectively and, if necessary, to launch

[42] Security Council Press Release SC/6313, 14 Jan. 1997.
[43] Information from UN Department of Public Information, New York, 10 Jan. 1997.
[44] *International Peacekeeping News*, vol. 2, no. 2 (May/June 1996), p. 23.
[45] Background Note: United Nations Peace-keeping Operations, UN Department of Public Information, New York, 16 Dec. 1996.

new operations'.[46] In 1996 the DPKO maintained about 400 staff, including 100 military officers seconded from governments.[47]

The UN role in the former Yugoslavia remained important, despite its presence in Bosnia and Herzegovina being secondary to that of IFOR and the civilian structure headed by High Representative Carl Bildt (both non-UN institutions established under the 1995 Dayton Agreement). The UN High Commissioner for Refugees (UNHCR) remained responsible for humanitarian relief and refugees. While the former declined in importance as a semblance of normal economic and commercial activity returned to the country, the latter should have increased as refugees returned to their previous places of residence—a right enshrined in the Dayton Agreement. While a trickle of refugees bravely made the attempt, for the most part return of refugees was the great unfulfilled promise of Dayton, precluded by continuing ethnic hatred and distrust and, at least on the part of the Republika Srpska, deliberate government policy.

The UN also provided the civilian police (CivPol) component for implementation of the Dayton Agreement, the International Police Task Force (IPTF). Hampered by slow recruitment of personnel and other teething problems, especially its relationship with IFOR, the IPTF gradually proved increasingly effective in monitoring the behaviour of local police and providing assistance and training. However, it clearly could not be ubiquitous and continuing violations of human rights occurred on all sides of the ethnic divide. It also became increasingly apparent that there was an operational gap between the functions and capabilities of the unarmed CivPols and those of the heavily armed but military-oriented IFOR in situations such as continuing ethnic cleansing, attempted large-scale return of displaced persons and refugees, and rioting crowds. It was not clear whether the follow-on force to IFOR would be able to fill this gap. The UN's activities in Bosnia and Herzegovina were coordinated by the UN Mission in Bosnia and Herzegovina (UNMIB), an umbrella structure rather than a peacekeeping operation in its own right.

On the other hand UNTAES, established in January, was a full-scale UN peacekeeping operation, with complex responsibilities for supervising and assisting in the demilitarization of the region and its transfer from local Serbian control to Croatian Government control in accordance with their 1995 Basic Agreement. Initially the UN Secretary-General and Secretariat were reluctant to take on the task because of their salutary experience with peace enforcement in Bosnia and Herzegovina and because of the unwillingness of the Security Council to provide the 11 300 troops believed necessary.[48] The UN was eventually placated by a NATO commitment to provide close air support to defend or help UNTAES withdraw (although this had proved

---

[46] United Nations, Comprehensive review of the whole question of peace-keeping operations in all their aspects: report of the Special Committee on Peace-keeping Operations, UN document A/51/130, 7 May 1996, p. 2.

[47] Year in Review 1996: United Nations Peace Missions, UN Department of Public Information, New York, Dec. 1996, p. 14.

[48] Bothe, M., 'The peace process in Eastern Slavonia', International Peacekeeping, vol. 3, no. 1 (Dec. 1995/Jan. 1996), pp. 6–7.

problematic in the Bosnia and Herzegovina case) and by providing the force with robust rules of engagement and substantial military capability, including attack helicopters, tanks and artillery.[49] In addition, an American, Jacques Klein, was appointed Transitional Administrator and a US Major-General, Jozef Schoups, Force Commander, ensuring that cooperation and coordination with IFOR in neighbouring Bosnia and Herzegovina would be more likely.

UNTAES performed well, using its military capability to good effect in bringing about demilitarization and ensuring steady progress towards eventual Croatian control. However, Croatia's unwillingness to provide funding for several aspects of the mission, as agreed, and its demand for an end to UNTAES after only a year strained relations with the operation and the Security Council.[50] By the end of the year it appeared that UNTAES would be withdrawn over three months beginning in mid-1997.[51]

UNMOP was established in March 1996 to permit UN observers who had been monitoring the situation on the Prevlaka peninsula under UNCRO's mandate to continue their operations. The situation there steadily improved as the Croatian military withdrew and partial demining was carried out in the UN zone on the Croatian side of the border and as heavy weapons were withdrawn and movement restrictions eased on both the Croatian and Montenegrin sides.[52] Meanwhile the UN's first preventive deployment, UNPREDEP in Macedonia, continued its unchallenged mission and had its mandate renewed but with a reduction to 300 troops by April 1997.[53] With Macedonia's border areas quiet, the mission expanded its role in internal conflict prevention and peace-building.

The UN Mission in Haiti (UNMIH) faced difficulties, not from the host government, which wished it to stay, but from China. In a fit of pique at the Haitian Government's continuing relationship with Taiwan and perhaps to exert its prerogatives in the Western-dominated Security Council, China first threatened to veto an extension of the mandate and then repeatedly attempted to force a reduction in the recommended troop level. Eventually Canada volunteered to provide 700 troops at its own expense to bring the force up to strength. The USA subsequently offered to pay for Pakistani troops and some of the Canadians. At the request of the Haitian Government UNMIH's mandate was altered to emphasize training and consolidation of the Haitian National Police and renamed the UN Support Mission (UNSMIH).[54] UNSMIH's mandate was renewed in December, probably for the last time in view of Chinese and Russian opposition to its extension. Ambassador Yuri Fedotov said that Russia did not believe the situation in Haiti was a threat to

---

[49] Information from Workshop on Implementation of the Dayton–Paris Peace Agreement and Options for Follow-on Forces to IFOR, organized by the Center for Defence Studies (CDI), London, the Swedish Foreign Ministry and Swedish Defence Research Organization, Stockholm, 28–29 Oct. 1996.

[50] United Nations, Report of the Secretary-General on the United Nations Transitional Administration for Eastern Slavonia, Baranja and Western Sirmium, UN document, S/1996/622, 5 Aug. 1996.

[51] *International Peacekeeping News*, vol. 2, no. 4 (Sep./Oct. 1996), p. 21.

[52] United Nations (note 6), pp. 297–98.

[53] UN Security Council resolution 1082 (1996), 27 Nov. 1996.

[54] *International Peacekeeping News*, vol. 2, no. 4 (June/Aug. 1996), p. 13. The USA deployed 49 marines to Haiti in Aug. outside of UNSMIH to provide additional security to the Haitian Government.

international peace and security and that UNSMIH represented the double standards of a Council which had rejected requests from Georgia, Tajikistan and other countries for peacekeepers.[55]

All four missions in the Middle East—the Iraq–Kuwait Observation Mission (UNIKOM), the UN Interim Force in Lebanon (UNIFIL), the UN Disengagement Observer Force (UNDOF) on the Israel–Syria border and the UN Truce Supervision Organization (UNTSO) in the Sinai—were down-sized and streamlined administratively and logistically by up to 20 per cent as a cost-cutting measure.[56] In UNIFIL's case this was despite continuing tension and occasional military exchanges in its mission area, including a devastating Israeli artillery attack on the Fijian battalion headquarters at Qana in April, which killed 100 refugees and injured several peacekeepers. A report by the Secretary-General's Military Advisor, Major-General Franklin Van Kappen, expressed doubts that the attack had been as accidental as the Israelis claimed.[57]

Also down-sized was the UN Mission for the Referendum in Western Sahara (MINURSO), not to cut costs but as a result of the faltering peace process there. Boutros-Ghali was finally forced to conclude by mid-year that the requisite cooperation of the parties did not exist to permit MINURSO to carry out its mandate to ensure the fair and efficient registration of voters for the proposed referendum on the future of the disputed territory. Registration was suspended and the Security Council agreed that the military component of the operation be reduced by 20 per cent (the rest would help stave off renewed armed conflict) and that most of the UN civilian officials and CivPols should be withdrawn.[58] The Identification Commission left the area and its records were transferred to the UN Office at Geneva for safekeeping.[59] Polisario leader Mohamed Abdelaziz threatened renewed violence, while Morocco's King Hassan declared that his country would retain the territory regardless of any referendum.[60] As the year ended continuing efforts were being made to induce the recalcitrant parties to cooperate.

One mission that increased in size was the UN Observer Mission in Georgia (UNOMIG), which acquired a Human Rights Office to monitor and encourage respect for human rights (although China warned that this should not set a precedent for all peacekeeping operations).[61] UNOMIG was also given new mine-detection and -clearance capabilities following mine-laying in the Gali region targeted specifically at the mission (which killed one military observer). Cooperation with the Collective Peace-keeping Forces of the Commonwealth

---

[55] *International Peacekeeping News*, vol. 2, no. 5 (Nov./Dec. 1996), p. 11.

[56] *International Peacekeeping News*, vol. 2, no. 3 (July/Aug. 1996), pp. 20–21; and United Nations (note 6), pp. 256–57.

[57] United Nations, Annex to Letter dated 7 May 1996 from the Secretary-General addressed to the President of the Security Council, UN document S/1996/337, 7 May 1996.

[58] United Nations, Question of Western Sahara: report of the Secretary-General, UN document A/51/428, 27 Sep. 1996.

[59] *UN Chronicle*, no. 2 (1996), p. 54.

[60] *International Peacekeeping News*, vol. 2, no. 3 (July/Aug. 1996), p. 21.

[61] *Daily Highlights* (UN Department of Public Information), 22 Oct. 1996.

of Independent States (CIS), which UNOMIG monitors, was reportedly only 'satisfactory'.[62]

The UN Peace-keeping Force in Cyprus (UNFICYP) had one of its most eventful years in decades, when protests on the 'Green Line' separating the Greek and Turkish parts of the island led to the deaths of several civilians and rising tension.[63] Increasing militarization of the island also caused concern.[64] Cypriot President Glafcos Clerides reiterated a long-standing proposal for demilitarization and replacement of UNFICYP with a multinational, NATO-led force which would include Greek and Turkish components.[65] The USA, the UK and the European Union (EU) all appointed special representatives. The USA dispatched UN Ambassador Madeleine Albright and the UK its Foreign Secretary Malcolm Rifkind to try to move the Cyprus situation towards resolution but without noticeable effect.[66] Cyprus' application to join the EU may provide leverage to effect moves towards a settlement in 1997.

UNAVEM III in Angola continued to confront the slow pace of implementation of the Lusaka Protocol, although the fighting appeared to be finally ended, with conflict moving to the political arena. By the end of the year the much-delayed quartering and disarming of the opposition UNITA (National Union for the Total Independence of Angola) forces was finally completed, although the formation of a government of national unity remained problematic. None the less the UN was planning to implement a phased reduction of its 7200-strong military force by February 1997.[67]

The projected withdrawal of UNAVEM III, UNMOP and UNTAES in 1997 would produce a further major drop in UN peacekeeping deployments and costs and leave the world organization with a collection of small, largely traditional observation and monitoring missions, ending, at least for the time being, the post-cold war boom in large, multi-component, nation-building peacekeeping operations.

Continuing peacekeeping reforms

Despite the decline in peacekeeping activity, planning continued during the year for establishment of a Rapidly Deployable Mission Headquarters (RDMH) to accelerate deployment of future peace operations. It is proposed that the RDMH be an integral part of the DPKO and be staffed by military and civilian personnel covering all aspects of each operation. Eight officers would be recruited by January 1997 for the core headquarters staff, while others would be drawn part-time from the DPKO.[68] These New York-based officers

---

[62] United Nations (note 6), p. 230.

[63] *International Herald Tribune*, 12 Aug. 1996, p. 6.

[64] *Financial Times*, 20 Sep. 1996, p. 2.

[65] 'Cyprus: prospects for a settlement', *Strategic Comments* (Institute of International and Strategic Studies, IISS), vol. 2, no. 8 (Oct. 1996), p. 1.

[66] *International Herald Tribune*, 18 July 1996, p. 6 and 19 Dec. 1996, p. 2.

[67] *Daily Highlights* (UN Department of Public Information), 11 Dec. 1996.

[68] Press Release, 'Peace-keeping committee reviews proposals to set up Rapidly Deployable Mission Headquarters', UN Information Centre for the Nordic Countries, Copenhagen, Special Committee on Peace-keeping Operations 139th Meeting, document GA/PK144, 24 Oct. 1996, p. 4.

would be supplemented by 24 designated national staff who would remain in their home countries until required for pre-deployment integration into the RDMH. For the more ambitious operations a staff of up to 61 is envisaged. Interested states have volunteered personnel on loan to staff the headquarters initially, but it is expected that staff would eventually be funded from the regular UN budget. To ensure broad geographical representation, the strongest proponents of the idea—Canada, Denmark and the Netherlands—offered to finance participation by developing countries.[69]

None the less, churlish criticism was heard from a small number of developing states, led by Pakistan, about the self-appointed nature of the 'Friends of Rapid Reaction' (Australia, Canada, Denmark, Jamaica, the Netherlands, New Zealand, Nigeria, Senegal and Ukraine) which had been promoting and influencing decisions on the RDMH.[70] The Secretary-General's rejoinder was that all UN member states were welcome to support improvements to UN peacekeeping operations in any way they saw fit. In any case the Friends included several developing states. More justifiable criticism was heard that the growing number of personnel seconded from member states to the DPKO had skewed the principle of equitable geographic representation in the UN Secretariat. The solution to this problem will only come with a return to regular funding of all positions, which in turn depends on a solution to the UN's financial difficulties.

The UN Stand-by Arrangements System (UNSAS), which permits states to make non-binding pledges of contributions to future peacekeeping missions, continued slowly to attract additional pledges.[71] By the end of November 62 member states had offered a total of 80 000 personnel (compared with 47 members offering 55 000 at the end of October 1995).[72] Three additional states—Austria, Ghana and Malaysia—joined Denmark and Jordan in signing a Memorandum of Understanding with the UN confirming their participation in the system.[73]

A significant extension of the UNSAS concept occurred outside, but for the benefit of, the UN, among a group of states led by Denmark.[74] The group had proposed to the General Assembly in February that selected UNSAS contributors voluntarily form a Multinational UN Stand-by Forces High Readiness Brigade (SHIRBRIG) for deployment in Chapter VI operations (peacekeeping rather than peace enforcement) for a maximum of six months

[69] Axworthy, L., van Mierlo, H. and Petersen, N. H. (foreign ministers of Canada, the Netherlands and Denmark), 'Let's team up to make UN peacekeeping work', *International Herald Tribune*, 22 Oct. 1996, p. 8.

[70] UN Information Centre for the Nordic Countries (note 68), p. 1.

[71] For background see Findlay, T., 'Conflict prevention, management and resolution', *SIPRI Yearbook 1995: Armaments, Disarmament and International Security* (Oxford University Press: Oxford, 1995), pp. 55–57.

[72] United Nations, Progress Report of the Secretary-General on Standby Arrangements for Peacekeeping, UN document S/1996/1067, 24 Dec. 1996, p. 1.

[73] *Jane's Defence Weekly*, 20 Nov. 1996, p. 6.

[74] Argentina, Austria, Belgium, Canada, Czech Republic, Denmark, Finland (observer), Ireland (observer), the Netherlands, New Zealand, Norway, Poland and Sweden.

until replaced by a regular UN peacekeeping force.[75] In December, Austria, Canada, Denmark, the Netherlands, Norway, Poland and Sweden signed a letter of intent to establish the brigade.[76] It is expected that SHIRBRIG will have an initial operational and logistical capacity by 1 January 1998. Denmark will host its headquarters.[77]

Other reforms within the Secretariat included implementation from 1 July of new arrangements to simplify and speed up reimbursements for the UN's use and depreciation of contingent-owned equipment (subject to the availability of funds).[78] Members of the High-level Group of Experts on Procurement continued to work directly with the DPKO's Procurement and Transportation Division to establish an integrated mechanism for purchasing equipment for peacekeeping operations and improved accountability and transparency.[79]

The Secretary-General reacted sharply to criticisms in a report of the UN's Joint Inspection Unit (JIU), denying outright what he called the 'blanket judgement' that the DHA and the Department of Political Affairs still did not participate sufficiently in the planning of peacekeeping operations and that their participation should be further institutionalized. He pointed to the so-called Framework for Coordination, a 'flow-chart of actions that range from routine monitoring and early analysis of developments worldwide to formulation of options for preventive-action, fact-finding, planning and implementation of field operations, and conduct of evaluations or lessons-learned exercises'.[80] This had been supplemented in December 1995 by a standing Oversight Group of senior officers which met weekly to review potential or current crisis situations and determine whether any warranted the interdepartmental consultations foreseen in the Framework for Coordination. Further improvement would come, the Secretary-General promised, when the DHA's Humanitarian Early Warning System was made available to the other two Framework departments—but the fact that this had not been done previously indicates the continuing need for tackling compartmentalization and turf-guarding at UN headquarters. Member states continued to call for further reform.

The 1994 Convention on the Safety of United Nations and Associated Personnel had by 29 June acquired 43 signatories and 6 ratifications (compared with 29 and 3, respectively, in mid-1995).[81] The convention requires 22 instruments of accession or ratification before it enters into force.

---

[75] United Nations, Report of the Working Group on a Multinational United Nations Stand-by Forces High Readiness Brigade, Annex to letter dated 29 February 1996 from the Permanent Representative of Denmark to the United Nations addressed to the Secretary-General, UN document A/51/75, 5 Mar. 1996.

[76] Letter of intent concerning cooperation on the Multinational United Nations Stand-by Forces High Readiness Brigade, Denmark, 15 Dec. 1996 (copy courtesy of the Danish Embassy, Stockholm).

[77] *International Peacekeeping News*, vol. 2, no. 5 (Nov./Dec. 1996), p. 27.

[78] Joint Inspection Unit, 'Military component of United Nations peace-keeping operations', Note by the Secretary-General, UN document A/50/576/Add. 1, 28 June 1996, p. 4.

[79] Joint Inspection Unit (note 78), p. 4.

[80] United Nations, The 50th Anniversary Annual Report on the Work of the Organization (UN Department of Public Information: New York, 1996), p. 192.

[81] Joint Inspection Unit (note 78), p. 3; and Kirsch, P., 'The Convention on the Safety of United Nations and Associated Personnel', *International Peacekeeping*, Aug./Sep. 1995, p. 103.

The Lessons-Learned Unit continued its studies of recent peacekeeping operations, adding a report on UNAMIR in Rwanda to its previous study on the UN Operation in Somalia (UNOSOM).[82] It will next tackle UNPROFOR in the former Yugoslavia. While UN members welcomed the unit's products, there has been criticism of the overly diplomatic and unfocused character of the expert meetings called to provide the raw material for the reports.[83] Invariably tension between the need for realistic and truthful findings on the one hand and, on the other, pressures to preserve the reputations of the civilian and military leadership of past operations and avoid criticism of individual member states (especially permanent members of the Security Council), makes such exercises less valuable than independent assessments.

Other initiatives included the holding of the final two UN regional peace-keeping workshops, in Africa and Asia, and the establishment in Oslo, Norway, at no cost to the UN for an initial five years, of a depot for medical supplies for peacekeeping operations.[84] The UN Office of Legal Affairs prepared directives for UN peacekeepers to ensure compliance with the 1949 Geneva Conventions (a need identified after gross violations in Somalia).[85] The Demining Standby Capacity scheme established in 1995 attracted offers of services and equipment from at least 13 states, while the UN Voluntary Fund for Assistance in Mine Clearance provided resources for demining in six countries.[86]

Peacekeeping finance

The UN's financial crisis began to ease by the end of 1996 owing to adoption of a zero-growth budget for the current biennium, increased efficiency and reform, and efforts by states to meet their financial obligations (97 had paid their regular contributions in full by the end of November compared with only 72 in 1995[87]). By the end of 1996 outstanding regular budget assessments had dropped significantly to $546 million, although the deficit for peacekeeping operations remained high at $1.7 billion.[88] The UN was still required to use funds from its peacekeeping accounts to meet the regular running expenses of the organization. This resulted by the end of the year in the UN owing member states some $675 million for troops and equipment provided for peace-keeping operations.[89] The largest peacekeeping contributor, Pakistan, was owed up to $67.5 million during the year.[90] Such a situation penalized con-

---

[82] Comprehensive Report on Lessons Learned from the United Nations Assistance Mission for Rwanda (UNAMIR) October 1993/April 1996, Lessons Learned Unit, Department of Peace-keeping Operations, UN, New York, Dec. 1996.

[83] Chopra, J., 'Fighting for truth at the UN', *Crosslines Global Report*, vol. 4 (8), no. 26 (Nov. 1996).

[84] United Nations, Comprehensive review of the whole question of peace-keeping operations in all their aspects: report of the Special Committee on Peace-keeping Operations, UN document A/51/130, 7 May 1996, pp. 4–5.

[85] United Nations (note 80), p. 40.

[86] United Nations (note 6), p. 321.

[87] *Daily Highlights* (UN Department of Public Information), 12 Dec. 1996.

[88] *Daily Highlights* (UN Department of Public Information), 13 Dec. 1996.

[89] United Nations (note 80), p. ix.

[90] *International Peacekeeping News*, vol. 2, no. 4. (Sep./Oct. 1996), p. 29.

tributors twice: first in making the sacrifice in the first place and second in effectively providing the UN with an interest-free loan for its normal operating expenses. Boutros-Ghali described the situation as absurd: 'our reward to countries, including some of the world's poorest, that send their sons and daughters into harm's way on behalf of the international community is to impose an added financial burden on them'.[91]

Sixty-nine per cent of the UN debt at the end of 1996 was owed by the USA.[92] In October the US Congress approved the Administration's request for regular dues ($314 million) and peacekeeping expenses ($282 million) for fiscal year 1997, but rejected its five-year $743 million plan to pay the backlog, agreeing to only $50 million for the current year.[93] Congress continued to withhold payment of the remainder until the UN met certain targets, including further budget savings, staff reductions and zero budgets.[94] The administration itself attempted to lower—whether unilaterally or by agreement remained unclear—US contributions to the regular budget from 25 per cent to 20 per cent and for peacekeeping from 30 per cent to 25 per cent. Boutros-Ghali seemed resigned to this outcome by promoting a ceiling of 20 or 15 per cent of the regular budget for any one member state, as a means of both lessening the UN's dependence on the world's remaining superpower and of universalizing the current UN financial predicament.

Other UN member states continued to be infuriated at the USA's violation of its legally binding financial obligations.[95] Russia, the second largest debtor, seized the moral high ground by adhering to its pledge to pay off its debt by regular annual amounts. It cleared its debt to the regular budget in 1996, although it still owed the peacekeeping account $300 million.[96]

Proposals made by Boutros-Ghali in January for measures to relieve the UN financial crisis, including an international tax, created a storm of protest among Republican members of the US Congress, who introduced bills barring US participation in such schemes.[97] There was evidence, however, of a domestic backlash against continuing US failure to meet its UN financial obligations. Both a confidential State Department study and a report by the Council on Foreign Relations concluded that damage was being done not just to the

---

[91] United Nations (note 80), p. 199.

[92] *Daily Highlights* (UN Department of Public Information), 13 Dec. 1996.

[93] *Wireless File* (US Information Service, US Embassy: Stockholm, 7 Oct. 1996).

[94] 'Congressional wrap-up for 1996: action on UN budget & peacekeeping issues', Fact Sheet, Oct. 1996, Project on Peacekeeping and the United Nations, Council for a Livable World Education Fund, New York, p. 2.

[95] Australia told the Special Committee on Peacekeeping Operations that: 'we cannot comprehend that the largest financial contributor can countenance the destabilization of the operations of this organisation which inevitably is the consequence of its failure to fulfil its legitimate financial obligations. We reject any unilateral decision by a Member State to alter its agreed level of assessment, in contravention of its Charter obligations.' Statement by the Australian Representative to the Special Committee on Peacekeeping Operations, 3 Apr. 1996, p. 3.

[96] 'Russia: government makes contribution to UN Peacekeeping budget', ITAR–TASS World Service (Moscow), 25 Sep. 1996, Foreign Broadcast Information Service, *Daily Report—Central Eurasia (FBIS-SOV)*, FBIS-SOV-96-188), 27 Sep. 1996.

[97] Browne, M. A. and Reintsma, M., *UN Funding: Global Tax Proposals*, Congressional Research Service Report for Congress, Washington DC, 14 Feb. 1996.

UN but to US national interests.[98] The latter report noted that public support for the UN is stronger than credited by US politicians. The State Department warned that US influence with other UN members was being eroded, making them increasingly reluctant to support US reform proposals.

The report of the High-level Open-ended Working Group on the Financial Situation of the United Nations presented to the General Assembly was unfortunately devoid of any practical, agreed ideas on rescuing the UN from its financial plight.[99]

National and additional cooperative efforts

New peacekeeping contributors continued to appear,[100] among them Latvia, which contributed 50 National Armed Forces personnel to IFOR as part of a joint Latvian–Swedish unit.[101] Albania also launched itself into peacekeeping for the first time by joining IFOR and offering troops for Zaire.[102] The Chief of the South African National Defence Force (SANDF), General Georg Meiring, announced that South Africa would be ready to consider joining peacekeeping operations by the end of 1996.[103] A small number of individual countries continued their long-standing but little noted contribution to almost all current peacekeeping operations. Among these were Uruguay, which in 1996 participated in six missions.[104] Meanwhile a joint Polish–Ukrainian mechanized battalion formed for participation in UN peacekeeping missions began training in Poland.[105] Russia announced that up to 22 000 Russian troops would form a dedicated force for 'maintaining or restoring international peace and security'.[106] Greek and Romanian troops conducted peacekeeping exercises in Romania in November.[107]

As often in the field of peacekeeping the Nordic countries led the way in innovative approaches to future needs. At a meeting in Sweden the defence ministers of Denmark, Finland, Norway and Sweden agreed on the establishment of the Nordic Coordinated Arrangement for Military Peace Support

---

[98] *International Herald Tribune*, 22 Aug. 1996, p. 5, and 4 Nov. 1996, p. 9.

[99] United Nations, Report of the High-level Open-ended Working Group on the Financial Situation of the United Nations, UN document A/50/43, 6 June 1996.

[100] For details of other new peacekeepers since the end of the cold war see Findlay, T. (ed.), *Challenges for the New Peacekeepers*, SIPRI Research Report no. 12 (Oxford University Press: Oxford, 1995).

[101] Radio Riga Network (Riga), 26 Sep. 1996 (in Latvian), in 'Latvia: Saeima decides to send peacekeepers to Bosnia', FBIS-SOV-96-190, 1 Oct. 1996.

[102] *International Peacekeeping News*, vol. 2, no. 4 (Sep./Oct. 1996), p. 15.

[103] Cilliers, J. and Malan, M., 'Regional peacekeeping role for South Africa: pressures, problems and prognosis', *African Security Review*, vol. 5, no. 3 (1996), p. 21.

[104] UNAVEM III, MINURSO, UNOMIG, UNIKOM, UNMOGIP and UNMOT. For further details of Uruguay's peacekeeping record see *El Ejercito Uruguayo En Misiones de Paz 1953–1993* [The Uruguayan Defence Forces in Peace Missions 1953–1993] (Ejercito Nacional Republica Oriental del Uruguay: La Paz, 1993).

[105] TV Polonia Network (Warsaw), 27 Sep. 1996 (in Polish), in 'Poland: Polish–Ukrainian battalion training for UN peacekeeping', Foreign Broadcast Information Service, *Daily Report–East Europe (FBIS-EEU)*, FBIS-EEU-96-190, 1 Oct. 1996.

[106] *Jane's Defence Weekly*, 8 May 1996, p. 4.

[107] ROMPRES (Bucharest), 28 Nov. 1996, in 'Romania: generals assess "Balkanic" peacekeeper drills', FBIS-EEU-96-234-A, 5 Dec. 1996.

(Nordcaps), which will make clear in advance which personnel and what types of *matériel* they would make available to a joint Nordic rapid reaction battalion of approximately 1000 personnel.[108] Sweden decided to improve its own ability to contribute to peace operations, including those 'that can involve greater risks and authority as regards the use of force', by establishing an International Command capable of deploying a rapid reaction force of 800–1400 personnel 15–30 days after a government decision.[109] The Baltic states, with the assistance of their Nordic neighbours, also moved to increase their peacekeeping capabilities by agreeing to establish a joint Estonian–Latvian–Lithuanian battalion by 1998 which would be available for peace missions as an independent unit.[110] Denmark included Baltic units in its battalion in Bosnia, while Norway incorporated Estonians in its UNIFIL contingent.[111] The Nordic states also sponsored the first Nordic/UN Peacekeeping Senior Management Seminar in Stockholm and New York in September–October.[112]

Argentina actively promoted the concept of the 'White Helmets', teams of volunteer non-military experts in reconstruction and development, to assist in pre- or post-conflict peace-building or humanitarian emergencies.[113] The DHA worked closely on this issue with the Argentine Government (which had already sent volunteers to Angola, Armenia, Gaza, Haiti and Jamaica to demonstrate the viability of the concept) and the UN Volunteers, now based in Bonn, Germany, who would be responsible for administering the scheme on behalf of the UN.

South Korea planned to become the first foreign country to send military personnel to the Malaysian Peacekeeping Training Centre, reinforcing Malaysia's pretensions to becoming the regional peacekeeping trainer.[114]

In both national and international efforts at reform there was a noticeably strong emphasis on the military aspects of peacekeeping but relatively little attention to civilian issues, despite the complaints of many force commanders about operating in a political vacuum without the necessary civilian underpinning to make comprehensive peace settlements work.

---

[108] 'Nordic common force goal', *Dagens Nyheter* (Stockholm), 9 Oct. 1996, p. 10, in 'Sweden: Nordics look at joint peacekeeping force', Foreign Broadcast Information Service, *Daily Report–West Europe (FBIS-WEU)*, FBIS-WEU-96-210, 30 Oct. 1996. For background and details of past Nordic cooperative efforts see Karhilo, J., 'Redesigning Nordic military contributions to multilateral peace operations', *SIPRI Yearbook 1996* (note 7), pp. 101–16.

[109] *Jane's Defence Weekly*, 18 Sep. 1996, p. 29.

[110] Estonian Television Network (Tallinn), 15 Oct. 1996 (in Estonian), in 'Baltics: Baltic states to assume control over peacekeeping battalion', FBIS-SOV-96-201, 17 Oct. 1996.

[111] *International Peacekeeping News*, vol. 2, no. 4 (Sep./Oct. 1996), p. 24.

[112] See Nordic/UN Peace-keeping Senior Management Seminar Stockholm–New York, 23 Sep.–3 Oct. 1996, Report of the First Seminar, National Defence College, Stockholm, 1996.

[113] United Nations (note 6), p. 163. For background see papers delivered at the International Colloquium on 'Le Concept des "Casque blancs": A-t-on besoin d'une nouvelle forme d'intervention internationale?' [The White Helmets concept: is there a need for a new form of international intervention?] organized by the Raoul-Dandurand Chair in Strategic and Diplomatic Studies, University of Quebec at Montreal, 19–20 June 1996.

[114] *International Peacekeeping News*, vol. 2, no. 3 (July/Aug. 1996), p. 12.

IV. UN peace-enforcement measures

The two principle means which the UN Charter envisages for 'enforcing' peace are sanctions and the threat or use of military force.[115]

Sanctions

Eight sanctions regimes were in place in 1996, against Angola, Iraq, Liberia, Libya, Rwanda, Somalia, Sudan and the former Yugoslavia, most of them administered in routine fashion by ad hoc committees of the Security Council.[116]

In the only new regime established during the year, the Security Council imposed diplomatic and certain other restrictions on Sudan in May after it failed to meet a demand to extradite to Ethiopia three suspects wanted in connection with the June 1995 assassination attempt on Egyptian President Hosni Mubarak.[117] Resolution 1070 (1996) of 16 August imposed further sanctions, notably against government-owned Sudan Airways.

The suspended arms embargo against the Rwandan Government was terminated on 1 September, but that against non-government forces remained fully operative.[118]

On 1 October, in Resolution 1074 (1996), the Council formally lifted economic, military and other sanctions imposed on the Federal Republic of Yugoslavia (Serbia and Montenegro) in a series of resolutions between 1992 and 1995.[119] This was done after the OSCE certified, controversially, that the 14 September elections in Bosnia and Herzegovina were democratic and in keeping with internationally accepted practices. The arms embargo imposed in 1991 against Croatia and Bosnia and Herzegovina expired automatically in 1996, 180 days after the signing of the Dayton Agreement. The Council warned that it would reimpose sanctions if any party failed significantly to meet its obligations under the Dayton Agreement. NATO and the Western European Union (WEU) consequently lifted their naval blockade in the Adriatic Sea that had been enforcing the sanctions. The combined force challenged 73 000 ships during its operation. More than 5800 were inspected at sea and nearly 1400 diverted and inspected in port.[120]

---

[115] 'Enforce' is used here in the sense of coercing a party to do something it would otherwise not wish to do or to refrain from doing something it does wish to do. The difference between an enforcement activity and a non-enforcement activity turns on the question of consent. If the consent of the party is not forthcoming then the action taken is necessarily an enforcement activity.

[116] For details see Findlay, T., 'Multilateral conflict prevention, management and resolution', *SIPRI Yearbook 1994* (Oxford University Press: Oxford, 1994); Findlay (note 71); and Findlay (note 22).

[117] Security Council resolutions 1044 (1996), 31 Jan. 1996 and 1054 (1996), 26 Apr. 1996. For background see *UN Chronicle*, no. 2 (1996), p. 55; and Waller, R., 'Sudanese security: rogue state in crisis', *Jane's Intelligence Review*, July 1996, pp. 311–15.

[118] In accordance with UN Security Council Resolution 1011 (1995), 16 Aug. 1996. See Security Council press release SC/6313, 14 Jan. 1997, p. 5.

[119] *Wireless File* (US Information Service, US Embassy: Stockholm, 2 Oct. 1996); and Security Council press release, SC/6274, 1 Oct. 1996.

[120] *International Herald Tribune*, 20 July 1996, p. 5.

While sanctions on Iraq resulting from the 1991 Persian Gulf War were retained, the UN and the Iraqi Government on 20 May 1996 signed an agreement permitting Iraq to sell $1 billion worth of petroleum and petroleum products every 90 days in order to meet the humanitarian needs of the Iraqi people.[121] The agreement came in response to criticism, including that by permanent Council members China, France and Russia and assessments by UN humanitarian agencies that UN sanctions were imposing intolerable hardships on the populace. Iraqi action against the Kurds and further arguments with the UN delayed implementation of the agreement until the end of the year.[122]

In September the Security Council gave Major Pierre Buyoya, who seized power in Burundi in a military coup, until 31 October to open negotiations with opposition leaders or face a UN embargo in addition to that imposed by regional states.[123] This threat had the desired effect and sanctions remained in abeyance.

The General Assembly meanwhile entrusted the Secretariat with ensuring that the unintended consequences of UN sanctions against innocent populations and countries were minimized. Proposed measures, based on recommendations of the Inter-Agency Standing Committee, included exemptions of humanitarian supplies from sanctions; establishment of a mechanism to provide timely information to the Security Council on the possible impact of sanctions; and development of methodology and indicators for the assessment of the humanitarian impact of sanctions.[124]

Use of military force

No UN forces were involved in the use of military force, other than in self-defence, in 1996. The USA argued that it used force in furtherance of Security Council Resolution 688 of 5 April 1991 when it undertook missile attacks in August/September against Iraqi air defences after Baghdad launched an offensive against its northern Kurdish enclave. However, that resolution, while it condemned Iraq's repression of its Kurdish minority, did not authorize the use of force. Moreover, the no-fly zone established over northern Iraq north of 36°N and south of 32°N (the latter was extended by the USA in September to south of 33°N) was never endorsed by the Security Council. The only Security Council-endorsed peace-enforcement operation in regard to Iraq is UNIKOM, the UN operation on the Iraq/Kuwait border, which after 1993 was authorized to use force to prevent violations of the Demilitarized Zone (DMZ) but not in the case of internal conflict within Iraq.[125]

---

[121] *UN Chronicle*, no. 2 (1996), p. 14. See Iraq–United Nations: Memorandum of Understanding on the sale of Iraqi oil, implementing Security Council Resolution 986 (1995), New York, 20 May 1996, UN document S/1996/356, 20 May 1996.

[122] *Jane's Defence Weekly*, 11 Sep. 1996, p. 5.

[123] *International Herald Tribune*, 6 Sep. 1996, p. 2; and United Nations, Report of the Secretary-General on the situation in Burundi, UN document S/1996/887, 29 Oct. 1996.

[124] United Nations (note 80), p. 162.

[125] *United Nations Peace-keeping* (UN Department of Public Information: New York, Sep. 1996), p. 67.

Three multilateral UN forces endorsed by the Security Council—IFOR, SFOR and the proposed Zaire/Rwanda humanitarian mission—were authorized under Chapter VII and acquired 'robust' rules of engagement giving them greater latitude in using force beyond self-defence. None used significant military force in 1996.

V. Regional and other multilateral organizations

In view of the reluctance of the Security Council to authorize large-scale interventions in dangerous circumstances, such as those which plagued the UN missions in Bosnia and Herzegovina, Rwanda and Somalia, increasing hope was being placed (some would say misplaced) in regional organizations. In February the UN Secretary-General convened the second high-level meeting (the first was in 1994) between the UN and 13 regional organizations with which it had cooperated in peacekeeping and peacemaking, in the hope that the UN's burden might be lessened.[126]

However, regional organizations are only gradually increasing their capacities to handle conflict prevention, management and resolution. Their political, military, financial and material resources are in most cases no match for those of the UN and, owing to the presence of a regional great power and/or entanglements in the very conflicts they are meant to address, they are often singularly ill-equipped to undertake disinterested, effective intervention. Broad regional organizations, such as in the Asia–Pacific, may have widely disparate membership with little in common. Sometimes small subregional organizations are more effective. Overall, however, regionalism is unlikely to be the panacea for the shortcomings of the United Nations for many years, if ever. What is required is cooperation, mutually supportive behaviour and burden-sharing between the global, regional and subregional levels.

Europe and the CIS

The most sophisticated regional organizations remained those based in Europe, although even these were of widely varying capability and effectiveness. NATO's first peace operation, IFOR in Bosnia and Herzegovina, proved, in military terms, highly successful. After taking over from UNPROFOR in December 1995, it quickly secured the cease-fire and began implementing the various stages of the peace plan negotiated in Dayton, Ohio, in November. Tasks included establishing a zone of separation between the parties, supervising the withdrawal of forces to barracks, cantonments or other areas, monitoring the withdrawal of heavy weapons to holding areas, contributing to the provision of a 'security environment' for other elements of the international presence and assisting the civilian elements in their tasks, including the holding of elections. The force numbered 60 000 at its peak (not including those on standby in Hungary) and comprised more than 20 000 US

---

[126] United Nations (note 80), p. 193.

troops and smaller forces from 32 other countries, including non-NATO members. Unlike UNPROFOR it was well equipped militarily and provided with 'robust' rules of engagement sufficient to cow the local parties to submit to its will. While shows of force were occasionally necessary, no actual use of force was required. IFOR was, however, heavily criticized in some quarters for its unwillingness to seize indicted war criminals, guard sites of suspected war crimes and protect civilians at risk. The Force Commander argued that these either lay beyond IFOR's mandate, would risk sustaining casualties or would detract from its primary tasks and lead to the much-feared 'mission creep'. Detractors argued, especially in relation to the arrest of war criminals, that it would be unheard of for civil police in normal societies to refuse to carry out certain tasks because of the danger of casualties.

Although President Bill Clinton had promised to end IFOR's deployment and withdraw all US troops after 20 December it was increasingly apparent as the year progressed that a 'follow-on' force to IFOR would be needed and that US participation was both essential and likely. After the US presidential election Clinton announced that the USA would join a post-IFOR force which would be smaller and more oriented towards non-military tasks. SFOR took over from IFOR in December, accompanied by an enlarged UN CivPol presence.

With a successful IFOR mission as exemplar, NATO leaders, after more than two and a half years of wrangling, agreed in June on the basic principles for so-called Combined Joint Task Forces (CJTF)—international ('combined'), inter-service ('joint') force packages tailored for specific missions ('task forces'), including peacekeeping, humanitarian or peace enforcement.[127] As a result of US concessions, CJTF may, with the agreement of the North Atlantic Council (NAC), be European-led, controlled by the WEU and deployed beyond NATO's borders using NATO military assets and US logistical and organizational support. Such deployments would be prepared in advance, with clear lines of political and military control, rather than established ad hoc. Complicating the situation, in November France, Italy, Portugal and Spain inaugurated a 20 000-strong, combined rapid deployment force for humanitarian and peacekeeping missions in the Mediterranean area. Headquartered in Florence, the force could act independently or under the auspices of NATO or the WEU.[128]

NATO's Partnership for Peace programme continued to carry out joint peacekeeping training exercises, including one in Lithuania in August involving troops from Denmark, Lithuania and Poland and one in Ukraine in June involving Bulgaria, the Czech Republic, Moldova, Poland, Romania, Russia, Ukraine and Slovakia.[129]

---

[127] 'NATO, CJTFs, and IFOR', *Strategic Comments*, International Institute of Strategic Studies (IISS), vol. 2, no. 5 (June 1996). For further discussion see chapter 5 in this volume.

[128] *Jane's Defence Weekly*, 20 Nov. 1996, p. 12.

[129] *International Herald Tribune*, 12 Aug. 1996, p. 6; and *International Peacekeeping News*, vol. 2, no. 2 (May/June 1996), p. 22.

The OSCE[130] maintained its various missions designed to prevent, manage or resolve conflict, adding new ones to Croatia and Serbia (the latter to attempt to resolve the impasse between the government and opposition over President Slobodan Milosevic's attempt to void opposition victories in the November municipal elections).[131] However, the organization, despite being prepared for its first peacekeeping mission, to Nagorno-Karabakh (Azerbaijan), was still unable to deploy it because of continuing disagreement between the warring parties.[132] The May 1994 cease-fire continued to hold despite occasional skirmishes. Besides the OSCE, the USA, Russia, Georgia and Turkey were also involved in peace efforts in regard to Nagorno-Karabakh.[133] As for Georgia's own conflicts, the OSCE and Russia mediated an accord between Georgian Foreign Minister Irakly Menagarishvili and South Ossetian leader Ludvig Chibirov which rejected the use of force or political or economic pressure but failed to address South Ossetia's claim to independence.[134] The OSCE's greatest challenge during the year was to oversee the holding of complex general elections in Bosnia and Herzegovina. It was out of its depth and the elections were widely criticized as being unfree, unfair and, had IFOR not provided last-minute unforeseen assistance, potentially disastrous.

Notwithstanding the failure of the EU to bring reconciliation and unity to the Bosnian city of Mostar, which had been under its tutelage even before the Dayton Agreement, efforts were made by the Union to increase its role in the military aspects of peacekeeping and humanitarian operations by incorporating such operations into the 1991 Maastricht Treaty as 'membership tasks'.[135] Meanwhile the EU appointed a Special Envoy for the Great Lakes Region, Aldo Ajello, to work with regional states and the OAU on resolving conflict in that part of Africa.[136]

The CIS continued to maintain two peacekeeping operations, in Abkhazia in Georgia and in Tajikistan, both monitored and assisted by accompanying UN missions, UNOMIG and UNMOT (the UN Mission of Observers in Tajikistan), respectively.[137] Russian budgetary pressures and Georgian parliamentary opposition to the continued presence of Russian peacekeepers in Abkhazia appeared to be leading in 1996 to consideration of a withdrawal of that mission.[138] The force in Tajikistan was meanwhile rendered less multinational than ever with the reported departure of the Kazakh and Uzbek contributions,

---

[130] For details on OSCE activities see chapter 5 in this volume.

[131] *International Peacekeeping News*, vol. 2, no. 3 (July/Aug. 1996), p. 18; and *Wireless File* (US Information Service, US Embassy: Stockholm, 16 Dec. 1996).

[132] For background see Nowak, J. M., 'The Organization for Security and Co-operation in Europe', ed. Findlay (note 100).

[133] *Jane's Defence Weekly*, 15 Oct. 1996, p. 27.

[134] *International Peacekeeping News*, vol. 2, no. 2 (May/June 1996), p. 20.

[135] 'EU "neutrals" to join defence initiative', *Financial Times*, 23 July 1996, p. 2.

[136] Opening statement at the EU–SADC Ministerial Conference, Windhoek, Namibia, 14 Oct. 1996, by Mr Dick Spring, President-in-Office of the Council of Ministers of the European Union, p. 5.

[137] For details of conflicts in all the former Soviet republics see chapter 4 in this volume.

[138] *International Peacekeeping News*, vol. 2, no. 2 (May/June 1996), p. 20.

leaving only a Kyrgyz battalion and the 201st Russian Motor Rifle Division.[139] There were reports that the Russian peacekeepers could switch to supporting regular Russian border troops along the Afghanistan border in view of the deteriorating situation in that country, a move which, according to the force commander, would be in accordance with their mandate.[140] This would leave UNMOT, which in 1996 sustained increasing harassment by both sides, without a credible role.[141] By the end of 1996 hopes were rising of a settlement in Tajikistan after an agreement was signed in Moscow by the government and opposition.[142]

Africa and the Middle East

Some progress was made on improving indigenous African capacities for conflict prevention, management and resolution, but it was agonizingly slow compared with the rapidly deteriorating conditions in Burundi and Zaire, and continuing strife in Liberia and Rwanda. There is a danger, moreover, that in the absence of strong regional mechanisms African states will increasingly resort to private security forces, such as those offered by South African-based Executive Outcomes which proved so 'effective' in Sierra Leone.[143]

The USA strongly pressed the case for an African Crisis Response Force (ACRF) comprising 10 000 troops from African states, endowed with US and other Western funding, training, logistics and material support, which could be deployed at short notice. While it would not be a standing force, it could be assembled quickly, would be led by Africans and would be deployed under OAU or UN mandate. The estimated start-up costs were $20–40 million, of which the USA offered half. Secretary of State Warren Christopher addressed the OAU and toured the continent in October seeking support. Only Ethiopia and Mali immediately offered to participate. A key potential contributor, South Africa, expressed caution, with President Nelson Mandela noting that to succeed the force would need the credibility of being established under UN rather than US auspices. Some African critics suspected the US proposal was intended to relieve the West of major responsibility for African security, particularly in providing peacekeeping forces, despite the fact that Africans had participated generously in peacekeeping operations in other regions of the world for the past 50 years. The Southern African Development Community (SADC) expressed concern that military assistance to selected states for peacekeeping could open a 'new window for militarization and arms build-up'

---

[139] Information from Alexei Arbatov, Member of the Russian Duma, presentation at SIPRI, 8 Oct. 1996.

[140] Gridneva, G., ITAR–TASS (Moscow), 1 Oct. 1996, in 'CIS: CIS peacekeepers stand by as Tajik border tension rises', FBIS-SOV-96-192, 3 Oct. 1996.

[141] See *Special Report: the War in Tajikistan Three Years on*, US Institute of Peace, Washington DC, Nov. 1995, p. 15.

[142] Interfax (Moscow), 23 Dec. 1996, in 'Tajikistan: president, opposition leader sign agreements in Moscow, FBIS-SOV-96-248, 26 Dec. 1996.

[143] 'Editorial comment: privatising peace enforcement', *African Security Review*, vol. 5, no. 6 (1996), pp. 1–3.

and sought close consultation in all aspects of the proposal.[144] France appeared to abandon its own plans for an African force after the President of Togo, General Gnassingbe Eyadema, who had been mandated by the 1995 Franco-African summit to prepare a blueprint for action, failed to do so.[145] France reportedly rebuffed US suggestions that it dovetail its proposal with that of the USA.

In June a meeting of African generals at OAU headquarters in Addis Ababa agreed on less startling measures to improve the continent's peacekeeping capabilities, including the earmarking by member states of rapidly deployable peacekeeping units and the establishment of a military staff unit at the OAU.[146] The OAU subsequently dispatched teams to assess the peacekeeping abilities of its member states. Among bilateral initiatives Ireland explored the possibility of assisting the Zambia Military Academy establish a peacekeeping wing.[147]

The OAU moved slowly to establish its Early Warning System on Conflict Situations in Africa, proposed by the OAU summit meeting in June 1995 as part of the OAU Conflict Resolution Mechanism. A seminar was convened in January in Addis Ababa to determine the modalities of the system.[148] It recommended, *inter alia*, that the system be modest, realistic and efficient and expanded on an incremental basis; that it draw on existing resources including the Pan-African Development Information System of the UN's Economic Commission for Africa (ECA) and the experience of NGOs; that it publish an annual survey of conflict in Africa; and that a strategy group be established to assist the OAU with strategic planning for the system.[149] Funding remained an obvious problem despite the US pledge to provide $1.5 million annually from 1995 to 1998 to assist the OAU's conflict resolution programme.

The first institutional mechanism for conflict prevention in Africa, the UN General Assembly's Standing Advisory Committee on Security Questions in Central Africa, which was established in May 1992, continued to prove useless in regard to the conflicts brewing in the Great Lakes region.[150] It has,

---

[144] SAPA (Johannesburg), 13 Oct. 1996, in 'SADC concerned over militarization of peacekeeping', Foreign Broadcast Information Service, *Daily Report–Sub-Saharan Africa (FBIS-AFR)*, FBIS-AFR-96-200, 17 Oct. 1996; and Lippman, T. W., 'US revises plans for African force', *International Herald Tribune*, 10 Feb. 1997, p. 4.

[145] *Jane's Defence Weekly*, vol. 26, no. 17 (23 Oct. 1996), p. 17. For background see Findlay (note 71), p. 76.

[146] *International Peacekeeping News*, vol. 2, no. 2 (May/June 1996), p. 3. The meeting was attended by military personnel from Algeria, Burkina Faso, Burundi, Cameroon, Congo, Djibouti, Egypt, Ethiopia, Gabon, Ghana, Guinea, Kenya, Lesotho, Malawi, Mali, Mauritania, Namibia, Nigeria, Senegal, South Africa, Sudan, Swaziland, Tunisia and Zimbabwe.

[147] *International Peacekeeping News*, vol. 2, no. 3 (July/Aug. 1996), p. 3.

[148] Martin, G., 'North of the border: conflict resolution in Africa', *Track Two*, vol. 5, no. 2 (June 1996), p. 15.

[149] Nhara, W. G., 'Early warning and conflict in Africa', *IDP Papers* (Institute for Defence Policy, Cape Town), no. 1 (Feb. 1996), p. 7.

[150] Ayafor, C. and Fomete, J.-P., 'Towards a subregional Agenda for Peace in Central Africa', *Disarmament*, vol. 19, no. 1 (1996), pp. 73–94. Its singular achievement has been the initialling in Yaoundé in Sep. 1994 of a Non-Aggression Pact between the 11 member states of the Economic Community of Central African States (ECCAS), whose members are Angola, Burundi, Cameroon, Central African Republic, Chad, Congo, Equatorial Guinea, Gabon, Rwanda, Sao Tomé and Principe, and Zaire.

however, conducted studies on a model national peacekeeping unit (such units subsequently were established by Chad, Equatorial Guinea and Zaire); a typology of the types of crises and conflicts likely to require the intervention of the subregional security mechanism; and a proposed general staff committee for crisis management in the sub-region.

Meanwhile the SADC resolved the previous year's political disagreements and, meeting in Gaborone, Botswana in June, agreed to establish an Organ for Politics, Defence and Security under the chairmanship of Prime Minister Robert Mugabe of Zimbabwe.[151] The organ is intended, *inter alia*, to handle conflict prevention, management and resolution and develop a peacekeeping capacity within national armies for use in the subregion or elsewhere in Africa. These tasks would be governed by an envisaged Protocol on Peace, Security and Conflict Resolution. Although the organ's principles contained the usual caveat about respect for sovereignty and territorial integrity they also, unprecedentedly for an African security organization, would permit military intervention after all possible political remedies had been exhausted in accordance with the OAU and UN charters. The organ began work almost immediately by holding a meeting at head of state level in Luanda, Angola, to give sustenance to the peace process slowly unfolding in that country.

African states made a landmark effort in 1996 to employ a peace-enforcement tool—economic sanctions—against another African state. On 31 July a second summit meeting (Arusha II) of the leaders of the states located in the Great Lakes Region imposed, under OAU auspices, economic sanctions on Burundi after the elected government was overthrown by former president Major Pierre Buyoya. Former Tanzanian President Julius Nyerere, who had been appointed by Arusha I as the group's mediator in Burundi, acted as the summit's facilitator. The aim of the sanctions was to bring Buyoya, along with the factions opposing him, to the negotiating table. Although Rwanda was tardy in implementing the sanctions regime against its neighbour, eventually all states of the region joined in, demonstrating a remarkable degree of unity. A third summit in October, Arusha III, dispatched a delegation to the Burundi capital Bujumbura, in an attempt to speed up the peace process. Towards the end of the year regional attention focused away from Burundi towards the even more pressing crisis on the Rwanda/Zaire border. A summit of African presidents and representatives of the OAU, convened in Nairobi in December, mandated the presidents of Cameroon, Kenya, South Africa and Zimbabwe to take initiatives to end the conflict, but Zaire failed to attend and its ailing president, Mobutu Sese Seko, appeared unmoved by such well-intentioned initiatives.[152]

West Africa's regional peacekeeping force, the Economic Community of West African States [ECOWAS] Monitoring Group (ECOMOG), remained on duty in Liberia, accompanied by the UN Observer Mission in Liberia

---

[151] Communique, Summit of heads of state or governments (sic) of the Southern African Development Community (SADC), Gaborone, Republic of Botswana, 28 June 1996 (document courtesy of the Namibian Embassy, Stockholm)

[152] *The Australian*, 18 Dec. 1998, p. 10.

(UNOMIL), even though the former lost control of the situation in April when renewed factional fighting devastated the capital Monrovia and destroyed the 1995 Abuja Agreement that had ended the five-year civil war.[153] More than 1500 people died in the fighting, while looting and bloodshed prompted the withdrawal of NGOs, UN agencies and most of UNOMIL. A cease-fire was eventually negotiated by representatives of UNOMIL, ECOWAS, UN Special Envoy James Jonah and the ambassadors of Guinea, Nigeria, Sierra Leone and the USA.[154] New talks in Abuja, Nigeria, hosted by ECOWAS, which deployed and has sustained ECOMOG, produced a revised version of the Abuja Agreement involving the formation of a new interim Council of State headed by former Liberian senator Ruth Perry.[155] The government will oversee preparations for elections scheduled for 30 May 1997. The six warring factions which signed the accord are pledged to disband their estimated 60 000 combatants by January. An assassination attempt on warlord Charles Taylor in November signalled that the peace process remained extremely fragile.[156]

More than a dozen Liberian peace agreements have been signed and violated since 1990.[157] Boutros-Ghali warned that the international community's previous failure to provide the promised resources to the Liberian peace process, including ECOMOG, had been partly responsible for such a situation. ECOMOG was due to be increased from 8500 to 18 000, including for the first time troops from Côte d'Ivoire and Burkina Faso, while part of the much promised US military aid to the force was finally delivered.[158]

Complementing the renewed Liberian peace process was an improving situation in neighbouring Sierra Leone, which held successful elections followed by a peace agreement signed in Abidjan, Côte d'Ivoire, on 30 November by the government and the Revolutionary United Front (RUF).[159] The government of Côte d'Ivoire, especially its foreign minister, Amara Essay, was credited with a key role in the successful talks to end the five-year conflict.[160]

Meanwhile a French–African summit meeting in December held in Ouagadougou, Burkina Faso, mandated an 'international follow-up committee' from the West African states of Burkina Faso, Chad, Gabon and Mali, led by Malian ex-President Amadou Toumani Toure, to negotiate an end to the third armed rebellion in eight months in the Central African Republic, which broke out in November.[161] French troops stationed there had earlier intervened to

---

[153] United Nations, Letter dated 25 August 1995 from the permanent Representative of Nigeria to the United Nations addressed to the President of the Security Council, Annex, Abuja Agreement to Supplement the Cotonou and Akosombo Agreements, UN document S/1995/742, 28 Aug. 1995.

[154] *UN Chronicle*, no. 2 (1996), p. 11.

[155] *International Herald Tribune*, 19 Aug. 1996, p. 9.

[156] *International Herald Tribune*, 1 Nov. 1996, p. 6.

[157] 'Conflict in Liberia and Sierra Leone', *Strategic Comments* (IISS), vol. 2, no. 8 (Oct. 1996), p. 1.

[158] *International Peacekeeping News*, vol. 2, no. 4 (Sep./Oct. 1996), pp. 7–8.

[159] *Daily Highlights* (UN Department of Public Information), 2 Dec. 1996.

[160] French, H. W., 'Amid a continent's chaos, Sierra Leone sets a peace example', *International Herald Tribune*, 1 Dec. 1996, p. 1.

[161] AFP (Paris), 6 Jan. 1997 (in French), in 'France: Defence Ministry denies French troops present in Kinsangani', FBIS-WEU-97-004, 8 Jan. 1997.

quell the fighting. The peace process initiated in nearby Niger in 1994 suffered a setback when the main Touareg resistance group, the Organization of the Armed Resistance, withdrew from the process.[162]

In the Middle East, in one of the few regional attempts at conflict resolution outside the Middle East peace process, the Gulf Cooperation Council attempted to mediate a territorial dispute between Qatar and Bahrain.[163]

Latin America

In Latin America the Caribbean Community (CARICOM) built on its involvement in UN peacekeeping (it had provided a contingent to UNMIH) by identifying at its May 1996 foreign ministers meeting in Jamaica ways of increasing cooperation with the UN in peacekeeping.[164] The Military Observer Mission Ecuador/Peru (MOMEP), comprising observers from the four guarantor parties to the 1942 Rio Protocol—Argentina, Brazil, Chile and the USA—continued to monitor the cease-fire, withdrawal and demilitarization agreement reached between Peru and Ecuador in February 1995 after their brief military clash earlier that year. They were joined during the year by observers from the two conflicting parties, but the USA warned it would withdraw if progress was not made in negotiating a settlement. Despite Ecuador's charges that Peru was violating the agreement, military manoeuvres by both sides and the purchase by Peru of 12 MiG-29 aircraft from Belarus, the two countries signed the Santiago Declaration on 29 October committing them to begin substantial negotiations in Brasilia by the end of the year.[165] In Nicaragua meanwhile the joint UN–OAS (Organization of American States) International Verification and Support Commission (Comisión Internacional de Apoyo y Verificación, CIAV), which had begun in May 1990 to help implement the Esquipulas and Tela agreements, continued the work of its second phase (1993–96), aimed at strengthening capacities for conflict mediation and resolution and human rights protection.[166]

VI. Other players

A multitude of other players continued to be active in 1996 in conflict prevention, management and resolution.

[162] Radio France International (Paris), 7 Jan. 1997 (in French), in 'Niger: Touareg rebel group rejoins peace process', FBIS-AFR-97-005, 9 Jan. 1997. It rejoined in Jan. 1997.

[163] 'Gulf Cooperation Council: the acceptable; the unacceptable', Riyadh-al Riyad, 13 Jan. 1997, pp. 1, 6 (in Arabic), in 'Saudi Arabia: editorial on Qatari-Bahraini dispute, GCC "future"', Foreign Broadcast Information Service, Daily Report–Near East and South Asia (FBIS-NES), FBIS-NES-97-013, 13 Jan. 1997.

[164] United Nations (note 6), pp. 308–309.

[165] Voz de los Andes (Quito), 29 Oct. 1996 (in Spanish), in 'Ecuador, Peru sign 4-point Santiago Agreement', Foreign Broadcast Information Service, Daily Report–Latin America (FBIS-LAT), FBIS-LAT-96-211, 31 Oct. 1996.

[166] Peace Process in Nicaragua: Human Rights Verification, Conflicts Resolution and Peacebuilding, Organization of American States—Nicaragua, Managua, Aug. 1996. For background see Baranyi, S., 'Central America: a firm and lasting peace?', SIPRI Yearbook 1995: Armaments, Disarmament and International Security (Oxford University Press: Oxford, 1996), pp. 147–70.

Individual countries were again the most prominent. Norway, for instance, active in a number of peace processes around the world, deployed 40 observers to Hebron to monitor a May accord between Israel and the Palestinian Liberation Organization on lowering tensions in the city.[167] In addition to its predominance in CIS missions, Russia continued its peacekeeping/peacemaking[168] efforts in two former Soviet republics: in Georgia's South Ossetia region and in eastern Moldova. With its regular troops withdrawing from the Trans-Dniester region of Moldova concerns were expressed that it might also withdraw its peacekeeping force.[169] Russia and Ukraine were involved in drafting the outline of a Moldova settlement but to no avail.[170] Russia also continued to attempt to broker settlements in other armed conflicts around the Russian periphery.

However, it was the USA which was again ubiquitous in peace processes worldwide. Its efforts included shoring up implementation of the Dayton Agreement in Bosnia and Herzegovina and encouraging a resumption of progress in the Middle East and Northern Ireland peace processes. Mediation by President Bill Clinton and his envoy Richard Holbrooke headed off confrontation between NATO allies Greece and Turkey over the Imia islets in the Aegean Sea in January.[171]

In April the USA and South Korea proposed quadripartite talks with North Korea and China on a new peace regime for the Korean peninsula, the first time the South had agreed to talks other than bilateral.[172] During the year North Korea put the 1953 Armistice Agreement under further stress by announcing that it was abandoning its 'duty' to help patrol the DMZ between North and South Korea and subsequently carrying out several minor incursions into the zone as well as an ill-fated submarine-launched spy mission into the South in September.[173] Although the USA and North Korea reached a landmark agreement on return of the remains of US missing-in-action (MIAs) from the Korean War, any possibility of quadripartite talks was scuttled by these incursions and South Korea's refusal to countenance food aid to the North unless Pyongyang apologized. The Neutral Nations Supervisory Commission (NNSC) for Korea continued its thankless task of attempting to monitor the so-called truce between the two Koreas.

An International Commission on Northern Ireland, chaired by former US Senator George Mitchell, whose other members were former Prime Minister of Finland Harri Holkeri and General John de Chastelain of Canada, delivered its report in late January. It concluded that paramilitary groups would not agree to decommission weapons in advance of all-party negotiations, as

[167] *International Peacekeeping News*, vol. 2, no. 4 (Sep./Oct. 1996), p. 24.

[168] Russian political parlance does not differentiate between peacekeeping, peace making and peace enforcement. The term used in Russia—*'mirotvorchestvo'*—means, if directly translated 'peace creation'; this could cover a very broad range of activities, from political mediation to combat operations aimed at 'imposing peace'.

[169] Information from Alexei Arbatov, Member of Russian Duma, presentation at SIPRI, 8 Oct. 1996.

[170] *The Economist*, 5 Oct. 1996, pp. 31–32.

[171] 'Greek–Turkish disputes', *Strategic Comments* (IISS), vol. 2, no. 2 (7 Mar. 1996), pp. 1–2.

[172] *Korea Newsreview*, vol. 25, no. 16 (20 Apr. 1996), pp. 6–8.

[173] *Jane's Defence Weekly*, 25 Sep. 1996, pp. 4–5.

demanded by the British Government.[174] The commission instead recommended six principles of non-violence and democracy to which, in the absence of decommissioning, all parties should commit themselves. In February the Irish Republican Army (IRA) broke the 1994 cease-fire with a bombing at London's Canary Wharf. None the less, following elections in Northern Ireland to choose representatives to an all-party peace forum, talks did eventually begin in Belfast in June under Senator Mitchell's chairmanship, with the assistance of the other members of his Commission. Sinn Fein, the political wing of the IRA, was refused a seat until the IRA agreed to reinstate the cease-fire. The talks continued dispiritedly throughout the year, without notable achievement, as further IRA bombings occurred.

The Commonwealth established a Ministerial Action Group (CMAG) to deal with Nigeria on issues of human rights and democracy after it was suspended from membership at the Commonwealth Heads of Government Meeting (CHOGM) in New Zealand in 1995 due to its summary execution of several human rights activists. CMAG had no notable effect on Nigerian policies during the year.

Ad hoc groups of countries, formed when action by the UN or formal regional organizations proved impossible, were popular in 1996. The proposal for the largest new peace operation of the year, to be deployed in eastern Zaire, emanated not from any international organization, whether global, regional or subregional, but from a group of interested countries led by Canada. Although unanimously endorsed by the Security Council on 15 November,[175] the Temporary Multinational Force in Eastern Zaire, a mix of Western and African states, was to be organized and paid for by the participating countries and in the case of the African states, by a trust fund established by the Security Council.[176] Its aim was to provide security and support to relief organizations to allow them to distribute humanitarian assistance and assist in creating conditions for the return of refugees from Zaire to Rwanda and Burundi in cooperation with UNHCR. The operation was called into question even before it began by the sudden defeat by Tutsi Zairean rebels of Hutu extremists, the Interehamwe, who had been intimidating Rwandan refugees into not returning home. Millions of refugees began pouring back into Rwanda, emptying the camps that had been the source of instability for over two years.[177] The deployment of the force was cancelled.

Another ad hoc arrangement operated in Bosnia and Herzegovina in the form of the High Representative, Carl Bildt, and the civilian organization thrown together for supervising the non-military aspects of the Dayton Agreement. This arrangement was slow to begin its work, cumbersome and, without integration with IFOR or the support of a parent international organization, lacking in political, military and economic leverage. Several international

---

[174] *The Independent*, 24 Jan. 1996, p. 1.
[175] Security Council Resolution 1080 (1996), 15 Nov. 1996.
[176] *Wireless File* (US Information Service, US Embassy: Stockholm, 14 Nov. 1996).
[177] For background see Karhilo, J., 'Case study on peacekeeping: Rwanda', *SIPRI Yearbook 1995* (note 166), appendix 2C, pp. 100–16.

gatherings convened during the year with the parties to the conflict kept the civilian aspects of the accord moving tortuously forward. However, by the end of the year the promise of Dayton that refugees and displaced persons be allowed to return to their place of origin had not been fulfilled and low-level 'ethnic cleansing' continued. Moreover, the new democratic structures intended to sustain a unitary Bosnia and Herzegovina were proving to be frustratingly difficult to inaugurate and sustain.

Resumed fighting between rival Kurdish forces in northern Iraq, a major violation of intra-Kurdish agreements reached in US-sponsored talks in Ireland in 1995,[178] prompted negotiation efforts by Iran,[179] Turkey, the UK and the USA. The efforts of the latter three resulted in a cease-fire and establishment of a Supervisory Peace Monitoring Group, which met in Ankara, Turkey, in November with plans to demarcate a cease-fire line and deploy a Peace Monitoring Group.[180] In Lebanon, a cease-fire monitoring committee comprising France, Israel, Lebanon, Syria, the USA and the Hezbollah was established after a formal agreement between Israel and Hezbollah in April to refrain from attacking each other.[181]

After years of negotiations supported by Indonesia and the Organization of the Islamic Conference (OIC) a landmark agreement was reached between the Philippines Government and the largest Muslim opposition faction, the Moro National Liberation Front (MNLF), ending 24 years of war in the southern Philippines.[182] President Fidel Ramos and rebel leader Nur Misuari personally finalized details of the agreement in August. Signed in Manila on 2 September, it establishes an autonomous Muslim council based in Davao City and covering about a quarter of Philippine territory which will dispense development funds over 14 provinces and 9 cities. The council will have neither legislative nor police powers and will be replaced by a permanent autonomous structure in 1999, when a plebiscite is held to determine which regions will belong to it. Hardline Christian elements and at least two Muslim extremist factions, including the Moro Islamic Liberation Front (MILF), continued to oppose the agreement.[183] Large-scale development funding, some promised by Japan and Malaysia, will be crucial in making the plan work. Meanwhile President Fidel Ramos announced a 60-day Christmas–New Year unilateral government cease-fire in its war against the Communist New People's Army, the longest ever declared.[184] The government and rebels began formal peace talks in the Netherlands in June.

Another ad hoc group of organizations and states helped the local parties in Guatemala produce a peace agreement ending 36 years of armed conflict. The UN, the Friends of the Guatemala Peace Process (Colombia, Mexico, Norway,

---

[178] For background see 'Kurdistan? Which one do you mean?', *The Economist*, 10 Aug. 1996, pp. 31–32.

[179] *International Herald Tribune*, 28 Aug. 1996, p. 8.

[180] *Wireless File* (US Information Service, US Embassy: Stockholm, 15 Nov. 1996).

[181] *International Peacekeeping News*, vol. 2, no. 4. (Sep./Oct. 1996), p. 24.

[182] Emerson, T., 'Pinch us, it's peace', *Newsweek*, 16 Sep. 1996, pp. 36–37.

[183] Clifton, T., 'Life on the last frontier', *Newsweek*, 27 May 1996, pp. 21–23.

[184] *Ichaleej Times* (Dubai), 29 Nov. 1996, p. 9.

Spain, the USA and Venezuela) and Sweden all contributed to the effort, although the basic impetus came, appropriately, from within Guatemala itself, including from the new democratically elected government of President Alvaro Arzu. In March both the government and the Unidad Revolucionaria Nacional Guatemaltec (URNG) announced a cessation of hostilities and on 6 May signed in Mexico City under UN auspices an Agreement on the Social and Economic Aspects and Agrarian Situation in Guatemala.[185] It was seen as a precursor to a full peace agreement. In September the parties signed a further agreement in Mexico City under UN auspices, on the future size and role of Guatemala's armed forces, reducing them by one-third by 1997.[186] US-trained counterinsurgency units, accused by the rebels of atrocities, would be disbanded. The UN Mission for the Verification of Human Rights (MINUGUA) continued, however, to report serious and repeated violations of human rights which were neither clarified nor punished.[187] By August Norwegian mediation had produced an Agreement on a Definitive Ceasefire, signed in Oslo in December, to be verified by UN monitors.[188] Further agreements were signed in December in Stockholm on constitutional and military reform[189] and in Madrid on integrating the guerrilla forces into the political life of the country.[190] Despite last-minute delays the parties signed the long-awaited, concluding Agreement on a Firm and Lasting Peace on 29 December in Guatemala City. Guatemala is a fascinating case of a deliberate, step-by-step, bottom-up approach to peacemaking, tended by a diverse array of states and organizations acting in a surprisingly integrated and cooperative fashion.

Again in 1996, the parties to conflicts themselves sometimes initiated a peace process, with or without external assistance, often in response to changing political or military fortunes. In the Sudan a shift in political alliances resulted in a so-called Peace Charter between the government and some of the southern factional leaders, although it did not involve the main rebel group, the Sudanese People's Liberation Army.[191] UN-mediated proximity talks between the factions, under DHA auspices, were directed solely at ensuring continuance of Operation Lifeline Sudan, which provides humanitarian assistance. In Cambodia rifts in the Khmer Rouge produced mass defections to the government and the opportunity to negotiate peace with the break-away faction.[192] The isolation suffered by the group since the UN peacekeeping operation, the UN Transitional Authority in Cambodia (UNTAC), in 1991–93 was clearly a factor in this development, which opened the possibility of an end to Cambodia's 18-year civil war.[193] In South Africa peace talks between the Zulu

[185] UN Chronicle, no. 2 (1996), p. 56.

[186] Jane's Defence Weekly, 25 Sep. 1996, p. 15; International Herald Tribune, 22 Sep. 1996, p. 1.

[187] United Nations (note 80); p. 233.

[188] International Peacekeeping News, vol. 2, no. 3 (July/Aug. 1996), p. 14; and Daily Highlights (UN Department of Public Information), 4 Dec. 1996.

[189] Dagens Nyheter, 18 Dec. 1996.

[190] Daily Highlights (UN Department of Public Information), 12 Dec. 1996.

[191] United Nations (note 80), p. 172; and International Herald Tibune, 18 Feb. 1997, p. 6.

[192] The Australian, 17 Aug. 1996, p. 9.

[193] For background see Findlay, T., Cambodia: The Legacy and Lessons of UNTAC, SIPRI Research Report no. 9 (Oxford University Press: Oxford, 1995).

organization Inkatha and the African National Congress led to a reduction in tribal violence that had killed more than 10 000 people since the 1980s and induced Inkatha to join multi-party negotiations on South Africa's new constitution.[194] The Bangladeshi Government held talks with India and rebel groups over its long-running Chittagong Hill Tracts conflict.[195]

Non-governmental organizations continued to increase their activity in conflict prevention and peacemaking, sometimes proving more effective than governments. The Roman Catholic Sant' Egidio community, which previously had attempted to negotiate in Algeria, helped devise a plan to end Burundi's conflict in cooperation with US special envoy Howard Wolpe and Tanzanian mediator Julius Nyerere.[196] International Alert took Sri Lankan parliamentarians to Belfast to meet representatives of the Liberation Tigers of Tamil Elam (LTTE) or Tamil Tigers.[197] In general NGOs are becoming better organized in such activities. The London-based International Crisis Group (ICG), with its board of political luminaries, pioneered high-level lobbying of governments to induce them to act in particular conflict situations, notably in Bosnia and Herzegovina, Burundi, Nigeria and Sierra Leone.[198] The Swedish UN Association established a so-called Peace Team Forum for Swedish NGOs interested in conflict prevention, while the World Federation of UN Associations (WFUNA) began investigating the establishment of a conflict prevention network among its member organizations.

VII. Conclusions

The year was notable for peace settlements in the Philippines, Sierra Leone and Guatemala, but progress was frustratingly slow in other better known cases such as the Middle East, Northern Ireland, and Bosnia and Herzegovina. Africa and an arc of instability around the Russian periphery remained the most troubled regions and those most targeted by conflict prevention, management and resolution efforts.

The UN remained prominent in such efforts even while its budget crisis continued and the Security Council remained shy, to the detriment of its credibility, about launching new initiatives, even in desperate situations like those of Burundi and Zaire. UN peacekeeping consequently continued its dramatic decline, the largest extant peacekeeping mission anywhere in 1996 being the non-UN NATO-led IFOR in Bosnia and Herzegovina and its successor, SFOR. With the remaining large-scale UN operations all due to end in 1997, the post-cold war era of large multi-component missions, aimed in

---

[194] *The Economist*, 5 Oct. 1996, pp. 49–50.

[195] Ahmed, S., 'Ethnic conflict in South Asia: the case of the Chittagong Hill Tracts', Paper presented to the conference on Conflict Resolution in the Post Cold War Era: Lessons for South Asia, University of Karachi, 1–2 Dec. 1996.

[196] *International Peacekeeping News*, vol. 2, no. 4 (Sep./Oct. 1996), p. 5.

[197] Saravanamuttu, P., 'Failure of state system in South Asia: a case study of Sri Lanka', Paper presented to conference on Conflict Resolution in the Post Cold War Era (note 195).

[198] International Crisis Group, ICG 1995–1996 Review: International Crisis Group Annual Review and Financial Statements, London, Dec. 1996.

effect at nation-building, appeared to be over. Peacekeeping reform continued regardless, partly through inertia but also in the expectation that sooner or later a pressing need will arise that only the UN can meet and for which the requisite political will can be garnered. The kaleidoscopic instabilities of the African Great Lakes region during 1996 were a continuing reminder that the 'end of history' is not nigh for peace operations. Rapid reaction capabilities were boosted considerably during the year in initiatives taken both within and outside the UN. With its leadership crisis over the UN could, at year's end, look forward to less uncertainty, more robust reform and, the US Congress willing, improved financial health.

None the less the debate about universalist versus regionalist approaches to conflict prevention, management and resolution continued during the year, heightened by attempts by the Security Council, the OAU and even some by the parties directly involved to shirk responsibility for dealing with the multiple Great Lakes crises. Only slight less pernicious was the continuing tendency of the UN, regional organizations and their member states—seen most tragically in 1994 in the Rwandan case—to define their responses to crisis situations by what they were willing to contribute rather than what was required. While needs will always outpace resources there still needs to be a recognition that conflict prevention, management and resolution, although less expensive than war, is not cheap. In the most difficult cases it requires major commitments of political and diplomatic attention, military power or its threatened use, human and material resources, and finance.

With regional organizations worldwide still struggling to create the capacity to deal with potential and actual conflicts in their own bailiwicks, competent subregional organizations only just emerging and the UN over-burdened, unreconstructed and under-funded, the clear answer was for cooperative and integrated approaches by all parties willing and able to contribute to a particular peace process, as demonstrated so felicitously in the Guatemala case. Effective early warning of impending crises especially demands the pooling of information and analysis from as many sources as possible. Embryonic efforts by the United Nations and governmental and non-governmental organizations to institutionalize coordination beyond information sharing are welcome. The most effective approach could be one that permits a flexible, varying mix of actors and contributors to be custom-built for the specific needs of each conflict prevention, management or resolution endeavour.

Appendix 2A. Multilateral peace missions, 1996

OLGA HARDARDÓTTIR

Table 2A lists multilateral observer, peacekeeping, peacebuilding and combined peacekeeping and peace-enforcement missions initiated, continuing or terminated in 1996 by international organization and by starting date. Five groups of missions are presented. The 26 missions run by the United Nations are divided into two sections. UN peacekeeping operations (19) are those so designated by the UN itself (see figure 2.1 in this volume), although they may include some missions more properly described as observer missions; the other UN operations comprise missions not officially described by the UN as peacekeeping operations (2 of these are operated in cooperation with the Organization of American States, OAS). Of the remaining missions 11 are run by the Organization for Security and Co-operation in Europe (OSCE), 4 by the Commonwealth of Independent States (CIS)/Russia and 10 by other organizations. Peace missions comprising individual negotiators or teams of negotiators not resident in the mission area are not included.

Legal instruments underlying the establishment of an operation, such as relevant resolutions of the UN Security Council, are cited in the first column.

Missions that ended in 1996 and individual countries that ended their participation in 1996 are italicized, while new missions and individual countries participating for the first time in 1996 are bolded. Numbers of civilian observers and international and local civilian staff are not included.

Mission fatalities are recorded from the beginning of the conflict until the last reported date for 1996 ('to date'), and as a total for the year ('in 1996'). Information on the approximate or estimated annual cost of the missions ('yearly') and the approximate outstanding contributions ('unpaid') to the operation fund at the close of the 1996 budget period (the date of which varies from operation to operation) is given in current US $m. In the case of UN missions, unless otherwise noted, UN data on contributing countries and on numbers of troops, military observers and civilian police as well as on fatalities and costs are as of 31 December 1996. UN data on total mission fatalities ('to date') are for all UN missions since 1948.

Figures on the number of personnel participating in OSCE missions are totals for each mission, and include both military and civilian staff in 1996. The OSCE Sanctions Assistance Missions (SAMs) in Albania, Bulgaria, Croatia, Hungary, the Former Yugoslav Republic of Macedonia, Romania and Ukraine, not listed in the table, were discontinued on 31 September 1996 as a result of UN Security Council Resolution 1047 (1 Oct. 1996), which terminated the sanctions.

Table 2A. Multilateral peace missions

Acronym/ (Legal instrument[a])	Name/type of mission (O: observer) (PK: peacekeeping)	Location	Start date	Countries contributing troops, military observers (mil. obs) and/or civilian police (civ. pol.) in 1996	Troops/ Mil. obs/ Civ. pol.	Deaths: To date / In 1996	Cost: Yearly / Unpaid
United Nations (UN) peacekeeping operations[1] (19 operations) (UN Charter, Chapters VI and VII)					20 787[2] / 1 347 / 2 739	1 502[3] / 52	1 200[4] / 1 700[5]
UNTSO (SCR 50)	UN Truce Supervision Organization (O)	Egypt/Israel/ Lebanon/Syria	June 1948	Argentina, Australia, Austria, Belgium, Canada, Chile, China, Denmark, Finland, France, Ireland, Italy, Netherlands, New Zealand, Norway, Russia, Sweden, Switzerland, USA	– / 163 / –	38 / –	27 / –
UNMOGIP (SCR 91)	UN Military Observer Group in India and Pakistan (O)	India/Pakistan (Kashmir)	Jan. 1949	Belgium, Chile, Denmark, Finland, Italy, South Korea, Sweden, Uruguay	45 / –	11 / 2	7 / –
UNFICYP (SCR 186)	UN Peace-keeping Force in Cyprus (PK)	Cyprus	Mar. 1964	Argentina, Australia, Austria, Canada, Finland, **Hungary,** Ireland, UK	1 162 / – / 35	168 / 1	45[6] / 13
UNDOF (SCR 350)	UN Disengagement Observer Force (O)	Syria (Golan Heights)	June 1974	Austria, Canada, **Japan,** Poland	1 046 / 7 / –	36 / –	32[8] / 9[9]
UNIFIL (SCR 425, 426)	UN Interim Force in Lebanon (PK)	Lebanon (Southern)	Mar. 1978	Fiji, Finland, France, Ghana, Ireland, Italy, Nepal, Norway, Poland	4 505 / –10 / –	214 / 5	126 / 177
UNIKOM (SCR 689)	UN Iraq–Kuwait Observation Mission (O)	Iraq/Kuwait (Khawr 'Abd Allah waterway and UN DMZ[11])	Apr. 1991	Argentina, Austria, Bangladesh, Canada, China, Denmark, Fiji, Finland, France, Germany, Ghana, Greece, Hungary, India, Indonesia, Ireland, Italy, Kenya, Malaysia, Nigeria, Pakistan, Poland, Romania, Russia, Senegal, Singapore, Sweden, Thailand, Turkey, UK, USA, Uruguay, Venezuela	905[12] / 197 / –	8 / 3	52[13] / 15

Acronym/ Legal instrument[a]	Name/type of mission (O: observer) (PK: peacekeeping)	Location	Start date	Countries contributing troops, military observers (mil. obs) and/or civilian police (civ. pol.) in 1996	Troops/ Mil. obs/ Civ. pol.	Deaths: To date In 1996	Cost: Yearly Unpaid
MINURSO (SCR 690)	UN Mission for the Referendum in Western Sahara (O)	Western Sahara	Sep. 1991	Argentina, Austria, Bangladesh, *Belgium*, China, Egypt, El Salvador, France, *Germany*, Ghana, Greece, Guinea, Honduras, Hungary, Ireland, Italy, Kenya, Malaysia, Nigeria, Norway, Pakistan, Poland, **Portugal**, Russia, South Korea, Togo, Tunisia, USA, Uruguay, *Venezuela*	27[14] 196 8	7 –	32 43
UNOMIG (SCR 849, 858)	UN Observer Mission in Georgia (O)	Georgia (Abkhazia)	Aug. 1993	Albania, Austria, Bangladesh, Cuba, Czech Rep., Denmark, Egypt, France, Germany, Greece, Hungary, Indonesia, Jordan, Pakistan, Poland, Russia, South Korea, Sweden, Switzerland, Turkey, UK, USA, Uruguay	– 124[15] –	1 –	17 7
UNOMIL (SCR 866)	UN Observer Mission in Liberia (O)	Liberia	Sep. 1993	Bangladesh, China, Czech Rep., Egypt, *Guinea-Bissau*, India, Jordan, Kenya, Malaysia, **Nepal**, Pakistan, Uruguay	7[16] 71[17] –	– –	14 5
UNMIH (SCR 867)	*UN Mission in Haiti* (PK)	*Haiti*	*Sep. 1993[18]*	*Algeria, Antigua & Barbuda, Argentina, Austria, Bahamas, Bangladesh, Barbados, Belize, Benin, Canada, Djibouti, France, Guatemala, Guinea-Bissau, Guyana, Honduras, India, Ireland, Jamaica, Jordan, Mali, Nepal, Netherlands, New Zealand, Pakistan, Philippines, Russia, St Kitts & Nevis, St. Lucia, Suriname, Togo, Trinidad & Tobago, Tunisia, USA*	1 831[19] – 414	8 6	.. 6
UNAMIR (SCR 872)	*UN Assistance Mission for Rwanda* (PK)	*Rwanda*	*Oct. 1993[20]*	*Argentina, Australia, Austria, Bangladesh, Canada, Chad, Congo, Djibouti, Ethiopia, Fiji, Germany, Ghana, Guinea, Guinea-Bissau, India, Jordan, Malawi, Mali, Niger, Nigeria, Pakistan, Poland, Russia, Senegal, Spain, Switzerland, Tunisia, UK, Uruguay, Zambia, Zimbabwe*	669[21] 19 –	26 –	.. 28[22]
UNMOT (SCR 968)	UN Mission of Observers in Tajikistan (O)	Tajikistan	Dec. 1994	Austria, Bangladesh, Bulgaria, Denmark, Jordan, Poland, Switzerland, Ukraine, Uruguay	– 43 –	1 –	7 1

Mission	Location	Date	Contributing countries							
UNAVEM III (SCR 976)	UN Angola Verification Mission III (O)	Angola	Feb. 1995	Algeria, Bangladesh, Brazil, Bulgaria, Congo, Egypt, *Fiji*, France, Guinea-Bissau, Hungary, India, *Italy*, Jordan, Kenya, Malaysia, Mali, *Namibia*, Netherlands, New Zealand, Nigeria, Norway, Pakistan, Poland, Portugal, Romania, Russia, Senegal, Slovakia, South Korea, Sweden, Tanzania, *UK*, **Ukraine**, Uruguay, Zambia, Zimbabwe	6 017[23] 345 246	33 27	323 113[24]
UNCRO (SCR 981)	*UN Confidence Restoration Operation in Croatia (PK)*	*Croatia*	*Mar. 1995*[25]	*Argentina, Bangladesh, Belgium, Brazil, Canada, Czech Rep., Denmark, Egypt, Estonia, Finland, France, Germany, Ghana, Indonesia, Ireland, Jordan, Kenya, Lithuania, Malaysia, Nepal, Netherlands, New Zealand, Nigeria, Norway, Pakistan, Poland, Portugal, Russia, Senegal, Slovakia, Spain, Sweden, Switzerland, Tunisia, Turkey, UK, Ukraine, USA*	3 294[26] 290 168	17 1	–_27
UNPREDEP (SCR 983)	UN Preventive Deployment Force (PK)	Macedonia	Mar. 1995	Argentina, Bangladesh, Belgium, Brazil, Canada, Czech Rep., Denmark, Egypt, Finland, *France*, Ghana, Indonesia, Ireland, Jordan, Kenya, Nepal, *Netherlands*, New Zealand, Nigeria, Norway, Pakistan, Poland, Portugal, Russia, *Spain*, Sweden, Switzerland, **Turkey**, *UK*, Ukraine, USA	1 040 35 26	– –	53 10
UNMIBH (SCR 1035)[28]	UN Mission in Bosnia and Herzegovina (O)	Bosnia and Herzegovina	Dec. 1995	**Argentina, Austria, Bangladesh, Bulgaria, Canada,** Denmark, Egypt, Estonia, Finland, France, Germany, **Ghana,** Greece, **Hungary, India,** Indonesia, Ireland, Jordan, *Kenya*, **Malaysia, Nepal, Netherlands, Nigeria, Norway, Pakistan,** Poland, Portugal, Russia, Senegal, Spain, Sweden, Switzerland, Tunisia, **Turkey, USA**	5 – 1 704[29]	3 3	161 13
UNTAES (SCR 1037)	UN Transitional Administration for Eastern Slavonia, Baranja and Western Sirmium	Croatia	Jan. 1996	**Argentina, Austria, Bangladesh, Belgium, Brazil, Czech Rep, Denmark, Egypt, Fiji, Finland,** *France*, **Ghana, Greece, Indonesia, Ireland, Jordan, Kenya, Lithuania, Nepal, Netherlands, New Zealand, Norway,** Pakistan, Poland, Portugal, Russia, *Senegal*, Slovakia, Sweden, Switzerland, Tunisia, *Turkey*, UK, Ukraine, USA	4 791 100 453	4 4	286 51
UNMOP (SCR 1038)[30]	UN Mission of Observers in Prevlaka	Croatia	Jan. 1996	Argentina, Bangladesh, Belgium, Brazil, Canada, Czech Rep, Denmark, Egypt, Finland, *France*, Ghana, Indonesia, Ireland, Jordan, Kenya, Nepal, New Zealand, Nigeria, Norway, Pakistan, Poland, Portugal, Russia, Sweden, Switzerland, *UK*, Ukraine	– 28 –	– –	–_31 ..

Acronym/ (Legal instrument[a])	Name/type of mission (O: observer) (PK: peacekeeping)	Location	Start date	Countries contributing troops, military observers (mil. obs) and/or civilian police (civ. pol.) in 1996	Troops/ Mil. obs/ Civ. pol.	Deaths: To date In 1996	Cost: Yearly Unpaid
UNSMIH (SCR 1063)	UN Support Mission in Haiti	Haiti	July 1996[32]	Algeria, Bangladesh, Canada, *Djibouti*, France, India, Mali, Pakistan, *Russia*, Togo, *Trinidad & Tobago*, USA	1 282[33] – 267	– –	57 15

Other United Nations (UN) operations (7 operations)[34]

Acronym/ (Legal instrument[a])	Name/type of mission (O: observer) (PK: peacekeeping)	Location	Start date	Countries contributing troops, military observers (mil. obs) and/or civilian police (civ. pol.) in 1996	Troops/ Mil. obs/ Civ. pol.	Deaths: To date In 1996	Cost: Yearly Unpaid
CIAV/OAS	International Commission for Support and Verification[35]	Nicaragua	May 1990	_[36]	_[37] – –	.. ..	.. ..
MICIVIH (GAR 47/20B[38])	International Civilian Mission to Haiti	Haiti	Feb. 1993	..	_[39] – –	.. ..	.. ..
UNSMA (GAR 48/208)	UN Special Mission to Afghanistan	Afghanistan/Pakistan[40]	Mar. 1994[41]	Ghana, Ireland	– 2[42] –	.. –	.. ..
MINUGUA[43] (GAR 48/267)	UN Mission for the Verification of Human Rights and of Compliance with the Commitments of the Comprehensive Agreement on Human Rights in Guatemala	Guatemala	Oct. 1994	Argentina, Brazil, Canada, Colombia, Italy, Spain, Sweden, Uruguay, Venezuela[44]	– 17 50	– –	34[45]
OSGA (SG Jan. 1995)[46]	*Office of the Secretary-General in Afghanistan*	*Afghanistan/Pakistan*[47]	*Jan. 1995*[48]	*Ghana, Ireland*	– 2[49] –	.. ..	.. ..
MINUSAL (SG Feb. 1995)[50]	*Mission of the UN in El Salvador*	*El Salvador*	*May 1995*[51]	..	– – ..	.. ..	.[52] ..

Operation	Location	Date		Members			Cost ($m.)
ONUV (GAR 50/226) / UN Office of Verification	El Salvador	May 1996[53]	—	3[54]	..	..	..

Organization for Security and Co-operation in Europe (OSCE) (11 operations)[55]

Operation	Location	Date		Members			Cost ($m.)
OSCE Spillover Mission to Skopje (O) (CSO 18 Sep. 1992[56])	Former Yugoslav Rep. of Macedonia	Sep. 1992	—	4[57]	—	—	0.5[58]
OSCE Mission to Georgia (O) (CSO 6 Nov. 1992[59])	Georgia (S. Ossetia; Abkhazia)	Dec. 1992	—	17	1	1	1.7[58]
OSCE Mission to Estonia (O) (CSO 13 Dec. 1992[60])	Estonia	Feb. 1993	—	6	—	—	0.4[58]
OSCE Mission to Moldova (O) (CSO 4 Feb. 1993[61])	Moldova	Apr. 1993	—	8	—	—	0.7[58]
OSCE Mission to Latvia (O) (CSO 23 Sep. 1993[62])	Latvia	Nov. 1993	—	7	—	—	0.6[58]
OSCE Mission to Tajikistan (O) (1 Dec. 1993[63])	Tajikistan	Feb. 1994	—	8	—	—	0.7[58]
OSCE Mission in Sarajevo (O) (2 June 1994[64])	Bosnia and Herzegovina	Oct. 1994	—	6	—	—	0.8[58]
OSCE Mission to Ukraine (O) (CSO 15 June 1994[65])	Ukraine	Nov. 1994	—	6	—	—	0.5[58]
OSCE Assistance Group to Chechnya (O) (11 Apr. 1995[66])	Chechnya	Apr. 1995	—	8	—	—	1.5[58]

Acronym/ (Legal instrument[a])	Name/type of mission (O: observer) (PK: peacekeeping)	Location	Start date	Countries contributing troops, military observers (mil. obs) and/or civilian police (civ. pol.) in 1996	Troops/ Mil. obs/ Civ. pol.	Deaths: To date In 1996	Cost: Yearly Unpaid
— (8 Dec. 1995[67])	OSCE Mission to Bosnia and Herzegovina (O)	Bosnia and Herzegovina	Dec. 1995[68]	..	8[69] —	— —	23.5[58] ..
— **(18 Apr. 1996)**[70]	**OSCE Mission to Croatia** (O)	**Croatia**	**July 1996**	..	—[71] —	— —	1[72] ..
CIS/Russia (4 operations)[73]							
— (Bilateral agreement[74])	'South Ossetia Joint Force' (PK)	Georgia (S. Ossetia)	July 1992	Georgia, Russia, North and South Ossetia	..[75] —	.. ..	.. ..
— (Bilateral agreement[76])	'Moldova Joint Force' (PK)	Moldova (Trans-Dniester)	July 1992	Moldova, Russia, 'Trans-Dniester Republic'	..[77] —	.. ..	.. ..
— (CIS 24 Sep. 1993[78])	CIS 'Tajikistan Buffer Force' (PK)	Tajikistan (Afghan border)[79]	Aug. 1993[80]	Kazakhstan, Kyrgyzstan, Russia, Uzbekistan[81]	..[82] —	..[83] ..	..[84] ..
— (CIS 15 Apr. 1994)[85]	CIS 'Peacekeeping Forces in Georgia' (PK)	Georgian– Abkhazian border	June 1994	Russia	..[86] —	.. ..	.. ..
Other (10 operations)							
NNSC (Armistice Agreement[87])	Neutral Nations Supervisory Commission (O)	North Korea/ South Korea	July 1953	Sweden, Switzerland[88]	— 10 —	— —	1.4[89] ..
MFO (Protocol to treaty[90])	Multinational Force and Observers in the Sinai (O)	Egypt (Sinai)	Apr. 1982	Australia, Canada, Colombia, Fiji, France, Hungary, Italy, New Zealand, Norway, Uruguay, USA	1 896[91] — —	.. ..	51[92] ..

Acronym	Name (type)	Location	Start date	Countries	Troops	Mil. obs.	Civ. police	Deaths	Cost
ECOMOG (ESMC 7 Aug. 1990[93])	ECOWAS[94] Monitoring Group (PK)	Liberia	Aug. 1990	Gambia, Ghana, Guinea, Mali, Nigeria, **Niger**, Sierra Leone, *Uganda*[95]	7 500[96]	–	–	..	..[97]
ECMM (Brioni Agreement[98])	European Community Monitoring Mission[99] (O)	Former Yugoslavia	July 1991	Austria, Belgium, Czech Rep., Denmark, Finland, France, Germany, Greece, Ireland, Italy, Netherlands, Norway, *Poland*, Portugal, Slovakia, Spain, Sweden, UK	211	–	–	6	19[100]
OMIB[101] (OAU 1993)	OAU Mission in Burundi (O)	Burundi	Dec. 1993	*Burkina Faso, Guinea, Mali, Niger, Tunisia*	–[102]	1	–	1	2.5[103]
WEUPF (Washington Agreement 16 Mar. 1994)[104]	Western European Union Police Force[105] (O)	Bosnia and Herzegovina (Mostar)	July 1994[106]	Austria, Belgium, Finland, France, Germany, Greece, India, Luxembourg, Netherlands, Portugal, Spain, Sweden, UK	–	–	180	–	..
– (Agreement Sep. 1994; SCR 943)	Mission of the International Conference on the Former Yugoslavia[107] (O)	Serbia/ Bosnia and Herzegovina border area	Sep. 1994[108]	Belgium, Canada, Czech Rep., Denmark, Finland, France, Germany, Greece, Ireland, Italy, Netherlands, Norway, Portugal, Russia, Spain, Sweden, UK, USA	–	..	–	–	..
MOMEP (Decl. of Itamaraty)[109]	Mission of Military Observers Ecuador/Peru (O)	Ecuador/Peru	Mar. 1995	Argentina, Brazil, Chile, **Ecuador, Peru**, USA	–	35	–	–	..
IFOR (SCR 1031)[110]	Implementation Force (PK)	Bosnia and Herzegovina	Dec. 1995[111]	**Albania**, Austria, Belgium, **Bulgaria**, Canada, Czech Rep., Denmark, Egypt, Estonia, Finland, France, Germany, Greece, Hungary, Italy, Jordan, Latvia, Lithuania, Luxembourg, Malaysia, Morocco, Netherlands, Norway, Poland, Portugal, Romania, Russia, Slovakia, Spain, Sweden, Turkey, UK, Ukraine, USA[112]	40 000[113]	–	–	52[114] / 52	5 000[115]
SFOR (SCR 1088)	Stabilization Force (PK)	Bosnia and Herzegovina	Dec. 1996[111]	Albania, Austria, Belgium, Bulgaria, Canada, Czech Rep., Denmark, Egypt, Estonia, Finland, France, Germany, Greece, Hungary, Italy, Jordan, Latvia, Lithuania, Luxembourg, Malaysia, Morocco, Netherlands, Norway, Poland, Portugal, Romania, Russia, Spain, Sweden, Turkey, UK, Ukraine, USA[116]	32 000[116]	–	–	..	..[117]

Notes for table 2A

[a] GAR = General Assembly Resolution; SCR = Security Council Resolution; SG = Secretary-General

[1] Sources for this section, unless otherwise noted: United Nations, Department of Peacekeeping Operations, Monthly summary of troop contributions to peace-keeping operations; United Nations, United Nations Peace-keeping Operations, Background Note, DPI/1634/Rev. 5, Dec. 1996; United Nations, Status of contributions as at 31 December 1996, UN document ST/ADM/SER.B/505, 8 Jan. 1997; and information from UN Department of Public Information, Peace and Security Section, New York.

[2] As of 31 Dec. 1996. Operational strength varies from month to month because of rotation.

[3] Casualty figures are valid 31 Dec. 1996 and include military, civilian police and civilian international and local staff. The figures, from the UN Situation Centre, are based on information from the Peace-Keeping Data-Base covering the period 1948–96. This database is still under review and some errors or omissions are possible.

[4] 17 of the 19 UN peacekeeping operations conducted or ongoing in 1996 are financed from their own separate accounts on the basis of legally binding assessments on all member states in accordance with Article 17 of the UN Charter. UNTSO and UNMOGIP are funded from the UN regular budget. Some missions, as noted in the relevant footnote, are partly funded by voluntary contributions. Figures are annualized budget estimates.

[5] Outstanding contributions to UN peacekeeping operations as of 30 Nov. 1996.

[6] With effect from 16 June 1993, the financing of UNFICYP is inclusive of voluntary contributions of $6.5 m. annually from the Government of Greece and of one-third of the cost from the Government of Cyprus. Thus only c. $23 m. is assessed on the UN member states annually. United Nations, Report of the Secretary-General on United Nations Operation in Cyprus, UN document S/1996/1016, 10 Dec. 1996, p. 7.

[7] UNDOF comprised 4 military observers seconded by UNTSO and was in addition assisted by 73 military observers of the Observer Group Golan (OGG) of UNTSO. United Nations, Report of the Secretary-General on the United Nations Disengagement Observer Force, UN document S/1996/959, 18 Nov. 1996, p. 2.

[8] Initially financed from a special account established for UNEF II (Second UN Emergency Force, Oct. 1973–July 1979). At the termination of UNEF II, the account remained open for UNDOF.

[9] Total approximate value of outstanding contributions to UNEF II and UNDOF.

[10] 57 UNTSO military observers assisted. United Nations, Report of the Secretary-General on the United Nations Interim Force in Lebanon, UN document S/1997/42, 20 Jan. 1997.

[11] SCR 687 (3 Apr. 1991) established a demilitarized zone (DMZ) stretching about 200 km along the Iraq–Kuwait border, extending 10 km into Iraq and 5 km into Kuwait.

[12] Authorized strength: 910 troops and 300 military observers. Financing of the activities arising from Security Council Resolution 687 (1991): United Nations Iraq–Kuwait Observation Mission, Report of the Secretary-General, UN document A/49/863, 20 Mar. 1995, p. 5.

[13] Two-thirds of the cost of the mission, equivalent to some $41 m., is funded through voluntary contributions from the Government of Kuwait. United Nations, Report of the Secretary-General on the United Nations Iraq–Kuwait Observation Mission, UN document S/1996/801, 27 Sep. 1996.

[14] SCR 1056 (29 May 1996) authorized reduction of strength of military component by 20%.

[15] Authorized strength: 136 military observers. SCR 937 (21 July 1994).

[16] Original authorized strength: 65 troops (20 military medical staff and 45 military engineers) and 303 military observers. United Nations, Report of the Secretary-General on Liberia, UN document S/26422/Add. 1, 17 Sep. 1993, p. 1.

[17] SCR 950 (21 Oct. 1994) authorized temporary reduction of observer force to 90 because of deteriorating security. SCR 1020 (10 Nov. 1995) decided that the number of military observers should not exceed 160.

[18] Replaced by UNSMIH when its mandate expired on 30 June 1996.

[19] As of 30 June 1996.

[20] SCR 1029 (12 Dec. 1995) extended mandate of UNAMIR for a final period to 8 Mar. 1996 and withdrawal was completed on 19 Apr.

21 As of 31 Mar. 1996.

22 Total approximate value of outstanding contributions to UNOMUR (June 1993–Jan. 1994) and UNAMIR.

23 Authorized strength pursuant to SCR 976 (8 Feb. 1995): 7000 military personnel, 350 military observers and 260 police observers.

24 Total approximate value of outstanding contributions to UNAVEM I (Jan. 1989–June 1991), UNAVEM II (June 1991–Feb. 1995) and UNAVEM III.

25 Pursuant to SCR 1025 (30 Nov. 1995), the mandate of UNCRO ended on 15 Jan. 1996.

26 As of 31 Dec. 1995. When UNCRO's mandate expired all civilian police officers redeployed to Bosnia and Herzegovina or to new operation in Eastern Slavonia, Baranja and Western Sirmium (UNTAES), established by SCR 1037 (15 Jan. 1996). United Nations, Further report of the Secretary-General pursuant to Security Council resolutions 1025 (1995) and 1026 (1995), UN document S/1996/83, 6 Feb. 1996.

27 Total approximate value of outstanding contributions to UNCRO, UNPROFOR and UNPF headquarters was $729 m.

28 SCR 1035 (21 Dec. 1995) authorized establishment of International Police Task Force (IPTF), in accordance with annex 11 to the General Framework Agreement for Peace in Bosnia and Herzegovina (the Dayton Agreement), plus a civilian mission as proposed in the Secretary-General's report of 13 Dec. 1995, S/1995/1031. The mission was later given the name UNMIBH. UN document S/1996/83 (note 26), p. 5.

29 Authorized strength of IPTF, the principal component of UNMIBH: 1721 police monitors.

30 The Security Council authorized UN military observers to continue monitoring the demilitarization of the Prevlaka peninsula which had previously been carried out by UNPROFOR and UNCRO since 1992.

31 Cost included in UNMIBH.

32 Replaced UNMIH when its mandate expired on 30 June 1996.

33 Authorized strength according to SCR 1063 (28 June 1996): 300 civilian police and 600 troops. An additional 700 military personnel are funded voluntarily by the United States and Canada. United Nations, Report of the Secretary-General on the United Nations Support Mission in Haiti, UN document S/1996/813, 1 Oct. 1996.

34 Comprises substantial UN peace missions (2 in cooperation with OAS) not officially described by the UN as peacekeeping.

35 Established jointly by UN and OAS, after a request from the 5 Central American presidents, to verify compliance with the Tela Agreement of 7 Aug. 1989 on a timetable for the dismantling of Contra camps in Nicaragua and repatriation of rebels.

36 Civilian staff from Argentina, Colombia, Nicaragua and Uruguay. Information from CIAV/OAS in Managua.

37 Total staff 91, of whom 87 are Nicaraguan.

38 Joint UN participation with OAS was authorized by the resolution.

39 UN component was 32 human rights officers at the end of 1996. United Nations, Year in Review 1996: United Nations peace missions, DPI/1861–96–93401–Dec. 1996–4M, p. 12.

40 Mission maintains an office in Islamabad, Pakistan.

41 UNSMA took over all activities of OSGA which ceased to exist at the end of June 1996 (see note 48).

42 There were also 5 political officers, a director and a deputy director as well as support staff. Information from UNSMA office in Islamabad.

43 Information concerning this mission from MINUGUA office in Guatemala.

44 Countries providing military observers and civilian police. In addition c. 30 countries were contributing civilian personnel.

45 $28 m. came from the UN regular budget and $6 m. were voluntary contributions to a Trust Fund, created by the Secretary-General.

46 Established by Secretary-General following discontinuation of the function of the Personal Representative of the Secretary-General for Afghanistan and Pakistan in Dec. 1994. United Nations, Strengthening of the coordination of humanitarian and disaster relief assistance of the United Nations, including special economic assistance: emergency international assistance for peace, normalcy and reconstruction of war-stricken Afghanistan, Report of the Secretary General, UN document A/50/737, 8 Nov. 1995, p. 2.

47 The headquarters were in Jalalabad in Afghanistan, but the mission also maintained an office in Pakistan.

48 According to the Secretary-General's decision OSGA ceased to exist with effect from end of June and all UN peacemaking activities in Afghanistan were integrated into the UNSMA. United Nations, The situation in Afghanistan and its implications for international peace and security, UN document A/50/908/Add.1, 16 July 1996, p. 1–2. See note 41.

49 As of Dec. 1995. There were also 3 political officers and the director. Information from OSGA office in Pakistan.

50 Established by the Secretary-General in response to a request from the Government of El Salvador and from FMLN. United Nations, Assistance for the reconstruction and development of El Salvador. Report of the Secretary-General, UN document A/50/455, 23 Oct. 1995, p. 4.

51 Terminated 30 Apr. 1996. Replaced by ONUV. See note 53.

52 Mission staff partly funded by voluntary contributions. In May 1995 the Secretary-General established Trust Fund for MINUSAL in order to support the mission's activities, United Nations, The situation in Central America: Procedures for the establishment of a firm and lasting peace, freedom, democracy and development. Report of the Secretary-General, UN document A/50/517, 6 Oct. 1995, pp. 1–2.

53 Replaced MINUSAL when it terminated 30 Apr. 1996. See note 51.

54 There were also 7 other international staff. UN (note 39), p. 12.

55 29 countries contributed personnel to OSCE long-term missions in 1996: Armenia, Austria, Azerbaijan, Belarus, Bulgaria, Canada, Czech Rep., Denmark, Finland, France, Georgia, Germany, Hungary, Ireland, Italy, Lithuania, Moldova, Netherlands, Norway, Poland, Romania, Russia, Slovakia, Spain, Sweden, Switzerland, Ukraine, UK, USA. As country representation is constantly changing there is no OSCE information on current mission composition. The mission to Kosovo, Sandjak and Vojvodina, expelled on 28 June 1993, could not be redeployed because of a lack of agreement on its extension. Sources: OSCE, *Survey of OSCE Long-Term Missions and other OSCE Field Activities* (Conflict Prevention Centre, CPC: Vienna, 26 Feb. 1997); OSCE, *Survey of OSCE Long-Term Missions and other OSCE Field Activities* (CPC: Vienna, 14 Sep. 1996); OSCE, *Survey of OSCE Long-Term Missions and other OSCE Field Activities* (CPC: Vienna, 15 Feb. 1996); and specific information from the CPC.

56 Decision to establish the mission taken at 16th CSO meeting, 18 Sep. 1992, Journal no. 3, Annex 1. Authorized by Government of FYROM through Articles of Understanding (corresponding to an MOU) agreed by exchange of letters, 7 Nov. 1992.

57 Authorized strength: 8 members. Supplemented by 2 monitors from the European Community Monitoring Mission (ECMM) (note 98) under operational command of OSCE Head of Mission.

58 Budget adopted for 1996.

59 Decision to establish the mission taken at 17th CSO meeting, 6 Nov. 1992, Journal no. 2, Annex 2. Authorized by Government of Georgia through MOU, 23 Jan. 1993 and by 'Leadership of the Republic of South Ossetia' by exchange of letters on 1 Mar. 1993. Mandate expanded in Mar. 1994 to include i.a. monitoring of Joint Peacekeeping Forces in South Ossetia.

60 Decision to establish the mission taken at 18th CSO meeting, 13 Dec. 1992, Journal no. 3, Annex 2. Authorized by Estonian Government through MOU, 15 Feb. 1993.

61 Decision to establish the mission taken at 19th CSO meeting, 4 Feb. 1993, Journal no. 3, Annex 3. Authorized by Government of Moldova through MOU, 7 May. An 'Understanding of the Activity of the CSCE Mission in the Pridnestrovian [Trans-Dniester] Region of the Republic of Moldova' came into force on 25 Aug. 1993 through exchange of letters between Head of Mission and 'President of the Pridnestrovian Moldovan Republic'.

62 Decision to establish the mission taken at 23rd CSO meeting, 23 Sep. 1993, Journal no. 3, Annex 3. Authorized by Government of Latvia through MOU, 13 Dec.

63 Decision to establish the mission taken at 4th meeting of the Council, Rome (CSCE/4-C/Dec. 1), Decision I.4, 1 Dec. 1993. No MOU signed.

64 Decision to establish the mission taken by Permanent Committee, 2 June 1994, Journal No. 23, Annex. According to Article 18 of 'Decision on OSCE Action for Peace, Democracy and Stability in Bosnia and Herzegovina' (MC(5).DEC/1) by the Budapest Ministerial Council on 8 Dec. 1995, the present OSCE Mission in Sarajevo is now a distinct section of the Mission to Bosnia and Herzegovina. See note 68.

65 Decision to establish the mission taken at 27th CSO meeting, 15 June 1994, Journal No. 3, Decision (c). Authorized by Government of Ukraine through MOU, 24 Jan. 1995.

66 Decision to establish the mission taken at 16th meeting of Permanent Council, 11 Apr. 1995, Decision (a). No MOU signed.

67 Decision to establish the mission taken at 5th meeting, Ministerial Council, Budapest, 8 Dec. 1995 (MC(5).DEC/1) in accordance with Annex 6 of the Dayton Agreement. OSCE cooperates closely with ECMM (note 98).

68 Head of Mission started work in Sarajevo 29 Dec. 1995, relying, initially, on infrastructure of existing mission in Sarajevo (note 64).

69 Planned strength for the initial period of 1997 was 194 internationally seconded members.

70 Decision to establish the mission taken by Permanent Council, 18 Apr. 1996, Journal No. 65 (PC.DEC/112).

71 The modalities (PC.DEC/112) foresee that the mission will be composed of up to 14 members.

72 Budget valid from 1 May to 31 Dec. 1996

73 Figures used in this section could not be verified by official sources. Russian-dominated peacekeeping efforts in South Ossetia and Moldova cannot be described as CIS peacekeeping operations as the agreements establishing them were bilateral, they are being undertaken by CIS and non-CIS forces, or came into being before general CIS peacekeeping agreements entered into force. See Crow, S., 'Russia promotes CIS as an international organization', RFE/RL Research Report, vol. 3, no. 11 (18 Mar. 1994), p. 35, note 11.

74 Agreement on the Principles Governing the Peaceful Settlement of the Conflict in South Ossetia, signed 24 June 1992 by Georgia and Russia. Under the Agreement, a 4-party Joint Monitoring Commission established with representatives of Russia, Georgia and North and South Ossetia. Force Commander is Russian.

75 700 Russian troops and 700 joint N/S Ossetian units in 1995. O'Prey, K., Henry L. Stimson Center, Keeping the peace in the Borderlands of Russia, Occasional paper no. 23 (Henry L. Stimson Center: Washington, DC, July 1995), p. 16.

76 Agreement on the Principles Governing the Peaceful Settlement of the Armed Conflict in the Trans-Dniester Region, signed 21 July 1992 by presidents of Moldova and Russia. 'Moldovan Peace Agreement signed', RFE/RL Research Report, vol. 1, no. 31 (31 July 1992), p. 73.

77 Originally reported to comprise: between 4 and 6 Russian battalions reportedly reduced to 640 troops in 1993–94; 3 Moldovan battalions (1200 troops); 3 Dniester battalions (1200 troops); and 10 military observers from each of the parties involved in the conflict. Gribincea, M., 'Rejecting a new role for the former 14th Russian Army', Transition, vol. 2, no. 6 (22 Mar. 1996), pp. 38–39.

78 CIS Agreement on the Collective Peace-keeping Forces and Joint Measures on their Logistical and Technical Maintenance, Moscow, 24 Sep. 1993. Tajikistan operation is first application of Agreement on Groups of Military Observers and Collective Peacekeeping Forces in the CIS, signed at Kiev 20 Mar. 1992.

79 Mandate limited to guarding Afghan border. Russian and other CIS forces stationed or operating elsewhere in Tajikistan are not part of this operation.

80 An earlier CIS operation in Tajikistan began Dec. 1992 as decided by meeting of CIS defence ministers, 30 Nov. 1992. O'Prey (note 75), p. 37.

81 'Tajik, Kyrgyz presidents hold talks', Open Media Research Institute (hereafter OMRI), OMRI Daily Digest, no. 135, part I (15 July 1996), URL <http://www.friends-partners.org> (hereafter, references to OMRI Daily Digest refer to the Internet edition at this URL address); 'Bishkek summit produces treaty on eternal friendship', OMRI Daily Digest, no. 8, part I (13 Jan. 1997).

82 Force reportedly consists mainly of Russian 201st Motor Rifle Division (MRD). Estimates of number of troops range from less than 10 000 to 25 000. 'Tajik fighting spreads' and 'Russian Tajik pks killed', International Peacekeeping News, vol. 2, no. 4 (Sep./Oct. 1996), p. 27; 'Tajik peace talks begin', International Peacekeeping News, vol. 2, no. 3 (July/Aug. 1996), p. 22.

83 As of 28 Sep. 1995. Masyuk, Y., Moscow NTV, video report, 23 Oct. 1995 (in Russian), Foreign Broadcast Information Service, Daily Report–Central Eurasia (FBIS-SOV), FBIS-SOV-95-207. 26 Oct. 1995, p. 14. By the end of Nov., more than 30 soldiers and officers had been killed in 1995. Gridneva, G., Moscow ITAR-TASS in English 30 Nov. 1995, FBIS–SOV-95-231, 1 Dec. 1995, p. 55. Fatal casualties in the 201st MRD reportedly numbered 39 in 1993, 35 in 1994 and 23 in 1995. Krasnaya Zvezda, 19 Jan. 1996, p. 2. According to an article in OMRI Daily Digest more than 60 Russians were killed during 1995–96. 'Suspect sentenced to death for killing Russian soldiers', OMRI Daily Digest, no. 24, part I (4 Feb. 1997).

[84] National contingents fully financed by the state sending them. Only command of the collective force and combat support units are financed from joint budget, shared as follows: Kyrgyzstan 10%; Tajikistan 10%; Kazakhstan 15%; Uzbekistan 15%; and Russia 50%. O'Prey (note 75), p. 38.

[85] CIS Council of Heads of States on 15 Apr. expressed readiness to send a 'peacemaking' force of military contingents from interested parties to the CIS Treaty on Collective Security. Georgian–Abkhazian Agreement on a Cease-fire and Separation of Forces, 14 May 1994, stipulated that Georgian and Abkhazian units move 12 km away from the Inguri river and a CIS peacekeeping contingent take up positions inside the 24-km buffer zone. In an unusual procedure not provided for in any CIS document, the Chairman of the Council, President Boris Yeltsin, decided to deploy the force in June following CIS Executive Secretary mission to other CIS states to obtain support. Mandate approved by Heads of States members of the CIS Council of Collective Security, 21 Oct. 1994.

[86] Estimates of number of troops range from 1400 to 3000. 'UN extends mandate of observer mission in Georgia', OMRI Daily Digest, no. 22, part I (31 Jan. 1997); 'Georgia demands Russian withdrawal', International Peacekeeping News, vol. 2, no. 4 (Sep./Oct. 1996), p. 25; Iberia (Tbilisi), 1 Nov. 1996 (in Georgian), in 'Georgia: Number of Russian peacekeeping troops in Abkhazia decreases', FBIS-SOV-96-214, 5 Nov. 1996.

[87] Agreement concerning a military armistice in Korea, signed at Panmunjom on 27 July 1953 by Commander-in-Chief, UN Command; Supreme Commander of the Korean People's Army; and Commander of the Chinese People's Volunteers. Entered into force 27 July 1953. US Department of State, Treaties in Force: A List of Treaties and Other International Agreements of the United States in Force on January 1, 1994, Department of State Publication 9433 (Department of State, Office of the Legal Adviser: Washington, DC, June 1994), p. 359.

[88] By end of 1996, Korean People's Army/Chinese People's Volunteers had not nominated replacement for the former Czechoslovak member of the Commission, whose nomination they had withdrawn in Jan. 1993 following the division of Czechoslovakia into two separate states. North Korea announced withdrawal of its consent to Polish participation in Nov. 1994. In diplomatic notes of 23 Jan. and 8 Feb. 1995 it demanded withdrawal of the Polish delegation by 28 Feb. 1995. Polish personnel left North Korea but Poland remains a Commission member. Information from Swedish Foreign Office; and United Nations, Letter dated 9 May 1995 from the Deputy Permanent Representative of the United States of America to the United Nations addressed to the President of the Security Council, UN document S/1995/378, 11 May 1995, p. 7.

[89] Approximate cost of Swedish and Swiss delegations. Information from Swedish Foreign Office and Swiss Embassy in Stockholm.

[90] 1981 Protocol to Peace Treaty between Egypt and Israel of 26 Mar. 1979. Established following withdrawal of Israeli forces from Sinai. Deployment began 20 Mar. and mission commenced 25 Apr. 1982. Multinational Force and Observers, Annual Report of the Director General (MFO: Rome, Jan. 1996).

[91] Strength as of Nov. 1996.

[92] Operating budget for FY 1996. Force funded by Egypt, Israel, and USA and voluntary contributions from Germany (since 1992), Japan (since 1989) and Switzerland (since 1994).

[93] Decision to establish force taken by the ECOWAS Standing Mediation Committee (ESMC) at its first session on 7 Aug. 1990. ESMC composed of Gambia, Ghana, Guinea, Nigeria, Sierra Leone and Mali.

[94] ECOWAS membership: Benin, Burkina Faso, Cape Verde, Côte d'Ivoire, Gambia, Ghana, Guinea, Guinea-Bissau, Liberia, Mali, Mauritania, Niger, Nigeria, Senegal, Sierra Leone and Togo.

[95] Pursuant to the Cotonou Peace Agreement of 25 July 1993 (UN document S/26272) signed by 3 Liberian parties, ECOMOG expanded to include troops from outside West Africa. Ugandan participation in 1996 could not be confirmed. AFP (Paris), 7 Apr. 1997, in 'Liberia: Burkinabe troops join ECOMOG peacekeeping force', Foreign Broadcast Information Service, Daily Report–Sub-Saharan Africa (FBIS-AFR), FBIS-AFR-97-097, 9 Apr. 1997.

[96] All ranks as of Jan 1997. United Nations, Twenty-first progress report of the Secretary-General on the United Nations Observer Mission in Liberia, UN document S/1997/90, 29 Jan. 1997. Estimated troop strength required to implement Accra Agreement of 21 Dec. 1994 (UN document S/1995/7, 5 Jan. 1995, annexes I and II): 12 000.

[97] Mainly financed by ECOWAS countries with additional voluntary contributions from UN member states through Trust Fund for the Implementation of the Cotonou Agreement. United Nations, Ninth progress report of the Secretary-General on the United Nations Observer Mission in Liberia, UN document S/1995/158, 24 Feb. 1995, p. 6.

[98] Mission established by Brioni Agreement, signed at Brioni (Croatia), 7 July 1991 by representatives of European Community (EC) and governments of Croatia, the Federal Republic of Yugoslavia (Serbia and Montenegro) and Slovenia. Mandate confirmed by EC foreign ministers meeting, The Hague, 10 July 1991. Mission authorized by governments of Croatia, Yugoslavia and Slovenia through MOU, 13 July 1991. Information from Swedish delegation to ECMM, Zagreb.

[99] EC established mission maintained with OSCE cooperation, including monitors from 3 non-EU OSCE participating states: Czech Republic, Poland and Slovakia.

[100] Not including national expenditures.

[101] In French MIOB: Mission de l'OUA au Burundi. Both names are official. *Source*: Permanent Delegation of the OAU in Geneva and OMIB Office in Bujumbura.

[102] Soon after the coup in Burundi (25 July 1996) the decision was taken by the OAU to withdraw the military component of OMIB. All military officers, except one medical doctor, left Burundi in Aug. 1996. At the same time as the OAU decided to withdraw the military component, it called for the reinforcement of the civilian component. This decision had not been implemented by Jan. 1997 when the number of civilian observers was 5.

[103] Funded by regular budget of the OAU and voluntary contributions.

[104] MOU from 23 July 1994 defined the goals of the three partners (Bosnians, Croats and the EU) to return the city of Mostar to normality to the greatest extent possible. Information from the Swedish Armed Forces International Centre (SWEDINT).

[105] WEUPF worked under the EUAM (European Union Administration in Mostar).

[106] Mandate ended in July 1996. Last police left in Oct. and transfer of authority from WEUPF to IPTF (see note 28) in Mostar occurred on 15 Oct. 1996. *Bosnia and Herzegovina—UNMIBH*. Version current on 25 Apr. 1997, URL <http://www.un.org:80/Depts/DPKO/Missions/unmibh_b.htm>.

[107] Established pursuant to exchange of letters 17 Sep. 1994 between Co-Chairmen of the Steering Committee of the International Conference on the Former Yugoslavia (ICFY) and Foreign Minister of Yugoslavia to monitor border closure between Yugoslavia and Bosnia and Herzegovina to all traffic except deliveries of humanitarian assistance. ICFY closed down on 31 Jan. 1996. Mission continued its work reporting to High Representative for Bosnia. Information from the ICFY in Geneva; Office of the High Representative in Brussels; and Operations of the Mission of the International Conference on the Former Yugoslavia to the Federal Republic of Yugoslavia (Serbia and Montenegro), reproduced as annex to United Nations, Letter dated 10 November 1995 from the Secretary-General addressed to the President of the Security Council, UN document S/1995/944, 10 Nov. 1995.

[108] Following the suspension of sanctions on Republika Srpska on 27 Feb. 1996, the ICFY mission closed down on 19 Mar. Report of the High Representative for Implementation of the Bosnian Peace Agreement to the Secretary-General of the United Nations, 14 Mar. 1996, Version current on 9 May 1997, URL <http://www.ohr.int/reports/r960314a.htm#2.2>.

[109] First article of Declaration, dated 17 Feb. 1995, states the willingness of the guarantor countries of the Protocol of Rio de Janeiro of 1942—Argentina, Brazil, Chile and USA—to send observer mission to the region in conflict, as well as the acceptance of this offer by the conflicting parties. Information from Brazilian Embassy in Stockholm.

[110] SCR 1031 authorized member states to establish a multinational military Implementation Force, under unified control and command and composed of ground, air and maritime units from NATO and non-NATO nations, to ensure compliance with the Dayton Agreement (UN document A/50/790-S/1995/999).

[111] Transfer of authority from IFOR to SFOR took place on 20 Dec. 1996. United Nations, Thirteenth Report to the UN Security Council on IFOR Operations, published as appendix to UN document S/1996/1066. 24 Dec. 1996, p. 5.

[112] Every NATO nation with armed forces committed troops to IFOR. Non-NATO participating states: Albania, Austria, Bulgaria, Czech Rep, Estonia, Finland, Hungary, Latvia, Lithuania, Poland, Romania, Russia, Slovakia, Sweden and Ukraine—all Partnership for Peace participants—plus, Egypt, Jordan, Malaysia and Morocco. NATO, *NATO's role in the implementation of the Bosnian Peace Agreement*, NATO Fact Sheet No. 11, Sep. 1996, p. 3. Version current on 28 Feb. 1997, URL <http://www.nato.int/docu/facts/fs11.htm>; UN document S/1996/1066 (note 111), p. 4.

[113] As of Dec. 1996. UN document S/1996/1066 (note 111), p. 4.

[114] UN document S/1996/1066 (note 111), p. 3.

115 Estimate for 1996. *International Peacekeeping News*, vol. 2, no. 4 (Sep./Oct. 1996), p. 28; International Institute for Strategic Studies, *The Military Balance 1996–97* (Oxford University Press: Oxford, 1996), p. 304. Mix of common and national funding. NATO common-funded costs are borne by the Military Budget and the NATO Security Investment Programme. Non-NATO countries pay their own national contributions to IFOR and SFOR, but NATO does not seek reimbursement from them for NATO common-funded costs. NATO (note 112), p. 4.

116 As of late Jan. 1997. United Nations, Monthly report to the United Nations Security Council on SFOR operations, appendix to UN document S/1997/81, 27 Jan. 1997, p. 3.

117 Mix of common and national funding. NATO common-funded costs are borne by the Military Budget and the NATO Security Investment Programme. Non-NATO countries pay their own national contributions to IFOR and SFOR, but NATO does not seek reimbursement from them for NATO common-funded costs. NATO (note 112), p. 4.

3. The Middle East peace process

PETER JONES

I. Introduction

The year 1996 was arduous for the Middle East peace process. After four years of peacemaking, resolution of the Arab–Israeli conflict was still elusive. Violent incidents occurred throughout the year with tragic consequences for hundreds of people. The new Israeli Government signalled its intent to review what many regard as the basic understandings of the peace process. This caused the process to grind to a halt for several months. Many regarded 1996 as a year in which the peace process moved backwards, before tentatively inching forward in the early weeks of 1997.

This chapter reviews events in the Middle East in 1996 and their impact on the peace process. The different tracks of the process are summarized in section III, and wider Middle East developments are discussed in section IV. Section V points to concerns which may affect the region in future.

II. Key events in 1996

The year began with progress on all tracks of the peace process. Israeli–Syrian talks had resumed in late 1995 in the USA. They continued into 1996, and US Secretary of State Warren Christopher travelled to the region to spur progress. Officials spoke of a good negotiating climate but cautioned that much remained to be done.[1] In addition, the USA formally offered to station troops on the Golan Heights as part of a peacekeeping force after a peace treaty had been signed. This proposal had been mentioned previously but never formally stated. By mid-January Israel was arguing that the Syrian negotiators needed fresh instructions if the talks were to progress.[2] Syrian President Hafez al-Assad reportedly agreed to this in January.[3]

Israeli withdrawals from Palestinian towns ceded to the Palestinian Authority (PA) were completed in early 1996, with the exception of the city of Hebron, which was seen by both sides as a special security concern. Hebron would become a critical issue as 1996 progressed. Other than these withdrawals, the Israeli–Palestinian track of the peace process was temporarily quiet as the Palestinians prepared for their historic election.

---

[1] 'Talks in Maryland were "very special," but short on substance—Beilin', *Mideast Mirror*, 5 Jan. 1996, pp. 2–8; and Ozanne, J., 'Israel sees Syrian talks improving relationship', *Financial Times*, 6–7 Jan. 1996, p. 3.

[2] Erlanger, S., 'Hussein and Christopher make twin visits to Israel', *New York Times*, 11 Jan. 1996.

[3] 'Syria said ready for bilateral tourism, regional cooperation and economic development', *Mideast Mirror*, 8 Jan. 1996, pp. 2–3; and Erlanger, S., 'Israel–Syria talks to re-open, focusing on military', *New York Times*, 13 Jan. 1996.

The Palestinian election

The Palestinian Authority held its first election on 20 January 1996. At stake were 88 seats in the new Palestinian Council and the post of President (Ra'ees) of the Executive Authority of the Council. Although one person did run against Yasser Arafat for the post of Ra'ees, the vote was essentially uncontested, and Arafat won by a wide margin. The Council vote was also won by Arafat supporters, but the voters 'sent a message' by backing a number of independent candidates. The final tally was 50 seats for Arafat supporters and 38 seats for independents. Many of the independents were community leaders during the intifada period who were displeased that most positions in the PA had gone to senior Palestine Liberation Organization (PLO) officials who had returned from exile with Arafat. This split between PLO officials and community-based leaders is becoming a characteristic of Palestinian politics.[4]

International monitors, organized and supervised by the European Union (EU), declared the election substantially fair, although there were some instances of fraud and intimidation. Several opposition candidates were subjected to harassment by the PA police, including interruptions of their campaigning on what were seen as specious technical grounds, physical detention and intimidation. It was also widely believed that access to the Palestinian media was controlled by Arafat forces for their own benefit.[5]

Nevertheless, the Palestinians and the international community accepted the election as a genuine expression of the desires of the Palestinians.[6] Calls for an election boycott by Islamic opponents of the peace process were ignored by Palestinians. With increased legitimacy, Arafat set about establishing a government and preparing the next step in the peace process.

The Israeli election

After assuming office following the assassination of Yitzhak Rabin, Israeli Prime Minister Shimon Peres faced a finely balanced choice. He had a mandate to hold office until the autumn of 1996, and his popularity in the wake of Rabin's murder was high. His choice was whether to hold elections sooner than scheduled in an attempt to take advantage of this standing or to wait until September and use the remaining time to strive for a peace deal with Syria.[7]

By 11 February Peres concluded that President Assad would not meet his timetable. Accordingly, he announced that Israel would go to the polls in late May. Although statements were made that the Israeli–Syrian talks would con-

---

[4] Ozanne, J., 'Independents can vent voters' anger', *Financial Times*, 8 Jan. 1996, p. 4.

[5] See, e.g., Brown, D., 'Arafat "tinkers with polls"', *The Guardian*, 2 Jan. 1996, p. 7; and Silver, E., 'Arafat's guards hold top rights activist', *The Independent*, 4 Jan. 1996, p. 10.

[6] See the round-up of Arab press coverage of the election in 'Arab press applauds Arafat for winning big, along with his Fateh loyalists and peace policies', *Mideast Mirror*, 22 Jan. 1996, pp. 7–13.

[7] 'Peres's dilemma: to KO Netanyahu in May or June or risk waiting for Syria', *Mideast Mirror*, 26 Jan. 1996, pp. 2–8; and Erlanger, S., 'Peres weighs pros (popularity) and cons (Syria talks) of early election', *International Herald Tribune*, 18 Jan. 1996.

tinue during the campaign, the talks were effectively brought to an end pending the outcome of the election.

Peres enjoyed a substantial lead in public opinion polls over Benjamin Netanyahu, leader of the right-wing Likud Party. This margin of personal popularity was crucial as a new system of direct voting for prime minister was introduced in this election. Israelis would cast two ballots: one for prime minister and one for the parliamentary party of their choice. The result would determine the number of seats the various parties would have in the Knesset (parliament) and the leader who would be given the right to attempt formation of a coalition government (even if his party did not win the greatest number of seats). It also meant that if the prime minister failed to form a coalition a new election would be called, rather than having the leader with the next highest number of seats try to form a government.

The positions of the two leaders on the eve of the election indicate how split the parties were on the peace process. Peres, in many ways the Israeli architect of the peace process, vowed to continue it to its logical conclusion: resolution of the so-called Final Status issues[8] with the Palestinians and a peace treaty with Syria. Although he did not expressly state it, this meant that Israel would have to cede more land and power to the PA (implying a permanent freeze on Jewish settlements on the West Bank and perhaps the dismantlement of some existing ones), eventually accept a politically independent Palestinian entity (perhaps a demilitarized state) and entertain a compromise on Jerusalem. This last issue became a battleground in the election. Peres never conceded the idea of dividing the city, but during the campaign it became known that academics with close ties to the Israeli Government had held talks with Palestinians at which ideas for joint control of certain areas were discussed. These talks closely resembled the academic discussions which began the 'Oslo process' that led to the Israeli–Palestinian Declaration of Principles (DOP) of 1993 (also known as the Oslo Agreement).[9]

Netanyahu seized on the discussions to show that 'secret' talks to 'divide' Jerusalem were under way.[10] In addition to refusing to discuss compromise on Jerusalem, he stated that the entire Oslo process was deeply flawed. He argued that Arafat was an unreformed terrorist who could not be trusted, that Israeli settlements should be allowed to expand and that any agreement which hinted at eventual Palestinian statehood would never be acceptable to Likud.

On the Syrian talks, Peres spent much of 1995 preparing Israel for what many regard as inevitable: that peace with Syria will require Israel to give up the Golan Heights. Although there was disagreement over the boundaries and

---

[8] These issues include: the status of the Palestinian Government, Jerusalem, Israeli settlement, borders, water, security arrangements and the rights of Palestinian refugees. Jones, P., 'The Middle East peace process', *SIPRI Yearbook 1996: Armaments, Disarmament and International Security* (Oxford University Press: Oxford, 1996), chapter 4, pp. 162–69.

[9] The text of the Declaration of Principles on Interim Self-Government Arrangements of 13 Sep. 1993 is reproduced in *SIPRI Yearbook 1994* (Oxford University Press: Oxford, 1994), appendix 3A, pp. 117–22.

[10] Ozanne, J., 'Jerusalem issue put at centre of election', *Financial Times*, 19 Feb. 1996, p. 5; and Silver, E., 'Likud hits out with poll attack on Peres', *The Independent*, 19 Feb. 1996, p. 11.

the security arrangements attending transfer of the Golan Heights, Peres seemed aware that the essential aspect of the Syrian track of the peace process was 'land for peace'.[11]

Netanyahu took the view that peace discussions with Syria should not proceed on the basis of land for peace and argued that peace was possible without territorial concessions. Although many regarded this claim as unworkable and expected Netanyahu to abandon it if he was elected, it underlined his approach to the Israeli–Syrian issue.

During the campaign both candidates realized that they could not win on the positions which were the foundation of their core support. Accordingly, Peres began to move to the right and Netanyahu to the left.[12] Peres promoted the candidacy of retired generals such as Foreign Minister Ehud Barak and took an increasingly firm line on Jerusalem. Netanyahu softened his positions, saying that, although deeply flawed, the DOP and the 1995 Interim Agreement[13] were signed and would be respected. He also said that he would meet Arafat if he were elected prime minister, even though he had previously claimed that he would never do so.

This phenomenon underlined the deep divisions over the peace process in Israel. Polls consistently showed that a majority of Israelis supported the process, but the same polls indicated that Israelis were suspicious of it and frightened for their personal security in the wake of several terrorist attacks. For each candidate the task became to demonstrate that he would continue the peace process, but would place greater emphasis on its security aspects.

The odds favoured Peres to win the election. He was the incumbent; there had been an unparalleled period of economic growth; and US President Bill Clinton strongly supported him. Indeed, many came to feel that Clinton went too far in his support of Peres and became involved in the election.[14] A Labour victory seemed assured until 25 February when another terrorist bombing campaign began with two bus bombs which killed 25 people.[15] The putative cause was retaliation for Israel's killing, on 5 January 1996, of Yahya Ayyash, a Palestinian known as 'the engineer' for his skill in manufacturing bombs.[16] Another bomb exploded in Jerusalem on 3 March, killing 19 people. On 4 March a Tel Aviv shopping centre was bombed; 20 people were killed and many wounded.[17] Despite swift action to punish Hamas—in which the PA

---

[11] Jones (note 8), pp. 175–80.

[12] 'Labour, Likud trying to woo the floating voters in the centre', *Mideast Mirror*, 8 May 1996, pp. 9–12.

[13] The 400-page Israeli–Palestinian Interim Agreement on the West Bank and the Gaza Strip was signed in Washington, DC, on 28 Sep. 1995. It is known as the Interim Agreement or Oslo II, and excerpts from it are reproduced in *SIPRI Yearbook 1996* (note 8), appendix 4A, pp. 191–202. Hereafter the DOP and the Interim Agreement are referred to as the 'Oslo agreements'.

[14] Ozanne, J., 'US denies Israeli political meddling', *Financial Times*, 1 May 1996, p. 4.

[15] Gellman, B., 'Two bombs in Israel kill 25, Peres jeered as "traitor"', *International Herald Tribune*, 26 Feb. 1996, pp. 1, 9.

[16] Brown, D., 'Israeli agents kill Hamas bombing chief', *The Guardian*, 6 Jan. 1996, p. 7. Hamas vowed revenge a few days later. Although Arafat publicly criticized Israel for killing Ayyash at the time, it later emerged that Israeli and Palestinian security services had collaborated in the attack. Royce, K., 'PLO and Israel "united to kill Hamas bomber"', *The Guardian*, 18 Jan. 1996, p. 2.

[17] Cornwell, R., 'Tel Aviv blast has peace on the ropes', *The Independent*, 5 Mar. 1996, p. 9.

cooperated—and new steps to seal off the occupied territories, support for Peres plummeted and never recovered. Israelis, tired of living with terrorism, were now receptive to Likud's message.[18]

The Sharm El Sheik summit meeting

In order to shore up Peres, President Clinton hastily organized a 'Summit of the Peacemakers' at the Egyptian resort of Sharm el Sheik. The summit meeting was based on a suggestion by Arafat, and it was co-hosted by Egyptian President Hosni Mubarak. It sought to demonstrate that the problem of terrorism was one faced by all nations committed to the peace process. The underlying message was that Israel was not alone.

Twenty-nine leaders met for four hours on 13 March 1996. The USA had hoped that the meeting would condemn Iran for what it alleged was Tehran's involvement in terrorism, but the meeting declined to do so.[19] Instead, a general statement was issued expressing support for the peace process, denouncing terrorism and committing the nations present at the meeting to continue the negotiations.[20] The only concrete outcome of the summit meeting was a pledge to hold regular meetings of senior officials from the participating countries to explore ways of cooperating against terrorism. In a unilateral move, the USA also promised to step up its anti-terrorism assistance to Israel.

Fighting in Lebanon

With the Israeli election moving into a more intense phase, the activities of the Hezbollah guerrillas in southern Lebanon stepped up. These Islamic guerrillas, supported by Iran and Syria, had fought against Israel's presence since 1982 in the self-proclaimed 'Security Zone' in southern Lebanon, and fighting had escalated before. After a substantial Israeli artillery and air campaign in 1993, known as 'Operation Accountability', a tacit understanding had been reached in which each side agreed not to purposely target the other's civilians or use them as shields.

The fighting continued, however. Many Israelis charged that it was supported by Syria as a way of putting pressure on Israel. The theory was that Hezbollah attacks against Israelis in Lebanon increased when the Israeli–Syrian talks were at an impasse. Syria denied this, stating that the activities of Hezbollah were the actions of a people wishing to rid themselves of an unwanted occupier.[21]

By early 1996 the fighting in southern Lebanon had accelerated considerably. Each side blamed the other for systematically undermining the tacit

---

[18] 'Barak rebuffs Hamas as Netanyahu closes gap on Peres in opinion polls', *Mideast Mirror*, 1 Mar. 1996, pp. 2–8.
[19] Brown, D., 'Summit lets Iran off hook', *The Guardian*, 14 Mar. 1996, p. 7.
[20] The Sharm al-Sheikh Declaration, 13 Mar. 1996.
[21] Jones (note 8), p. 179.

understanding of 1993.[22] Hezbollah attacks against Israeli positions increased in March and April 1996,[23] leading Lebanese officials to publicly express fear that Israel could again unleash its military might in Lebanon.[24]

On 11 April, aware of the need to be firm against terrorism during the election, Peres launched 'Operation Grapes of Wrath' which involved a large-scale air and artillery bombardment as far north as Beirut. In addition to punishing Hezbollah, Israel appears to have wanted to show the Lebanese and Syrian governments that they could not permit or conduct a proxy war with impunity.[25] This meant considerable suffering for the Lebanese people, who were again caught in the crossfire of their neighbour's conflict.

Polls showed that a majority of Israelis initially supported Grapes of Wrath, and were glad to be striking back.[26] Netanyahu also expressed support. Within 24 hours it became clear that the fighting could not be limited to Lebanon. Hezbollah was able to secure its Katyusha rockets from bombardment and began to fire them into northern Israel.[27] Although not widespread, the resulting death and damage had a profound impact on Israeli public sentiment. Moreover, international opinion was roundly critical of Israel's actions.

Criticism increased on 18 April, when Israeli gunners shelled a UN position at Qana in southern Lebanon, where refugees had taken shelter. Over 100 people were killed, many of them women and children, and the images shocked the world. Conflicting claims as to whether the shelling was accidental or not further damaged Israel's standing internationally.[28]

Warren Christopher's ongoing diplomatic efforts intensified. Peres sought a more binding agreement on Hezbollah activity than had resulted from the 1993 tacit understanding: effectively, written assurances that civilians in the north of Israel would not be targeted in future. Such assurances required Lebanese and, more importantly, Syrian approval.[29] Christopher spent much time in Damascus, including one trip during which Assad said that he was unable to meet with him because of a conflicting meeting with another dignitary. As the crisis wore on, it became clear that Assad wanted both Israel and

[22] Brown, D., 'Lebanon accord in jeopardy', *The Guardian*, 10 Apr. 1996, p. 6.

[23] See, e.g., Haddadin, H., 'Hizbullah blasts posts in Lebanon', *The Guardian*, 14 Mar. 1996, p. 7.

[24] These fears were publicly expressed in 'Israel's revenge seen targeting Iran, Syria and/or Lebanon', *Mideast Mirror*, 7 Mar. 1996, pp. 8–10; and Fisk, R., 'Lebanon's fear: "they're coming"', *The Independent*, 16 Mar. 1996, p. 11.

[25] 'IDF offensive aims to change the "rules of play" with Hizbollah', *Mideast Mirror*, 11 Apr. 1996, pp. 2–9; Hirst, D. and Brown, D., 'Israel bombs Beirut to punish Hizbollah', *The Guardian*, 12 Apr. 1996, p. 3; and Dennis, M., 'Peres wants good harvest from grapes of wrath', *Financial Times*, 16 Apr. 1996, p. 4.

[26] Gellman, B., 'For Israelis, there is no downside to raids on Lebanon', *International Herald Tribune*, 16 Apr. 1996, pp. 1, 7.

[27] Cockburn, P., 'Peres warns as rockets strike Israeli town', *The Independent*, 13 Apr. 1996, p. 10.

[28] Israel called the shelling a tragic accident of war and immediately apologized. The UN investigated the incident, and its study raised questions as to whether the shelling had been accidental. See the report by the Military Advisor to the Secretary-General: von Kappen, F. (Maj.-Gen.), 'Report on the shelling of the United Nations compound at Qana, 18 April, 1996', New York, 1 May 1996 (and subsequent addendum of 7 May 1996). Israel angrily dismissed the UN report, and Israeli Chief of Staff Lt.-Gen. Amnon Shahak said that only a 'twisted mind' would suggest that the attack had been deliberate.

[29] 'Peres wants "written" document of understandings with Syria on Hizbollah', *Mideast Mirror*, 17 Apr. 1996, pp. 2–9; and Ozanne, J. and Gardner, D., 'Israelis demand formal truce with Hizbullah', *Financial Times*, 18 Apr. 1996, p. 4.

the USA to 'pay a price' in return for his agreement to a cease-fire.[30] This was unfortunate for the Lebanese, as it meant that Syria wanted the fighting to continue until the pressure became intolerable for Israel.

Christopher was not alone in his efforts. French President Jacques Chirac, angered by what he saw as US refusal to allow France and the EU to play what Paris believed to be its rightful roles in the region, dispatched his foreign minister to the area.[31] Israel and the USA were upset at what they viewed as unhelpful interference, but the Arab states were positive. They saw a chance to balance what they regarded as the USA's blatantly pro-Israel stance.

Also present in Damascus, to the irritation of the USA, was the Iranian Foreign Minister, Ali Akbar Velayati. Although he did not take part in any meetings with Christopher, Velayati's presence underscored his country's sponsorship of Hezbollah,[32] its relationship with Syria and its desire to play a role in broader Middle East questions.[33]

After several meetings, including one at which Christopher apparently threatened to leave after Assad reopened an agreed text, a cease-fire was agreed on 26 April.[34] It listed the earlier understandings in written form and created a committee to oversee them. Israel and Hezbollah are members of the committee, as are France, Lebanon, Syria and the USA. The committee meets infrequently, and its sessions have been inconclusive, although they do help to keep the situation in southern Lebanon under control diplomatically.

Revision of the PLO Charter

While fighting continued in Lebanon the Palestinians met in Gaza to fulfil a long-standing promise: removal of the elements of the PLO Charter of 1964 calling for the destruction of Israel. Arafat had promised to do this immediately after the signing of the DOP, but had not. Right-wing Israelis pointed to this as evidence of his lack of enthusiasm for the peace process and argued that the PLO had not accepted the existence of Israel. Although Arafat said that the DOP effectively rendered the 'end of Israel' clauses of the Charter null and void and that Palestinian political opinion would not allow him to revise the Charter more quickly, the charge that he had reneged on a key understanding of the Oslo process was a powerful one in Israel.

Revision of the Charter required a full meeting of the Palestinian National Council (PNC). This body is often referred to as the Palestinian parliament in exile. With the election of the Palestinian Council, the relationship between

[30] Hirst, D. and Brown, D., 'Syrian leader raises price of ceasefire', *The Guardian*, 23 Apr. 1996, p. 7.

[31] Buchan, D., 'France presses on with peace efforts', *Financial Times*, 20–21 Apr. 1996, p. 3.

[32] Throughout the crisis, Iran reportedly continued to supply Hizbollah, via Syria. Wright, R., 'Iran rearms Hizbullah during clash', *International Herald Tribune*, 19 Apr. 1996, p. 5.

[33] Gardner, D., 'Iran gains stronger role in Mideast peace process', *Financial Times*, 22 Apr. 1996, p. 3.

[34] 'Christopher clinches cease-fire agreement and written understandings', *Mideast Mirror* 26 Apr. 1996, p. 2; Ozanne, J. and Gardner, D., 'Lebanon ceasefire deal reached', *Financial Times*, 27–28 Apr. 1996, pp. 1, 22; and 'Israel and Lebanon agree to halt border shellings; a safeguard for civilians', *New York Times*, 27 Apr. 1996.

the two is in flux, but it appears that the PNC represents the Palestinian diaspora, while the Council represents the self-rule areas. The PNC is not elected, consisting of the leaders of the factions of the Palestinian resistance. Arafat is its leader because he leads the largest movement (Fatah), but the PNC also comprises several groups which are opponents of the peace process.

Israeli security forces agreed to allow leaders of Palestinian groups in exile to return to Gaza for the vote, but some hard-line leaders refused to attend. After much debate, Arafat won a significant victory on 24 April when 504 PNC members voted to remove references to the destruction of Israel from the Charter, while 54 were opposed. (Fourteen members abstained, and 107 reportedly did not attend the meeting.) Peres was pleased, as were other world leaders.[35] Indeed, the next day the Israeli Labour Party agreed to drop its opposition in principle to the eventual formation of a Palestinian state.[36] Netanyahu was not satisfied with the PNC resolution, arguing that it did not actually revoke the offending clauses but only empowered a judicial committee to make the changes.[37]

The Israeli vote

By the end of April the Israeli election had grown closer. Polls predicted a Labour victory, but Likud was gaining with its message of security first. Many believed another bombing would tip the balance, and Israeli security went on higher alert, enforcing particularly tight restrictions on Palestinians. Many were annoyed, especially as restrictions had been placed on their freedom of movement for several years, but Arafat appeared willing to endure these restrictions to help Peres win the election. The level of anti-terrorism cooperation between Israeli forces and those of the PA increased during the election, continuing a trend established in the latter half of 1995. Polls revealed that the gap between Peres and Netanyahu was narrowing in a nasty campaign.[38] Most believed that Peres would win, but the result was no longer assured.

Israel went to the polls on 29 May. At first Peres held a slight lead, but Netanyahu won the direct election for prime minister with 50.3 per cent of the vote to Peres' 49.7 per cent. Almost 3 million Israelis cast ballots, and Netanyahu received fewer than 25 000 more votes than Peres.

Labour won 34 Knesset seats to 31 for the Likud bloc (Netanyahu had made a deal with the other right-wing parties to present themselves as a bloc). Although Labour had more seats, Netanyahu was supported by other parties and was able to achieve a majority after a difficult period of coalition forma-

---

[35] 'Revoked charter gives Peres a "gift worth more than gold" from Arafat', *Mideast Mirror*, 25 Apr. 1996, pp. 2–6; 'Palestinians revoke "end of Israel" clauses', *International Herald Tribune*, 25 Apr. 1996, p. 1; and Cockburn, P., 'Arafat wins historic vote', *The Independent*, 25 Apr. 1996, p. 12.

[36] Greenberg, J., 'Israel's Labor Party, in switch, lends support to Palestinian state', *New York Times*, 26 Apr. 1996. Arafat is quoted as telling PNC delegates: 'This is the first reaction from the other side to your decision yesterday'.

[37] Netanyahu's remarks were broadcast in an Israel Radio interview and quoted in *Mideast Mirror*, 25 Apr. 1996, p. 2.

[38] Bhatia, S., 'Israeli election battle turns nasty', *The Guardian*, 13 May 1996, p. 6.

tion. He was supported by the religious parties, which had won a larger number of seats than ever before.[39]

The Arab summit meeting

In response to the Likud victory, the leaders of the Arab states quickly undertook a round of calls and visits.[40] President Mubarak of Egypt then called for an Arab summit meeting to review the peace process, the first such summit meeting since the Iraqi invasion of Kuwait. Pointedly, Iraq was not invited.[41]

The summit meeting was a calculated risk. In addition to the Arab–Israeli dispute, there were inter-Arab tensions. Wounds opened by the 1991 Persian Gulf War had not yet healed completely; Jordan and Syria had a continuing dispute over the latter's alleged support of groups wishing to undermine King Hussein's rule; and Libya remained problematic because of its standing in the world after the 1988 Lockerbie bombing. Despite these potential difficulties, Mubarak believed that much stood to be gained from a summit meeting.[42]

The leaders met on 21–23 June in Cairo. Despite calls for a harsh anti-Israeli line, Mubarak was able to secure a seemingly moderate statement. It said that the Arab countries looked forward to continuation of the peace process and remained willing to pursue the 'Madrid process'[43] to what they regarded as its logical conclusion: the establishment of a Palestinian state with at least part of Jerusalem as its capital, and the return of the Golan Heights to Syria in exchange for peace. However, the statement also said that any abrogation of this process would cause the Arab leaders to revise their stand on normalization of relations with Israel. The threat was clear but not made in a belligerent fashion.[44]

Inter-Arab differences were kept largely to bilateral meetings between the leaders concerned, although they did spill over into some of the items on the larger agenda. The summit meeting's characterization of the need to control terrorism, for example, created difficulties since the approach of states which felt that terrorism was directed at them differed from the stance of states that tolerate it or use it as an instrument of policy.

The Israeli response

Netanyahu called the summit meeting statement unacceptable and said that it was an attempt to impose preconditions on the peace process, which he argued

[39] Ozanne, J., 'Israel braces for retreat from secularisation', *Financial Times*, 13 June 1996, p. 4.

[40] Jehl, D., 'Arab leaders seem ready to search for a new unity', *New York Times*, 1 June 1996.

[41] Reuter, 'Iraq complains at exclusion from Arab summitry', *The Guardian*, 10 June 1996, p. 7.

[42] He was also doubtless interested in shoring up Egypt's position as leader of the Arab world. Whittington, J., 'Mubarak back at centre stage', *Financial Times*, 12 June 1996, p. 4.

[43] The Middle East peace talks began at an international conference in Madrid on 30 Oct.–1 Nov. 1991. Eisendorf, R., 'The Middle East: the peace and security-building process', *SIPRI Yearbook 1994* (note 9), chapter 3, pp. 101–102.

[44] A translation of the summit meeting statement appears in *Mideast Mirror*, 24 June 1996, pp. 8–19. See also Lancaster, J., 'Arabs warn Israel it must withdraw', *International Herald Tribune*, 24 June 1996, p. 1; and Whittington, J., 'Arabs call for new peace process', *Financial Times*, 24 June 1996, p. 1.

was intolerable.[45] He then made his own preconditions. Perhaps the most important was that 'land for peace' would not be the basis of his government's approach to the peace process. He did not say that Israel would *not* trade land for peace but did state that such trades would neither be automatic nor necessarily involve all the land taken by Israel in 1967.

Netanyahu also said that Israel would not discuss Jerusalem, that a Palestinian state was out of the question (although both issues were clearly open for negotiation in the Oslo agreements) and that expansion of Israeli settlements would resume.[46] Netanyahu reiterated that Israel would not return the Golan Heights, saying that peace should be possible without it.[47] Finally, Netanyahu made it clear that he would not soon redeploy the Israeli Army in Hebron.[48]

Of all the towns covered under the Interim Agreement Hebron presented the greatest difficulties. The site of a religious tomb revered by both Judaism and Islam, Hebron boasts a small settlement of 400 militant Jews in the midst of a population of more than 100 000 Palestinians. The redeployment of the Israeli Army in Hebron was different from the case of other Arab towns covered under the DOP. The Israeli Army completely withdrew from the other towns, but Hebron is the only town which has an Israeli settlement within the municipal boundary. The Army therefore remained in part of Hebron to guard the settlers but redeployed from most of the city. Netanyahu questioned these arrangements, saying he needed more time to study the issue. Although Peres had made the same point in delaying redeployment, many Palestinians felt that Netanyahu was using the security issue to reopen the Hebron agreement, which set the stage for a summer of mounting frustration.

Not all the developments were negative. Netanyahu began talks with Arafat as soon as he took office, sending an emissary, Dore Gold, to open up contacts soon after the election and meeting Arafat on 4 September.[49] Netanyahu also began easing restrictions on Palestinians entering Israel to work.[50]

The USA, smarting after the defeat of Peres and in the midst of a presidential election, appealed for calm, hinting that Netanyahu needed time. Washington's 'honest broker' status was at an all-time low because of what the Arabs saw as excessive support for Israel. Throughout 1996 European leaders, particularly President Chirac, argued that more voices were needed in the peace process and that the EU should play a greater role. Arab states supported this

[45] On 24 June Netanyahu told Israel Radio that 'peace can be achieved without preconditions . . . The attempt to create facts and dictate preconditions, which undermine the security of Israel, does not conform with a true peace process'. Quoted in *Mideast Mirror*, 24 June 1996, p. 2.

[46] MacFarquhar, N., 'Israel is lifting freeze on Jewish settlements', *New York Times*, 3 Aug. 1996; and Machlis, A., 'Threat to peace as Israel signals settlement drive', *Financial Times*, 4 Aug. 1996, p. 3.

[47] 'Netanyahu holds firm on Golan', *International Herald Tribune*, 7 June 1996, p. 2.

[48] Cody, E., 'Israel drives home hard line during Christopher's visit', *International Herald Tribune*, 26 June 1996, p. 1.

[49] 'Netanyahu and Arafat commit to peace after historic handshake at Erez', *Mideast Mirror*, 4 Sep. 1996, pp. 2–6.

[50] 'Israel says it will relax blockade of West Bank and Gaza', *International Herald Tribune*, 17 July 1996, p. 9.

argument, while Israel and the USA were cautious about the danger of involving too many additional actors.[51]

Syrian redeployments and an Egyptian military exercise

As the peace process deteriorated in the months after Netanyahu's election, troubling signs emerged that Syria was undertaking extensive redeployment of its military forces in Lebanon and on the Israeli border.[52] Syria also engaged in a much-publicized test of a long-range Scud C missile during the summer.[53] Official statements indicated that the redeployments were routine, but the moves contributed to concern in Israel that war with Syria was a possibility.[54] In late summer and autumn, Israel redeployed troops and conducted military exercises in the Golan Heights area, and tension was heightened further.[55] By late 1996, however, official commentators on both sides were saying that the possibility of conflict was slight, although Israel expressed the opinion that an increase in Syrian-sponsored terrorism was likely if the peace process broke down irretrievably.

Perhaps even more disturbing was a major Egyptian military exercise in September, code-named 'Badr-96'. Israelis charged that the manoeuvres bore a striking resemblance to the opening moves of the 1973 Middle East War and that the publicity which surrounded the exercise was inflammatory. Egypt dismissed the concerns, but only half-heartedly. It seemed clear that at least one purpose of the exercise was to send an unmistakable message to Israel that its peace with Egypt was not irreversible.[56]

The Jerusalem tunnel

By September tension in the region was high. As often before, Jerusalem provided the impetus for it to boil over. For several years a tunnel beneath part of the wall surrounding the ancient Temple Mount, the most holy site in Judaism (upon which sits the Dome of the Rock, Islam's third holiest site), had been open to tourists. Plans existed to extend the tunnel slightly and create an exit

---

[51] 'Arab outrage at Christopher's "parroting" of Netanyahu's line', *Mideast Mirror*, 26 June 1996, pp. 8–9; and Hirst, D., 'Arabs look to Europe to break peace impasse', *The Guardian*, 2 Aug. 1996, p. 7.

[52] Schmemann, S., 'Syrian troop movements near Golan have Israelis nervous (and baffled)', *New York Times*, 18 Sep. 1996.

[53] 'Israel says Syria is missile-rattling', *International Herald Tribune*, 21 Aug. 1996, p. 8.

[54] 'Probability of war with Syria is no longer low', *Mideast Mirror*, 18 Sep. 1996, pp. 2–7. By late Nov. 'senior military sources' in Israel were saying that 'Syria has been seriously preparing an offensive option against Israel for quite some time'. *Yedi'ot Aharonot* (Tel Aviv), 24 Nov. 1996, in 'Military sources: Syria preparing offensive option', Foreign Broadcast Information Service, *Daily Report–Near East and South Asia (FBIS-NES)*, FBIS-NES-96-228, 2 Dec. 1996.

[55] Radio Monte Carlo (Paris), 3 Nov. 1996, in 'Syria: authoritative sources say limited Israeli attack possible', FBIS-NES-96-214, 5 Nov. 1996. President Mubarak stated that Egypt would not stand 'idle' if Syria was attacked. *Al-Nahar* (Beirut), 21 Nov. 1996, in 'Egypt, Lebanon: Mubarak says Egypt not to stand idle if Syria attacked', FBIS-NES-96-228, 26 Nov. 1996.

[56] Faraj, C. and Finnegan, P., 'Egyptians send a message with largest military exercise', *Defense News*, vol. 11, no. 37 (16–22 Sep. 1996), p. 60.

in a predominantly Arab area of the old city. Because of local sensitivities, successive Israeli governments had shelved the plans for more than a decade.

Taking pains to have the work done quietly at night and without informing the security services, who reportedly would have counselled against it,[57] Netanyahu opened the exit on 24 September. This action did not physically undermine the Dome of the Rock (as some Arabs claimed) or radically alter the balance of Arab and Israeli influence in the old city.[58] However, coming as it did after a summer of increasing frustration with Netanyahu's approach to the peace process and his government's strident tone on the issue of Palestinian rights in Jerusalem, the opening of the tunnel was the cause of terrible rioting. Over 65 people were killed and hundreds more wounded in confrontations on the West Bank. Of greatest concern to Israel was the fact that PA police fired at the Israeli Army as it deployed around and then into Palestinian towns. Netanyahu was angered that the PA police were firing on Israeli soldiers with guns provided by Israel and said that this was totally unacceptable. He accused Arafat of being behind the shooting and of having given 'secret' orders to his police to fire on the Israelis.[59]

Arafat denied the charge. He responded that the PA police were defending people from Israeli aggression and warned that he could not restrain the Palestinians in the face of provocation and broken promises. Perhaps Arafat believed that the peace process was failing and that he had nothing to lose by resorting to violence to force Israel to the table. For their part, the PA police may have felt that they needed to fire to maintain whatever credibility they had with the Palestinian people, many of whom saw the police as collaborators because of their crack-downs on opponents of the peace process. Many Palestinians seemed to agree that to have stood by and allowed Israeli troops to enter the Palestinian towns without a fight would have destroyed the legitimacy of the PA police in the eyes of the Palestinian people.[60]

The Washington summit meeting

With the peace process in tatters, and one of the accomplishments of his administration with it, Clinton called a 'snap' summit meeting in Washington. It was designed to allow Netanyahu and Arafat to meet on neutral ground, together with King Hussein, who had been helpful in the past. Expectations were low. Mubarak refused the invitation, saying that continuation of the peace process required Israel to live up to its past commitments and re-embrace the land for peace formula as the basis of that process.[61]

---

[57] 'Israel: "crisis of confidence" between PM, defense establishment', *Yedi'ot Aharonot* (Tel Aviv), 11 Oct. 1996, in FBIS-NES-96-199, 15 Oct. 1996.

[58] Schmemann, S., 'Beneath the battle, a historic tunnel', *New York Times*, 27 Sep. 1996.

[59] Brown, D., 'Israelis stunned as Palestine rises in bloody revolt', *The Guardian*, 27 Sep. 1996, p. 7. For more on the idea that Arafat might have issued secret orders months before, see Cockburn, P., 'PLO: we're ready to shoot at Israelis', *The Independent*, 12 Mar. 1996, p. 1.

[60] Bhatia, S., 'Palestinian police: despised by their people, the ex-guerrillas can now redeem themselves', *The Guardian*, 27 Sep. 1996, p. 6.

[61] A summary of Arab comment on the summit meeting is presented in 'The Washington summit and Mubarak's reservations', *Mideast Mirror*, 30 Sep. 1996, pp. 15–22.

The Washington summit meeting began on 1 October and continued for two days. Little of substance emerged, but apparently frank discussions took place during hours of one-on-one talks between Arafat and Netanyahu. It was also reported that King Hussein, the Arab leader who has moved closest to a 'warm peace' with Israel, was blunt in his criticism of Netanyahu during their private discussions. Ultimately, however, no decisions were reached, although all the participants spoke of a new appreciation of each other's difficulties.

The participants returned home voicing renewed determination to resume talks and agreeing that the Hebron issue should be the first priority. However, neither side was willing to appear to be flexible, and Arafat warned that the situation could rapidly become uncontrollable.[62]

III. The tracks of the peace process

Israeli–Palestinian and Israeli–Syrian bilateral relations are described in the above section. In 1996 that there was little progress on the official tracks of the peace process that deal with Israeli–Palestinian and Israeli–Syrian relations, for the reasons outlined above. However, some official meetings took place before the situation soured dramatically, and after the Washington summit meeting. This section describes those meetings and the multilateral track of the peace process in 1996.

The Israeli–Palestinian talks

The Israeli–Palestinian talks were dormant by mutual agreement during the Palestinian and subsequent Israeli elections. On 5 May senior negotiators from both sides did meet at Taba, Egypt, to formally begin the Final Status talks, as required by the schedule established in the Oslo agreements. Recognizing that no progress could be made until after the elections, the meeting was pro forma, with the participants promising to convene after the voting.[63]

With the election of Netanyahu the Final Status talks did not resume. Instead, acrimonious discussion of the fulfilment of the commitments arising from the first round of the Oslo agreements consumed the remainder of 1996. Chief among these was Hebron.

Under the Interim Agreement Israel agreed to withdraw from the greater part of the city of Hebron, although Peres delayed redeployment during the election.[64] Upon taking office Netanyahu continued the delay in order to study the issue, particularly the security arrangements for the remaining Jewish settlers in Hebron. The Palestinians accused Israel of trying to reopen the negotiations or even postponing redeployment indefinitely. They feared that giving in on this issue would cause the process to unravel and suspected that this was

---

[62] Gardner, D., 'A poor and mangled peace', *Financial Times*, 4 Oct. 1996, p. 21.

[63] Pathfinder News Service, 'Israel, PLO begin journey toward final peace', 6 May 1996. URL <http://pathfinder.com/@@dO8krQcAUbLwXsHD/news/>.

[64] 'Peres wrestling with Hebron redeployment and disaffected Arab voters', *Mideast Mirror*, 3 May 1996, pp. 2–8.

Netanyahu's real purpose. This issue would become an acid test of Netanyahu's willingness to advance the peace process and would not be resolved until early 1997.

The talks were complex, involving both technical and political issues. Israel wanted to increase the powers of its security forces remaining in the city and to limit those of the PA police. Heated arguments took place over the size and shape of the area to be patrolled by Israeli forces. Individual streets were the subject of intense discussion. Israel also wanted to limit the rights of the PA police to carry weapons in areas near the Jewish enclave and to gain the right of 'hot pursuit' for Israeli forces into Palestinian areas of the city. The Palestinians resisted. Intensive US mediation failed to resolve the impasse.[65]

Throughout the autumn of 1996 agreement appeared close on several occasions, but the talks broke down each time. By December, Israel accused Arafat of deliberately postponing agreement to increase tension and gain concessions on other issues. Israel hinted that Egypt was pushing Arafat to take difficult positions to increase pressure on Israel throughout the region. Egypt denied the charge, but relations, already frosty, worsened. Meanwhile the Palestinians claimed that Israel was using the Hebron dispute to revise Israel's commitment to redeploy troops from the so-called Area C (the remainder of that area of the West Bank which was to be handed over to the PA starting in 1997).[66]

During the first days of 1997, with the entire peace process stalled, Jordan's King Hussein again demonstrated his commitment to the peace process by personally intervening with a compromise suggestion for completion of the withdrawal from Area C by March 1998. With Hussein's assistance, the issue was finally resolved on 14 January 1997.[67]

The Israeli–Syrian talks

Although these talks continued after the call for elections in Israel, little was accomplished as both sides awaited the outcome. After the March bombings in Israel, Peres withdrew the Israeli team from the talks as a gesture apparently aimed at Israeli voters. They did not return in 1996.

Netanyahu's repudiation of 'land for peace' killed the talks. However, he did present the idea of a 'Lebanon first' approach—an agreement between

---

[65] See, e.g., IDF Radio (Tel Aviv), 0500 GMT, 28 Oct. 1996 (in Hebrew), in 'Arab–Israeli talks: talks on Hebron stuck; sides blame each other', FBIS-NES-96-210, 30 Oct. 1996; *Al-Sharq Al-Awsat* (London), 15 Nov. 1996, p. 2 (in Arabic), in 'Arab–Israeli talks: Arafat spokesman on 3 points obstructing Hebron deal', FBIS-NES-96-223, 19 Nov. 1996; and Israel Television, channel 1 (Jerusalem), 1700 GMT, 3 Dec. 1996 (in Arabic), in 'West Bank: negotiator blames Netanyahu for impasse in Hebron talks', FBIS-NES-96-234, 5 Dec. 1996.

[66] 'Arafat adviser cited on "outstanding" points with Israelis', *Al-Dustur* (Amman), 8 Dec. 1996, in FBIS-NES-96-237, 10 Dec. 1996. Netanyahu subsequently made a suggestion to this effect, arguing that Israeli redeployment from Area C be postponed until 1999. Arafat rejected the idea.

[67] The Hebron Protocol specifies in detail the relationship between the Israeli forces remaining in Hebron and the PA police taking over those areas of the city from which the Israeli Army will redeploy. The Protocol also deals with the civil administration of the city. Attached to the Protocol is a Note for Record concerning future steps in the process. Israel pledged to begin further redeployments by March 1997 to resolve other outstanding issues and to resume the Final Status talks. The PA agreed to complete the revision of the PLO Charter and to fight terrorism.

Israel and Syria to ease the situation in Lebanon and allow the Israeli Army to withdraw. Syria rejected the idea, since stopping the fighting in southern Lebanon, and thereby allowing Israel to withdraw from Lebanon, would have benefited Israel without giving Syria anything in return.[68]

Various US and European officials visited both Jerusalem and Damascus in 1996 seeking ways to restart the talks, but to no avail. Throughout the summer word leaked that 'secret channels' were open between Israel and Syria and that the two sides were sending messages to each other. Whatever the content of these messages may have been, they did not contain ideas for the resumption of the talks which met with acceptance on both sides.[69]

Rumours surfaced in early 1997 that an agreement in principle on the broad issues had been reached by the Peres Government before its defeat. If such an agreement had been reached, however, it is not known how detailed it was. Statements of principle tend to unravel when the details have to be filled in.[70] If there was such a tacit agreement, Netanyahu made clear that he would not abide by it in his approach to the Syrian talks.

The multilateral track

An integral component of the peace process, the multilateral track comprises five working groups intended to address pan-regional concerns which go beyond the Arab–Israeli talks.[71] A 'subtext' of the multilateral track is that it is intended to normalize relations between Israel and the region as progress is made in defusing the Arab–Israeli dispute. Although the multilateral negotiations are technically independent of the bilateral talks, it is recognized that they are politically subservient to them. The Arab states (with varying degrees of firmness) maintain that progress in the multilateral negotiations must follow progress in the bilateral negotiations. Syria and Lebanon hold the view that the multilateral negotiations should not take place at all until bilateral issues are resolved, and they do not participate.

Not surprisingly, with the general slow-down on the bilateral front in 1996, the multilateral negotiations were also affected. By the autumn the Palestinian delegation was boycotting all multilateral sessions in protest at the impasse over Hebron. Generally speaking, the five working groups met less frequently and undertook fewer projects in 1996 than in the past.

---

[68] Gardner, D., 'Netanyahu toys with "Lebanon first" policy', *Financial Times*, 1 Aug. 1996, p. 4.

[69] The Israeli newspaper *Ha'aretz*, e.g., broke the story that a Syrian envoy had travelled to Jerusalem in July to meet Netanyahu. Both sides denied the story, but only half-heartedly. Linzer, D., 'Israeli PM "in secret talks with Syria on Lebanon"', *The Guardian*, 2 Aug. 1996, p. 7.

[70] In 1997 a detailed report surfaced that Peres believed that a peace treaty might be possible by Oct. 1996 and that the framework of such a treaty had been achieved by Feb. 1996. However, Peres decided that it could not be completed before the election. *Yedi'ot Aharonot* (Tel Aviv), 4 Feb. 1997, p. 2 (in Hebrew), in 'Israel: peace treaty with Syria nearly signed in October 1996', FBIS-NES-97-024, 6 Feb. 1997; and Lippman, T., 'Election cited for derailing Mideast peace move', *Washington Post*, 29 Jan. 1997.

[71] For more on the multilateral talks, see Peters, J., *Pathways to Peace: The Multilateral Arab–Israeli Peace Talks* (Royal Institute for International Affairs: London, 1996); and Jones (note 8), pp. 181–88.

The *Arms Control and Regional Security Working Group* (ACRS) did not meet at all in 1996. This group had been making progress on the elaboration of regional confidence-building measures (CBMs) and the creation of a regional Conflict Prevention Centre until it stalled over a dispute between Israel and the Arab participants (especially Egypt) over Israel's nuclear status. The last plenary meeting was held in December 1994, and a few intersessional activities took place in 1995 before the group came to a halt. Given the depth of bad feeling within the group over the nuclear issue it is questionable whether progress would have been possible in 1996 even if the broader peace process had not been in such difficulty. The combination of the two problems, however, made meetings impossible.[72] Academic meetings took place at which some officials participated (in their private capacities).

The activity of the *Refugee Working Group* (RWG) also slowed down in 1996. Nevertheless, meetings and activities were carried out under its auspices. For example, the Gavel's mission to Jordan took place on 12–14 May. The mission was intended to open and develop dialogue with Palestinian refugees in Jordan, to raise their awareness of the RWG's activities and to consult them on the group's future plans.

An intersessional meeting on the refugee database was held in Oslo on 12–13 June 1996. This was a technical meeting designed to take stock of database activities and to consider ideas for future work, but little was accomplished. The refugee database, initiated by Norway, is a controversial project as Israel is suspicious of initiatives which might compromise its position on the question of possible compensation to Palestinians displaced in the conflict with Israel. For this reason the database is intended solely to compile an accurate picture of the living conditions of refugees and efforts to assist them.

In addition, the Jordan Living Conditions Survey is largely completed, but the release of the data presents political difficulties. Essentially, the question of the living conditions of Palestinian refugees in Jordan is sensitive for the Jordanian Government. At a meeting in Amman on 27–28 November, a decision was taken to release the data. Efforts are now under way to analyse these data.

An informal coordination meeting was held in Rome on 15 May 1996 and was largely devoted to preparing an intersessional meeting on the question of the adaptation of Palestinians in the West Bank and Gaza to the changes which are occurring as a result of the peace process—particularly those brought about by refugees who may return to the West Bank and Gaza. The planned intersessional meeting was postponed for political reasons after the Israeli election.

Another informal coordination meeting was held in Jordan on 24–26 November 1996 to assess the work of the RWG and to prepare future activities. Expectations of the meeting were low, particularly in view of ten-

---

[72] For more on ACRS, see Jentleson, B., *The Middle East Arms Control and Regional Security (ACRS) Talks: Progress, Problems, and Prospects*, Institute on Global Conflict and Cooperation (IGCC) Policy Paper 26 (University of California, San Diego: La Jolla, Calif., Sep. 1996); and Jones, P., 'Arms control in the Middle East: some reflections on ACRS', *Security Dialogue*, vol. 28, no. 1 (Mar. 1997).

sions in the region. Arab delegations argued that the international community should become more active in the refugee issue as it pertains to the Final Status talks, while Israel insisted that the RWG stick to issues concerning the health and well-being of refugees. The meeting was able to agree to hold intersessional meetings on public health among refugees (scheduled to take place in Tunis in early 1997 but subsequently postponed) and family reunification (no date set). There was no agreement as to when the next plenary meeting should be held.

The *Working Group on Water Resources* held few meetings in 1996. Jordan, the PLO (on behalf of the Palestinian Authority) and Israel initialed an agreement in Oslo on 13 February 1996 which dealt with the serious and chronic water problems in the region. The Steering Committee of the Group held an intersessional meeting in Boppard, Germany, on 1 March 1996. Various plans for technical projects were discussed and approved, but no date could be set for the next plenary meeting. A meeting in Hammamet, Tunisia, in May reached a number of decisions including the establishment of an EU-funded water data bank project to begin in January 1997 and a Norwegian-funded project to assist the Palestinian Water Authority in developing infrastructure and staff. In addition, a number of reports and decisions were considered which are designed to improve communication and data sharing on water resources among regional parties. Finally, a working-level technical meeting took place in Cyprus on 28–29 November. Although the Palestinian Authority announced at approximately the same time that it intended to boycott multilateral meetings until the Hebron issue was resolved, the Palestinian delegates did attend the Cyprus meeting.

The *Environment Working Group* held an intersessional meeting in Muscat, Oman, on 26–27 June 1996. Participants agreed to establish a regional environment centre in Amman, Jordan, that would provide vocational training and disseminate information on environmental matters. A plenary meeting was scheduled to take place in November 1996 but was rescheduled for December, and then postponed. Dates for a workshop on the Environmental Code of Conduct were to have been set at this plenary meeting.

Finally, the *Regional Economic Development Working Group* (REDWG) was not able to hold a plenary meeting in 1996. However, some technical committees dealing with regional economic infrastructure met during the year. The Monitoring Committee established by Egypt, Israel, Jordan and the Palestinians to oversee specific projects met in Cairo on 10 June and on 12 August. It was supposed to meet in December, but the meeting was cancelled for political reasons.

Closely associated with the REDWG are the meetings of the Middle East and North Africa Economic Summit. The first of these was held in Casablanca, Morocco, in 1994, and the second took place in Amman in 1995. The 1996 meeting was held in Cairo on 12–14 November. The purpose of these meetings is to stimulate contacts throughout the Middle East and between regional businessmen and international investors. Previous meetings featured high-level political involvement and discussion of regional infrastructure and trade projects.

Reflecting the poor atmosphere in the peace process generally, the Cairo Conference shied away from the intense discussion of regional projects which had characterized previous summit meetings. Instead, led by Egypt, regional countries used the meeting as an opportunity to try to attract foreign investment. Few high-level leaders from the region attended. The Israeli foreign minister flew to Cairo but left without entering the conference hall because of his anger at anti-Israeli statements in the Egyptian press. There was little interplay between Arab businessmen and their Israeli counterparts.

Finally, although it is not formally a part of the peace process, the European Union's 'Barcelona Initiative' (also known as the 'Euro-Med process') was active in 1996. Efforts at the political level centred on the development of a Political and Security Partnership. As of the end of 1996 work on a document was in the initial stages, but participants were also still defining the purpose of the exercise. Efforts were also under way to hold low-key events to discuss various aspects of confidence-building and political cooperation. On the other front of the process, greater economic cooperation, many countries, including Egypt and Jordan, are critical of the EU's unwillingness to allow them to export such items as agricultural produce, one of the region's few viable sources of income, while insisting that regional partners eliminate tariff barriers to manufactured goods from Europe.

IV. Wider regional issues

The Middle East peace process played out against a backdrop of wider trends and developments in the region. Unrest in several Gulf states, much of it blamed on Iran, continued throughout 1996. Saudi Arabia saw its ruler temporarily step down for health reasons and then return to the throne.

Other tensions continued to mount in the area. Iraq staged its most substantial military campaign since the 1991 Persian Gulf War, striking at Kurdish areas in northern Iraq in support of a friendly faction. This brought about an armed US response. Internal dissent was also evident in the region, with violence against both civilian and military targets in Algeria, Bahrain, Egypt and Saudi Arabia. Although, with some justification, the governments of these states blamed outside interference (particularly by Iran) for the bloodshed, it is clear that internal factors were also at work. These have largely to do with dissatisfaction with the policies of the governments of these countries.

In Iran parliamentary elections seemed to herald a more moderate government, but it is difficult to be certain as many opposition movements were denied the right to take part. Presidential elections are scheduled for 1997, and the incumbent, Hashemi Rafsanjani, is ineligible to run again, having served two terms, unless the law is temporarily altered to allow him to run a third time. With the re-election of President Clinton, there were signals from Washington that a broad consensus may emerge that the US policy of dual-containment in the Gulf is not working and that a new *modus vivendi* must be found for relations with Iran. However, early indications in 1997 are that this change will be slow in coming, if it comes at all.

Israel and Turkey signed a landmark military cooperation agreement in 1996. Although both countries are adamant that the agreement simply allows the Israeli Air Force to use Turkish airspace for training (Israel's skies are too small and crowded to permit realistic training flights), it appears that the two are inching towards a strategic partnership of a sort. The idea that Israel might form a partnership with the non-Arab Muslim states on the periphery of the region was an idea put forward by former Israeli Prime Minister David Ben Gurion, and many Arab states saw in the Israeli–Turkish agreement the first step in that direction. For Turkey, the agreement appears to have been slargely by its military, which is reportedly worried at the growing level of Islamic fundamentalism in the countries around Turkey, and even within Turkey. Whatever the reason, most Arab states were concerned about the new Israeli–Turkish relationship and called upon Turkey to reconsider.[73]

V. Conclusions

In 1996 the peace process began to face a number of critical issues: whether or not the Palestinians will get a state and what its powers and boundaries will be; whether Israel will accept curtailment of settlements in the occupied territories; whether a compromise of some sort can be achieved on Jerusalem; and whether a suitable exchange of the Golan Heights for peace with Syria can be worked out. These issues remain the crux of the peace process. Rabin and Peres seemed to believe that Israel would have to compromise on these issues to achieve peace. Despite a tough bargaining stance, both seemed inclined to make the required compromises, if they could be sure that Israel's security would be enhanced.

As 1996 progressed Netanyahu's attitudes towards the peace process came under intense scrutiny. It was known that some senior ministers, such as Ariel Sharon and Raful Eitan, were steadfastly opposed to any compromise. Others, such as David Levy and Natan Sharansky, were seen as more moderate, but of the opinions of Netanyahu himself little is known. He has repeatedly stated that he is committed to the peace process, but he has also taken steps seemingly inimical to that end. Several of his public statements, and the actions of his government, indicate that he is not convinced that the compromises implicit in the Madrid conference formula of land for peace and in the UN Security Council resolutions, upon which the peace process is based, are in Israel's interest. It is difficult to know whether he has launched himself on this course as a tactical gambit (designed to force more from his negotiating partners at the table), whether he is walking a fine line in terms of his domestic political partners or whether he believes that through the sheer force of his

---

[73] Pomfret, J., 'Nervous Turks tilt towards Israel', *International Herald Tribune*, 4 June 1996, p. 2.

own personality and Israel's strengths he can unilaterally impose a fundamental change on the peace process

The year 1997 may be decisive for the Middle East peace process. Either the process will get back on track or a new dynamic will emerge to replace it. The troubled history of the region is such that any dynamic which replaces the peace process is more likely than not to be a bloody one.

4. Russia: conflicts and its security environment

VLADIMIR BARANOVSKY*

I. Introduction

In 1996, five years after the dissolution of the Soviet Union, the new post-Soviet states continued to face numerous security-related challenges. As in the past, they were closely interlinked with domestic developments, conflict-settlement efforts and organization of the post-Soviet geopolitical space.

This chapter outlines conflict developments and settlement efforts on the territory of the former USSR, with a special focus on Russia. Section II presents an overview of domestic political trends. Section III analyses developments in Chechnya and section IV those in four other conflict areas (Abkhazia, Nagorno-Karabakh, South Ossetia and the Trans-Dniester region) where political settlements of separatist conflicts are under negotiation. Section V deals with the civil war in Tajikistan and the attempts to promote a peace process. Russia's policy towards the Commonwealth of Independent States (CIS) and its relations with its immediate European neighbours—the Baltic states, Belarus and Ukraine—are discussed in section VI. Section VII presents the conclusions.

II. The domestic context

In Russia, presidential elections were held in two rounds on 16 June and 3 July 1996. Most observers claim that they were held in basic accordance with democratic requirements,[1] although the governing élite used all the means at its disposal not to lose power and to ensure that Boris Yeltsin would continue as President of the Russian Federation. His re-election was influenced by several factors: (a) the consolidation of political forces which associated their interests with the new regime (including most of the local élites);[2] (b) the mobilization of huge financial resources—those of new private businesses and government allocations to meet the immediate demands of the population

---

[1] It is widely recognized, however, that the fairness of the elections was undermined by the predominantly pro-Yeltsin orientation of the electronic mass media. See the report of the European Institute for the Media, as cited in Open Media Research Institute (OMRI), *OMRI Russian Presidential Survey*, no. 15 (19 July 1996).

[2] During the election campaign, power-sharing treaties were signed between the Russian Administration and dozens of 'subjects of the Federation' (autonomous republics and administrative regions) which provided local élites with more power.

* In the data collection for this chapter the author was assisted by Boris Nevelev, whose contribution is gratefully acknowledged.

SIPRI Yearbook 1997: Armaments, Disarmament and International Security

(especially payment of wage and pension arrears); (c) an aggressive professional campaign by the mass media, especially the electronic media, which combined Soviet-style propaganda with US-style political advertising; (d) a dramatic 'black and white' presentation of the voters' choice, with the main challenger to Yeltsin, Communist Party leader Gennadiy Zyuganov, portrayed as advocating the restoration of totalitarian political order and a state-controlled economy; and (e) a skilful 'appropriation' of the most popular slogans, promises and arguments of the opposition (such as to provide reforms with a stronger 'social orientation', halt the unprecedentedly widespread corruption, fight crime and end the war in Chechnya). The decisive factor was Yeltsin's temporary alliance with one of the most popular candidates, General Alexander Lebed, who received the third highest share of the votes (nearly 15 per cent) in the first round and was invited to join the administration as Secretary of the Russian Security Council and become the president's national security adviser.[3]

The victory of Yeltsin, with 54 per cent of the vote, may have prevented a new period of political destabilization in Russia. It did not, however, decisively consolidate democracy. Rather, the political system is gradually turning into an oligarchy with a growing role for corporate financial–industrial structures, an increasingly corrupt bureaucracy, a highly monopolized private sector that flourishes only when it can extract favours from the state, and criminalization of political power in the provinces and 'the centre'. The weakness of this regime stems from: the ruthless and seemingly anarchic struggle between competing power groups, which is becoming more threatening in view of Yeltsin's poor health; the non-development of a 'middle class' as a stability-providing social force; persisting tension generated by social disparities and the scandalously low living standards of the majority of the population; the disappointing macroeconomic results of reforms (despite claims to the contrary by the government); and the continuing risk of fragmentation because of the growing power of local élites.

In most of the other European post-Soviet states, elections are recognized by the major domestic actors as the main tool in their power struggles. Indeed, since the demise of the USSR, a non-violent transfer of power to the political opponents of incumbent leaders occurred in the three Baltic states and in Belarus (1994), Ukraine (1994) and Moldova (1996).

Developments in Belarus in 1996 represented a clear departure from this trend. The authoritarian policy of President Alexander Lukashenko provoked a fierce confrontation with the parliament, demonstrations of protest in the capital and an attempt by the parliament to start the process of impeachment of the president. Having openly threatened to use force, the president organized a controversial referendum on 24 November 1996 (carried out in flagrant violation of the fundamental criteria for a democratic system), proclaimed the par-

---

[3] In Oct. Lebed was dismissed from both posts, having managed in a period of several months to bring crucial votes to Yeltsin, stop the hostilities in Chechnya and provoke the furious opposition of Moscow's élites by his determination not to observe 'the rules of the game' in the top power echelons and by his ambition to become the next president, which he may have good chances of realizing.

liament dissolved and introduced a new constitution legitimizing the de facto *coup d'état* and establishing one-man rule in practically all spheres of public life.[4]

Domestic trends in the non-European post-Soviet states were even more controversial. Political stabilization was often achieved by new power élites establishing effective control over purportedly democratic procedures. Instances of presidential manipulation and distortion of democratic institutions have become something of a norm. In many states (for example, Kazakhstan, Turkmenistan, Uzbekistan and even Armenia, with a much better past democratic record) there were egregious examples of electoral manipulation or overstepping of presidential powers in the name of stability, efficiency and better economic performance.

III. War and peace in Chechnya

The year 1996 witnessed the cessation of the war in Chechnya—the most serious in terms of casualties and armed conflict on former Soviet territory[5] and the most dramatic challenge experienced by post-Soviet Russia. The process of ending hostilities and promoting political settlement was both difficult and contradictory.

Basic approaches

The year started with a dramatic crisis in which Chechen separatists took hostages in Dagestan, an adjacent autonomous republic. This incident illustrated the major features of the conflict: the continuing separatist strategy of selective retaliation in response to offensive Russian operations; Russia's inability to contain the guerrillas within Chechnya and the possibility of the conflict spilling over into neighbouring north Caucasian republics; substantial

---

[4] Although Lukashenko based his strategies on those of Yeltsin in his confrontation with the Russian Supreme Soviet, Belarus avoided armed clashes (in contrast to the autumn 1993 events in Moscow, when tanks fired on the parliament building). Another difference between the Belarussian and the 'earlier Yeltsin' case is the strong negative reaction of the international community, which put Belarus at risk of becoming a pariah in Europe. The Organization for Security and Co-operation in Europe, the Council of Europe, the European Union and a number of leading states have openly condemned the legitimacy of the 'new order' established in the country.

[5] During hostilities, 3826 Russian federal troops were killed, 17 892 wounded and 1906 reported missing in action. The total number of casualties was assessed by Russian Security Council Secretary Alexander Lebed at 80 000–100 000; about 3 times as many were wounded. *Kommersant-Daily*, 3 Oct. 1996, p. 1; and *Russia Reform Monitor* (American Foreign Policy Council, Washington, DC), no. 182 (5 Sep. 1996), URL <http.//www.afpc.org>. According to the non-governmental 'Memorial' association, 4379 Russian servicemen were killed. Rutland, P., 'Russian losses in Chechen war', Open Media Research Institute (OMRI), *OMRI Daily Digest*, no. 9, part I (14 Jan. 1997), URL <http://www.omri.cz> (hereafter, references to *OMRI Daily Digest* refer to the Internet edition at this URL address). Lebed's earlier assessment of the number of Russian troop casualties was 6000–7000. *Argumenty i Fakty*, no. 17 (1996), p. 4. In Mar. 1996 the Russian General Staff assessed the number of Chechen fighters killed at 15 500. *Izvestiya*, 16 Mar. 1996, p. 1. The Chechen side reported 78 000 civilian deaths and 238 000 wounded. *Nezavisimaya Gazeta*, 22 Mar. 1996, p. 3.

civilian casualties;[6] the poor performance of the Russian 'force structures' (*siloviye vedomstva*)[7] and unprofessionalism of their leadership;[8] and distorted information flows from the conflict area to the Kremlin and its inadequate political reaction (including that of President Yeltsin).[9]

Meanwhile, the morale of the armed forces was deteriorating because of a dramatic lack of supplies owing to insufficient financing, poor organization and large-scale abuses and to increasingly critical public opinion and mass media. The latter acquired crucial importance in the presidential campaign. Indeed, Yeltsin had to openly recognize that a continuation of the war would prevent his re-election.[10] He needed either a victory or peace and, since it was unrealistic to expect victory before the elections, pressure increased within the administration to reach a quick political settlement.[11] Settlement was apparently also promoted by powerful economic actors with considerable stakes in the multi-billion dollar Caspian shelf oil transport projects and interests in stabilization of the entire northern Caucasus area.

In a parallel development the proponents of a solution 'by force' argued that a decisive victory over the separatists was within reach and only a final blow was needed to crush them. Offensive operations were repeatedly resumed. The failures of the federal troops[12] were explained by their insufficiently resolute action, attributed to the lack of a clear political mandate to use unrestrained force. This logic continued to receive support in Russian political quarters even after the crucial decisions on political settlement were announced. Moreover, some influential politicians, analysts and officers who rejected or did not believe in the prospect of a 'total' military victory considered that at least some spectacular successes by federal troops were needed—as a face-saving

---

[6] In Mar. 1996 a report by the head of the OSCE mission in Chechnya, Swiss diplomat Tim Guldimann, condemned Dudayev's fighters for repeatedly taking civilian hostages, while the Russian forces were accused of waging 'warfare against the civilian population', engaging in 'wanton destruction and systematic looting' and extorting money from villages in return for not attacking them. Rutland, P., 'OSCE report condemns conduct of Chechen war', *OMRI Daily Digest*, no. 62, part I (27 Mar. 1996).

[7] In Russian political parlance this refers to ministries and other state institutions possessing armed units—the Ministry of Defence, the Federal Security Service, the Ministry of the Interior, etc.

[8] The operation against 200–250 terrorists involved *c.* 2500 Russian troops with armoured combat vehicles, artillery and aircraft and was headed by 2 army generals—Minister of the Interior Anatoliy Kulikov and Head of the Federal Security Service Mikhail Barsukov. The operation resulted in many civilian casualties and the escape of most of the Chechen fighters. *Izvestiya*, 10 Jan. 1997, p. 2.

[9] Reported by Russian television, Yeltsin's comments on '38 snipers' from the security services who were allegedly extremely efficient in targeting Chechen fighters in the area of hostage-taking were mocked throughout the country—especially in the light of the subsequent spectacular failure of the military operation against the terrorists.

[10] Belin, L., 'Yeltsin instructs Chernomyrdin to find Chechnya solution', *OMRI Daily Digest*, no. 29, part I (9 Feb. 1996).

[11] In Feb. 1996, 7 options for ending the war in Chechnya were reportedly discussed at a Russian Federation Security Council meeting. Belin (note 10).

[12] Evidence points to the scandalously poor performance of the Russian top military command in Chechnya. See, e.g., the report of the Chairman of the State Duma Committee on Defence, Lev Rokhlin, published in *Nezavisimaya Gazeta*, 27 Apr. 1996, pp. 1, 3. Unable to effectively fight guerrilla combatants, the federal troops were often reported to retaliate ruthlessly against the civilian population. Even the pro-Moscow Chechen Supreme Soviet backed by the Russian Administration accused the federal troops of engaging in looting, pillaging and reprisals. Fuller, L., 'Chechen leadership accuses federal troops', *OMRI Daily Digest*, no. 57, part I (20 Mar. 1996).

device and to provide a better bargaining position for Russia in the negotiations.

These two contradictory lines of reasoning dominated the difficult search for ways out of the Chechnya deadlock from early 1996. Combat operations were carried out in parallel with increasingly strong signals of Russia's readiness to reach a political compromise.

Ending the war

Yeltsin's 'peace plan' was announced on 31 March 1996. It contained two new elements in Russia's approach: a gradual withdrawal of federal troops from Chechnya and a readiness to negotiate, via mediators, with Dzhokhar Dudayev, president of the breakaway republic.[13] While combat operations continued, the most important obstacle (in the eyes of Russia) to negotiations was removed three weeks later, when Dudayev, the personal symbol of Chechen separatism, was reported to have been killed in a rocket attack on 21 April.[14] Yeltsin invited Dudayev's successor, President Zelimkhan Yandarbiyev, to a meeting in Moscow on 27 May at which the Russian and separatist delegations agreed on a total cease-fire from midnight on 31 May. On 10 June two protocols were signed in Nazran, capital of the neighbouring Ingush republic, by Russian Nationalities Minister Vyacheslav Mikhailov and Chechen Chief of Staff Aslan Maskhadov—one on the withdrawal of Russian troops by the end of August 1996 and the surrender of weapons by Chechen militants, and the second on the release of all hostages and prisoners of war (POWs). Thus, just a few weeks before the Russian presidential elections, the process of political settlement in Chechnya started to take shape.

Soon after the Russian elections the process was at the point of collapsing. On 10 July, just one week after Yeltsin was re-elected, Russian armed forces renewed combat operations. Once again the military 'hawks' had succeeded in promoting the argument that a 'decisive blow' was both needed (because of the violations of the Nazran protocols by the Chechen side[15]) and possible (because there were no longer Russian electoral constraints[16]). Heavy damage

---

[13] For the text of the presidential decree 'On the programme of crisis settlement in the Chechen Republic' and Yeltsin's statement on this issue see *Krasnaya Zvezda*, 2 Apr. 1996, pp. 1, 3.

[14] Dudayev was successfully located and targeted by satellite communication while speaking on a cellular telephone with a Russian lawmaker about Yeltsin's peace initiative. *Russia Reform Monitor*, no. 130 (26 Apr. 1996), URL <http.//www.afpc.org>.

[15] Whatever violations by the Chechen separatists took place, the non-compliance of the Russian side was also obvious. The essential element of the Nazran agreements was the decision on the postponement of the election to a new People's Assembly (scheduled for 16 June by the pro-Moscow loyalists in Chechnya) until after the withdrawal of all Russian troops. However, the election was held—not openly obstructed by the separatists but described by the OSCE as 'manipulated' and 'a parody of democracy'. Fuller, L., 'Truce in Chechnya', *OMRI Daily Digest*, no. 118, part I (18 June 1996); *Segodnya*, 19 June 1996, p. 2; *Izvestiya*, 20 June 1996, p. 3; *Nezavisimaya Gazeta*, 5 July 1996, p. 3; and 'Ingushi president frustrated by Russian policy in Chechnya', Interfax, 10 July 1996.

[16] This was after General Lebed had been appointed Secretary of the Security Council and entrusted with authority to control the 'force structures', including the military, and with 'special powers' to terminate the war in Chechnya.

was inflicted on several villages and considerable civilian casualties were reported.[17]

The separatists responded with their most spectacular victory of the 20-month war: on 6 August 1996 they attacked and established control of Grozny, the capital of Chechnya, threatening the lives of all the Russian troops deployed there, who had apparently been taken by surprise. The Russian command in the area issued a controversial 48-hour ultimatum that the civilian population leave Grozny because a counter-attack was going to be made by Russian troops, who would presumably use heavy artillery and air strikes. The ultimatum provoked panic in Grozny and confusion in Moscow; in the end Russia cancelled the deadline for the 'exodus' and agreed to withdraw Russian troops. These events marked a crucial military and psychological victory for the separatist fighters[18] and a turning-point in the settlement process in at least two respects.

On the one hand, the loss of Grozny shattered any illusions about the ability of the Russian armed forces to defeat the guerrilla forces,[19] causing the 'Party of War' in Moscow and in the military establishment to stop advocating continued hostilities. Implementation of agreements reached in May and June 1996 began to look realistic. The shuttle diplomacy of Alexander Lebed,[20] whatever its concrete results, seemed to be the only way to facilitate the process. On 31 August Lebed and Maskhadov signed an agreement in Khasaviurt, Dagestan, that finally ended the war in Chechnya.[21]

On the other hand, the defeat in Grozny was so spectacular that the Russian Government was forced to negotiate from a position of weakness. The price was acceptance of the separatists' control over Chechnya and abandonment of previous Russian demands,[22] except insistence on the principle of Russia's territorial integrity. This considerably complicated the reaction of Russian political circles and mass media to the settlement.

Although the urgent need to stop hostilities was generally recognized, Lebed was none the less accused of having brokered a peace agreement which amounted to Russia's capitulation and de facto recognition of Chechnya's

[17] The Chechen side announced that Russian troops had used chemical weapons, which was denied by the Russian military. *Izvestiya*, 24 July 1996, p. 1.

[18] In a humiliating recognition of defeat, the Russian President declared 10 Aug., the day after his official inauguration, a day of state mourning for those who had perished in Grozny after the separatists' attack.

[19] The Russian mass media often pointed out the spectacular failures of the regular armed forces and interior troops operating in Chechnya. In numerous localities officially reported as 'liberated' by the federal troops, it took small guerrilla-type groups of separatists only a matter of hours to re-establish control. Yakov, V., 'Kto zhe khozyain v Chechne?' [Who is in control of Chechnya?], *Izvestiya*, 29 July 1996, pp. 1–2.

[20] Lebed made 7 peace-making trips to the northern Caucasus. *Nezavisimaya Gazeta*, 28 Dec. 1996, p. 3.

[21] For the text of the Agreement on the Principles for Clarifying the Basis for Mutual Relations between the Russian Federation and the Chechen Republic see *Nezavisimaya Gazeta*, 3 Sep. 1996, p. 3.

[22] Some previously negotiated provisions were abandoned, to the obvious disadvantage of Russia. If Russia initially interpreted the agreements on federal troop withdrawal as conditional on Chechnya's complete demilitarization, after the events in Grozny any discussions of disarmament of the separatists became pointless. Russia also intended to keep 2 brigades permanently deployed on the territory of Chechnya; however, on 23 Nov. Yeltsin had to sign a decree on their withdrawal on the demand of the separatist leaders.

secession. The legal terms of the agreement were openly questioned by some top Russian officials, and the Ministry of Justice claimed that it was a 'political declaration' with 'no state–legal significance'.[23] However, its implementation proceeded quickly and efficiently, contrary to expectations.

The settlement process

In early 1997 the key elements of a settlement in Chechnya were the following.

Troop withdrawal and exchange of prisoners of war

Russian troops (totalling over 40 000 in mid-1996) started to leave Grozny on 23 August 1996. All combat units were withdrawn by 31 December and the last Russian soldiers were officially announced to have left Chechnya by 5 January 1997.[24]

The three basic Russian–Chechen agreements (those signed in 1996 in Moscow, Nazran and Khasaviurt) stipulated the release of all POWs, hostages and other persons forcibly detained during the hostilities. By the end of October approximately 200 had been released,[25] after which the process practically stopped and both sides blamed each other for detaining 1000–2000 persons.[26] In Russia this raised intense criticism.

Chechnya's status

The signatories to the Khasaviurt agreement agreed to postpone any definition of Chechnya's status until 31 December 2001 but failed to define how its future status would be decided. This 'deferred' status allowed both sides to persist with their official rhetoric: Chechnya could continue to insist on its independence (although with a kind of 'special relationship' with Russia) and Russia on its territorial integrity (although with the possibility of granting Chechnya a 'special status' within the Russian Federation).

Surprisingly, both sides seem to prefer to engage in practical cooperation rather than to address the divisive issue of status. However, there are opponents to such an approach in both Russia and Chechnya; if their arguments prevail, the fragile foundation of the settlement process may be eroded. In

---

[23] ITAR-TASS (Moscow), 12 Sep. 1996, in 'Russia: Justice Ministry says Lebed "incapable" of assessing accord', Foreign Broadcast Information Service, *Daily Report–Central Eurasia (FBIS-SOV)*, FBIS-SOV-96-178, 13 Sep. 1996.

[24] *Nezavisimaya Gazeta*, 24 Aug. 1996, p. 1; Rutland, P., 'Chechnya free of Russian troops', *OMRI Daily Digest*, no. 3, part I (6 Jan. 1997); and Russian television news programme 'Vremya', 6 Jan. 1997.

[25] Federal authorities had released 35 militants and the Chechens had released 100 civilians and 51 soldiers. Rutland, P., 'Chechnya prisoner exchange going slowly', *OMRI Daily Digest*, no. 214, part I (5 Nov. 1996).

[26] More moderate assessments give the figure of *c.* 200 Russian soldiers held captive. Rutland, P., 'Russian captives in Chechnya', *OMRI Daily Digest*, no. 7, part I (10 Jan. 1997). Many Russian servicemen were believed to be held captive by field commanders or private citizens who demanded ransom or hoped to 'exchange' them for Chechens detained as convicted criminals by Russian legal authorities. An amnesty was required for the release of the Russian captives.

terms of the Russian constitutional order, Chechnya will represent a 'grey zone' during a transitional period, with numerous and inevitable politico-legal collisions.

Political power

None of the three agreements defines who will govern Chechnya until its status is decided. However, by withdrawing, Russia recognized the separatists as being de facto in exclusive control. The establishment of joint bodies[27] does not represent even the rudiments of power-sharing. No Russian laws, taxes or institutions operate in Chechnya today.

Russia, which was interested in incorporating pro-Russian individuals and groups into the new Chechen political system, for a time provided support to its most recent client, the 'legitimate head of state' Doku Zavgayev,[28] but later withdrew its support.[29] Whether a consolidation of anti-Dudayev forces in Chechnya is possible remains an open question.[30] The Chechen presidential and parliamentary elections scheduled for 27 January 1997 were endorsed by Russia as legitimizing political power in the republic, although all the leading Chechen candidates strongly favoured independence.

Law and order

With attempts to demilitarize Chechnya abandoned and the basic elements of state organization still to be reconstructed, the large number of weapons in the possession of individuals has resulted in a considerable increase in crime. The new authorities are facing serious difficulties in controlling the situation; some field commanders have continued to operate independently, their paramilitary units engaging in criminal and terrorist activities.

Once installed in Grozny, the separatist authorities announced their intention to promote Islamic law (sharia). Stern measures to halt the consumption of alcohol were adopted and spectacularly harsh punishment was inflicted.[31] However, fears of a fundamentalist Islamic order being introduced throughout Chechnya seem to have been exaggerated.

[27] The Khasaviurt agreement, e.g., established a joint commission to monitor the Russian troop withdrawal and coordinate measures to prevent crime and terrorist activities.

[28] Russia promoted the participation of the pro-Moscow Zavgayev Government in the 'intra-Chechen dialogue' but the separatists resolutely rejected it as a puppet regime. Baranovsky, V., 'Conflicts in and around Russia', *SIPRI Yearbook 1996: Armaments, Disarmament and International Security* (Oxford University Press: Oxford, 1996), pp. 257–59.

[29] In the light of Moscow's new policy for dealing with new partners, the loyalty of 'old' clients appeared increasingly counterproductive. Furthermore, they tried to openly challenge this line of policy, insisting on continuation of the war. Mamaladze, T., 'Svoya igra Doku Zavgayeva' [Doku Zavgayev plays his own game], *Izvestiya*, 13 June 1996, p. 2; and Dementyeva, I., 'Voyna miru' [War to peace], *Izvestiya*, 20 June 1996, p. 3.

[30] Already in Sep. 1996 Zavgayev's local administrators and police (who had been in control of the Nadterechniy district in northern Chechnya) were reported to have either joined the separatists or disappeared. However, some reports testified to the continuation of the anti-Dudayev opposition.

[31] In one district of Grozny, in Sep. up to 30 people a day were punished and drunkards were subject to 40 strokes with a cane. Rutland, P., '. . . As new authorities clamp down on alcohol', *OMRI Daily Digest*, no. 176, part I (11 Sep. 1996).

Refugees and Russians in Chechnya

In contrast to the settlement efforts in other areas of the former USSR (Abkhazia and Nagorno-Karabakh), the return of refugees (totalling approximately 300 000, or a quarter to one-third of the pre-war Chechen population) was not addressed in the settlement process. Russia insisted only that refugees be allowed to take part in the January 1997 elections. Most of the refugees are Russians[32] and apparently do not intend to return to Chechnya, fearing insecurity, discrimination and other pressure to leave. Russia has no programme to support Russian refugees from Chechnya. The Russian/ Cossack population in the northern areas of the republic and in the neighbouring territories of Russia is becoming increasingly radical in its demands that Russia protect its interests, even through the use of force.

Economic restoration

After the Khasaviurt agreement was signed, Chechen President Yandarbiyev raised the issue of the 'contribution' (war reparations) to be paid by Russia. The request, for a total of 100 trillion roubles,[33] seemed to have little chance of being officially negotiated by the Russian and Chechen authorities.

Rather, both sides have engaged in practical cooperation to address the region's urgent economic needs, including the restoration of transport links with Chechnya, the extraction and processing of Chechen oil, the security of oil pipelines transiting Chechnya, and social and humanitarian problems (payment of wages and pensions). A new agreement on economic relations between Chechnya and Russia was expected to be signed soon after the January 1997 Chechen elections.

Both sides are interested in resuming normal economic activities in Chechnya.[34] Russian private business has become active,[35] hoping to reap immense gains from the appropriation of economic assets in the region, from its 'special economic status' and from huge Russian Government allocations.[36]

---

[32] According to the 1989 census, there were 290 000 Russians in the Chechen Republic, 210 000 of them residents of Grozny. By the end of 1996 no more than 50 000 remained in Grozny (figures for the whole of Chechnya are not available). Grafova, L., 'Kak spasti russkikh, ostayushchikhsya v Chechne?' [How to save Russians remaining in Chechnya?], *Izvestiya*, 26 Dec. 1996, p. 5.

[33] This sum is equivalent to *c.* $18 billion, calculated on the basis of $100 000 in compensation per family who had suffered damage. *Argumenty i Fakty*, no. 40 (3 Oct. 1996), p. 2.

[34] Both during the war and after its cessation, the 'shadow economy', such as illegal oil extraction and processing, has become a universal phenomenon in the republic, providing for both the survival of most of its population and widespread crime.

[35] The deep involvement in the settlement process of Boris Berezovskiy, one of the 'heavyweights' of the Russian financial oligarchy appointed Deputy Secretary of the Russian Security Council in Oct., may be a reflection of this trend.

[36] Exact figures for current Russian spending on Chechnya are not available; different sources assess the 1995 allocations for reconstruction at 8–11 trillion roubles ($1.5–2 billion). According to Lebed, 90% of the money had been misused or stolen. Morvant, P., 'Lebed on Chechnya reconstruction losses', *OMRI Daily Digest*, no. 181, part I (18 Sep. 1996).

The international dimension

As compensation for its military and political defeat, Russia has adopted a firm position on not tolerating international recognition of Chechnya or independent international contacts by Chechnya. External involvement is acceptable to Russia only if it does not undermine the official position that Chechnya is part of Russia. Russia therefore welcomed the mediation role of the Organization for Security and Co-operation in Europe (OSCE) mission in Chechnya and did not bar (although it expressed dissatisfaction concerning) external financial assistance for the Chechen elections.[37] However, Russia strongly opposed the Council of Europe hearings on the Chechnya peace plan scheduled for 23 September 1996 with the participation of Maskhadov.

Prospects

The traumatic experience of the war seems to have made the prospect of eventual Chechen secession less unacceptable to Russian public opinion. Some analysts, however, argue in favour of such an option under two conditions: (*a*) that all those wishing to leave Chechnya to reside permanently in Russia should be allowed and financially assisted to do so; and (*b*) that the current borders between Chechnya and the neighbouring administrative entities of the Russian Federation should be altered.[38] The opposing argument stresses that this would legitimize the use of force in the quest for secession and could produce a 'contaminating effect' with extremely destabilizing consequences in other regions (such as the neighbouring autonomous republic of Dagestan).

The strategy of the Russian Government seems to aim at consolidating Russian interdependence with Chechnya so that the latter's eventual formal withdrawal would in practical terms be meaningless. The Chechen authorities apparently recognize that without Russia the republic cannot prosper economically or fight crime effectively. Their strong rhetoric on independence might eventually evolve into a mutually acceptable, pragmatic pattern of relations with Russia.[39]

---

[37] External financial assistance for the elections in Chechnya (mainly from the USA and the EU) channelled via the OSCE was reported to total $600 000. Parrish, S., 'Russian foreign minister criticizes OSCE funding of Chechen elections', *OMRI Daily Digest*, no. 16, part I (23 Jan. 1997).

[38] During the Soviet period, the 'historical' territory of Chechnya (Ichkeria) was enlarged twice: in 1922 and in 1956–57, when some districts with a Cossack (Russian) population were annexed from the neighbouring administrative regions.

[39] Note the remarks of a key separatist leader, Movladi Udugov: 'The terms like "independence, sovereignty, territorial integrity" are the reason for much speculation. They are toyed with by people who want to continue in the war. . . . For both the Chechen Republic and Russia, what form of mutual relations they choose is important. The Bashkiriyan Constitution [Bashkortostan is one of the autonomous republics in the Russian Federation] says that it is an independent, sovereign state that has bilateral relations with the Russian Federation. There is no other mention of the Russian Federation in the Constitution. I believe it to be the Constitution of an independent state, and it does not cause any excitement in Russia'. Prochazkova, P. and Stetina, J., 'It was a struggle for physical survival', *Lidove Noviny* (Prague), 10 Sep. 1996, p. 6 (in Czech), in 'Russia: Minister Udugov views situation in Chechnya', FBIS-SOV-96-178, 13 Sep. 1996. As another example of a possible workable pattern, the new Chechen President will reportedly not take the seat in the upper house of the Russian Parliament which is auto-

IV. Conflicts in abeyance

In four other conflict areas that have recently been the arena of armed clashes, the situation remained relatively stable in 1996 although political settlements were not reached. Russia continued to be the most important outside player in these regions.

Nagorno-Karabakh (Azerbaijan)

The dispute over the claim to independence by the enclave of Nagorno-Karabakh in Azerbaijan, populated by ethnic Armenians, is the longest-running conflict in the former Soviet Union; in 1996 it entered its ninth year. The cease-fire agreement reached in May 1994 has been observed by both conflicting parties, but the prospects for political settlement remain unclear. The positions of the parties are far apart on such principal issues as: (*a*) the political status of Nagorno-Karabakh and its relationship to Azerbaijan; (*b*) the return of refugees who, according to Azerbaijani estimates, number up to 1 million; (*c*) the liberation of the 20 per cent of Azerbaijan's territory occupied by Karabakh forces outside the enclave, such as the Lachin corridor linking the rebellious region with Armenia; and (*d*) guarantees to Karabakh that there would be no resumption of hostilities.

Azerbaijan maintains that the conflict is a direct consequence of aggression by Armenia. Azerbaijan's essential demands are recognition by Armenia of Azerbaijan's territorial integrity, a complete and unconditional withdrawal of Armenian combatants from its territory and the return of refugees. If these conditions are met, Azerbaijan would be prepared to grant a significant degree of autonomy to Nagorno-Karabakh.

The Karabakh leadership continues to consolidate the enclave's de facto independence and strengthen its armed forces. Five years after the unilateral declaration of independence from Azerbaijan, the Karabakh presidential election was held on 24 November 1996.[40]

---

matically granted to him, as head of a constituent autonomous republic, by the Russian Constitution. However, Chechnya may send a commissioner, who will have the right to vote, to the Russian Parliament for the next 5 years. Rutland, P., 'Chechen government plans', *OMRI Daily Digest*, no. 3, part I (6 Jan. 1997).

[40] The election produced a 76% turnout and a convincing victory (86%) for incumbent President Robert Kocharyan. Danielyan, E., 'Kocharyan reelected president of Nagorno-Karabakh', *OMRI Daily Digest*, no. 228 (25 Nov. 1996); and Sytaya, Ye., 'Izbran prezident NKR' [The president of NKR is elected], *Nezavisimaya Gazeta*, 26 Nov. 1996, p. 3. Azerbaijan portrayed the elections as 'an attempt to legalize a puppet regime'. They were also condemned by Russia and the USA as undermining the prospects for a political settlement. Armenia was the only country that characterized the elections as legal, arguing that, given the invitation by the OSCE Council of Ministers on 24 Mar. 1992 to Karabakh's elected representatives to participate in a Minsk peace conference, it was preferable for the population of the enclave to choose its representatives in a fair election. Moreover, with no control by the Azerbaijani Administration over Karabakh, it is believed in Armenia that some authority should govern the area and ensure that the cease-fire holds until a settlement is achieved.

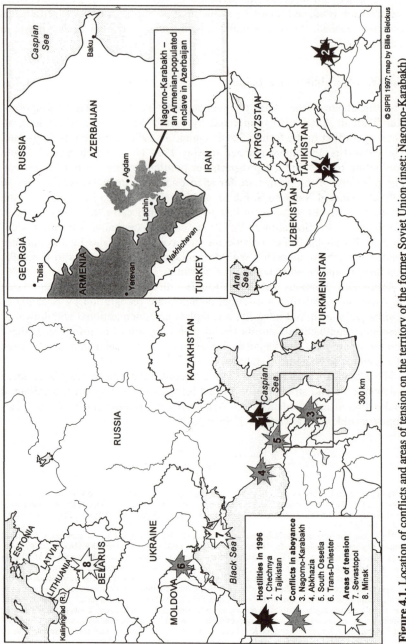

Figure 4.1. Location of conflicts and areas of tension on the territory of the former Soviet Union (inset: Nagorno-Karabakh)

Armenia denies military involvement in the conflict, is ambivalent towards the territorial integrity of Azerbaijan,[41] and threatens to recognize Karabakh's statehood if progress towards a political settlement is not made.

Searching for more Russian involvement in a political settlement, Russian Foreign Minister Yevgeniy Primakov played an important role in mediating between President Heidar Aliev of Azerbaijan, President Levon Ter-Petrosyan of Armenia and the leadership of Nagorno-Karabakh on the exchange of POWs and hostages.[42] This was one of the few (if not the only) areas where substantial progress was achieved in 1996.

Talks mediated by the OSCE-sponsored Minsk Group continued in 1996, without producing a breakthrough. The issue of Nagorno-Karabakh produced a mini-crisis at the OSCE summit meeting in Lisbon in December 1996 when Azerbaijan threatened to veto the final document unless it contained an unambiguous statement of recognition of the territorial integrity principle, while Armenia resolutely objected to this as a guiding principle for settling the Nagorno-Karabakh conflict.[43]

Abkhazia (Georgia)

Three years after the fall to the rebels of the Abkhazian capital, Sukhumi, negotiations between Georgia and the separatist government of Abkhazia are deadlocked. Abkhazian President Vladislav Ardzinba continues to insist that Abkhazia can accept nothing short of equal status with Georgia within a federation or confederation.[44] Georgian President Eduard Shevardnadze refuses to entertain any serious discussion of Abkhazia's future status as long as the Abkhazian leadership does not unequivocally recognize Georgia's territorial integrity. If this condition is complied with, Georgia would be prepared to grant the broadest autonomy to Abkhazia envisaged in international practice.

The refugee problem has become the central obstacle to a settlement. Albeit a titular nationality, the Abkhaz constituted a minority of 17 per cent in this autonomous republic of Georgia before the conflict flared up in the summer of 1992. Hostilities and ethnic cleansing precipitated an exodus of Georgian refugees who were driven from their homes in Abkhazia, thus tilting the inter-ethnic balance in favour of the Abkhaz. Rejecting Georgia's claim that the

---

[41] Armenia has proposed that both sides recognize Azerbaijan's right to maintain its territorial integrity to the same degree as Nagorno-Karabakh has the right to establish its independence. In practice, this would mean that the enclave would legally remain a part of Azerbaijan, while its autonomy would be equivalent to independence.

[42] Over 100 POWs were released and repatriated in May 1996. While this affected all the POWs registered by the International Committee of the Red Cross, Azerbaijan claims that 850 POWs are still being held in Armenia. *Agence France-Presse International News*, 8 May 1996, cited in *International Peacekeeping News*, vol. 2, no. 2 (May–June 1996), p. 20.

[43] As the result of a last-minute compromise, the contentious language was removed from the final communiqué of the OSCE summit meeting and it was adopted as a separate document.

[44] Abkhaz Foreign Minister Konstantin Ozgan stated that Abkhazia would never return to Georgia's jurisdiction and that its independence would be recognized by the world community in 2 or 3 years. *Georgia Profile*, vol. 1, no. 7–8 (1996), p. 7.

majority of Abkhazia's pre-war population live outside Abkhazia,[45] the separatist government organized elections to the parliament on 23 November 1996. Georgia claimed that the elections were illegal and conducted an alternative plebiscite among refugees.[46]

Since 1994 Shevardnadze's strategy has been aimed at bringing Abkhazia back into Georgia's fold by politically and militarily aligning the country with Russia.[47] Georgia insists that Russian peacekeepers,[48] deployed in August 1993 as an allegedly CIS peacekeeping operation (only Russia offered troops),[49] should be entrusted with police powers for organizing the safe return of the refugees. However, their mandate, extended until 31 January 1997, instructs them to prevent acts of terrorism and sabotage in the zones of their responsibility and, if requested, to protect UN personnel. Abkhaz consent is required for any accord that gives additional authority to the peacekeepers. Abkhazia rejects demands that the peacekeepers, now controlling half of the Gali district (once home to about 100 000 Georgians), be authorized to oversee the whole district. Because of Russia's unwillingness to give a more robust mission to its peacekeepers,[50] which is also opposed by the Abkhaz Government, Georgia has repeatedly threatened to refuse an extension of their mandate. Indeed, the continuing status of peacekeepers as a disengagement force is increasingly perceived by Georgia as perpetuating Abkhazia's de facto independence. Another source of irritation for Georgia is the fact that the Russian State Duma, dominated by enemies of Shevardnadze,[51] has so far refused to consider ratification of the 1994 Georgian–Russian treaty.[52]

To retain leverage over its powerful neighbour, the Georgian leadership attempted to diversify its sources of external support and play on Russia's sensitivities towards foreign influence in the Transcaucasus. The Shevardnadze Government has attempted to show that there are alternatives to Russian mediation by engaging other states (such as Turkey, Russia's perennial rival in the region) and international organizations (such as the UN) in the peace pro-

[45] Abkhaz sources claim that as many as 320 000, the majority of the 525 000-strong population registered in the 1989 census, now live in Abkhazia. According to Georgian sources, there are currently only 180 000 inhabitants, constituting one-third of the pre-war population of 540 000. Globachev, M., 'Prazdnik blokadnogo optimizma [Festive blockade optimism], *Nezavisimaya Gazeta*, 27 Nov. 1996, p. 3; Strugovets, V., 'Parad suverenitetov-2' [Parade of sovereignties 2], *Krasnaya Zvezda*, 21 Nov. 1996, p. 3; and Grankina, V., 'Bezhentsy gotoviatsa k referendumu' [Refugees are preparing themselves for referendum], *Nezavisimaya Gazeta*, 21 Nov. 1996, p. 3.

[46] The participation of 230 000 refugees was reported by the Georgian side. 'Abkhazia vote goes ahead as Tbilisi, Moscow protest', *New Europe*, 1–7 Dec. 1996, p. 34.

[47] It was hoped that Russia would bring its influence to bear on Georgia's unity once Georgia offered to allow Russia to retain 4 military bases in Georgia for 25 years. The very possibility of Russia's military presence there is unequivocally linked by Georgia to Russia's role in the conflict in Abkhazia.

[48] A total of 1500 Russian troops are stationed in the 24-km security zone and the 20-km restricted-weapons zone on both banks of the Inguri River separating Georgia and Abkhazia. Blotskiy, O., 'Mirotvortsy sozdayut usloviya dlya normalizatsii dostanovki' [Peacekeepers create conditions for normalization], *Nezavisimaya Gazeta*, 29 Oct. 1996, p. 3.

[49] See also appendix 2A in this volume.

[50] See chapter 2 and appendix 2A for details of the UN Observer Mission in Georgia (UNOMIG).

[51] Many Russian communist-, nationalist- and 'patriotic'-oriented politicians blame the decline and collapse of the USSR on Shevardnadze, who was Foreign Minister under President Mikail Gorbachev.

[52] The Treaty between Georgia and the Russian Federation on Friendship, Neighbourly Relations, and Cooperation was signed on 3 Feb. 1994. *Diplomaticheskiy Vestnik*, no. 5–6 (Mar. 1994), p. 33.

cess. Furthermore, the Georgian Parliament has delayed ratification of the 1994 Russian–Georgian agreement on protection of the Georgian–Turkish border, which is strategically important for Russia.[53] At the same time, Georgia has signalled to both the separatists and Russia that, with its patience running out, it might consider resort to military means.

South Ossetia (Georgia)

In contrast to the conflict in Abkhazia, some progress was made in 1996 towards resolution of the stand-off in the South Ossetian region of Georgia. With a truce holding for four years and many intransigent leaders replaced by more moderate politicians, the parties were able to move forward and agree in a memorandum of 16 May 1996 on renouncing the use or threat of force and political and economic pressure against each other, a gradual demilitarization of the conflict zone, the need to address the refugee problem and the non-persecution of combatants who have not committed war crimes.[54]

The reaction of Georgia's leadership to the South Ossetian Parliament's decision to introduce the presidency and hold a presidential election on 10 November 1996 was more reserved than its response to the Abkhazian election.[55] The election of Ludvig Chibirov as President of South Ossetia, with 65 per cent of the vote, weakened the influence of hard-liners advocating South Ossetia's secession from Georgia and its unification with North Ossetia within the Russian Federation.

A number of more fundamental issues, however, are still unresolved. They include such problems as the status of South Ossetia within Georgia, the division of power between the Georgian and South Ossetian governments, repatriation of Georgian refugees, and the relationship between the two states of South and North Ossetia.[56]

The Trans-Dniester region (Moldova)

The situation in the Trans-Dniester region of Moldova was basically 'frozen' in 1996. It is still uncertain whether a political compromise can be reached because the aim of the separatists is to preserve the de facto independence of Trans-Dniester and Moldova is resolutely opposed to recognizing the region as enjoying statehood. The separatist authorities prohibited balloting on the territory of the Trans-Dniester region in Moldova's presidential elections of

---

[53] The Agreement on the Status and Conditions of Presence of the Russian Border Troops in Georgia. *Diplomaticheskiy Vestnik*, no. 5–6 (Mar. 1994), p. 33. The external border of Georgia is currently guarded on land and at sea by 8000 Russian border troops. Blotskiy, O., 'Rossiyskie pogranichniki, vozmozhno, pokinut Gruziyu' [Russian border controllers may leave Georgia], *Nezavisimaya Gazeta*, 1 Nov. 1996, p. 3.

[54] For the text of the memorandum see *Diplomaticheskiy Vestnik*, no. 6 (June 1996), pp. 52–53.

[55] However, Georgia registered its condemnation of the election, echoed by Russian officials, as undermining the bilateral commitment not to undertake unilateral steps that would affect the peace process.

[56] A non-CIS peacekeeping force is deployed in South Ossetia. See appendix 2A in this volume.

17 November and 1 December. In another move that undermined the prospects for a political settlement, presidential elections were held in the separatist region on 22 December. After Igor Smirnov was re-elected, with 72 per cent of the votes (and a 57 per cent turnout), he reiterated that he intends to continue working to strengthen Trans-Dniestrian independence from Moldova.

Russia favours a special status for Trans-Dniester within Moldova but not full independence. Although Smirnov has sought Russia's support for Trans-Dniestrian statehood, the Russian Government clearly prefers to develop its relations with Moldova.[57] The victory of Petru Lucinschi in the Moldovan presidential elections may open the way for further *rapprochement* with Russia. However, some political forces in Russia seem to consider the Trans-Dniester issue as a litmus test for a policy aimed at consolidating Russia's stance in the CIS area—or at least as a lever to be used against Moldova.[58]

Against this background, the issue of the withdrawal of Russian troops from Trans-Dniester may again trigger political tension.[59] The agreement between Moldova and Russia, signed in 1994 and envisaging a three-year withdrawal period, has still not been ratified.[60]

V. Tajikistan

For most of the year, the civil war in Tajikistan between the government and opposition forces was a low- to mid-intensity conflict, with neither side able to achieve a decisive victory. Occasional heavy fighting took place involving the use of artillery and tanks by both sides. The Tajik Government was unable to control more than one-third of the country's territory and attacks by the opposition were reported as close as 13 km from the capital, Dushanbe. Anti-government fighters consolidated their positions in the mountainous Pamir area (Gorno-Badakhshan), which might become an important bridgehead for attacks against Dushanbe, allowing the establishment of an alternative government or precipitating the region's separation from Tajikistan.

Russia, concerned with the prospect of destabilization in and around Tajikistan and reluctant to have its influence throughout Central Asia weakened, has continued to be involved. In addition to providing political and economic support to the Tajik Government, Russia notably also pressured it to find a

---

[57] On 8 Oct., 11 cooperation accords were signed by the prime ministers of the 2 countries. It is noteworthy that Smirnov—although president of the self-proclaimed Trans-Dniester Republic—took part in the talks as a member of the Moldovan delegation.

[58] On 14 Nov. the Russian State Duma adopted Resolution 284-29, declaring the Trans-Dniester region a 'zone of special strategic interest for Russia'.

[59] Lucinschi, the newly elected President of Moldova, immediately reiterated Moldova's demand for early withdrawal of the remaining Russian troops. The separatist leadership wants to keep Russian troops in the region until there are 'firm guarantees' that the Trans-Dniestrian problem will not be solved by force.

[60] For the text of the agreement on withdrawal see *Diplomaticheskiy Vestnik*, no. 21–22 (Nov. 1994), pp. 47–51. The above-mentioned resolution of the Russian State Duma contained an appeal to consider establishing a permanent Russian military base in the region—an option that Moldova rejects and Ukraine openly opposes.

negotiated settlement.[61] Russian troops deployed in the country within the formal framework of a CIS peacekeeping force (accompanied by a UN observer force, the UN Mission of Observers in Tajikistan, UNMOT) were supposedly neutral and were to refrain from interfering in the civil war; failure to do so might result in heavy Russian casualties.[62]

Another factor which contributed to making a political settlement in Tajikistan urgent was continuing instability in neighbouring Afghanistan, where the opposition has its bases. The success of the Islamic Taleban movement in Afghanistan, which took control of Kabul on 26 September 1996 and proclaimed an Islamic state, has dramatically increased Russia's fear of a fundamentalist threat from the south and of thousands of refugees streaming across the Tajik frontier. The initial Russian reaction was one of alarm and reportedly included consideration of possible responses, ranging from establishing contacts with the Taleban in order to stabilize the frontier by mutual guarantees to providing their opponents with military support. Russia initiated an extraordinary summit meeting with the other Central Asian CIS states in Almaty, Kazakhstan, on 4 October 1996 to discuss a more active role for them in preventing a spillover of the conflict.[63]

By the end of the year a breakthrough was achieved in the process of political settlement. On 23 December 1996 Tajik President Imomali Rakhmonov and United Tajik Opposition leader Said Abdullo Nuri, with mediation by representatives of Russia and UN Secretary-General Boutros Boutros-Ghali, signed an agreement in Moscow which went much further than the cessation of hostilities. In addition to confirming the previous decision on a cease-fire, it provided for a general amnesty, an exchange of all prisoners and a promise by both sides to create the necessary conditions for the return of Tajik refugees. Most importantly, it was agreed to establish for a 'transitional' 12- to 18-month period a two-party National Reconciliation Council headed by a representative of the opposition and provided with significant responsibilities. This amounted to providing the opposition with access to power; its representatives may also be appointed to executive posts.

If the agreement is fulfilled (despite considerable opposition from both sides to reconciliation and inevitable disagreement about power-sharing) this may be a significant step towards a political settlement. However, establishing a viable political regime still requires the creation of a stable balance between

[61] In 1996 it was manifested that the policy of supporting one side in the civil war was becoming increasingly unpopular in Russia—especially since this side neither appeared to be victorious nor enjoyed sufficient political support even among non-Islamist groups in the country. President Rakhmonov's nepotism, cronyism and unwillingness to share power with representatives of areas other than his native Kulyab region are believed to be among the main reasons preventing the government from building a solid domestic power base.

[62] See also chapter 2 and appendix 2A in this volume. The leaders of the opposition threatened to retaliate against Russian servicemen 'in case of Russian aircraft participation in the operations of government forces'. Sporadic attacks against the Russian military were reported during the year which were interpreted by Russia as attempts to provoke retaliation in order to blame Russia for interference.

[63] The option of direct interference in Afghan affairs was reportedly rejected, but the CIS Defence Ministers Council, meeting in Dushanbe on 29 Oct., adopted an unspecified 'comprehensive plan' for dealing with the situation on the Tajik–Afghan border.

the numerous local power clans in the country. More than anywhere else on the former Soviet territory, the four-year war has destroyed the social fabric, transforming it into a patchwork of entrenched and increasingly independent factions, with warlords involved in illegal trading in opium, weapons and metals and uninterested in normalization.

VI. Russia's western vicinity

In 1996 security-related developments in the European part of the former USSR continued to be predominantly (but not exclusively) a function of Russia's relations with other post-Soviet states in this area. Furthermore, Russia increasingly assesses these relations in the context of its overall policy in Europe—particularly against the background of an enlargement of NATO.

Promoting the CIS

The appointment in January 1996 of Yevgeniy Primakov as Russian Foreign Minister brought a stronger emphasis on 'the near abroad' in Russia's policy, with the proclaimed aim of fostering integrative tendencies within the CIS. Developments in 1996 also manifested a tendency to create a 'core area' within this structure. The 'Treaty of Four' was signed on 29 March 1996 by Russia, Belarus, Kazakhstan and Kyrgyzstan,[64] and four days later another 'big treaty' was signed by Russia and Belarus.[65]

These two 'breakthroughs' overshadowed the lack of significant progress by the CIS, which continues basically as a framework for multilateral interaction rather than as a mechanism for integration. The exchange of information and mutual accommodation on practical matters, important as they are, are still far from becoming common CIS policy. The divergent interests of the members predominate over their declared 'integration' goals. Many adopted documents are in fact dead letters; whenever cooperation is assessed as desirable, bilateral channels are clearly preferred to multilateral ones.

In addition, the reaction of Russia's partners to its proclaimed 'CIS first' policy has not been entirely enthusiastic. First, they proceed from the necessity of maintaining and further developing economic links with Russia, which are often vital for their future development, but this factor is not as important as it was several years ago.[66] Second, Russian pro-CIS rhetoric and 'more balanced' diplomacy notwithstanding, it is not yet clear to what extent Russia would be ready to seriously de-prioritize its relations with the West in favour of its post-Soviet neighbours. Third, suspicions and apprehensions continue

[64] For the text of the Treaty on Deepening Integration in Economic and Humanitarian Spheres see *Diplomaticheskiy Vestnik*, no. 4 (1996), pp. 56–60.

[65] For the text of the Agreement on the Formation of a Community see *Diplomaticheskiy Vestnik*, no. 5 (1996), pp. 39–42.

[66] On the one hand, Russia has proved both reluctant to take upon itself the economic burdens of the CIS partners and not particularly impressive in its own performance; on the other hand, the other CIS states may have alternative (and sometimes better) options in developing ties with other international actors.

(although they are not always openly expressed) that the CIS is mainly needed by Russia in order to be able to pressure the other participants, strengthen its own positions within this area and consolidate it into a kind of 'velvet empire'.

It is significant that Russia's CIS partners were reluctant to accept some of the decisions that Russia might have considered natural and self-evident.[67] Nor have they attempted to transform the CIS into a military alliance as a response to NATO enlargement eastward. Russia, on the other hand, appears to be irritated over bilateral and subregional cooperation between the CIS states when it takes place without Russian participation. In fact, although continuing its pro-CIS rhetoric, Russia no longer seems to consider the goal of 'reintegration' as realistic. It is noteworthy that the only new post in the government given to the opposition after the 1995 elections to the parliament was the ministry with responsibility for CIS affairs—which may be interpreted as an indication that no significant breakthrough is expected in this area.

Ukraine and Belarus

Russian–Ukrainian relations were less complicated by crisis in 1996 than in the preceding years. The official Russian line highlighted the importance of cooperative relations with Ukraine and avoiding confrontation—by promoting economic relations and agreeing to restructure Ukraine's debt and by refraining from interference in some sensitive areas, such as the status of Crimea. The Ukrainian leadership also downplayed divisive issues.

However, intensive behind-the-scenes struggle continued. The long-proclaimed goal of signing a Russian–Ukrainian friendship and cooperation treaty was not reached in 1996 because settlement of the Black Sea Fleet issue was blocked by differences in approach to the basing rights of both sides.[68] By the end of 1996 criticism of the very idea of sharing the fleet again became vociferous, dramatically highlighting the inability of the fleet to play any strategic role in the Black Sea area.[69] The Russian Parliament demanded that the division of the fleet be halted and called on the government to use 'the principle of a single Black Sea Fleet as the position of the Russian side'. Furthermore, Ukraine regards the continuing claims in some Russian political circles (although not endorsed by the Russian Government) that Sevastopol is a city under Russian jurisdiction as a dangerous manifestation of Russian neo-imperial tendencies. Ukraine emphasizes that any Russian military presence there could be tolerated only temporarily.[70]

---

[67] In Oct. Moscow failed to impose the appointment of General Kolesnikov as Chief of the CIS Military Cooperation Staff.

[68] Russia insisted on having Sevastopol at the exclusive disposal of its fleet, with basing facilities to be rented on a long-term lease, whereas Ukraine was reluctant to accept either demand.

[69] After the dissolution of the USSR, the number of surface ships in the Black Sea Fleet was reduced by 50%, submarines by 75% and aircraft armed with missiles by 100%. Medvedko, L., 'Rossiya i Ukraina dolzhny soglasovat' pozitsii' [Russia and Ukraine must coordinate positions], Nezavisimaya Gazeta, 28 Nov. 1996, p. 3.

[70] The concern over Sevastopol was strongly promoted by the spectacular claims of Moscow Mayor Yuri Luzhkov (a potential candidate for the presidency in 2000), backed by the Federation Council.

In a positive development, the transfer to Russia of the remaining former Soviet strategic nuclear warheads based on Ukrainian territory was completed by 1 June 1996. This finally ended Russia's concerns regarding the possibility of Ukraine's 'going nuclear'. None the less, the general uncertainties about longer-term Russian–Ukrainian relations persisted. Ukraine is irritated by what it resents as the Russian élites' (and public opinion's) reluctance to accept the irreversibility of Ukraine's independence. Russia is increasingly concerned with the expansion of contacts between Ukraine and the West. Growing Western attention to Ukraine is regarded as a challenge to Russia's interests and implementation of the strategy of 'geopolitical pluralism' within the post-Soviet space. Ukraine is seen as competing with Russia for a privileged relationship with the West; indeed, Ukraine preceded Russia in signing a partnership agreement with the European Union, accepting the NATO Partnership for Peace (PFP) framework and joining the Council of Europe.

In the context of Russia's strong opposition to NATO enlargement, any actual or perceived ambiguity in Ukraine's attitude towards the Atlantic Alliance[71] is of particular concern to Russia, while Ukraine fears that it may be more strongly pressured by Russia as a 'responsive measure'. In a broader sense, Ukraine may become the main cause of discord in (and eventually the main victim of) a renewed bipolarization of Europe.

While Ukraine continues to be a serious concern for Russia, the latter's attention is increasingly focused on Belarus. Geopolitically oriented Russian politicians, analysts and government executives seem to consider Belarus as a safe buffer zone against the eastward expansion of NATO and as the only reliable supporter of Russia's opposition to this process. Furthermore, a number of obvious strategic stakes lie behind Russia's interest in Belarus—most importantly, those related to the westward lines of communication (and pipelines) and to the air-defence system. Not surprisingly, at the final stage of the 1996 political crisis in Belarus, a key role was played by the active 'mediation' efforts of Russia, which was apparently more interested in preserving the pro-Russian orientation of Belarussian President Lukashenko than in his democratic credentials.

Russia's relationship with Belarus has become one of the most controversial subjects of political debate in Russia. On the one hand, Belarus' integration with (or even incorporation into) Russia is regarded as responding to basic interests in preserving and consolidating the historical ties between the two Slavic peoples; the treaty on establishing a community (commonwealth) of two states of 2 April 1996 is widely claimed to represent the highest level of

---

[71] The option of joining NATO has become a matter of public debate in Ukraine, with some politicians (including influential parliamentarians) arguing that 'Ukraine should strive for NATO membership in order not to become a buffer zone between Russia and the alliance's member countries'. Rudyuk, O., 'Bridges are not only burnt but also captured', *Holos Ukrayiny* (Kiev), 7 Dec. 1996, p. 3 (in Ukrainian), in 'Ukraine: lawmakers discuss European security, urge joining NATO', FBIS-SOV-96-240, 13 Dec. 1996.

integration within the CIS.[72] On the other hand, political élites in Russia seem basically to distrust Lukashenko, who effectively used the popular idea of *rapprochement* with Russia to outmanoeuvre his domestic opponents as well as Russia. Supporting the Belarussian leader may also have negative international implications for Russia because of Lukashenko's record on human rights and the democratic process as well as his controversial anti-Western stance[73] (although it would be easier to present Russia as a loyal partner and democratically oriented state by comparison with Belarus). The economic burden of 'reintegration' is also considered by many in Russia as prohibitively high, especially in view of Lukashenko's extremely poor performance in developing market reforms. Last but not least, the primitive and assertive populism of Lukashenko makes him an unpredictable partner even for Russia.

The Baltic states

Three issues feature prominently in Russia's relations with Estonia, Latvia and Lithuania: the determination of borders, the plight of the Russian-speaking minorities and the shift of the Baltic states away from Russia's sphere of influence towards the West.

Lithuania and Russia have negotiated for three years and reached agreement on 90 per cent of the 300-km border; some difficulties persist[74] although there seem to be good prospects for a cooperative approach to prevail. With respect to Latvia, Russia threatens to demarcate the border unilaterally if Riga refuses to drop demands that are interpreted by Russia as territorial claims.[75] As regards the frontier problem with Estonia, the two countries were reported to have struck a bargain in which Estonia would drop its demand to include a reference to the 1920 Tartu Peace Treaty in a bilateral border agreement, thus accepting, with minor exceptions, the current border. Russia would reciprocate

[72] The treaty aims at 'uniting their [Russian and Belarussian] material and intellectual potentials' and envisages a joint economic space, foreign policy coordination, interaction in ensuring security, border protection, a fight against crime, and a unification of currency and budget systems (to create conditions for a joint currency). See note 65. However, the practical results of this course are assessed as very modest.

[73] Among the many eccentric statements of Lukashenko was his threat to use nuclear missiles to prevent the eastward expansion of NATO. Freeland, C., 'Lukashenko takes his case to Russia', *Financial Times*, 14 Nov. 1996, p. 4. However, Lukashenko completed the removal of the remaining nuclear warheads to Russia on 27 Nov. 1996, supposedly in order to ease the international community's concerns and signal his cooperativeness towards Moscow.

[74] The remaining problems concern the delimitation of 3 border segments—along Lake Vistytis, at the mouth of the Nemunas River and at the Lagoon of Kursiu Marios. The negotiations on determining the exclusive economic zones and continental shelf came to a halt because of disagreements on the D-6 oil field located in neutral territory in the Baltic Sea.

[75] Three communes of Latvia's Abrene district were incorporated into the Pytalovskiy district of the RSFSR Pskov region on 23 Aug. 1944. Russia claims that the 1920 Tartu Peace Treaty, which recognized Latvia's sovereignty over the contested territory, was invalidated when Latvia was incorporated into the USSR in 1940. Latvia argues that the illegal Soviet occupation did not modify the treaty's effect. However, some prominent politicians in Latvia contend that it is more interested than Russia in concluding a border agreement, since better border control could reduce smuggling and illegal movement of refugees. It is also pointed out that there are almost no Latvian inhabitants in the contested district. Latvian President Guntis Ulmanis recently hinted that Latvia might agree that Abrene is under temporary Russian authority.

by withdrawing its demands for Estonian compliance with the 1990 agreement obliging Tallinn to grant citizenship to all residents of the country.[76] The more flexible approach of the Baltic states towards the border issue was motivated, among other things, by their desire to remove potential obstacles to prospective NATO membership.

The plight of the ethnic Slavs in Estonia and Latvia has been at the centre of Russia's policy towards these states ever since their independence. In 1996 Russia continued to accuse Latvia and even more so Estonia[77] of discrimination against their Russian minorities. However, in November 1996 the UN General Assembly decided to stop discussing Estonian and Latvian human rights issues, having assessed that they are adequately respected. At the same time OSCE High Commissioner on National Minorities (HCNM) Max van der Stoel expressed his concern that 28 per cent of the permanent residents of Latvia do not have citizenship.[78] By and large, the issue seemed less conflict-prone in 1996, although it has not been removed from the agenda.

In 1996 the Baltic states repeatedly expressed concern over not being included in the first round of NATO enlargement, fearing they might be trapped in a 'grey zone' between Russia and the West. Against this background, seeking security guarantees from Western countries has become a prominent theme of Baltic policy, which in turn causes serious concern on the part of Russia. The possible involvement of the Baltic states in Western security structures may become a serious problem, fraught with considerable consequences for both the northern Europe/Baltic Sea area and relations between Russia and the West generally. The prospects for admission of these countries to NATO, although not immediate, will be a constant disturbing factor for Russian politics, provoking suspicion and sporadic nervousness in Moscow.

VII. Conclusions

On the territory of the former USSR, 1996 opened with continuing open hostilities in two conflict zones: Chechnya and Tajikistan. By the end of the year combat operations were over in the first case, and the political dialogue between the conflicting sides in the second had received a significant boost.

Developments in the post-Soviet areas where conflict is triggered by separatist demands—Chechnya, the Trans-Dniester region, Abkhazia, Nagorno-Karabakh and South Ossetia—have revealed a number of common features. First, it has proved impossible to halt separatism by force. Second, separatist

---

[76] It should be noted, however, that the high level of mutual hostility in the legislatures in Tallinn and Moscow may obstruct ratification of any accord reached by the executive branches of the 2 countries.

[77] The Estonian Government failed to comply with a timetable set for issuing aliens' passports to non-citizens—which prompted Moscow to strongly criticize Estonia for putting a large number of Russians in the category of stateless persons.

[78] Latvian authorities countered that non-citizens had been passive in seeking Latvian citizenship; indeed, fewer than 1000 residents were naturalized in 1996, although 33 000 were eligible to apply. Similarly, while non-citizens in Estonia are eligible to vote in the municipal elections, only one-third of them registered to participate. Girnius, S., 'OSCE commissioner visits Latvia', *OMRI Daily Digest*, no. 196, part I (9 Oct. 1996); and *Krasnaya Zvezda*, 25 Oct. 1996, p. 3.

areas have achieved de facto independence from the 'centres'. Third, separatist leaderships have successfully legitimized their power through elections. Fourth, political dialogues were initiated or continued—with different patterns, varying intensity, often on the basis of mediation or involvement of third parties and/or international organizations, and in some cases in spite of the clear reluctance of the direct participants. Fifth, 'centres' may manifest considerable flexibility in accepting a high level of autonomy for breakaway regions but refuse to compromise on the principle of territorial integrity. Sixth, parties seem to prefer perpetuation of the status quo to reaching a comprehensive solution—because of the efforts required, the costs and the political repercussions. A relatively peaceful balance—with the 'centre' militarily defeated and unable to resume military activities and the separatists enjoying a sense of victory and not wishing to continue fighting—can be maintained for a relatively long time.[79]

Each conflict pattern has specific aspects. Moldova seems to have basically renounced pressure against the Trans-Dniester region, while Georgia has repeatedly threatened to use force against Abkhazia. Developments in South Ossetia are apparently moving towards a settlement, which is not the case in Nagorno-Karabakh. The issue of the return of refugees is of special relevance to the settlements in Abkhazia and Nagorno-Karabakh. Peacekeepers have played a stabilizing role in the Trans-Dniester region, South Ossetia and Abkhazia. In the case of Abkhazia, Georgia insists on providing them with peace-enforcement functions, whereas Azerbaijan objects to any peacekeeping mission in Nagorno-Karabakh having an exclusively or a predominantly Russian/CIS composition. The case of Chechnya will probably continue to be unique: this conflict has produced both the heaviest casualties and an unprecedented post-war cooperativeness between Russia and the leadership of the breakaway republic (in no other post-Soviet conflict would the 'centre' support elections as a tool for legitimizing separatist power).

The CIS area has become a special focus of Russia's attention, with any indication of outside influence causing concern in Russia. However, Russia has neither the resources nor the political will to reintegrate the post-Soviet space on the basis of the 'USSR minus the Baltics' formula. Moreover, it cannot count on the support of most of its CIS partners. While the CIS does not appear to be moving towards a military alliance, its very existence as a forum embracing 12 former republics of the USSR does provide a useful framework for multilateral interaction, also in security-related areas.

The 1996 record of Russia's post-Soviet neighbourhood has shown that Ukraine is persistent in pursuing an independent policy, with Azerbaijan gradually becoming more alienated in the Transcaucasus and Uzbekistan in Central Asia. Against this background, the activism of Russia in some directions is being promoted by broader strategic considerations, with Belarus—its domestic record notwithstanding—appreciated as the most 'pro-Russian' state,

---

[79] This thesis is developed by Russian Presidential Council member Emil Payin in *Rossiyskie Vesti*, 19 Sep. 1996.

Georgia viewed as potentially important (even more so as a submissive partner in the Transcaucasus) and Tajikistan regarded as requiring considerable efforts to achieve a peace settlement that will consolidate this forward-based outpost against the threat of Islamic fundamentalism and the illegal movement of drugs, weapons and migrants.

5. Europe: in search of cooperative security

ADAM DANIEL ROTFELD

I. Introduction

In 1996 three basic issues remained on the European security agenda: (*a*) the transformation and eastward enlargement of NATO and the European Union (EU); (*b*) the Atlantic partnership, notably the changing nature and role of the United States in the new security system taking shape in Europe, on the one hand, and the European pillar of NATO, on the other; and (*c*) agreement on the conceptual framework of the Organization for Security and Co-operation in Europe (OSCE) model for European security for the 21st century. Some headway was made on all these questions in 1996, but no definitive agreements were reached.

Since insecurity in Europe no longer stems from external threats, but rather from domestic developments in individual countries, the existing security structures, mechanisms and procedures are only partly adequate to the new circumstances. Unambiguous identification of potential military threats is essential for the normal and effective operation of a military alliance and the proper definition of its mandate.[1] In the post-cold war environment these threats are unpredictable. The debate and the decisions made in 1996 reflect an attempt to accommodate NATO and other structures to the new security environment, one in which there is no definite 'enemy' or clear-cut 'threat'. Vaguely defined terms such as 'uncertainty', 'instability', 'risks' and 'challenges' have characterized the debate. The paradox of the post-cold war situation is that the old military instruments have relatively easily been transformed into new confidence- and security-building tools. This is for the simple reason that on the one hand they are available, well organized, deployable and manageable, and on the other hand military instruments have lost their excessive political significance.

This chapter reviews the main developments, concepts and arrangements aimed at shaping a new Atlantic community, enlarging NATO and the EU, and creating a common European security space.[2]

---

[1] Cornish, P., 'European security: the end of architecture and the new NATO', *International Affairs* (London), vol. 42, no. 4 (Oct. 1996), p. 751.

[2] The European security debate is reflected in the documents of the Berlin and Brussels Ministerial Meetings of the North Atlantic Council (NAC, 3 June, 10 Dec. and 17–18 Dec. 1996), the EU Council and Summit meetings (Turin, 29 Mar.; Florence, 21–22 June; and Dublin, 13–14 Dec. 1996) and the OSCE Summit (Lisbon, 2–3 Dec. 1996). These and some other 1996 documents contain the catalogue of ideas, concepts and decisions which are part of the multilateral process of searching for a European security system to face the post-cold war realities. Identifying a new agenda for conventional arms control and adapting the obligations of the 1990 Treaty on Conventional Armed Forces in Europe (the CFE Treaty) to the new politico-military environment are analysed in chapter 14 in this volume.

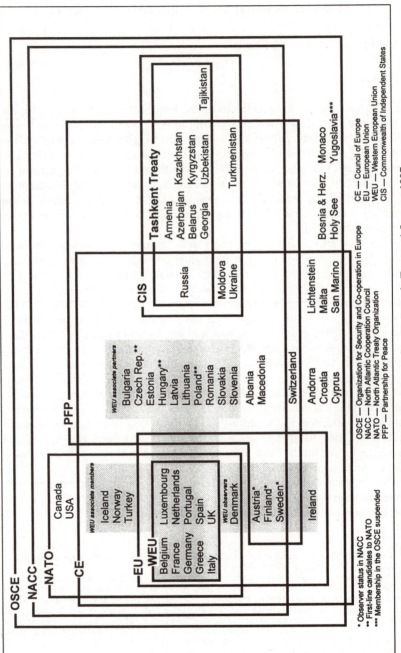

Figure 5.1. Membership of intergovernmental multilateral security structures in Europe, 1 January 1997

II. NATO: transformation and enlargement

There was a clear shift of emphasis in developments in 1996. Although the need for a new type of pan-European system is repeatedly acknowledged in numerous official documents, in practice priority has been given to the US concept of a new Atlantic community and to the enlargement of NATO and the EU.

A US vision of Euro-American relations and a new Atlantic community for the 21st century was presented in Stuttgart by US Secretary of State Warren Christopher on 6 September 1996. The Secretary of State outlined the concept of a new Atlantic community with NATO as a security pillar, a democratic Russia as a full partner and economies that are increasingly integrated and thriving.[3] President Bill Clinton defined his view in Detroit on 22 October, saying that NATO should remain open to all of Europe's emerging democracies that are ready to 'shoulder the responsibilities of membership'. The new NATO will be both an alliance of security and 'an alliance of values with Europe'. The US policy 'to build a new NATO for a new era' has three elements: (*a*) giving NATO new capabilities for new missions; (*b*) opening NATO to new members among Europe's emerging democracies; and (*c*) building a strong and cooperative relationship between NATO and Russia.[4]

In 1996 the debate and decisions made focused on the internal transformation of the Alliance, its enlargement to the east and a formula of accord between NATO and Russia. These issues are closely interrelated. Since the changes in the international security environment have been fundamental, they should be accompanied by a corresponding transformation of the military Alliance in order to retain its effectiveness, covering both external relations and internal mechanisms. Steps in this process have been the creation of the North Atlantic Cooperation Council (NACC) in 1991 as a new institution comprising both NATO and former Warsaw Treaty Organization (WTO) states (although it ran out of steam in organizing a new security regime in Europe); and the Partnership for Peace (PFP), the programme launched in 1994, addressed to all non-NATO states and built upon bilateral Individual Partnership Programmes with the Alliance aimed at peacekeeping and crisis

---

[3] His address was delivered on the 50th anniversary of the speech by US Secretary of State James Byrnes, 6 Sep. 1946 in Stuttgart, which determined the foundations of transatlantic relations. In the New Atlantic Community, NATO should remain the central pillar of the US security engagement in Europe. Christopher said: 'It will be a new NATO, adapted to meet emerging challenges, with the full participation of all current Allies and several new members from the East. NATO's Partnership for Peace and the OSCE will give us the tools to prevent conflict and assure freedom for all our citizens. In our vision for this New Atlantic Community, a democratic Russia will be a full partner. Europe and America will be taking joint actions against the global threats we can only overcome by working together'. US Secretary of State Warren Christopher's speech on a new Atlantic community for the 21st century, Stuttgart, 6 Sep. 1996.

[4] 'But for NATO to fulfil its real promise of peace and democracy in Europe it will not be enough simply to take on new missions as the need arises. NATO must also take in new members, including those from among its former adversaries. It must reach out to all the new democracies in Central Europe, the Baltics and the New Independent States of the former Soviet Union.' White House transcript, Clinton remarks to people of Detroit, 22 Oct. 1996. Version current on 23 Oct. 1996, URL <gopher://198.80.36.82:70/0R44030763-44063001-range/archives/1996/pdq.96>.

management. The PFP programme constructed a military-to-military bridge between NATO, Central Europe, Russia and other non-NATO members, fostering cooperation and building confidence among the participants.[5] At the NATO Ministerial Meeting on 10 December 1996, agreement was reached on the establishment of a political multilateral Atlantic Partnership Council.[6] Its main function will be to engage non-members in the planning and execution of NATO missions.

The ultimate enlargement of the Alliance and the institutionalization of relations between NATO and Russia are two longer-term components of the process aimed at establishing a non-exclusive security order in Europe. If Central European countries that bordered on the former Soviet Union enter the Alliance, the internal transformation and reformulation of its mandate will accelerate. Decisions on enlargement require agreement with Russia on a formula for cooperation with NATO, to neutralize fears that the process might lead to a new division in Europe and to the isolation of Russia.

The internal transformation of NATO

The internal transformation of NATO has been affected more by the operational requirements of NATO-led Implementation Force (IFOR) operations in Bosnia and Herzegovina than by the abstractions offered by various schemes and plans. As the new NATO Secretary General, Javier Solana, has stated: 'The scale of the operation and number of participating nations, the unprecedented level and range of coordination between the Implementation Force and the reconstruction effort—this is new ground we have broken in putting our concept of cooperative security to work'.[7]

NATO's task in Bosnia involves facilitating implementation of the military aspects of the 1995 Dayton Agreement and ensuring that hostilities are not renewed. Carrying out that mandate broke the ground for implementation of the agreements regarding the construction of a democratic state. NATO's role in Bosnia is the greatest, most difficult and most complex in its history, and one not usually played by military alliances.[8] IFOR replaced the struggling UN Protection Force (UNPROFOR) with a mandate to enforce peace in Bosnia, if necessary by military means.[9] However, the transformation of NATO was not determined by that mission.

---

[5] Mendelsohn, J., 'NATO expansion and the future of European security', *Focus* (Center for Post-Soviet Studies, Arms Control Association, Washington, DC), vol. 3, no. 3 (Mar. 1996).

[6] NATO Final Communiqué, Ministerial Meeting of the North Atlantic Council, Brussels, 9–10 Dec. 1996, Press Communiqué M-NAC-2(96)165. Version current on 10 Dec. 1996, URL <http://www.nato.int/docu/pr/1996/p96-165e.htm>.

[7] Solana, J., 'NATO in transition', *Perceptions*, vol. 1, no. 1 (Mar./May 1996), p. 9.

[8] The chief role in implementing the civilian, or political, economic, legal and humanitarian tasks was given to the EU and the OSCE. The High Representative, Carl Bildt, rightly noted: 'The military and civilian components of the Peace Agreement were two sides of the same coin'. Bildt, C., 'Implementing the civilian tasks of the Bosnian Peace Agreement', *NATO Review*, no. 5 (Sep. 1996), p. 3.

[9] Seidt, H. U., 'Lessons learnt from the crisis in the Balkans', *European Security*, vol. 5, no. 1 (spring 1996), p. 68.

The key question for the future of the Alliance is the relationship between the USA and its European allies. This is based on the following premises: on the one hand, NATO remains of prime importance to the United States as the foundation of its security engagement in Europe; on the other hand, the end of the hegemonic threat to Europe means that the US role will become 'more uncertain and less central'.[10] Although far from isolationist, the United States is becoming increasingly preoccupied with its own domestic priorities and with geostrategic and economic interests in Asia. Since the primary mission of NATO, that is, collective defence under Article 5 of the 1949 North Atlantic Treaty, has declined in importance and the Alliance has turned 'into a motor of European security cooperation and a catalyst for political change',[11] the European members of the Alliance have been pursuing a more cohesive and independent European defence pillar, although without undermining the US commitment.

In this respect, the decisions taken at the Ministerial Meeting of the North Atlantic Council (NAC) in Berlin (3 June 1996) offered practical meaning to the Western European Union (WEU) commitments as defined in Petersberg (19 June 1992). Regarding the concept of the Combined Joint Task Forces (CJTF) the Berlin decisions were highly symbolic: 'By permitting a more flexible and mobile deployment of forces including for new missions, this concept will facilitate the mounting of NATO contingency operations, the use of *separable but not separate* military capabilities in operations led by the WEU, and the participation of nations outside the Alliance in operations such as IFOR'.[12] In order to adapt the Alliance's capability to its new role and missions, the North Atlantic Council defined three fundamental objectives: to ensure NATO's military effectiveness in the changing security environment; to preserve the transatlantic link; and to develop the European Security and Defence Identity (ESDI) within the Alliance. The ESDI would be based on an 'elaboration of appropriate multinational European command arrangements within NATO, consistent with and taking full advantage of the CJTF concept, able to prepare, support, command and conduct the WEU-led operations'. This implies 'double-hatting' appropriate personnel within the NATO command structure to perform these dual functions. In fact, the concept of subsidiarity has been established as a cornerstone of European integration.[13]

The general formulations and detailed solutions agreed in Berlin ended a significant phase of internal NATO discussion on the future role of the USA

[10] Szabo, S. F., 'The United States and new European security challenges', ed. G. Herolf, *Europe: Creating Security through International Organization*, Conference Papers 17 (The Swedish War College and the Swedish Institute for International Affairs: Stockholm, 1996), p. 21.

[11] Speech by NATO Secretary General Javier Solana, 'The new NATO and the European security architecture', delivered before the Federation of Austrian Industries, Vienna, 16 Jan. 1997.

[12] NATO Final Communiqué, Ministerial Meeting of the North Atlantic Council, Berlin, 3 June 1996, Press Communiqué M-NAC-(96)63, para. 6 [emphasis added]. Version current in Mar. 1997, URL <http://www.nato.int/docu/pr/1996/p96-063e.htm>.

[13] Lenzi, G. S. and Martin, L. (eds), 'The European security space', Working papers by the European Strategy Group and the Institute for Security Studies of the Western European Union, Paris, 1996, p. 1. See also 'The European security and defence identity', *NATO Factsheet*, no. 3 (Mar. 1997), Version current in Mar. 1996, URL <http://www.nato.int/docu/facts/fs3e.htm>.

in the Alliance and on the military and financial commitment of the European allies. The evolution of the positions of France and the USA, anticipated at the end of 1995, was particularly notable:[14] (a) declarations by France that it would participate in NATO's Strategy Review Group (1991), established at the 1990 NATO summit meeting in London; (b) a call for the development of the WEU as a European security pillar (1992); and (c) various French proposals for a European army free from US control and subordinated to the EU (December 1995–March 1996). After the end of the cold war, competition for primacy in European security started to unfold between NATO, led by the United States, and the WEU, led by France. This resulted in the WEU obtaining formal competence regarding common defence. It still lacks adequate assets and resources to pursue this goal, however, while NATO enjoys both. France aims to bridge this gap, seeing NATO renewal as still incomplete.[15] The French concept of a 'new Alliance' calls for the transformation of NATO's command structure, an increased role for the 16 defence and foreign ministers in the Alliance's political and military decision-making process, and the definition of mechanisms allowing the Europeans to use NATO assets for joint military operations. This would ensure a more visible and active role for the WEU. The USA, however, is not willing to give up command of the 6th Fleet, despite the French demand that a European general should run NATO's Southern Command.[16]

Another significant event in 1996 was the Spanish Parliament's endorsement of Spain's decision to join the military structure of the Alliance.

Three aspects of NATO's adaptation

The conceptual thinking reflected in NATO documents in 1996 was aimed at the rapid constitution of a militarily coherent and effective European force within the Alliance.[17] However, many questions remain. Detailed planning will be needed to identify and free NATO capabilities and assets for use by the WEU, including NATO monitoring of their use. The implementation of the CJTF concept is seen as the first and essential element of the Alliance's adaptation.[18] Meeting in Ostend on 19 November 1996, the WEU Ministers

[14] French Foreign Minister Hervé de Charette commented on the outcome of the Berlin meeting: 'For the first time in the history of the Atlantic Alliance, Europe can express its defence identity'. 'Defence deal keeps all the parties happy', *The Independent*, 4 June 1996. See also Rotfeld, A. D., 'Europe: towards new security arrangements', *SIPRI Yearbook 1996: Armaments, Disarmament and International Security* (Oxford University Press: Oxford, 1996), p. 294; and Grant, R. P., 'France's new relationships with NATO', *Survival*, vol. 38, no. 1 (spring 1996), pp. 58–80.

[15] Millon, C., 'France and the renewal of the Atlantic Alliance', *NATO Review*, vol. 44, no. 3 (1996); and Boyer, Y., 'Security through international organizations: A French perspective', ed. Herolf (note 10), p. 49.

[16] Note 15. See also speech delivered by French Foreign Minister Hervé de Charette at the meeting of ambassadors in Paris, 28 Aug. 1996; and Erlanger, S., 'Albright and France call end to verbal war: secretary of state hopes to bridge gap over NATO', *International Herald Tribune*, 18 Feb. 1997, p. 1.

[17] In Berlin it was noted: 'the Alliance will support the development of the ESDI within NATO by conducting at the request of and in coordination with the WEU, military planning and exercises for illustrative WEU missions identified by WEU'. NATO Final Communiqué (note 12), para. 7.

[18] The CJTF is being developed primarily for military (i.e., peacekeeping) operations beyond those mandated for in Article 5 of the UN Charter, including operations in which nations outside the Alliance

agreed that it would be valuable for the WEU to become actively involved in NATO's defence planning and expressed their readiness to participate. Participation by all European NATO members in WEU-led operations (using NATO assets and capabilities) would be decisive for the development of the ESDI.

The second aspect of NATO's adaptation to the new security requirements is seen in new roles and missions such as Operation Joint Endeavour in Bosnia and Herzegovina. IFOR brought together NATO and 17 non-NATO countries from Europe, North Africa, the Middle East and Asia, including the 12 NACC and PFP partners. The IFOR activities in 1996 resulted in the successful separation of the forces of the former warring factions and in their demobilization and confinement to cantonments. In the broader perspective, they are an example of cooperative multinational interventionism in Europe.

The defence ministers' session of the NAC in Brussels on 17–18 December 1996 authorized the Supreme Allied Commander, Europe (SACEUR) to replace IFOR by the Stabilization Force (SFOR) under UN Security Council Resolution 1088.[19] The new force was activated on 20 December 1996. Its mandate is to deter renewed hostilities and to stabilize and consolidate the peace in Bosnia and Herzegovina 'in order to contribute to a secure environment in which civil implementation plans can be pursued'.[20] SFOR will also stand ready to provide emergency support to the UN Transitional Administration for Eastern Slavonia (UNTAES). The SFOR operation is to be conducted in phases over a period of 18 months.[21] The new force retains the same unity of command, robust rules of engagement, enforcement authority and status of forces as IFOR, but initially comprised about 30 000 troops, half the size of IFOR. It will cooperate closely with the High Representative, civil organizations and the OSCE, and it should also support the implementation of arms control agreements and the International Police Task Force (IPTF) in promoting a climate of law and order in Bosnia and Herzegovina. The IFOR/SFOR experience has stimulated thinking about NATO's new missions, fostered close cooperation with non-member states and other international institutions, and hastened the restructuring of NATO command to permit flexible and quick peacekeeping deployments into a crisis area.

The third important aspect of NATO's adaptation to the new security environment is an intensified effort to address the potential proliferation of nuclear, biological and chemical (NBC) weapons. The NAC defence ministers reaffirmed in Brussels (18 December 1996) that defence planning should guard against the risks posed by the possible use of NBC weapons and their means of delivery[22] and committed themselves to develop policies based

could participate. However, the employment of the CJTF for Article 5 operations is not excluded. NATO Communiqué, Meeting of the North Atlantic Council in Defence Ministers Session held in Brussels on 17 and 18 Dec. 1996, Press Communiqué M-NAC(DM)-3(96)172, Brussels, 18 Dec. 1996. Version current in Apr. 1997, URL <http://www.nato.int/docu/pr/1996/p96-172e.htm>.

[19] See chapter 2 in this volume.

[20] Note 18, para. 7.

[21] Note 18, para. 7.

[22] Carter, A., 'Countering the proliferation risks: adapting the Alliance to the new security environment', *NATO Review*, no. 5 (Sep. 1996), pp. 10–15.

on the Guiding Principles of the Senior Defence Group on Proliferation (DGP).

Enlarging NATO

In 1996 the central issue in the debates on the internal transformation and external adaptation of NATO was the accession of new members. NATO enlargement featured in statements by politicians at sessions of the main NATO bodies and in deliberations of experts on European security.[23] Arguments raised in 1996 added little to those heard for and against NATO enlargement in previous years,[24] but there were some new elements in the sphere of political decisions. The *Study on NATO Enlargement,* published in September 1995, announced an intensification of the dialogue with individual countries interested in joining the 1949 North Atlantic Treaty, and since the spring of 1996 interested states have started presenting their respective positions on matters raised in the study.[25] The US position was described by US Secretary of State Warren Christopher in Prague on 20 March 1996:

Today, our goal is to extend eastward the same structure of values and institutions that enabled Western Europe to overcome its own legacy of conflict and division. These institutions, NATO and the European Union among them, are not ends in themselves. . . . NATO enlargement is not a step we will take lightly. It involves the most solemn commitments that one nation can make to another. New allies will be full members of NATO, with all the benefits that entails. But they must be ready to assume the full risks, costs, and responsibilities as well.[26]

In the summer of 1996 both Houses of the US Congress passed, by overwhelming majorities, a NATO Enlargement Facilitation Act.[27] The act stated that US policy should be to ensure that all Central and East European (CEE) countries are fully aware of the costs and responsibilities of NATO membership and to work to define 'a constructive and cooperative political and security relationship' between an enlarged NATO and the Russian Federa-

[23] See more on this in Haglund, D. G. (ed.), *Will NATO Go East? The Debate over Enlarging the NATO Alliance* (Centre for International Relations: Kingston, Ontario, 1996).

[24] These arguments are analysed in detail in past *SIPRI Yearbooks.* Rotfeld, A. D., 'Europe: towards a new regional security regime', *SIPRI Yearbook 1994* (Oxford University Press: Oxford, 1994), pp. 205–37; Rotfeld, A. D., 'Europe: the multilateral security process', *SIPRI Yearbook 1995: Armaments, Disarmament and International Security* (Oxford University Press: Oxford, 1995), pp. 278–81; and Rotfeld (note 14), pp. 279–322.

[25] NATO, *Study on NATO Enlargement* (NATO: Brussels, Sep. 1995), was prepared by the special NATO Working Group. See Rotfeld (note 14).

[26] Christopher, W., 'A democratic and undivided Europe in our time', Address delivered at Cernin Palace, Prague (US Department of State, Office of the Spokesman, Washington, DC, 20 Mar. 1996).

[27] Among the 24 findings made by Congress there are those defining the criteria for NATO membership (i.a., 'Democratic civilian control of defense forces is an essential element in the process of preparation for those states interested in possible NATO membership', para. 27, p. H8117) and enumerating the specific states who have made 'the most progress toward achieving the stated criteria and should be eligible for additional assistance described in this bill' (Poland, Hungary and the Czech Republic, para. 23, p. H8117). The Bill—H.R. 3564, *Congressional Record—House,* 23 July 1996, pp. H8116-8118. Congress has enacted the NATO Participation Act in 1994—Title II of Public Law 103-447; 22 U.S.C. 1928 note; and in 1995 the NATO Participation Act Amendments (section 585 of Public Law 104-107).

tion.[28] In the view of Congress, the enlargement process should not stop with the admission of Poland, Hungary and the Czech Republic.[29]

In his October speech in Detroit President Clinton declared that NATO remains 'the bedrock of our common security' and that it can and should do for Central and Eastern Europe what it did in the past for the Western part of Europe: prevent a return to local rivalries, strengthen democracy against future threats, and create conditions for economic and social prosperity. He announced that a first group of future NATO members would be named in the spring or early summer of 1997 and that the next NATO summit meeting should invite them to begin accession talks. He anticipated that by 1999, at NATO's 50th anniversary and 10 years after the fall of the Berlin Wall, 'the first group of countries we invite to join should be full-fledged members of NATO'.[30] This would mean extending security guarantees to new allies and sharing the costs of enlarging NATO.

This position was reflected in the document adopted by the North Atlantic Council in Brussels. It recommended that a summit meeting be convened in Madrid on 8–9 July 1997 and that the agenda include 'inviting one or more of the countries which have expressed interest in joining the Alliance to begin accession negotiations'.[31] In response to Russian objections and reservations, assurances were given that NATO enlargement would not require a change in the current nuclear posture: 'NATO countries have no intention, no plan and no reason to deploy nuclear weapons on the territory of new members nor any need to change any aspect of NATO's nuclear posture or nuclear policy—and we do not foresee any future need to do so'.[32] To avoid criticism that the enlargement of NATO would introduce new lines of division into Europe, the ministers pledged that the Alliance would remain open to accession by additional members in accordance with Article 10 of the North Atlantic Treaty. However, this failed to convince US critics of enlargement.[33]

US critics of enlargement

Arguments against the decision to enlarge NATO focused on the costs involved, the fear that a US commitment to provide security guarantees to the CEE states (whose security can never be identical to that of the USA) may be detrimental to the vital security interests of the USA and other NATO states, and the risk of inciting paranoia, nationalism and militarism in Russia. Two underlying motives for these arguments are of particular significance: first, a

---

[28] The Bill (note 27), section 3, para. 3 and 4, p. H8117.

[29] The Bill (note 27), section 6, para. (b), p. 8117.

[30] Clinton remarks (note 4).

[31] NATO (note 6).

[32] NATO (note 6).

[33] This is illustrated in articles by prominent commentators in the *International Herald Tribune*, e.g., Pfaff, W., 'Eastward expansion of NATO looks like a dangerous idea', 15 May 1996, p. 16; 'A bigger NATO would create the problems it seeks to prevent', 19 Dec. 1996; Friedman, T. L., 'Eastward expansion of NATO doesn't look like a good idea', 28 Nov. 1996, p. 8; and Cohen, R., 'A bad night in New York for NATO enlargement', 13 Dec. 1996, p. 9.

preference for Russian interests *vis-à-vis* those of the CEE states;[34] and, second, a fear of a fundamental change which might dilute NATO and ultimately destabilize Central and Eastern Europe.[35]

The arguments of the US critics were addressed in 1996 not so much to the Administration as to Congress, aiming to slow down the process, limit the group of potential newcomers and differentiate the commitments that would be undertaken *vis-à-vis* new members. NATO should proceed so slowly that, in the end, enlargement might be found unnecessary, suggested one of the opponents.[36] Others claimed that neither the US Senate nor the parliaments of the other 15 member states would ratify the decision to admit new members.[37]

The cost of NATO enlargement

The cost of implementing the enlargement decision is a significant factor in the debate and depends on the exact form of NATO enlargement, the countries included and, more important, how soon it will take place. In March the Congressional Budget Office (CBO) examined five options to provide a defence for the Visegrad states (the Czech Republic, Hungary, Poland and Slovakia).[38] Each option built on the previous one in scope and cost. It was estimated that the cost for all five options during 1996–2010 would be in the range $61–$125 billion,[39] and it was assumed that about 70 per cent of this would be borne by the Visegrad countries themselves. With the current low levels of threat to this region much lower estimated costs can also be considered for the same 15-year period.[40] The CBO report concludes that the costs of enlargement for the

[34] 'By anchoring NATO expansion on the needs of Poland, Hungary and the Czech Republic, as important as those countries are, the administration has obscured the most important issue for European peace and prosperity. That issue is the consolidation of reform in Russia. The timing, shape and even need for NATO expansion should be determined by how much it helps or hinders Russia's reform. Washington has not given nearly enough attention to that question.' Cohen (note 33), p. 8.

[35] It 'could provoke the most severe conflict between Russia and the West since the end of the cold war'. Steel, R., 'The hard questions', *New Republic*, 25 Nov. 1996, p. 29.

[36] Cohen (note 33), p. 9. The Brussels decision of 10 Dec. 1996 was commented by the *New York Times* as follows: 'fortunately, as part of an international treaty, none of this can happen without the approval of a two-thirds majority in the US Senate, as well as the endorsement of the Parliaments of the alliance's 15 European members'. 'NATO expansion?' *New York Times*, editorial reproduced in *International Herald Tribune*, 13 Dec. 1996, p. 8. A few days later William Pfaff noted: 'From the beginning of the debate over NATO enlargement, critics have maintained that it is most unlikely that a two-third's majority of the US Senate would agree to extend unconditional US nuclear guarantees to NATO's new members'. Pfaff (note 33, 19 Dec. 1996).

[37] A study published by the Program on International Policy Attitudes found, however, that the majority of Americans generally support NATO extension; at the same time, they strongly favour pacing this process so as to accommodate Russian concerns. Kull, S., *Americans on Expanding NATO*, A Study of US Public Attitudes, Program on International Policy Attitudes (School of Public Affairs (CISSM), University of Maryland: College Park, Md., 1 Oct. 1996).

[38] These 5 options are to: (*a*) enhance Visegrad defence forces and facilitate NATO reinforcement; (*b*) project NATO air power eastwards to defend the Visegrad states; (*c*) project power eastwards with ground forces based in Germany; (*d*) move stocks of prepositioned equipment eastwards; and (*e*) station a limited number of forces forward. Congressional Budget Office, *The Costs of Expanding the NATO Alliance*, CBO papers (Congressional Budget Office: Washington, DC, Mar. 1996), pp. XII–XXI.

[39] Figures are in billions of 1997 dollars. CBO (note 38), summary table I, p. XIV.

[40] The subset of option *a* is estimated to cost $21.2 billion (instead of $60.6 billion) and of that amount the Visegrad nations would cover $15.6 billion, the USA $1.9 billion and other NATO allies $3.7 billion. CBO (note 38), p. XVI.

USA and other NATO states might be manageable, but only if new members pay a substantial portion of the expenses.[41] The authors concluded that newcomers might be able to assume such a burden but that the USA and other NATO states would need to make higher financial contributions to the process. 'If they did not do so, even basic tasks needed to undertake expansion might not be completed, leading to a NATO security guarantee of questionable effectiveness'.[42] On the other hand, the estimated cost of enlargement is confused with the cost of internal NATO adaptation. While Central European officials declared their readiness to meet their share of the costs of enlargement, their estimates are much lower than those of the Congressional Budget Office.[43]

A report of the Euro-Atlantic Association, published in Warsaw, estimates that Poland will have to spend $1.5 billion over 15 years on integration with NATO.[44] The authors of the Polish report, while criticizing the CBO study, compared the cost that would have to be incurred to prepare Poland's armed forces for cooperation with NATO and that necessary to modernize the army regardless of possible Alliance membership. The latter would be five times higher than the direct costs of integration with NATO, which will comprise the adaptation of command, control and communication systems, air defence and the modernization of airports.[45]

Russia and NATO enlargement

In Russia, the issue of NATO enlargement featured significantly in the 1996 presidential election campaign. Ignoring rhetoric designed for domestic consumption, a certain shift in Russia's standpoint could be discerned in 1996. Foreign Minister Yevgeniy Primakov, followed by other Russian representatives, has repeatedly made statements to the effect that, although Russia continues to oppose NATO enlargement, it does not have any right of veto on the matter.[46] Furthermore, in June 1996, during his meeting with the NATO foreign ministers in Berlin, Primakov made another new point by declaring that

---

[41] 'Accounts can only be made once we know who is becoming a member. Moreover, the eastward enlargement should not primarily be viewed under the cost aspect. The common costs are small anyway, they amount to an average 0.1 percent of national defense budgets.' Inacker, M. J., 'We must help Russia remove its old weapons', Interview with General Klaus Naumann, chairman of the NATO Military Committee, *Welt am Sonntag* (Hamburg), 29 Dec. 1996 (in German), in 'NATO: Naumann announces lean command structures', Foreign Broadcast Information Service, *Daily Report–West Europe (FBIS-WEU)*, FBIS-WEU-96-252, 29 Dec. 1996.

[42] CBO (note 38), p. XXI.

[43] In his address at Chatham House, Poland's President Kwasniewski noted in this respect: 'They coincide in time, but in reality have little to do with actual enlargement'. President Aleksander Kwasniewski's address at the Royal Institute of International Affairs, Chatham House, London, on 24 Oct. 1996, and before the WEU Assembly in Paris on 4 Dec. 1996.

[44] 'Estimated cost of NATO enlargement: a contribution to the debate', Euro-Atlantic Association, Warsaw, 20 Jan. 1997. See also Urbanowicz, J., 'NATO. A question of billions', *Warsaw Voice*, 2 Feb. 1997, p. 7; and 'Poles claim West overstates expense of NATO expansion', *Defense News*, no. 5 (3–9 Feb. 1997), p. 10.

[45] Note 43; see also Fitchett, J., 'The cost of NATO expansion? Washington is aiming very low', *International Herald Tribune*, 15–16 Feb. 1997.

[46] *Nezavisimaya Gazeta*, 1 Mar. 1996, p. 2; and *Segodnya*, 6 Mar. 1996, p. 2.

Russia understands some countries' drive to join the Atlantic Alliance, but does not accept NATO's military structures coming closer to its borders.[47] In this context, Russia also raised the matter of guarantees that military bases and nuclear weapons would not be deployed on the territories of new NATO members. In a confidential letter to the US President, leaked to the Russian press, President Boris Yeltsin warned that extending NATO to the Baltic states is absolutely unacceptable.[48] This opposition can be interpreted as Russia reconciling itself to the possibility of a limited group of Central European states being admitted to the Alliance.

Contacts have been established between NATO and Russia with the aim of reaching a partnership agreement. Soon after the Russian election, Yeltsin publicly demanded that a charter governing relations between NATO and Russia be signed prior to a decision on extending the Alliance.[49] Similar statements made by the new Secretary of the Russian National Security Council, General Aleksander Lebed, in Brussels in October 1996,[50] aimed at postponing the decision on admission of new members. An outline of the desired Russian–NATO agreement was submitted by the Secretary of the newly established Council for Defence, Yuriy Baturin. It called for a fundamental transformation of NATO in the spheres of doctrine and strategic and operational planning. The essence of a treaty between Russia and NATO would be joint decisions on European security, collaboration on implementing these decisions, and joint responsibility for the decisions adopted and the effects of their implementation.[51] Leading Russian politicians discounted signing a document of a 'purely declarative character'.[52]

US Vice-President Al Gore declared that it is essential, as enlargement proceeds, that 'we work in parallel to build a strong and cooperative NATO–Russian relationship'.[53] This was in response to the statement by Russian Prime Minister Viktor Chernomyrdin at the opening of the OSCE Summit in

[47] *Izvestiya*, 6 June 1996, p. 3. In an address to the Moscow Institute of International Relations, Primakov said: 'There must be a dialogue, solutions and a compromise. But there cannot be a compromise on one issue—plans to bring NATO's infrastructure closer to our borders. On all the other issues we should seek agreement'. *Trud*, 25 June 1996.

[48] The letter, excerpts of which were made public by the Russian press, reads: 'Even a hypothetical possibility of extending NATO's zone of operation to the Baltic states is out of the question. Such a prospect is categorically unacceptable to Russia, and any steps in this direction would be assessed as an open challenge to our national security interests, an undermining of the foundations on which European stability rests.' *Izvestiya*, 6 July 1996, pp. 1–3.

[49] This postulate was put forward by Boris Yeltsin on 28 Sep. 1996 at the end of his meeting with the new Defence Minister of Russia, Igor Rodionov. See also ITAR-TASS in English, 1 Oct. 1996.

[50] General Lebed also acknowledged that, 'politically and legally', Russia could not exercise a veto over the membership of a 'legitimate organization' such as NATO or the choice of 'any independent nation to join such an alliance'. *International Herald Tribune*, 8 Oct. 1996, pp. 1, 10.

[51] Having presented his concept in the Duma during the seminar on The Future of European Security, Yuriy Baturin concluded: 'The envisaged treaty between Russia and the North Atlantic bloc is not a compensation for the latter's expansion. It is not a means of countervailing NATO enlargement. It is necessary of itself or by itself for the creation of a common European security area'. *Nezavisimaya Gazeta*, 28 Nov. 1996, pp. 1–2.

[52] Yevgeniy Primakov's statement of 11 Oct. 1996, ITAR-TASS report, Open Media Research Institute (OMRI), *OMRI Daily Digest*, no. 198 (11 Oct. 1996), URL <http:www.omri.cz>.

[53] 'Vice-President Gore praises role of OSCE', Al Gore's speech at OSCE Lisbon summit meeting. Version current on 2 Dec. 1996. URL <gopher://198.80.36.82:70/0R50884240-50897913-range/rchives/1996/pdq.96>.

Lisbon,[54] which although implying agreement to the eastward extension of NATO political structures indicated firm opposition to bringing NATO military infrastructure closer to Russia's frontiers. The stances of Russian representatives, although addressed to their Western partners, have a clear domestic dimension and purpose[55] even though this debate is conducted within the political élites.[56] Four possible options for Russia in the event that enlargement is neither stopped nor slowed down are considered: (a) a redivision of Europe; (b) the OSCE as a pan-European security order alternative and superior to NATO; (c) Russian partnership with NATO: institutionalization of Russia–NATO relations aimed at joint decision making and implementation of decisions; and—the least likely—(d) Russian membership of NATO.[57] Russia will most likely continue to fluctuate between the first three options according to different internal and external factors. In 1996 NATO enlargement was opposed by almost the entire spectrum of the political élite and all significant parties in Russia. It would, however, be illusory to conclude that their attitude to the issue indicates consensus in matters of Russia's national security.[58] The fact that—despite earlier announcements—the NAC Defence Ministers' session in Brussels did not name candidates with whom NATO will enter into negotiations on admission testifies to a reluctance to ignore Russia's position. Moreover, a document is being prepared on political and military cooperation between Russia and NATO.[59]

Central European arguments

The main Central European aspirants to NATO membership—the Czech Republic, Hungary and Poland—proceed from the assumption that both the enlargement debate and the political process have already passed the point of

[54] The Russian Prime Minister stated in Lisbon on 2 Dec.: 'We clearly declare our firm opposition to plans for moving the military infrastructure of the North Atlantic Alliance closer to our territory. The appearance of new lines of division in Europe would lead to a worsening of the geopolitical situation in the world as a whole. Russia has no veto over enlargement of the Alliance, but neither has anybody a veto over our right to protect our national interests. There is still time and reason to consider where NATO enlargement might lead.' *Krasnaya Zvezda*, 3 Dec. 1996, p. 3.

[55] 'V Lisabone Moskva okazalas' v izolatstii' [In Lisbon, Moscow turned out to be in isolation], *Izvestiya*, 4 Dec. 1996.

[56] 'The overwhelming majority of Russians do not care much about NATO. . . . Even for the minority of Russians who do care about foreign policy, NATO remains mostly irrelevant.' Kortunov, A., 'NATO enlargement and Russia: in search of an adequate response', ed. D. G. Haglund, *Will NATO go East? The Debate over Enlarging the Atlantic Alliance* (Centre for International Relations, Queen's University: Kingston, Ontario, 1996), p. 69.

[57] Kortunov (note 56), p. 88.

[58] 'If Russia really intends to develop its democratic reforms consistently, it need not be afraid of an alliance of states united by their adherence to the system of democratic values.' Parkhalina, T., 'Stoit li boyatsya rasshireniya NATO' [Do we need to be afraid of NATO enlargement?], *Segodnya*, 28 Aug. 1996, p. 5.

[59] 'We welcome the aim to conclude a document which could take the form of a Charter between NATO and Russia. We believe that our relations with Russia can and should be more broader, more intensive and more substantive and that they can and should be placed on a more permanent institutional basis . . . we invite the Council in Permanent Session to task the NATO Military Authorities to make proposals ' or the development of closer military relationships with Russia and to identify concrete areas for military cooperation'. NATO Communiqué (note 18).

no return. To initiate their individual dialogues with the Atlantic Alliance, they each presented official position papers and undertook to meet the criteria of NATO membership as defined in the *Study on NATO Enlargement*.[60] These states have also regulated relations with their neighbours through treaties and cleared up matters of particular dispute.[61] They have also developed their cooperation within such subregional organizations as the Central European Initiative (CEI), the Council of the Baltic Sea States (CBSS) and the Central European Free Trade Agreement (CEFTA), and established contacts and cooperation within NACC and the PFP. Individual PFP programmes and the Planning and Review Process (PARP) were seen by the CEE states as a preparatory stage for NATO membership and full integration with the political and military structures of the Atlantic Alliance. Their efforts in 1996 were focused on three areas: civilian and democratic control of the armed forces; a comprehensive programme of restructuring their armed forces to ensure interoperability with NATO forces; and adaptation of defence budgets to the Alliance requirements. Their main motives for joining NATO, as presented in numerous statements, are:[62] (*a*) the Atlantic Alliance is the central and crucial collective defence organization in Europe; (*b*) it is a key stabilizing factor in the Euro-Atlantic region and an instrument of promotion and consolidation of democratic transformation; and (*c*) enlargement will 'help to handle conflicts among the new member states themselves'.[63] According to the CEE states, NATO enlargement should be accompanied by a partnership agreement between Russia and NATO and similar arrangements between Ukraine and the Baltic states.[64]

III. The European Union: negotiations in 1996

Some opponents of NATO enlargement in Western Europe, the USA and Russia favour enlarging and enhancing the EU and its defence arm, the WEU, as a possible and desirable alternative. In fact, it is not an alternative but a parallel process, and one with important security implications. In some non-aligned countries (e.g., Austria, Finland and Sweden) membership in itself is seen as promoting security and widening thus most directly corresponds to 'security building through international organization'.[65] Enlargement of the Union will be subject to negotiations in 1998, after the expected conclusion of

---

[60] On the *Study on NATO Enlargement*, see Rotfeld (note 14), pp. 285–86.

[61] In 1996 Hungary settled its relations with Romania, and the Czech Republic reached a long-negotiated agreement with Germany. Poland stabilized its relations with all 7 neighbours and concluded relevant agreements in 1991–95 (particularly regarding its relations with Belarus, the Czech Republic, Germany, Lithuania, Russia, Slovakia and Ukraine).

[62] Regarding Poland's accession to NATO, see, e.g., Kwasniewski at Chatham House (note 43).

[63] Valky, L., *NATO Enlargement—Divergent Approaches. A View from Hungary*, SWP-AP 2984, Ebenhausen, Munich, Nov. 1996, p. 11.

[64] Kwasniewski's statement at Chatham House (note 43).

[65] Huldt, B., 'Sweden and security in a New Europe', ed. Herolf (note 10), p. 119. See also Hoagland, J., 'Expand the European Union instead of NATO', *International Herald Tribune*, 5 Aug. 1996, p. 6; and Heisbourg, F., 'At this point, only Washington can slow the reckless pace', *International Herald Tribune*, 28 Nov. 1996.

the Intergovernmental Conference (IGC) in 1997. The IGC initiated on 29 March 1996 has a mandate to reassess and revise the Maastricht Treaty, including the part on a Common Foreign and Security Policy (CFSP). One of the main tasks of the IGC is to reform the CFSP to give it real meaning in shaping a common security policy for member states. This was the chief subject of negotiations in 1996, reflected in the Presidency Conclusions of the Florence European Council (21–22 June).[66] Two aspects of the CFSP were given particular attention: along with synergy with the external activities of EU competence, security aspects, including 'a deeper examination of the issue of the European Union's relationship with the Western European Union', were addressed.

To enhance the role of the EU and its capabilities in conflict management, Finland and Sweden submitted a joint proposal on 25 April 1996. The driving force behind their initiative was the conviction that the Union can and must take stronger action to prevent and handle conflicts. EU competence in military crisis management would be enhanced by a reinforced institutional link between the EU and the WEU,[67] assuming that in the foreseeable future the WEU will concentrate on peacekeeping actions, crisis management and humanitarian aid. On the other hand, because of their policies of military non-alignment, Finland and Sweden are not prepared to take part in cooperation on common defence, envisaged in the Maastricht Treaty as a possible future area for the CFSP.[68]

Constituting a wide network supplementing the large European structures, these subregional arrangements, with various tasks and roles, are of particular importance for those countries which are not members of the 'hard-core' security organizations. In this context the specific role of regional and subregional organizations should be noted, although they cannot substitute for collective defence structures or security guarantees. Subregional security arrangements, such as the Visegrad Group, the Central European Initiative, or the Council of Baltic Sea States and the Barents Euro-Arctic Council in the north, complement and reinforce the wider European security structures and are of special significance for those countries which are not members of hard-core security arrangements.

The Presidency Conclusions of the Florence European Council summarized the initial stage of the IGC. The Council asked that a general outline for a draft revision of the Maastricht Treaty be prepared by the Irish Presidency for the Dublin meeting (13–14 December), which should be oriented to 'greater consistency and efficiency'. Specific recommendations were also made to relax the stringency of the unanimity rule of the decision-making procedures

---

[66] The Italian Foreign Minister presented the priorities of the Italian Presidency of the Council of the EU in different capitals between 18 Dec. 1995 and 16 Jan. 1996. See Info—Note, no. 2/96, Secretariat of the European Commission, Brussels, 30 Jan. 1996.

[67] The IGC and the security and defence dimension towards an enhanced EU role in crisis management. Memorandum from Finland and Sweden, 25 Apr. 1996.

[68] Address by Ulf Hjertonsson, Director General for Political Affairs, Ministry for Foreign Affairs of Sweden, at the Swedish Institute of International Affairs Conference, 14 Mar. 1996.

and to establish closer links between the EU and the WEU as the result of the June 1996 NATO meeting in Berlin.

In fact the European security structures constitute an overlapping, multi-layered system, as shown in figure 2.1. At its heart, the EU and the WEU are trying to define themselves 'as security actors, setting up machinery for planning and decision making, creating the rudiments of a security policy and assembling some capacity for joint activities'.[69]

The text submitted by the Irish Presidency proposed the strengthening of the CFSP in a number of significant and practical ways: the Secretary-General of the Council would be given a new standing and visibility in foreign policy (with responsibility for policy planning and an early-warning capability); the Commission would be associated in an enhanced way with CFSP policy implementation; and diplomatic meetings with third countries would be conducted by the Presidency, supported by the Council's Secretary-General and the Commission.

The proposed solutions deal with procedural and competence matters.[70] These may be more significant for joint representation in matters of foreign policy than for its shaping. Institutional reform of the EU in the sphere of common security may at best mean some procedural innovations in the decision-making process but will be of little practical importance in the promotion of conflict prevention and peaceful dispute resolution in Europe.[71] The fact that the EU could in principle be involved in such activity was evidenced by its role in the implementation of the Dayton Agreement.[72]

IV. The OSCE: the common security framework

The concept of mutually reinforcing and interlocking European and trans-atlantic organizations and institutions, as defined in the 1992 Helsinki Summit Declaration,[73] was implemented at different levels in 1996. The OSCE is seen as a primary instrument in preventive diplomacy, conflict prevention, post-conflict rehabilitation and regional cooperation.[74] Its involvement in Bosnia and Herzegovina posed the greatest challenge ever confronted by the OSCE and tested its preparedness to take on more complex tasks in the post-cold war

[69] Lenzi and Martin (note 13), p. 1. See also Bailes, A. J. K., 'Sub-regional organizations: the Cinderellas of European security', *NATO Review*, no. 2 (Mar. 1997), pp. 27–31.

[70] Decision-making procedures would be improved in 2 ways: (*a*) although unanimity would still apply, it would be possible to make a declaration of constructive abstention (a member state which made such a declaration would not be obliged to apply the decision); and (*b*) qualified majority voting would be introduced for all decisions under CFSP other than the adoption of Joint Actions and all decisions with a military/defence dimension. Note 66.

[71] Rummel, R., *Common Foreign and Security Policy and Conflict Prevention: Priorities for the Intergovernmental Conference* (Safer World and International Alert Report: London, May 1996).

[72] The Conclusions of the Peace Implementation Council—Review Conference in Florence, 14 June 1996, and of the Ministerial Meeting of the Steering Board with the Presidency of Bosnia and Herzegovina in Paris, 14 Nov. 1996; and the London Peace Implementation Conference Report, London, 4–5 Dec. 1996. See chapter 2 in this volume.

[73] Helsinki Document 1992: The Challenge of Change, Helsinki, 10 July 1992. The text is reproduced in *SIPRI Yearbook 1993: World Armaments and Disarmament* (Oxford University Press: Oxford, 1993), pp. 190–209.

[74] NATO (note 6), para. 20.

multi-institutional set-up.[75] The OSCE was actively involved and assisted in three different types of activity: supervision and monitoring of elections; negotiations on confidence- and security-building measures (CSBMs); and arms control talks, crowned with the Agreement on Sub-Regional Arms Control (the Florence Agreement).[76] In Chechnya the OSCE Assistance Group was involved in and contributed to the ending of the armed conflict.[77]

Consultations, negotiations, missions

In 1996 the central role within the new OSCE structure was played by the Permanent Council (PC) as an organ and forum for consultations and enhancing the OSCE's operational capabilities. It provided political guidance for missions in the field.

OSCE missions

Eleven missions of long duration and other field activities served to provide early warning, conflict prevention and crisis management during the year.[78] The active missions within the OSCE are:[79]

1. *The spill-over monitoring mission to Skopje* (1992). In close cooperation with the United Nations Preventive Deployment Force (UNPREDEP), this mission continued to monitor the situation, both internally and externally.

2. *The mission to Georgia* (1992). The primary task of the mission is to facilitate a settlement of the South Ossetian conflict.[80] The main activities in 1996 were: the signing in May in the Kremlin of the memorandum 'to enhance security and CSBMs'; the revitalization on 23 July of the Joint Control Commission established in 1994 to find practical solutions to the problems arising from the conflict; continued activity in Abkhazia (another conflict zone in Georgia), notably the opening on 10 December of a human rights office in Sukhumi; and access to detained persons on both sides of the conflict and humanitarian aid.

3. *The mission to Estonia* (1993). In 1996, the main task of the mission was to monitor the citizenship examinations and residence permit processing.[81] It continued to deal with issues relating to Estonian language training for Russophone inhabitants.

---

[75] OSCE, *Annual Report on OSCE Activities* (OSCE: Vienna, Nov. 1996).

[76] See chapter 14 in this volume. The Florence Agreement is reproduced in appendix 14B.

[77] See chapter 4 in this volume.

[78] The mission of long duration in Kosovo, Sanjak and Vojvodina has been characterized by the OSCE Secretary General as 'non-operational' because the government of the Federal Republic of Yugoslavia (Serbia and Montenegro), suspended since 1992, has made its reactivation conditional on the country's return to the OSCE.

[79] For a detailed presentation of the mandates and activities of the missions, see Rotfeld 1995 (note 24), pp. 290–95. See also appendix 2A in this volume.

[80] In his Annual Report for 1996 the OSCE Secretary General mentioned the mission's threefold task: to help preserve the cease-fire; to act as an intermediary between President Eduard Shevardnadze of Georgia and the South Ossetian leader Chibirov; and to facilitate a Georgian–Ossetian flow of information. OSCE (note 75).

[81] The examinations began in Dec. 1995 pursuant to Estonia's Citizenship Law.

4. *The mission to Latvia* (1993). The activities of the mission were focused on monitoring the implementation of the 1994 Citizenship Law and the 1995 Law on Non-Citizens and the conduct of naturalization examinations.

5. *The mission to Moldova* (1993). The main achievement in 1996 was the signing of the memorandum on the principles of settlement of relations between Moldova and the Trans-Dniester region, prepared with support and assistance from the OSCE mission.

6. *The mission to Tajikistan* (1994). In cooperation with the UN High Commissioner for Refugees, this mission mainly monitored the human rights situation of returned refugees.[82] On 24–26 April the OSCE organized a regional seminar on confidence-building measures (CBMs), the first of its kind in Tajikistan, with the participation of the five Central Asian countries and senior OSCE representatives and delegations from other participating states.[83]

7. *The mission to Ukraine* (1994). The mission focused in 1996 on the elaboration and adoption of a Crimean constitution. The Constitution of Ukraine adopted on 28 June 1996 recognized an Autonomous Republic of Crimea.[84] The mission was also concerned with deportees, particularly the Crimean Tatars.

8. *The mission to Sarajevo* (1994) was expanded in early 1996 and reorganized into a section of the OSCE mission to Bosnia and Herzegovina.

9. *The mission to Bosnia and Herzegovina* (1995). With 233 members, this is by far the biggest OSCE field mission (headed by Ambassador Robert Frowick of the USA). Its task is to supervise the preparation and conduct of free and fair elections; to monitor human rights;[85] and to facilitate the monitoring of arms control and CSBM arrangements in Bosnia and Herzegovina. In 1996 more than 1200 election supervisors from OSCE states assisted the authorities, and about 900 international observers monitored the elections on 14 September.[86]

---

[82] On 22 Feb. 1996, the OSCE Permanent Council approved financial support for the establishment of an ombudsman office. However, the Tajik Government continues to postpone the establishment of the institution.

[83] The inter-Tajik talks took place under UN auspices and with the direct involvement of the Russian Federation as a mediator.

[84] The Ukrainian Parliament adopted on 4 Apr. 1996 a partial constitution for Crimea—some 20 critical articles in the document must be correlated with Ukrainian law. OSCE (note 75).

[85] As a follow-up to the Dayton Peace Agreement, the Human Rights Commission was established as a national body which will have an international character for the first 5 years of its existence. It consists of the Human Rights Chamber and the Human Rights Ombudsman (Gret Haller of Switzerland). A new important element in the work of the mission was close cooperation with various international institutions and bodies, including the European Monitoring Mission (ECMM), IFOR, the Office of the High Representative (OHR), the Office of the Coordinator for International Monitoring (CIM) and the International Criminal Tribunal for the former Yugoslavia (ICTY).

[86] On 29 Sep. the Provisional Elections Commission certified that elections had taken place in accordance with internationally accepted standards of eligibility, access, participation and transparency. This assessment met with critical comments in the mass media. One can assume that owing to the displacement of people and lack of experience, as well the scope of the tasks assigned to the OSCE in Bosnia, it was unavoidable that some shortcomings occurred, particularly in checking the lists of those eligible for voting against those who voted.

Two agreements were concluded under OSCE auspices: on CSBMs, between the Bosnian Government, the Bosnian-Croat Federation and the Republika Srpska (26 January 1996—implementation started on 1 March); and an agreement designed to assist the parties in achieving balanced and stable defence force levels at the lowest possible numbers consistent with their respective security needs (14 June).

10. *The mission to Croatia* (1996).[87] The task of the mission is to provide assistance and expertise to the Croatian authorities at all levels in the field of protection of human rights and of minorities' rights.

11. *The Assistance Group to Chechnya* (1996).[88] The mandate of the Group is to facilitate contacts between the conflicting parties. Its mediation contributed to achieving the Moscow cease-fire agreement and two protocols signed in Nasran.

Activities in Nagorno-Karabakh. The OSCE is involved in the search for a peaceful solution by the Personal Representative of the Chairman-in-Office (CIO) on the conflict, dealt with by the Minsk Conference. The Personal Representative held monthly meetings with the authorities of Armenia and Azerbaijan and the leaders of Nagorno-Karabakh[89] and, in cooperation with the conflicting parties, introduced a 'mechanism of crisis monitoring' for the verification of allegations of cease-fire violations. However, no peace agreement has been reached and no OSCE peacekeeping force, for which plans have been drawn up, has yet been deployed.

Other OSCE activities

Other OSCE activities were connected with the implementation of some bilateral agreements (e.g., between Latvia and Russia on military pensioners) in the framework of the Joint Committee on the Skrunda Radar Station and with the Estonian Government Commission on Military Pensioners.[90]

The High Commissioner on National Minorities (HCNM). Max van der Stoel, appointed as the first OSCE HCNM in 1993, became involved in minority questions in Albania, Croatia, Estonia, the Former Yugoslav Republic of Macedonia, Hungary, Kazakhstan, Kyrgyzstan, Latvia, Romania, Slovakia and Ukraine.[91] His main concerns were inter-ethnic relations and respect for national minority rights.[92]

---

[87] Established on the basis of the OSCE Permanent Council decision of 17 Apr. 1996, pursuant to a report of an OSCE Fact-finding Mission to Croatia (Oct. 1995) and a Report of the Personal Representative of the Chairman-in-Office, Feb. 1996.

[88] The OSCE group started its work on 4 Jan. 1996. See also chapter 4 in this volume.

[89] In July 1996 the CIO appointed Andrzej Kasprzyk as his new Representative.

[90] The Estonian Government Commission, tasked with the review of applications for residence permits by former Soviet career officers (now of foreign, mainly Russian, nationality) had managed to deal with the bulk of the applications by 12 July 1996. Some 5000 additional cases not previously reviewed were to be dealt with in early 1997. OSCE (note 75).

[91] In recognition of the HCNM's contribution to the defusing of inter-ethnic tension, his mandate was extended in the autumn of 1995 for the second 3-year term.

[92] Report by Mr Max van der Stoel, OSCE HCNM, Vienna, 4 Nov. 1996; and OSCE (note 75).

Activities of the Office for Democratic Institutions and Human Rights (ODIHR). Under the Dayton Agreement in 1996 three major roles in Bosnia and Herzegovina were added to the normal workload of the ODIHR: supervision of the electoral process; assistance to the ombudspersons; and assistance in the process of creating modern legislation. Apart from the Assistance Programme for the Recovery and Development of Bosnia and Herzegovina, the ODIHR has developed an election monitoring framework, produced the Election Observation Handbook and observed the parliamentary elections in many member countries.[93] Moreover, the ODIHR has compiled a number of Early Warning Reports, coordinated Legal Support (training programmes) and contributed to the building of civil society. A number of seminars, symposia and meetings were held under ODIHR auspices: a symposium on the rule of law and democratic institution building;[94] a professional training programme for Russian judges (Orel, 10–13 July) on how to implement the international human rights commitments; a programme for Belarus Government Migration Officials (Warsaw, 15–19 July); a project for the Georgian Ministry of Justice focused on prison reform and the application of international standards to the Georgian penal system (6–8 September); and other workshops.[95]

Division of labour

In his address to the OSCE Implementation Meeting (Vienna, 22 November 1996), Swiss Foreign Minister and OSCE Chairman-in-Office Flavio Cotti proposed a 'fundamental division of labour' between the Council of Europe and the OSCE. He said that the dramatic shortage of resources, common to other multilateral European organizations, forced the OSCE to tackle the problem in a concrete manner: 'All around us we can hear allusions being made daily about the necessity of coordination among international organizations. If we want to be taken seriously, we must transform words into deeds'.[96] Cotti's proposals received little support. Division of labour among different European institutions is one of the most difficult problems and no tangible success was achieved in 1996.

---

[93] OSCE ODIHR, *Annual Report for 1996*, Warsaw, 1996.

[94] The Third ODIHR Annual Judicial Symposium, Warsaw, 10–14 June 1996.

[95] Seminars and workshops were held on human rights and international standards in Dushanbe, Tajikistan, on 28–30 May 1996, Erevan, Armenia, on 16–19 Feb.; a Round Table on Legal Aspects of the Ombudsman Institution took place in Tbilisi on 11–12 Mar.; a meeting on constitutional, legal and administrative aspects of the freedom of religion was held in Warsaw on 16–19 Apr.; and many training programmes were organized for NGOs and journalists on the role of independent mass media. Other activities were focused on the integration of recently admitted participating states, on the economic dimension (the first implementation review meeting in Geneva, 22–23 Jan., and the fourth OSCE Economic Forum in Prague, 27–29 Mar., and seminars organized in cooperation with the UN Economic Commission for Europe, the OECD, the CIS, etc.) and inter-institutional cooperation. A new important aspect of OSCE activities is the interaction with its Partners for Cooperation: Japan and the Republic of Korea in the Far East, and its Mediterranean partners: Algeria, Egypt, Israel, Morocco and Tunisia.

[96] Declaration of the Chairman-in-Office, Federal Councillor Flavio Cotti, to the OSCE Implementation Meeting, Vienna, 22 Nov. 1996.

Assessment

In assessing the effectiveness of an organization an essential criterion is whether the means and instruments at its disposal are adequate to the allotted tasks. The means demonstrate the commitment of states to the implementation of the declared goals. The fact that the OSCE's mandate and tasks remain in blatant disproportion to its means suggests two things: (a) the OSCE is a moderately bureaucratized structure that makes economic and effective use of its modest budget;[97] and (b) the OSCE participating states do not provide the appropriate resources. For example, the OSCE was justifiably criticized for mistakes made in the planning for and organization of the supervision of elections in Albania and Bosnia and Herzegovina. While over 3000 individuals were deployed by the OSCE on election day in the latter case, including election supervisors and observers, the operation revealed both financial limitations and inadequate staff training.

The greatest disappointment, however, stems not so much from the fact that, despite numerous agreements, the existing security structures in Europe continue to operate in a badly coordinated way and duplicate each other's functions, as from the fact that during the chief political meeting of 1996 there was no critical reflection on the fundamental question of why these structures fail to effectively meet the existing security threats and challenges.[98]

The Lisbon Summit decisions

The main result of the OSCE Lisbon Summit (2–3 December 1996) was agreement on negotiations in early 1997 with the aim of adapting the 1990 Treaty on Conventional Armed Forces in Europe (the CFE Treaty) to the changing security environment in Europe.[99] Another decision was reflected in the Lisbon Declaration on a Common and Comprehensive Security Model for Europe for the Twenty-First Century.[100] Both decisions are seen as initiatives aimed at defusing Russian fears about NATO enlargement.

The decisions of the December 1995 Budapest Ministerial Council[101] took the work on a security model to an operational stage. The memorandum submitted by the Russian Federation on 21 March 1996 proposed that the future security system in Europe be based on: (a) the elaboration of a European Security Charter comparable to the Helsinki Final Act; (b) new legal foundations for the security system in the OSCE region, including security guarantees for the states concerned and a network of agreements to coordinate

---

[97] The OSCE budget for 1996 was initially established at a level of 310.1 million Austrian schillings (c. $28.3 million), and with additional tasks in Bosnia and Herzegovina, the budget was revised and established at the level of 546.1 million Austrian schillings ($49.837 million).

[98] The critical remarks of Flavio Cotti (note 96) remain in stark dissonance with the tone of self-satisfaction demonstrated by representatives of other international organizations who usually appreciate the activity of their own bureaucratic structures highly.

[99] See chapter 14 in this volume.

[100] OSCE, Lisbon Document 1996, OSCE document DOC.S/1/96, 3 Dec. 1996. Excerpts are reproduced in appendix 5A in this volume.

[101] Rotfeld (note 14).

functions among existing European and Euro-Atlantic institutions and structures; and (c) the establishment of a Security Council for Europe (or an OSCE Executive Committee). These proposals and the initiative to revise the CFE Treaty, to define national ceilings in place of the original bloc-to-bloc entitlements, were aimed at neutralizing possible NATO enlargement. On both accounts, the Western countries showed an understanding for Russia's demands and expectations.[102]

Within the established Security Model Committee, 28 states have submitted specific proposals.[103] The Lisbon Declaration identified the common elements for shaping a cooperative security system in Europe as being respect for human rights, fundamental freedoms and the rule of law, market economy and social justice. This also implies mutual confidence and the peaceful settlement of disputes, and excludes any quest for domination. The new political commitments undertaken in the Lisbon Security Model Declaration can be summarized as follows: 'to act in solidarity' to promote full implementation of the principles and norms adopted in different basic documents of the Helsinki process;[104] to consult promptly with a participating state whose security is threatened and to consider 'jointly actions that may have to be undertaken in defence of our common values'; not to support those who are acting 'in violation of international law against the territorial integrity or political independence of any participating State'; and to attach importance to the security concerns of all participating States 'irrespective of whether they belong to military structures or arrangements'.[105] The commitments to *act in solidarity* and to consider the undertaking of *joint actions* constitute a positive response to the proposal, addressed to the OSCE, to define new principles of solidarity and the right to 'cooperative intervention'.[106] In the context of the debate on NATO enlargement the Lisbon Declaration reaffirmed 'the inherent right of each and every participating State to be free to choose or change its security arrangements, including treaties of alliance, as they evolve'. On the other hand, the OSCE states committed themselves not to strengthen their security 'at the expense of the security of other States'. Under the Lisbon Security Model Declaration participating states are obliged to respect transparency in their actions: their security arrangements should be of 'a public nature, predictable and open, and should correspond to the needs of individual and collective security'. The heads of state or government instructed their representa-

---

[102] Report of the Chairman-in-Office to the Lisbon Summit on the Security Model Discussion 1995–1996; and Drozdiak, W., 'NATO aims to sweeten deal on ties with Russia', *International Herald Tribune*, 16 Jan. 1997, pp. 1–6.

[103] The Security Model Committee began its work on 19 Jan. 1996 and held 18 meetings throughout 1996. In cooperation with the CIO, an Independent Working Group on A Future Security Agenda was established under SIPRI auspices and conducted its work from 2 Dec. 1995 to 3 Oct. 1996. The results of its work were presented at the Committee's session on 28 June 1996 and published as *A Future Security Agenda for Europe* (SIPRI: Stockholm, Oct. 1996). This contribution was taken note of in the CIO's report to the Lisbon Summit (note 102).

[104] That is: the Helsinki Final Act of 1975; the Charter of Paris of 1990; the Helsinki Summit Decisions of 1992; the Budapest Summit Decisions of 1995 and other CSCE/OSCE documents.

[105] OSCE, Lisbon Document 1996 (note 100).

[106] The Independent Working Group report (note 103), p. 1–12.

tives 'to work energetically on the Security Model' and to report on the progress made to the next Ministerial Council in Copenhagen in December 1997. The recommended agenda in this respect should be focused, for example, on enhancing instruments of joint cooperative action in the event of non-compliance with the OSCE commitments; further developing the concepts and principles included in the Lisbon Declaration; and recommending any 'new commitments, structures or arrangements' which would reinforce security in Europe.[107]

V. Conclusions

1. Of all the regions in the world Europe has achieved the highest degree of institutionalized security cooperation. Consequently, the focus is too often on organizational and procedural matters.[108] The real problems, which call for a common approach, are often relegated to second place.

2. No single organization—whether NATO, the EU, the OSCE or the Council of Europe—can handle the whole European security process. The issue at stake is not so much how to enlarge NATO or the EU, but how to establish an efficient new security system in Europe which will correspond to the new international security environment. The focus should therefore be more on the cooperation between security-related organizations and institutions than on their structures and procedures.

3. The internal transformation and enlargement of initially Western institutions, such as the Council of Europe, the Organisation for Economic Co-operation and Development (OECD), the EU and NATO, is often perceived as a contradiction: deepening *versus* widening, and as creating new divisions. It should rather be seen as a natural process and a part of 'a larger package' that could provide credible safeguards for Russia's legitimate security interests and give Russia a responsible role in managing European security.[109] The process of unifying Europe should be based on accepting common democratic security values and building security networks that can help prevent conflicts and find solutions to both common and individual security problems.

---

[107] OSCE, Lisbon Document 1996 (note 100), paras 6–12.
[108] See, e.g., Herolf (note 10), pp. 13–17.
[109] Blackwill, R., Horelick, A. and Nunn, S., *Stopping the Decline in US–Russian Relations*, RAND Report P-7986 (RAND Corporation: Santa Monica, Calif., 1996).

Appendix 5A. Documents on European security

LISBON SUMMIT DECLARATION

1. We, the Heads of State or Government of the participating States of the Organization for Security and Co-operation in Europe, have met in Lisbon to assess the situation in the OSCE region and to establish a co-operative foundation for our common security. As we approach the new century, it is more important than ever that we build together a peaceful OSCE region where all our nations and individuals feel secure.

2. We today adopt the Lisbon Declaration on a Common and Comprehensive Security Model for Europe for the twenty-first century to strengthen security and stability throughout the OSCE region. We welcome the historic decision of OSCE participating States signatory to the CFE Treaty to begin negotiations in early 1997 with a view towards adapting the Treaty to the changing security environment in Europe. We intend to realize our full potential for consolidating peace and prosperity in the entire OSCE region, as demonstrated by our combined efforts—through the OSCE and other relevant institutions—to forge a sustainable peace in Bosnia and Herzegovina.

3. We reaffirm the OSCE principles as set forth in the Helsinki Final Act and other OSCE commitments. We believe that observance of all these principles and implementation of all commitments need to be improved and constantly reviewed. We recognize that serious risks and challenges, such as those to our security and sovereignty, continue to be of major concern. We are committed to address them.

4. Respect for human rights remains fundamental to our concept of democracy and to the democratization process enshrined in the Charter of Paris. We are determined to consolidate the democratic gains of the changes that have occurred since 1989 and peacefully manage their further development in the OSCE region. We will co-operate in strengthening democratic institutions.

5. The OSCE has a key role to play in fostering security and stability in all their dimensions. We decide to continue our efforts to further enhance its efficiency as a primary instrument for early warning, conflict prevention, crisis management and post-conflict rehabilitation capabilities. We ask the Chairman-in-Office to report on progress achieved to the 1997 Ministerial Council.

6. The Lisbon Declaration on a Common and Comprehensive Security Model for Europe for the twenty-first century is a comprehensive expression of our endeavour to strengthen security and stability in the OSCE region; as such, it complements the mutually reinforcing efforts of other European and transatlantic institutions and organizations in this field.

7. Arms control constitutes an important element of our common security. The CFE Treaty, in particular, is and will remain key to our security and stability. The Forum for Security Co-operation (FSC), the work of which is also important to our security, has adopted two decisions defining new directions for further work, 'A Framework for Arms Control' and 'Development of the Agenda of the Forum for Security Co-operation'. As an example of co-operative security, the Open Skies Treaty, covering the territory from Vancouver to Vladivostok, aims at increased transparency among all Parties. Recalling the Budapest Decision of 1994, we once again strongly emphasize the significance of the entry into force and implementation of this Treaty. In addition, ending illegal arms supplies, in particular to zones of conflict, would make a major contribution to not only regional, but also global security.

8. We welcome the fulfilment by Kazakhstan, Ukraine and Belarus of their commitment to remove from their territory all nuclear warheads. This is an historic contribution to reducing the nuclear threat and to the creation of a common security space in Europe.

9. The OSCE's comprehensive approach to security requires improvement in the implementation of all commitments in the human dimension, in particular with respect to human rights and fundamental freedoms. This will further anchor the common values of a free and democratic society in all participating States, which is an essential foundation for our common security. Among the acute problems within the human dimension, the continuing violations of human rights, such

as involuntary migration, and the lack of full democratization, threats to independent media, electoral fraud, manifestations of aggressive nationalism, racism, chauvinism, xenophobia and anti-Semitism, continue to endanger stability in the OSCE region. We are committed to continuing to address these problems.

10. Against the background of recent refugee tragedies in the OSCE region and taking into account the issue of forced migration, we again condemn and pledge to refrain from any policy of 'ethnic cleansing' or mass expulsion. Our States will facilitate the return, in safety and in dignity, of refugees and internally displaced persons, according to international standards. Their reintegration into their places of origin must be pursued without discrimination. We commend the work of the ODIHR Migration Advisor and express support for his continuing activities to follow up on the Programme of Action agreed at the May 1996 Regional Conference to address the problems of refugees, displaced persons, other forms of involuntary displacement and returnees in the relevant States.

11. Freedom of the press and media are among the basic prerequisites for truly democratic and civil societies. In the Helsinki Final Act, we have pledged ourselves to respect this principle. There is a need to strengthen the implementation of OSCE commitments in the field of the media, taking into account, as appropriate, the work of other international organizations. We therefore task the Permanent Council to consider ways to increase the focus on implementation of OSCE commitments in the field of the media, as well as to elaborate a mandate for the appointment of an OSCE representative on freedom of the media to be submitted not later than to the 1997 Ministerial Council.

12. The same comprehensive approach to security requires continued efforts in the implementation of OSCE commitments in the economic dimension and an adequate development of OSCE activities dealing with security-related economic, social and environmental issues. The OSCE should focus on identifying the risks to security arising from economic, social and environmental problems, discussing their causes and potential consequences, and draw the attention of relevant international institutions to the need to take appropriate measures to alleviate the difficulties stemming from those risks. With this aim, the OSCE should further enhance its

ties to mutually-reinforcing international economic and financial institutions, including regular consultations at appropriate levels aimed at improving the ability to identify and assess at an early stage the security relevance of economic, social and environmental developments. Interaction with regional, sub-regional and transborder co-operative initiatives in the economic and environmental field should be enhanced, as they contribute to the promotion of good-neighbourly relations and security. We therefore task the Permanent Council to review the role of the OSCE Secretariat in the economic dimension, and to elaborate a mandate for a co-ordinator within the OSCE Secretariat on OSCE economic and environmental activities, to be submitted not later than the 1997 Ministerial Council.

13. We pay tribute to the achievements of the OSCE Mission to Bosnia and Herzegovina in helping to implement the General Framework Agreement for Peace in Bosnia and Herzegovina. Pragmatic co-operation with international institutions and IFOR, as well as the role of the High Representative, have contributed greatly to this success, thus demonstrating in a tangible way the kinds of co-operative undertakings on which security can be built through the action of mutually reinforcing institutions.

14. We welcome the agreement by the Presidency of Bosnia and Herzegovina on the establishment of the Council of Ministers, which represents an important step in forming fully effective joint institutions. Reaffirming the need for the full implementation of the Peace Agreement, we welcome the guiding principles agreed at the Meeting of the Ministerial Steering Board and the Presidency of Bosnia and Herzegovina in Paris on 14 November 1996, and the OSCE decision to extend its Mission's mandate to Bosnia and Herzegovina for 1997, noting its possible prolongation in the framework of the two-year consolidation period. We pledge ourselves to provide all necessary resources, financial and personnel, for the Mission to fulfil its mandate.

15. The OSCE will continue to play an important role in the promotion and consolidation of peace in Bosnia and Herzegovina based on OSCE principles and commitments. We confirm that we will supervise the preparation and conduct of elections for the municipal governing authorities in 1997, and welcome the agreement of the Parties to Annex 3 of the Peace Agreement in this regard. We will fully support the Mission's

work and its contribution to implementation of the election results. We will assist in democracy building through concrete programmes and be active in human rights promotion and monitoring. We will continue assisting in the implementation of subregional stabilization measures among the Parties to the Peace Agreement.

16. Recalling that the prime responsibility for implementing the Peace Agreement lies with the Parties themselves, we call upon them to co-operate in good faith with the OSCE and other institutions in implementing the civilian aspects of the Peace Agreement. The role of the High Representative will remain of particular importance in this context. We call upon the Parties to co-operate fully with the International Criminal Tribunal for the former Yugoslavia.

17. The Agreement on Confidence- and Security-Building Measures in Bosnia and Herzegovina and the Sub-Regional Arms Control Agreement will continue to play an important role in promoting and consolidating military stability in and around Bosnia and Herzegovina. Favourable conditions for full implementation of these Agreements should be fostered. Failure to meet the commitments under these Agreements remains, however, a serious concern. We support the November 1996 reaffirmation in Paris by the Ministerial Steering Board and the Presidency of Bosnia and Herzegovina of the necessity for full implementation and strict avoidance of circumvention of both Agreements. We call upon the Parties to fulfil their commitments through co-operation in good faith. With respect to regional arms control, and depending on satisfactory progress on the implementation of Articles II and IV, efforts undertaken to promote the implementation of Article V of Annex 1-B of the Peace Agreement will continue.

18. The implementation of the Peace Agreement for Bosnia and Herzegovina has opened the way for efforts at the regional and subregional levels aimed at the achievement of durable peace, stability and good neighbourliness in Southeastern Europe. We welcome the development of various initiatives fostering subregional dialogue and co-operation, such as the Stability Process initiated at Royaumont, the Southeastern European Co-operation Initiative, the Central European Initiative and the comprehensive process of stability, security and co-operation reactivated by the Sofia Declaration of the Ministers of Foreign Affairs of the countries of Southeastern Europe. The OSCE could contribute to using fully the potential of the various regional co-operative efforts in a mutually supportive and reinforcing way.

19. We welcome the OSCE's continuing focus on the Federal Republic of Yugoslavia. We express our expectation that the OSCE Mission of Long Duration to Kosovo, Sandjak and Vojvodina will be able to resume its work as soon as possible. In fulfilling its mandate, such a Mission should actively contribute, among other things, to following developments and fostering dialogue with a view to overcoming the existing difficulties. Other forms of OSCE involvement would also be desirable. They should include efforts to accelerate democratization, promote independent media and ensure free and fair elections. Recalling our previous declarations, we call for the development of a substantial dialogue between the Federal Authorities and the Albanian representatives of Kosovo in order to solve all pending problems there.

20. We reaffirm our utmost support for the sovereignty and territorial integrity of Georgia within its internationally recognized borders. We condemn the 'ethnic cleansing' resulting in mass destruction and forcible expulsion of predominantly Georgian population in Abkhazia. Destructive acts of separatists, including obstruction of the return of refugees and displaced persons and the decision to hold elections in Abkhazia and in the Tskhinvali region/South Ossetia, undermine the positive efforts undertaken to promote political settlement of these conflicts. We are convinced that the international community, in particular the United Nations and the OSCE with participation of the Russian Federation as a facilitator, should continue to contribute actively to the search for a peaceful settlement.

21. We note that some progress has been made towards a political settlement in Moldova. Real political will is needed now to overcome the remaining difficulties in order to achieve a solution based on the sovereignty and territorial integrity of the Republic of Moldova. We call on all sides to increase their efforts to that end. Recalling the Budapest Summit Decision, we reiterate our concern over the lack of progress in bringing into force and implementing the Moldo-Russian Agreement of 21 October 1994 on the withdrawal of Russian troops. We expect an early, orderly and complete withdrawal of the Russian troops. In fulfilment of the mandate

of the Mission and other relevant OSCE decisions, we confirm the commitment of the OSCE, including through its Mission, to follow closely the implementation of this process, as well as to assist in achieving a settlement in the eastern part of Moldova, in close co-operation with the Russian and Ukrainian mediators. The Chairman-in-Office will report on progress achieved to the next meeting of the Ministerial Council.

22. We welcome the recent steps towards a peaceful settlement in Chechnya, Russian Federation. We recognize the valuable role played by the OSCE Assistance Group in facilitating dialogue towards political resolution of the crisis. We believe that the Assistance Group should continue to play its role in the future, in particular with a view towards a lasting peaceful settlement, monitoring human rights and supporting humanitarian organizations.

23. We emphasize the importance of the Central Asian States in the OSCE. We are committed to increasing OSCE efforts aimed at developing democratic structures and the rule of law, maintaining stability and preventing conflicts in this area.

24. We are committed to further developing the dialogue with our Mediterranean partners for co-operation, Japan, and the Republic of Korea. In this context, strengthening security and co-operation in the Mediterranean is important for stability in the OSCE region. We welcome the continued interest displayed by the Mediterranean partners for co-operation, Japan, and the Republic of Korea in the OSCE, and the deepening of dialogue and co-operation with them. We invite them to participate in our activities, including meetings as appropriate.

25. The next Ministerial Council will take place in Copenhagen in December 1997.

26. We take note of the invitation by Turkey to host the next OSCE Summit in Istanbul.

27. Poland will exercise the function of Chairman-in-Office in 1998.

LISBON DECLARATION ON A COMMON AND COMPREHENSIVE SECURITY MODEL FOR EUROPE FOR THE TWENTY-FIRST CENTURY

Excerpts

1. We, the Heads of State or Government of the States participating in the OSCE and meeting in Lisbon, believe that history has offered us an unprecedented opportunity. Freedom, democracy and co-operation among our nations and peoples are now the foundation for our common security. We are determined to learn from the tragedies of the past and to translate our vision of a co-operative future into reality by creating a common security space free of dividing lines in which all States are equal partners.

(...)

6. We jointly commit ourselves:
– to act in solidarity to promote full implementation of the principles and commitments of the OSCE enshrined in the Helsinki Final Act, the Charter of Paris and other CSCE/OSCE documents;
– to consult promptly—in conformity with our OSCE responsibilities and making full use of the OSCE's procedures and instruments—with a participating State whose security is threatened and to consider jointly actions that may have to be undertaken in defence of our common values;
– not to support participating States that threaten or use force in violation of international law against the territorial integrity or political independence of any participating State;
– to attach importance to security concerns of all participating States irrespective of whether they belong to military structures or arrangements.

7. We reaffirm the inherent right of each and every participating State to be free to choose or change its security arrangements, including treaties of alliance, as they evolve. Each participating State will respect the rights of all others in this regard. They will not strengthen their security at the expense of the security of other States. Within the OSCE, no State, organization or grouping can have any superior responsibility for maintaining peace and stability in the OSCE region, or regard any part of the OSCE region as its sphere of influence.

8. We shall ensure that the presence of foreign troops on the territory of a participating State is in conformity with international law, the freely expressed consent of the host State, or a relevant decision of the United Nations Security Council.

9. We are committed to transparency in our actions and in our relations with one another. All our States participating in security arrangements will take into consideration that such arrangements should be of a public

nature, predictable and open, and should correspond to the needs of individual and collective security. These arrangements must not infringe upon the sovereign rights of other States and will take into account their legitimate security concerns.

We may use the OSCE as a repository for declarations and agreements in regard to our security arrangements.

(...)

– We commit ourselves to the continuation of the arms control process as a central security issue in the OSCE region.

The further strengthening of stability through conventional arms control will be decisive for future European security. We reaffirm the importance of the CFE Treaty and welcome the decision of the CFE States Parties to adapt it to a changing security environment in Europe so as to contribute to common and indivisible security.

We welcome the decisions on the 'Framework for Arms Control' and on the 'Development of the Agenda of the Forum for Security Co-operation' adopted by the Forum for Security Co-operation. We are determined to make further efforts in this Forum in order to jointly address common security concerns of participating States and to pursue the OSCE's comprehensive and co-operative concept of indivisible security.

In this context, we reaffirm that we shall maintain only such military capabilities as are commensurate with individual or collective legitimate security needs, taking into account rights and obligations under international law. We shall determine our military capabilities on the basis of national democratic procedures, in a transparent manner, bearing in mind the legitimate security concerns of other States as well as the need to contribute to international security and stability.

– We reaffirm that European security requires the widest co-operation and co-ordination among participating States and European and transatlantic organizations. The OSCE is the inclusive and comprehensive organization for consultation, decision-making and co-operation in its region and a regional arrangement under Chapter VIII of the United Nations Charter. As such it is particularly well suited as a forum to enhance co-operation and complementarity among such organizations and institutions. The OSCE will act in partnership with them, in order to respond effectively to threats and challenges in its area.

In exceptional circumstances the participating States may jointly decide to refer a matter to the United Nations Security Council on behalf of the OSCE whenever, in their judgement, action by the Security Council may be required under the relevant provisions of Chapter VII of the Charter of the United Nations.

– The OSCE will strengthen co-operation with other security organizations which are transparent and predictable in their actions, whose members individually and collectively adhere to OSCE principles and commitments, and whose membership is based on open and voluntary commitments.

11. Our work on the Security Model is well under way and will actively continue. We instruct our representatives to work energetically on the Security Model and invite the Chairman-in-Office to report to the next Ministerial Council in Copenhagen. The agenda for their work will include the following:

– continuing review of the observance of OSCE principles and implementation of commitments to ensure progress toward the goals of the OSCE and towards the work outlined in this agenda;

– enhancing instruments of joint co-operative action within the OSCE framework in the event of non-compliance with the OSCE commitments by a participating State;

– defining in a Platform for Co-operative Security modalities for co-operation between the OSCE and other security organizations as set out above;

– based on the experience of OSCE instruments for preventive diplomacy and conflict prevention, refining the existing tools and developing additional ones in order to encourage participating States to make greater use of the OSCE in advancing their security;

– enhancing co-operation among participating States to develop further the concepts and principles included in this Declaration and to improve our ability to meet specific risks and challenges to security;

– recommending any new commitments, structures or arrangements within the OSCE framework which would reinforce security and stability in Europe.

Drawing on this work, remaining committed to the Helsinki Final Act and recalling the Charter of Paris, we will consider developing a Charter on European Security which can serve the needs of our peoples in the new century.

12. Our goal is to transform our search for greater security into a mutual effort to

achieve the aspirations and improve the lives of all our citizens. This quest, grounded in pragmatic achievements as well as ideals, will draw on the flexible and dynamic nature of the OSCE and its central role in ensuring security and stability.

A FRAMEWORK FOR ARMS CONTROL (FSC.DEC/8/96)

Excerpts

I. INTRODUCTION

1. Arms control, including disarmament and confidence- and security-building, is integral to the OSCE's comprehensive and co-operative concept of security. The strong commitment of the OSCE participating States to full implementation and further development of arms control agreements is essential for enhancing military and political stability within the OSCE area. The positive trends of co-operation, transparency and predictability need to be strengthened.

2. Building on existing arms control measures, the OSCE will seek to develop new ways to deal with security concerns affecting all States in the OSCE area. Such security concerns include inter- or intra-State tensions and conflicts which might spread to affect the security of other States. The goal should be to develop a concept and structure that will support a range of arms control efforts, including on regional matters. At all times it will be important to ensure complementarity between OSCE-wide and regional approaches. Regional arms control efforts should be based *inter alia* on specific military security issues.

3. In order to provide this conceptual and structural coherence to the OSCE's efforts, the participating States have decided to establish a Framework for Arms Control, designed to create a web of interlocking and mutually reinforcing arms control obligations and commitments. The Framework will link current and future arms control efforts into a comprehensive structure. It will serve as a guide for future arms control negotiations amongst the participating States, and as a basis for the establishment of a flexible agenda for future work on arms control. The Framework will be an important contribution to wider OSCE efforts in the security field, and will complement ongoing work in the OSCE on a security model for the twenty-first century.

4. The basis for such a web already exists.

The CFE Treaty establishes a core of military stability and predictability, which is fundamental to the security of all participating States of the OSCE. The Vienna Document has brought about increased transparency and mutual confidence as regards the military forces and military activities of all OSCE participating States. The Code of Conduct has defined important norms for politico-military aspects of security. These existing obligations and commitments lie at the heart of the OSCE's concept of co-operative security.

The Treaty on Open Skies, which should enter into force as soon as possible, can make a major contribution to transparency and openness.

The arms control process under OSCE auspices initiated by the General Framework Agreement for Peace in Bosnia and Herzegovina is an important part of the OSCE's efforts to strengthen security and stability.

In addition to continued emphasis on the full implementation and appropriate further development of existing agreements, new negotiations and efforts are needed to complement their contribution in order to provide effective responses to the military challenges to the security of the OSCE participating States.

5. The lessons and achievements of past efforts, as well as the purposes, methods and negotiating principles set out in this document together form the basis for addressing the challenges and risks to military security in the OSCE area. Thus, subsequent negotiations and resulting agreements will be related conceptually to existing agreements within the Framework. The Forum for Security Co-operation has a key role to play in the way in which the OSCE links the many separate endeavours that individually and collectively contribute to the security and well-being of all participating States.

6. The purpose of the Framework is:

– to contribute to the further development of the OSCE area as an indivisible common security space by, *inter alia*, stimulating the elaboration of further arms control measures;

– to provide a basis for strengthening security and stability through tangible steps aimed at enhancing the security partnership among OSCE participating States;

– to enable OSCE participating States to deal with specific security problems in appropriate ways, not in isolation but as part of an overall OSCE undertaking to which all are committed;

– to create a web of interlocking and mutually reinforcing arms control obligations and commitments that will give expression to the principle that security is indivisible for all OSCE participating States;

– to provide structural coherence to the interrelationship between existing and future agreements;

– to provide a basis for the establishment of a flexible agenda for future arms control in the OSCE.

II. CHALLENGES AND RISKS

7. Challenges and risks in the field of military security still exist in the OSCE area and others may arise in the future. The Framework will help to promote co-operative responses to challenges and risks that may be dealt with through arms control measures. In doing so, the following issues, *inter alia*, should be addressed:

– military imbalances that may contribute to instabilities;

– inter-State tensions and conflicts, in particular in border areas, that affect military security;

– internal disputes with the potential to lead to military tensions or conflicts between States;

– enhancing transparency and predictability as regards the military intentions of States;

– helping to ensure democratic political control and guidance of military, paramilitary and security forces by constitutionally established authorities and the rule of law;

– ensuring that the evolution or establishment of multinational military and political organizations is fully compatible with the OSCE's comprehensive and co-operative concept of security, and is also fully consistent with arms control goals and objectives;

– ensuring that no participating State, organization or grouping strengthens its security at the expense of the security of others, or regards any part of the OSCE area as a particular sphere of influence;

– ensuring that the presence of foreign troops on the territory of a participating State is in conformity with international law, the freely expressed consent of the host State, or a relevant decision of the United Nations Security Council;

– ensuring full implementation of arms control agreements at all times, including times of crisis;

– ensuring through a process of regular review undertaken in the spirit of co-operative security, that arms control agreements continue to respond to security needs in the OSCE area;

– ensuring full co-operation, including co-operation in the implementation of existing commitments, in combating terrorism in all its forms and practices.

III. NEGOTIATING PRINCIPLES

8. Interlocking and mutually reinforcing arms control agreements are the logical consequence of the principle of the indivisibility of security. Accordingly, both negotiation of and implementation within the OSCE area of regional or other agreements not binding on all OSCE participating States are a matter of direct interest to all participating States. The OSCE participating States will continue efforts to build confidence and stability through freely negotiated arms control agreements. Arms control regimes will take into account the specific characteristics of the armed forces of individual participating States as well as already agreed commitments and obligations. Drawing on past experience, the OSCE participating States have developed the following principles, to serve as a guide for future negotiations. The applicability of each of these principles will depend on the particular security needs being addressed:

– *Sufficiency.* Arms control regimes should contain measures designed to ensure that each participating State will maintain only such military capabilities as are commensurate with legitimate individual or collective security needs, and will not attempt to impose military domination over any other participating State.

– *Transparency through information exchange.* A key element of an effective arms control regime is provision for complete, accurate and timely exchange of relevant information, including the size, structure, location and military doctrine of military forces as well as their activities.

– *Verification.* The measures adopted should be combined, as appropriate, with verification that is commensurate with their substance and significance. This should include verification sufficiently intrusive to permit an assessment of information exchanged and of the implementation of agreed measures subject to verification, thereby enhancing confidence.

– *Limitations on forces.* Limitations and, where necessary, reductions are an important element in the continuing search for security and stability at lower levels of forces. Other constraining provisions on armed forces and security-building measures continue to be significant elements in the quest for stability.

IV. GOALS AND METHODS FOR THE FURTHER DEVELOPMENT OF ARMS CONTROL

9. Among the goals of arms control and the methods to help strengthen stability and security and increase transparency, co-operation and confidence within the OSCE area should be the following:

– to strengthen the concept of the indivisibility of security;

– to improve existing OSCE-wide measures, based on a continuing evaluation of their effectiveness, and to develop as appropriate new ones, to deal with future and continuing security challenges;

– to move the discussion of regional security issues to a more practical and concrete plane, in order to devise measures aimed at reducing regional instability and military imbalances among OSCE participating States;

– to devise arms control measures for stabilizing specific crisis situations, including by making appropriate use of any relevant existing measures;

– to examine, as appropriate, the issue of limitations on armed forces and constraints on their activities;

– to take due account, in elaborating arms control measures, of the legitimate security interests of each participating State, irrespective of whether it belongs to a politico-military alliance;

– to develop transparency, consultation and co-operation in the evolution or establishment of multinational military and political organizations, recognizing in this context the inherent right of each participating State to choose or change its own security arrangements, including treaties of alliance;

– to ensure greater transparency by providing information to all participating States on the implementation within the OSCE area of regional or other agreements not binding on all OSCE participating States, as agreed by the signatories of such agreements;

– to improve existing verification provisions and to develop new ones, as necessary.

10. The participating States recognize that the full implementation, at all times, of the obligations and commitments they have agreed to makes an indispensable contribu-tion to the achievement of these goals. They intend to continue to follow that implementation closely on a regular basis, and to seek more effective methods of reviewing implementation, including by making the best use of existing expertise and resources.

V. BUILDING A WEB OF ARMS CONTROL AGREEMENTS

11. The participating States have undertaken a variety of obligations and commitments in the field of arms control. Such obligations and commitments are legally or politically binding, and vary in their substance and geographical scope, being global, OSCE-wide, regional or bilateral. The agreements listed in the Annex to this document constitute a basis for a web of interlocking and mutually-reinforcing agreements. The full implementation of the agreements listed is essential for building the collective and individual security of the participating States, irrespective of whether or not they are a party or signatory to these agreements.

12. Building on the results achieved, future work on arms control will address emerging and new challenges as well as further developing transparency, openness and co-operation in the military field. Future arms control agreements may be negotiated separately but would be integral to the web.

(...)

___

DOCUMENT ADOPTED BY THE STATES PARTIES TO THE TREATY ON CONVENTIONAL ARMED FORCES IN EUROPE ON THE SCOPE AND PARAMETERS OF THE PROCESS COMMISSIONED IN PARAGRAPH 19 OF THE FINAL DOCUMENT OF THE FIRST CFE TREATY REVIEW CONFERENCE

1 December 1996

I. INTRODUCTION

1. The States Parties have defined the following scope and parameters for the process commissioned in paragraph 19 of the Final Document of the First CFE Treaty Review Conference.

II. AIMS AND OBJECTIVES

2. The States Parties intend to improve the operation of the Treaty in a changing environ-

ment and, through that, the security of each State Party, irrespective of whether it belongs to a politico-military alliance. The character of this process should be such as to permit the Treaty to sustain its key role in the European security architecture, in conditions existing and foreseen.

3. The process should strengthen the Treaty's system of limitations, verification and information exchange. It should promote the Treaty's objectives and enhance its viability and effectiveness as the cornerstone of European security, introducing such new elements and making such adaptations, revisions or adjustments to existing elements as may be agreed to be necessary.

4. The process should preserve and strengthen overall and zonal stability and continue to prevent destabilizing accumulations of forces anywhere within the Treaty's area of application.

5. The process should further develop and consolidate the emerging new co-operative pattern of relationships between States Parties, based on mutual confidence, transparency, stability and predictability. It will aim to promote equally the security of all CFE States Parties. Acting within the context of the Treaty, States Parties will address new security risks and challenges through binding mechanisms, while taking into account the legitimate security interests of each State Party.

III. PRINCIPLES

6. The following principles will guide the process:

– arms control obligations, freely entered into, must be fully met;

– the integrity of the Treaty and its associated Documents must be preserved, that is to say a common commitment to the Treaty's objectives, achievements and efficient functioning;

– the results of the process must be internally consistent, coherent and an integrated whole;

– the States Parties will avoid a wholesale renegotiation of the Treaty, adopting specific adaptations for specific purposes;

– the process must be consistent with the OSCE's concept of comprehensive, indivisible and co-operative security, while bearing in mind States Parties' other security arrangements and obligations, their inherent right to choose or change security arrangements, the legitimate security interests of other States Parties, and the fundamental

right of each State Party to protect its national security individually;

– the existing Treaty and its associated Documents must remain fully in force and be implemented in good faith until such measures and adaptations as may be decided upon through this process have themselves come into operation;

– the States Parties will maintain, individually or in association with others, only such military capabilities as are commensurate with individual or collective legitimate security needs, taking into account their obligations under international law;

– the process should not result in any adverse effect on the legitimate security interests of any CFE State Party or other OSCE participating State;

– the process should recognize the importance of the CFE Treaty's adaptation for:

– the broader OSCE security context, in particular the ongoing dialogue in the Forum for Security Co-operation (FSC);

– the work on a common and comprehensive security model for the twenty-first century;

– separate regional arms control arrangements and negotiations, both existing and as they occur, will be taken into account.

IV. SCOPE

7. To meet the aims and objectives set out in Section II, and committed to the Principles recorded in Section III of this Document, the States Parties will consider and elaborate, as appropriate, specific measures and adaptations to the Treaty.

8. The scope of this process will be consistent with the original CFE mandate, taking account of developments since Treaty signature, and with agreements reached at the First CFE Treaty Review Conference, and will retain:

– all existing categories of Treaty-Limited Equipment (TLE) established by the Treaty and will not result in an increase in total numbers of TLE within the Treaty's area of application;

– all the scope and detail of the information and verification arrangements established by the Treaty;

– the area of application established by the Treaty.

9. Specific aspects of this process will involve, *inter alia*, consideration of the following:

– evolution of the group structure of the Treaty, as well as elaboration of provisions addressing participation of States Parties in the Treaty other than as members of a group;

– the functioning of the Treaty's system of limitations and its individual elements, that is:

– development of the Treaty's system of maximum levels for holdings, including the possibility to establish a system of national limits for TLE;

– in this context the development of the redistribution mechanisms in Article VII;

– the zonal provisions in Article IV of the Treaty, preserving the principle of zonal limitations, so that no destabilizing accumulations of forces should occur;

– the provisions in Article IV of the Treaty limiting aggregate numbers for a group of States Parties, preserving the principle that no destabilizing accumulations of forces should occur;

– the Treaty's provisions in relation to stationing forces;

– Article XIV and related provisions on Verification, the Protocol on Notification and Exchange of Information and the possibility of promoting further co-operation in the spheres of Information Exchange and Verification;

– the Treaty's provisions on designated permanent storage sites (DPSS);

– the possibility of accession to the Treaty by individual States who might request it, and related modalities;

– means to assure the full functioning of the Treaty in cases of crisis and conflict;

– the possibility of incorporating provisions designed to facilitate the involvement and co-operation of States Parties in peace-keeping operations conducted under the mandate of the United Nations or the OSCE;

– the possibility of extending the Treaty's coverage so as to include new, or expanded, categories of conventional armaments and equipment;

– provisions on temporary deployments.

10. Further measures and adaptations, additional to those listed in paragraph 9 above, may be taken under consideration as part of this process as it evolves.

V. TIMETABLE, MODALITIES AND MISCELLANEOUS

11. The States Parties have decided that:

– in order to permit the next phase of this process to commence promptly in 1997, in accordance with the scope and parameters defined in Sections II-IV above, the Joint Consultative Group (JCG), in Vienna, in parallel with its ongoing tasks, will take responsibility for these negotiations when it resumes work in January 1997;

– they will work in good faith with the aim of completing these negotiations as expeditiously as those conducted under the original Treaty mandate;

– they will consider a report on results achieved at the time of the OSCE Ministerial Meeting in Copenhagen;

– during these negotiations, the Chairman of the JCG should, on a frequent and regular basis, at the FSC inform all other OSCE participating States of the work done and progress made; and that States Parties should exchange views with other OSCE participating States and take into consideration the views expressed by the latter concerning their own security.

12. They also recall that:

– the JCG should, in parallel with these negotiations, intensively continue efforts directed at resolving the implementation issues contained in the Review Conference Final Document, recognizing that such efforts will contribute substantially to the success of the negotiating process;

– the existence of this negotiating process will not prevent the JCG from adopting concurrently additional measures for enhancing the operational functioning of the current Treaty.

VI. UNDERPINNING THE PROCESS

13. Building on the achievements of the Treaty on Conventional Armed Forces in Europe, States Parties commit themselves to exercise restraint during the period of negotiations as foreseen in the document in relation to the current postures and capabilities of their conventional armed forces—in particular with respect to their levels of forces and deployments—in the Treaty's area of application, in order to avoid that developments in the security situation in Europe would diminish the security of any State Party. This commitment is without prejudice to the outcome of the negotiations, or to voluntary decisions by the individual States Parties to reduce their force levels or deployments, or to their legitimate security interests.

Source: OSCE, Lisbon Document 1996, DOC.S/1/96, 3 Dec. 1996.

Part II. Military spending and armaments, 1996

Chapter 6. Military expenditure

Chapter 7. Military research and development

Chapter 8. Arms production

Chapter 9. The trade in major conventional weapons

6. Military expenditure

PAUL GEORGE, AGNÈS COURADES ALLEBECK and
EVAMARIA LOOSE-WEINTRAUB*

I. Introduction

Military spending by the NATO countries and members of the former Soviet bloc continued to decline in 1996, with expenditure in the United States alone falling by 5 per cent in real terms over the previous year. Overall NATO expenditure fell by 2.9 per cent in 1996, indicating a levelling off from the average reduction of 4.8 per cent for the previous three years. Expenditure for the European NATO countries remained virtually the same as the previous year, compared with a fall of more than 3 per cent per year in the period 1992–95.

Given the lack of reliable information on defence spending for Russia and many countries in the developing regions, it is infeasible to attempt to determine a meaningful global figure for military expenditure. China poses a particular problem for analysis because of the lack of transparency in defence spending as well as the difficulty of factoring in the many commercial activities of the military.[1] As NATO expenditure is the dominant component of overall world military spending, it is clear that the decline in aggregate global military expenditure noted in recent years was maintained in 1996. Nevertheless, analysis of regional trends in military expenditure for 1987–96 shows that the decline in NATO expenditure has not been matched in two important regions, the Middle East and South-East Asia.

In real terms, the three dominant spenders in South-East Asia, Malaysia (with an increase of more than 15 per cent), Singapore (an increase of 7 per cent) and Thailand (an increase of almost 23 per cent), in 1996 maintained the region's reputation as the fastest-growing defence spender. In North-East Asia, military expenditure grew by 2 per cent in real terms in Japan and by some 5 per cent in South Korea from 1995 to 1996. Because of the lack of data for 1996 for some important countries, it is not possible to provide comparable data for the Middle East region. However, there is no evidence that defence spending declined in the Middle East in 1996.

---

[1] Ball, N. *et al.*, 'World military expenditure', *SIPRI Yearbook 1994* (Oxford University Press: Oxford, 1994), pp. 441–48.

* Sections I, VI and VII were written by P. George; section II by A. Courades Allebeck; and sections III–V by E. Loose-Weintraub. The authors were assisted by Eva Jenkner and Boris Nevelev, whose contributions are gratefully acknowledged.

The levelling out of defence spending in South Asia, noted in the *SIPRI Yearbook 1996*,[2] continued in 1996. Aggregate expenditure in the region remained stable in real terms from 1995 to 1996. However the dominance of India and the lack of growth in official Indian defence spending in real terms distort the overall picture for South Asia. Military expenditure grew in real terms by some 2 per cent in Pakistan and by almost 29 per cent in Sri Lanka in the same period.

Although the lack of data makes it difficult to provide broad comparisons of trends in other regions, a subregional assessment of military expenditure in South America shows spending in Argentina and Paraguay being maintained at virtual parity with 1995 in real terms and increasing by more than 34 per cent in Chile. In other parts of the continent, tensions between Ecuador and Peru have probably led to upward pressure on their defence budgets, but neither country has provided information on its defence spending to SIPRI in 1996. In Ecuador, the military's receipt of 15 per cent of oil revenues was reconfirmed in 1995 for another 15 years. Colombia imposed a special war tax in 1996, which raised some $500 million for the purchase of transport and communications equipment to counter narcotics trafficking. In Central America, the establishment of democracy, at least formally, in all the Central American states, as well as the end of civil wars in both El Salvador and Nicaragua and the cease-fire in Guatemala, are reflected in declining military spending. Military spending in the major southern African states has declined in real terms since the collapse of apartheid, the end of the cold war and the remarkable improvement in the regional security environment.

Section II of this chapter examines developments in NATO, with particular emphasis on France. Section III provides an overview of defence budget developments in Russia and examines the process of military reform. Section IV deals with the 1996 defence budget of Ukraine, and Section V provides disaggregated military spending data for five countries in Central and Eastern Europe. Section VI analyses the impact of the end of conflict in Ethiopia on military spending levels and examines the 'peace dividend' resulting from the shift in resources from the military to the social sector. Section VII presents the conclusions.

II. NATO

By 1996 total NATO military spending had fallen by more than 25 per cent in real terms from its peak level in 1987.[3] However, there were indications that this trend was bottoming out, with a decline of 2.9 per cent in 1996 compared to the average annual decline of 4.8 per cent in the period 1993–95.

In 1996 the military spending of the United States and Canada continued to fall—by 5.0 and 7.7 per cent, respectively. While total European NATO spending increased in real terms by 0.4 per cent, it declined in Belgium, Den-

[2] George, P. *et al.*, 'Military expenditure', *SIPRI Yearbook 1996: Armaments, Disarmament and International Security* (Oxford University Press: Oxford, 1996), p. 325.

[3] See appendix 6B, table 6B.2, which provides military expenditure figures in constant 1990 dollars.

mark, Luxembourg and Spain and in the three biggest European defence spenders—France (by 2 per cent), Germany (3.1 per cent) and the United Kingdom (1.5 per cent).

From 1991 to 1996 German military expenditure declined in real terms by more than 22 per cent. In 1996 the entire cut was made in personnel costs and other operating expenditure,[4] while spending for equipment procurement rose by 2 per cent following an increase of 4 per cent in 1995. The 1997 German defence budget planned a further cut from 48.2 billion DM ($32 billion) to 46.3 billion DM ($31 billion), or a decline of 3.9 per cent.[5] Although the new Eurofighter aircraft was included in the budget plan, the decision about its funding was further postponed until 1997.[6]

The United Kingdom slowed the rate of decline in its military spending in 1996 following four years of major cuts especially focused on procurement. On 23 October 1996, British Defence Secretary Michael Portillo, underlining the widening gap in military capability between Europe and the United States, urged the NATO European partners to stop decreasing their defence budgets.[7] The 1997 budget for major equipment acquisitions increased by £1.2 billion ($1.9 billion) to about £6.5 billion ($10.1 billion).[8]

A few NATO countries—Greece, Italy, Norway and Portugal—deviated from the overall declining trend by noticeably increasing their military expenditure in 1996. Italy showed 11.9 per cent growth in real terms, nearly all of which was for personnel costs. Following two years of moderate growth, Greece increased its defence spending in real terms by 5.8 per cent in 1996, returning to its 1988 level. On 14 November 1996 a major Greek armament programme aimed at maintaining the military balance with Turkey was adopted.[9] Spared the tough budget cuts experienced by civil departments, the five-year defence programme amounted to 4 trillion drachmas ($16.6 billion), to be partially funded by US military loans (Foreign Military Financing, FMF) and loans sought in foreign capital markets. In spite of a moderate growth of 1.7 per cent in defence expenditure, Turkey increased equipment procurement by more than 20 per cent, while cutting personnel costs by almost 15 per cent. Turkey has planned a further increase in defence spending in 1997, mainly for

---

[4] See appendix 6A, table 6A.1, which shows the distribution of NATO military expenditure among different categories: personnel; other operating expenditures; and equipment for NATO member countries except France.

[5] Figures for 1997 budgets in this section do not follow the same definition as appendix 6B, which provides data on defence spending as defined by NATO. For further details on sources and methods, see appendix 6C. 'False notes at Ruehe's budget-cutting recital—SPD criticizes lack of clarity in the Defense Minister's budget', *Die Welt*, 16 Nov. 1996 (in German), in 'Germany: SPD questions defense budget proposals', Foreign Broadcast Information Service, *Daily Report–West Europe (FBIS-WEU)*, FBIS-WEU-62-224, 20 Nov. 1996.

[6] 'Coalition won't decide on Eurofighter until 1997—Ruehe demands sound fighter financing', *Die Welt*, 13 Nov. 1996 (in German), in 'Germany: Eurofighter funding delayed until 1997', FBIS-WEU-96-221, 15 Nov. 1996.

[7] Press Association, 23 Oct. 1996, in 'United Kingdom: defense secretary criticizes European defense cuts', FBIS-WEU-96-206, 24 Oct. 1996.

[8] *Defense News*, 2–8 Dec. 1996, p. 4.

[9] 'Greece: "mammoth" defense program unveiled', *Athens Ta Nea*, 14 Nov. 1996 (in Greek), in 'Our expensive defense', FBIS-WEU-96-224, 17 Dec. 1996.

weapon procurement.[10] In 1995 the shares of military expenditure in the gross domestic product (GDP) of Greece and Turkey were 4.4 and 4.0 per cent, respectively—slightly more than that of the United States and far above the average 1995 share of other NATO partners.[11]

While the decline in NATO defence spending was initially induced by the end of the cold war, the financial situation of member states was the second crucial factor. In the United States and France, discussed in the sections below, the budget deficit is a major focus of the debate on defence spending. For France, which until recently claimed that defence was so crucial that its policy should be defined only in terms of strategic requirements, regardless of the costs involved, the official acknowledgement of the financial limitations of defence spending is a novelty. Although the voted defence budgets have suffered from regular cuts since the beginning of the 1990s, the decline in expenditure was never planned as such.[12]

All the European Union (EU) members which are willing to join the European Monetary Union (EMU) have committed themselves to budget discipline, striving to conform to the single-currency criterion of a budget deficit ceiling of 3 per cent of GDP.[13] The countries concerned are now facing the challenge of setting priorities between meeting the EMU criteria and conducting their domestic affairs, including their defence policies.

The United States

The United States remains by far the largest spender within NATO, its military expenditure accounting for 57.7 per cent of total NATO spending in 1996.[14] For the fourth year, US military spending declined by 5 per cent in real terms in 1996, contributing to a drop of 32 per cent since 1987. This was the largest reduction of all the NATO members for this period. In 1996 US spending on equipment declined for the second year running by over 10 per cent.[15] By the end of 1996 US military forces were reduced to 1.46 million men and women from a total of 2.17 million in 1987.[16] In terms of the share of GDP, US defence spending fell from 6.3 per cent in 1987 to 3.8 per cent in 1995.[17]

---

[10] *Defense News*, 28 Oct.–3 Nov. 1996, pp. 1 and 32.

[11] See appendix 6B, table 6B.3, on the share of military expenditure in GDP.

[12] See the discussion on France below.

[13] According to Article 104c, Title VI, of the Treaty Establishing the European Community, Title II of the Treaty on European Union. *Treaty on European Union* (Office for Official Publications of the European Communities: Luxembourg, 1992), p. 27.

[14] This share, calculated in current prices and exchange rates, better reflects reality than a share calculated with constant values. It is based on data provided by NATO in *Financial and Economic Data Relating to NATO Defence*, Press release (96)168, 17 Dec. 1996.

[15] See appendix 6A, table 6A.1.

[16] William J. Perry, Secretary of Defense, US Department of Defense, *Annual Report to the President and the Congress* (US Government Printing Office: Washington, DC, Mar. 1996), Personnel tables, appendix C, p. C-1; and *Congressional Quarterly*, vol. 54, no. 10 (9 Mar. 1996), p. 627.

[17] See appendix 6B, table 6B.3.

The fiscal year 1997 defence budget

As in recent years, the fall in military expenditure was the subject of intensive budgetary debates between the US President and the Congress.[18]

In its fiscal year (FY) 1997 budget, released on 4 March 1996, the Clinton Administration requested $254.4 billion in budget authority for national defence, of which $242.6 billion was for the Department of Defense (DOD). This meant a 5.8 per cent decline in real terms in comparison to the previous fiscal year for the total budget authority.[19] According to a new, six-year, $1.55 trillion defence plan beginning in 1997 and running through 2002, the DOD budget would start rising again in FY 2000.[20] However, critics questioned the feasibility of increasing defence spending given the government's commitment to balance the federal budget by 2002. The US federal deficit for the fiscal year ending 30 September 1996 was $107 billion, the lowest annual deficit in 15 years.[21]

Congress added $11.2 billion to the Administration's 1997 budget request; $9.7 billion of the increase was for military procurement and research projects. The Administration's request of $2.80 billion for anti-missile defence was increased by 31 per cent to $3.65 billion. Despite earlier threats of a veto, President Clinton signed the Defence Appropriations Bill of $244.3 billion on 23 September 1996 and the Defence Authorization Bill of $265.6 billion on 30 September.[22]

In spite of Congress' amendments, procurement of new weapons was deferred again in the FY 1997 budget. According to a new modernization plan aimed at increasing force readiness in the next century, equipment funding would rise in FY 1998 with the goal of 40 per cent growth in real terms by 2001.[23]

As requested, the bill included a 3 per cent military pay rise. The reduction in military personnel was expected to be nearly completed by the end of FY 1997, although reductions in civilian personnel were still projected for the years ahead.

France

In 1996 France made its greatest changes in defence policy and subsequently in military spending since the major modernization plans of the early 1960s initiated by President Charles de Gaulle. A six-year military spending pro-

---

[18] For a background description of the US defence budget debate, see *SIPRI Yearbook 1996* (note 2), pp. 330–33.

[19] 'Clinton's Administration's FY 1997 Budget for National Defense', Press release, Center for Strategic and Budgetary Assessments, Washington, DC, 22 Mar. 1996.

[20] 'US defense budget goals: deterrence, fighting capability (Perry calls forward deployment, power projection key)', *European Wireless File* (United States Information Service, US Embassy: Stockholm). Version current on 4 Mar. 1996, URL <http://www.usia.usemb.se>.

[21] Schaffer, J., 'US fiscal deficit lowest in 15 years ($107.331 million deficit registered in 1996)', *European Wireless File,* United States Information Service, US Embassy: Stockholm. Version current on 28 Oct. 1996, URL <http://www.usia.usemb.se>.

[22] *Congressional Quarterly*, vol. 54, no. 44 (2 Nov. 1996), p. 3125.

[23] 'US defense budget goals . . .' (note 20).

gramme for the period 1997–2002, the first step in the reassessment of France's military requirements for the next 20 years, was presented to the National Assembly on 13 May 1996.[24] The plan for 1995–2000, adopted as late as 1994 but considered too expensive by the new government, was swept away. The budget of the Ministry of Defence for 1996 was purely transitional. It was reduced at mid-term by 3.7 billion francs ($726 million) and actual spending in 1996 amounted to 191.3 billion francs ($37.5 billion).[25]

As mentioned above, the crucial economic factor which led to the decision to plan for a decrease in military spending was the French budget deficit. During the period 1992–96 cumulated budget deficits almost tripled in comparison to the period 1987–91.[26] France plans to reduce its budget deficit share of GDP from 4.15 per cent in 1995 to 2 per cent in 1999 in order to conform to the EMU criterion. During the 1990s the defence budget has often been the object of mid-term adjustments because the budget could not accommodate the former military plan. In 1990–95 the defence budget accounted for the largest share (28.7 per cent) of the total budget freeze and cancellations, although it accounted for only 13 per cent of the total budget.[27] The main cuts were made in weapon procurement. Additional costs of penalties paid to industry for order delays and cancellations further burdened the budget. In 1996 alone 8 billion francs ($1.6 billion) in payments were carried over and penalties were imposed.[28]

Along with a major reduction in planned military spending, the proposed programme brought about fundamental changes in French defence policy. The three major reforms planned were the gradual transition from conscription to a completely professional army, the elimination of the land-based constituents of nuclear deterrence and the overhauling of the military industry. The underlying ambition of the new plan was to enable France to play a major role in the definition of a European defence policy.[29] On 5 December 1995 France decided to rejoin NATO's Military Committee as a part of a broader effort to reintegrate NATO.[30] The aim of the 1997–2002 plan is to adapt France's military capability in that perspective.

In order to facilitate the adoption of the 1997–2002 plan, President Jacques Chirac, whose term will end in May 2002, has given a commitment that the

[24] Assemblée Nationale, *Projet de loi relatif à la programmation militaire pour les années 1997–2002*, Document no. 2766 (Assemblée Nationale: Paris, 13 May 1996).

[25] The budget for the Ministry of Defence does not include pensions. This is the case for all budget figures discussed in this section. Assemblée Nationale, *Avis présenté par M. Arthur Paecht au nom de la commission des finances, de l'économie générale et du plan sur le projet de loi relatif à la programmation militaire pour les années 1997–2002*, Document no. 2826 (Assemblée Nationale: Paris, 29 May 1996), p. 29.

[26] Assemblée Nationale, Document no. 2826 (note 25), p. 30.

[27] Assemblée Nationale, Document no. 2826 (note 25), p. 31.

[28] These penalties amounted to 550 million francs ($110 million) in 1995 and 351 million francs ($70 million) in 1994. Assemblée Nationale, Document no. 2826 (note 25), p. 27.

[29] Assemblée Nationale, Document no. 2766 (note 24), p. 7.

[30] France withdrew from NATO's integrated military command in 1966. 'Intervention du Ministre des Affaires Etrangères lors de la session ministérielle du Conseil de l'Atlantique Nord', 5 Dec. 1995. *Propos sur la Défense*, Document no. 55 (Ministère de la Défense, Service d'Information et de Relations Publiques des Armées (SIRPA): Paris, Dec. 1995), p. 25.

defence budget will not be the object of further cuts. As former head of the Rassemblement pour la République (RPR) Gaullist party, he was ironically the best placed to make fundamental changes in French doctrine and policy without provoking a storm of opposition. The government's determination to resume a final series of nuclear tests in September 1995 was seen by some observers as a concession to the military establishment before undertaking cuts in the defence budget and the restructuring of the armed forces.

The 1997–2002 military spending programme

The military spending programme for 1997–2002, planning a 14 per cent cut in spending, provides a yearly allocation of 185 billion francs, at 1995 prices, ($37 billion), including 99 billion francs ($19.8 billion) for operating costs and 86 billion francs ($17.2 billion) for equipment.[31] Although it was planned to reduce manpower by 28 per cent by 2015, the cost of force restructuring will not allow savings before the next six-year plan.[32]

Between 1991 and 1996, equipment expenditure by France fell by 27 per cent in real terms.[33] It was planned to reduce equipment expenditure by 17 per cent in comparison with the previous six-year plan. Nuclear programme allocations would be cut by almost 20 per cent, to 105.8 billion francs ($21.2 billion).[34]

The implementation of the 1997–2002 military spending programme is expected to have consequences both for the armed forces and for the defence industry.

France has finally opted for a smaller professional army. The transition from a conscript to a professional army by 2002 will entail a reduction of 23 per cent in the number of civil and military personnel of the Ministry of Defence. The three services will be affected differently by the restructuring. Manpower will be down-sized by 36 per cent for the Army, 24 per cent for the Air Force and 19.2 per cent for the Navy.[35] Worst hit, the Army will see 38 regiments disbanded, of which 11 are in Germany. Germany expressed regret that France planned to reduce its presence on German territory without prior consultation.[36] The German concern over the future of the Eurocorps was not officially discussed before the Franco-German summit in Nuremberg on 9 December 1996.[37]

---

[31] Assemblée Nationale, Document no. 2766 (note 24), p. 9.

[32] Assemblée Nationale, Document no. 2826 (note 25), p. 41.

[33] See appendix 6A, table 6A.2.

[34] Assemblée Nationale, Document no. 2826 (note 25), p. 93.

[35] Assemblée Nationale, *Rapport fait par M. Michel Voisin au nom de la commission de la défense nationale et des forces armées sur le projet de loi relatif aux mesures en faveur du personnel militaire dans le cadre de la professionnalisation des armées,* Document no. 3003 (Assemblée Nationale: Paris, 2 Oct. 1996), p. 12.

[36] *Le Monde,* 15 Feb. 1996, p. 6.

[37] 'Common Franco-German concept on security and defence', text reproduced in *Le Monde,* 30 Jan. 1997, p. 13.

Table 6.1. Personnel of the French Ministry of Defence according to the 1997–2002 plan

	1996		2002	
	No. personnel	Share (%)	No. personnel	Share (%)
Professional soldiers	297 836	*52*	330 012	*75*
Civilian personnel	73 747	*13*	83 023	*19*
Conscripts/volunteers	201 498	*35*	27 171	*6*
Total	**573 081**	*100*	**440 206**	*100*

Source: Assemblée Nationale, *Rapport fait au nom de la commission des Affaires Etrangères, de la Défense et des forces armées sur le projet de loi relatif à la programmation militaire pour les années 1997–2002 relatif aux mesures en faveur du personnel militaire dans le cadre de la professionnalisation des armées*, Document no. 3003 (Assemblée Nationale: Paris, 2 Oct. 1996), p. 10.

As procurement was the main object of the planned budgetary cuts almost all the programmes were down-sized and/or delayed,[38] although no major programme was cancelled. The most criticized programme revision was that of the Rafale fighter aircraft. In the 1997–2002 plan, the Rafale programme, which had been suspended in early 1996 and for which there were orders for the Navy and the Air Force, was to be further postponed for three years, bringing the total programme delay to 10 years. A few weeks after the plan was adopted, the government signed a contract with Dassault for 48 Rafale aircraft, of which 10 were for export. Development was to be finished by the end of 1997 and the first deliveries brought forward to 2001 instead of 2005. As the contract remains secret, it is not known if the company accepted the 10 per cent decrease in costs requested by the government. The Ministry of Defence acknowledged that orders were placed because Dassault finally agreed to the principle of its fusion with Aérospatiale. It was not specified where the extra funding for the new order (17–20 billion francs, or $3.4–5 billion) would come from.[39]

The restructuring of the French defence industry, in order to make it more competitive, was one of the main objectives of the 1997–2002 plan. The planned reforms are the hoped-for merger of Dassault and Aérospatiale, the privatization of Thomson CSF and the restructuring of the state-owned GIAT Industries and Direction des Constructions Navales (DCN).[40] The first attempt to privatize Thomson-CSF failed in 1996 and plans for concentration in the aerospace industry were not discussed seriously until early 1997.[41] The gov-

---

[38] See chapter 7 in this volume for a detailed list of cancelled and modified programmes; and Assemblée Nationale, Document no. 2826 (note 25), pp. 153–55.

[39] *Le Monde*, 25 Jan. 1997, p. 16.

[40] Assemblée Nationale, Document no. 2826 (note 25), p. 95.

[41] For a discussion on developments in the French defence industry, see Sköns, E., 'Arms production', *SIPRI Yearbook 1996* (note 2), pp. 427–28.

ernment planned procurement funding on the assumption of a 30 per cent decrease in programme costs within six years.[42]

The French defence industry has experienced severe reductions in personnel since 1990. Of 252 500 direct jobs provided by the defence sector in 1990, only 193 000 remained in 1996.[43] To fulfil the 30 per cent cost decrease, a further 50 000–75 000 of approximately 250 000 direct and indirect defence jobs should disappear by 2002.[44] State-controlled companies, long protected by their status, are the most concerned for their future. As a consequence of the 1997–2002 plan, GIAT Industries planned to cut 2570 of 11 000 jobs. DCN, the warship builder, announced that, of 24 000 employees, 6730 would have to leave. The Délégation Générale pour l'Armement (DGA), France's armaments board, accountable for 10 per cent of the programme cost, was also asked to reduce its costs and personnel.[45]

III. Russia

The debate over the 1996 defence budget of the Russian Federation was in many respects a repetition of the 1995 budget debate. The main difference was that the overriding government aim was to have the 1996 budget in place by 1 January 1996, the start of the fiscal year. The twin purposes of this were to improve budget implementation and to ensure that the 1996 budget was passed by the outgoing parliament, which was perceived to be more supportive of the government's economic reform strategy.

Fiscal policy in the Russian Federation is still impaired by problems with tax collection, made even more acute by improvised tax measures, the granting of tax concessions to large companies, and the resurgence of wage and tax arrears caused by unsustainable promises to the electorate.

The 1996 defence budget process

The 1996 federal budget was approved by the State Duma[46] on 19 December 1995. It provided for an increase in defence expenditure from 59.4 trillion roubles[47] in 1995 to 80.2 trillion roubles in 1996, which was 24 per cent of the

---

[42] Assemblée Nationale, *Rapport fait par M. Jacques Boyon au nom de la commission de la défense nationale et des forces armées sur le projet de loi relatif à la programmation militaires pour les années 1997–2002*, Document no. 2827 (Assemblée Nationale: Paris, 30 May 1996), p. 136.

[43] Assemblée Nationale, *Avis présenté par M. Jean-Guy Branger au nom de la commission de la défense nationale et des forces armées sur le projet de loi de finances de 1992—défense, recherche et industrie de l'armement*, Document no. 2258 (Assemblée Nationale: Paris, 9 Oct. 1991), p. 14; and *La Tribune Desfossés*, 15 Feb. 1996.

[44] *Le Monde*, 5 Oct. 1996, p. 1.

[45] Assemblée Nationale, *Rapport fait par M. Philippe Auberger au nom de la commission des finances, de l'économie générale et du plan sur le projet de loi de finances de 1997*, Document no. 3030 (Assemblée Nationale: Paris, 10 Oct. 1996), p. 65.

[46] Under the new constitution the Russian Parliament consists of 2 chambers: upper (the Federation Council) and lower (the State Duma).

[47] Figures for Russian military expenditure are not converted to US dollars because none of the available rouble–dollar exchange rates is as yet appropriate for international comparisons.

federal budget or 3.5 per cent of GDP (see table 6.2).[48] In 1995 actual spending on 'national defence' was 47.6 trillion roubles, or 2.9 per cent of GDP.[49] The initial 1996 defence budget allocation was for about 78 trillion roubles,[50] but the confirmed budget plan for outlays on 'national defence' shows a slightly higher allocation of 80.2 trillion roubles, which indicates that the 1996 defence budget was eventually implemented in full.

Russian military expenditure dropped drastically over the period 1991–96. In 1991, at the end of the Soviet era, defence spending accounted for 8.6 per cent of GDP—a much greater share than in 1996. As in previous years, in 1996 the military's opening bid was far in excess of the sum the government was prepared to accept, and even the proposal by the Defence Committee of the Duma was turned down.[51] According to Deputy Defence Minister Andrey Kokoshin, Russia's military expenditure should reach at least 5–6 per cent of GDP 'to ensure a worthy life for the Armed Forces and rescue the defence industry'.[52] However, the government's publicly declared aim remained to preserve 1996 defence spending at the 1995 level.[53]

Russian defence officials had claimed that the entire industry was facing 'absolute disaster' unless extra financing was provided. The government responded on 3 August 1995 and a revised budget was agreed, setting defence spending slightly above the initial budget—at about 79 trillion roubles.[54]

The government's inflation forecast for 1996 was based on an unrealistic assumption that the rate of growth would be 1.2 per cent per month. After a Conciliatory Commission met to discuss the issue and the government revised the figures in October, with the crucial inflation forecast being raised to 1.9 per cent a month, the draft budget was submitted to the Duma and finally signed by President Boris Yeltsin on 31 December 1995.

The 1996 defence budget

Even though Russia has started to publish more figures under six major categories in the federal budget, these figures are highly aggregated.[55] Many addi-

---

[48] *Rossiyskaya Gazeta*, 10 Jan. 1996, p. 3.

[49] *Rossiyskaya Ekonomika v Pervom Polugody 1996 Goda* (Institute for the Economy in Transition: Moscow, Sep. 1996), p. 12.

[50] 'Russia: 1997 budget expenditures detailed, 1997 federal budget outlays (from an explanatory memorandum of the Ministry of Finance to the 1997 draft federal budget)', *Rossiyskaya Gazeta*, 21 Sep. 1996, pp. 8–10 (in Russian), in Foreign Broadcast Information Service, *Daily Report–Central Eurasia (FBIS-SOV)*, FBIS-SOV-96-211-S, 21 Sep. 1996, p. 1.

[51] The Ministry of Defence had asked for 135 trillion roubles; the Defence Committee's proposal of 110 trillion roubles was turned down. Interfax (Moscow), 3 Oct. 1995, in 'Duma Defence Committee demands raise in 1996 budget', FBIS-SOV-95-192, 4 Oct. 1995, p. 29.

[52] ITAR-TASS (Moscow), 27 Oct. 1995, in 'Military calls on Duma to raise defence expenditure', FBIS-SOV-95-209, 30 Oct. 1995, p. 42.

[53] *Rossiyskaya Gazeta*, 29 June 1995, p. 1 (in Russian), in 'Military issues: Yeltsin on security issues, military reform', FBIS-SOV-95-125, 29 June 1995, pp. 25–27.

[54] *Delovoy Mir*, 28 Sep. 1995; BBC, *Summary of World Broadcasts*, SU/2412 S1/3, 19 Sep. 1995; *Krasnaya Zvezda*, 4 Oct. 1995; and *Voprosy Ekonomiki*, no. 9 (1995), p. 151 (GDP forecast).

[55] In 1995 Russia provided the OSCE with a defence planning document which included a table of defence budget data for 1995. OSCE document AC/127-D/808, 5 July 1996, annex V. The submission of such data remains erratic, however, despite the commitment under the Vienna Document 1994 to provide

tional costs associated with defence appear in other areas of the federal budget, while a number of military-related agencies are considered to be semi-autonomous and 'civilian' for budgetary purposes.[56] Some points about the total figure should be made. There is a distinction between (a) the official defence budget allocation, the 'national defence' article of the budget law, which covers the basic allocations to the Ministry of Defence and the nuclear weapon-related activities of the Ministry of Atomic Energy (Minatom), and (b) various defence-related allocations included under other chapters of the budget. According to the NATO definition, applied by SIPRI, 'other forces', for example, internal troops and border guards, are also included in defence expenditure. They are shown in table 6.2 in 'total military budget'.

The budget for 1996 was prepared on the basis of a Ministry of Economics forecast for the GDP of 2300 trillion roubles. If the budget for 'other forces' of 12.7 trillion roubles is included in the confirmed budget figure of 80.2 trillion roubles, the total military budget amounts to 92.7 trillion roubles, or 4 per cent of GDP. In reality it is impossible to tell what the precise figure is because financial data are not yet available or unreliable and because only some of the defence off-budget items can be discerned in the federal budget.

The bulk, or 51.3 per cent, of the defence budget went to personnel and operation and maintenance (O&M) spending—salaries, operations, pensions and infrastructure, mainly housing—while only 16.5 per cent was allocated for procurement. The Ministry of Defence Industries considers this wholly insufficient and has requested a supplementary budget of 7 trillion roubles for procurement.[57] Procurement fell by 2.4 per cent over the figure for 1995. Notwithstanding Yeltsin's concern and the commitment to a 10 per cent share for research and development (R&D), its proportion of total expenditure of about 8 per cent in 1996 is roughly the same as in 1995. The contraction of the science base of the defence industry and progressive erosion of its capacity are giving rise to mounting concern within the military.

Mobilization allocations in 1996 were very low—only 0.4 per cent of the budget. This is surprising since the war in Chechnya, with the final cease-fire agreement in August 1996, was undoubtedly a major strain on the defence budget, especially when the cost of the Russian troop withdrawal is taken into account. The draft budget for 1996 apparently does not contain any special allocation for the military in connection with Chechnya. Very little information has been released on funding of the Chechnya war. The cost must have been absorbed within the budget, with no evidence of any additional funding through other channels. In December 1996 Defence Minister Igor Rodionov and Prime Minister Viktor Chernomyrdin together with the Finance Ministry discussed the funding of the armed forces and in particular the Russian troop withdrawal from Chechnya. A decision was taken to allocate 100 billion

such information no later than 2 months after the budget has been formally approved. Thus, at the time of writing, no 1996 budget breakdown has been provided. Sections of the federal budget still remain secret as does the detail in long-term planning documents.

[56] For example, the Defence Federal Road Building Directorate, formerly the Construction Troops and the Federal Administration of Railway Troops, has been attached to the Railway Ministry.

[57] Zhigulsky, A., 'Russia slashes weapon buys', *Defense News*, vol. 11, no. 9 (4–20 Mar. 1996), p. 3.

Table 6.2. Russia's defence budget, 1996[a]

	Budget (tr. current roubles)	Share of total official defence budget (%)	Share of total military budget (%)[b]
Operations and maintenance (O&M)	41.1	51.3	44.3
Procurement	13.2[c]	16.5	14.2
Research and development (R&D)	6.5	8.1	7.0
Construction	7.6	9.5	8.2
Pensions	9.9	12.3	10.7
Ministry of Defence total	**78.3**		
Minatom (nuclear weapons)	1.5	1.9	1.6
Mobilization	0.3	0.4	0.3
Other	0.1	–	0.1
Total official defence budget	**80.2**	**100.0**	
Internal troops of the Ministry of Interior	3.3		3.6
State security organs	5.1		5.5
Border troops	4.1		4.4
Total military budget	**92.7**		**100.0**
Total expenditure (tr. roubles)		347.2	
Total official defence budget as share of GDP (%)		3.5[d]	
Total military budget as share of GDP (%)		4.0	

[a] As approved by President Boris Yeltsin on 31 Dec. 1995 and published on 10 Jan. 1996.

[b] Figures may not add up to totals due to rounding.

[c] Including 2.1 trillion roubles to settle debts from 1995.

[d] The GDP forecast for 1996 on which the budget is based is 2300 trillion roubles.

Sources: *Rossiyskaya Gazeta*, 10 Jan. 1996; and *Sobranie zakonodatel'stva Rossiyskoy Federatsii* [Collected legislation of the Russian Federation] (Moscow), no. 1 (1996), article 21. Background material was provided by Julian Cooper, Centre for Russian and East European Studies, University of Birmingham.

roubles to the Defence Ministry to settle its units in their new bases; the Interior Ministry will receive an additional 60 billion roubles and the Federal Security Service 10 billion roubles.[58]

Despite years of debate about military reform and President Yeltsin's May 1996 decree to establish a professional army, Russia is no closer to its goal of creating a streamlined, professional force by the year 2000.[59] The defence budget covers only 35 per cent of the military's existing expenses and Yeltsin has not provided the funds professionalization would require.

On the contrary, Lev Rokhlin, chairman of the State Duma Defence Committee, stated that the government's debt overhang from previous years to the

---

[58] *NTV 'Segodnya' Newscast* (Moscow), 21 Dec. 1996 (in Russian), in 'Russia: Chernomyrdin, Rodionov, officials discuss army funding', FBIS-SOV-96-247, 24 Dec. 1996, p. 1.

[59] The Russian Federation budget specified 1 469 900 servicemen in the federal armed services, with a further 600 000 civilian staff (not including manpower of the Border Service, the Interior Ministry or other law-enforcement agencies).

armed forces (e.g., to enterprises for equipment that was ordered but never paid for) amounted to more than 15 trillion roubles.[60]

The 1997 defence budget

The 1997 defence budget of 101 trillion roubles was passed on 24 January 1997.[61] It represents 19.1 per cent of total government expenditure, or 3.7 per cent of Russia's estimated GDP.[62] If spending on 'other forces' of 16.3 trillion roubles is included, the total military budget is 117.4 trillion roubles (table 6.3). According to Defence Minister Rodionov, the 1997 budget covers only one-third of the necessary expenses for the armed forces, and the package of measures to prepare for and implement military reform has not been fulfilled. After losing an internal government battle with the Finance Ministry (the Defence Ministry proposed 260 trillion roubles),[63] Rodionov took the unusual step of issuing a press release to protest against the budget package before it was released publicly.[64]

At the time of writing, the federal budget indicated separately allocations of 6.5 trillion roubles for military reform, including 396 billion roubles that will be saved from a reduction of spending on the 'national defence' article and 2.1 trillion roubles to be saved by cutting the capital spending envisaged by the Defence Ministry estimate. In addition 2.8 trillion roubles are being allocated to implement the housing programme for servicemen, and expenditure for financing the investment programmes linked with the conversion of the defence industry is to be increased from 2 trillion to 2.5 trillion roubles.[65] Efforts to gain more than a marginal real increase in one component of defence outlays necessarily force difficult choices over concomitant cuts in other parts of the budget. However, it looks for the first time as if spending on military reform and personnel cuts in the army will be specially fixed in the budget. According to Russian First Deputy Finance Minister Vladimir Petrov, about 50 000 officers will be discharged in 1997 as a result of military reform and personnel cuts. The draft 1997 federal budget envisages over 6.5 trillion roubles in discharge benefits, spending on relocation, housing and pensions, and additional compensation for discharged officers.[66]

---

[60] Corley, F., 'Russia phases out conscription', *Jane's Intelligence Review & Jane's Sentinel Pointer*, vol. 3, no. 7 (July 1996), p. 3.

[61] Open Media Research Institute, *OMRI Daily Digest*, part I, no. 18 (27 Jan 1997).

[62] 'Russia: 1997 budget expenditures detailed . . .' (note 50).

[63] Interfax (Moscow), 23 Aug. 1996, in 'Russia: Rodionov says proposed defence expenditures inadequate', FBIS-SOV-96-165, 23 Aug. 1996, p. 14.

[64] Yudin, P., 'Russian Parliament prepares for defence budget battle', *Defense News*, vol. 11, no. 38 (23–29 Sep. 1996), p. 20.

[65] ITAR-TASS (Moscow), 28 Oct. 1996, in 'Russia: government submits finalized 1997 draft budget to Duma', FBIS-SOV-96-209, 29 Oct. 1996.

[66] Interfax (Moscow), 24 Oct. 1996, in 'Russia: deficit figures included in modified draft federal budget', FBIS-SOV-96-207, 25 Oct. 1996.

Table 6.3. Russia's defence budget, 1997[a]

	Budget (tr. current roubles)	Share of total official defence budget (%)	Share of total military budget (%)[b]
Operations and maintenance (O&M)	48.0	47.5	40.9
Procurement	23.0	22.8	19.6
R&D	6.4	6.3	5.5
Construction	3.2	3.2	2.7
Pensions	18.0	17.8	15.3
Ministry of Defence total	**98.6**		
Minatom military programmes	2.4	2.4	2.0
Total official defence budget	**101.0**	*100.0*	
Internal troops of the Ministry of Interior	3.9		3.3
State security organs	6.6		5.6
Border troops	5.9		5.0
Total military budget	**117.4**		*100.0*

[a] As submitted by the government to the State Duma, the lower house of parliament, Sep. 1996.

[b] Figures may not add up to totals due to rounding.

Sources: Institute for Defense and Disarmament Studies (IDDS), *Arms Control Reporter*, Brookline, Mass.), sheet 240.B-1.70, Nov. 1996; 'Russia: defence budget prospects seen as bad dream', *Krasnaya Zvezda*, 29 Aug. 1996, p. 1 (in Russian), in FBIS-SOV-96-169, 29 Aug. 1996, pp. 14–15; and 'Russia: 1997 budget expenditures detailed', *Delovoy Mir*, 21 Sep. 1996, p. 1 (in Russian), in FBIS-SOV-96-211-5, 21 Sep. 1996, p. 1.

IV. Ukraine

Overall, the economic performance of Ukraine after independence has been worse than that of Russia. When it was part of the USSR, Ukraine was heavily industrialized, with large parts of its industry oriented, directly or indirectly, towards military production. Economic reform has been slow, particularly in the financial sector and in privatization. Ukraine lacks Russia's huge reserve of energy and raw-material supplies and is therefore highly dependent on natural gas and crude oil imports from Russia and Turkmenistan. The enormous increase in the cost of these imports since 1991 has been a major factor contributing to Ukraine's subsequent economic decline. The official decline in GDP between 1990 and 1995 was as massive as 58.5 per cent.[67] Inflation, at times hyper-inflation, has been a chronic problem since independence and inflation remained high, at 180 per cent, in 1995.[68]

[67] *Eastern Europe and the Commonwealth of Independent States 1997: A Political and Economic Survey* (Europa Publications: London, 1997), p. 802.

[68] Organisation for Economic Co-operation and Development (OECD), *OECD Economic Outlook*, no. 60 (Dec. 1996), p. 125.

The 1996 defence budget

While the Chechnya operation highlighted the crisis affecting the Russian armed forces, a similar crisis affecting the Ukrainian armed forces appears to be as bad, if not worse. The decline in discipline has been blamed on the general economic malaise which has produced a large number of social problems as well as low salaries and low prestige. Approximately 80 000 officers are without housing in spite of the fact that the situation was to have been corrected by the construction of accommodations with funds received from sales of surplus equipment. (Ukraine's arms stockpiles are colossal, much being inherited from the former USSR when the then Soviet republic was in the front line against NATO.)[69]

In 1994 the Ministry of Defence had asked for 631 billion karbovanets (c. $1.9 billion) but was allocated only about 280 billion karbovanets (c. $855 million).[70]

In April 1995 the Ukrainian Parliament voted in favour of a large International Monetary Fund (IMF) stabilization loan which was essential for President Leonid Kuchma's reform programme. As a result, government expenditure was reduced by 4 per cent and the largest cut was made in the armed forces. Total defence expenditure in 1995 was 106 billion karbovanets (c. $721 million), of which the army received 960 million karbovanets (c. $657 million).[71] This represents only 6.5 per cent of total government expenditure compared with 18.9 per cent in Russia.[72]

In March 1996 the parliament approved total expenditure for defence purposes as proposed in the draft budget—187 billion karbovanets (c. $1.1 billion), or 2.5 per cent of GDP. If expenditure for 'other forces' of 64 billion karbovanets (c. $349.6 million) is included in conformity with the NATO definition, the military budget amounts to 244 billion karbovanets (c. $1.3 billion), or 3.3 per cent of GDP (table 6.4).

Although the armed forces asked for about 270 billion karbovanets (c. $1.5 billion) only 138 billion karbovanets (c. $748 million) were approved. This represents a substantial fall in real terms given the persistence of high inflation and only 54 per cent had been received by the Ministry of Defence by November 1996.[73] The budget allocation was insufficient to allow for even elementary modernization of weapons and equipment, procurement was only 10 per cent and the share of R&D 1.7 per cent.[74] Even though the largest share, 65 per cent, was allocated for O&M, this will cover only the most basic items

---

[69] Kuzio, T., 'The Ukrainian armed forces in crisis', *Jane's Intelligence Review*, vol. 7, no. 7 (July 1995), p. 305.

[70] *Vidomosti Verkhovnoi Radi Ukraini* [Register of the Supreme Rada (parliament) of Ukraine], no. 50 (1994), article 439, p. 1287.

[71] *Vidomosti Verkhovnoi Radi Ukraini* [Register of the Supreme Rada (parliament) of Ukraine], no. 16 (1995), article 111, p. 353.

[72] *Kommersant-Daily*, 21 Dec. 1995.

[73] Interfax (Moscow), 22 Nov. 1996, in 'Ukraine: government sends amendment of budget bill 1997 to parliament', FBIS-SOV-96-228, 26 Nov. 1996.

[74] Ukraine inherited from the former Soviet Union a sizeable military establishment which was estimated at 400 800 personnel in 1996. International Institute for Strategic Studies, *The Military Balance 1996/97* (Oxford University Press: Oxford, 1996), p. 101.

Table 6.4. Ukraine's defence budget, 1996

	Budget (current b. karbovanets)	Share of total official defence budget (%)	Share of total military budget (%)[a]
Operations and maintenance (O&M)	117	*65.0*	*48.0*
Procurement	18	*10.0*	*7.4*
Research and development (R&D)	3	*1.7*	*1.2*
Ministry of Defence total	**138**		
Construction[b]	11	*6.1*	*4.5*
Pensions	31	*17.2*	*12.7*
Total official defence budget	**180**	*100.0*	
Internal troops of the Ministry of Interior	49		*20.1*
Border troops	15		*6.1*
Total military budget	**244**		*100.0*

[a] Figures may not add up to totals due to rounding.

[b] Construction of housing for servicemen of Ministry of Defence.

Source: *Vidomosti Verkhovnoi Radi Ukraini* [Register of the Supreme Rada (parliament) of Ukraine], no. 16 (1996), article 71, p. 151.

such as food, salaries and communal utilities. Ukraine has decided to slow down a planned reduction in its army because of the severe lack of funding; the Defence Council approved a State Military Programme to achieve that goal by 2005. The programme envisages cutting the army from about 453 000 (excluding Strategic Nuclear Forces and the Black Sea Fleet) to about 350 000 by 2005, not by the end of 1996 as initially planned.[75] The state budget allocated only 1.43 billion hryvnya[76] (*c.* $817 million) for the armed forces in 1997. This means that the stagnation of the army will continue and so far no allocation for army reform has been made.

Plans announced by the Interior Ministry to reduce its troops from 52 000 to 30 000 by 1998 will depend on substantial defence expenditure increases. Increased provision for defence budgets is unlikely to be affordable for the near future since the lack of progress with economic reform is unlikely to be corrected quickly.

V. Central and Eastern Europe

The Central and East European (CEE) countries—Bulgaria, the Czech Republic, Hungary, Poland, Romania and Slovakia—have all reduced their military expenditure in real terms since the beginning of 1990, primarily for economic

[75] 'Army reduction to slow down due to lack of cash' (combined reports), *New Europe (East Europe)*, 5–12 Jan. 1997, p. 22.

[76] In Sep. 1996 Ukraine introduced a new currency, the hryvnya, at a rate of 100 000 karbovanets per 1 hryvnya; the exchange rate at the time was 1.75 hryvnya : $1.

reasons.[77] The military problems, shared to varying degrees by all the former Warsaw Treaty Organization (WTO) countries, revolve around the nationalization of defence; the redeployment, restructuring and depoliticization of the armed forces; the redefinition of national military doctrines; the preponderance of former Soviet equipment; and the excessive dependence on Russia and other republics of the former Soviet Union for the supply of spare parts.

Table 6.5 provides data on the distribution of military expenditure for personnel, operating costs, procurement, construction and R&D for Bulgaria, the Czech Republic, Hungary, Poland and Romania for 1990 and 1996. Spending on procurement of arms has declined remarkably for most of the countries, especially for Romania, which allocated about 45 percentage points less for procurement in 1996 compared to 1990. Personnel costs, on the other hand, increased, mostly in Poland, which spent about 33 percentage points more on personnel compared to 1990. R&D expenditure has decreased, especially in Poland, which had technologically one of the most advanced arms industries in the region.

In January 1994 NATO stated that it would welcome expansion of its membership to include the democratic states in the East.[78] NATO will name its first new members for almost two decades at a special summit meeting in Madrid in July 1997. If any of the four Visegrad nations eventually are admitted, the cost of adjusting for NATO membership[79] will have an impact on their forthcoming equipment priorities[80] as well as on their military expenditure.

While President Vaclav Havel initiated a campaign to increase the Czech Republic's proposed 1997 defence budget to 32 billion Czech korunas (c. $1.2 billion),[81] the adaptation of the Czech Army to NATO standards continues, particularly in the modernization of communications, computer and command systems. Hungary's defence budget is expected to increase nominally by about 20 per cent in 1997. The 96.2 billion forints (c. $604.7 million) defence budget proposal before parliament at the time of writing represents the first budget increase, after accounting for inflation, since the fall of the Berlin Wall in 1989. The budget includes a doubling of the share for procurement, from less

---

[77] See appendix 6B.

[78] See also chapter 5 in this volume.

[79] During 1996 there have been US studies by RAND, Santa Monica, Calif., and the US Congressional Budget Office (CBO) on the costs of expanding the NATO alliance. RAND estimated that to project NATO's air and ground defence capabilities to the Czech Republic, Hungary, Poland and the Slovak Republic would cost $42 billion over a 15-year period. The CBO study stated that costs would reach $125 billion. A third report by the Polish defence and foreign affairs ministries, 'Estimating cost of NATO enlargement: a contribution to the debate', described the CBO figure of $125 billion as 'unrealistic to the point of fantasy'. According to the Polish document there are 6 areas where Poland should aim to achieve compatibility with NATO forces. The report asserted that the overall cost to Poland of implementing interoperability measures would be c. $1.26 billion. Even adding on a yearly contribution to the alliance's operating budget, which all NATO members are required to make, Poland's total cost would still amount to less than $1.5 billion. Finally, in Feb. 1997 another US report to the Congress on the enlargement of NATO was released by the Bureau of European and Canadian Affairs, US Department of State. It estimated that the total cost associated with enlargement from 1997 to 2009 will be about $2.1–2.7 billion per year, or a total of about $27–35 billion.

[80] See chapter 9 in this volume.

[81] McNally, B., 'Czech's Havel decries cut in buying power', *Defense News,* vol. 11, no. 46 (18–24 Nov. 1996), pp. 3 and 32.

Table 6.5. Disaggregated military expenditure data for Bulgaria, the Czech Republic, Hungary, Poland and Romania, 1990 and 1996

Figures are percentages.

	Bulgaria		Czech Rep.		Hungary		Poland		Romania	
	1990	1996	1993[a]	1996	1990	1996	1990	1996	1990	1996
Personnel	28.9	35.4	36.8	47.8	36.9	55.9	32.9	65.7	17.5	44.1
O&M[b]	30.5	41.2	53.5	30.1	41.4	41.2	33.7	18.3	17.0	36.4
Procurement	36.3	21.5	2.4	14.5	11.1	1.3	22.8	13.1	62.6	17.2
Construction	3.6	1.5	6.1	4.8	0.5	1.5	8.8	1.2	1.6	1.2
R&D	0.8	0.5	1.2	3.0	0.5	0.1	2.4	0.8	1.3	1.0
Total[c]	100.0	100.0	100.0	100.0	100.0	100.0	100.0	100.0	100.0	100.0

[a] The Czech Republic was formed after the breakup of Czechoslovakia on 1 Jan. 1993.

[b] Operations and maintenance (includes civilian personnel cost).

[c] Figures may not add up to totals due to rounding.

Source: SIPRI military expenditure database.

than 5 per cent in 1996 to 10 per cent in 1997.[82] Poland's 1997 draft defence budget envisions a 5 per cent increase in real terms.[83]

VI. Ethiopia

Defence spending dominated the Ethiopian economy during the rule of the Dergue regime (1974–91). Military expenditure as a share of central government expenditure (CGE) averaged about 35 per cent during the last three full years of the civil war (1988–90) and never went below 25 per cent of CGE in the five years preceding the end of hostilities.[84] The end of the war raised the possibility that the excessive resources once devoted to the military could be shifted to more productive use in social sector development. Although there is not always a clear correlation between reductions in defence expenditure and greater investments in areas such as education and health, in the case of Ethiopia available data suggest that there has been a potential 'peace dividend' as a result of the end of the war.

The victory of the Ethiopian Popular Revolutionary Democratic Front (EPRDF), an alliance of various opposition parties and guerrilla groups, over the Dergue regime in May 1991 ended almost 30 years of civil war in Ethiopia and led to the independence of Eritrea.[85] Military spending has declined

[82] Dennis, S. *et al.,* 'Central European budgets are at cross-roads: Hungary sees first increase since 1989', *Defense News,* vol. 11, no. 46 (18–24 Nov. 1996), pp. 3–34.

[83] *Polska Zbrojna* (Warsaw), 8 Nov. 1996 (in Polish), in 'Poland: defense official on military budget', Foreign Broadcast Information Service, *Daily Report–East Europe (FBIS-EEU),* FBIS-EEU-96-224, 11 Nov. 1996, pp. 1–3.

[84] US Arms Control and Disarmament Agency, *World Military Expenditures and Arms Transfers 1995* (US Government Printing Office: Washington, DC, 1995), p. 73.

[85] Eritrea became an independent state in May 1993 and was admitted as the 182nd member of the United Nations on 28 May 1993.

Table 6.6. Ethiopian military expenditure, 1987–95

Figures for birr are in current prices; US$ figures are at 1990 prices and exchange rates.

	1987	1988	1989	1990	1991	1992	1993	1994	1995
Birr m.	1 174	1 508	1 751	1 740	1 121	667	703	710	726
US$ m.	689	826	890	840	399	215	219	205	191
Share of GDP (%)	7.8	9.6	10.6	10.0	5.9	3.3	3.1	2.7	2.5

Note: The rapid decline in defence spending after 1991 coincides with the breakaway of Eritrea to form an independent country.

Source: Appendix 6B, tables 6B.1–6B.3.

dramatically in Ethiopia since 1990–92 (see table 6.6). Ethiopia's military expenditure peaked at almost $900 million in 1989, declining to $191 million in 1995 (at 1990 prices and exchange rates). Military spending represented 2.5 per cent of Ethiopia's GDP in 1995, down from almost 11 per cent in 1989.[86]

Information on military spending in 1996 is not yet available but there is no indication that there will soon be a return to the high levels of defence spending seen in Ethiopia in the past. Although Ethiopian Prime Minister Meles Zenawi has claimed that Ethiopia's defence budget in terms of GDP is 'the lowest in Africa or anywhere else in the world',[87] assuming that the trends identified by SIPRI continue, the prime minister is underestimating Ethiopia's actual defence budget situation. Nevertheless, he is justified in drawing attention to the significant spending reductions which have occurred in recent years.

The composition of the defence budget in Ethiopia is classified so it is not possible to provide disaggregated figures showing the proportion of expenditure devoted to personnel, procurement and other items. However, personnel costs almost certainly constitute the greater part of the defence budget as there has been no arms procurement activity since the end of the war.

Force levels

At the end of the war in 1991, Ethiopia had the largest standing army in Africa, with about 500 000 soldiers under arms. It is estimated that some 455 000 of the Dergue regime's troops either were captured by the EPRDF, or returned autonomously to their home villages or sought sanctuary in remote regions of Ethiopia and in neighbouring countries. The new Transitional Government of Ethiopia (TGE) moved quickly to neutralize the potential security

[86] Total military spending in Ethiopia during the war years was higher than shown in official statistics, which do not include expenditure by the various opposition forces. Comparable data are not yet available for Eritrea.

[87] *Press Release*, vol. 1, no. 2 (Apr. 1996), Press and Public Relations Department, Office of the House of People's Representatives, House of Federation, Addis Ababa, p. 5.

threat posed by so many suddenly unemployed soldiers. One of the biggest demobilization and reintegration programmes ever seen was established with the formation of the Commission for the Rehabilitation of Members of the Former Army and Disabled War Veterans three weeks after the TGE took power. The demobilization process has led to the restructuring of the military and the establishment of a more professional force.

The policy of the government is to create an army that reflects the country's ethnic and regional diversity. To achieve this, a second demobilization programme has been under way since the end of 1994. Some 20 000 Tigrayan soldiers have reportedly already been demobilized and replaced by new recruits from the Oromo, Amhara and Southern Peoples ethnic groups. The training requirements for the new troops from ethnic groups and regions currently under-represented in the defence forces will probably lead to a short-term increase in defence spending. Parliament has authorized armed forces of 120 000 (of which the air force component is about 3000), but current force levels are believed to be running somewhat higher, at around 150 000–160 000.

The peace dividend

Recurrent defence expenditure declined from an average of 8.2 per cent of GDP for the period 1986–91 to 2.7 per cent of GDP in 1994. According to a study prepared for the Ministry of Finance, in the same period social sector expenditures increased slightly. Recurrent expenditure on education grew from an annual average of 2.4 per cent of GDP in the period 1986–91 to some 2.6 per cent in 1994, and spending on health increased from an annual average of 0.7 per cent of GDP in the same period to approximately 1.0 per cent in 1994. Figure 6.1 provides a clear comparison of the shift in resources from the military to the social sector in nominal terms since the end of the civil war. Growth in the social sector has been more marked in capital expenditure terms than it has been for recurrent expenditures since 1986–91, with spending on education more than doubling as a share of the capital budget by 1994.[88]

The transformation from the priorities of a war-based economy to post-conflict reconstruction and development is reflected in the fiscal record. The massive reduction in expenditures on the military has enabled the government to transfer resources to more productive sectors. The effects are clearly seen from the economic growth achieved by the country since the end of the civil war. The approximately 10 per cent of GDP which the government spent on defence in each of the last three full years of the war (1988–90) had a serious impact on an already weak economy. The impact of the end of the war combined with the introduction of economic reform on the economy in Ethiopia is evident. From FY 1992/93 to FY 1995/96 GDP grew at an average of 6.5 per cent annually and inflation has been brought under control. Annual inflation

[88] Peterson, S. B., 'Financial management issues of the Government of Ethiopia', Report prepared for the Ministry of Finance, Government of Ethiopia and the Ethiopia Mission, United States Agency for International Development, 18 June 1996, pp. 9–13.

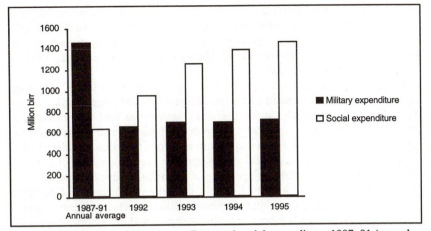

Figure 6.1. Ethiopian military expenditure and social expenditure, 1987–91 (annual average) and 1992–95 (m. birr, current prices)

peaked in FY 1990/91 at about 21 per cent and was as low as 1.2 per cent in FY 1995/96.[89] This performance clearly supports the contention that there has been a potential peace dividend in Ethiopia as a result of the end of the conflict.[90]

VII. Conclusions

The continuing decline in world military spending in 1996 largely reflects the ongoing consolidation of the defence forces and reductions in equipment purchases of the NATO members and the countries of the former Soviet bloc as a result of the end of the cold war. Although the overall downward trend in military spending patterns appears positive, military spending seems poised to start to increase in several countries and regions. The prospect of the expansion of NATO to the east has generated considerable debate about the potential cost of integrating new members. Although there is no definitive figure, it is likely that potential new members of NATO will have to increase their defence budgets to meet the force-modernization and infrastructural requirements of admission.

In the developing world the termination of conflicts in many countries, notably in Africa and Central America, has led to reductions in military spending and freed scarce resources for more productive use in sectors such as health and education. However, the collapse of traditional markets has driven

[89] 'Supply response to economic reform in Ethiopia', Paper presented by the Global Coalition for Africa at the Economic Committee Meeting hosted by the Government of the Federal Democratic Republic of Ethiopia, Addis Ababa, 26–27 Aug. 1996, p. 9.

[90] Although the social sector appears to have directly benefited from the major reductions in military spending that have occurred since 1991, this should be seen as a positive trend only. Confirmation that the identifiable increases in aggregate levels of spending in health and education have led to an improvement also in service delivery in these sectors would require further study.

all the major arms suppliers to actively seek new customers in the developing countries. Pressures are growing on countries in regions such as South America and South Asia to purchase new advanced weapon systems from the major suppliers in the former Soviet Union and the West and may lead to increases in defence budgets.

The general lack of accountability and transparency in defence budgeting can encourage corruption and undermine the principles of a democratic society as well as feed concerns about the size, capabilities and intentions of a country's armed forces. In order to help develop confidence between states, such developments must be closely monitored. As a first step, priority should be given to improving statistical information on the components of defence expenditure. Often, if military spending is specifically identified at all, it is shown as a single line item in a state's budget. A breakdown of military expenditure into its main functional classifications—personnel costs, operations and maintenance, procurement, and research and development—would permit more comprehensive analysis. Transparency will draw attention to military spending decisions and reduce the potential for uncertainty and misunderstanding to lead to conflict. It remains essential, therefore, that countries provide reliable information on their military spending.

Appendix 6A. Tables of NATO military expenditure

Table 6A.1. NATO distribution of military expenditure by category, 1987–96

Figures are in US $m. at 1990 prices and exchange rates. Figures in italics are percentage changes from previous year.

State	Item	1987	1988	1989	1990	1991	1992	1993	1994	1995	1996
North America											
Canada	Personnel	5 296	5 280	5 526	5 773	5 144	5 231	4 976	5 238	4 565	4 162
	Other oper. exp.	3 435	3 675	3 461	3 718	3 353	2 966	3 119	2 925	2 999	2 707
	Equipment	2 458	2 338	2 123	1 963	1 885	1 950	2 003	1 773	1 767	1 666
	Equip. change	*8.3*	*–4.9*	*–9.2*	*–7.5*	*–4.0*	*3.4*	*2.7*	*–11.5*	*–0.4*	*–5.7*
USA	Personnel	118 906	121 771	122 403	112 058	116 206	111 658	104 415	99 075	94 318	88 737
	Other oper. exp.	117 581	115 294	111 829	122 468	84 195	103 418	101 186	76 465	71 691	73 570
	Equipment	87 772	80 317	81 068	75 930	73 435	65 063	59 204	74 179	66 213	58 630
	Equip. change	*1.5*	*–8.5*	*0.9*	*–6.3*	*–3.3*	*–11.4*	*–9.0*	*25.3*	*–10.7*	*–11.5*
Europe											
Belgium	Personnel	3 116	3 061	3 175	3 177	3 155	2 455	2 485	2 461	2 474	2 372
	Other oper. exp.	1 018	980	946	924	920	797	732	721	682	747
	Equipment	657	577	468	367	375	308	250	277	188	172
	Equip. change	*2.2*	*–12.3*	*–18.8*	*–21.7*	*2.3*	*–17.9*	*–18.9*	*10.8*	*–32.2*	*–8.4*
Denmark	Personnel	1 469	1 574	1 584	1 547	1 543	1 502	1 507	1 519	1 549	1 526
	Other oper. exp.	721	657	612	620	612	577	693	590	625	621
	Equipment	397	391	347	395	426	471	387	411	320	323
	Equip. change	*12.4*	*–1.5*	*–11.2*	*13.8*	*7.9*	*10.6*	*–17.8*	*6.2*	*–22.2*	*0.9*
Germany	Personnel	19 960	20 000	20 515	22 049	22 196	22 090	20 197	19 226	19 390	18 457
	Other oper. exp.	10 102	10 262	9 635	8 041	7 059	8 896	8 466	7 463	7 020	6 590
	Equipment	8 155	7 767	7 628	7 491	6 118	5 014	3 774	3 447	3 588	3 661
	Equip. change	*0.2*	*–4.8*	*–1.8*	*–1.8*	*–18.3*	*–18.0*	*–24.7*	*–8.7*	*4.1*	*2.0*

State	Item	1987	1988	1989	1990	1991	1992	1993	1994	1995	1996
Greece	Personnel	2 379	2 373	2 349	2 476	2 359	2 338	2 311	2 381	2 436	2 492
	Other oper. exp.	740	656	535	475	498	487	390	454	574	660
	Equipment	663	950	836	827	744	891	918	922	762	859
	Equip. change	8.7	43.2	-12.0	-1.2	-10.1	19.8	3.0	0.5	-17.4	12.7
Italy	Personnel	13 393	13 938	14 266	14 400	15 195	14 666	14 559	14 809	13 892	16 395
	Other oper. exp.	4 086	4 630	4 496	4 231	4 077	4 259	4 028	3 838	3 422	3 390
	Equipment	4 676	4 943	4 982	4 091	3 864	3 454	3 981	3 499	3 092	3 067
	Equip. change	25.9	5.7	0.8	-17.9	-5.5	-10.6	15.3	-12.1	-11.6	-0.8
Luxembourg	Personnel	68	76	72	77	75	84	79	87	88	86
	Other oper. exp.	9	17	11	10	10	10	8	12	12	13
	Equipment	3	3	4	3	6	5	3	2	3	5
	Equip. change	43.9	-18.1	24.4	-12.4	86.4	-11.1	-44.5	-7.4	11.3	75.9
Netherlands	Personnel	4 072	4 106	4 101	4 000	3 984	4 125	3 914	3 707	3 705	3 430
	Other oper. exp.	1 816	1 520	1 695	1 655	1 653	1 621	1 450	1 329	1 321	1 316
	Equipment	1 352	1 542	1 344	1 328	1 126	1 019	923	1 068	963	1 149
	Equip. change	-10.7	14.1	-12.9	-1.2	-15.2	-9.5	-9.4	15.8	-9.8	19.3
Norway	Personnel	1 490	1 495	1 435	1 470	1 525	1 563	1 197	1 220	1 177	1 190
	Other oper. exp.	912	899	809	825	734	789	938	972	966	957
	Equipment	702	617	836	767	724	871	918	996	802	960
	Equip. change	7.5	-12.2	35.5	-8.2	-5.6	20.2	5.4	8.5	-19.5	19.7
Portugal	Personnel	1 027	1 153	1 302	1 371	1 442	1 592	1 523	1 465	1 556	1 621
	Other oper. exp.	322	330	255	246	248	237	277	305	294	231
	Equipment	158	183	217	193	164	44	137	78	118	267
	Equip. change	66.6	15.6	18.9	-11.0	-15.3	-73.4	215.8	-43.1	51.0	126.6
Spain	Personnel	4 968	5 093	5 540	5 613	5 677	5 639	5 497	5 256	5 407	5 415
	Other oper. exp.	2 159	2 018	2 059	2 082	1 825	1 517	2 047	1 644	1 646	1 505
	Equipment	2 469	1 934	1 769	1 150	1 132	884	1 191	969	1 119	1 125
	Equip. change	18.5	-21.7	-8.5	-35.0	-1.6	-21.9	34.7	-18.7	15.5	0.5

Turkey Personnel	1 498	1 354	2 027	2 567	2 650	2 799	3 463	3 169	3 156	2 693
Other oper. exp.	1 653	1 426	1 447	1 515	1 420	1 322	1 252	1 062	1 048	1 236
Equipment	911	856	756	1 063	1 240	1 425	1 455	1 820	1 841	2 213
Equip. change	12.3	– 6.1	– 11.6	40.5	16.7	14.9	2.1	25.1	1.2	20.2
UK Personnel	16 599	16 543	16 113	16 149	17 133	16 268	15 796	14 538	13 360	12 968
Other oper. exp.	13 875	12 072	14 032	14 478	14 175	13 073	8 606	8 779	9 780	9 411
Equipment	10 513	10 324	8 974	7 120	7 971	6 722	9 441	8 744	7 031	6 956
Equip. change	– 2.7	– 1.8	– 13.1	– 20.7	12.0	– 15.7	40.4	– 7.4	– 19.6	– 1.1
NATO Europe Personnel	70 040	70 765	72 478	74 896	76 933	75 122	72 529	69 837	68 191	68 645
Other oper. exp.	37 414	35 467	36 533	35 102	33 233	33 588	28 886	27 167	27 389	26 676
Equipment	30 656	30 086	28 162	24 794	23 889	21 108	23 379	22 234	19 828	20 758
Equip. change	4.2	– 1.9	– 6.4	– 12.0	– 3.6	– 11.6	10.8	– 4.9	– 10.8	4.7
NATO total Personnel	194 242	197 817	200 407	192 727	198 283	192 010	181 921	174 150	167 074	161 543
Other oper. exp.	158 430	154 436	151 823	161 288	120 781	139 973	133 192	106 557	102 078	102 953
Equipment	120 886	112 741	111 352	102 688	99 210	88 121	84 587	98 186	87 808	81 054
Equip. change	2.3	– 6.7	– 1.2	– 7.8	– 3.4	– 11.2	– 4.0	16.1	– 10.6	– 7.7

Note: France does not return figures giving this breakdown to NATO. NATO data on the distribution between the different spending categories include a fourth category—infrastructure—which is of minor importance and has been excluded. The NATO data show percentage shares; the dollar figures have been calculated using these percentages and the total expenditures shown in table 6B.2. Calculations are based on rounded input data.

Sources: NATO, Financial and economic data relating to NATO defence, Press release (96)168, 17 Dec. 1996. Version current on 18 Dec. 1996, URL <http://www.nato.int/docu/pr/1996/p96-168e.htm>.

Table 6A.2. Military equipment expenditure of France, 1987–96

Figures are in US $m. at 1990 prices and exchange rates. Figures in italics are percentage changes from previous year.

Item	1987	1988	1989	1990	1991	1992	1993	1994	1995	1996
Equipment	17 315	17 893	18 270	18 295	18 161	16 980	16 312	15 943	13 740	13 298
Equipment change	*9.7*	*3.3*	*2.1*	*0.1*	*–0.7*	*–6.5*	*–3.9*	*–2.3*	*–13.8*	*–3.2*

Note: This table was compiled on the basis of domestic data on equipment expenditure as presented in the French defence budget. These figures refer to expenditure which actually took place. Budgetary freezes and cancellations are taken into account. Equipment expenditure includes all items covered by Titles V and VI of the French defence budget (i.e., research and development, prototype construction, procurement of finished equipment, infrastructure and technical and industrial investments, and investment subsidies). This equipment expenditure is not comparable to the equipment expenditure as defined by NATO and presented in table 6A.1. Equipment maintenance and munitions, which fall under operating costs according to the NATO definition, are included in Titles V and VI of the French budget. French equipment expenditure in 1996, according to the NATO definition, has been estimated as 20% lower than the figure given above. The data in this table should therefore be used with caution.

Sources: Assemblée Nationale, *Rapport fait par M. Phillippe Auberger, au nom de la Commission des Finances, de l'Economie Générale et du Plan sur le projet de loi de finances pour 1997 (no. 2993)*, Document no. 3030 (Assemblée Nationale: Paris, 10 Oct. 1996), p. 18; Assemblée Nationale, *Avis présenté, par M. Arthur Paecht, au nom de la Commission des Finances, de l'Economie Générale et du Plan sur le projet de loi (no. 2766) relatif à la programmation militaire pour les années 1997 à 2002*, Document no. 2826 (Assemblée Nationale: Paris, 29 May 1996), p. 25; and Assemblée Nationale, *Avis présenté, par M. Arthur Paecht, au nom de la Commission des Finances, de l'Economie Générale et du Plan sur le projet de loi (no. 1153) relatif à la programmation militaire pour les années 1995 à 2000*, Document no. 1217 (Assemblée Nationale: Paris, 10 May 1994), p. 30.

Table 6A.2 was prepared by Agnès Courades Allebeck.

Appendix 6B. Tables of military expenditure

PAUL GEORGE, AGNÈS COURADES ALLEBECK and EVAMARIA LOOSE-WEINTRAUB

Sources and methods are explained in appendix 6C. Notes and explanations of the conventions used appear below table 6B.3.

Table 6B.1. World military expenditure, in current price figures, 1987–96

Figures are in local currency, current prices.

State	Currency	1987	1988	1989	1990	1991	1992	1993	1994	1995	1996
NATO[1]											
North America											
Canada	m. C. dollars	11 715	12 336	12 854	13 473	12 830	13 111	13 293	13 008	12 457	11 677
USA	m. dollars	288 157	293 093	304 085	306 170	280 292	305 141	297 637	288 079	277 813	271 417
Europe											
Belgium	m. francs	155 422	150 647	152 917	155 205	157 919	132 819	129 602	131 955	131 156	132 448
Denmark	m. kroner	14 647	15 620	15 963	16 399	17 091	17 129	17 390	17 293	17 468	17 633
France	m. francs	209 525	215 073	225 331	231 911	240 936	238 874	241 199	246 469	238 432	238 364
Germany[2]	m. D. marks	61 354	61 638	63 178	68 376	65 579	65 536	61 529	58 957	59 982	59 049
Greece	m. drachmas	393 052	471 820	503 032	612 344	693 846	835 458	932 995	1 052 760	1 171 377	1 343 276
Italy	b. lire	22 872	25 539	27 342	28 007	30 191	30 813	32 364	32 835	31 561	36 688
Luxembourg	m. francs	2 730	3 163	2 995	3 233	3 681	3 963	3 740	4 214	4 194	4 189
Netherlands	m. guilders	13 254	13 300	13 571	13 513	13 548	13 900	13 103	12 990	12 864	13 201
Norway	m. kroner	18 551	18 865	20 248	21 251	21 313	23 638	22 528	24 019	22 224	24 292
Portugal	m. escudos	159 288	194 036	229 344	267 299	305 643	341 904	352 504	360 811	403 478	449 359
Spain	m. pesetas	852 767	835 353	923 375	922 808	947 173	927 852	1 054 902	994 689	1 078 805	1 097 301
Turkey	b. lira	2 477	3 789	7 158	13 866	23 657	42 320	77 717	156 724	302 864	569 822
UK	m. pounds	19 269	19 290	20 868	22 287	24 380	22 850	22 686	22 490	21 163	21 410

State	Currency	1987	1988	1989	1990	1991	1992	1993	1994	1995	1996
Other Europe											
Albania	m. leks	1 011	955	965	990	..	3 200	3 776	4 416	5 085	5 086
Austria	m. schillings	16 972	16 597	17 849	17 537	18 208	18 419	19 350	19 744	20 300	21 700
Bulgaria	m. leva	(1 741)	1 752	1 605	1 615	4 434	5 748	8 113	12 920	24 000	37 966
Croatia[3]	m. kuna						191	3 044	7 083	7 893	..
Cyprus[4]	m. C. pounds	64.7	76.7	81.7	127	131	191	90.1	98.7	169	175
Czech Rep.[5]	m. korunas							24 151	27 515	26 900	30 500
Czechoslovakia[6]	m. korunas	28 496	29 236	43 784	41 900	43 037	48 503				
Estonia[7]	m. kroons						68	174	327	417	483
Finland[8]	m. markkaa	5 816	6 445	6 853	7 405	8 903	9 298	9 225	9 175	8 336	9 157
German DR	m. marks	20 897	21 647								
Hungary	b. forints	28	38	48	47	50	58	166	73	68	71
Ireland[9]	m. I. pounds	252	255	263	290	314	324	332	350	430	456
Latvia[10]	m. lati							10.7	17.1	19.9	20.5
Lithuania[11]	m. roubles/m. litai						2 721	85.4	79.3	130	180
Malta[12]	m. liri	6 479	7 998	7 426	6 722	7 029	8 513	9 419	10 533	10 996	11 645
Poland	b. zlotys	468	742	2 146	14 945	18 300	26 237	39 803	51 170	65 945	82 721
Romania	b. lei	(25)	(28)	(29)	30	80	196	420	1 185	1 538	1 959
Slovak Rep.[13]	m. korunas							8 629	10 400	12 932	14 100
Slovenia[14]	m. tolars						18 229	20 864	24 520	31 730	29 823
Sweden	m. kronor	26 039	28 035	31 037	34 974	35 744	35 302	36 309	37 608	39 908	40 973
Switzerland	m. francs	4 716	4 956	5 431	5 947	6 104	6 249	5 753	5 935	5 952	5 711
Yugoslavia[15]	m. new dinars	197	568	6 113	5 180	..	..	678	1 200	1 611	4 210
CIS[16]											
Armenia	m. roubles									..	..
Azerbaijan	m. manats						1 642	13 290		..	..
Belarus[17]	m. B. roubles							177 303	365 148	1 723 179	2 231 533
Georgia	m. lary							..		..	76 371
Kazakhstan[18]	b. roubles/b. tenge						24	0.7	14	28	..
Kyrgyzstan	m. som							38	(105)	151	..
Moldova	m. lei							9.7	36.7	60.0	72.2

Country	Currency										
Russia[19]	b. roubles						855	7118	28 018	59 400	80 185
Tajikistan	m. roubles							256	24 338	34 700	:
Turkmenistan	b.manats									4.6	:
Ukraine[20]	b. roubles/b. karbovanets						112	547	280	106	244
Uzbekistan[21]	b. roubles/m. sum						12	164	991	3 400	:
Middle East											
Bahrain	m. dinars	60.3	70.4	73.6	81.2	89.2	94.6	94.4	96.3	95	:
Egypt	m. E. pounds	3 309	3 258	3 143	3 106	3 523	4 015	4 458	5 933	:	:
Iran[22]	b. rials	645	703	812	1 010	1 235	1 482	2 328	(2 860)	(4 215)	(5 587)
Iraq	m. dinars	:	:	:	:	:	:	:	:	:	:
Israel	m. new shekels	8 379	9 121	10 566	12 940	[15 709]	18 478	18 288	29 290	31 800	27 800
Jordan	m. dinars	253	257	252	205	260	221	281	284	308	283
Kuwait	m. dinars	377	375	476	560	2 543	2 682	1 783	1 350	944	:
Lebanon	b.L. pounds		5 458	10 573	97 874	139 979	498 541	518 482	703 981	795 168	759 944
Oman	m. riyals	584	589	601	742	643	778	738	779	776	:
Saudi Arabia	m. riyals	54 226	50 080	47 812	(50 000)	(100 000)	54 000	61 636	(61 800)	(50 600)	(45 300)
Syria	m. S. pounds	14 327	14 612	16 654	18 429	32 483	33 412	29 948	[34 964]	(39 980)	(36 460)
UAE	m. dirhams	5 827	(5 827)	(5 827)	(5 827)	(5 827)	7 163	[7 391]	7 342	7 159	[14 318]
Yemen[23]	m. rials	3 124	5 533	6 030	12 062	13 227	16 812	19 752	:	:	:
South Asia											
Bangladesh	m. taka	9 080	9 290	10 750	11 450	11 965	13 980	16 095	17 290	18 080	19 110
India	b. rupees	108	122	135	146	156	165	184	220	240	261
Nepal	m. rupees	664	737	775	919	1 019	:	:	:	:	:
Pakistan	m. rupees	43 315	46 808	50 261	57 898	69 682	81 604	90 610	97 816	(108 425)	(123 000)
Sri Lanka	m. rupees	6 001	4 732	4 073	6 736	10 317	12 876	15 413	19 415	(32 000)	(50 000)
Far East											
Brunei[24]	m. B. dollars	220	359	363	419	:	:	:	:	:	:
China, P. R.[25]	b. yuan	21	22	25	29	33	38	43	55	63	75
Cambodia	b. riels	:	:	:	:	:	:	:	:	:	298
Indonesia	b. new rupiahs	(2 385)	(2 618)	(3 057)	(3 581)	(4 170)	(4 784)	(5 932)	(7 337)	(7 641)	(8 238)
Japan	b. yen	3 563	3 789	4 041	4 130	4 330	4 511	4 619	4 673	4 714	4 816
Korea, North	m. won	3 971	3 863	4 060	4 314	4 466	4 582	4 692	4 817	:	:

State	Currency	1987	1988	1989	1990	1991	1992	1993	1994	1995	1996
Korea, South	b. won	4 683	5 316	6 022	6 797	8 040	8 857	9 177	10 553	11 597	12 838
Malaysia	m. ringgits	3 611	2 241	2 761	3 043	4 323	4 500	4 951	5 367	5 980	(7 176)
Mongolia	m. tugriks	793	900	850	592	[888]	1 184	4 795	7 017	9 339	11 663
Myanmar	m. kyats	1 355	1 632	3 656	4 991	5 813	8 297	..	..	..	..
Philippines	m. pesos	10 186	14 906	15 907	14 707	15 898	17 461	20 130	23 271	27 793	30 183
Singapore	m. S. dollars	2 157	2 414	2 735	3 159	3 340	3 684	3 846	4 112	5 226	5 686
Taiwan	b. T. dollars	149	160	188	211	227	239	255	257	(265)	(273)
Thailand	m. baht	42 812	44 831	48 846	55 502	64 961	64 536	78 900	85 400	82 824	107 900
Viet Nam	b. dong	103	792	2 047	3 319	4 292	3 730	3 168	4 730	..	..
Oceania											
Australia	m. A. dollars	7 667	7 963	8 538	9 206	9 665	10 385	11 098	11 381	9 871	10 019
Fiji[26]	m. F. dollars	31.2	35.2	43.1	45.2	47.9	45.9	49.4	40.8	41	..
New Zealand[27]	m. NZ dollars	1 173	1 336	1 341	1 300	1 210	1 097	1 111	1 118	1 317	(1 383)
Papua New Guinea	m. kina	38.4	40.1	45.5	65.6	50.1	56.5	67.1	(69.0)	..	..
Tonga	th. pa'anga	1 115	1 138	1 565	1 980	2 269	..	..	..	..	..
Africa											
Algeria[28]	m. dinars	5 805	6 084	6 500	[8 470]	10 439	[20 125]	29 810	46 800	58 847	79 519
Angola[29]	m. Kz/Kz rdj.	36 585	43 961	58 267	52 391	101 597	387 446	7 204 161	..	1 141 640	..
Benin	m. francs	10 700	11 000	9 100	8 935	..	376	..	..	..	..
Botswana	m. pulas	124	171	207	291	348	..	..	..	..	..
Burkina Faso	m. francs	15 241	17 033	21 315	22 997	19 608	18 824	17 139	17 372	..	..
Burundi	m. francs	3 804	4 809	6 014	6 782	..	..	..	..	10 126	..
Cameroon[30]	m. francs	48 165	45 118	48 749	49 674	47 597	49 550	50 811	54 082	..	..
Cape Verde	m. escudos	360	366	..	..	..	..	220	..	..	..
Central African R.[31]	m. francs	5 610	..	..	..	6 093	6 137	5 421	5 935	6 496	(6 239)
Chad	m. francs	20 307	..	..	..	..	..	..	..	..	..
Congo	m. francs	30 208	..	..	..	..	..	..	..	..	..
Côte d'Ivoire	m. francs	36 900	38 155	41 368	39 199	40 671	41 503	42 088	46 677	..	..
Djibouti	m. D. francs	4 664	4 701	4 705	4 709	4 809	..	..	..	..	..
Eritrea[32]	m. birr	..	..	..	..	..	..	185	..	..	..
Ethiopia[32]	m. birr	1 174	1 508	1 751	1 740	1 121	667	703	710	726	..

Country	Currency									
Gabon	m. francs	43 407	:	:	:	:	:	:	:	:
Gambia	m. dalasis	:	:	20.6	31.0	31.2	23.4	22.2	30.1	40.9
Ghana	m. cedis	6 659	4 603	9 006	15 230	23 242	39 481	:	:	:
Guinea-Bissau	m. pesos	2 168	8 027	:	:	:	:	:	:	:
Kenya[33]	m. shillings	3 770	4 350	5 240	4 890	5 170	4 290	6 570	7 580	:
Lesotho	th. maloti	36 836	59 321	62 505	62 393	[76 600]	[65 493]	87 875	99 500	:
Liberia	m. dollars	25.8	[27.4]	28.3	21.7	37.3	23.6	41.3	:	:
Libya	m. dinars	549	582	:	:	:	:	:	:	:
Madagascar	m. francs	39.2	48.5	56.7	63.7	72.4	68.9	84.6	104	135
Malawi	m. kwachas	47.8	62.9	66.3	66.5	69.6	67.8	151	232	259
Mali	m. francs	13.3	14.7	14.2	:	:	:	:	:	:
Mauritania	m. ouguiyas	3 230	3 229	3 239	3 232	3 640	3 427	3 640	3 750	:
Mauritius	m. rupees	46.9	96.1	136.3	164.3	190.2	177.9	211.0	238.0	246.0
Morocco	m. dirhams	6 816	8 407	8 816	9 999	11 640	10 488	12 565	12 246	:
Mozambique[34]	m. meticais	41 700	102 400	136 000	178 000	416 800	259 300	508 000	626 000	704 000
Namibia[35]	m. rand	190	147	144	309	229	355	202	226	312
Niger	m. francs	5 300	5 749	12 315	:	:	:	:	:	:
Nigeria	m. nairas	(749)	(2 220)	(2 286)	(3 554)	(6 382)	(4 822)	(6 608)	(7 747)	(15 500)
Rwanda	m. francs	2 979	3 336	7 964	13 184	11 863	11 863	:	:	:
Senegal	m. francs	29 200	31 300	31 300	29 928	29 056	29 056	:	:	:
Seychelles	m. rupees	63.4	73.6	79.2	87.6	67.1	55.2	35.2	:	:
Sierra Leone	m. leones	156	577	1 369	4 792	10 081	105	230	:	:
Somalia	m. shillings	3 000	4 200	:	:	:	:	:	:	:
South Africa	m. rand	7 474	9 971	9 850	9 316	9 613	9 797	11 021	10 830	11 050
Sudan	m. S. pounds	791	3 050	4 420	7 420	13 750	29 500	49 900	51 256	:
Swaziland	m. emalangeni	16.0	22.2	35.8	40.6	58.2	73.6	85.5	99.7	107
Tanzania	m. shillings	7 418	10 823	12 196	16 130	13 000	:	:	:	:
Togo	m. francs	13 047	13 354	13 817	12 950	13 000	14 200	14 100	:	:
Tunisia[36]	m. dinars	161.1	269.3	287.2	314.6	318.6	347.3	364.0	326.0	342.7
Uganda	m. shillings	4 298	25 740	37 509	50 034	60 799	63 063	:	:	:
Zaire[37]	m./b. new zaires	3 178	26 055	41 549	703 657	33	1 258	10 816	(202 716)	(224 678)
Zambia[38]	m. kwachas	637	2 315	4 220	5 575	16 835	23 149	22 907	37 388	45 000
Zimbabwe	m. Z. dollars	655	803	954	1 117	1 793	2 015	1 826	2 071	:

State	Currency	1987	1988	1989	1990	1991	1992	1993	1994	1995	1996
Caribbean											
Bahamas	m. B. dollars	13.2	16.6	18.1	19.9	19.2	19.3	17.8	20.3	21.5	..
Barbados	m. B. dollars	15.8	19.1	24.2	27.9	26.2	24.5	26.2	27.0	..	..
Cuba	m. pesos	1 242	1 274	1 377	1 380	1 160	.	(300)	..	..	..
Dominican Rep.	m. pesos	191	242	284	341	431	593	780	..	..	..
Haiti	m. gourdes	..	..	..	(262)	(242)	(602)	(768)	..	..	..
Jamaica	m. dollars	132	163	613	811	894	937	989	1 023	..	..
Central America											
Belize[39]	th. B. dollars	8 000	(8 332)	8 837	9 771	9 364	10 991	13 684	(18 425)	..	..
Costa Rica[40]	b. colones	(2)	2	9	11	13	16	23	..	..	..
El Salvador	m. colones	768	777	926	975	1 011	975	888	829	886	..
Guatemala	m. quetzals	310	337	368	593	600	795	814	880	(1 112)	..
Honduras	m. lempiras	141	150	247	276	(252)	(280)	(290)	(385)	(445)	..
Mexico	m. new pesos	1 043	2 077	2 642	2 665	3 661	4 530	5 445	7 554	7 860	9 904
Nicaragua[41]	m. gold córdoba	..	50.6	1 802	218 002	401	211	224	232	242	..
Panama[42]	m. balboas	104	102	101	74.1	80.1	86.7	94.6	98.7	96.8	..
South America											
Argentina[43]	m. australes/pesos	5 863	27 355	786	12 483	23 354	4 270	4 247	4 712	4 683	4 593
Bolivia	m. bolivianos	174	180	225	357	440	473	537	569	632	371
Brazil[44]	m. reais	42	429	6 786	142	448	4 882	(3 561)	(5 723)	(10.0)	(14.0)
Chile[45]	b. pesos	126	136	167	203	254	304	351	396	430	(611)
Colombia	b. pesos	100	155	207	289	345	396	548	790	646	..
Ecuador	b. sucres	35.4	61.3	102	156	273	532	841	982	..	..
Guyana[46]	m. G. dollars	..	137	..	142	227	454	562	759	801	780
Paraguay	b. guaranies	26.9	32.6	59.7	81.4	142	159	181	202	240	(266)
Peru[47]	b. intis/m. soles	21 702	90 500	2 046	130	480	1 001	[1 390]	(1 778)	(2 200)	..
Uruguay	m. new pesos	31	58	114	233	363	813	974	2 083	..	..
Venezuela[48]	m. bolivares	9 005	12 934	14 110	24 350	46 896	(110 769)	[110 885]	(137 960)	(212 427)	(286 754)

Table 6B.2. World military expenditure, in constant price figures, 1987–96

Figures are in US $m., at 1990 prices (CPI-deflated) and exchange rates unless otherwise noted. All notes appear below table 6B.3.

State	1987	1988	1989	1990	1991	1992	1993	1994	1995	1996
NATO[1]										
North America										
Canada	11 488	11 631	11 536	11 547	10 413	10 482	10 433	10 191	9 549	8 817
USA	331 215	323 860	320 427	306 170	268 994	284 116	269 111	254 038	238 176	226 369
Europe										
Belgium	5 017	4 806	4 732	4 644	4 579	3 760	3 571	3 551	3 479	3 443
Denmark	2 662	2 714	2 648	2 650	2 697	2 648	2 653	2 587	2 561	2 544
France	42 284	42 243	42 793	42 589	42 875	41 502	41 052	41 260	39 234	38 432
Germany[2]	40 570	40 242	40 146	42 320	39 216	37 697	34 002	31 621	31 478	30 507
Greece	3 856	4 078	3 819	3 863	3 663	3 808	3 716	3 780	3 849	4 072
Italy	22 699	24 113	24 304	23 376	23 706	23 024	23 147	22 575	20 612	23 059
Luxembourg	89	101	93	97	107	111	102	112	109	107
Netherlands	7 598	7 561	7 636	7 421	7 217	7 174	6 590	6 358	6 175	6 180
Norway	3 442	3 279	3 369	3 395	3 293	3 569	3 326	3 495	3 156	3 380
Portugal	1 563	1 738	1 824	1 875	1 925	1 977	1 908	1 861	2 000	2 156
Spain	9 995	9 345	9 668	9 053	8 775	8 113	8 823	7 940	8 230	8 094
Turkey	4 316	3 802	4 398	5 315	5 463	5 747	6 355	6 213	6 200	6 306
UK	42 561	40 646	40 792	39 776	41 087	37 141	36 312	35 116	31 961	31 475
NATO Europe	*186 653*	*184 668*	*186 223*	*186 375*	*184 601*	*176 273*	*171 556*	*166 469*	*159 046*	*159 756*
NATO Total	*529 356*	*520 159*	*518 185*	*504 092*	*464 008*	*470 872*	*451 100*	*430 698*	*406 771*	*394 943*
Other Europe										
Albania	..	..	..	66	..	46	28	30	31	28
Austria	1 612	1 546	1 622	1 542	1 543	1 507	1 528	1 514	1 522	1 586
Bulgaria	(592)	(588)	(507)	544	344	244	209	223	256	234
Croatia[3] 1993 prices/ER						[845]	[851]	[956]	[1 023]	..
Cyprus[4]	159	182	187	277	272	373	168	176	293	286

State	1987	1988	1989	1990	1991	1992	1993	1994	1995	1996
Czech Rep.[5] 1993 prices/ER							828	857	762	793
Czechoslovakia[6]	1 762	1 774	1 816	2 683	2 334	1 520				
Estonia[7] 1993 prices/ER						10	13	17	17	[15]
Finland[8]	1 809	1 907	1 903	1 937	2 237	2 277	2 211	2 176	1 959	2 133
German DR	..	..	..	..						
Hungary	570	659	707	540	428	404	944	349	(254)	(216)
Ireland[9]	460	455	452	480	505	505	510	525	630	653
Latvia[10] 1993 prices/ER						3	16	19	(17)	(18)
Lithuania[11] 1993 prices/ER							20	11	(12)	(13)
Malta[12]	21	26	24	21	22	26	27	29		
Poland	1 758	1 776	1 477	1 573	1 090	1 075	1 192	1 150	1 158	1 220
Romania	(1 202)	(1 310)	(1 347)	1 337	1 300	1 023	617	(735)	(722)	748
Slovak Rep.[13] 1993 prices/ER							280	298	337	347
Slovenia[14] 1993 prices/ER						212	184	181	208	177
Sweden	5 499	5 572	5 762	5 909	5 540	5 325	5 243	5 295	5 477	5 619
Switzerland	3 759	3 878	4 120	4 281	4 153	4 086	3 639	3 725	3 669	3 493
Yugoslavia[15]	4 351	4 562	3 699	458	..	..	..	..	..	..
CIS[16]										
Middle East										
Bahrain	165	192	215	216	235	250	244	246	245	..
Egypt	2 758	2 307	1 836	1 553	1 472	1 475	1 462	[1 787]	..	..
Iran[22]	16 053	13 601	12 835	14 831	15 487	14 784	19 162	(17 902)	(17 629)	(18 231)
Iraq	..	..			..					
Israel	6 808	6 374	6 141	6 418	[6 547]	6 879	6 137	8 751	8 633	6 619
Jordan	593	566	440	309	362	296	359	351	372	327
Kuwait 1989 prices/ER	1 371	1 344	1 650	1 907	7 936	8 417	5 575	4 119	2 852	..
Lebanon										
Oman	1 743	1 913	1 823	1 931	1 888	2 164	1 672	1 597	1 559	..
Saudi Arabia	15 067	13 786	13 027	(13 351)	(25 455)	13 759	15 541	(15 619)	(15 697)	(15 776)
Syria	2 283	1 731	1 770	1 642	2 655	2 460	1 947	1 971	(2 116)	..

UAE	1 662	(1 662)	(1 653)	(1 587)	(1 589)	1 945	[2 007]	1 994	1 944	[3 889]
Yemen[23]	:	:	:	349	191	76	62	:	:	:
South Asia										
Bangladesh	342	320	336	331	323	362	416	432	427	420
India	7 810	8 080	8 403	8 314	7 800	7 421	7 747	8 416	8 345	8 333
Nepal	29	29	28	31	30	:	:	:	:	:
Pakistan	2 555	2 537	2 525	2 667	2 871	3 071	3 101	2 978	(2 938)	(3 003)
Sri Lanka	232	160	124	168	230	257	276	320	(490)	(630)
Far East										
Brunei[24]	127	205	204	231	:	:	:	:	:	:
Cambodia	:	:	:	:	:	:	:	:	:	:
China, P. R.[25]	6 363	5 558	5 410	6 063	6 666	7 184	7 063	7 505	7 487	8 162
Indonesia	(1 604)	(1 629)	(1 788)	(1 943)	(2 068)	(2 206)	(2 495)	(2 844)	(2 706)	(2 674)
Japan	26 123	27 572	28 773	28 524	28 950	29 644	29 982	30 135	30 428	31 028
Korea, North	:	:	:	:	:	:	:	:	:	:
Korea, South	8 139	8 624	9 238	9 603	10 393	10 779	10 654	11 531	12 133	(12 765)
Malaysia	1 445	874	1 048	1 125	1 531	1 522	1 617	1 690	1 821	[2 101]
Mongolia	:	:	:	:	:	812	:	:	:	:
Myanmar	371	385	679	787	693	555	595	631	697	698
Philippines	584	785	747	605	551	:	:	:	:	:
Singapore	1 280	1 411	1 560	1 743	1 782	1 921	1 961	2 035	2 540	2 718
Taiwan	6 045	6 430	7 213	7 782	8 086	8 154	8 444	8 172	(8 134)	(8 101)
Thailand	1 939	1 956	2 022	2 169	2 402	2 293	2 712	2 793	2 563	3 150
Viet Nam	:	:	:	781	552	408	301	393	:	:
Oceania										
Australia	6 830	6 611	6 594	6 627	6 742	7 174	7 390	7 237	6 735	5 423
Fiji[26]	27	27	32	31	30	28	28	23	23	:
New Zealand[27]	835	894	(849)	(776)	704	632	632	625	710	718
Papua New Guinea	48	48	52	70	50	54	61	(61)	:	:
Tonga	1.1	1.0	1.3	1.6	1.6	:	:	:	:	:

State	1987	1988	1989	1990	1991	1992	1993	1994	1995	1996
Africa										
Algeria[28]	875	866	847	[945]	926	[1 355]	1 666	2 027	(1 963)	(2 187)
Angola[29]	..	..	..	(1 752)	(1 788)	(1 709)	(2 147)	..	(1 221)	..
Benin	..	..	..	33	..	..	..	..	..	..
Botswana	90	114	124	156	167	(156)	..	..	..	..
Burkina Faso	58	62	78	84	70	69	62	50	..	..
Burundi	28	34	38	40	..	..	..	..	35	..
Cameroon[30]	179	178	182	182	175	182	193	191	..	..
Cape Verde	6.2	6.1	..	..	..	..	2.5	..	..	..
Central African Rep.[31]	20	..	..	..	23	23	21	(19)	(17)	..
Chad	82	..	..	..	..	..	..	..	..	..
Congo	115	..	..	..	..	..	..	..	..	..
Côte d'Ivoire	145	140	151	144	147	145	143	126	..	..
Djibouti	..	..	..	26	22	..	..	..	..	..
Eritrea[32]	..	..	..	..	..	..	55	..	..	..
Ethiopia[32]	689	826	890	840	399	215	219	205	191	..
Gabon	167	..	..	..	..	..	..	..	..	..
Gambia	..	..	..	3	4	3	2	2	3	4
Ghana	46	24	26	28	40	55	75	..	..	..
Guinea-Bissau	4	..	5	..	..	..	..	..	..	..
Kenya[33]	239	233	219	229	178	121	100	98	112	..
Lesotho	20	19	26	24	20	[18]	[19]	20	21	..
Liberia	123	..	..	..	..	..	..	..	..	..
Libya	..	..	..	..	..	..	..	..	..	..
Madagascar	41	38	36	38	39	37	35	30	30	25
Malawi	29	24	26	24	22	18	15	25	25	25
Mali	..	53	54	52	38	(37)	(36)	(34)	(34)	(33)
Mauritania	..	..	..	..	..	..	..	..	..	..
Mauritius	..	5	7	9	10	11	10	11	11	11
Morocco	933	1 007	1 091	1 070	1 123	1 114	1 176	1 207	1 207	1 109
Mozambique[34]	123	114	143	129	127	127	144	144	(108)	(86)

Namibia[35]	107	109	64	56	107	104	62	49	(50)	(68)
Niger	19	19	21	45	[391]	..	..	..	..	..
Nigeria	(232)	(346)	(297)	(284)	133	110	..	..	..	..
Rwanda	39	36	42	96	112	109	..	..	..	..
Senegal	106	112	115	115	16	19	12	6	..	..
Seychelles	13	13	14	15	16	20	..	..	10	..
Sierra Leone	5	5	8	9	16	..	..	..	..	..
Somalia	44	63	..	..	..	..	..	..	..	..
South Africa	4 275	4 757	4 411	3 809	3 124	2 831	2 631	2 714	2 455	(2 330)
Sudan	..	794	1 120	982	737	628	669	..	..	..
Swaziland	8	9	10	14	14	19	20	21	21	..
Tanzania	85	78	75	63	64	..	..	..	..	..
Togo	48	47	50	51	47	47	52	38	..	..
Tunisia[36]	226	306	327	327	331	317	332	332	280	(281)
Uganda	64	58	80	87	91	73	71	..	(191)	(202)
Zaire[37]	29	204	66	58	43	..	..	..	..	..
Zambia[38]	169	122	174	146	100	101	48	31	38	..
Zimbabwe	381	383	385	390	370	418	368	273	238	..
Caribbean										
Bahamas	15	18	19	20	18	17	15	17	18	..
Barbados	9	10	12	14	12	11	11	12	..	..
Cuba	..	..	..	..	..	..	..	..	..	..
Dominican Rep.	75	66	53	40	33	43	..	..	..	..
Haiti	..	..	..	..	..	..	..	..	..	..
Jamaica	28	32	104	113	82	49	42	32	..	..
Central America										
Belize[39]	..	(4)	5	5	5	5	6	(8)	..	..
Costa Rica[40]	(30)	28	119	117	112	112	147	..	..	..
El Salvador	167	141	143	121	110	95	73	62	60	..
Guatemala	120	118	116	132	100	121	111	126	(126)	..
Honduras	100	102	152	138	(94)	(96)	(90)	(98)	(86)	..
Mexico	1 208	1 122	1 189	947	1 061	1 137	1 245	1 615	1 245	1 197

State	1987	1988	1989	1990	1991	1992	1993	1994	1995	1996
Nicaragua[41]	. .	. .	. .	. .	. .	. .	. .	. .	. .	. .
Panama[42]	105	102	101	74	79	84	91	94	91	. .
South America										
Argentina[43]	4 146	4 316	3 893	2 560	1 761	2 583	2 323	2 471	2 377	2 330
Bolivia	86	76	83	112	114	109	115	(115)	(114)	(60)
Brazil[44]	1 961	2 580	2 945	2 031	1 279	1 162	. .	. .	. .	. .
Chile[45]	702	656	692	665	684	707	728	733	(738)	(991)
Colombia	417	502	531	576	527	444	537	625	(423)	. .
Ecuador	191	208	197	203	239	301	329	301	. .	. .
Guyana[46]	. .	4	. .	4	6	11	13	15	14	13
Paraguay	47	46	67	66	93	90	87	(81)	(84)	(85)
Peru[47]	2 350	1 279	826	691	501	603	[563]	(582)	. .	. .
Uruguay	164	190	207	199	153	204	159	234	(174)	. .
Venezuela[48]	644	716	423	519	745	(1 339)	[971]	(751)	(723)	(588)

Table 6B.3. World military expenditure as a percentage of gross domestic product, 1987–95[49]

Notes appear below this table.

State	1987	1988	1989	1990	1991	1992	1993	1994	1995
NATO[1]									
North America									
Canada	2.1	2.0	2.0	2.0	1.9	1.9	1.9	1.7	1.6
USA	6.3	6.0	5.8	5.5	4.9	4.9	4.5	4.2	3.8
Europe									
Belgium	3.0	2.7	2.5	2.4	2.3	1.9	1.8	1.7	1.7
Denmark	2.1	2.1	2.1	2.1	2.1	2.0	2.0	1.9	1.8
France	3.9	3.8	3.7	3.6	3.6	3.4	3.4	3.3	3.1
Germany[2]	3.1	2.9	2.8	2.8	2.3	2.1	2.0	1.8	1.7
Greece	6.3	6.2	4.6	4.7	4.3	4.4	4.4	4.4	4.4
Italy	2.3	2.3	2.3	2.1	2.1	2.0	2.1	2.0	1.8
Luxembourg	1.2	1.3	1.1	1.1	1.2	1.2	1.0	1.0	1.0
Netherlands	3.0	2.9	2.8	2.6	2.5	2.5	2.3	2.1	2.0
Norway	3.3	2.9	3.0	2.9	2.8	3.0	2.7	2.8	2.4
Portugal	3.1	3.2	2.8	2.8	2.8	2.8	2.7	2.6	2.7
Spain	2.4	2.1	2.0	1.8	1.7	1.6	1.7	1.5	1.5
Turkey	3.3	3.0	3.3	3.5	3.7	3.9	4.0	4.0	4.0
UK	4.6	4.1	4.0	4.0	4.2	3.8	3.6	3.4	3.0
Other Europe									
Albania	5.9	5.6	5.2	5.9	. .	2.6	3.8	3.7	4.4
Austria	1.1	1.1	1.1	1.0	0.9	0.9	0.9	0.9	0.9
Bulgaria	(4.8)	4.6	4.1	3.6	3.4	2.9	2.8	3.4	3.8
Croatia[3]						. .	. .	13.9	14.7
Cyprus[4]	3.6	3.8	3.6	5.0	4.9	6.2	2.8	2.8	4.4
Czech Rep.[5]							2.7	2.7	2.2
Czechoslovakia[6]	4.1	4.0	4.0	5.8	5.2	4.4			
Estonia[7]						0.5	0.8	1.0	0.9

State	1987	1988	1989	1990	1991	1992	1993	1994	1995
Finland[8]	1.5	1.5	1.4	1.4	1.8	2.0	1.9	1.8	1.5
German DR									
Hungary	2.3	2.6	2.8	2.2	2.0	2.0	4.7	(1.7)	(1.4)
Ireland[9]	1.2	1.1	1.0	1.1	1.1	1.1	1.0	1.0	1.1
Latvia[10]							0.7	0.9	(0.8)
Lithuania[11]							0.8	0.5	(0.6)
Malta[12]	1.2	1.3	1.1	0.9	0.9	1.0	1.0	1.0	..
Poland	2.8	2.5	1.8	2.5	2.2	2.3	2.6	2.3	2.3
Romania	(3.0)	(3.3)	(3.6)	3.5	3.6	3.3	2.1	(2.4)	(2.7)
Slovak Rep.[13]							2.3	2.4	2.5
Slovenia[14]						(1.9)	(1.5)	(1.4)	(1.5)
Sweden	2.5	2.5	2.5	2.6	2.5	2.4	2.5	2.5	2.4
Switzerland	1.9	1.8	1.9	1.9	1.8	1.8	1.7	1.7	1.7
Yugoslavia[15]	3.9	3.7	2.2	..	..	..	..	..	..
CIS[16]									
Russia									3.5
Middle East									
Bahrain	5.1	5.5	5.5	5.4	5.6	5.7	5.4	5.3	5.6
Egypt	6.4	5.3	4.1	3.2	3.2	2.9	2.8	[3.7]	..
Iran[22]	3.4	3.2	3.1	2.9	2.6	2.4	2.7	(2.4)	(2.3)
Iraq	..	13.0	..	..	[11.6]	..	..	..	..
Israel	14.7	13.0	12.3	12.3	9.1	11.5	9.9	14.9	15.1
Jordan	11.4	11.4	10.6	7.7	9.1	6.3	7.4	6.8	6.7
Kuwait	6.0	6.5	6.7	10.5	81.2	46.0	25.0	18.9	13.0
Lebanon	..	..	..	..	..	..	..	..	..
Oman	19.4	20.1	18.6	18.3	16.4	17.9	15.7	14.7	13.3
Saudi Arabia	19.7	17.6	15.4	(12.8)	(23.2)	11.9	13.9	(13.9)	(11.5)
Syria	11.2	7.9	8.0	6.9	10.4	9.0	7.2	7.0	..
UAE	6.7	(6.7)	(5.8)	(4.7)	(4.7)	5.5	[5.7]	5.5	..
Yemen[23]	7.2	..	..	..	19.8	18.1	16.9	..	..

South Asia									
Bangladesh	1.6	1.5	1.5	1.5	1.4	1.5	1.6	1.7	1.5
India	3.3	3.2	3.1	2.8	2.6	2.4	2.4	2.7	2.8
Nepal	1.1	1.0	0.9	1.0	0.9	:	:	:	:
Pakistan	8.0	7.5	7.0	7.1	7.4	7.3	7.4	(7.7)	(8.1)
Sri Lanka	3.1	2.1	1.6	2.1	2.8	3.0	3.1	(3.4)	(4.8)
Far East									
Brunei[24]	3.7	6.2	6.2	6.4	:	:	:	:	:
Cambodia	:	:	:	:	:	:	:	:	:
China, P. R.[25]	1.9	1.5	1.6	1.6	1.6	1.6	1.4	1.6	1.6
Indonesia	(2.0)	(1.9)	(1.9)	(1.9)	(1.9)	(1.9)	(1.9)	(2.0)	(2.0)
Japan	1.0	1.0	1.0	1.0	1.0	1.0	1.0	1.0	1.0
Korea, North	:	:	:	:	:	:	:	:	:
Korea, South	4.2	4.0	4.0	3.8	3.7	3.7	3.4	3.6	3.7
Malaysia	4.5	2.5	2.7	2.6	3.3	3.0	3.0	3.0	(3.1)
Mongolia	:	:	:	:	:	:	:	:	:
Myanmar	2.1	2.3	3.6	3.6	3.4	3.6	:	:	:
Philippines	1.5	1.9	1.7	1.4	1.3	1.3	1.4	2.0	1.7
Singapore	5.1	4.9	4.8	4.9	4.6	4.7	4.3	4.2	5.0
Taiwan	4.6	4.6	4.8	5.0	4.8	4.6	4.5	4.2	(4.1)
Thailand	3.6	3.3	3.0	2.9	3.1	2.8	3.2	3.1	2.8
Viet Nam	:	:	:	8.7	6.1	3.7	2.9	3.9	:
Oceania									
Australia	2.7	2.5	2.4	2.4	2.5	2.6	2.7	2.6	2.1
Fiji[26]	2.1	2.2	2.3	2.2	2.2	1.9	1.9	1.5	1.4
New Zealand[27]	2.1	1.8	(1.8)	(1.8)	1.7	1.5	1.4	1.3	1.5
Papua New Guinea	1.3	1.3	1.5	2.1	1.4	1.4	1.3	(1.3)	:
Tonga	0.8	0.8	1.0	1.1	1.1	:	:	:	:
Africa									
Algeria[28]	1.9	1.9	1.8	[1.6]	1.3	[2.1]	2.7	3.3	3.1
Angola[29]	:	:	:	:	:	(9.7)	(24.3)	:	(11.4)

State	1987	1988	1989	1990	1991	1992	1993	1994	1995
Benin	2.3	2.3	1.9	1.8	..	..	..	..	..
Botswana	3.8	3.7	3.6	4.4	4.7	(4.8)	..	..	..
Burkina Faso	2.5	2.3	3.1	3.3	2.5	2.4	(2.2)	(1.7)	..
Burundi	2.6	3.1	3.3	3.4	..	..	..	..	(3.1)
Cameroon[30]	1.2	1.2	1.4	1.5	1.4	1.6	1.6	1.6	..
Cape Verde	2.7	2.4	..	..	..	..	(0.8)	..	..
Central African Rep.[31]	1.6	..	..	..	1.5	1.6	1.4	(1.2)	(1.1)
Chad	8.3	..	..	..	..	—	..	..	..
Congo	4.4	..	..	..	..	..	..	..	..
Côte d'Ivoire	1.2	1.2	1.3	1.3	1.4	1.4	1.4	1.2	..
Djibouti	..	..	..	6.3	6.1	..	..	..	..
Eritrea[32]	..	..	..	..	..	—	(0.5)	..	..
Ethiopia[32]	7.8	9.6	10.6	10.0	5.9	3.3	3.1	2.7	2.5
Gabon	4.2	..	..	..	..	..	..	..	..
Gambia	..	..	..	0.8	1.1	1.1	0.9	0.8	1.1
Ghana	0.9	0.4	0.4	0.4	0.6	0.8	1.0	..	..
Guinea-Bissau	2.3	2.7	2.2	..	..	..	..	..	..
Kenya[33]	2.9	2.7	2.5	2.7	2.2	1.7	1.6	1.7	1.6
Lesotho	5.1	4.0	4.8	4.0	3.8	[3.5]	[3.4]	3.3	3.2
Liberia	2.3	2.3	..	..	(1.5)	(1.4)	(2.0)	(2.0)	..
Libya	..	..	..	—	..	..	..	..	..
Madagascar	1.4	1.3	1.2	1.2	1.3	1.2	1.1	0.9	0.8
Malawi	1.8	1.5	1.5	1.3	1.1	1.0	0.8	1.3	1.0
Mali	..	..	..	2.1	..	..	..	..	..
Mauritania	..	..	4.0	3.8	3.5	(3.7)	(3.8)	(3.5)	(3.2)
Mauritius	0.2	0.2	0.3	0.4	0.4	0.4	0.3	0.3	0.3
Morocco	4.3	4.1	4.3	4.1	4.2	4.3	4.6	(4.2)	(4.1)
Mozambique[34]	10.6	9.2	10.3	10.1	8.7	8.3	7.6	(5.9)	(4.6)
Namibia[35]	5.4	4.9	2.8	2.4	4.9	4.5	2.7	2.0	(2.0)
Niger	0.8	0.8	0.9	1.9	[1.1]	(0.9)	(1.1)	(1.0)	..
Nigeria	(0.7)	(1.2)	(1.0)	(0.9)	..	..	..	..	..

Rwanda	1.7	1.5	1.7	4.1	6.2	5.5	:	:	:
Senegal	2.1	2.0	2.1	2.0	1.9	1.8	:	:	:
Seychelles	4.5	4.3	4.3	4.0	4.4	4.7	2.8	1.5	2.3
Sierra Leone	0.6	0.5	0.8	0.9	1.8	2.5	:	:	:
Somalia	1.8	:	:	:	:	:	:	:	:
South Africa	4.5	4.7	4.1	3.6	3.0	2.8	2.6	2.6	2.2
Sudan	1.9	2.0	3.2	2.9	2.4	3.1	6.1	9.5	(4.3)
Swaziland	1.2	1.1	1.1	1.5	1.6	2.0	2.3	2.1	2.2
Tanzania	3.6	2.4	1.9	1.6	1.7	:	:	:	:
Togo	3.5	3.1	3.1	3.1	2.8	2.9	3.9	2.7	:
Tunisia[36]	2.0	2.7	2.8	2.7	2.6	2.3	2.4	2.3	1.9
Uganda	1.9	1.8	2.2	2.5	2.4	1.7	1.7	:	(3.7)
Zaire[37]	0.4	2.4	0.8	:	:	:	:	:	:
Zambia[38]	3.2	2.4	4.2	3.7	2.5	3.0	(1.6)	(1.1)	(1.4)
Zimbabwe	7.1	6.5	6.1	6.3	7.6	(7.6)	(6.5)	(4.6)	(4.3)
Caribbean									
Bahamas	0.6	0.6	0.6	0.7	0.6	0.6	0.6	0.6	0.6
Barbados	0.5	0.6	0.7	0.8	0.8	0.8	0.8	0.8	:
Cuba	:	:	7.0	:	3.7	:	(1.0)	:	:
Dominican Rep.	1.0	0.9	0.7	0.5	0.4	0.5	0.6	:	:
Haiti	:	:	:	(1.9)	(1.5)	(3.5)	(3.4)	:	:
Jamaica	0.8	0.8	2.6	2.7	2.0	1.2	0.9	0.7	:
Central America									
Belize[39]	:	(1.3)	1.2	1.2	1.1	1.1	1.3	(1.7)	:
Costa Rica[40]	(0.6)	0.5	2.2	2.1	1.9	1.8	2.2	:	:
El Salvador	3.3	2.8	2.9	2.7	2.4	2.0	1.5	1.2	1.1
Guatemala	1.7	1.6	1.6	1.7	1.3	1.5	1.3	1.2	(1.3)
Honduras	0.8	0.7	1.0	0.8	(0.5)	(0.5)	(0.5)	(0.5)	:
Mexico	0.5	0.5	0.5	0.4	0.4	0.4	0.5	0.6	:
Nicaragua[41]	:	:	:	:	:	:	:	:	:
Panama[42]	1.9	2.1	2.0	1.4	1.4	1.3	1.3	1.3	1.3

State	1987	1988	1989	1990	1991	1992	1993	1994	1995
South America									
Argentina[43]	2.5	2.5	2.4	1.8	1.3	1.9	1.6	1.7	1.6
Bolivia	1.7	1.6	1.6	2.3	2.3	2.1	2.1	2.0	1.9
Brazil[44]	..	..	..	..	..	..	..	..	..
Chile[45]	2.8	2.3	2.2	2.2	2.1	2.0	1.9	1.8	1.6
Colombia	1.1	1.3	1.4	1.4	1.3	1.1	1.2	1.4	0.9
Ecuador	2.0	2.0	2.0	1.9	2.2	2.7	3.1	2.7	..
Guyana[46]	..	3.3	..	4.7	0.6	1.0	1.0	1.0	0.9
Paraguay	1.1	1.0	1.3	1.3	1.7	1.6	1.5	1.4	1.4
Peru[47]	3.0	2.1	..	2.0	1.3	1.9	..	..	..
Uruguay	1.9	2.1	2.4	2.4	1.8	2.3	1.9	..	..
Venezuela[48]	1.3	1.5	0.9	1.1	1.5	(2.7)	(2.0)	(1.6)	(1.6)

1 Official NATO publications provide the data for member countries and reflect NATO's definition of military spending rather than domestic budgetary information.
2 Figures on German military expenditure refer to West Germany up to and including 1990 and to the united Germany from 1991 onward.
3 Croatia declared its independence from the former Yugoslavia in June 1991 and was recognized by the European Community on Jan. 1992 and the United Nations in May 1992.
4 Figures up to and including 1992 may not include full procurement costs.
5 The Czech Republic became independent after the breakup of Czechoslovakia on 1 Jan. 1993.
6 Czechoslovakia split into the Czech Republic and the Republic of Slovakia on 1 Jan. 1993.
7 Estonia became independent in Sep. 1991.
8 Excluding expenditure for border guards and peacekeeping activities. Figures from 1991 onward include pensions.
9 Excluding military pensions.
10 Latvia became independent in Sep. 1991. Frontier and home guards are included in total military expenditure.
11 Lithuania became independent in Sep. 1991. Figures up to 1992 are in million roubles, from 1993 onward in million litai.
12 Figures up to 1991 are recurrent expenditure only, from 1992 onward recurrent and capital expenditure.
13 The Slovak Republic became independent after the breakup of Czechoslovakia on 1 Jan. 1993.
14 Slovenia declared its independence from the former Yugoslavia in June 1991 and was recognized by the European Community in Jan. 1992 and by the United Nations in May 1992.
15 Serbia and Montenegro announced the creation of the Federal Republic of Yugoslavia in Apr. 1992. Figures prior to 1992 are for the former Yugoslavia.
16 All the CIS states declared their independence during 1991. Because of high inflation, volatile exchange rates and the absence of reliable national statistics for most of the CIS countries, it is difficult to calculate military expenditure in constant US dollars and as a percentage of GDP (tables 6A.2 and 6A.3). In table 6A.1 figures are provided, where possible, for all the CIS states.
17 Pensions and internal security are not included.

18 Figures cover spending for both the armed forces and law enforcement.

19 Up to and including 1994 figures represent expenditure and are taken from Institut ekonomicheskogo analiza, *Finansovaya stabilizatsiya v Rossii* (Moscow, June 1995), p. 213. Figures for 1995 and 1996 are budget figures. All exclude the costs of paramilitary forces.

20 Figures up to 1993 are in billion roubles, from 1994 onwards in billion karbovanets. The 1996 figure includes the cost of paramilitary forces.

21 Figures up to 1992 are in billion roubles, from 1993 onward in billion sum.

22 Figures include public order and safety expenditure.

23 The People's Democratic Republic of Yemen (South Yemen) and the Yemen Arab Republic (North Yemen) merged in May 1990 to form the Republic of Yemen. Figures up to 1989 refer to North Yemen and from 1990 onward to the unified state.

24 Figures include allocations made to the Royal Brunei Armed Forces only.

25 Figures are official figures only. The official figure for the Chinese defence budget is only a fraction of the revenue available to the People's Liberation Army and falls far short of actual expenditure.

26 Military pensions are not included.

27 Figures for New Zealand do not include superannuation payments for ex-servicemen or civilian employees of the Ministry of Defence.

28 Recurrent expenditure only.

29 Figures up to 1994 are in million new kwanzas, from 1995 onward in million kwanzas readjusted (1 kwanza readjusted = 1000 new kwanzas). Figures include public order and safety expenditure.

30 Recurrent expenditure only.

31 Recurrent expenditure only from 1993 onward.

32 Eritrea became independent from Ethiopia in May 1993.

33 Recurrent expenditure only.

34 From 1994 onward, costs of demobilization of government and Renamo forces and the formation of a new unified army are included.

35 Namibia became independent on 21 Mar. 1990. From 1991 onward figures include recurrent and capital expenditure.

36 From 1988 onward figures include recurrent and capital expenditure.

37 Figures up to 1991 are in million zaïres, from 1992 onward in billion new zaïres (1 new zaïre = 3 million zaïres).

38 From 1989 onward, public order and safety expenditure included.

39 Public order and safety expenditure included.

40 Costa Rica abolished its armed forces in 1948 but the security services have a military function, i.e., the maintenance of the country's territorial integrity. Figures include spending on the Guardia de Assistencia Rural (the Rural Guard) which forms part of the police service, expenditure within the ministry of Public Security and pensions for its personnel.

41 Because Nicaragua experienced hyper-inflation from 1985 to 1991, it is difficult to calculate military expenditure in constant US dollars and as a percentage of GDP (tables 6B.2 and 6B.3).

42 Panama's army was abolished by the National Assembly in Aug. 1994.

43 Excluding intelligence, including gendarmería and coast guard. The full amount of pension payments is not covered by the budget and payments on the military debt have not been identified. Because of hyper-inflation and currency changes, figures are unreliable. Figures for 1987–88 are in million australes, for 1989–91 in billion australes and from 1992 onward in million pesos.

44 Estimating Brazilian military expenditure is complicated because published data do not match the size and activity of the armed forces. Military spending falls under a number of other budget headings in addition to the army, navy and air force. These include the Presidential budget, the Ministry of Justice, which is responsible, among other things, for the paramilitary, federal police and military pensions.

[45] Figures do not include expenditure for public order and security (Carabineros and Investigaciones) or supporting services, military industries and military pensions.
[46] Military pensions and internal security included.
[47] Figures up to 1988 are in billion intis and from 1989 onward in million soles.
[48] These figures are essentially operating budgets; special credits for military equipment not included.

Conventions in tables

. .	Data not available or not applicable
–	Nil or a negligible figure
( )	Uncertain data
[ ]	SIPRI estimate
—	Series break when data not comparable.

ER	exchange rate
m.	million
b.	billion (thousand million)
rdj.	readjusted

Appendix 6C. Sources and methods

The military expenditure project collects information on and monitors trends in global military spending. The data provide a solid basis for comparisons and evaluations of military spending and of the economic burden of such expenditure.

Tables of military expenditure in current and constant prices, as well as military spending as a share of gross domestic product (GDP), are published annually in the *SIPRI Yearbook,* where they are presented as a 10-year time-series of military spending for individual countries. It is important to note that the tables are updated each year and the revisions can be quite extensive—not only are significant changes made in figures which were previously estimates, but entire series are revised when new and better sources come to light. As a result there is sometimes a considerable variation between data sets for individual countries in different *Yearbooks.*

I. Methods and definitions

All figures in the tables in appendix 6B are presented on a calendar-year basis on the assumption that military expenditure occurs evenly throughout the fiscal year. This permits the provision of a uniform picture of trends in military expenditure even though there is no common fiscal year for the budgetary information reported by individual countries. The consumer price index (CPI) is used to deflate current prices into constant values, and period-average market exchange rates are used to convert domestic currencies to US dollars using the base year (currently 1990) exchange rate. The ratio of military expenditure to GDP is calculated in domestic currency (at current prices).

The data for NATO countries are estimates made by NATO to correspond to a common definition of military expenditure. These include: all current and capital expenditure on the armed forces and in the running of defence departments and other government agencies engaged in defence projects and space activities; the cost of paramilitary forces, border guards and gendarmerie when judged to be trained and equipped for military operations; military research and development, testing and evaluation costs; and costs of retirement pensions of service personnel and civilian employees. Items on civilian defence, interest on war debts and veterans' payments are excluded.

The NATO definition is used as a guideline for all countries but in practice it is not possible to adhere to a common definition of military expenditure for all countries since this would require much more detailed information than is available about the content of military budgets and off-budget military expenditure items. For example, although information on the sums expended on paramilitary forces is available for many countries, it is not always clear whether such expenditure is included in defence budgets or if it appears under some other budget heading. In many cases, the budgets of the defence and interior ministries are combined in official statistics without any information about their relationship or the content of the internal security budget.

The figures for 'constant price' military expenditure become more unreliable when inflation is rapid and unpredictable. Supplementary allocations, made during the course of the year to cover losses in purchasing power, often go unreported and recent military expenditure can appear to be falling in real terms. This is a particular problem in countries in economic transition and in much of Latin America.

Where accurate data are not available, and when possible, estimates are made based on analysis of the political and economic conditions in individual countries. Estimated figures are presented in square brackets in the tables. When economic indicators are projections and/or when a preliminary figure for defence spending is given, the figures are presented in round brackets, signifying 'uncertain data'.

II. Sources

The estimates of military expenditure for NATO countries are taken from official information published yearly in *NATO Review*.

Data for the Central and East European countries are taken primarily from domestic budgets provided by their respective embassies in Stockholm or by the ministries of defence or finance in certain countries.

For the remaining countries, the military expenditure project submits a questionnaire to all countries with diplomatic accreditation in Stockholm every year to request current defence budget information. The same request is made to the ministry of defence, the ministry of finance, the statistical office and the central bank of each country, especially in the developing world. In many cases SIPRI does receive useful material from this effort but, unfortunately, very often information is not forthcoming.

For all countries, data are collected from national and international publications such as defence budgets, government financial statistics and other economic information and are stored in a computerized database. Information on the CPI, exchange rates and GDP are taken from the International Monetary Fund (IMF) *International Financial Statistics Yearbook*. Other sources consulted include the IMF publication, *World Economic Outlook*, the UN publication *National Accounts Statistics: Main Aggregates and Detailed Tables* and *Economic Outlook*, published by the Organisation for Economic Co-operation and Development (OECD). Other sources regularly consulted include: *Länderbericht* of the German Statistical Office, *Europa World Yearbook* and Economist Intelligence Unit publications. Supplementary material on military expenditure is collected through systematic scanning and analysis of a wide range of journals, magazines and newspapers. This information is integrated into the database to provide the broadest possible overview of developments in global military expenditure.

7. Military research and development

ERIC ARNETT

I. Introduction

Global military research and development (R&D) expenditure continues to decline, although two major investors with plans for growth—Japan and South Korea—continue their programmed increases. Total expenditure had decreased to a level of about $49 billion by the end of 1996, of which $32 billion is accounted for by the USA, $43 billion by NATO and $45 billion by the Organisation for Economic Co-operation and Development (OECD) countries. The most notable development in 1996 was the continuity in policy among the most important technology bases despite several elections and defence reviews.

The nuclear weapon states are adjusting to declining military R&D budgets in markedly different ways: the USA and more so the UK are shifting strongly towards research on conventional weapons while maintaining their extant nuclear arsenals; China and Russia appear to be retaining a nuclear emphasis without neglecting conventional systems entirely; and France occupies a position somewhere between, deciding in 1996 to continue all its military modernization programmes.

Among the most advanced states, aircraft projects are still claiming the lion's share of effort. A comparable US initiative in the field of ballistic missile defence (BMD) has gained the cooperation of Germany, Israel and Italy, but France and the UK remain aloof and US security partners in the Pacific apparently prefer for now to purchase BMD technology off the shelf as appropriate. Russian development of more capable theatre missile defences continues, but with a lower priority than in the USA, while China has expressed misgivings about BMD.

This chapter investigates these developments in more detail. After a description of global trends with special attention paid to the nuclear weapon states and India in section II, section III examines the R&D programmes of three military establishments in North-East Asia: those of Japan and South Korea, the two states that continue to expand their military technology bases, and that of Taiwan, which has similar economic conditions but on a smaller scale and with more limited access to technology. It is found that the Japanese and South Korean build-ups are only explicable if the development of an independent arms industry is desirable as an end in itself, despite economic and political trends to the contrary. In contrast, Taiwan's build-up during the 1970s and 1980s was apparently intended primarily as a cover for politically sensitive technology transfers following the mainland government's

Table 7.1. Official estimates of government military R&D expenditure, 1993–96[a]

Country	Military R&D expenditure		Year	Percentage of total military expenditure	Source
	(Current local currency)	(1990 US $m.)			
Nuclear weapon states					
USA (m. dollars)	38 000	32 000	1996	*14*	OECD
France (b. francs)	29	4 800	1995	*12*	OECD
UK (b. pounds)	2.0	3 200	1994	*9.1*	OECD
Russia (tr. roubles)	2.73	1 200[b]	1994	*6.4*	UN
China[c]	..	1 000	1994	*<4*	PRC Govt
Non-nuclear weapon and threshold states					
Germany (m. D. mark)	2 900	1 500	1995	*4.8*	OECD
Japan (b. yen)	170	1 100	1996	*3.4*	OECD
India (b. rupees)	14.9	570	1994	*6.5*	Indian Govt
Sweden (b. kronor)	4.1	560	1995	*10.3*	OECD
South Korea (b. won)	373	370	1996	*3.0*	ROK Govt
Italy (b. lire)	480	320	1995	*1.4*	OECD
Spain (b. pesetas)	37	280	1995	*3.5*	OECD
Taiwan (b. T. dollars)	8.9	280	1994	*3.3*	ROC Govt
Canada (m. C. dollars)	190	150	1995	*1.6*	OECD
Australia (m. A. dollars)	220	150	1994	*2.0*	OECD
Switzerland (m. francs)	117	140	1995	*2.0*	UN
South Africa (m. rand)	579	130	1995	*5.2*	RSA Govt
Netherlands (m. guilders)	170	78	1996	*1.3*	OECD
Norway (m. kroner)	430	61	1995	*1.8*	OECD
Brazil (m. reais)	45.4	49[b]	1995	*0.5*	UN
Finland (m. markaa)	120	27	1995	*1.3*	OECD
Poland (m. new zlotys)	101	18	1995	*1.5*	UN
Ukraine (b. karbonavets)	416	13[d]	1994	*2.3*	UN
Argentina (m. pesos)	17.1	8.6	1995	*0.4*	UN
Czech Republic (m. korunas)	278	8.6[d]	1994	*1.2*	UN
Philippines (b. pesos)	249	6.7	1994	*1.2*	UN
Turkey (b. lira)	140	5.6	1994	*0.1*	UN
Denmark (m. kroner)	37	5.3	1995	*0.2*	OECD
Portugal (b. escudos)	1.2	5.1	1994	*0.2*	OECD
Slovakia (m. korunas)	150	3.9[d]	1995	*1.2*	UN
Belgium (m. francs)	150	3.9	1995	*0.1*	OECD
New Zealand (m. NZ dollars)	6.3	3.6	1993	*0.6*	OECD
Greece (b. drachmas)	1.0	3.4	1995	*0.1*	OECD
Colombia (m. pesos)	770	1.8	1995	*0.1*	UN
Hungary (m. forints)	164	1.1	1994	*0.2*	UN

[a] Includes only states spending more than $1 million on military R&D.
[b] Figures derived using current exchange rates.
[c] Figures for China are accurate to only one significant digit.
[d] Figures in 1993 US $m.

Sources: OECD Main Science and Technology Indicators, no. 2 (1996) and no. 2 (1995); UN documents A/49/190, 29 June 1994; A/49/190/Add. 1, 30 Aug. 1994; A/50/277, 20 July 1995; A/50/277/Add. 1, 11 Oct. 1995; A/50/277/Add. 2, 20 Feb. 1996; and A/51/209, 24 July 1996; and other data provided by national governments as cited below.

Table 7.2. Government expenditure on military R&D in the Group of Seven (G7) industrialized countries, 1994–97

Country	Year	Military R&D expenditure (1990 US $m.)	Military R&D as a percentage of			
			Total military expenditure	Military equipment expenditure	Govt R&D expenditure	National R&D expenditure
USA	1996	32 000	14	54	54.7	20
France	1995	4 800	12	39	33.3	16
UK	1994	3 200	9.1	37	40.8	14
Germany	1995	1 500	4.8	44	9.1	3.6
Japan	1995	1 000	3.3	14	6.2	1.0
Italy	1995	320	1.4	10	4.7	2.4
Canada	1995	150	1.6	10	4.8	2.6

Sources: *OECD Main Science and Technology Indicators*, no. 2 (1996) and no. 2 (1995); UN document A/49/190, 29 June 1994, pp. 34–35; Defense Agency, *Defense of Japan 1996* (Japan Times: Tokyo, 1996); and chapter 6 in this volume.

re-emergence into the international system. Taiwan may be scaling back its military technology base in response to exporters' new willingness to supply it with arms over Beijing's objections.

II. Global trends

Global military R&D expenditure in the mid-1990s has fallen to about $49 billion,[1] a decrease of about 60 per cent from the estimate for 1986 given in the *SIPRI Yearbook 1987*.[2] Of the former Warsaw Treaty Organization

[1] This estimate is based on government figures for all the 20 largest investors with the possible exception of Israel. The Israeli figure for 1994 is $59 million for all but special projects. One special project is the Arrow ballistic missile defence (BMD) system, to which Israel has committed $350 million for the 6 years beginning in 1996. Thailand, which has also been among the top 20, has not provided information since 1991, and so is not included in table 7.1. Thailand's R&D budget at that time was 2.89 billion baht (about $110 million). Arnett, E., 'Military research and development', *SIPRI Yearbook 1996: Armaments, Disarmament and International Security* (Oxford University Press: Oxford, 1996), pp. 382–83; and Morrocco, J. D., 'Arrow on target for initial, limited capability in 1998', *Aviation Week & Space Technology*, 3 Mar. 1997, p. 58.

[2] This figure is derived from the sum of best publicly known estimates and 1% of military expenditure in states where no figure for military R&D is publicly known. The estimate of China's expenditure is elaborated in Arnett, E., 'Military technology: the case of China', *SIPRI Yearbook 1995: Armaments, Disarmament and International Security* (Oxford University Press: Oxford, 1995), pp. 375–77. The estimate that China spends on the order of $1 billion to one significant digit is meant to imply that it spends between $0.5 and $1.5 billion, but no more precise estimate is possible. A 'military researcher', Dai Shizheng, is cited giving an estimate of 4.3 billion yuan for 1993 ($670 million in 1990 dollars) in Lai, A., 'Preparation for high-tech regional wars', *China Strategic Review*, Aug. 1996. Researchers from the Chinese Academy of Military Science stated in 1996 that R&D constituted less than 4% of military expenditure. Wu Fangming and Wu Xizhi, 'On dealing correctly with the relations of our defence establishment to our economic construction', *National Defence*, 15 Feb. 1996, pp. 4–6 (in Chinese), in 'PRC: AMS journal views military role in economic development', Foreign Broadcast Information Service, *Daily Report–China (FBIS-CHI)*, FBIS-CHI-96-203, 21 Oct. 1996. See Arnett (note 1), pp. 382 and 384 on the reduction in the global figure since the 1986 estimate in Tullberg, R. and Hagmeyer-Gaverus, G., 'World military expenditure', *SIPRI Yearbook 1987: World Armaments and Disarmament* (Oxford University Press: Oxford, 1997), p. 153.

(WTO) states, only Russia spends more than $100 million on military R&D. Only India, Japan and South Korea continue with plans to increase their military R&D spending significantly, although India has not funded the planned increases for the past two years. In the cases of India and South Korea, the plans are interesting not only in their own right, but also because one of the reasons given for increasing the budget for military R&D is emulation of putative Western defence policies, where R&D is said by proponents of increased spending to be typically 10 per cent of military expenditure. In fact, as shown in tables 7.1 and 7.2, only the NATO nuclear weapon states and Sweden spend at this level.

A note on sources of information

As discussed more comprehensively in the *SIPRI Yearbook 1996*,[3] information on military R&D in the public domain has improved since the mid-1980s but is still quite limited. The most complete information is available from certain national governments, in particular that of the USA. Data from any one state, however, are not easily compared with those from another. Often only R&D undertaken by the defence ministry is counted, neglecting other projects of military importance. The largest set of comparable data on military R&D comes from the OECD, which compiles a survey of national budgets to produce the most comparable aggregate figures for total civil and military R&D investment in member states.[4] (NATO data are also comparable, but cover only the 16 member states.[5]) As the OECD has expanded—recent additions include Mexico, South Korea, and several Central and East European states[6]—so has the coverage of its science and technology indicators database.

Although considerable effort was put into making the UN register of military budgets comparable, it is difficult to know how governments derive the figures they submit, and some give only a single figure for military R&D without disaggregating at all. Moreover, although the register still enjoys unanimous support in the First Committee of the UN General Assembly, only 63 states have submitted R&D data in any one year since the register was started in 1980, 16 of these (mainly African and Latin American states) have only filed nil reports and only 31 have given figures for any year since 1993. The USA has not made a submission since 1990, and Indonesia, an original promoter of the register, stopped submitting data in 1982. Of the 20 largest

---

[3] Arnett (note 1), pp. 387–88.
[4] Definitions and methods are described in OECD, *Frascati Manual 1993* (OECD: Paris, 1993). Data generally refer to expenditures by organizations carrying out R&D, but may include budgeted disbursements from funding organizations. Some OECD members report figures to the UN as military R&D that are excluded from that category by OECD methods because they relate more closely to education and training or other objectives. In cases where the OECD method gives a nil return for a member, table 7.1 gives the figure submitted to the UN when it is greater than $2 million.
[5] See chapter 6 in this volume.
[6] A list of members of the OECD is given in the Glossary.

Table 7.3. Trends in government expenditure on military R&D in selected countries, 1989–96

US$ figures are at 1990 prices and exchange rates.

Country	1989	1990	1991	1992	1993	1994	1995	1996	1989–94
USA	43 000	40 000	38 000	37 000	37 000	33 000	32 000	32 000	228 000
France	5 900	6 800	6 000	5 600	5 100	5 000	4 800	..	34 400
UK	4 000	3 900	3 700	3 400	3 600	3 200	3 400	..	17 900
Germany	1 900	2 100	1 900	1 800	1 500	1 400	1 500	..	10 600
Japan	660	720	770	830	900	920	1 000	1 100	4 800
Sweden	670	650	780	680	640	490	560	..	3 910
Italy	800	490	670	640	650	630	320	..	3 880
India	460	430	420	430	520	570	..	..	2 830
Spain	440	490	470	390	320	270	280	..	2 380
South Korea	150	230	240	270	320	320	350	370	1 530
South Africa	390	310	220	180	130	130	130	..	1 360
Canada	250	230	190	200	180	180	150	..	1 230
Australia	180	170	160	160	160	150	..	..	980

Sources: *OECD Main Science and Technology Indicators*, no. 2 (1996) and no. 2 (1995); Government of India, Department of Science and Technology, *Research and Development Statistics*, various years; Cilliers, J., 'Defence research and development in South Africa', *African Security Review*, vol. 5, no. 5 (1996), p. 42; and table 7.10.

investors in military R&D among UN members, China, India, South Africa and South Korea have never filed a return.[7]

This chapter uses OECD figures where possible, falling back when necessary on submissions to the UN and other national data in that order. Independent R&D undertaken by firms with the expectation that it will be reimbursed during procurement is not included, although it may constitute more than half of all military R&D investment in some cases.

In general, this chapter seeks to evaluate and compare the results of R&D programmes rather than the opportunity cost to governments of the relevant expenditures and human resources. Nevertheless, current figures are deflated using the local consumer price index and converted to US dollars at the 1990 exchange rate in order to facilitate comparisons between figures in this chapter and chapter 6. Purchasing power parity (PPP) conversions are usually preferable for comparing R&D figures, but are difficult to derive for military goods. Using PPP would tend to give lower results for some currencies (by about 20 per cent for the yen and the Deutschmark, and over 35 per cent in the case of the Swedish krona) and may increase results by as much as a factor of four for currencies like the rouble, yuan and rupee.

---

[7] Israel has filed once, but aggregated military R&D with procurement: 6.4084 billion new shekels (about $4 billion in 1990 dollars) for FY 1988. If the technological intensity (R&D/equipment) of Israeli equipment expenditure is comparable to that of non-nuclear NATO members, as much as one-third of this amount could have been R&D spending. UN document A/INF/45/5, 18 Oct. 1990.

Table 7.4. Recent combat aircraft programmes in selected countries

Country	Programme	Full-scale development begun	Expected date of initial operation	Expected govt R&D funds (constant US $b.)	No.
USA	F-22	1991	2004	17	442
UK/Germany/Italy/Spain	EF2000	1988	2001	12	620
France	Rafale	1987	2002	7	294
Japan	F-2	1988	1999	3	130
Taiwan	Ching-kuo	1982	1995	3	130
South Korea	KTX-2	1997	2004	2	100
USA	F/A-18E/F	1991	2001	2	1 000
India	LCA	1983	2002	2	220
Sweden	JAS-39	1982	1996	2	200

Source: Compiled by the author.

Areas of emphasis: combat aircraft and missile defence

The main expense for many of the states with major military R&D efforts continues to be combat aircraft. Recent programmes are summarized in table 7.4. For smaller budgets, combat aircraft can account for most of the R&D expenditure. In the most extreme case, Spain's contribution to the Eurofighter consortium consumed over 90 per cent of the R&D budget during its peak years in the early 1990s.[8] Almost one-third of the funding authorized for R&D in 1997 for major weapon systems in the USA goes to seven programmes for combat aircraft, as seen in table 7.5. Western governments are already moving to a new generation of aircraft: the USA has launched its Joint Strike Fighter (JSF) project with $2.2 billion for competitive 'Concept Demonstration'. The winning industrial team will build more than 3000 aircraft beginning in 2008. European governments are studying a Future Offensive Aircraft for initial operation in 2015. The dominance of Western firms in relevant technologies is such that new projects are justified more on the basis of new air-defence missiles than hostile aircraft.[9] Russia appears to be the only major aircraft-producing state to be de-emphasizing its effort, as described below.

[8] Arnett (note 1), pp. 398–400. For 1997, 23.7 billion pesetas are allocated for Spain's contribution to the Eurofighter, 84% of the Defence Ministry's R&D budget. Del Vado, S. F., 'Presupuesto con crecimiento cero' [Budget with zero growth], *Revista Española de Defensa*, Nov. 1996, p. 10. In a similar case on a smaller scale, Pakistan has committed $6 million to its share of the Chinese K-8 trainer, despite having an annual military R&D budget of only some 130 million rupees (*c.* $4 million). Siddiqa, A., 'Ad hocracy, decision-making and Pakistan's arms production and nuclear projects', *Indian Defence Review*, no. 3 (1996), pp. 18, 22; and Arnett, E., 'Military research and development in southern Asia', ed. E. Arnett, SIPRI, *Military Capacity and the Risk of War: China, India, Pakistan and Iran* (Oxford University Press: Oxford, 1997).

[9] A US Air Force official attributed the need for the JSF to 'increasing proliferation of things like SA-10s, 12s, 15s, 17s'. Department of Defense news briefing, 16 Nov. 1996. A RAND study for the Air Force advised against justifying the F-22 with possible future Russian fighters. Lambeth, B. S., *Russia's Air Power at the Crossroads* (RAND: Santa Monica, Calif., 1996).

Table 7.5. Appropriations for major US R&D programmes, 1997[a]

Figures are in current US $m.

Programme	R&D budget	Service or agency
Aircraft and associated weapons		
F-22 fighter	1 906	Air Force
B-2 bomber	624	Air Force
V-22 tilt-rotor utility aircraft	577	Navy
Joint Strike Fighter	534	Air Force, Navy
F/A-18E/F fighter-bomber	441	Navy
RAH-66 attack helicopter	339	Army
E-8A JSTARS surveillance aircraft	243	Air Force, Army, Navy
B-1B bomber upgrades	228	Air Force
Endurance unpiloted aerial vehicles	176	DARPA
Joint Air-to-Surface Stand-off Missile (JASSM)	169	Air Force
F-15E fighter-bomber	158	Air Force
F-16 fighter	156	Air Force
Tomahawk cruise missile and mission planning system	146	Navy
Joint Stand-Off Weapon (JSOW) smart bomb	110	Navy, Air Force
Subtotal	**5 807**	
Missile defence		
National Missile Defense	833	BMDO
Theater High-Altitude Area Defense (THAAD)	622	BMDO
Patriot Advanced Capability (PAC)-3	597	BMDO
Joint tactical missile defence	528	BMDO
Space Based Infrared (SBIR) satellite	448	Air Force
Navy Area Defense (Lower Tier)	311	BMDO
Navy Theater Wide (Upper Tier)	304	BMDO
Subtotal	**3 643**	
Other strategic programmes		
Nuclear weapon research, development and testing	1 600	Department of Energy
Milstar communications satellite	720	Air Force
Intercontinental ballistic missile	230	Air Force
Subtotal	**2 550**	
Other		
NSSN attack submarine	389	Navy
Brilliant Anti-armour Technology (BAT) submunition	165	Army
Arsenal ship	125	Navy
SSN-23 Seawolf attack submarine	118	Navy
Grand total	**12 797**	

[a] Includes only those programmes allocated more than $100 million.

Sources: US Senate, *Conference Report on Department of Defense Appropriations Act, 1997* (US Government Printing Office: Washington, DC, 1996); and US Senate, Committee on Armed Services, *National Defense Authorization Act for Fiscal Year 1997* (US Government Printing Office: Washington, DC, 1996).

The three states that plan significant increases in their R&D budgets—India, Japan and South Korea—are devoting the main share of those budgets to aircraft projects. The small production runs over which such large R&D expenditures can be amortized combined with the surplus capacity of established exporters willing to offer lavish inducements to potential customers suggests that much of this effort is not strictly necessary from the perspective of economical military planning.

A second area of major interest in some states is BMD. Others have been reluctant to invest heavily in this technology, preferring either to avoid undercutting the viability of missile forces or to allow major investors to assume the technological risk, demonstrated in 1996 and early 1997 by a string of six failures and several postponements in the US Theater High-Altitude Area Defense (THAAD) and Navy Theater Wide/Upper Tier development programmes.[10]

The greatest enthusiasm for BMD has been evident in the USA, which is not only investing heavily in its own projects but also underwriting co-development elsewhere. Israel has been the most eager collaborator, its research being subsidized heavily by the USA. US efforts to interest the other NATO nuclear weapon states in BMD have to date been largely unsuccessful, although Germany and Italy have shown some interest.[11] The Franco-Italian Aster 30 air-defence system has a very limited BMD capability and may be improved, but France and the UK are apparently uncomfortable with the implications of BMD for the viability of their nuclear arsenals vis-à-vis Russia, which is developing an advanced theatre-range interceptor, the S-400.[12] As discussed in section III, Japan and South Korea, the USA's main security partners in North-East Asia, have so far declined the opportunity to get involved in developing BMD technology. China has been the most critical of Western BMD programmes, but has imported the Russian S-300 system.

The nuclear weapon states

Having prepared for the Comprehensive Nuclear Test-Ban Treaty (CTBT),[13] the nuclear weapon states show radically divergent approaches to their military technology bases. At one end of the spectrum, R&D on new nuclear weapons has practically ended in the UK, and the budget is dominated by conventional systems, particularly aircraft and air-launched missiles. Similarly,

---

[10] See chapter 11 in this volume for a discussion of the distinction between tactical and strategic systems and the implications of ambiguities for arms control.

[11] Differences of emphasis and interpretation with respect to the concept of counter-proliferation account for some of the controversy. A NATO report claiming Europe faced a threat from the ballistic missiles of Algeria, Iran, Iraq or Libya within the decade was dismissed by Eduardo Serra, Spain's Defence Minister: 'I am absolutely sure there is no threat of imminent danger', Television Española, 25 Nov. 1996, in 'Spain: Defense Minister on NATO, Libya, Zaire', Foreign Broadcast Information Service, *Daily Report–West Europe (FBIS-WEU)*, FBIS-WEU-96-228, 26 Nov. 1996.

[12] Russia's S-400 is said to be comparable to the US THAAD. A. Arbatov, personal communication, 5 Oct. 1996. See also Kravtsev, A., 'A global myth', *Air Defense Digest*, no. 9 (1992), p. 25, cited in Arbatov, A., 'The ABM Treaty and theatre missile defence', *SIPRI Yearbook 1995* (note 2), p. 687.

[13] See also chapter 12 in this volume.

the USA, while working on modifications to existing designs that might give the nuclear forces new capabilities, has forsworn development of entirely new systems. In contrast, strategic modernization apparently continues to take the lion's share of funding in Russia and China.[14] France, which completed a review of the military budget in 1996, has again decided not to terminate any R&D programmes and to proceed with new nuclear forces despite the ban on nuclear testing. The rest of this subsection briefly discusses the USA, France and Russia.

The United States

The USA continues to spend nearly two-thirds of the government funds invested globally in military R&D, $32 billion of $49 billion. This is a decrease of more than 25 per cent from 1989, and the budget is expected to decrease by an additional 10 per cent in gross terms by the end of fiscal year (FY) 2002, despite President Bill Clinton's 1992 election campaign promise to increase it.[15] Not only is this level of effort almost seven times that of France (as seen in table 7.3), the nearest competitor, but there is also reason to believe that the amounts involved are administered more effectively than the smaller budgets characteristic of other countries. In addition to major projects sponsored by the armed services, a total of $3.7 billion was allocated to the Pentagon's Ballistic Missile Defense Organization for R&D.[16] Above and beyond the BMD programmes listed in table 7.5, $56.8 million was allocated for the Air Force's Airborne Laser for boost-phase interception,[17] and $30 million was allocated for Medium Extended Area Defense System (MEADS), a project to involve European partners in Corps SAM, a highly mobile system which otherwise would have been cancelled.[18]

[14] China discontinued most of its conventional R&D programmes after 1979, retaining a strong emphasis on the nuclear programmes. Independent R&D on conventional programmes continued in the interest of developing export products, but most were not successful. Arnett (note 2). Lack of government funding is still constraining efforts to develop, *inter alia,* the LY-60 SAM and a medium-range air-to-air missile. Opall, B., 'Chinese strive to boost range, aim of missiles', *Defense News,* 9–15 Dec. 1996, p. 1; and Mecham, M., 'China displays export air defense missile', *Aviation Week & Space Technology,* 2 Dec. 1996, p. 61.

[15] Arnett, E. H. and Kokoski, R., 'Military technology and international security: the case of the USA', *SIPRI Yearbook 1993: World Armaments and Disarmament* (Oxford University Press: Oxford, 1993), p. 309. Reports from the American Association for the Advancement of Science (AAAS) project a 32% decline in military R&D between 1995 and 2002, compared with a decline of 20% in civilian R&D for the same period. Although the USA has the highest ratio of military to civilian R&D of the OECD states—55% in FY 1997—the ratio for basic research is only 7%. AAAS, *Congressional Action on Research and Development in the FY 1997 Budget* (AAAS: Washington, DC, 1996); AAAS, *Projected Spending on Nondefense R&D, FY 1995–2002* (AAAS: Washington, DC, 1996); and AAAS, *President's FY 1997 Budget: Projections for Defense R&D* (AAAS: Washington, DC, 1996).

[16] After a 1995 review found that funding was too high, BMD funding was reduced by 30% over the next 5 years. Some of the reduction was reinstated by Congress. Kaminski, P. G., 'Dark clouds of nuclear war threat fading, but not gone', *Defense Issues,* vol. 11, no. 92 (1996).

[17] A $1.1 billion contract for the prototype was awarded in 1996. Total programme costs were estimated at $5.6 billion for 7 aircraft. Fulghum, D. A., 'Boeing team tapped to build laser aircraft', *Aviation Week & Space Technology,* 18 Nov. 1996, p. 22.

[18] Total development costs for MEADS are expected to exceed $3 billion, and US officials are not certain that the programme will reach completion. Anselmo, J., 'MEADS faces tough sell', *Aviation Week & Space Technology,* 3 Mar. 1997, p. 57.

Table 7.6. French expenditure on military R&D

Expenditures are given in billion current francs. Figures in italics are percentages.

| Year | Sector of R&D expenditure | | | |
	Nuclear	Space	Conventional	Total
1991	10.8 (*36*)	2.4 (*8*)	16.7 (*56*)	29.9 (*100*)
1992	10.0 (*34*)	3.0 (*10*)	16.3 (*55*)	29.4 (*100*)
1993	8.7 (*30*)	3.1 (*11*)	17.0 (*59*)	28.8 (*100*)
1994	7.9 (*29*)	3.2 (*12*)	16.5 (*60*)	27.6 (*100*)
1995	8.0 (*30*)	3.8 (*14*)	15.2 (*56*)	27.1 (*100*)
1996	6.9 (*28*)	3.9 (*16*)	13.9 (*56*)	24.7 (*100*)
1997	6.3 (*28*)	2.0 (*9*)	13.9 (*62*)	22.3 (*100*)

Source: Assemblée Nationale, Défense équipement, Document no. 3030, Annexe no. 40 (Assemblée Nationale: Paris, 1996), p. 20.

France

France's defence review was completed in June 1996. While the implications for the armed forces and industrial base were profound,[19] no major R&D programmes were terminated. The exception was an equivocal threat to withdraw from the multi-nation Future Large Aircraft (FLA) project, for which France would not allocate R&D funds but continued to express interest in producing.[20] Continued pressure on the French budget and those of its partners in collaborative projects—especially Germany—suggest that some projects will eventually be terminated, making it possible to reduce R&D funding further.[21] Those seen as most threatened were the Hélios 2 surveillance satellite, the Tigre attack helicopter and the FLA, which was supported independently with the industry's own funds after the French and German governments declined to provide any money in 1996.[22]

France continued its ambitious attempt to maintain indigenous design capability for a range of conventional and nuclear weapons. As seen in table 7.6, nuclear systems are expected to retain a major portion of the R&D budget at the expense of the military space programme. Despite speculation to the contrary, the 1996 review approved funding for both a new submarine-launched

---

[19] See chapter 6 in this volume.

[20] France had already withdrawn from MEADS, a programme to which it had never really been committed, and officials expect Germany to do the same in 1997 or early 1998. France claimed it could not afford to participate, and its own effort to give the Aster a capability against missiles is funded largely (1 billion francs) by Aérospatiale independently. Provost, O., *Tribune Desfossés*, 2 Dec. 1996, p. 13 (in French), in 'France: prospects for armament program with Germany examined', FBIS-WEU-96-233, 4 Dec. 1996.

[21] France's military R&D budget has already decreased by 29.4% since 1990, as seen in table 7.3. In the same period, arms-producing companies have increased their military R&D budgets by an average of more than 20% to compensate. Sparaco, P., 'French industry upturn continues, at slow pace', *Aviation Week & Space Technology*, 10 Mar. 1997, p. 33.

[22] German plans are also short on funding for Eurofighter and Hélios, and the production decision on the Tigre has been postponed.

ballistic missile (SLBM), the M-51, and a new air-launched cruise missile (ALCM), the ASMP-A (Air-Sol Moyenne Portée Amélioré).[23]

Russia

In 1995 Russia reported its military expenditure to the United Nations for the first time.[24] Among the figures submitted for the years 1992 to 1994 were military R&D expenditures broken down into the standard UN format (table 7.7).[25] While it is uncertain exactly how the figures were derived, which programmes are under which headings and how they should be compared to Western R&D statistics, some trends can be observed.

Most importantly, the continuing high priority ascribed to the strategic forces (nuclear weapons and national air defence) is clear. Weapons for all three legs of the triad are being developed: the SS-X-27 intercontinental ballistic missile (ICBM), the SS-NX-28 SLBM, the Borey Class strategic ballistic missile submarine (SSBN) and a new ALCM.[26] In addition, the only fighter project being funded by the air force is an upgrade of the MiG-31, an interceptor designed for strategic air defence.[27]

Since production of surface warships has nearly ceased,[28] the naval R&D budget is probably spent primarily on the new strategic systems, other weapons (missiles, torpedoes, etc.) and tactical submarine research. Russia is known to be developing new nuclear and diesel attack submarines, the Severodvinsk and Lada classes respectively, which are expected to enter

---

[23] Both of these appear to be derived from existing systems, the M-45 and the ASMP, rather than being entirely new. Friedman, N., 'French navy restructures', *USNI Proceedings*, Sep. 1996, p. 100. Nevertheless, development of the M-51 is expected to cost 30 billion francs. France gives green light to nuclear missile', *Jane's Defence Weekly*, 8 May 1996, p. 14.

[24] UN document A/50/277, 20 July 1995, pp. 66–75.

[25] Although time series are difficult to derive from Soviet and Russian data, the R&D budget appears to have decreased by more than a factor of 10 since the mid-1980s. Arnett (note 1). The capacity of the technology base to apply these funds effectively has dramatically decreased. The aggregate R&D figure for 1995 is 4.94 trillion roubles according to Leiter, S., *Prospects for Russian Military R&D*, MR-709-A (RAND: Santa Monica, Calif., 1996), p. 9. The figures for 1996 and 1997 are 6.5 and 6.4 trillion roubles respectively according to chapter 6 in this volume.

[26] According to US officials, only the ICBM—essentially an all-Russian SS-25—is on schedule. Starr, B., 'Russian nuclear modernization in slow-down', *Jane's Defence Weekly*, 28 Aug. 1996, p. 5; and Holzer, R., 'Subs benefit from separate Russian navy budget', *Defense News*, 9–15 Sep. 1996, p. 14. The first SSBN is under construction, ending a 10-year break in SSBN building. It is thought to carry 12–16 ten-warhead missiles. Interfax, 3 Nov. 1996, in 'Russia: building of new strategic nuclear submarine class begins', Foreign Broadcast Information Service, *Daily Report–Central Eurasia (FBIS-SOV)*, FBIS-SOV-96-214, 5 Nov. 1996; and Handler, J., 'Russia seeks to refloat a decaying fleet', *Jane's International Defence Review*, Jan. 1997, p. 43. There is also a new tactical missile, the SS-X-26 with a range of 400 km. Norris, R. S. and Arkin, W. M., 'Estimated Russian stockpile, September 1996', *Bulletin of the Atomic Scientists*, vol. 52, no. 5 (Sep./Oct. 1996), p. 62.

[27] Lambeth (note 9), p. 94. Despite energetic work at Sukhoi to develop variants of the Su-27, no government money was spent on any of them, at least up to 1993 (p. 255). Chinese and Indian orders for the Su-27 and Su-30 will no doubt be used to pay off some R&D debts. On the use of export revenues to fund R&D, see chapter 8 in this volume.

[28] This is the conclusion of the British Ministry of Defence. International Institute for Strategic Studies (IISS), *The Military Balance 1995–96* (Oxford University Press: Oxford, 1995), p. 110. Nevertheless, a new missile cruiser, *Peter the Great*, was launched in Oct. 1996. Frolov, L., ITAR-TASS, 1 Oct. 1996.

Table 7.7. Soviet and Russian expenditure on military R&D as reported to the UN
Figures are in billion current roubles. Figures in italics are percentages.

Year	Land		Naval		Air		Strategic[a]		Total	
USSR										
1989	0.97	*(7)*	2.16	*(15)*	2.734	*(19)*	7.48	*(53)*	14.1	*(100)*
1990	0.85	*(7)*	1.50	*(12)*	2.488	*(19)*	7.52	*(58)*	12.9	*(100)*
Russia										
1992	4.72	*(6)*	11.6	*(16)*	13.6	*(18)*	35.4	*(47)*	74.7	*(100)*
1993	25.1	*(6)*	58.5	*(14)*	66.7	*(16)*	189	*(45)*	417	*(100)*
1994	214	*(8)*	332	*(12)*	418	*(15)*	1 380	*(50)*	2 730	*(100)*

[a] Includes only the 'strategic missile forces' (the ICBMs) and 'anti-aircraft forces' (national air defence). The strategic submarine and bomber forces are included under the naval and air forces respectively.

Sources: UN documents A/INF/45/5 Add. 1, 1 Nov. 1990; A/46/381 Add. 1, 22 Oct. 1991; and A/50/277, 20 July 1995, pp. 66–75.

service after 2000.[29] The lack of funding for modernization of land forces is consistent with earlier information that production of armoured vehicles has practically stopped. Strategic bombers are apparently not being modernized, and investment in aviation R&D is probably destined for the general-purpose forces, complemented by independently funded R&D on products for export. In addition to government funding for the MiG-31M, a new air-to-air radar (Zhuk or 'Beetle') and missile (R-77/AA-12 'Adder') and two new conventionally armed cruise missiles,[30] funding for the S-400 air-defence missile may be counted against the air force's total if it is intended for air-base defence. Most estimates agree that Russian R&D projects are being stretched out and many are likely to peter out as a result of indifference.[31]

India

India's Plan 2005—under which the allotment for the military R&D (that is, R&D funded by the Defence Research and Development Organisation,

---

[29] The President of the US Naval War College, Rear Admiral James Stark, claims that Russia 'is pouring billions into submarines'. Ljunggren, D., 'Suspicious West asks what Russia is doing with subs', Reuter, 8 July 1996. Weapons research appears to focus on submarine-launched anti-ship cruise missiles. Friedman, N., 'Russians display technology', *USNI Proceedings*, Jan. 1997, p. 94; and Norris and Arkin (note 26), p. 62. The Lada may be independently funded and offered for export under the name Amur. Associated Press, 'Russia–Air Force', 3 Dec. 1996; and Starr, B., 'USA reports new SSBNs, details Sang-O intruder', *Jane's Defence Weekly*, 26 Feb. 1997, p. 5.

[30] Norris and Arkin (note 26), p. 62; and Lambeth (note 9), p. 249.

[31] A pessimistic reading of the tank and AWACS programmes in particular is given in IISS, *Strategic Survey 1995/96* (Oxford University Press: Oxford, 1996), p. 25. Deputy Defence Minister Andrei Kokoshin has stated that R&D should concentrate on upgrades of proven designs, particularly in the fields of reconnaissance, command and control, supply, and guidance. Mamchur, Y., 'If we preserve the defence complex, we will preserve Russia', *Krasnaya Zvezda*, 29 Oct. 1992; and ITAR-TASS, 24 Dec. 1993, cited in Lambeth (note 9), pp. 250, 252.

Table 7.8. Trends in India's DRDO expenditure, 1981–97[a]

Year	DRDO budget (current billion rupees)	(1990 billion rupees)	(1990 US $m.)	R&D share in MOD budget	Comments[b]
1981–82	0.96	2.0	110	2.8	
1982–83	1.18	2.3	130	2.7	
1983–84	1.64	2.8	160	3.5	LCA and IGMDP begun
1984–85	2.12	3.3	190	4.4	ATV begun
1985–86	3.14	4.7	270	4.9	
1986–87	4.31	5.9	340	4.7	
1987–88	5.49	6.9	400	5.3	First Trishul test
1988–89	5.78	6.7	380	5.1	First Prithvi test
1989–90	6.08	6.7	380	5.0	First Agni test
1990–91	6.70	6.7	380	4.9	
1991–92	6.83	6.0	340	5.2	
1992–93	7.88	6.2	350	5.4	Second Agni test
1993–94	10.46	7.7	440	5.7	Arjun prototypes delivered
1994–95	12.41	8.3	490	6.5	Plan 2005 launched
1995–96	13.59	8.3	490	..	'Incomplete' LCA prototype rolled out
1996–97	14.09	8.0	450	..	Akash, Arjun, Nag, Trishul begin low-rate initial production

[a] Figures for 1995–96 and 1996–97 are revised estimates and best estimates respectively.

[b] LCA = Light Combat Aircraft; IGMDP = Integrated-Guided Missile Development Plan; ATV = Advanced Technology Vessel.

Source: Government of India, Ministry of Defence, *Annual Report* (various years); and Government of India, Department of Science and Technology, *Research and Development Statistics*, various years.

DRDO, and the armed services) would be doubled to 10 per cent of the defence budget[32]—enjoyed consensus support during a change of government in 1996. The new United Front government led by Prime Minister H. D. Deve Gowda endorsed the plan, as did the new parliament's Standing Committee on Defence. Despite the rhetoric, the DRDO's budget decreased in real terms and as a fraction of the defence budget for a second year, as seen in table 7.8. At 6.5 per cent of total military expenditure, the total military R&D budget for 1994 was nevertheless 24 per cent higher than at the peak of Rajiv Gandhi's build-up in the 1980s.[33]

[32] Plan 2005 was proposed by DRDO Director General A. P. J. Abdul Kalam in Nov. 1994 and approved by the government and parliament in 1995. 'India to have 70 pc indigenous defence inventory', *Indian Express* (Madras), 16 Nov. 1994; and Lok Sabha, Committee on Defence, *Defence Research and Development: Major Projects* (Lok Sabha Secretariat: New Delhi, 1995). The 10% figure has long been a demand of the DRDO and its promoters. See, e.g., Singh, J., 'Self-reliance in defence equipment', *Economic Times* (Bombay), 6 Jan. 1994.

[33] These figures may not include military projects undertaken by the Department of Atomic Energy at the Bhabha Atomic Research Centre (BARC), which account for a small portion of BARC's annual R&D budget—probably on the order of tens of millions of rupees annually. Indian space projects have military applications, but these are secondary. Total Indian Government expenditure on military R&D is

Plan 2005 is meant to bring a small number of major projects—the Light Combat Aircraft (LCA), the Arjun tank and four tactical missiles developed under the Integrated Guided-Missile Development Plan (IGMDP)—from full-scale development to production.[34] So far only the Arjun and the Prithvi short-range ballistic missile have entered low-rate production, but the Nag anti-tank missile and the Akash and Trishul surface-to-air missiles (SAMs) are due to enter low-rate production in 1997.[35] A full-scale production decision on the Prithvi awaits a requirement for more than the 100 ordered in the initial batch.[36] The first flight of the LCA was postponed from 1996 until November 1997.[37]

Less clear is the fate of a number of lower-priority projects. In the furore over India's decision not to sign the CTBT, the Government expressed its willingness to move forward with more tests of the Agni ballistic missile, which has been tested to a range of 1000 km and pronounced complete in early 1994, but quickly equivocated.[38] In October, the Ministry of Defence decided not to provide further funding for the programme unless there was a change for the worse in India's security environment,[39] but DRDO Director General A. P. J. Abdul Kalam said in December that he had requested approval from the government to resume testing in 1997.[40]

---

typically 20% more than the DRDO budget, the additional amount being funded directly by the armed services. Private investment adds less than another 3% on average. Government of India, Department of Science and Technology, *Research and Development Statistics*, various years; and Ghosh, A. K., *India's Defence Budget and Expenditure Management in a Wider Context* (Lancer: New Delhi, 1996), p. 304.

[34] These programmes are discussed in more detail in Arnett, E., 'Military technology: the case of India', *SIPRI Yearbook 1994* (Oxford University Press: Oxford, 1994), pp. 346–50. In addition to the IGMDP missiles, the DRDO is researching a submarine-launched missile, Sagarika; a medium-range air-to-air missile, Astra; and a laser-guided bomb.

[35] Plan 2005 allocates 2.5 billion rupees a year for the Arjun project for 5 years. Lok Sabha (note 32), p. 5. A retired deputy chief of the Army Staff claims that the procurement budget cannot accommodate more than 60 tanks a year, and that the army remains sceptical of the tank's performance. Other reports suggest that no more than 125 Arjuns will be produced. Singh, H., 'The second coming of Arjun', *The Tribune* (Chandigarh), 29 Mar. 1996; and Bedi, R., 'Army must rethink financial priorities', *Jane's Defence Weekly*, 12 Feb. 1997, p. 25. Two good status reports are given in Bedi, R., 'Expensive tinkering?', *Indian Express*, 1 Jan. 1997; and Sawhney, P., 'Arjun MBT still in technical and fiscal mire', *Jane's International Defence Review*, Nov. 1996, p. 15.

[36] The Army ordered the Prithvi only under duress. Joshi, M., 'Vehicles of war', *Frontline* (Madras), 25 Sep. 1992. Plan 2005 allocates 2.5 billion rupees a year to the IGMDP for 5 years. Lok Sabha (note 32), p. 5.

[37] 'LCA prototype test flight postponed till Nov '97', *Times of India*, 18 Dec. 1996. Although the first LCA prototype was rolled out on 17 Nov. 1995 with the prime minister present, it was 'an incomplete aircraft', according to an official working in the project. Singh, A., 'LCA taken back to complete fabrication', *Hindustan Times* (New Delhi), 22 Nov. 1995.

[38] 'Deve Gowda approved in principle DRDO's proposal to fund 5 tests'. Raghuvanshi, V., 'India's DRDO awaits approval for Agni flight tests', *Defense News*, 26 Aug.–1 Sep. 1996, p. 14. 'Foreign Minister Inder Kumar Gujral said testing of the Agni was not on the cards'. Reuter, 'India missile tests "not on the cards"', 21 Aug. 1996.

[39] Cooper, K. J., 'India halts mid-range missile plans', *Washington Post*, 6 Dec. 1996, p. A46. No further funding has been forthcoming since the first 550 million rupees were used for 3 tests. An additional 500 million rupees would be required for 5 more tests. The Agni was to serve as the basis for the Surya ICBM project, which was still active in Dec. 1995 but was not tested in 1996 as Abdul Kalam claimed it would be. 'Agni, Prithvi not shelved', *The Pioneer* (Delhi), 22 Dec. 1995; and Mahapatra, R., 'Surya, India's ICBM project', *Probe* (Allahabad), May 1994.

[40] Srikanth, B. R., 'Preparations for Agni test belie capping reports', *Asian Age*, 30 Dec. 1996, p. 1.

Major funding was also not forthcoming for the Advanced Technology Vessel (ATV), an indigenous nuclear submarine.[41] The Ministry of Defence and the Director General of Civil Aviation turned down applications to certify the Advanced Light Helicopter despite four years of test flights.[42] A number of new projects were proposed or launched at the December India Aero '96 show, but the process by which decisions will be made about which should be funded is not publicly known.[43] Indeed, the current practice of planning to increase R&D funds while actually decreasing them in real terms suggests a decision-making process in turmoil.

III. North-East Asia

The market economies of North-East Asia are developing expertise in dual-use electronics and process technologies and experiencing rapid economic growth, which is helping finance increased military expenditure. In the cases of Japan and South Korea, military R&D expenditure is increasing even more quickly than defence budgets, making them the only states with large military industrial bases to sustain significant increases in military R&D spending since the end of the cold war.

As elsewhere, indigenous R&D is meant to foster strategic independence or freedom of action. Japan, South Korea and Taiwan have all been dependent on the USA for military technology throughout the post-war period (and are still among the ten leading arms importers[44]), but seek a degree of self-reliance to secure bargaining leverage in negotiations with Washington, if not insurance against sudden shifts in policy. For its part, the USA has encouraged all three to bear a greater share of their defence burdens since the Nixon era, but expresses reservations when it appears to be losing political or economic advantages. Since US guidance has kept the force postures of all three states largely defensive, a side effect of greater independence could be the ability to develop offensive capabilities.[45]

---

[41] Most design work has been done on the reactor, which is still too large. The Navy leadership reportedly opposes the project, which is primarily the responsibility of the DRDO and the Department of Atomic Energy, mainly on grounds of cost. According to an unnamed DRDO official, the ATV requires at least another 25 billion rupees for development. 'Indigenous n-sub's energy plant to be land tested soon', Economic Times, 10 Mar. 1996; Aneja, A., 'N-sub era may dawn only after a decade', The Hindu (Madras), 10 July 1996, p. 14; and 'The nuclear submarine', The Hindu, 12 July 1996, p. 12.

[42] Siddiqui, H., 'Light helicopter design fails to get govt's okay', Indian Express, 10 Oct. 1996; and Bedi, R., 'Advanced Light Helicopter still far from taking off', Indian Express, 3 Nov. 1996.

[43] India's procurement process is described and critiqued in Singh, R. P., 'India', ed. R. P. Singh, SIPRI, Arms Procurement Decision-Making Processes: China, India, Israel, Japan and South Korea (Oxford University Press: Oxford, forthcoming 1997).

[44] See chapter 11 in this volume.

[45] Nolan, J. E., Military Industry in Taiwan and South Korea (Macmillan: London, 1986), p. 14.

Japan

Two decades after launching its 1976 National Defense Program Outline (NDPO),[46] Japan has emerged as one of the major investors in military R&D and now spends more than any other non-nuclear weapon state except Germany. By and large, the 20-year build-up is a technological success story: Japanese firms with important indigenous technologies to offer have used plentiful government funding, good management practices and access to US technology to create an arms industry that is advanced in important niches and produces most of Japan's military goods while spinning off technologies to the civilian sector. With the end of the cold war, however, questions arise regarding the necessity for an independent arms industry that does its job expensively, excites suspicion among neighbours and antagonizes the USA, with which Japan has an unusually close security partnership. Nevertheless, Japan's commitment to an independent military technology base was reiterated in 1995, when it adopted a new NDPO, its first post-cold war reappraisal of the security situation.[47]

Japanese officials justify their R&D programme on the familiar grounds of self-reliance: 'Indigenous defense equipment using Japan's own technology is advantageous because it is suited to the country's geographical conditions and national situation, and can be easily improved, modified, maintained and replenished.'[48]

Most US arms are appropriate for use in Japan's region. One line of thinking has it that US arms are actually *too* capable—even unconstitutional—given Japan's 'exclusively defensive defence' posture. From this point of view, Japan's arms must be designed to be less capable than imported alternatives.[49] Japanese military technology is limited by the current interpretation of Article IX of the Constitution to 'the minimum necessary for self-defence'.[50] US requests for Japan to deploy refuelling aircraft and over-the-horizon radars in order to protect sea lanes to a distance of 1000 km were initially rebuffed by the Japanese Government as potentially offensive, but finally accepted in 1981. In practice, Japan's Self-Defense Forces are barely capable of offensive

[46] High levels of R&D and production were sustained in the 1950s and 1960s as well. The failure of the first indigenous fighter aircraft, the F-1, to fulfil expectations precipitated the renewed build-up in the military technology base under the NDPO. See Defense Agency, *Defense of Japan 1996* (Japan Times: Tokyo, 1996), pp. 270–74 for the text of the NRDO; and Tomohisa Sakanaka, 'Japan's changing defence policy', eds R. Matthews and Keisuke Matsuyama, *Japan's Military Renaissance?* (St. Martin's Press: New York, 1993), p. 78.

[47] It was adopted on 28 Nov. 1995 and is reproduced in Defense Agency (note 46), pp. 276–83. The main requirements established for R&D involve a medium-range SAM and an improved flying boat (p. 291).

[48] Defense Agency, *Defense of Japan 1995* (Japan Times: Tokyo, 1995), p. 164.

[49] Green, M. J., *Arming Japan: Defense Production, Alliance Politics, and the Postwar Search for Autonomy* (Columbia University Press: New York, 1995), p. 29.

[50] A corollary restriction prohibits weapons that 'from their performance, are to be used exclusively for the total destruction of other countries', including strategic missiles and bombers and 'offensive aircraft carriers'. Defense Agency, *Defense of Japan 1994* (Japan Times: Tokyo, 1994), p. 62. Defense Agency officials told Samuels in 1992 that in order to comply with the constitution Japan's forces had to be 'nonnuclear, tactical, and defensive'. Samuels, R. J., *'Rich Nation, Strong Army': National Security and the Technological Transformation of Japan* (Cornell University Press: Ithaca, N. Y., 1994), p. 191.

action against the territory of other states.[51] In addition, the Diet has imposed other limits on conventional weapons, when their capabilities were perceived to be greater than 'the minimum necessary'. This issue is becoming more salient as the possibilities of building ships capable of embarking aircraft and nuclear submarines for anti-submarine operations are considered.[52]

Another important aspect of the Japanese 'national situation' is the desire to protect Japanese technology.[53] Indigenous design allows Japanese firms to introduce locally developed dual-use technology—mainly electronics and process technologies—into military systems without sharing commercial secrets, as might be necessary in upgrading license-produced systems.[54]

Finally, Japanese military R&D is seen as providing bargaining leverage in negotiations with the USA on arms transfers. When Japan's military power was seen by both the Japanese and US governments as crucial to the strategy of containment, its technology base was not yet sufficiently highly developed to make credible the threat to develop major systems indigenously. Although Japan is continuing to increase its military R&D budget in the 1990s and its military technology is making important advances, it is unlikely to gain any more leverage in its negotiations with Washington, in part because there is no longer a consensus between Washington and Tokyo about security policy and the arms industry. Indeed, few observers expect any state ever again to enjoy a co-development arrangement as favourable to the junior partner as the F-2 (see below). With the leverage argument for increased military R&D spending weakened, Japan's persistence in building up the military technology base suggests it is pursuing a local arms industry for ideological reasons.[55]

Resources

Military R&D is coordinated by the Technical Research and Development Institute (TRDI). Of the three cases under consideration in this section, Japan provides the most complete information about its military spending and technology base, but this is limited to a single figure for military R&D in the defence budget and descriptions of major programmes.[56] The difficulty of characterizing Japanese R&D is aggravated by a high fraction of independent R&D conducted by industry. Typically, TRDI funds R&D only up to the prototype stage, and industry funds the remainder of development with

---

[51] Attack aircraft are capable of strikes against land targets, but the Air Self-Defense Force has no modern air-to-ground missiles and is configured primarily for air defence and anti-ship missions. Levin, N. D., Lorell, M. and Alexander, A., *The Wary Warriors: Future Directions in Japanese Security Politics*, MR-101-AF (RAND: Santa Monica, Calif., 1993), p. 59.

[52] Levin *et al.* (note 51), p. 54.

[53] Green concludes that political support for R&D in the 1990s derives in part from resentment of the conflict with the USA over this issue in the context of the F-2 fighter. Green (note 49), p. 124.

[54] Green (note 49, p. 79) dates this approach to the 1976 NDPO.

[55] For an elucidation of the ideological justification, which includes a definition of national security that stresses technological independence, see Samuels (note 50) and for a sympathetic critique see Green (note 49).

[56] Japan's submissions to the UN reporting mechanism for military budgets count all R&D funds as 'support', with none allocated to the constituent services. UN document A/50/277/Add. 1, 11 Oct. 1995, pp. 34–40.

Table 7.9. Trends in Japanese expenditure on military R&D[a]

Year	R&D budget			R&D budget as % of		Comments
	(current b. yen)	(1990 b. yen)	(1990 US $m.)	MoD budget	Equipment funds	
1976	13.5	21	140	0.89	5.2	National Defense Program Outline
1981	25.0	29	200	1.0	4.3	T-4 trainer begun
1986	57.7	61	420	1.7	5.9	
1987	65.4	69	480	1.9	6.5	T-4, Type 88 AShM completed
1988	73.3	77	530	2.0	6.6	FS-X (later F-2) fighter begun
1989	82.8	85	590	2.1	7.0	Type 90 tank completed
1990	92.9	93	640	2.2	7.4	
1991	102.9	100	690	2.3	7.7	
1992	114.8	110	750	2.5	9.1	OH-1 begun
1993	123.8	120	800	2.7	10	
1994	125.5	120	810	2.7	11	AAM-4 begun
1995	140.1	130	910	3.0	14	
1996	149.6	140	1 000	3.1	14	Medium-range SAM begun

[a] Figures given are corrected expenditures, not budgets for the TRDI.

Source: Defense Agency, *Defense of Japan* (various years).

expenses being recouped during procurement. Independent R&D probably accounts for more than half of Japanese military R&D.[57]

Although Japanese military R&D is a relatively small percentage of military expenditure and total government and national R&D expenditure (as seen in table 7.2), the gross figure is still high in comparative terms.[58] As seen in table 7.9, the portion of the military equipment budget given over to R&D has more than doubled in the past decade,[59] and plans are for R&D to reach 5 per cent of the defence budget.[60] The steady increase in R&D funding as a portion of total equipment funding since 1983 suggests that R&D programmes are not prompting greater procurement (sometimes called 'technology push' and blamed as a cause of arms racing), and may in fact be inhibiting procurement under a capped defence budget.[61]

[57] Chinworth, M. W., *Financing Japan's Defense Build-up* (Massachusetts Institute of Technology, Center for International Studies: Cambridge, Mass., 1992), p. 4; Green (note 49), p. 16; and Samuels (note 50), p. 192.

[58] Recall that using PPP rather than exchange-rate figures would decrease this by roughly 20%.

[59] At 14%, it is comparable to Italy's and still far below those of the USA, the UK, France and Germany, as seen in table 7.2. This suggests a continuing high reliance on imported technology, despite the politically important fact that more than 90% of Japanese arms have been 'produced' in Japan since 1983. Defense Agency, *Defense of Japan 1989* (Japan Times: Tokyo, 1989); and Defense Agency (note 46).

[60] US Congress, Office of Technology Assessment, *Global Arms Trade*, OTA-ISC-460 (US Government Printing Office: Washington, 1991), p. 116; and Levin *et al.* (note 51), p. 75. TRDI's budget for 1997 is 178.5 million yen, or 3.6% of the defence budget.

[61] Indeed, the decline in procurement is given by one author as evidence of Japan's decision to avoid post-cold war arms racing. Hummel, H., 'Japan's military expenditures after the cold war: the "Realism" of the peace dividend', *Australian Journal of International Affairs*, vol. 50, no. 2 (1996), pp. 144–46.

Since Japan does not export arms, there is no opportunity to defray increasing R&D costs through foreign sales. Real equipment costs are high because R&D investment must be amortized across short production runs stretched out over several years, and production is generally less efficient than might otherwise be possible because of low volume and idiosyncratic industry practices. Further, major military R&D projects are often begun because of industrial interest in a new technology that later turns out to be infeasible or too expensive to include in the finished product.[62] As a result, Japan's indigenous systems are the most expensive in the world.

Programmes

Although aircraft account for only 35 per cent of procurement, they dominate the military technology base. Foremost among recent aircraft projects have been the F-2 fighter and the OH-1 scout helicopter, which together have accounted for three-quarters of the TRDI budget in recent years (60 per cent for the F-2 and 15 per cent for the OH-1).[63] The F-2 is a modified F-16 being developed cooperatively by Japanese and US firms (primarily Lockheed Martin), with at least 40 per cent of R&D funding (about $1 billion) going to the US firms.[64] A total of 130 F-2s are planned. The programme cost more than 320 billion yen between 1989 and early 1995, peaking at 97 billion yen in the years 1993 and 1994.[65] At an expected average cost of 12.8 billion yen, the F-2s are three to four times as expensive as F-16Cs bought off the shelf.[66]

The military justification for the additional 1.3 trillion yen that could have been saved if F-16Cs had been bought instead of F-2s is the contribution made to the F-2's performance by unique Japanese technologies. So far Japan has identified nine innovations in the F-2 programme that replace US components without being derivative. Five of these have been made public: the fire control radar, the mission computer hardware, the navigation system, the electronic

---

[62] Japanese planning is often criticized for being more responsive to industrial policy than military requirements, which sometimes are not even specified. This case is made most pointedly in Twigg, J. L., *'To Fly and Fight': Norms, Institutions, and Fighter Aircraft Procurement in the United States, Russia, and Japan*, doctoral dissertation (Massachusetts Institute of Technology, Department of Political Science: Cambridge, Mass., 1994). See also Alexander, A. J., *Of Tanks and Toyotas: An Assessment of Japan's Defense Industry*, N-3542-AF (RAND: Santa Monica, Calif., 1993), pp. 52–56; and Chinworth, M. W., *Inside Japan's Defense: Technology, Economics & Strategy* (Brassey's: New York, 1992), p. 139.

[63] 'Defense research boost', *Aviation Week & Space Technology*, 2 Nov. 1992, p. 15. In addition, TRDI spent 19.2 billion yen between 1973 and 1989 on technologies destined for the F-2, primarily electronics and materials. Samuels (note 50), p. 236.

[64] For good brief descriptions of Japan's decision to build an F-16 variant rather than an indigenous design, see Chinworth (note 62), pp. 132–61, especially 153, 158; and Samuels (note 50), pp. 237–44. Chinworth and Samuels both conclude that the F-16 was chosen over more militarily appropriate aircraft because it offered better opportunities to develop and apply Japanese technology. Developing a relationship with a new US supplier can also be seen as a means of gaining technology transfer.

[65] Usui, N., 'Japanese defense spending stays flat', *Defence News*, 11–17 Jan. 1993, p. 8; and Usui, N., 'Japanese R&D gains windfall', *Defence News*, 6–12 Feb. 1995, p. 44. Increases in the F-2 R&D budget, which nearly doubled as problems arose, displaced and delayed several other projects.

[66] There is hope that unit costs will drop by as much as 33%. Even then they will cost more than the EF2000, Rafale and F-22, all of which have 2 engines to the F-2's one. Sekigawa, E., 'Japan begins F-2 production in $246-billion budget plan', *Aviation Week & Space Technology*, 1 Jan. 1996, p. 23.

warfare system and radar absorbing materials (and related manufacturing processes).[67] While these demonstrate Japanese technological aptitude and create high-wage jobs, it is difficult to accept the claim that they represent dramatic improvements or address unique characteristics of Japan's security environment.

When the F-2 prototype was completed in 1994, funding was freed for the TRDI's next priority: the OH-1 scout helicopter.[68] The OH-1 cost 90 billion yen through the production of prototypes.[69] The emphasis of aviation R&D should now shift to maritime patrol: in the year 2000 a team led by Kawasaki is expected to begin developing a maritime patrol aircraft to replace the P-3.[70] In the meantime, any slack in the aviation technology base will be drawn taut by a technology demonstrator for the next-generation fighter.[71] Prototypes are expected in 2003.[72] In addition, a helicopter, the RP-1, was funded to maintain Mitsubishi's expertise, since its role in the OH-1 was limited. This led to a commercial helicopter, the MH2000.

After aviation, the TRDI puts the greatest emphasis on missiles. Japan's missile sector was built through indigenization of foreign designs. After an effort second in scale only to the F-2 project, Japanese firms can now produce all-Japanese first-generation Patriot air-defence missiles.[73] The AAM-4, intended to have roughly the capability of the US AMRAAM (advanced medium-range air-to-air missile), was accorded third priority behind the F-2 and OH-1 in 1993, but has not enjoyed the expected crescendo of funding as the other two projects moved into pre-production, presumably because initial investigations into the technology were unsuccessful and the AMRAAM was already available.[74] Instead, the 1997 budget funds the medium-range Chu SAM as the highest priority at 29.3 billion yen.[75]

The TRDI's third priority is land warfare, but given that the sole project is a self-propelled howitzer funded to the tune of 18 billion yen in 1995, it is a distant third.[76] Similarly, although naval procurement accounts for 39 per cent

[67] These 9 are the only ones that the US Government agrees are 'non-derived'. Japan claims that another 8 are, too. The 5 technologies are evaluated in US General Accounting Office (GAO), *US–Japan Fighter Aircraft: Agreement on F-2 Production* (GAO: Gaithersburg, Md., 1997), pp. 14–15; and Chinworth (note 62), pp. 150–51. TRDI has said a total of 46 items are indigenously developed. *Nikkei Shimbun*, 23 Feb. 1993, cited in Green (note 49), p. 127.

[68] Usui 1995 (note 65), p. 4. R&D on the F-2 continued through 1996, but at a lower level.

[69] Ebata, K., 'OH-X, first all-Japanese helicopter, is rolled out', *Jane's Defence Weekly*, 27 Mar. 1996, p. 13. OH-1 R&D continued in 1996 and procurement begins in 1997.

[70] 'A costly step', *World Aerospace and Defense Intelligence*, 1 Mar. 1996, p. 5.

[71] 'Japanese consider platform for future stealth fighter', *Aviation Week & Space Technology*, 5 Aug. 1996, p. 22. Technology-base research for combat aircraft continues in the form of 12.7 billion yen in funding for engine design and test facilities in FY 1997. Ebata, K., 'Japan seeks a bigger budget for R&D', *Jane's Defence Weekly*, 13 Nov. 1996, p. 17.

[72] Proctor, P., 'Japan building stealthy jet', *Aviation Week & Space Technology*, 2 Dec. 1996, p. 13.

[73] Some units will be retrofit to the second-generation standard used by the USA in the Persian Gulf War. Chinworth (note 62), p. 95. Others may have been upgraded with Japanese technology. Chinworth, M. W., 'Technology leakage and US-Japan security relations', eds Matthews and Matsuyama (note 46), p. 213; and Samuels (note 50), pp. 187, 274.

[74] 'Japan defence spending capped', *Military Affairs*, 17 Aug. 1993, p. 4.

[75] Ebata (note 71).

[76] The Type 90 tank, Japan's biggest land warfare project to date, was developed for 29 billion yen. 'Slow seppuku', *The Economist*, 10 June 1995, p. 66.

of total procurement, little of the TRDI's effort is devoted to ships. Japan's ship designs are simple and rely heavily on imported electronics. Even the new helicopter carrier, which has been politically sensitive, is a relatively unsophisticated design and should cost only 20 billion yen.[77]

Finally, despite assiduous courting from the USA, Japan has remained cool to cooperative efforts in the field of BMD.[78] Nevertheless, Japan has concluded a two-year 20-million yen study and earmarked a total of 440 million yen to the THAAD project for 1996 and 1997. The Defense Agency has promised to decide before the summer of 1997 whether to join the project or simply to import US systems as they become available.[79] In addition to concerns about cost, division of labour and technological risk, the TRDI may see THAAD as a competing with the Chu SAM, its current highest priority.[80]

South Korea

With the US presence in Korea being reduced to 37 000 troops and US nuclear weapons having been removed from the peninsula, South Korea is increasing its efforts to defend against an invasion from the north. The US commitment to South Korea remains strong even as the ability of North Korea to launch an attack has atrophied with the loss of support from China and the Soviet Union. Nevertheless, with the Ministry of National Defense (MND) requesting 3.6 per cent of the defence budget for R&D, or about $670 million (in 1990 US dollars) in FY 1997, South Korea has become one of the 10 largest investors in military R&D.[81] It is also one of only three states known to be planning a significant increase in its military R&D budget.

Resources

The MND's main justification for the R&D build-up is imitation of the industrial policies of the Group of Seven (G7) leading industrialized countries and hopes that technology will spin off to the civilian sector.[82] For this reason, the R&D budget is to be increased as a fraction of the total military expenditure, which in turn is expected to increase by 12.9 per cent annually

---

[77] 'Japan starts new LPH', *World Aerospace and Defense Intelligence*, 23 Sep. 1994, p. 18; and Beaver, P., 'Amphibious craft planned by Japan', *Jane's Defence Weekly*, 5 Sep. 1992, p. 23. The 5500-ton ship was laid down in 1995 without much fanfare.

[78] The US BMDO had encouraged Japan to invest $4.5 billion to $16.3 billion in R&D. Beaver, P., 'Japan weighs up missile defence options', *Jane's Defence Weekly*, 13 Aug. 1994, p. 21. See also 'Japan–US anti-missile effort urged', *International Herald Tribune*, 17 Sep. 1993, p. 2.

[79] *Kyodo* (Tokyo), 28 Oct. 1996, in 'Japan: defense agency comments on missile defense talks with US', Foreign Broadcast Information Service, *Daily Report–East Asia (FBIS-EAS)*, FBIS-EAS-96-209, 29 Oct. 1996.

[80] Green (note 49), p. 124.

[81] Sullivan, K., 'The cost of guarding South Korea: for the US, billions', *International Herald Tribune*, 11 Apr. 1996, p. 4; and Karniol, R., 'South Korean budget seeks 16.7% increase', *Jane's Defence Weekly*, 19 June 1996, p. 23.

[82] Republic of Korea, *Defense White Paper 1995–1996* (Ministry of National Defense: Seoul, 1996), p. 100.

Table 7.10. Trends in South Korean expenditure on military R&D[a]

Year	R&D budget (current b. won)	(1990 b. won)	(1990 US $m.)	R&D budget as % of MND budget	Equip.[b] budget as % of MND budget	R&D budget as % of funds for equipment	Comments
1971	0.34	2	3	0.2	10.9	1.8	
1976	36.0	130	170	5.1	35.1	15	Nuclear project ended
1981	66.5	100	140	2.5	33.5	7.5	Frigate prod. began 1980
1986	56.2	71	100	1.3	33.5	3.8	Submarine prod. began 1983
1987	56.9	70	100	1.2	38.8	3.1	K1 tank production begins
1988	82.8	95	130	1.5	39.0	3.8	KTX-1 R&D begins
1989	90.2	98	150	1.5	38.1	3.9	
1990	166	166	230	2.5	36.8	6.8	
1991	186	170	240	2.5	34.9	7.2	
1992	219	190	270	2.6	33.0	7.9	
1993	276	230	320	3.0	31.6	9.5	
1994	292	230	320	2.9	30.2	9.6	
1995	[330]	[250]	[350]	[3.0]	29.1	[10]	
1996	373	270	370	3.0	28.3	11	

[a] Figures in square brackets are author's estimates.

[b] For 1986–93, the figure given is that for 'force improvement'. From 1994, the figure given is that for 'maintenance of force capacity'.

Sources: Republic of Korea, *Defense White Paper* (various years). Figures for 1987, 1988 and 1990 derived from Korean Institute of Defense Analysis report cited in Reed, C. *et al.*, 'South Korean business: diversify for survival', *Jane's Defence Weekly*, 31 July 1993, p. 18. Figures before 1986 from *Whitebook on National Defense* (Ministry of National Defense: Seoul, 1988) cited in Chung-in Moon and In-taek Hyun, 'Muddling through security, growth, and welfare: the political economy of defense spending in South Korea', eds S. Chan and A. Mintz, *Defense, Welfare and Growth* (Routledge: London, 1992), p. 143.

during the 1998–2002 five-year plan.[83] South Korea's military R&D budget has increased by a factor of 6.7 in real terms in the 10 years since 1987, when the USA stopped Foreign Military Sales credits and thereby stimulated a redoubling of the indigenous effort.[84]

The R&D budget is expected to increase by a further factor of 2–5 in the next decade. In 1992, it was decided to increase the portion of the defence budget devoted to R&D from 2.6 per cent to 'between five and ten percent by the 2000s',[85] suggesting the budget could reach as much as $2–3 billion. In April 1993, it was decided to increase R&D from 3 per cent to 5 per cent by 1998. This programme has continued after the election of reform-minded Kim Young Sam in 1993.

[83] *Korea Herald*, 11 Dec. 1996, p. 3, in 'South Korea: Ministry announces midterm defense plan 1998–2002', FBIS-EAS-96-239, 12 Dec. 1996.

[84] Sköns, E. and Gill, B., 'Arms production', in *SIPRI Yearbook 1996* (note 1), p. 451.

[85] Republic of Korea, *Defense White Paper 1992–1993* (Ministry of National Defense: Seoul, 1993), p. 132. The following European countries spend 5–10% of the defence budget on R&D: France, Russia, Sweden and the UK.

Programmes

South Korea began a process of modernization and indigenization in 1974 as a response to US President Richard Nixon's 1969 policy of shifting primary responsibility for the defence of US security partners in Asia. A three-stage strategy for developing the military technology and industrial base took it from licensed production to indigenous design in less than 15 years, and one-third of military expenditure since 1974 has been devoted to modernization. After some difficulty setting priorities in the 1970s,[86] development of the technology base has proceeded more smoothly, albeit with exaggerated claims of success. With US support Korea quickly began producing systems with at least a measure of local content, including tanks, armoured vehicles, frigates, submarines and helicopters, and began local production of F-5 and F-16 fighters.

Most R&D is carried out by the Agency for Defense Development (ADD). Little information is given in the annual white paper on specific projects. Korea's top goal for the military technology and industrial base in the 1990s has been to develop a 'self-sufficient' aircraft industry—defined as 75 per cent of the capacity of major firms in Europe and the USA—by the turn of the century. To this end, ADD is leading a team of Korea's largest firms to build and design civilian and military aircraft of increasing domestic content, meant to culminate in an indigenous fighter soon after 2000.

The team's achievements so far have been limited. A turboprop trainer—the KTX-1—has been developed by the team members, but the government was apparently reluctant in ordering 100 and has not offered additional development funding. The goal of creating an indigenous fighter has been scaled back for the time being. Instead, a jet trainer with limited combat capabilities, the KTX-2, will go into full-scale development in 1997 or 1998 and not enter production before 2004. R&D costs are estimated at $2 billion.[87] The KTX-2 was to be followed by a new fighter, the FX. Originally intended to be completely indigenous, the FX is now expected to be imported or produced under licence. Candidates include the F-15, F-22, Rafale and Su-37. Acquisition is expected to begin in 2002.[88]

Indigenous development of armoured vehicles has also been limited. The Hyundai K1 already in service is derived from the US M1 with a German

[86] Initially, the Park Chung Hee Administration (1963–79) was overly enthusiastic about prestige projects that diverted resources but did not benefit modernization of the general-purpose forces. Chief among the status projects was one for a ballistic missile capable of reaching Pyongyang, the 160-km range NH-K, developed from the US-supplied Nike-Hercules. Nolan (note 45), pp. 65–66, 74, 174. See also Nolan, J. E., 'South Korea: an ambitious client of the United States', eds M. Brzoska and T. Ohlson, SIPRI, *Arms Production in the Third World* (Taylor & Francis: London, 1986), p. 224.

[87] 'Team is announced for KTX-II advanced trainer', *Jane's Defence Weekly*, 14 Jan. 1995, p. 6. Total government support for the aerospace self-sufficiency initiative amounts to $5 billion. Mecham, M., 'South Korea seeks slice of world's aerospace pie', *Aviation Week & Space Technology*, 14 Oct. 1996, p. 42.

[88] 'Seoul air show '96 takes to the skies', *Newsreview* (Seoul), 26 Oct. 1996, pp. 12–13; and Proctor, P., 'Quick F-22 exports?', *Aviation Week & Space Technology*, 4 Nov. 1996, p. 17.

power pack.[89] An upgrade of the K1 entered production in 1996 and initial planning for a follow-on design, the K2, began. Daewoo produces the K200 Korean Infantry Fighting Vehicle (KIFV), a variant of the US M-113/AIFV (armoured infantry fighting vehicle) powered by a German-designed engine. Some K200s are equipped with French-designed air-defence guns and missiles—the Mistral and the Crotale NG. A variant of the latter is the basis of the Chon-ma or Pegasus system.[90] A similar arrangement will probably characterize the project to develop a longer-range SAM, K-SAM, to replace the current I-Hawk.[91]

The extent of US intervention in Korean military technology planning was a sore point during bilateral discussions of Korea's ballistic missile programmes in 1996. Washington and Seoul agreed in 1979 that the USA would supply Korea with technology for the 160-km NH-K ballistic missile in exchange for Korea's promise not to deploy missiles of range greater than 180 km. While Washington has championed Korea's application to join the Missile Technology Control Regime, an export cartel, it has rebuffed Korean requests to waive the 1979 limit on Korea's own missiles.[92] A December bilateral meeting was complicated by reports in the Korean media that US satellites had observed the test of a Korean cruise missile with a range greater than 300 km, a report denied by both sides.[93]

Assessment

Korea's apparent ambition is a military technology base comparable to that of Japan, despite a shorter history of military R&D and production and a weaker national technology base on which to build[94] as well as more limited access to US technology. In 1990, when Japan's military R&D budget was comparable in size to that expected for South Korea in 1997, the military industrial base and the defence budget were both larger and therefore better able to accommodate the build-up. Further, Japan had already developed several relevant technologies and had arranged a partnership to co-develop a fighter, having

[89] A Korean official has characterized the K1 as an M1 assembled by cheaper Korean labour. Yi Chong-hun, 'Exporting is the only way to survive', *SISA Journal*, 29 Aug. 1996, p. 34 (in Korean), in 'ROK: journal says exporting only way defense firms can survive', FBIS-EAS-96-172, 5 Sep. 1996. The K1 also includes subsystems imported from elsewhere and has been criticized on the grounds that the entire package has not been integrated successfully. Glain, S., 'South Korea slows down arms purchases', *Wall Street Journal*, 29 Dec. 1993, pp. 1, 4.

[90] Electronics are provided by Thomson and the missile is developed from the US LTV VT-1. 'Crotale SAM plans', *Milavnews*, Aug. 1990, p. 19.

[91] O Yong-chin, *Korea Times*, 1 Jan. 1997, p. 21; and 'South Korea to develop medium-range SAM', *Jane's Defence Weekly*, 24 July 1996, p. 12.

[92] According to Korean Minister of National Defense Kim Tong-chin: 'The US side recognized the ROK's need for an upward readjustment of the range to 300 km . . . However, an additional agreement is necessary'. *Chungang Ilbo*, 23 Dec. 1996, p. 17. On the Missile Technology Control Regime (MTCR), see chapter 10 in this volume.

[93] Kim Kyong-ho, 'Seoul, Washington clash on South's missile aspirations', *Korea Herald*, 9 Dec. 1996, p. 2; and O Yong-chin (note 91).

[94] South Korea's weak technology base is ascribed to structural problems and dependence on Japanese components in Simon, D. F. and Changrok Soh, 'Korea's technological development', *Pacific Review*, vol. 7, no. 1 (1994), pp. 94, 97–98.

Table 7.11. Taiwan Ministry of National Defense budget for 'science', 1993–94

Figures are in billion current new Taiwan (NT) dollars and 1990 US $m. Figures in italics are percentages.

Year	MND 'science' budget		MND 'science' budget as percentage of			
	(current NT $b.)	(1990 US $m.)	Govt R&D expenditure	National R&D expenditure	MND budget	MND investment
1993	9.7	320	*19*	*8.6*	*3.1*	*8.4*
1994	8.9	280	*17*	*7.2*	*3.3*	*9.2*

Sources: Republic of China, *National Defense Report, 1993–94*; *Statistical Yearbook of the Republic of China 1995*; and *Monthly Bulletin of Statistics of the Republic of China*, Dec. 1996.

achieved a number of earlier design milestones.[95] This suggests that South Korea may already be overreaching itself in its effort to build a military technology base, in which case further increases in the military R&D budget would bring diminishing returns. At best, it seems likely that following the Japanese model will yield a similar result: very expensive systems with less than state-of-the-art capabilities and the loss of offset countertrade.

Taiwan

Taiwan's military R&D effort has been intended primarily to redress weaknesses caused by the reluctance of arms exporters to offend the Beijing government by supplying complete systems. Many of the projects portrayed as indigenously developed are actually licensed copies of foreign systems or assemblages of imported components, suggesting that Taiwanese military R&D is in effect a sort of technology laundering scheme.[96] The extent to which Taiwan and its foreign suppliers have succeeded in skirting constraints on the transfer of complete systems is suggestive of how other states could escape limits on arms transfers imposed for other reasons, albeit only with the cooperation of other national governments.

[95] Given the harsh congressional criticism of US technology transfer in the F-2 project, South Korea is unlikely to get a comparable deal. The controversy is detailed in Shear, J., *The Keys to the Kingdom: The FS-X Deal and the Selling of America's Future to Japan* (Doubleday: New York, 1994). See also US Senate, Committee on Armed Services, *Implications of the FS-X Aircraft Agreement between the United States and Japan*, S. Hrg 101-324 (US Government Printing Office: Washington, DC, 1989). A similar conflict was provoked by the Israeli Lavi, reviewed in Zakheim, D. S., *Flight of the Lavi: Inside a US–Israeli Crisis* (Brassey's: Washington, DC, 1996).

[96] The Beijing government has not been fooled, although it has played along. As a pro-Beijing magazine put it: 'To say that Taiwan develops and produces sophisticated weapons is not as accurate as saying that Taiwan assembles sophisticated weapons..... [V]olume production still requires United States permission'. Yuan Lin, 'Taiwan's surface-to-surface guided missiles', *Wide Angle* (Hong Kong), 16 Oct. 1996, pp. 76–77 (in Chinese), in 'Taiwan: surface-to-surface missile development capabilities viewed', FBIS-CHI-97-029, 14 Feb. 1997.

Table 7.12. CIST missile programmes

Project name	Type[a]	Initial operational capability	Comments
Tien-chien (Sky Sword) I	AAM	1992	Early Sidewinder copy, 5000 bought
Tien-chien II	AAM	1996	AMRAAM substitute, Israeli advice
Hsiung-feng (Proud Wind) I	AShM	1980	Modified, licensed Gabriel II
Hsiung-feng II	AShM	1996	Harpoon substitute
Hsiung-feng III	AShM	after 2000	Possibly submarine-launched
Tien-kung (Sky Bow) I	SAM	1993	Copy of Patriot with local electronics
Tien-kung II	SAM	1996	Boosted TK I, $700 million for R&D Production begins in 1997
Tien-kung III	SAM	1997	Licensed Patriot Local propulsion, control & warhead
Tien-ji (Sky Halberd)	SSM	late 1990s	Modified TK II
Ching-feng (Green Bee)	SSM	1981	Copy of Lance, Israeli advice
Tien-ma (Sky Horse)	SSM	. .	Suspended under US pressure in 1982
Kun-wu I	ATM	1980	Copy of AT-3

[a] AAM = air-to-air missile; AShM = anti-ship missile; SSM = surface-to-surface missile; ATM = anti-tank missile.

Source: Compiled by the author.

Resources

The Taiwanese Ministry of National Defense's budget for 'science' in 1994 was 8.9 billion new Taiwan dollars, a 12 per cent decrease from 1993 as seen in table 7.11.[97] Although it is not clear what is included under this heading, it appears to represent military R&D funding. This figure and its fraction of military expenditure and capital investment are comparable with those of South Korea in recent years. The proportion of military R&D in government and national R&D is high for a non-nuclear weapon state (compare with table 7.2), as might be expected.

Programmes

Two organizations have been responsible for most of Taiwan's military R&D projects: the Aero Industry Development Center (AIDC) and the Chung-shan (Sun Yat-sen) Institute of Science and Technology (CIST). In addition, Taiwan has an active shipbuilding industry.

The main military project undertaken by the AIDC has been the Ching-kuo fighter aircraft, named after the son of and successor to Chiang Kai-shek. The Ching-kuo was developed for roughly $3 billion, half of the $6 billion pro-

---

[97] Republic of China, *National Defense Report, 1993–94* (Ministry of National Defense: Taipei, 1994), pp. 117, 120. Military R&D figures are specifically excluded from *Statistical Yearbook of the Republic of China 1995*, p. 71. The government's portion of national R&D expenditure in table 7.11 is extrapolated from previous years.

gramme cost. After declining to supply F-16 or F-20 fighters, the US Government in 1983 allowed US firms to develop a new design using US technology for production in Taiwan. Ten years into the programme, just before the first 10 Ching-kuos were delivered in 1993, France and the USA reversed course and allowed Mirage 2000 and F-16 fighters to be exported to Taiwan, reducing both the demand and the funding available for the Ching-kuo.[98] The production run was reduced from 250 to 130, which may be the number for which important components had already been delivered. Forty-seven production Ching-kuos were delivered (in addition to four prototypes) before production was stopped late in 1995 because of concerns about the fuel system.[99] Decreasing defence business led to a decision in 1995 to partially privatize AIDC and encourage greater emphasis on civilian markets.

The CIST is Taiwan's government-owned missile-design firm. It has overseen the production of a diverse range of missiles, as summarized in table 7.12. The first generation of air-to-air, surface-to-air and anti-ship missiles was developed after the USA refused to transfer AIM-9L Sidewinder, Patriot and Harpoon missiles.[100] Design work continues on a radar-guided air-to-air missile, a new anti-ship missile, and two new surface-to-air missiles. As with the Ching-kuo, the availability and cost of better imported products will cut into the support for local projects.[101] The CIST began reducing its level of R&D effort in 1994,[102] but continued limitations on technology transfers—including the US decision in 1996 not to sell Taiwan the AMRAAM[103]—have since reinvigorated some programmes. The CIST has also asked the government for 2.6 billion new Taiwan dollars (US $100 million) to develop a ballistic missile warning radar.[104]

Assessment

Taiwan's military technology base appears to be atrophying, having played its role during the years when direct transfers of advanced weapon systems were

---

[98] Procurement of the F-16 and Mirage 2000 will cost 300 billion new Taiwan dollars (US $12 billion) over 7 years from 1993 to 1999. Republic of China (note 97), p. 126.

[99] 'Taiwan to halt fighter jet production—report', *Air Letter*, 20 Oct. 1995, p. 1. Production has since resumed.

[100] Nolan (note 45), p. 57.

[101] For example, the Sky Bow II project was curtailed when Patriot technology became available, despite $700 million in development investment. 'RoC Sky Bow deployment cut', *World Aerospace and Defense Intelligence*, 11 Feb. 1994, pp. 12–13. An indigenous project to copy the Swedish RBS70 seems to have been put aside after the US Stinger was made available. Opall, B., 'China concerns stall Taiwan Stinger deal', *Defense News*, 12–18 Aug. 1996, p. 1.

[102] 'Taiwan institute cutting back sharply due to foreign supply', *The Estimate*, 10–23 June 1994, p. 4; and Republic of China (note 97), pp. 152–53.

[103] 400 Sky Sword IIs, an indigenous missile more comparable to the US Sparrow, will be bought instead. 'Tien Chien 2 post-scriptum', *Military Technology*, Apr. 1996, p. 93. Taiwan will be the first recipient of the comparable French MICA, which will arm its Mirage 2000s. AMRAAM and MICA are seen by US officials as a particularly effective technology of the sort that should not be sold in some cases, despite the existence of similar missiles (the Russian AA-12) in the region. Agmon, M. *et al.*, *Arms Proliferation Policy: Support to the Presidential Advisory Board* MR-771-OSD (RAND: Santa Monica, Calif., 1996), pp. 40, 42. The USA has since shown a greater willingness to sell the AMRAAM in East Asia.

[104] Reuter, 'Taiwan army hopes to develop anti-missile radar', 6 May 1996.

politically difficult, if not impossible for most suppliers. For the present, Taiwan is able to import most of the arms its forces require, so a technology base is no longer as important.

8. Arms production

ELISABETH SKÖNS and JULIAN COOPER*

I. Introduction

During 1996 it became increasingly clear that the arms industry is undergoing profound structural and commercial changes which are likely to have an important political impact in the long term.

The pace of consolidation in the US arms industry was extremely rapid, resulting in a strengthening of industry's influence over weapon prices and greater US dominance in arms production and in the international arms trade. In Europe, the restructuring process continued at a slower rate and seems to have led to less rationalization. It is predicted that the Russian arms industry will become more competitive with the trend towards new corporate structures and a strong concentration in fewer and larger arms-producing enterprises.

For the first time this chapter presents a series of company data. The total volume of arms production by the companies on the SIPRI list of the 'top 100' arms-producing companies in the Organisation for Economic Co-operation and Development (OECD) and developing countries fell by one-third in 1990–95 (table 8.4). This decline is now levelling out in the OECD countries, and this may soon be the case in Russia and Ukraine too.

During the same six-year period, 29 companies left the top 100 list altogether, an indication of the radical structural change in the arms industry (table 8.5). The number of companies which reduced their dependence on defence sales significantly was not very high (table 8.6). The share of exports in company sales is still high in many companies, and the scarce data available show that surprisingly many of the remaining companies in the top 100 list have even increased this share significantly (table 8.7).

It has been government policy in most of the major arms-producing centres to have a market-led restructuring process. This has resulted in high profitability and stock values, especially in the US and British arms industries. For successful completion of the down-sizing of industry, it is important that these earnings be reinvested into civilian production. It is now being called into question whether civilian reinvestment is taking place, but as yet there are no comprehensive studies to indicate the extent to which this is the case.

Military exports have become an important company strategy, and governments are increasingly involved in the promotion of arms exports. The renewed offensive in military exports is partly supported by public expenditures, the extent of which is not known, however, since this is an area of little transparency in most countries.

* Section IV on Russia was contributed by Julian Cooper.

SIPRI Yearbook 1997: Armaments, Disarmament and International Security

Table 8.1. Regional/national shares of arms sales[a] for the top 100 arms-producing companies in the OECD and the developing countries, 1995 compared to 1994[b]

Number of companies, 1995	Region/ country	Percentage of total arms sales		Arms sales 1995 (US $b.)
		1994	1995	
40	USA	58.8	57.0	87.7
40	*West European OECD*	*32.9*	*34.4*	53.0
12	France	*12.5*	*13.2*	20.4
12	UK	*10.5*	*11.5*	17.7
8	Germany	*5.2*	*5.1*	7.8
2	Italy	*1.8*	*2.1*	3.3
3	Sweden	*1.2*	*1.2*	1.9
2	Switzerland	*1.0*	*0.9*	1.3
1	Spain	*0.7*	*0.4*	0.7
12	*Other OECD*	*5.5*	*5.9*	9.1
10	Japan[c]	*5.1*	*5.5*	8.4
1	Turkey	*0.2*	*0.2*	0.4
1	Canada	*0.2*	*0.2*	0.3
8	*Non-OECD countries*	*2.8*	*2.7*	4.2
5	Israel	*1.7*	*1.6*	2.5
2	India	*0.6*	*0.6*	1.0
1	South Africa	*0.4*	*0.4*	0.7
100		*100.0*	*100.0*	**154.0**

[a] Arms sales include both sales for domestic procurement and exports.

[b] China is not included because of the lack of data. Four companies in South Korea would be among the top 100 if data were available for 1995. *SIPRI Yearbook 1996: Armaments, Disarmament and International Security* (Oxford University Press: Oxford, 1996), table 10.14.

[c] For Japanese companies data in the arms sales column represent new military contracts rather than arms sales.

Source: Appendix 8A.

II. The SIPRI top 100

After several years of declining arms sales among the top 100 arms-producing companies in the OECD and developing world except China, their combined arms sales, as expressed in current prices, increased in 1995.[1] Their total arms sales of $154 billion in 1995[2] (table 8.1) represented an increase of $7 billion or almost 5 per cent compared to the previous year. The actual volume increase in their arms sales was smaller, however, since this increase includes the effect of inflation and fluctuations in exchange rates. Using the trend for the top 100 companies as an indicator for developments in the arms industry

---

[1] In 1994 the decline was 2% in current prices; in 1993 the decline was 6%. Sköns, E. and Gill. B., 'Arms production', *SIPRI Yearbook 1996: Armaments, Disarmament and International Security* (Oxford University Press: Oxford, 1996), p. 413.

[2] Because the companies in the 'top 100' differ from year to year, this figure cannot be directly compared with the figure reported in the *SIPRI Yearbook 1996* for the combined top 100 arms sales in 1994, which was $148 billion. Sköns and Gill (note 1), p. 413.

Table 8.2. Companies whose arms sales changed the most in 1995[a]
Companies are ranked according to the volume change in their arms sales.

Company/subsidiary	Country	Sector[b]	Arms sales (US$ m.)		Change 1994–95	
			1994	1995	(US $m.)	(%)
Companies with decreased arms sales						
Unisys	USA	El	1 400	260	− 1 140	− 81
Lockheed Martin	USA	Ac El Mi	14 400	13 800	− 600	− 4
Teneo/INI[c]	Spain	A Ac El MV Sh	1 020	670	− 350	− 34
British Aerospace	UK	A Ac El Mi SA/O	7 030	6 720	− 310	− 4
Mitsubishi Heavy Ind.[d]	Japan	Ac MV Mi Sh	2 730	2 440	− 290	− 11
Oshkosh Truck	USA	MV	430	260	− 170	− 40
TAAS	Israel	A MV SA/O	400	270	− 130	− 33
Thiokol	USA	Eng SA/O	370	260	− 110	− 30
Companies with increased arms sales						
Loral	USA	El Mi	5 100	6 500	+ 1 400	+ 27
GEC	UK	El Sh	3 190	4 100	+ 910	+ 29
Rolls Royce	UK	Eng	1 360	2 050	+ 690	+ 51
GKN	UK	Ac MV	550	1 180	+ 630	+ 115
DCN	France	Sh	2 730	3 290	+ 560	+ 21
IRI	Italy	Ac El Eng Mi Sh	2 070	2 620	+ 550	+ 27
Alliant Tech Systems	USA	SA/O	760	1 190	+ 430	+ 57
Raytheon	USA	El Mi	3 550	3 960	+ 410	+ 12
McDonnell Douglas	USA	Ac El Mi	9 230	9 620	+ 390	+ 4
Thomson	France	El	4 270	4 630	+ 360	+ 8
General Motors	USA	El Eng Mi	5 900	6 250	+ 350	+ 6
TRW	USA	Other	2 480	2 800	+ 320	+ 13
Vickers	UK	Eng MV SA/O	260	560	+ 300	+ 115
NEC[d]	Japan	El	520	780	+ 260	+ 50
GIAT Industries	France	A MV SA/O	1 030	1 280	+ 250	+ 24
Japan Steel Works[d]	Japan	SA/O	190	350	+ 160	+ 84
Tracor	USA	Comp	560	720	+ 160	+ 29
Toshiba[d]	Japan	El Mi	400	540	+ 140	+ 35
Rafael	Israel	SA/O Oth	360	490	+ 130	+ 36
Saab	Sweden	Ac El Mi Oth	350	470	+ 120	+ 34
Olin	USA	SA/O	320	440	+ 120	+ 38
UNC	USA	Comp	210	280	+ 70	+ 33

[a] The table includes all parent companies among the top 100 in 1995 which had a change in arms sales of at least ± $250 million or ± 30%.
[b] Abbreviations are explained in appendix 8A.
[c] Arms sales data for 1994 are for INI, the predecessor of Teneo as a state holding company for most of the Spanish government-controlled arms-producing companies.
[d] For Japanese companies data in the arms sales column represent new military contracts.
Source: Appendix 8A.

as a whole, the realistic interpretation is that there was a slow-down rather than an increase in the decline in arms sales, since the increasing concentration in arms production means that the arms sales of the 100 leading companies represent an increasing share of total arms production in these countries.

This interpretation is confirmed by table 8.2. Most of the companies with the most pronounced increases in arms sales in this table had acquired major arms production units in 1994 and 1995.[3]

The United States

The rate of acquisition in the US arms industry was quite spectacular in 1996 and the first month of 1997. Between January 1996 and January 1997 there were six huge acquisitions with a combined value of more than $40 billion, in addition to several smaller ones (table 8.3).

As a result, the structure of the US arms industry changed significantly. Its 14 leading prime military contractors were reduced to nine. The degree of concentration became very high, with the four leading companies at least three times as big as the next in rank. In order of arms sales volume these are Boeing, Lockheed Martin, Raytheon and Northrop Grumman, all aerospace and electronics firms.

Concentration, which has been a marked feature of the US defence industrial adjustment process, has been associated with consolidation, rationalization and capacity reductions. Companies have realized that in order to survive they must combine resources. The direction of the merger and acquisition process appears to be increasingly influenced by three factors: (a) the short-term effects that decide whether companies win or lose in the competition for large domestic arms procurement programmes; (b) the prospect of building up a systems integration capability in order to be able to become prime contractors for the fewer and larger military contracts in the longer term; and possibly (c) the capacity of the company to take greater responsibility for the financial risk of major weapon programmes in the future.

Acquisitions within the US arms industry have been supported by subsidies from the US Department of Defense (DOD). The rationale behind this policy has been to promote rationalization and thereby reduce the costs of arms production and lower prices for acquisitions by the DOD.[4] According to a decision in July 1993 by the then under-secretary of defence for acquisition, arms-producing companies are eligible to be reimbursed for part of the costs of mergers and acquisitions.[5] The total size of the subsidy programme is not publicly known, but known examples indicate that substantial sums are involved, ranging between the $25–133 million for four acquisition agreements in the

[3] Major international and US acquisitions in 1994–95 are listed in Sköns and Gill (note 1), tables 10.3 and 10.4 respectively.
[4] For a critique of the subsidies and their rationale, see Korb, L. J., 'Merger mania', *Brookings Review*, summer 1996, pp. 22–25; and Hartung, W. D., 'Saint Augustine's rules', *World Policy Journal*, summer 1996.
[5] According to section 818 of the National Defense Authorization Act for Fiscal Year 1995 (and DOD interim regulations effective from 29 Dec. 1994), DOD payments to contractors for costs associated with business combinations, e.g., costs associated with closing facilities and eliminating jobs, can be made if a senior DOD official certifies that projected savings from the restructuring are based on audited data and should result in overall reduced costs (net savings) to the DOD. US General Accounting Office (GAO), *Defense Contractor Restructuring: First Application of Cost and Savings Regulations*, GAO/NSIAD-96-80 (GAO: Gaithersburg, Md., Apr. 1996).

Table 8.3. Major take-overs in the US arms industry, agreed between 1 January 1996 and 31 January 1997

Take-overs are listed by size of acquisition.

Buyer	Seller	Acquired unit	Production of acquired units	Comments
Boeing	McDonnell Douglas	McDonnell Douglas	Aerospace	Price: $13 300 m.
Raytheon	General Motors	Hughes Electronics' defence division (Hughes Aircraft)	Missiles, radars and electronics	Price: $9500 m. agreed Jan. 1997
Lockheed Martin	Loral	All military businesses and 20% of space	Electronics, incl. communications	Price: $9100 m.
Northrop Grumman	Westing-house	Electronic Systems Group	Radars, command and control systems	Price: $3600 m.
Boeing	Rockwell	Aerospace	Aerospace	Price: $3200 m.
Raytheon	Texas Instruments	Defence Systems and Electronics Group	Missiles, radars and communications	Price: $2950 m. agreed Jan. 1997
Raytheon	Chrysler	Electrospace Systems; Chrysler Technologies Airborne Systems	Electronics	Price: $475 m.
General Dynamics	Lockheed Martin	LM Defense Systems; LM Armament Systems	Combat vehicle gun systems	Price: $450 m.
Litton	Black & Decker	PRC Inc.	Communications	Price: $425 m.

Source: SIPRI arms industry database.

period 1992–95[6] and the agreement to subsidize the Lockheed Martin merger with up to $1.8 billion.

The size and potential market shares of the merged US companies may have important implications in at least two broad areas: weapon prices and inter-national military–industrial relations.

Increased concentration of production can lead to cost reduction through less duplication, longer production runs and economies of scale. At the same time, however, it is feared that the deterioration in competition which may follow the concentration process may lead to higher weapon prices through monopolistic pricing.[7] Whereas competition was already limited in some seg-ments of shipbuilding, and in the production of armoured vehicles, these ten-dencies will now become stronger in aerospace and electronics too.

The exact nature of the impact on international military–industrial relations is not yet clear. One realistic scenario is that the US defence industrial base

[6] These were the Hughes acquisition of General Dynamics divisions, Martin Marietta's acquisition of General Electric units, Northrop's merger with Grumman, and the formation of United Defense LP by FMC and Harsco. 'DoD: merger savings justify costs', *Defense News*, 29 July–4 Aug. 1996, p. 4.

[7] Bischak, G., 'Market drives merger urge', *Defense News*, 14–20 Oct. 1996, p. 60.

transforms into a two-tiered system, in which a small group of large defence conglomerates (which have already been formed) act as more or less single-source systems integrators for final weapon systems, and another group of commercialized firms act as component suppliers, especially in fast-moving technologies such as electronics.[8] This would lead to an expansion of inter-nationalization at the component level, but very limited international coopera-tion at the systems level, since these conglomerates would be protected from competition by the government.

As the pace of concentration is much faster in the USA than anywhere else in the world, and since US companies have by far the largest domestic market, the competitiveness of US companies is rapidly increasing. It is feared that this will lead to US dominance not only in the international arms trade but also in high technology trade in general and therefore also in economic and political relations.[9]

Although the decline in US arms production has been enormous since its peak in 1987,[10] companies have not suffered significantly, at least not the prime contractor firms. Profits in the US arms industry are high and share values are rising.[11] Despite continuing over-capacity in the US arms industry and the expectation that consolidation will continue for some years,[12] the industry is optimistic about future sales.[13]

Western Europe

In Western Europe, the process is slower than in the USA, both as regards cuts in military production capacity and as regards consolidation of continued arms production—although there are great national variations. The possibilities for further national horizontal integration are being exhausted in most countries, and several of the recent major national acquisitions were actually vertical take-overs.[14] The process of internationalization through acquisitions and joint ventures does not contribute much to rationalization, partly because there are few cases but also because the integration process in many of the existing

[8] Pages, E. R., 'The future US defense industry: smaller markets, bigger companies, and closed doors', *SAIS Review*, vol. 15, no. 1 (winter/spring 1995), pp. 135–51.

[9] See, e.g., van Scherpenberg, J., 'Transatlantic competition and European defence industries: a new look at the trade-defence linkage', *International Affairs*, vol. 73, no. 1 (1997), pp. 99–122.

[10] One indicator often used to illustrate this, although not perfect, is the decline in defence-related employment. The US Department of Labor estimates that 1.8 million jobs were lost in 1987–97, and the DOD estimates a decrease of 39% during 1989–97. The level of US defence-related industrial employ-ment was about 2.3 million in FY 1995. US General Accounting Office, *Defense Industry—Trends in DOD Spending, Industrial Productivity, and Competition*, GAO/PEMD-97-3 (GAO: Gaithersburg, Md., Jan. 1997), pp. 2, 5 and 14.

[11] The only negative indicator reported in the press is the increasing debt levels of prime contractors. See, e.g., 'Soaring debt may tether industry', *Defense News*, 15–21 Jan. 1996, p. 9.

[12] *Interavia*, Jan./Feb. 1996, p. 5.

[13] See, e.g., US Aerospace Industries Association (AIA), *1996 Year-End Review and Forecast—An Analysis* (1996); and 'EIA: Electronic component spending to rise over decade', *Defense News*, 21–27 Oct. 1996, p. 16.

[14] Examples include the take-over in 1996 by the electronics company GEC of the VSEL shipbuilding company, and that in 1995 by the GKN automotive company of the Westland aerospace company.

cases is drawn-out and limited in itself.[15] The planned privatization and rationalization of the French arms industry, widely expected to contribute to an acceleration of international consolidation,[16] failed to take place in 1996. At company level efforts are now concentrated on the aerospace industry, with the restructuring of Airbus Industrie[17] and the creation of a 'military' division of Airbus, and with the start in 1996 of more general negotiations for cooperation in the production of the next-generation fighter aircraft in Europe.

The continued and considerable duplication of weapon systems produced in Europe is often noted. All governments therefore declare support for Europe-wide consolidation, but there are great differences in their policy recommendations to this end. Achieving the declared common goal of establishing a European armaments market is, therefore, a slow process, and it is still not clear whether it will be reached in the form originally envisioned.

Efforts to achieve the goal of a European Armaments Agency within the framework of the Western European Union (WEU) have taken a new direction with the establishment of a looser structure for armaments cooperation. Originally agreed on a bilateral Franco-German basis in December 1995, it was expanded into a quadrilateral initiative by the inclusion of Italy and the UK in the 12 November 1996 agreement to establish a Joint Armaments Cooperation Organization (JACO)[18] outside the framework of the WEU.[19] Although these four countries managed to agree on a common text, their main differences seem to have survived the process.[20] These divisive issues are (a) *juste retour:* should political considerations of national work shares be eliminated altogether, or should they remain a basic principle although not applied to each weapon programme?; (b) supranational decision making in arms procurement: should it be the long-term goal or not?; (c) European preferences: does the agreed principle on preference[21] allow for a policy of European preferences or of European protection, and what is the agreed difference

[15] See Bäcklund, K. and Sandström, M., *The Integration of Acquired Companies into the Defence Industry—Experiences from Western Europe*, Report by the FIND-Programme of the Swedish Defence Research Establishment, FOA-R-96 00312-1.3-SE (FOA: Stockholm, Oct. 1996), which examines the integration of 5 acquired companies in the West European defence industry: GEC-Marconi's acquisition of parts of Plessey and Ferranti International; Siemens' acquisition of another part of Plessey; Thomson CSF's acquisition of Hollandse Signaalapparaten and part of Ferranti International; and Daimler-Benz's acquisition of Telefunken.

[16] See, e.g., 'France sees Thomson sale as consolidation catalyst', *Defense News*, 21–27 Oct. 1996.

[17] The 4 original partners in Airbus Industrie agreed in Jan. 1997 to transform the consortium into an autonomous corporation by the year 1999, which would take over all aircraft businesses (commercial and civilian) of its 4 owner companies—Aérospatiale, BAe, Casa and Dasa—and Alenia, which decided in 1996 to join. 'Airbus agrees restructuring deal', *Interavia Air Letter*, 14 Jan. 1997, p. 1.

[18] Its French acronym is OCCAR (Organisation Conjointe de Coopération pour l'Armement).

[19] The Western European Armaments Organization (WEAO), also established within the WEU in Nov. 1996, is yet another organization with the more limited mandate of coordinating armaments, research projects and requirements.

[20] These differences were outlined by the official representatives of British and French procurement agencies in their speeches at the symposium 'Nordic Defence Industry in an International Perspective During the Coming Decades' organized by the Royal Swedish Academy of War Sciences, 13 Nov. 1996, in Stockholm.

[21] This formulation is 'preferring, when meeting the requirements of their armed forces, products in whose development they have participated'. 'Arms Agency evades buy-European issue', *Defense News*, 18–24 Nov. 1996, p. 4.

between the two?; and (d) transatlantic cooperation: is the common aim to establish true transatlantic cooperation or to ensure compensation in industrial offsets and technology transfer? Discussions within the Inter-Governmental Conference of the European Union of its Common and Foreign Security Policy may have some implications for the future restructuring of the European arms industry, although probably on a rather limited scale.

III. Company behaviour in 1990–95

When arms procurement budgets started to fall in the late 1980s, and it was possible to forecast continued cuts during the 1990s, it was foreseen by analysts that there would be deep future cuts in arms production, problems for the arms industry and increased pressure to export weapons as a substitute for lost domestic procurement. It should now be possible to start looking at what actually happened and why. Data from the SIPRI arms industry database provide some indications and lead to some hypotheses for subsequent case studies on which to base more definite conclusions.

The findings of an overall survey for the period 1990–95 are presented here, showing trends in the level of arms production, in dependence on arms sales by individual companies, in company profitability and in exports. Only the top 100 companies in the OECD and developing countries are included, as systematic data have not been compiled for many more than these. Although the conclusions cannot be automatically applied to the entire arms industry, they should provide some indication of general trends.

Table 8.4 shows a decline in arms sales during this period. The combined arms sales of the top 100 companies in 1990 fell by one-third to $148 billion in 1995. The combined arms sales of those included in the top 100 in 1995—a different set of companies—declined by one-fifth to $154 billion in 1995. This is not too different from the decline in government expenditure on arms procurement for the aggregate NATO countries excluding France, which was around one-quarter between 1987 and 1995.[22]

The number of US companies among the top 100 has declined from 46 to 40, largely as a result of the concentration of the US arms industry into fewer companies, while the number of companies in OECD countries other than the USA and Western Europe has increased from 7 to 12, as a result of the increase in the number of Japanese companies among the top 100. In all country groups there was a fall in average company arms sales.

The set of companies included among the top 100 has shifted considerably during the period. Companies leaving the list have mainly ceased military production or existence as an independent company, while companies being added to the list have risen from below the top 100 threshold. The arms sales threshold for inclusion among the top 100 has therefore declined over the period—from $360 million in 1990 to $260 million in 1995. Companies taken

---

[22] See table 6A.1 (NATO distribution of military expenditure) in appendix 6A in this volume. In 1996, the decline in NATO arms procurement expenditures was another 8%.

Table 8.4. Regional/national arms sales for the top 100 arms-producing companies in the OECD and the developing countries, 1995 compared to 1990

Figures for arms sales are in US $b., at constant (1995) prices and exchange rates.

Region/ country	Top 100 companies in 1990			Top 100 companies in 1995		
	Number of companies	Arms sales		Number of companies	Arms sales	
		1990	1995		1990	1995
USA	46	129.1	88.1	40	111.6	87.7
West European OECD	41	71.0	49.0	40	66.5	53.0
Other OECD	7	10.6	7.4	12	11.5	9.1
Developing countries	6	5.6	3.4	8	6.2	4.2
Total	**100**	**216.3**	**147.9**	**100**	**195.8**	**154.0**

Source: Appendix 8A and the SIPRI arms industry database.

off the list can be grouped into four categories (see table 8.5): (*a*) those that have left the arms industry altogether by selling off their arms-producing units; (*b*) those that have merged with or been acquired as subsidiaries by other companies; (*c*) state holding companies which no longer have a central role in state manufacturing of weapons; and (*d*) those which have slipped from the list as a result of declining arms sales.

Dependence on military sales

Table 8.6 suggests that the reduction of arms sales has not taken place primarily through diversification into civilian production. Only 18 companies among the top 100 companies in 1995 have decreased the military share in their total sales by 10 per cent or more. For most of these companies, the decreased military share in their sales was the combined effect of increased civilian sales and decreased arms sales, and all but two increased their civilian sales.[23] Most of the companies with a decreased dependence on military sales are based within the electronics sector. Surprisingly many of these companies are based in France and Israel, countries where companies have not adopted strong diversification or conversion strategies.

Few systematic studies are available on company strategies in response to changes in the demand for military equipment.[24] A recent study of 175 companies in south-west England indicated that of three strategy alternatives—rationalization, diversification and focusing upon new defence markets—most companies reported that they attached most importance to diversification, and the next most favoured option was new defence markets. A possible explana-

[23] The exceptions are Unisys and Smiths Industries.
[24] For more general studies, see Latham, A. and Hooper, N. (eds), *The Future of the Defence Firm: New Challenges, New Directions*, NATO ASI Series (Kluwer: Dordrecht, Boston and London, 1995).

Table 8.5. Companies leaving the top 100 list between 1990 and 1995[a]

Figures for arms sales are given in US $m.

Company	Country	Sector[b] 1990	Arms sales 1990	Comments
(a) Companies that left the arms industry altogether				
Nobel Industries	Sweden	El Mi SA/O	930	Military business sold to Celsius
Ferranti-International	UK	El	440	Bankruptcy; military business sold; now parts of GEC and Thomson
Thorn EMI	UK	El	450	Military business sold to Racal and Thomson
Emerson Electric	USA	EL	610	Military business spun off into Esco
Ford Motor	USA	Ac El MV Mi	700	Military business sold to Loral
Hercules	USA	Ac Mi	800	Military business sold to Alliant Tech
IBM	USA	El	1 600	Military business sold to Loral
LTV	USA	Ac El Mi	1 490	Military business sold to Carlyle/ Northrop Grumman and Loral
Teledyne	USA	Eng El Mi	500	Military business sold to Litton
Unisys	USA	El	2 000	Military business sold to Loral
(b) Companies that merged or were acquired as subsidiaries by other companies				
Matra	FRA	El Mi	1 180	Became subsidiary of Lagardère
Dowty	UK	Ac El	520	Became subsidiary of TI
Hawker Siddeley	UK	Ac	480	Became subsidiary of BTR
VSEL	UK	Sh	930	Became subsidiary of GEC
Westland	UK	Ac	510	Became subsidiary of GKN
Bath Iron Works	USA	Sh	550	Became subsidiary of General Dyn.
E-Systems	USA	El	1 400	Became subsidiary of Raytheon
Grumman	USA	Ac El	2 900	Merged into Northrop Grumman
Martin Marietta	USA	Mi	4 600	Merged into Lockheed Martin
Northrop	USA	Ac	4 930	Merged into Northrop Grumman
(c) State holdings that no longer have a central role in state manufacturing of weapons				
EFIM	Italy	Ac El MV	1 710	Military production transferred to IRI
Armscor	S. Africa	A Ac El MV SA/O	1 330	Military production transferred to Denel
INI	Spain	Ac A El MV Sh	1 560	Military production transferred to Teneo
(d) Companies leaving the list because of declining arms sales				
CAE	Canada	El	640	Part of military business sold
Mannesmann	Germany	MV	420	Declining sales of Krauss-Maffei
FFV	Sweden	A El SA/O	500	Most military business sold; now part of Celsius and Volvo Aero
Morrison Knudsen	USA	MV	380	Declining arms sales
Sequa	USA	El Eng	700	Declining arms sales
Sundstrand	USA	Ac	390	Declining arms sales

[a] The table includes all companies which are included as parent companies in the top 100 list for 1990 but not for 1995.

[b] Abbreviations are explained in appendix 8A.

Source: Appendix 8A and the SIPRI arms industry database.

tion for the low importance attached to rationalization strategies, in apparent contradiction to the significant employment reductions being made, was that these redundancies were mainly to reduce costs, not to reduce capacity.[25] Ten companies, that is, 10 per cent of the top 100, increased their military share of production significantly during this period of general downsizing. With the exception of Celsius, which acquired a large proportion of the Swedish arms-producing companies, all these companies are located in the UK and the USA, countries in which the rate of concentration and restructuring has been very fast. All but two of the companies listed in table 8.6 as among those with the greatest increase in the military share of sales increased not only their share but also their volume of military sales during the period, several as a result of acquisitions. BAe and General Dynamics are the exceptions which had an increased military share in spite of decreased volumes of military sales. In both cases this was the result primarily of divestitures of production units with higher than average civilian production. Among the companies with a significantly increasing military share, there is a stronger representation of firms producing military vehicles, small arms and ordnance and ships.

Profitability

In general the profitability of the arms industry has not suffered from the sharp reductions in the demand for military equipment since 1987. On the contrary, although with some important exceptions, companies have been able to avoid losses and even increase their profitability.

As regards national variations in profitability, it is often said that US arms companies were highly profitable during the adjustment process of the 1990s, while the profits of European companies were modest. The forecast is that this pattern will continue because of the fragmentation of the European defence market and the slow pace of cost-cutting.[26] Although the arguments may appear convincing, this cannot be confirmed by a strict national statistical comparison of profitability. It is possible to derive any result from such a comparison, depending on the companies included in each country's sample.[27] When calculating a profitability average for European companies, the inclusion of companies with very high losses, such as many of the French companies, pulls down the average profitability for Europe considerably.

While there are no firm statistics, a few general observations can be made. By and large, US companies seem to have gone through the adjustment process without substantial losses, and most of them have seen high and rising

[25] Bishop, P. and Williams, T., 'Strategic options for change in the UK defense sector', *Defense Analysis*, vol. 12, no. 2 (1996), pp. 259–61. This survey was carried out during the summer of 1995.

[26] See, e.g., the summary of a report by Moody's Investor Service in *Interavia*, Dec. 1995, p. 10, showing a one-line graph for US and European defence company profitability respectively, and specifying US profitability at 9%, while European profitability was mediocre at 4%.

[27] Since arms-producing companies are seldom 100% dependent on arms sales, an important selection criterion is the share of arms sales. When elaborating with different shares, the results vary widely. There is also the question of how to derive an average for a country, that is, how each company should be weighted in the average.

Table 8.6. Changes in the military share of total sales, 1990–95[a]

Figures are percentages.

Company[b]	Country	Industry	Military share of total sales		
			1990	1995	1990–95
Companies which had the sharpest decrease in the military share					
TAAS/IMI	Israel	A MV SA/O	97	66	– 31
Thiokol	USA	Eng SA/O	52	27	– 25
Raytheon	USA	El Mi	57	34	– 23
Gencorp	USA	El Eng	49	28	– 21
GIAT Industries	France	A MV SA/O	97	77	– 20
Texas Instruments	USA	El	32	13	– 19
Aérospatiale Groupe[c]	France	Ac Mi	44	26	– 18
Rheinmetall	Germany	A El MV SA/O	41	23	– 18
Esco Electronics	USA	El	96	78	– 18
Oerlikon–Bührle	Switzerland	A Ac El Mi SA/O	40	23	– 17
Unisys	USA	El	20	4	– 16
Lockheed Martin	USA	Ac El Mi	75	60	– 15
Logicon[c]	USA	El Oth	99	85	– 14
Rockwell International	USA	El Mi	33	19	– 14
Elbit	Israel	El	45	31	– 14
Smiths Industries	UK	El	41	29	– 12
Dassault Aviation	France	Ac	66	55	– 11
SNPE Groupe	France	A SA/O	45	35	– 10
Companies which had the largest increase in the military share					
Celsius	Sweden	A El SA/O Sh	14	55	+ 41
Litton	USA	El Sh	58	91	+ 33
BAe	UK	A Ac El Mi SA/O	44	74	+ 30
Racal Electronics	UK	El	13	33	+ 20
GKN	UK	Ac MV	4	23	+ 19
Ceridian/Control Data	USA	El Oth	20	38	+ 18
General Dynamics	USA	MV Sh	82	96	+ 14
Hunting	UK	SA/O	28	38	+ 10
Dyncorp	USA	Comp (Ac)	50	60	+ 10
AlliantTech Systems	USA	SA/O	90	100	+ 10

[a] The table includes all parent companies among the top 100 in 1995 which had a change in their arms sales share of total sales of ± 10 percentage points or more.

[b] Companies with two names separated by a slash (/) have changed their names.

[c] For Aérospatiale and Logicon, the data listed in the 1990 column are for 1991.

Source: Appendix 8A and SIPRI arms industry database.

profits during the period.[28] On average, British companies appear to have been even more profitable than US companies, although the rate of profits has decreased and there have been dips over the period, while French companies have experienced increasing losses, particularly GIAT Industries, and the losses of

---

[28] There are numerous reports on the spectacular (double-digit) profit rates of US defence companies. 'Sustained efficiency push reflected in profit momentum', *Aviation Week & Space Technology*, 5 Aug. 1996, pp. 49–50; and 'US industry rides profit momentum', *Aviation Week & Space Technology*, 3 Feb. 1997, pp. 36–41.

Thomson-CSF and Aérospatiale had decreased to a rather low level by 1995. The losses of the main German arms-producing company, Daimler Aerospace (DASA), had a great impact on the German average, but several other German companies have fared better.

However, the important question is how to interpret profitability trends. The most obvious conclusion is that the companies have proved well able to protect themselves from the adverse effects of arms industry restructuring, at least in the short run. Whether this will be true in the long run depends on whether their investments have been adjusted to future challenges. This is sometimes questioned. It is often claimed that companies which have diversified into civilian production have better growth prospects than those which continued with arms production. The examples most often quoted are Raytheon and Hughes Electronics, on the one hand, and Northrop Grumman, General Dynamics and Lockheed Martin, on the other.[29]

Military exports

The reduction in arms procurement in the domestic markets of the world's main arms-producing centres has resulted in strong competition in world export markets.[30] In a shrinking market for arms exports, companies compete fiercely for the often very large orders. Export contracts can involve billions of dollars over a number of years. For many companies, especially those with a high ratio of exports to sales, winning an export contract of this size could mean the key to long-term survival as an arms producer. To the extent that the government has paid the research and development (R&D) and other fixed costs, exports can be more profitable than domestic sales, and companies tend to calculate in export earnings in their contract bids. Governments can also have an incentive to export if this allows them to recoup some of their military R&D investments in the programme.[31]

Few companies provide information on their military export sales. Listing a selection of the few that have, table 8.7 shows that arms exports account for a high and growing share of total arms sales in most of these companies.

In the heightened competition for fewer and larger military export contracts, companies request financial and other support from their governments. Most governments in arms-producing countries are therefore actively involved in the business of exporting military equipment, and some of the costs of arms exports are paid by the national budget in supplier countries. Failure of the arms industry to adjust to lower procurement budgets therefore also means costs for the general public in arms-producing countries.

---

[29] See, e.g., 'Zivile Produktion bringt früheren Rüstungskonzernen Kurspotential' [Civil production brings earlier growth prospects for defence firms], *Frankfurter Allgemeine Zeitung,* 31 Aug. 1996, p. 20.
[30] See chapter 9 in this volume.
[31] This is not the only government motive for arms exports. Apart from the traditional motive of wider foreign policy interests, it has also been suggested that, at least in the British case, their impact on the prospects for civil exports of greater economic value is an explanatory factor. Miller, D., *Export or Die: Britain's Defence Trade with Iran and Iraq* (Cassell: London, 1996).

Table 8.7. Company military exports, 1990 and 1995

Figures are percentages.

Company	Country	Industry	Military exports in total arms sales	
			1990	1995
Dassault Aviation	France	Ac	61[a]	29
Dassault Electronique	France	El	20	58
GIAT Industries	France	A MV SA/O	36 (1988)	40
Matra Défense	France	Mi	13	45
SAGEM	France	El	. .	43
SNECMA	France	Eng	35 (1992)	. .
Thomson-CSF	France	El	. .	51
Diehl	Germany	SA/O	17	21
Dynamit Nobel	Germany	SA/O Oth	43 (1992)	39 (1994)
Rheinmetall	Germany	A El MV SA/O	. .	9 (1994)
BAe	UK	A Ac El Mi SA/O	76	82 (1994)
GKN	UK	Ac MV	. .	55
Rolls Royce[b]	UK	Eng	60	54
VSEL[b]	UK	Sh	1 (1989)	2 (1993)
Vosper Thornycroft[b]	UK	Sh	48	72
Alliant Tech Systems	USA	SA/O	4 (1992)	10
BDM International	USA	El Oth	3 (1991)	42 (1994)
Boeing	USA	Ac El Mi	21	25
E-Systems	USA	El	9	7 (1994)
General Dynamics	USA	MV Sh	13	. .
Loral[b]	USA	El Mi	20 (1991)	14 (1993)
McDonnell Douglas[b]	USA	Ac El Mi	19	37
Raytheon	USA	El Mi	9 (1991)	15
Texas Instruments	USA	El	. .	19 (1993)

[a] For 1991 the share for Dassault Aviation was down to 25%.

[b] Figures are for total exports as a share of total sales for these companies, most of which have a high military share in total sales: Loral, VSEL, and Vosper more than 90%, McDonnell Douglas 60–70%, and Rolls Royce only around 30%.

Source: Appendix 8A and the SIPRI arms industry database.

The magnitude of the cost of supporting military exports is difficult to assess, although some preliminary estimates are beginning to emerge.[32] There are few data and it is not easy to decide which costs should be included. Government support to military exports takes a variety of forms, the most important being: grant military aid, loans, interest rate subsidies and credit guarantees for arms exports, the net costs of various forms of compensation offers offsetting the import costs of the recipient country (offsets), contribu-

---

[32] It has been estimated that government subsidies to British arms exports amount to at least £384 m. a year, one-fifth of the total value of British arms exports. World Development Movement, *Gunrunners' Gold: How the Public's Money Finances Arms Sales* (London, May 1995), p. 15. See also Cooper, N., *The Business of Death: Britain's Arms Trade at Home and Abroad* (Tauris Academic Studies: London, 1997), chapter 6. For the USA, the corresponding figure is $6.3 billion in fiscal year 1994. 'Economic costs of arms exports: subsidies and offsets', testimony of Lora Lumpe to the Subcommittee on Foreign Operations of the US Senate Appropriations Committee, 23 May 1995.

tion to military exhibitions, and a range of government services linked to arms export deals.

Although financial support for military exports has been little discussed, mainly because of lack of transparency, there are indications that it is an important factor in arms exports.[33]

The governments of France, Germany, the UK and the USA provide differing levels of financial support for arms exports. Shares of total export credits going to military sales in 1993 were 1 per cent in Germany, 21 per cent in France and 48 per cent in the UK.[34] In France, the UK and the USA this support is being strengthened in several ways. In France the Government had planned to announce decisions on an improved policy to promote French arms exports before the end of 1996, but this was postponed because of the delays in restructuring the French arms industry.[35] During the period 1990–94, the French credit agency, COFACE, signed credit guarantees for 65 per cent of French defence exports, valued at 115 billion francs ($23 billion) and provided customer credit for one-third of these deals, for a total of 90 billion francs ($18.2 billion).[36] British government credit guarantees for military exports have increased considerably over the past 10 years, from an annual average of £365 million in the five-year period up to 1989/90 to £1005 million in the following five years.[37] Credit guarantees become government costs if the customer fails to deliver credit payments. For the UK, this share of actual government payments was about one-quarter of the level of guarantees during the period 1989/90–1993/94.[38]

In the USA the main support for arms exports has been the Foreign Military Financing (FMF) programme, providing grants and loans for military exports. However, this programme has been limited to arms exports to a few allied countries, mainly Egypt, Israel, Greece and Turkey. In 1996 two new arms export subsidy programmes were created in the USA, an export loan guarantee fund, amounting to $15 billion and administered by the Department of Defense, and the possibility for importers of US weapons to waive R&D fees to the US Government.[39]

The costs to the taxpayers for defence industrial policies relying on arms exports are likely to increase in the near future.

[33] The provision of credit was judged by British defence attachés to be the most important factor in securing arms sales, according to a 1989 report by the National Audit Office, cited in Miller, D., 'The Scott Report and the future of British defense sales', *Defense Analysis*, vol. 12, no. 3 (1996), p. 368.

[34] US General Accounting Office, *Export Finance: Comparative Analysis of US and European Union Export Credit Agencies'*, GAO/GGD-96-1 (GAO: Gaithersburg, Md., Oct. 1995), p. 9. The defence share can vary considerably from one year to another. The average defence share in the UK was 30% in the 5 years up to 1994/95. See Cooper (note 32), based on data in House of Commons Defence Committee and House of Commons Trade and Industry Committee, *Aspects of Defence Procurement and Industrial Policy*, Memoranda, Session 1994–95, HC 333 (Her Majesty's Stationary Office: London, July 1995), p. 103.

[35] 'Millon veut doper les exportations en 1997', *La Tribune*, 27 Dec. 1996, p. 8.

[36] 'France shuns export aid hike', *Defense News*, 9–15 Oct. 1995, p. 30.

[37] House of Commons 1994–95 (note 34), p. 103.

[38] House of Commons 1994–95 (note 34), p. 91.

[39] Hartung, W., D., 'Saint Augustine's rules', *World Policy Journal*, vol. 13, no. 2 (summer 1996), pp. 65–73.

IV. Russia and Ukraine

Russia

From the end of 1995, for the first time since the collapse of the Soviet Union, the Russian defence industry began to receive more attention from President Boris Yeltsin and the government. This development was not unconnected to the Presidential election campaign in the first half of 1996. In January Yeltsin replaced Viktor Glukhikh, Chairman of the State Committee for the Defence Branches of Industry, by Zinoviy Pak, one of the most energetic advocates in Russia of the development of dual-use technologies.[40] In May 1996 Pak had his first significant success: the State Committee was upgraded to become the Ministry of the Defence Industry (Minoboronprom). With ministerial status, Pak was now a full member of the government with the same formal standing as the Minister of Atomic Energy.

His success proved to be short-lived. In March 1997 Minoboronprom was dissolved and responsibility for oversight of the defence industry was transferred to the Ministry of Economics. The Minister, Yakov Urinson, exercised overall leadership, assisted by three deputy ministers. This change was opposed by many within the industry, but welcomed by 'Rosvooruzhenie', the state company for arms exports, which believed that it would facilitate restructuring.

Ownership

By the end of 1996 the ownership structure of the defence industry had undergone substantial change. In April Yeltsin established a Federal Commission to review privatization in the defence sector and in July a government decree approved a list of 480 industrial enterprises and R&D organizations that would remain in full state ownership.[41] By that time Minoboronprom had 1700 enterprises and organizations under its control, or cooperating with it, employing a total of 3 million people.[42] Several hundred other privatized companies have left the defence sector altogether.

Output trends

Notwithstanding the enhanced formal status of the industry, there was no reversal of the fall in output (table 8.8). By the end of 1996 military output

---

[40] Pak was the general director of the Federal Centre for Dual-Use Technologies, founded in 1995. Pak's views are developed in *Izvestiya*, 9 Feb. 1996; *Krasnaya Zvezda*, 18 May 1996; *Kommersant Daily*, 25 May 1996; and *Business in Russia*, Mar. 1996, pp. 28–29 and July 1996, pp. 20–22. These policy options were also favoured by two other leading figures, Andrei Kokoshin, First Deputy Defence Minister, and Boris Kuzyk, Yeltsin's personal adviser on the arms trade and defence industry matters.

[41] The largest number of state units were in the munitions and special chemicals industry (93), the lowest in electronics (44) and the aviation industry (45). *Rossiyskaya Gazeta*, 30 July 1996.

[42] Of the total, 41% were in full state ownership, 32% were joint stock companies with state participation (either a federal shareholding of up to 51%, or a single golden share with veto rights), and the remaining 27% were fully privatized companies retaining links with the ministry. *Rossiyskii Vesti*, 30 July 1996.

Table 8.8. Output of the Russian defence industry (Minoboronprom), 1991–96[a]
Index, 1991=100, constant prices.[b]

	1991	1992	1993	1994	1995	1996
Military	100.0	49.5	32.5	19.9	16.6	12.3
Civilian	100.0	99.6	85.6	52.6	41.3	29.1
Total	**100.0**	**80.4**	**64.6**	**39.2**	**31.2**	**22.7**

[a] Defence industry is defined here as enterprises belonging to the Ministry of the Defence Industry (the State Committee for the Defence Branches of Industry prior to May 1996).

[b] Data refer to production (not sales) in rouble terms. Constant prices are calculated with the use of specific price indices for each type of product, military and civilian. Adjustments are made to the series so that it is unaffected by enterprises leaving the group belonging to the Ministry. Output data for the Minoboronprom defence industry are considered to be reasonably reliable.

Source: *Krasnaya Zvezda*, 25 Jan. 1997.

was just one-eighth of the 1991 level and civilian production was down by 70 per cent.

The decline was not uniform across the branches of the industry. To the end of 1995 the electronics and communications equipment industries suffered the largest falls of almost 80 per cent in relation to 1991, with shipbuilding, protected by foreign orders for civilian vessels, the least affected with a fall of only one-third.[43] In 1996 this pattern was largely unchanged except that the shipbuilding industry also experienced a more pronounced downturn.[44] In the nuclear industry under Minatom, military output fell by two-thirds between 1991 and 1994 and by a further 30 per cent in 1995; the military share of the Ministry's total output declined to only 8 per cent in 1996.[45] The contraction of the labour force of the defence industry also continued. From a total of 6.4 million employees in 1991, less than 3 million remained within the Minoboronprom system by the end of 1996, a year in which employment in the industry declined by approximately 13 per cent.

A number of factors accounted for the decline and its differential impact. First, in circumstances of severe budgetary constraint, procurement for the Russian armed forces has been cut back drastically.[46] Second, the output of

[43] Centre for Economic Analysis of the Government of the Russian Federation, *Rossiya-1994*, no. 1 (1994), p. 193 and *Rossiya-1995*, no. 1 (1995), p. 139; and *Segodnya*, 27 Dec. 1995.

[44] *Krasnaya Zvezda*, 7 Dec. 1996.

[45] BBC, *Summary of World Broadcasts*, SU/2395 C/1, 30 Aug. 1995; *Konversiya*, no. 3 (1996), p. 32; and RIA Novosti, 13 Jan. 1997.

[46] Whereas 414 military aircraft (fixed-wing planes and helicopters) were supplied to the forces in 1991, the number in 1995 was a mere 7 and in 1996 the air forces of the country received no new aircraft at all. *Security Dialogue*, no. 1 (1995), p. 81; and BBC, *Summary of World Broadcasts*, SU/2769 S1/1, 14 Nov. 1996 and SU/2787 S1/1, 5 Dec. 1996. Since 1991 no new large naval surface ships have been laid down. The Navy received 28 new submarines and surface ships in 1992, but only 3 in 1995. *Krasnaya Zvezda*, 17 Apr. 1993; and *Pravda*, 2 Mar. 1996. Similarly, the order for new tanks (domestic procurement plus exports) in 1996 was 58 units, compared with 570 tanks received by the forces in 1991. *Security Dialogue*, no. 1 (1995), p. 81; and *Krasnaya Zvezda*, 7 Sep. 1996.

many of the civilian goods produced by the defence industry has fallen sharply in the face of foreign competition and depressed domestic demand. Third, manufacturers have been experiencing severe problems of insufficient working capital, a lack of investment finance and delayed payment from the Ministry of Defence and other customers resulting in severe problems of wage arrears. The decline in output would have been even more pronounced if it were not for exports, however.

Exports

Russian exports of weapons and other military equipment, as reported by the state arms export corporation Rosvooruzhenie, are shown in table 8.9. These data include the delivery of spares, technology and services relating to military purposes as well as actual weapon systems.

There is no doubt that since the establishment of Rosvooruzhenie in November 1993 Russia's approach to the arms trade has become more professional and serious attention is now being devoted to the supply of spares and back-up services. There is also a new realization of the gains to be made from the modernization of older-generation Soviet weapons, in particular combat aircraft. The aviation industry makes the largest contribution: in 1995 more than half of total exports were aircraft. One-quarter were infantry weapons, while naval equipment and air defence systems each accounted for one-tenth of total sales.[47] A limited number of suppliers of end-product systems dominate the export trade: according to Pak, in 1995 a mere 18 companies accounted for 80 per cent of total export sales.[48] However, this understates the impact of exports on the Russian defence industry as a much larger number of supplier firms also benefit. Overall, in 1994 exports were reported to account for almost half of the total military output, rising to 55 per cent in the first half of 1996.[49] Looking to the future, Rosvooruzhenie has drafted a programme for Russia's military–technical collaboration with foreign states to the year 2005, providing for what Pak has termed a 'dramatic increase' in arms exports. This will be considered by the government during the first half of 1997.[50]

To an increasing extent, export possibilities have been driving the process of restructuring. Export earnings are helping to fund new development programmes and some new investment. Rosvooruzhenie itself is playing an active role. Part of its profits are used to fund investment projects and it also provides guarantees for bank loans. In 1994 Rosvooruzhenie investment amounted to $150 million; in 1995, $420 million.[51]

---

[47] *Finansovye Izvestiya*, 13 Feb. 1996.

[48] The Jamestown Foundation, *Monitor*, 30 May 1996.

[49] *Delovaya Sibir*, no. 38 (Sep. 1996), p. 5.

[50] *Nezavisimaya Gazeta*, 19 Nov. 1996; and BBC, *Summary of World Broadcasts*, SUW/0468 WD/15, 10 Jan. 1997.

[51] Including $172 million from its own resources, the balance taking the form of bank loans in hard currency at heavily subsidized annual rates of interest of 12–15%. *Finansovye Izvestiya*, 4 Apr. 1996; BBC, *Summary of World Broadcasts*, SUW/0430 WD/13, 12 Apr. 1996; and *Business in Russia*, Sep. 1995, p. 78.

Table 8.9. Exports of military equipment, 1991–96

Figures are in US $b., at current prices.

	1991	1992	1993	1994	1995	1996 (Provisional)
Value of exports	7.1	2.3	2.5	1.7	3.1	3.5

Sources: For 1991–95: *Izvestiya*, 24 Dec. 1996 (Rosvooruzhenie data); and for 1996: BBC, *Summary of World Broadcasts*, SUW/0468 WD/1, 10 Jan. 1997.

New corporate structures

However, it is the trend towards the creation of large, more competitive corporate structures that is the most significant. What is new since the end of 1995 is the willingness of the state to intervene to accelerate the process. A stimulus to this policy has undoubtedly been developments in the United States and Western Europe: the rapid consolidation of the US aerospace industry has been followed with great attention and has been seen as an example to be emulated if Russia is not to be marginalized in the increasingly competitive world aerospace business.

The most notable examples of new corporate structures are the so-called military–industrial companies MAPO and Sukhoi, both established by Presidential decree. The former, employing 100 000 people, includes the MiG design organization and a set of manufacturing companies concerned with the final assembly of MiG aircraft, aero engines and components. Significantly, it also includes the Kamov helicopter design bureau.[52] The Sukhoi company, formed in late 1996, includes the design organization and several production enterprises, including the Komsomol'sk-na-Amure, Novosibirsk and Irkutsk plants responsible for most export deliveries of 'Su' combat aircraft, and also the Beriev aircraft design organization of Taganrog.[53]

A looser form of organization is the financial–industrial group (FIG), linking enterprises, R&D organization, trading companies and banks. Officially registered FIGs undergo a tough inter-agency approval process; registration provides eligibility for state support in the form of tax relief, preferential credit terms, accelerated depreciation or the right of the central company of the group to take over state shareholdings on a trust basis. In practice, the extent of state support has proved to be limited. Other FIGs have been formed on an informal basis, usually by large commercial banks. By the end of 1996 there were 45 officially registered FIGs in the Russian economy, several of which related to the defence industry.[54]

Another form of state-supported group is the Federal Research and Production Centre (FNPTs), created on the basis of R&D and manufacturing facilities concerned with what are considered to be the most important types

---

[52] *Krasnaya Zvezda*, 2 June 1996; and *Kommersant Daily*, 28 May 1996.

[53] *Kommersant Daily*, 4 and 6 Dec. 1996; and *Krasnaya Zvezda*, 6 Jan. 1997. It has been rumoured that the Mil helicopter design bureau may also join and that the new company may link with the Tupolev and Yakovlev organization to form a very large financial–industrial group.

[54] *Segodnya*, 21 Dec. 1996.

of military hardware. Five had been created by the end of 1996.[55] This form of organization, which is designed to guarantee special state support, is likely to prove important for the production of types of weapon not expected to find export markets. Other important R&D facilities have been granted the status of State Research Centre (GNT), providing access to regular state budget funding. Of the 61 GNTs by the end of 1996, 25 were in, or closely related to, the defence industry.[56]

If the present trend is maintained—and there is no sign that it will be reversed—it can be predicted that within the next one or two years the development and manufacture of armaments in Russia will be concentrated heavily in a relatively small number of large corporations and groups.

Diversification and conversion

While conversion remains official policy and was boosted in 1996 by the approval of new programmes and the creation of a conversion fund, progress has been limited by the lack of investment. By October the planned level of state budget funding for conversion had been met to only 30 per cent and later in the year it was reported that not one of 250 conversion programmes approved by Minoboronprom had been started.[57] Attention has increasingly turned to projects for which there are potential customers able to afford the new civilian goods. Above all it is the oil and gas industry which meets this criterion and the supply of equipment to the fuel and energy sector has become the most dynamic direction of conversion activity, involving a growing range of facilities of the shipbuilding, aviation and ground forces equipment industries. However, even in this promising market many producers are experiencing problems of sales as the fuel and energy industry shows a preference for imported equipment.

By the end of 1996, prompted by the newly created Defence Council and a heightened concern with questions of military reform, there were signs that the government and Ministry of Defence were preparing new policy measures to protect and strengthen the ability of the defence industry to develop new weapons and to respond to the planned expansion of procurement within the framework of a long-term programme of armaments to the year 2005 prepared during the year. The process of creating large corporations is likely to be accelerated, more FNPTs created, the system of mobilization preparedness further reformed, measures taken to enhance the effectiveness of budget funding for military R&D programmes, and a new impetus given to international collaboration—within the Commonwealth of Independent States (CIS) and with other foreign partners.[58]

---

[55] Including such major facilities as the Severodvinsk Centre for Atomic Shipbuilding (nuclear submarines), the Miass (Urals) Makeev Centre (submarine-launched strategic missiles), and the Moscow Khrunichev and Samara 'Progress' Centres (space launchers and satellites).

[56] *Konversiya*, no. 12 (1995), pp. 11–13; and Scientific and Technical Complex of Russia: Outline of Development, Moscow, 1995, pp. 52–53.

[57] *Krasnaya Zvezda*, 7 Dec. 1996; and *Rossiyskaya Gazeta*, 28 Nov. 1996.

[58] *Krasnaya Zvezda*, 7 and 20 Dec. 1996; BBC, *Summary of World Broadcasts*, SUW/0459 WD/11, 1 Nov. 1996 and SU/2803 S1/5, 24 Dec. 1996; and *Inzhenernaya Gazeta*, no. 108 (Nov. 1996).

Ukraine

Prior to the country's independence, Ukraine was responsible for approximately one-fifth of the total output of the Soviet defence industry and 15 per cent of deliveries of end-product weapons.[59] Particular strengths were shipbuilding, the missile space industry, tank building, Antonov transport aircraft, aero engines, radar and optical systems. Notable gaps in Ukrainian military production included small arms, tank guns and other artillery systems, combat aircraft and submarines.

After independence the defence industry and the civilian engineering industry were brought together under a single Ministry of Machine Building, Military-Industrial Complex and Conversion (Minmashprom). The contraction of the defence industry has been remarkable. While the reliability of data for the Ukrainian defence industry is uncertain,[60] the following numbers provide at least an indication of the magnitude of the reductions. By 1995 military production had declined to only 10 per cent of its 1991 level.[61] The size of the core defence industry has declined from around 700 enterprises and a similar number of R&D organizations in 1991 with a total of 1.5 million people employed[62] to only 139 enterprises in 1995 employing 63 000 people in military production, 11 per cent of the defence industry's total labour force of almost 600 000.[63]

A number of factors account for this contraction of the Ukrainian defence industry. Severe budgetary limits have reduced the share of defence ministry expenditure in GDP to less than 2 per cent and within the defence ministry's budget there has been hardly any funding for procurement or R&D.[64] Second, arms exports have been at a very modest level. Third, Ukrainian producers of armaments and other military hardware are heavily dependent on the supply of systems and components from Russia and other CIS states. Efforts have been made to maintain defence sector supply links, including Russian–Ukrainian intergovernmental and inter-ministerial agreements in 1994 and August 1996, but many problems remain.[65] Finally, the Ukrainian defence industry has experienced severe difficulties typical of industry in general, including wage arrears, an acute shortage of working capital and a lack of investment finance.

[59] Safiulin, Y. and Manachinskii, A., 'Voenno-promyshlenniy kompleks Ukrainy: sostoyanie i perspektivy konversii' [Ukraine's military–industrial complex: the state and prospects for conversion], *Finansovaya Ukraina*, 3 Jan. 1996, p. 28.

[60] Some confusion arises from the fact that enterprises of the military sector form only a subset of the total number of enterprises under the Minmashprom and it is not always clear whether figures refer only to the subset or to the whole Ministry.

[61] *Finansovaya Ukraina*, 3 Jan. 1996. The production of actual weapons and other military hardware accounted for a mere 3% of total output by 1994. BBC, *Summary of World Broadcasts*, SUW/0403 WD/10, 29 Sep. 1995; and *Ekonomika Ukrainy*, no. 7 (1995), p. 30.

[62] Safiulin and Manachinskii (note 59).

[63] *Moskovskie Novosti*, no. 22 (30 May 1993), p. 11b; *Narodnaya Armiya*, 13 June 1996; and BBC, *Summary of World Broadcasts*, SU/2638 S/1, 14 June 1996.

[64] According to the Minister of Defence, the 1997 draft budget provides no money at all for procurement. Markus, U., 'Ukrainian Defense Minister on armed forces' meager budget', Open Media Research Institute (OMRI), *OMRI Daily Digest*, 17 Jan. 1997, URL <http://www.omri.cz>.

[65] *Sobranie zakonov*, no. 35 (1994), Article 3716; and BBC, *Summary of World Broadcasts*, SU/2704 D/5, 30 Aug. 1996.

Arms exports have been seen as a means of preserving an arms production capability, and there are signs that Ukraine is trying to become a more significant actor on the world market.[66] During 1995 and 1996 Ukraine concluded a number of cooperation agreements with other countries, including China, Germany, Israel and Poland.[67] While these agreements are of a general character, they provide a framework which could be exploited if the parties find a common interest in doing so. Such cooperation could provide Ukraine with a relatively quick way of filling in some gaps in its military production capability.

It was Ukraine's fortune that much modern military hardware was inherited from the USSR, lessening the urgency of new procurement for the armed forces. However, there is evidence of a firm intention to satisfy most of the requirements of the forces from domestic sources of supply as budgetary constraints ease. An import substitution policy is being pursued, reducing dependence on Russian supplies, and new relationships are being forged with arms-producing firms outside the former Soviet Union. Export earnings, while still modest, will assist the restructuring process. If present trends are maintained, Ukraine could emerge as a relatively strong arms-producing country by the end of the century.

---

[66] See chapter 9 in this volume.
[67] BBC, *Summary of World Broadcasts*, SU/2410 S1/1, 16 Sep. 1995; SUW/0379 D/2, 12 Apr. 1996; SU/2598 D/6, 29 Apr. 1996; and SU/2331 S1/2, 16 June 1996.

Appendix 8A. The 100 largest arms-producing companies, 1995

ELISABETH SKÖNS, RENAUD BELLAIS and the SIPRI ARMS
INDUSTRY NETWORK*

Table 8A contains information on the 100 largest arms-producing companies in the
OECD and the developing countries ranked by their arms sales in 1995.[1] Companies
with the designation *S* in the column for rank in 1994 are subsidiaries; their arms
sales are included in the figure in column 6 for the holding company. Subsidiaries are
listed in the position in which they would appear if they were independent companies.
In order to facilitate comparison with data for the previous year, the rank order and
arms sales figures for 1994 are also given. Where new data for 1994 have become
available, this information is included in the table; thus the 1994 rank order and the
arms sales figures for some companies which appeared in table 10A in the *SIPRI
Yearbook 1996* have been revised.

Sources and methods

Sources of data. The data in the table are based on the following sources: company
reports, a questionnaire sent to over 400 companies, and corporation news published
in the business sections of newspapers, military journals and on the Internet.
Company archives, marketing reports, government publication of prime contracts and
country surveys were also consulted. In many cases exact figures on arms sales were
not available, mainly because companies often do not report their arms sales or lump
them together with other activities. Estimates were therefore made.

Definitions. Data on total sales, profits and employment are for the entire company,
not for the arms-producing sector alone. Profit data are after taxes in all cases when
the company provides such data. Employment data are either a year-end or a yearly
average figure as reported by the company. Data are reported on the fiscal year basis
reported by the company in its annual report.

Exchange rates. The period-average of market exchange rates of the International
Monetary Fund, *International Financial Statistics* is used for conversion to US
dollars.

Key to abbreviations in column 5. A = artillery, Ac = aircraft, El = electronics,
Eng = engines, Mi = missiles, MV = military vehicles, SA/O = small arms/ordnance,
Sh = ships, and Oth = other. Comp ( ) = components of the product within the paren-
theses. It is used only for companies which do not produce any final systems.

---

[1] For the membership of the Organisation for Economic Co-operation and Development, see the
Glossary. For countries in the developing world, see notes to appendix 9A.

* Participants in the SIPRI Arms Industry Network: Peter Batchelor, Centre for Conflict
Resolution (Cape Town), Paul Dunne, Middlesex University (London), Ken Epps (Ontario),
Jean-Paul Hébert, CIRPES (Paris), Peter Hug (Bern), Masako Ikegami (Uppsala), Christos
Kollias, Center of Planning and Economic Research (Athens), Rudi Leo (Vienna), Rita
Manchanda (New Delhi), Arcadi Oliveres, Centre d'Estudis sobre la Pau i el Desarmament
(Barcelona), Ton van Oosterhout, University of Twente (Enschede), Reuven Pedatzur (Tel
Aviv), Giulio Perani (Rome), Gülay Günlük-Senesen (Istanbul) and Werner Voß (Bremen).

Table 8A. The 100 largest arms-producing companies in the OECD and developing countries, 1995

Figures in columns 6, 7, 8 and 10 are in US $m.

1	2	3	4	5	6	7	8	9	10	11
Rank[a]					Arms sales					
1995	1994	Company[b]	Country	Sector[c]	1995	1994	Total sales 1995	Col. 6 as % of col. 8	Profit 1995	Employment 1995
1	1	Lockheed Martin	USA	Ac El Mi	13 800	14 400	22 853	60	682	160 000
2	2	McDonnell Douglas	USA	Ac El Mi	9 620	9 230	14 332	67	−416	63 610
3	3	British Aerospace	UK	A Ac El Mi SA/O	6 720	7 030	9 062	74	218	44 000
4	6	Loral	USA	El Mi	6 500	5 100	6 700	97	..	38 000
5	4	General Motors, GM	USA	El Eng Mi	6 250	5 900	168 800	4	6 900	709 000
S	S	Hughes Electronics (GM)	USA	El Mi	5 950	5 590	14 772	40	948	84 000
6	5	Northrop Grumman	USA	Ac El Mi SA/O	5 700	5 670	6 818	84	252	37 300
7	7	Thomson	France	El	4 630	4 270	14 388	32	−545	96 040
S	S	Thomson–CSF (Thomson)	France	El	4 620	4 260	7 111	65	−158	48 860
8	8	Boeing	USA	Ac El Mi	4 200	4 050	19 515	22	393	109 400
9	12	GEC	UK	El Sh	4 100	3 190	17 348	24	983	82 970
10	10	Raytheon	USA	El Mi	3 960	3 550	11 716	34	793	73 200
11	9	United Technologies, UTC	USA	El Eng	3 650	3 800	22 624	16	750	170 600
12	11	Daimler Benz, DB	FRG	Ac El Eng MV Mi	3 350	3 510	72 255	5	−4 001	310 990
13	15	DCN	France	Sh	3 280	2 730	3 352	98	..	22 440
S	S	Daimler–Benz Aerospace (DB)	FRG	Ac El Eng Mi	3 250	3 430	10 493	31	−2 918	50 780
14	13	Litton	USA	El Sh	3 030	3 160	3 320	91	135	29 100
15	14	General Dynamics, GD	USA	MV Sh	2 930	2 860	3 067	96	315	27 700
16	18	TRW	USA	Oth	2 800	2 480	10 172	28	446	66 520
17	21	IRI	Italy	Ac El Eng Mi Sh	2 620	2 070	41 904	6	392	263 060
18	20	Westinghouse Electric	USA	El	2 600	2 450	9 605	27	15	77 810
19	19	Aérospatiale Groupe	France	Ac Mi	2 550	2 450	9 862	26	−289	38 670

		Company	Country							
20	16	Mitsubishi Heavy Industries[d]	Japan	Ac MV Mi Sh	2 430	2 730	32 067	*8*	1 103	67 370
21	17	Rockwell International	USA	El Mi	2 430	2 550	12 981	*19*	742	82 670
S	S	Finmeccanica (IRI)	Italy	Ac El Eng Mi	2 380	1 860	6 326	*38*	25	52 590
22	32	Rolls Royce	UK	Eng	2 050	1 360	5 678	*36*	224	43 200
23	24	Alcatel Alsthom	France	El	2 000	1 800	32 138	*6*	-5 125	191 800
S	S	Pratt & Whitney (UTC)	USA	Eng	1 840	:	6 170	*30*	530	29 900
24	29	CEA	France	Oth	1 740	1 540	3 854	*45*	:	17 260
25	27	Texas Instruments	USA	El	1 740	1 710	13 128	*13*	1 088	59 570
26	25	General Electric	USA	Eng	1 700	1 800	70 028	*2*	6 573	222 000
27	30	Kawasaki Heavy Industries[d]	Japan	Ac Eng Mi Sh	1 670	1 450	11 548	*14*	175	24 460
28	26	Tenneco	USA	Sh	1 670	1 750	8 899	*19*	735	60 000
S	S	Newport News (Tenneco)	USA	Sh	1 670	1 750	1 670	*100*	:	18 200
29	28	Textron	USA	Ac El Eng MV	1 600	1 600	9 973	*16*	479	57 000
30	39	GIAT Industries	France	A MV SA/O	1 280	1 030	1 671	*77*	-2 062	16 000
31	33	Dassault Aviation Groupe	France	Ac	1 270	1 340	2 323	*55*	105	11 860
32	34	Allied Signal	USA	Ac El	1 220	1 300	14 346	*9*	875	88 500
33	50	Alliant Tech Systems	USA	SA/O	1 190	760	1 190	*100*	48	7 700
34	63	GKN	UK	Ac MV	1 180	550	5 217	*23*	319	31 100
35	42	Mitsubishi Electric[d]	Japan	El Mi	1 150	940	37 331	*3*	629	111 590
36	35	Celsius	Sweden	A El SA/O Sh	1 150	1 190	2 079	*55*	-59	16 240
37	38	SNECMA Groupe	France	Eng	1 080	1 060	3 605	*30*	-198	21 940
38	36	Israel Aircraft Industries	Israel	Ac El Mi	1 050	1 150	1 400	*75*	-46	13 000
39	41	ITT Industries	USA	El	1 000	1 000	8 884	*11*	708	58 000
40	46	Lagardère Groupe	France	Mi	980	820	10 534	*9*	126	43 620
41	37	FMC	USA	A MV	970	1 100	4 567	*21*	216	22 160
42	43	Siemens	FRG	El	910	870	61 938	*1*	1 454	373 000
43	48	AT&T	USA	El	900	790	79 609	*1*	139	299 300
44	53	Diehl	FRG	SA/O	870	740	2 191	*40*	:	13 640
45	57	Thyssen	FRG	MV Sh	780	640	28 032	*3*	512	126 440
46	67	NEC[d]	Japan	El	780	520	46 749	*2*	820	152 720
S	S	Matra Défense (Lagardère)	France	Mi	750	680	765	*97*	:	2 860

1	2	3	4	5	6	7	8	9	10	11
Rank[a]					Arms sales		Total sales	Col. 6 as	Profit	Employment
1995	1994	Company[b]	Country	Sector[c]	1995	1994	1995	% of col. 8	1995	1995
47	51	Oerlikon–Bührle	Switzerl.	A Ac El Mi SA/O	730	750	3 225	23	3	17 120
48	44	GTE	USA	El	730	850	19 957	4	−2 144	106 000
49	45	Harris	USA	El	720	840	3 444	21	155	26 600
50	62	Tracor	USA	Comp (Ac El Mi)	720	560	887	81	28	9 400
51	52	Bremer Vulkan, BV	FRG	El Sh	690	740	4 187	16	−488	23 000
52	40	Teneo[e]	Spain	A Ac El MV Sh	670	1 020	17 884	4	571	77 000
53	54	Hunting	UK	Comp (El Mi)	670	690	1 780	38	25	12 680
54	64	SAGEM Groupe	France	El	650	540	3 020	21	128	14 680
55	59	Denel	S. Africa	A Ac El MV Mi SA/O	650	600	938	69	104	14 150
56	58	FIAT	Italy	Eng MV	640	620	42 845	1	1 580	237 430
S	S	SNECMA (SNECMA Groupe)	France	Eng	630	650	1 735	36	−249	12 010
S	S	STN Atlas Elektronik (BV)	FRG	El	620	680	1 012	61	4	4 530
57	68	Dassault Electronique	France	El	610	490	852	72	−4	4 110
58	55	Eidgenössische Rüstungsbetriebe	Switzerl.	A Ac Eng SA/O	610	660	666	91	9	3 420
59	66	Ishikawajima–Harima[d]	Japan	Eng Sh	600	520	11 537	5	208	26 570
60	65	Ordnance Factories	India	A SA/O	590	520	719	82	..	..
S	49	Bath Iron Works (GD)	USA	Sh	590	770	640	92	..	8 300
61	–	Vickers	UK	Eng MV SA/O	560	260	1 806	31	82	9 630
62	70	Rheinmetall	FRG	A El MV SA/O	550	480	2 384	23	2	14 570
63	84	Toshiba[d]	Japan	El Mi	540	400	54 434	1	961	186 000
64	74	Racal Electronics	UK	El	540	450	1 661	33	72	12 860
65	72	Dyncorp	USA	Comp (Ac)	540	470	909	60	2	16 900
66	73	Ceridian	USA	El	510	460	1 333	38	59	10 200
S	56	VSEL (GEC)	UK	Sh	510	650	..	..	..	..
67	88	Rafael	Israel	SA/O Oth	490	360	500	98	−65	4 500
68	60	Gencorp	USA	El Eng	490	580	1 772	28	38	11 700
S	S	CASA (Teneo)	Spain	Ac	490	440	866	56	31	8 200

		Company	Country						
S	S	Aerojet (Gencorp)	USA	El Eng	490	580	520	*94*	30	3 070
69	S	BDM International	USA	El Oth	480	430	890	*54*	18	7 000
70	89	Saab	Sweden	Ac El Mi	470	350	1 111	*42*	26	8 430
71	69	Lucas Industries	UK	Comp (Ac)	460	490	4 629	*10*	−47	48 500
72	75	Honeywell	USA	El Mi	460	450	6 731	*7*	334	50 100
73	86	Avondale Industries	USA	Sh	450	380	576	*78*	28	5 300
74	76	Motorola	USA	El	450	450	27 040	*2*	1 780	142 000
75	96	Olin	USA	SA/O	440	320	3 150	*14*	140	13 000
S	S	SAGEM (SAGEM Groupe)	France	El	430	360	1 659	*26*	69	6 830
76	77	Mitre	USA	Oth	420	430	576	*73*	..	5 250
77	90	Koor Industries	Israel	A El	410	340	3 390	*12*	163	20 500
78	71	Smiths Industries	UK	Comp (Ac)	410	470	1 420	*29*	148	11 720
79	93	Logicon	USA	El Oth	410	340	476	*85*	25	..
80	80	Hindustan Aeronautics	India	Ac Mi	400	410	433	*92*	..	..
S	S	Hollandse Signaalapparaten (Thomson-CSF, France)	Netherl.	El	400	360	410	*99*	32	2 730
S	S	Agusta (Finmeccanica)	Italy	Ac	390	450	499	*77*	..	4 080
81	91	MKEK[f]	Turkey	SA/O	380	340	640	*59*	56	11 340
S	S	Tadiran (Koor Industries)	Israel	El	370	310	1 049	*35*	28	8 200
82	–	Wegmann Group	FRG	MV	350	280	424	*82*	..	960
83	–	The Japan Steel Works[d]	Japan	SA/O	350	190	1 253	*28*	−17	..
84	85	Esco Electronics	USA	El	350	390	441	*78*	−30	3 350
85	95	Devonport Management	UK	Sh	340	330	354	*97*	..	4 000
S	S	Sextant Avionique (Thomson-CSF)	France	El	340	330	978	*35*	..	..
86	98	Bombardier	Canada	El Mi	330	310	5 190	*6*	112	40 000
87	92	Vosper Thornycroft	UK	Sh	330	340	376	*87*	29	2 310
S	S	FIAT Aviazione (FIAT)	Italy	Eng	330	350	946	*35*	..	4 710
S	S	Allison (Rolls Royce, UK)	USA	Eng	330	..	750	*44*	49	..
88	79	Preussag	FRG	Sh	320	410	18 389	*2*	244	65 230
S	S	HDW (Preussag)	FRG	Sh	320	410	732	*44*	29	3 830

1	2	3	4	5	6	7	8	9	10	11
Rank^a					Arms sales					
1995	1994	Company^b	Country	Sector^c	1995	1994	Total sales 1995	Col. 6 as % of col. 8	Profit 1995	Employment 1995
89	–	Nissan Motor^d	Japan	A MV	310	290	64 216	..	–940	139 860
S	S	Oto Melara (Finmeccanica)	Italy	A MV Mi	310	270	310	100	..	1 520
90	100	SNPE Groupe	France	A SA/O	300	290	877	35	7	5 730
91	–	Elbit	Israel	EI	300	290	968	31	18	5 440
92	–	Fuji Heavy Industries^d	Japan	Ac	300	240	11 453	3	206	15 080
93	–	Babcock International Group	UK	Sh	290	280	..	..	..	..
S	–	Thomson Sintra (Thomson-CSF)	France	EI	290	..	307	96	..	1 400
94	–	UNC	USA	Comp (Ac)	280	210	536	52	2	..
S	S	Saab Military Aircraft (Saab)	Sweden	Ac	280	180	357	78	..	3 490
95	83	TAAS	Israel	A MV SA/O	270	400	405	66	–31	4 200
96	–	Ericsson	Sweden	EI	270	270	13 848	2	763	84 510
S	S	Ericsson Microwave (Ericsson)	Sweden	EI	270	270	516	52	..	3 710
97	87	Thiokol	USA	Eng SA/O	260	370	957	27	48	7 200
98	78	Oshkosh Truck	USA	MV	260	430	438	60	9	..
99	31	Unisys	USA	EI	260	1 400	6 202	4	–625	37 400
100	–	Komatsu	Japan	MV SA/O	260	230	10 624	2	149	27 920

^a The rank designation in the column for 1994 may not always correspond to that given in table 10A in the *SIPRI Yearbook 1996* because of subsequent revisions. A dash (–) in this column indicates either that the company did not produce arms in 1994, or that it did not exist as it was structured in 1995, in which case there is a zero (0) in column 7, or that it did not rank among the 100 largest companies in 1994. Companies with the designation S in the column for rank are subsidiaries.

^b Names in brackets are names of parent companies.

^c A key to abbreviations in column 5 is provided on page 261.

^d For Japanese companies data in the arms sales column represent new military contracts rather than arms sales.

^e Data for Teneo in the arms sales column for 1994 are for INI, the predecessor of Teneo as a state holding company for most of the government-controlled Spanish arms-producing companies.

^f Data for MKEK in the arms sales column for 1994 are for 1993.

9. The trade in major conventional weapons

IAN ANTHONY, PIETER D. WEZEMAN and
SIEMON T. WEZEMAN

I. Introduction

The SIPRI global trend-indicator value of international transfers of major
conventional weapons in 1996 was $22 980 million in constant (1990) US
dollars,[1] down from the revised estimate of the trend-indicator value for 1995
of $23 189 million.[2]

Section II surveys the dominant trends in the international arms trade based
both on official government data and SIPRI data. In 1996 the United States
accounted for 44 per cent of deliveries of major conventional weapons—the
largest share of any single supplier. As in 1995, Russia—with a share of
20 per cent of total deliveries—was the second largest exporter. In 1996
France, with a share of 9 per cent of total deliveries, was the third largest
exporter. Among the importers, five recipients—China, South Korea, Kuwait,
Taiwan and Saudi Arabia—together accounted for 43 per cent of total deliveries. Three recipients in North-East Asia—China, South Korea and Taiwan—
together accounted for over 30 per cent of the total.

In 1997 a decision is expected regarding the enlargement of the NATO
Alliance through the accession of new members from Central and Eastern
Europe. Section II includes a brief evaluation of the market for conventional
arms in the Czech Republic, Hungary, Poland and Slovakia as well as
observations on arms exports from Ukraine.

In 1997 a group of government experts will evaluate the returns to the
United Nations Register of Conventional Arms during its first five years of
operation with a view to recommending further steps in the development of
the register. One aspect of possible future development of the register—the
inclusion of information from UN member states on their procurement
through national production—is evaluated in section III.

---

[1] The index produced using the SIPRI valuation system enables the aggregation of data on physical
arms transfers. The SIPRI system for evaluating the arms trade was designed as a *trend-measuring
device*, to permit the measurement of changes in the total flow of major weapons and its geographical
pattern. A description of the method used in calculating the trend-indicator value is given in
appendix 9C.
[2] It is usual for figures for the most recent years to be revised upwards as new and better data become
available. For this reason it is advisable for readers who require time series data for periods longer than
the 5 years covered in this Yearbook to contact SIPRI. The figure for 1995 given here is slightly higher
than the estimate of $22 797 million given in Anthony, I., Wezeman, P. D. and Wezeman, S. T., 'The
trade in major conventional weapons', *SIPRI Yearbook 1996: Armaments, Disarmament and
International Security* (Oxford University Press: Oxford, 1996), p. 463.

Table 9.1. The 30 leading suppliers of major conventional weapons, 1992–96

The countries are ranked according to 1992–96 aggregate exports. Figures are trend-indicator values expressed in US $m., at constant (1990) prices.

Rank 1992–96	1991–95[a]	Supplier	1992	1993	1994	1995	1996	1992–96
1	1	USA	14 187	14 270	12 029	10 972	10 228	61 686
2	2	Russia	2 918	3 773	763	3 505	4 512	15 471
3	3	Germany	1 527	1 727	2 448	1 549	1 464	8 715
4	4	UK	1 315	1 300	1 346	1 568	1 773	7 302
5	5	France	1 302	1 308	971	785	2 101	6 467
6	6	China	883	1 234	718	949	573	4 357
7	7	Netherlands	333	395	581	430	450	2 189
8	8	Italy	434	447	330	377	158	1 746
9	9	Czech Rep.[b]	214	267	371	195	152	1 199
10	10	Israel	192	271	207	352	168	1 190
11	11	Canada	131	146	330	387	157	1 151
12	14	Ukraine	256	119	178	193	185	931
13	13	Uzbekistan	0	0	406	464	0	870
14	12	Switzerland	363	75	37	95	105	675
15	17	Sweden	123	45	54	174	274	670
16	15	Korea, North	86	423	48	48	21	626
17	21	Belgium	0	0	55	310	110	475
18	19	Spain	64	53	138	78	57	390
19	20	Poland	0	1	117	178	60	356
20	18	Norway	0	93	186	52	0	331
21	22	Slovakia	..	145	29	76	0	250
22	38	Belarus	20	0	5	24	190	239
23	23	Brazil	60	25	45	33	47	210
24	25	Nicaragua	110	56	0	0	0	166
25	27	Qatar	0	49	61	27	9	146
26	26	South Africa	57	34	25	10	9	135
27	28	Austria	44	13	23	33	3	116
28	29	Korea, South	0	33	11	46	23	113
29	24	Bulgaria	61	21	29	0	0	111
30	31	Egypt	24	20	30	19	4	97
		Others	142	101	256	263	146	909
		Total	**24 840**	**26 444**	**21 820**	**23 189**	**22 980**	**119 273**

[a] The rank order for suppliers in 1991–95 may differ from that published in the *SIPRI Yearbook 1996* (p. 465) because of the subsequent revision of figures for these years.

[b] For the year 1992 the data refer to the former Czechoslovakia; for 1993–96 the data refer to the Czech Republic.

Note: The index produced using the SIPRI valuation system is not comparable to official economic statistics such as gross domestic product, public expenditure or export/import figures. The purpose of the valuation system is to enable the aggregation of data on physical arms transfers. Similar weapon systems require similar values and SIPRI has created an index of trend-indicator values which can be aggregated in a number of different ways. The SIPRI system for evaluating the arms trade was designed as a *trend-measuring device*, to permit the measurement of changes in the total flow of major weapons and its geographical pattern. For a description of the method used in calculating the trend-indicator value see appendix 9C.

Source: SIPRI arms transfers database.

II. Main developments in 1996

Among the exporters there were relatively few changes in 1996 compared with the revised estimates for 1995. While the United States remained the largest supplier, its share of deliveries was reduced from an estimated 47 per cent in 1995 to 44 per cent in 1996. Russia, France and the United Kingdom all increased their share of total deliveries slightly. Comparing 1995 with 1996, Russia's share of deliveries increased from 15 per cent to 20 per cent and France increased its share of deliveries from 4 per cent to 9 per cent. The United Kingdom recorded a smaller increase, from 7 per cent to 8 per cent.

In the United States in 1996 the Clinton Administration was conducting an internal review of arms transfer policies towards countries in South America.[3] One element of the Clinton Administration conventional arms transfer policy is the potential impact of a sale on regional stability. The policy deliberately avoids a global approach and is weighted towards considering the military relations between states rather than other aspects of security.[4]

In the 1970s the United States initiated a restrictive policy regarding weapon sales to Latin America. The policy stated that the USA would not introduce certain types of advanced system—notably attack helicopters and fighter aircraft—into the region.[5] On 26 April 1996 a group of 79 members of the US House of Representatives sent President Bill Clinton a letter suggesting that this policy was no longer appropriate in prevailing conditions.[6] In 1995, in response to requests from the governments of Argentina and Chile as well as from US contractors, the Departments of State, Commerce and Defense had initiated a review of the policy. In late 1996 and January 1997, the White House confirmed that the review had not yet led to any formal proposal being sent to President Clinton for consideration.[7]

The arms transfer policy took place in the context of a wider initiative to strengthen the regional security dialogue in the Americas. In Santiago, Chile, in November 1995 the members of the Organization of American States agreed to formulate confidence- and security-building measures based on increased transparency and consultation.[8] Political change in South America

---

[3] The Clinton Administration established its conventional arms transfer policy in Feb. 1995 in Presidential Decision Directive 34, which is a classified document. However, the elements of the policy are described in 'Conventional arms transfer policy' (text of a White House fact sheet), *Wireless File* (United States Information Service, US Embassy: Stockholm, 17 Feb. 1995). The policy is discussed in Anthony, I., Wezeman, P. D. and Wezeman, S. T., *SIPRI Yearbook 1995: Armaments, Disarmament and International Security* (Oxford University Press: Oxford, 1995), pp. 497–99.

[4] The policy is discussed at length in Agmon, M., *et al.*, *Arms Proliferation Policy: Support to the Presidential Advisory Board*, RAND MR-771-OSD (RAND Corporation: Santa Monica, Calif., 1996).

[5] Voice of America Newswire, 24 Feb. 1997. Version current on 24 Feb. 1997 URL <gopher://gopher.voa.gov:70/00/newswire/mon/U-S_-_LATAM_ARMS_SALES

[6] *Jane's Defence Weekly*, 15 May 1996, p. 5.

[7] *Gazeta Mercantil* (São Pãolo), 8 Oct. 1996, p. A6 (in Portuguese), in 'Inter-American affairs: Perry quoted on liberalization of US arms sales', Foreign Broadcast Information Service, *Daily Report–Latin America (FBIS-LAT)*, FBIS-LAT-96-198, 11 Oct. 1996; and White House press briefing, transcript from the Office of the Press Secretary, Washington, DC, 16 Jan. 1997.

[8] 'Final Declaration of Santiago on Confidence- and Security-Building Measures', Santiago, 10 Nov. 1995, *Special Wireless File* (United States Information Service, US Embassy: Stockholm, 14 Nov. 1995.

Table 9.2. Official data on arms exports, 1991–95

Country	Currency unit	1991	1992	1993	1994	1995	1995 (US $m.)
Australia	m. A. dollars	..	57	67.3	28.3	..	21
Belgium	b. B. francs	15.371	15.112	11.684	11.403	8.230	279
Canada	m. C. dollars	189.2	361.8	335.9	497.4	447.3	326
Czech Rep.	m. US dollars	..	..	167	194	154	154
France	b. francs[a]	20.6	20.8	14.6	11.6	10.9	2 184
	b. francs[b]	..	29	20.6	16.8	19	3 806
Germany	m. D. marks	4 135	2 638	2 577	2 131	1 982	1 383
Italy	b. lire	..	1 246	979	915	1 227	754
Netherlands	m. guilders	691	1 007	1 475	1 006	1 029	641
Poland	m. US dollars	396.2	67.3	..	..	..	..
Russia	b. US dollars	7.1	2.3	2.5	1.7	3.1	3 100
South Africa	m. rand	752	463	798	854	1033	285
Sweden[c]	m. kronor	2 705	2 753	2863	3181	3313	464
Switzerland	m. S. francs	..	258.8	260.3	221	..	162
UK[c]	m. pounds	1 862	1 530	1 914	1 798	2 076	3 277
USA[d]	b. dollars[e]	8.6	10.1	10.9	9.3	11.6	11 616
	b. dollars[f]	5.2	2.7	3.8	2.1	3.6	3 620

[a] Value of exports of defence equipment.
[b] Value of deliveries of defence equipment and associated services.
[c] Changes in the coverage of data occurred in 1992–93.
[d] Data for the USA refer to fiscal years.
[e] Value of transfers made through the US Government.
[f] Value of military and certain dual-use equipment transfers from US commercial suppliers.

Sources: Annual Report: Exports of Defence and Related and Dual-Use Goods from Australia, Industry Involvement and Contracting Division, Department of Defence, Canberra, June 1996; official Belgian arms export data published in Rapport van de regering aan het parlement over de toepassing van de wet van 5 augustus 1991 betreffende de in-, de uit-, en de doorvoer van wapens, munitie, en speciaal voor militair gebruik dienstig materieel en de daaraan verbonden technologie, 1 januari 1995 tot 31 december 1995, Ministry of Foreign Affairs, Brussels, 1996; Annual Reports: Export of Military Goods from Canada, 1991, 1993, 1994, 1995, Exports Controls Division, Export and Import Controls Bureau, Department of Foreign Affairs and International Trade, Ottawa; Ministry of Economics, Bonn; Assemblée Nationale, nr 3030, Rapport fait au nom de la commission des finances, annexe nr 40, Paris, 4 Oct. 1996, p. 76; Letter from the Minister of Foreign Affairs to the Chairman of the Second Chamber, DAV/PC-N184/96 appendix 2, The Hague, 18 Jun. 1996; official Italian arms export data published in Elaborazioni sui dati Presidente del Consiglio dei Ministri, 'Relazione sulle operazioni autorizatte e svolte per il controllo dell'esportazione, importazione e transito dei materiali di armamento' (dal 1993: 'nonchè dell'esportazione e del transito dei prodotti ad alta tecnologia'), Rome; ARMSCOR Annual Report, 1995/96, p. 28; Regeringens skrivelse 1995/96:204, Redogörelse för den svenska krigsmaterielexporten år 1995 [1995 Report on Swedish exports of military equipment], Stockholm; Österreichische Militärische Zeitschrift, no. 3 (1995), p. 357; 'Czech armaments industry wants to draw on tradtition', Narodna Obroda, 27 Mar. 1997, in FBIS-EEU-97-090, 31 Mar. 1997; Rosvooruzheniye, in Segodnya, 1 Nov. 1996; Military Technology, Oct. 1995, p. 89; Foreign Military Sales, Foreign Military Construction Sales and Military Assistance Facts, as of September 30, 1995 Process Analysis Integration Division Comptroller, DSAA, Washington, DC; UK Defence Statistics, 1996 edn, Government Statistical Service, London.

in the past decade has seen a reduction in the role of the military in domestic politics in many countries of the region. At the same time the military have become increasingly engaged in bilateral and multilateral discussions with their counterparts in other countries in the region.[9] Finally, Argentina and Brazil have put in place national export control systems, reducing the risk of diversion to unauthorized third parties of any systems or technologies supplied.[10]

The main constraint on transfers of major conventional weapons to South America has been the low level of military expenditure combined with the absence of major disputes between states in the region.[11] At the same time, the inventories of air forces and navies in the region consist mainly of older equipment. The Clinton Administration has had to take into account the probability that countries will modernize at least some of their equipment and the desirability of achieving this modernization without a deterioration in the regional security environment. By contrast, the policy of European countries has been motivated more by possible market opportunity than considerations of regional stability.

The policy review has focused mainly on Argentina, Brazil and Chile as the three countries in the region most likely to purchase major equipment to which the earlier policy applied.[12] Given that in 1995 and 1996 European arms suppliers as well as Israel and Russia have marketed major systems in South America, the Clinton Administration has questioned whether US companies should still be prevented from bidding in major equipment programmes in South America.

The increases in French arms exports recorded in SIPRI data for 1996 reflect the fact that equipment has been delivered in the framework of several programmes that have been under way for some years. France has two major programmes in progress in Taiwan. In 1996 the delivery of 60 Mirage-2000-5 fighter aircraft with associated armament began. Among the arms delivered in the framework of this programme was the MICA air-to-air missile, for which Taiwan is the first customer. In addition, Taiwan commissioned the first of six La Fayette Class frigates. Elsewhere, France has begun to deliver equipment to several of the smaller states on the Arabian Peninsula—Oman, Qatar and the United Arab Emirates.

---

[9] In Oct. 1996 the Defence Ministers of the countries of the Western Hemisphere met in Bariloche, Argentina. This was their second meeting (the first was in the United States in mid-1995). The issues raised included confidence-building measures, cooperation in peacekeeping, the impact of crime and drugs on security, the threat posed by the illegal trade in arms and the impact of economic issues on security. 'Final Declaration of Bariloche Hemispheric Defense Ministerial', 9 Oct. 1996, *Wireless File* (United States Information Service, US Embassy: Stockholm, 10 Oct. 1996).

[10] See also chapter 10 in this volume.

[11] See also chapter 6 in this volume.

[12] State Department press briefing, 16 Jan. 1997. There has never been a US policy of blanket embargo on arms sales to South America. The USA has both sold arms and military equipment of various kinds into the region and provided significant military assistance, notably in the framework of the Andean Initiative, a cooperative effort to interdict drug shipments from Central and South America to the United States.

Table 9.3. The 50 leading recipients of major conventional weapons, 1992–96

Rank 1992–96	Rank 1991–95[a]	Recipient	1992	1993	1994	1995	1996	1992–96
1	1	Saudi Arabia	1 105	2 889	1 577	1 401	1 611	8 583
2	4	Turkey	1 590	2 171	1 591	1 015	1 066	7 433
3	3	Egypt	1 255	1 339	1 773	2 150	803	7 320
4	11	Taiwan	211	1 058	835	1 305	3 234	6 643
5	2	Japan	2 016	1 992	621	925	679	6 233
6	9	China	1 172	1 277	529	935	1 957	5 870
7	6	Greece	2 467	893	1 055	737	274	5 426
8	10	Korea, South	387	483	611	1 909	1 727	5 117
9	7	India	1 417	604	429	1 092	1 317	4 859
10	5	Germany	1 677	1 636	797	178	96	4 384
11	12	Kuwait	998	657	44	1 048	1 363	4 110
12	8	Israel	1 343	613	905	246	48	3 155
13	14	Thailand	866	152	807	785	355	2 965
14	15	USA	489	626	689	552	130	2 486
15	18	Spain	190	602	768	465	458	2 483
16	16	Iran	239	1 151	327	235	437	2 389
17	22	Indonesia	69	367	792	483	537	2 248
18	19	Finland	698	785	385	155	192	2 215
19	13	Canada	876	350	673	155	137	2 191
20	20	UAE	163	618	591	368	271	2 011
21	25	Australia	354	487	435	60	554	1 890
22	23	Malaysia	36	21	294	1 289	143	1 783
23	17	UK	1 141	45	37	122	230	1 575
24	26	Hungary	0	1 190	4	67	311	1 572
25	27	Chile	260	122	158	540	124	1 204
26	36	Brazil	48	55	258	248	490	1 099
27	46	Oman	14	60	144	141	478	837
28	35	Italy	67	243	149	210	166	835
29	21	Portugal	3	379	431	17	0	830
30	31	Switzerland	293	81	116	106	212	808
31	33	Myanmar	36	366	0	255	123	780
32	30	Netherlands	173	113	263	68	162	779
33	24	France	385	137	49	82	49	702
34	37	Peru	143	92	160	89	204	688
35	34	Norway	193	150	77	151	106	677
36	32	Singapore	80	106	167	215	104	672
37	29	Syria	342	188	55	43	21	649
38	38	Slovakia	0	211	36	260	71	578
39	28	Algeria	46	28	175	323	0	572
40	62	Qatar	76	16	16	16	393	517
41	40	Sweden	5	36	324	92	59	516
42	42	Morocco	24	118	181	50	109	482
43	43	Philippines	52	96	192	69	31	440
44	52	Kazakhstan	0	0	0	272	138	410
45	54	Viet Nam	0	0	0	265	118	383
46	41	Denmark	53	42	56	164	24	339
47	56	Cyprus	46	0	61	28	195	330

Rank								
1992–96	1991–95[a]	Recipient	1992	1993	1994	1995	1996	1992–96
48	47	Mexico	13	124	140	32	18	327
49	50	South Africa	240	0	16	31	39	326
50	53	Argentina	15	3	66	186	45	315
		Others	1 474	1 672	1 961	1 559	1 571	8 237
		Total	**24 840**	**26 444**	**21 820**	**23 189**	**22 980**	**119 273**

[a] The rank order for recipients in 1991–95 may differ from that published in the *SIPRI Yearbook 1996* because of the subsequent revision of figures for these years.

Note: The index produced using the SIPRI valuation system is not comparable to official economic statistics such as gross domestic product, public expenditure or export/import figures. The purpose of the valuation system is to enable the aggregation of data on physical arms transfers. Similar weapon systems require similar values and SIPRI has created an index of trend-indicator values which can be aggregated in a number of different ways. The SIPRI system for evaluating the arms trade was designed as a *trend-measuring device*, to permit the measurement of changes in the total flow of major weapons and its geographic pattern. For a description of the method used in calculating the trend-indicator value see appendix 9C.

Source: SIPRI arms transfers database

As reported in the *SIPRI Yearbook 1996*, Russia has once again become an important arms supplier following the turbulent period which followed the dissolution of the Soviet Union. In 1996 further changes were made to the procedures for regulating Russian conventional arms transfers. In October the State Committee on Military–Technical Policy was disbanded and licensing authority was transferred to the Ministry of Foreign Economic Relations.[13] This was expected to increase the importance of the advice given by the Ministry of Defence and the Ministry of Defence Industry.

Among the smaller supplier countries there were some which recorded significant increases in percentage terms but which nevertheless account for a small share of international transfers of major conventional weapons. The largest percentage increase is recorded for Belarus, largely reflecting the delivery of second-hand MiG-29 fighter aircraft to Peru and second-hand T-72 tanks to Hungary.

As in previous yearbooks, government data on the value of arms exports are presented above. The data in table 9.2 are useful because of their official character. However, several observations are necessary to alert readers to the limits on using these data in analysis. The data are for those governments which responded to requests for information or for which data were available in published documents. The table does not attempt to be comprehensive and certainly there are other countries whose arms exports would be as large as those from some of the countries represented in the table. The data presented in table 9.2 are as recorded by governments in their official documents and

---

[13] *Collection of Laws and Regulations of the Russian Federation*, no. 34 (1996), pp. 4081–82.

statements. No attempt has been made to compensate for differences in the national definitions of arms exports. A time series of data is presented to illustrate the trend in exports as recorded in official data. However, the definitions of arms exports used by governments are not consistent across countries. Moreover, they are not necessarily consistent within countries across time. No attempt has been made to compensate for these inconsistencies.

Arms recipients

Among the importers the data for 1996 tend to reinforce the main trends identified in 1995. Three regions—Asia, Europe and the Middle East—remain the predominant centres of demand for imported major conventional weapons (the total demand for major conventional weapons is heavily concentrated in North America and Western Europe). However, the relative importance of the three regions is changing. While demand from European countries has been decreasing, that from Asian countries has been growing.

The share of the European countries declined from 38 per cent of the total global deliveries of major conventional weapons in 1992 to 18 per cent in 1996. Over the same period the share of deliveries to Asian countries rose from 28 per cent to 48 per cent. The share of deliveries to the Middle East remained constant at around 25 per cent of the global total.

Reduced procurement expenditure by many European countries after 1990 has led to the slowing down, postponement or deferment of equipment modernization programmes, which has had an impact both on domestic production and on arms imports. At the same time within Asia—and in particular in North-East Asia—several countries initiated equipment programmes in the early 1990s which are now being reflected in the data on equipment deliveries. In 1996 three of the largest recipients of major conventional weapons—China, South Korea and Taiwan—were located in North-East Asia.[14]

Among the smaller arms-importing countries there were some noteworthy deliveries of naval systems in 1996. The Australian Navy began to commission Swedish-designed Type-471 submarines and German-designed Meko-200 Type frigates. The Meko-200 frigate acquisition is part of a larger collaborative programme involving the procurement of 10 ships, eight of which are for Australia and two of which are New Zealand. The Qatari Navy is in the process of taking delivery of four Vita Class fast attack craft.

Arms exports from Ukraine

The gradual recovery of Russian arms exports has been described in the past two *SIPRI Yearbooks*.[15] While Russia is overwhelmingly the most important

[14] For a discussion of the implications of defence modernization by China and Taiwan see Gill, B. and Bitzinger, R., *Gearing up for High-Tech Warfare? Chinese and Taiwanese Defense Modernization and Implications for Military Confrontation across the Taiwan Strait, 1995–2005*, CAPS paper no. 11 (Chinese Council of Advanced Policy Studies: Taipei, 1996). See also Arnett, E. (ed.), SIPRI, *Military Capacity and the Risk of War: China, India, Pakistan and Iran* (Oxford University Press: Oxford, 1997).
[15] See Anthony *et al.* (note 2); and Anthony *et al.* (note 3).

arms supplier among the newly independent states that have succeeded the Soviet Union, some others have concluded significant contracts for arms exports. Of these non-Russian suppliers the most important is Ukraine.

In 1996 several Ukrainian arms exports attracted international attention. Aside from alleged missile sales,[16] most attention was paid to the agreement with Pakistan for the supply of around 320 T-80UD main battle tanks.[17]

After the dissolution of the Soviet Union several of the newly independent states inherited significant defence industrial capabilities. The most important of these were in Ukraine.[18] Ukraine inherited major missile development and production facilities as well as significant capabilities to design and manufacture transport aircraft and armoured vehicles.

After being severed from the integrated Soviet arms production system, Ukraine made very few foreign sales. At the enterprise level managers had little or no expertise in marketing and few if any foreign contacts. Meanwhile, within the government the main priorities for the new Ukrainian state were to establish the basic elements of government. According to public sources, Ukraine sold $28 million worth of arms abroad in 1993, rising to $43 million in 1994.[19] In 1995, according to Ukrainian estimates, this figure rose to around $100 million.[20]

Ukraine has conducted several different forms of military–technical cooperation. Some sales have been made via Russia. Ukraine has supplied the air-to-air missile armament for fighter aircraft supplied by Russia to China, Malaysia, Slovakia and Viet Nam. Ukraine has also supplied surface-to-air missiles to Bulgaria and Iran. Ties between Russian and Ukrainian arms producers remain important to both countries. For example, elements of the T-80UD tank produced at the Malyshev plant in Kharkov are bought from Russian suppliers.[21]

A second element of Ukrainian arms transfers has been the disposal of parts of Ukraine's weapon inventory. Under the division of equipment agreed after the dissolution of the USSR, Ukraine inherited a large amount of relatively advanced equipment as well as some older platforms. Of these platforms some T-55 tanks, BMP-1 infantry fighting vehicles, An-32 transport aircraft and Mi-17 transport helicopters have been disposed of through exports in the past three years.

[16] Alleged missile sales by Ukraine are discussed in chapter 10 in this volume.

[17] *Military Technology*, Sep. 1996, p. 75; Shaikh, S., '$80 m. down payment for T-80 tanks next month', *The News* (Islamabad), 11 Sep. 1996, p. 5, in 'Pakistan: downpayment for T-80 tanks due 15 Oct', Foreign Broadcast Information Service, *Daily Report–Near East and South Asia (FBIS-NES)*, FBIS-NES-96-178, 13 Sep. 1996; and *Moscow News*, no. 34 (29 Aug.–4 Sep. 1996), p. 5.

[18] Recent defence industrial developments in Ukraine are discussed in chapter 8 in this volume.

[19] *Jane's Intelligence Review*, July 1996, p. 292.

[20] 'Ukraine sets up single arms export firm', *OMRI Daily Digest*, no. 215, part II (6 Nov. 1996), URL <http://www.omri.cz> (hereafter, references to the *OMRI Daily Digest* refer to the Internet edition at this URL address).

[21] Mostova, Y., 'Arms trade—in one hand! But whose?', *Zerkalo Nedeli* (Kiev), 3–9 Aug. 1996, pp. 1–2 (in Russian), in 'Ukraine: arms trade achievements, prospects discussed', Foreign Broadcast Information Service, *Daily Report–Central Eurasia (FBIS-SOV)*, FBIS-SOV-96-155, 9 Aug. 1996, pp. 38–41.

Ukraine has also sought to take advantage of its industrial capacities to repair and maintain equipment of Soviet origin. For example, 10 Egyptian MiG-21 fighter aircraft have been repaired by Ukraine.[22] China, Poland, Slovakia and Yugoslavia have explored military–technical cooperation with Ukraine.

There is evidence that Ukrainian policy began to emphasize the benefits of arms transfers in 1995 and 1996. In 1995 Ukrainian officials were prominent at the arms exhibition in Dubai. In February 1996, Deputy Defence Minister Lev Hnatenko suggested that revenues from arms exports would be the only viable means to enable the Ukrainian Ministry of Defence to modernize its own equipment.[23] However, the Ministry of Defence seems unlikely to receive much if any of the proceeds of weapon sales, which are more likely to be divided between the producing enterprises and the Ministry of Finance.[24]

In order to organize arms export activity Ukraine has made some adjustments to its national export procedures. In November 1996 three state trading agencies—Progress, Ukrinmash and Ukroboronservis—were combined into a single state trading agency, Ukrspetsexport.[25] These three trading agencies— the only ones legally entitled to conduct foreign military technical cooperation—were previously responsible to different state agencies. Progress was part of the State Security Service, Ukrinmash was part of the Ministry of Defence while Ukrspetsexport was part of the Ministry of Foreign Economic Relations. The combination into one agency forced inter-agency cooperation in the sphere of arms export policy.

The Central and East European arms market

In 1996 increased attention was paid to the prospect that countries in Central and Eastern Europe would emerge as a significant market for defence equipment including major platforms such as fighter aircraft. This section gives a brief overview of the current procurement plans of four Central and East European countries.

The background to this discussion has been the application of a number of countries to join NATO.[26] Among the studies conducted in and after 1993 (when the possibility that new members would be accepted assumed greater importance within the NATO Alliance) one consistent theme has been that any prospective member must be ready to share 'roles, risks, responsibilities,

[22] *New Europe*, 4–10 Aug. 1996, p. 18.

[23] Pukhov, O., 'Special to Intelnews', Intelnews (Kiev), 20 Feb. 1996, in 'Ukraine: Deputy Defense Minister encourages arms sales', FBIS-SOV-96-035, 21 Feb. 1996, p. 44.

[24] Interfax (Moscow), 26 Jan. 1996, in 'Ukraine seen "struggling" in world arms market', FBIS-SOV-96-019, 29 Jan. 1996, p. 45; and Chepalov, A., 'Our tanks by southern seas', Trud-7 (Kiev), 16–22 Aug. 1996, p. 11 (in Russian), in 'Ukraine: Kharkiv plant director hails Pakistani tank sales deal', FBIS-SOV-162, 20 Aug. 1996, pp. 29–30.

[25] *New Europe*, 10–16 Nov. 1996, p. 22; and Interfax (Moscow), 13 Nov. 1996, in 'Ukraine: new state-run international arms exporter under formation', FBIS-SOV-96-221, 15 Nov. 1996. This process is similar to the process of reorganization which occurred in Russia in 1994–95 with the creation of the state arms trading company Rosvooruzheniye.

[26] See chapter 5 in this volume.

costs and benefits' to ensure common security goals and objectives.[27] However, these discussions have tended to focus on the political dimension of NATO enlargement rather than the economic or cost considerations.

After the end of the cold war levels of military expenditure in Central and East European countries fell dramatically as a proportion of overall economic activity. According to SIPRI estimates, the Visegrad countries (the Czech Republic, Hungary, Poland and Slovakia) typically spend between 2 and 3 per cent of their gross domestic product on defence.[28] While the national ministries of defence in each of the Visegrad countries have consistently argued for an increased share of national resources, in the more benign post-cold war security environment, and with pressing spending priorities elsewhere, these resources have not been provided.

It is of great importance, therefore, whether membership of NATO would change the balance of this discussion and increase the likelihood that governments will raise the levels of their military expenditure.[29]

The NATO force structure is defined by the 1991 Alliance Strategic Concept.[30] The main emphasis of the Strategic Concept was to move away from a linear defence running along the 'Iron Curtain' towards more flexible formations that could be deployed anywhere within the NATO area of operations. At the time the new Strategic Concept was designed it was already clear that enhanced mobility would be one feature of the new military formations. Exactly what role new allies would play in this concept or whether the concept itself would need to be revised with the accession of new members is an issue which will be addressed during the bilateral discussions between NATO and those countries which are to be accepted into the alliance.

Subsequent events have required important changes to the Strategic Concept. Two changes stand out as particularly important. First, NATO forces have been deployed in new tasks outside the traditional area of operations—in particular in the former Yugoslavia.[31] Second, NATO forces now expect to participate in multilateral formations that include troops from countries that are not members of NATO.

New allies could expect to contribute to two different NATO activities. First, they would contribute to a modified force structure to provide collective defence. Second, new members might contribute to the new tasks of NATO. The full cost implications of NATO membership are outside the scope of this section, which is confined to the issue of equipment procurement.

---

[27] NATO, *Study on NATO Enlargement* (NATO: Brussels, Sep. 1995), p. 3.

[28] See the table of world military expenditure as share of gross domestic product, appendix 6B, table 6B.3 in this volume.

[29] Visegrad countries which have applied to join the EU as well as NATO are likely to come under cross-pressures because as they join the EU they will accept the criteria guiding public expenditure contained in the Maastricht Treaty.

[30] The basic elements of the new force structure were in place by the end of 1996.

[31] These operations are discussed in chapter 2 in this volume.

Equipment procurement is not decided collectively by NATO. However, in their national decision making allies try to take NATO functions into consideration in their procurement plans.[32]

NATO membership requires that the military forces of the allies can operate together. Countries must agree, for example, on common interfaces between aircraft fuel tanks and aircraft fuel pumps, or radio transmission on common frequencies. However, standard equipment is not required and the equipment operated by the current members of NATO is extremely diverse.

NATO has already established interoperability standards in command, control and communications equipment which new allies would have to accept and this would generate some new equipment requirements.[33] In a 1996 report, the Congressional Budget Office (CBO) has estimated the cost of full command, control and communications compatibility for the four Visegrad countries should they join NATO to be $7.1 billion.[34]

As indicated below, some of the required programmes are already budgeted for and are being implemented by some countries in response to the fact that the armed forces of non-NATO countries are already operating alongside NATO forces in the Stabilization Force (SFOR) or are exercising together in the framework of the Partnership for Peace in anticipation of possible joint peacekeeping missions.[35]

The CBO study suggested that new allies would probably want to undertake some programmes, notably the refitting of existing platforms (particularly combat aircraft), to permit the delivery of Western precision-guided munitions and the purchase of new air defence systems. A modern air defence environment would include comprehensive air surveillance, specialized centres for command of air operations and systems to distinguish between NATO and non-NATO aircraft (Identification, Friend or Foe or IFF systems). Assuming that no new combat aircraft are purchased the CBO estimated the costs of these new equipment programmes at approximately $6 billion.[36] Accepting the assumptions behind the CBO estimates, the total equipment costs for the four Visegrad countries would be roughly $13 billion.

[32] The most recent planning guidelines were agreed in Dec. 1996. *Ministerial Meetings of the Defence Planning Group and the Nuclear Planning Group on 17th December 1996*, Press Communiqué M-DPC/NPG-2(96)173, 17 Dec. 1996.

[33] See, e.g., Rose, C., Roth, W. and Voight, K., *The Enlargement of the Alliance*, North Atlantic Assembly report, Brussels, May 1994.

[34] *The Costs of Expanding the NATO Alliance* (Congressional Budget Office: Washington, DC, Mar. 1996), p. 30.

[35] A 1997 report by a group of Polish researchers suggested that the costs of restructuring the armed forces and buying new equipment should not be considered as part of the cost of NATO enlargement, since these measures will be undertaken regardless of the outcome of that decision. *Estimated Cost of NATO Enlargement: A Contribution to the Debate*, unpublished manuscript, 17 Feb. 1997, p. 6.

[36] *The Costs of Expanding the NATO Alliance* (note 34), p. 35. Three Visegrad countries—the Czech Republic, Hungary and Poland—have stated that they may introduce new fighter aircraft into their inventories, but in 1996 none took a decision on whether to pursue such an option or which aircraft to buy.

Armaments priorities of the Visegrad countries

In 1996 the Visegrad countries published in broad outline their forthcoming equipment priorities.

In the Czech Republic a five-year defence modernization plan had been agreed by the government and approved by the parliament in 1994.[37] The main elements were the development of a command and control system compatible with that of NATO, the upgrading of MiG-21 fighter aircraft in the Czech Air Force and the modernization of the T-72 main battle tanks of the Czech Army. In addition, the Aero Vodochody company was to develop, in collaboration with foreign partners, a new lightweight fighter, the L-159, based on the L-39 jet trainer aircraft already produced by Aero. These priorities have been translated into the defence budget programme.[38]

A new Czech command and control system, which is being developed with the French company Alcatel, is the most expensive single programme in the equipment budget. The Czech Republic is also in the process of increasing the number of radar sites for air defence and integrating these into a new air defence environment.[39]

In October 1996 the Defence and Security Committee of the Parliament recommended terminating the programme to modernize the T-72 tank. However, funding for the T-72 modernization was included in the 1997 budget.[40] The upgrading of avionics in the Czech MiG-21 fighter aircraft—which was to be carried out with Israeli cooperation—has never been initiated and has been opposed by parliamentarians.[41]

The L-159 is being developed together with the US company Rockwell Collins, which was awarded a contract in 1995 to develop an avionics suite for the aircraft.[42] The engine for the aircraft will also be supplied by a US company, Allied Signal, and production for the Czech Air Force is expected from 1998.

The Czech Minister of Defence has also stated that the replacement of MiG-21 fighter aircraft in the Czech Air Force is under consideration. However, the current budget contains no funds for such a programme.

[37] *Defense News,* 29 Aug.–4 Sep. 1994, p. 3.

[38] 'The Army of the Czech Republic will further converge to NATO standards', *Hospodarske Noviny* (Prague), 13 Jan. 1997, p. 4 (in Czech), in 'Czech Republic: article views army investment plans for 1997', Foreign Broadcast Information Service, *Daily Report—East Europe (FBIS-EEU),* FBIS-EEU-97-009, 15 Jan. 1997.

[39] The Czech Republic is carrying out this programme alongside the development of a new civilian air traffic control system.

[40] Horejsi, T., 'Food first, fighter aircraft later; the defense ministry's draft budget provides for the departure of thousands of employees from the sector', *Tyden* (Prague), 14 Oct. 1996, pp. 32–34 (in Czech), in 'Czech Republic: budget foresees 30-percent cut in army', FBIS-EEU-96-206, 24 Oct. 1996. The upgrading is being carried out with assistance from companies in Israel, Italy and the UK. *Defense News,* 28 Aug.–3 Sep. 1995, p. 8; and *Defense News,* 9–15 Oct. 1995, p. 20.

[41] Parliamentarians have argued that if the aircraft may soon be replaced with new models any investment in upgrading will be wasted. Pehe, J., 'Czech Army to modernize MiG-21 jets', *OMRI Daily Digest,* no. 142, part II (24 July 1995); and Kettle, S., 'Czech minister denies decision taken to modernize jets', *OMRI Daily Digest,* no. 143, part II (25 July 1995).

[42] *Jane's All the World's Aircraft, 1996–97* (Jane's Information Group: Coulsdon, UK, 1996), pp. 75–76. Rockwell has in turn subcontracted with Italian and British companies to supply important sub-systems such as the radars and passive defensive systems.

In Hungary the top priority has been accorded to air defence. The main programmes anticipated are the replacement of short-range air defence missiles and the purchase of long-range air surveillance radars. In addition, Hungary is studying the possible options for replacing MiG-21 and MiG-23 fighter aircraft, which form the core of the Hungarian Air Force. Modernization of the armoured vehicles of the land forces is also a priority in Hungary.[43] However, this is being achieved through the acquisition of surplus vehicles from former allies—notably Belarus and Russia—which is financed through a clearing arrangement based on the debts owed within the now defunct Council for Mutual Economic Assistance (CMEA). In 1996 Hungary took delivery of a large number of Russian BTR-80 wheeled armoured personnel carriers.

Hungary has acquired a NATO-compatible IFF system for 82 of its aircraft, including MiG-21, MiG-23 and Su-22 fighters. As funding becomes available, Hungarian MiG-29 fighters will also acquire these systems. In addition, airfields and other locations have been equipped with communications and other equipment to create compatibility with the NATO-led foreign military presence in the former Yugoslavia.[44]

In Poland current procurement plans centre on three programmes. First, the production of the PT-91 Twardy tank is under way. In 1997 the Polish armed forces are expected to order the first 20 serial production versions of this tank. Second, an existing Polish helicopter (the W-3 Sokol) is being developed into an anti-tank helicopter; this is known as the Huzar programme. The Polish Air Force hopes to buy 6–8 helicopters each year. Third, there is a plan to upgrade the Polish land-based air defence system, probably including the purchase of new surface-to-air missiles at some point.

At present none of these projects has a firm funding commitment in the budget. The Ministry of Defence has requested a doubling of equipment expenditure (to c. 10 billion zlotys per year) after 1998 to accommodate these plans.[45]

An additional plan which has not been included in this figure is the possible purchase of fighter aircraft equipped with medium-range air-to-air missiles for the Polish Air Force. A separate decision will be taken by the government on this programme (which would be by far the largest economic commitment among current plans), probably in mid-1997.

Poland has awarded a contract to the French company Thomson-CSF to provide new military communications systems, parts of which will be produced at the Radmor plant in Gdynia, Poland.[46]

In Slovakia the main priority of the Ministry of Defence is to ensure the repair and maintenance of equipment in current inventories. Regarding new equipment, it is government policy to favour procurement of domestic designs

[43] C+D97: The Third Central European Defence Equipment and Aviation Exhibition and Conference, Hungexpo, Budapest, 5 Dec. 1996.

[44] 'Hungarian crossroads', Air Force Monthly, Nov. 1995, pp. 22–29.

[45] Zukrowska, K., 'Poland: labour force in the transition period', Economic Developments and Reforms in Cooperation Partner Countries: The Social and Human Dimension, NATO Economics Colloquium 1996, Brussels, 26–28 June 1996.

[46] 'MON: more amendments', Warsaw Rzeczpospolita (Warsaw), 19 Dec. 1996, p. 2 (in Polish), in 'Poland: ministry officials discuss army structure, Israeli missiles', FBIS-EEU-96-247, 24 Dec. 1996.

from Slovak production.[47] Current plans focus on the acquisition of the Zuzana 155-mm howitzer produced in Slovakia along with the acquisition of new attack helicopters—probably the Russian Ka-50.[48] The Zuzana will enter series production for the Slovak armed forces in 1997. The Ka-50 would be provided by Russia in the framework of the clearing arrangement associated with the CMEA debt, and so the initial acquisition cost would not be reflected in the Slovak budget.

The primary motivating factors in the procurement programmes of the Visegrad countries are not potential NATO membership but rather domestic factors. Three seem particularly important. The first factor is the government approach to fiscal policy and public expenditure.[49] The second is the need to deal with the crisis in national defence industries.[50] While each of the Visegrad countries has involved foreign contractors in equipment procurement programmes, it has usually been in collaboration with a domestic supplier. Western suppliers are playing a significant role in some of the most important current programmes through the addition of sub-systems and technical assistance rather than through sales of major platforms. Procurement of major platforms from Western companies will require either a significant increase in defence spending in the Visegrad countries or very advantageous financing arrangements by suppliers.[51] The third factor concerns the constraints imposed by the domination of systems of Soviet-origin in the current equipment inventory. All the Visegrad countries continue to devote a large part of their resources to maintaining existing equipment.

Programmes are already under way in the Czech Republic, Hungary and Poland which will create compatibility with NATO command, control and communications operations. These programmes are already taken into account in national budgets and will proceed regardless of whether or not these countries join NATO. Equipment decisions regarding major platforms such as fighter aircraft have not been taken. However, these are not necessary elements of NATO enlargement and, in the absence of a significant change in threat perceptions, probably not a pressing spending priority.[52]

III. The continuing operation of the UN Register of Conventional Arms

As of 21 April 1997, 92 countries had responded to the request for information from the UN Secretary-General. This is the highest level of participation

---

[47] Interview with Jan Sitek, Slovak Defence Minister and Slovak National Party Deputy Chairman, by Pavol Vitko, 'We are waiting for Slovak weapons', *Pravda* (Bratislava), 19 Dec. 1996, p. 4 (in Slovakian), in 'Slovakia: Sitek views arms supplies, budget issues', FBIS-EEU-96-248, 26 Dec. 1996.

[48] TASR (Bratislava), 12 Dec. 1996, in 'Defense Minister discusses planned arms procurement', FBIS-EEU-96-247A, 24 Dec. 1996.

[49] See chapter 6 in this volume.

[50] The defence industries of the Visegrad countries are analysed in Kiss, Y., SIPRI, *The Defence Industry in East–Central Europe: Restructuring and Conversion* (Oxford University Press: Oxford, forthcoming, 1997).

[51] See chapter 6 in this volume for Central and East European defence budget data.

[52] *Warsaw Voice*, 2 Feb. 1997, p. 7; and *International Herald Tribune*, 15–16 Feb. 1997, p. 2.

Table 9.4. Government returns to the UN Register for calendar years 1992, 1993, 1994 and 1995 as of 21 April 1997

	Data on imports				Data on exports				Explanation in *note verbale*				Background information			
	1992	1993	1994	1995	1992	1993	1994	1995	1992	1993	1994	1995	1992	1993	1994	1995
Afghanistan	–	–	–	–	–	–	–	–	–	yes	–	–	–	no	–	–
Albania	nil	–	–	–	nil	–	–	nil	–	–	–	–	–	no	–	no
Antigua & Barbuda	nil	nil	–	–	nil	nil	–	–	–	–	–	yes	no	–	no	–
Andorra	–	–	nil	nil	–	–	–	nil	–	–	nil	–	–	–	no	no
Argentina	nil	yes	yes	yes	yes	nil	nil	yes	–	–	–	–	no	yes	yes	yes
Armenia	–	nil	nil	nil	–	nil	nil	nil	–	–	–	–	–	no	yes	yes
Australia	yes	yes	yes	yes	nil	nil	nil	nil	–	–	–	–	yes	yes	yes	no
Austria	–	nil	yes	yes	yes	–	–	nil	–	–	yes	–	yes	yes	yes	yes
Azerbaijan	–	–	–	nil	–	–	–	nil	–	–	–	–	–	–	–	yes
Bahamas	–	–	nil	nil	–	–	nil	nil	–	–	–	–	–	–	no	no
Barbados	–	–	nil	nil	–	–	nil	nil	–	–	–	–	–	–	no	no
Belarus	nil	nil	–	yes	yes	yes	–	–	–	–	–	–	no	yes	no	yes
Belgium	yes	yes	nil	nil	nil	–	yes	yes	yes	–	–	–	yes	yes	yes	yes
Belize	–	–	nil	–	–	–	nil	–	–	–	–	–	–	–	no	yes
Benin	–	–	nil	–	–	–	–	–	–	–	–	–	–	–	–	–
Bhutan	nil	nil	nil	nil	nil	nil	nil	nil	–	–	–	–	no	no	no	no
Bolivia	yes	–	–	–	–	–	–	–	–	–	–	–	no	–	–	–
Brazil	yes	yes	yes	yes	yes	nil	nil	nil	–	–	–	–	yes	yes	yes	yes
Bulgaria	yes	nil	–	nil	yes	yes	yes	nil	–	–	–	–	yes	yes	yes	yes
Burkina Faso	–	nil	nil	nil	–	nil	nil	–	–	–	–	–	–	no	no	no
Cameroon	–	–	nil	–	–	–	nil	–	–	–	–	–	–	–	no	–
Canada	yes	yes	yes	yes	yes	yes	yes	yes	–	–	–	–	yes	yes	yes	yes
Central African Rep.	–	–	–	nil	–	–	–	–	–	–	–	–	–	–	–	no
Chad	–	–	nil	–	–	yes	nil	–	–	–	–	–	–	no	no	–
Chile	yes	nil	yes	yes	nil	nil	nil	nil	–	–	–	–	yes	yes	no	no

Country	1	2	3	4	5	6	7	8	9	10	11	12	13	14	15	16
China	yes	yes	nil	yes	yes	yes	yes	yes	yes	yes	–	–	–	–	no	no
Colombia	yes	–	–	–	–	–	nil	–	–	–	–	–	no	no	no	no
Comoros	–	–	nil	–	–	–	–	–	–	yes	–	–	–	yes	–	–
Côte d'Ivoire	–	–	nil	–	–	–	–	–	–	yes	yes	yes	–	yes	–	–
Croatia	nil	nil	nil	nil	nil	nil	nil	nil	nil	–	–	–	–	yes	no	–
Cuba	nil	nil	nil	nil	nil	nil	nil	nil	nil	yes	–	–	no	yes	no	no
Cyprus	nil	–	–	nil	yes	yes	–	yes	–	–	–	–	–	–	no	no
Czech Republic	yes	yes	yes	yes	yes	yes	yes	yes	yes	–	–	–	yes.	yes	yes	yes
Denmark	nil	nil	yes	nil	yes	yes	yes	yes	yes	–	–	–	yes	yes	yes	yes
Dominica	nil	yes	nil	nil	nil	nil	nil	nil	nil	–	–	–	no	no	no	no
Dominican Rep.	nil	nil	nil	–	–	nil	nil	nil	–	–	–	–	–	–	–	–
Ecuador	–	–	–	–	–	–	–	–	–	–	–	–	no	no	–	–
Egypt	yes	yes	yes	yes	yes	yes	yes	yes	yes	–	–	–	no	–	–	–
El Salvador	–	nil	–	–	–	–	–	–	–	–	–	–	–	yes	yes	yes
Estonia	–	–	yes	–	nil	nil	–	nil	–	–	–	–	no	no	–	no
Ethiopia	–	nil	–	nil	nil	nil	nil	nil	nil	–	–	yes	–	–	–	–
Fiji	nil	nil	nil	nil	yes	yes	yes	yes	yes	yes	–	–	no	no	no	no
Finland	yes	yes	yes	yes	yes	yes	yes	yes	yes	–	–	–	yes	yes	yes	yes
France	nil	yes	yes	nil	nil	nil	nil	nil	yes	–	–	–	yes	yes	yes	yes
Gabon	–	–	–	–	nil	nil	–	nil	–	–	–	–	no	–	no	no
Georgia	nil	nil	nil	nil	yes	yes	nil	yes	yes	–	–	–	no	no	no	–
Germany	yes	yes	yes	yes	yes	yes	yes	yes	yes	–	–	–	yes	yes	yes	yes
Greece	yes	yes	nil	yes	yes	yes	–	bl.	nil	–	–	–	yes	yes	yes	yes
Grenada	nil	nil	–	–	–	nil	nil	nil	nil	–	–	–	no	no	no	no
Guyana	–	–	nil	–	–	yes	–	nil	nil	–	–	–	–	–	–	–
Hungary	nil	yes	yes	yes	yes	yes	yes	nil	nil	–	–	–	yes	no	yes	no
Iceland	nil	nil	nil	nil	nil	nil	nil	nil	nil	–	–	–	no	no	no	no
India	yes	yes	nil	yes	yes	yes	yes	nil	nil	–	–	–	no	no	no	no
Indonesia	nil	nil	yes	yes	yes	yes	–	nil	nil	yes	–	–	no	no	no	no
Iran	yes	yes	yes	yes	yes	–	nil	nil	nil	–	–	–	no	no	–	–
Ireland	nil	nil	yes	nil	nil	nil	nil	nil	nil	–	–	–	no	no	no	yes

	Data on imports				Data on exports				Explanation in *note verbale*				Background information			
	1992	1993	1994	1995	1992	1993	1994	1995	1992	1993	1994	1995	1992	1993	1994	1995
Israel	yes	yes	yes	yes	yes	yes	yes	yes	–	–	–	–	yes	yes	no	no
Italy	yes	–	yes	yes	yes	yes	yes	yes	–	–	–	–	yes	yes	yes	yes
Jamaica	–	–	nil	nil	–	–	nil	nil	yes	yes	yes	–	no	no	yes	no
Japan	yes	yes	yes	yes	nil	nil	nil	nil	yes	yes	yes	–	yes	yes	yes	yes
Jordan	–	nil	–	nil	–	nil	–	nil	–	–	–	–	–	no	–	no
Kazakhstan	nil	–	nil	yes	nil	–	nil	yes	yes	–	–	–	no	–	no	no
Kenya	–	nil	–	–	–	nil	–	–	–	–	–	–	–	no	–	–
Korea, South	yes	yes	yes	yes	nil	yes	yes	yes	–	–	–	–	yes	yes	yes	yes
Kyrgyzstan	–	–	–	nil	–	–	–	nil	–	–	–	yes	–	–	–	no
Latvia	–	–	–	yes	–	–	–	nil	–	–	–	–	–	–	–	no
Lebanon	nil	–	–	–	nil	–	–	–	yes	–	–	–	no	–	–	–
Lesotho	nil	–	–	–	nil	–	–	–	yes	–	no	–	no	–	–	–
Libya	nil	–	–	nil	nil	–	nil	nil	yes	–	–	–	no	no	–	no
Liechtenstein	nil	nil	nil	nil	nil	nil	nil	nil	yes	–	yes	–	no	–	–	no
Lithuania	yes	–	–	yes	yes	–	–	nil	–	–	–	–	no	–	no	no
Luxembourg	nil	nil	–	nil	nil	nil	–	nil	–	–	–	–	no	no	no	no
Madagascar	–	nil	–	–	–	nil	–	–	–	–	–	–	–	no	–	–
Malawi	–	nil	–	–	–	nil	–	–	–	–	–	–	–	no	–	no
Malaysia	nil	yes	yes	yes	nil	nil	nil	–	yes	–	–	–	no	no	no	no
Maldives	nil	nil	nil	nil	nil	nil	nil	nil	–	–	–	–	no	no	no	no
Malta	yes	nil	–	–	nil	nil	nil	nil	–	–	–	–	no	no	yes	no
Marshall Islands	–	–	–	–	–	–	–	–	–	–	–	–	–	no	yes	–
Mauritania	–	nil	nil	–	–	nil	nil	–	–	–	–	–	no	no	no	no
Mauritius	–	nil	–	nil	–	nil	–	nil	yes	–	–	–	no	no	–	no
Mexico	–	–	yes	yes	–	–	–	nil	yes	–	–	–	no	yes	no	yes
Moldova	–	–	yes	yes	–	–	yes	nil	–	–	–	–	–	yes	no	no
Monaco	–	–	–	nil	–	–	–	nil	–	–	–	–	–	–	–	no

Mongolia	nil	nil	nil	nil	nil	nil	nil	yes	–	–	–	no	no	no	no
Namibia	nil	–	–	–	–	–	–	–	–	–	–	no	no	no	no
Nepal	yes	nil	nil	nil	nil	nil	nil	–	–	–	–	yes	yes	yes	no
Netherlands	yes	yes	yes	yes	yes	yes	yes	yes	yes	–	yes	yes	yes	yes	yes
New Zealand	yes	yes	nil	nil	nil	nil	nil	yes	–	–	yes	yes	yes	yes	yes
Nicaragua	–	–	–	–	–	–	–	–	–	–	yes	–	–	–	–
Niger	–	–	–	–	–	–	–	yes	–	–	no	yes	yes	yes	–
Nigeria	–	–	–	–	–	–	–	yes	–	–	no	–	–	–	–
Norway	yes	yes	yes	yes	yes	nil	nil	yes	–	–	yes	yes	no	no	no
Oman	–	–	–	–	–	–	–	yes	–	–	no	–	–	–	–
Pakistan	yes	yes	nil	nil	nil	nil	nil	yes	–	–	yes	no	no	no	no
Panama	–	–	–	–	–	–	–	–	–	–	–	no	no	–	–
Papua New Guinea	nil	–	–	nil	nil	nil	nil	yes	–	yes	no	no	–	–	–
Paraguay	–	–	–	–	–	–	–	yes	–	–	no	yes	yes	yes	no
Peru	yes	yes	yes	nil	yes	nil	yes	yes	–	–	no	no	no	no	no
Philippines	yes	yes	yes	yes	yes	yes	nil	nil	–	–	no	no	no	no	no
Poland	yes	nil	nil	nil	yes	yes	yes	yes	–	–	yes	yes	yes	yes	yes
Portugal	yes	yes	yes	yes	nil	nil	nil	yes	–	–	yes	yes	yes	yes	yes
Qatar	–	–	–	–	–	–	–	–	–	–	yes	–	–	–	–
Romania	yes	nil	yes	yes	yes	yes	yes	–	–	–	no	no	no	–	no
Russian Fed.	nil	nil	yes	yes	yes	yes	yes	–	–	–	no	no	no	no	no
Saint Kitts & Nevis	–	–	–	–	–	nil	–	–	–	–	–	–	–	–	no
Saint Lucia	nil	nil	nil	nil	nil	nil	nil	–	–	–	–	no	no	no	–
Saint Vincent & the Grenadines	–	–	–	–	–	–	–	–	–	–	–	–	–	–	–
Samoa	–	nil	nil	nil	nil	nil	nil	yes	–	–	–	no	no	no	no
Senegal	nil	–	–	–	–	–	–	–	–	–	no	–	–	–	–
Seychelles	nil	–	–	–	–	–	–	–	–	–	no	yes	–	no	–
Sierra Leone	–	–	–	–	–	–	–	–	–	–	no	–	–	–	–
Singapore	yes	yes	yes	yes	yes	yes	yes	yes	yes	–	no	no	no	no	no
Slovakia	nil	yes	yes	yes	yes	yes	yes	yes	yes	yes	no	no	no	no	no

	Data on imports				Data on exports				Explanation in *note verbale*				Background information			
	1992	1993	1994	1995	1992	1993	1994	1995	1992	1993	1994	1995	1992	1993	1994	1995
Slovenia	nil	nil	nil	nil	nil	nil	nil	nil	yes	–	–	–	no	no	no	no
Solomon Islands	nil	–	nil	–	nil	–	nil	–	yes	–	–	–	no	–	no	–
South Africa	–	–	nil	nil	–	–	yes	yes	yes	–	–	–	no	–	yes	yes
Spain	yes	yes	yes	yes	nil	nil	nil	nil	–	–	–	–	yes	yes	yes	yes
Sri Lanka	yes	yes	yes	yes	–	–	–	–	yes	–	–	–	no	no	no	no
Sweden	yes	yes	yes	yes	yes	yes	nil	nil	–	–	–	–	yes	yes	yes	yes
Switzerland	nil	nil	nil	nil	–	yes	nil	yes	–	–	–	–	yes	yes	yes	yes
Tajikistan	–	–	nil	nil	nil	–	–	nil	–	–	–	–	–	–	no	no
Tanzania	nil	nil	nil	nil	–	–	nil	nil	–	–	–	–	no	no	no	no
Thailand	–	yes	yes	yes	–	nil	nil	–	–	–	–	–	–	no	no	no
Trinidad & Tobago	–	nil	–	nil	–	–	–	nil	–	–	–	–	–	no	–	no
Tunisia	–	–	–	–	yes	–	–	–	yes	–	–	–	no	–	–	–
Turkey	yes	yes	yes	yes	–	nil	nil	nil	–	–	–	–	yes	no	no	yes
Turkmenistan	–	–	–	nil	–	–	–	–	–	–	–	–	–	–	–	no
UK	yes	nil	yes	yes	yes	yes	yes	yes	–	–	–	–	yes	yes	yes	yes
Ukraine	nil	nil	nil	nil	nil	yes	yes	yes	–	yes	yes	–	no	no	no	no
USA	yes	yes	yes	yes	yes	nil	yes	yes	yes	–	–	–	yes	yes	yes	yes
Vanuatu	nil	nil	–	nil	–	–	–	nil	yes	–	–	–	no	no	–	no
Viet Nam	–	–	nil	yes	nil	nil	nil	nil	–	yes	yes	–	–	–	no	no
Yugoslavia (Serbia & Montenegro)	nil	nil	nil	–	nil	nil	nil	–	yes	–	–	–	yes	no	no	–

Note: '–' indicates that no information was returned.

Source: The composite table of replies of governments to the UN Register, supplied by the United Nations Centre for Disarmament Affairs, 21 Apr. 1997; and additional information supplied by the United Nations Centre for Disarmament Affairs.

recorded since the first year of reporting in 1992 and suggests that regular participation in the Register has been accepted as a responsibility by many governments.[53] The geographical pattern of participation in 1996 was very similar to that recorded in previous years. While participation was relatively high among Organization for Security and Co-operation in Europe (OSCE) participating states, in the Americas and in Asia, the Middle East and Africa stand out as virtual non-participating regions. As of 2 January 1997 only Israel and Jordan of the countries in the Middle East had submitted returns for 1995. At that time Iran, which had submitted data for each of the three previous years, had not yet done so for 1996. However, in previous years Iran subsequently provided data for the past calendar year.

Ten countries submitted returns to the register for the first time in 1996, for calendar year 1995. These were Andorra, Azerbaijan, the Central African Republic, Ethiopia, Gabon, Kyrgyzstan, Latvia, Monaco, Saint Kitts and Nevis, and Turkmenistan.

Seventeen countries which submitted returns to the register in 1995 did not do so in 1996. These were Belize, Benin, Cameroon, Chad, Croatia, Ecuador, Georgia, Grenada, Guyana, Iran, Libya, the Marshall Islands, Mauritania, Niger, Panama, Saint Lucia and the Solomon Islands. As noted above for Iran, some of these countries are likely to supply information at a later date.

In addition to the slight increase in the number of states participating in the register, there has also been a greater willingness to go beyond the minimum reporting requirements.[54] It is still the case, however, that there are widespread discrepancies between the information submitted by exporting and importing states for their bilateral transfers in the same calendar year. These discrepancies make the data in the register difficult to interpret.[55]

Expansion to include procurement through national production

In 1997 a Group of Government Experts will convene to prepare a report on the continuing operation of the register and its further development.[56] The objective is to develop a register 'which is capable of attracting the widest possible participation' among member states. The group of experts has not been given a more specific mandate and many issues may be introduced during their discussions. However, in UN General Assembly Resolution 46/36 L

[53] By comparison, at the same stage in 1993 the UN had received 82 replies from members; in 1994, 84 replies; and in 1995, 87 replies. However, it has been normal for some countries to submit information retrospectively for calendar years other than that requested by the Secretary-General. For example, by Feb. 1997 the UN had received 95 country returns for calendar year 1994.

[54] Chalmers, M. and Greene, O., *The UN Register in its Fourth Year*, Bradford Arms Register Studies, Working Paper no. 2 (Bradford University: Bradford, Nov. 1996), pp. 11–12.

[55] The problem of discrepancies led some government experts to suggest the creation of a consultative mechanism by which the UN Secretariat could question member states about the contents of their annual returns with a view to harmonizing the information presented by exporters and importers. However, there was no consensus supporting this idea.

[56] As required in UN General Assembly Resolution A/RES/49/75 C, 9 Jan. 1995. A comprehensive documentary history of the development of the United Nations Register of Conventional Arms is contained in Miller, C. D., *The United Nations Register of Conventional Arms: A Document History* (3 vols) (Monterey Institute of International Studies: Monterey, Calif., 1995).

(the resolution which established the UN Register of Conventional Arms) the member states requested the Secretary-General to 'prepare a report on the modalities for early expansion of the scope of the register by the addition of further categories of equipment and inclusion of data on military holdings and procurement through national production'.[57] This request has not been complied with by the Secretary-General. In the previous review by government experts it proved impossible to recommend any changes in the scope of the register by consensus and no action has been taken on either issue. It is likely, therefore, that both issues will feature in the discussions of the 1997 Panel of Government Experts.

This section is confined to a discussion of possible obstacles to the reporting of procurement through national production using the same seven categories of conventional arms that the register has already defined. The obstacles can be divided into several different types. There are problems of definition, problems of compilation and problems of verification. In some cases these problems are already unresolved in the existing register. In some cases they would be new problems that are not relevant for international transfers.

Problems of definition

In the framework of the UN Register of Conventional Arms member states are requested to report on equipment 'imported into or exported from their territory'. In his 1992 Report on the Register of Conventional Arms the Secretary-General provided some clarification of what this required by stating that international arms transfers involve, 'in addition to the physical movement of equipment into or from national territory, the transfer of title to and control over the equipment'.[58] However, the UN has never provided member states with a specific definition of an arms transfer. Two aspects of a transfer which were not clarified have proved to be problematic in the operation of the register. First, the identity of the recipient and second, the point at which a transfer is considered to have taken place.

Some items which clearly fall into the categories of equipment which are to be registered are bought not only by national armed forces but also by police, customs, border guards and other paramilitary forces. Under a literal interpretation, all items which fall into the categories of equipment specified in the annex to Resolution 46/36 L should be reported. However, the intent of the resolution is clearly linked to military use and in other data exercises it is usual to exclude forces other than the armed forces unless they are trained in military tactics and planned to operate under military authority in the event of war.[59]

An additional category of user which may become more important in the future comprises private companies which provide services to national minis-

---

[57] UN General Assembly Resolution A/RES/46/36 L, 3 Jan. 1992.

[58] Report of the United Nations Secretary-General on the Register of Conventional Arms, UN General Assembly document A/47/342, 14 Aug. 1992, para. 10. In the context of arms transfers this has had the effect of excluding equipment leased by one state to another.

[59] For example, NATO countries apply these criteria in compiling data on defence expenditure.

tries of defence. As ministries of defence review their procurement practices there is growing interest in the idea of contracting out services previously performed by government employees. Of possible relevance to the UN Register could be pilot or driver training or equipment maintenance if it emerges that private companies hold significant quantities of items falling in the categories of equipment to be registered.[60]

The problem of how to report equipment acquired for forces other than the armed forces would also face governments compiling data on procurement through national production.

The second aspect of an arms transfer which was not clarified by the UN was the point in time at which transfer of title and control takes place. For some complex items of equipment there can be extended periods of field trials before equipment is accepted into the armed forces. For example, the first Type 471 submarine (produced in Australia under licence from a Swedish company) was not commissioned into the Australian Navy for two and a half years after completion by the shipyard.[61] However, equipment which has not been accepted by the armed forces may be fully combat-capable and there are cases where such equipment has been pressed into service at short notice.

A third problem of definition which could reduce the usefulness of the register is that of separating procurement through national production from international transfers for the purposes of reporting.

For the purposes of the UN Register weapons acquisition can be considered as a continuum with international transfers at one end and national production at the other. However, very few major complex systems are entirely national in origin. If the UN Register is to retain a distinction between equipment procured by import and equipment procured by national production it will be necessary for member states to develop a method for classifying equipment with significant foreign content into one of these two categories.

Most major systems of the type included in the UN Register contain some foreign components. One solution might be to define the equipment to be reported as national production as that which is designed and developed in the country of production. However, even systems which are nominally designed and developed by one country may have very significant foreign inputs. It is extremely unlikely that the United Nations could devise a system for monitoring transfers of large sub-systems (such as engines and radars) and almost inconceivable that transfers of smaller components could be registered successfully. Therefore, it is logical to identify the country of final assembly and say that this country is responsible for reporting the acquisition to the UN.

One potential difficulty arises where an item is produced in one country under a licence obtained from another. In some cases a country of final assembly will be provided with complete knock-down (CKD) kits in which case comparatively little production is required from the end-user. SIPRI has traditionally defined this kind of acquisition as an international transfer and

---

[60] These could be, e.g., aircraft used for training which are combat-capable in the sense of being fitted with all sub-systems and wiring necessary to be armed.

[61] *Jane's Fighting Ships, 1996–97* (Jane's Information Group: Coulsdon, UK, 1996), p. 24.

reported on it in the annual SIPRI registers in the category 'licensed production'.

This can produce some problems in reporting where the number of kits delivered is different from the number of items ordered by the armed forces. An illustrative example is the programme to acquire armoured infantry fighting vehicles (AIFV) for the Indian Army.[62] Under the current system of reporting in the UN Register this programme does not meet the understanding of an international transfer. As noted above, this kind of programme is regarded by SIPRI as trade. However, if in future a programme of this kind were to be reported as procurement through national production the issue of what such a report might contain would arise.

In March 1981 the Government of India agreed with the former USSR on a licensing agreement covering the production in India of the BMP-1 AIFV. In 1984 the Government of India sanctioned the production of infantry combat vehicles by the Indian Ordnance Factories. In February 1985 a new licensing agreement was signed covering the production in India of 1250 BMP-2 AIFVs. In August 1987 a new sanction was agreed by the government providing funds for the construction of the BMP-2 AIFV by Indian Ordnance Factories. However, in 1991–92 and 1992–93, citing budget constraints, the Indian Ministry of Defence reduced its requirement to 800 BMP-2 armoured vehicles, but by this time the Indian Ordnance Factories had already imported additional vehicle sets from the Soviet Union. In March 1992, 143 vehicle sets had been ordered (of which 93 were already at the factory in India) for which there were no firm orders from the Ministry of Defence.

If the programme in question were to be treated as international trade then it could be argued that the number of vehicle sets physically transferred between countries would be the correct number to report. However, if the programme were reported as procurement through national production, it could be argued that only those sets acquired by the Ministry of Defence should be reported.

Problems of compilation

Developing the reporting procedures for the UN Register of Conventional Arms inevitably involved more than one agency in each country. At a minimum, liaison would be required between the Ministry of Foreign Affairs, the Ministry of Defence (or equivalent), the armed forces command and the customs service.

It is possible that the expansion to include reporting on procurement through national production could require additional procedures (because of the acquisition of equipment by forces other than the national armed forces referred to above). However, most or all of the information required would probably be held by the national command authority—usually the Ministry of Defence or equivalent.

---

[62] The following information is taken from the *Union Government–Defence Services*, Report of the Comptroller and Auditor General of India no. 8 of 1993, section 36 'Infantry Combat Vehicle', 7 May 1993.

More difficult would be any effort to resolve the definitions (noted above) of when acquisition has taken place. The experience in registering international arms transfers was that national authorities prefer to maintain their existing procedures and rarely wish to modify them in response to requests from other national agencies or international bodies such as the UN. Most useful in this respect would be an instruction from the highest political authority rather than horizontal inter-agency discussion.

Problems of verification

One of the most valuable aspects of the UN Register of Conventional Arms was the cross-checking procedure created by the separate reporting by each country of both imports and exports. However, this would not be available for reports on procurement through national production.

Historically, there have been cases where countries have developed and procured major systems in secret. For example, in the USA the F-117 stealth fighter and a stealth ship (Sea Shadow) were 'black' programmes whose existence was not acknowledged until they had already been acquired.[63]

The objective of the UN Register of Conventional Arms is to increase openness and transparency on the assumption that this will enhance confidence, ease tensions and contribute to restraint in production and transfers of arms. Clearly, the register could not survive long if states deliberately provided inaccurate and misleading information. However, since the register is a voluntary exercise undertaken in response to a request from the UN Secretary-General, member states are under no obligation to provide full reports. While it is seen as an act of good faith to provide information to the register, it is likely that most states regard the data received as one of a range of useful indicators of weapon acquisition, but no more than that.

---

[63] Since the end of the cold war there have been suggestions that systems exist in the inventory of the United States which are not known to the public. For example, there have been several suggestions that an aircraft known as 'Aurora' exists, although this has never been confirmed.

Appendix 9A. Tables of the volume of the trade in major conventional weapons, 1987–96

IAN ANTHONY, GERD HAGMEYER-GAVERUS, PIETER D. WEZEMAN and SIEMON T. WEZEMAN

Table 9A.1. Volume of imports of major conventional weapons

Figures are SIPRI trend-indicator values, as expressed in US $m., at constant (1990) prices.

	1987	1988	1989	1990	1991	1992	1993	1994	1995	1996
World total	44 185	38 055	37 360	30 899	26 494	24 840	26 444	21 820	23 189	22 980
Developing world	29 823	22 341	21 277	18 673	14 147	11 603	13 881	12 966	16 953	17 425
LDCs	1 117	1 935	2 919	2 805	1 507	112	424	182	445	231
Industrialized world	14 363	15 714	16 083	12 226	12 348	13 237	12 563	8 855	6 236	5 554
Africa	3 242	2 318	2 036	1 661	779	492	294	634	571	427
Sub-Saharan	2 668	1 887	603	1 166	138	407	147	263	154	255
Americas	3 425	1 829	2 107	1 684	2 619	1 994	1 485	2 323	1 898	1 220
North	1 500	981	553	462	1 623	1 376	1 099	1 501	738	285
Central	330	214	394	408	145	3	6	..	..	..
South	1 595	634	1 160	814	851	616	380	822	1 160	935
Asia	10 987	11 629	13 274	10 493	8 591	6 843	7 536	6 383	10 354	11 064
Europe	11 310	13 013	13 035	10 078	8 469	9 473	9 061	6 458	4 299	4 107
Middle East	14 629	8 331	5 986	6 585	5 774	5 597	7 532	5 567	6 001	5 603
Oceania	593	935	922	399	262	441	535	455	66	559
ASEAN	1 431	1 306	888	1 187	1 043	1 103	741	2 252	2 841	1 170
CSCE	12 645	13 764	13 551	10 497	10 074	10 836	9 825	7 808	5 016	4 359
EU	2 872	4 327	4 808	4 070	5 681	6 242	4 204	3 696	2 362	1 753
NATO	5 875	6 717	6 833	5 630	8 491	9 390	7 500	6 701	3 934	2 922
OECD	8 046	9 303	9 814	7 923	11 369	12 834	10 940	8 818	5 361	6 839
OPEC	9 739	5 646	6 187	5 912	3 420	2 817	5 818	3 750	3 879	4 616

Note: Tables 9A.1 and 9A.2 show the volume of trade for the different regional groupings to which countries are assigned in the SIPRI arms trade database. Since many countries are included in more than one group totals cannot be derived from the tables. The following countries are included in each group.

Developing world: Afghanistan, Algeria, Angola, Argentina, Bahamas, Bahrain, Bangladesh, Barbados, Belize, Benin, Bhutan, Bolivia, Botswana, Brazil, Brunei, Burkina Faso, Burundi, Cambodia, Cameroon, Cape Verde, Central African Republic, Chad, Chile, China, Colombia, Comoros, Congo, Costa Rica, Côte d'Ivoire, Cuba, Cyprus, Djibouti, Dominica, Dominican Republic, Ecuador, Egypt, El Salvador, Equatorial Guinea, Eritrea, Ethiopia, Fiji, Gabon, Gambia, Ghana, Guatemala, Guinea, Guinea-Bissau, Guyana, Haiti, Honduras, India, Indonesia, Iran, Iraq, Israel, Jamaica, Jordan, Kenya, Kiribati, North Korea, South Korea, Kuwait, Laos, Lebanon, Lesotho, Liberia, Libya, Madagascar, Malawi, Malaysia, Maldives, Mali, Marshall Islands, Mauritania, Mauritius, Mexico, Micronesia, Mongolia, Morocco, Mozambique, Myanmar, Namibia, Nepal, Nicaragua, Niger, Nigeria, Oman, Pakistan, Palau, Panama, Papua New Guinea, Paraguay, Peru, Philippines, Qatar, Rwanda, Samoa, Saudi Arabia, Senegal, Seychelles, Sierra Leone, Singapore, Solomon Islands, Somalia, South Africa, Sri Lanka, St Vincent & the Grenadines, Sudan, Suriname, Swaziland, Syria, Taiwan, Tanzania, Thailand, Togo, Tonga, Trinidad & Tobago, Tunisia, Tuvalu, Uganda, United Arab Emirates, Uruguay, Vanuatu, Venezuela, Viet Nam, North Yemen (–1990), South Yemen (–1990), Yemen (1991–), Zaire, Zambia, Zimbabwe.

Least developed countries (LDCs): Afghanistan, Bangladesh, Benin, Bhutan, Botswana, Burkina Faso, Burundi, Cape Verde, Central African Republic, Chad, Comoros, Djibouti, Equatorial Guinea, Eritrea, Ethiopia, Gambia, Guinea, Guinea-Bissau, Haiti, Laos, Lesotho, Liberia, Malawi, Maldives,

Table 9A.2. Volume of exports of major conventional weapons

Figures are SIPRI trend-indicator values, as expressed in US $m., at constant (1990) prices.

	1987	1988	1989	1990	1991	1992	1993	1994	1995	1996
World total	44 185	38 055	37 360	30 899	26 494	24 840	26 444	21 820	23 189	22 980
Developing world	4 250	3 198	2 055	1 648	1 499	1 470	2 162	1 203	1 543	976
LDCs	87	3	..	..	..	0	..	..	..	..
Industrialized world	39 936	34 857	35 305	29 250	24 995	23 371	24 282	20 617	21 646	22 004
Africa	216	117	4	46	35	78	34	24	10	9
Sub-Saharan	138	55	4	16	35	78	34	24	10	9
Americas	13 489	10 982	10 373	9 982	13 000	14 501	14 495	12 403	11 394	10 481
North	13 162	10 703	10 300	9 898	12 950	14 319	14 415	12 358	11 358	10 384
Central	..	..	1	4	2	110	56	..	..	..
South	326	278	72	79	49	73	24	45	36	97
Asia	3 385	2 358	1 605	1 378	1 252	1 006	1 721	1 233	1 661	668
Europe	26 769	24 148	24 997	19 244	11 980	9 038	9 842	7 825	9 678	11 638
Middle East	322	445	373	141	165	216	341	324	433	183
Oceania	4	6	9	108	62	2	10	12	14	1
ASEAN	36	24	23	6	6	24	14	32	16	24
CSCE	39 931	34 851	35 296	29 142	24 902	23 356	24 112	20 560	21 541	22 031
EU	6 846	6 010	6 904	6 239	5 597	4 998	5 261	5 907	5 343	6 391
NATO	20 059	16 733	17 306	16 151	18 686	19 317	19 768	18 452	16 505	16 499
OECD	20 488	17 436	17 987	16 970	19 309	19 863	19 945	18 609	17 074	17 131
OPEC	84	221	30	41	18	..	57	69	74	35

Mali, Mauritania, Mozambique, Myanmar, Nepal, Niger, Rwanda, Samoa, Sierra Leone, Somalia, Sudan, Tanzania, Togo, Uganda, Vanuatu, Yemen (1991–), North Yemen (–1990), South Yemen (–1990).

Industrialized world: Albania, Armenia (1992–), Australia, Austria, Azerbaijan (1992–), Belarus (1992–), Belgium, Bosnia and Herzegovina (1992–), Bulgaria, Canada, Croatia (1992–), Czechoslovakia (–1992), Czech Republic (1993–), Denmark, Estonia (1991–), Finland, France, Georgia (1992–), Germany, German DR (–1990), Greece, Hungary, Iceland, Ireland, Italy, Japan, Kazakhstan (1992–), Kyrgyzstan (1992–), Latvia (1991–), Liechtenstein, Lithuania (1991–), Luxembourg, Macedonia (1992–), Malta, Moldova (1992–), Monaco, Netherlands, New Zealand, Norway, Poland, Portugal, Romania, Russia (1992–), Slovakia (1993–), Slovenia (1992–), Spain, Sweden, Switzerland, Tajikistan (1992–), Turkey, Turkmenistan (1992–), UK, Ukraine (1992–), USA, USSR (–1991), Uzbekistan (1992–), Yugoslavia (–1991), Yugoslavia (Serbia and Montenegro) (1992–).

Africa: Algeria, Angola, Benin, Botswana, Burkina Faso, Burundi, Cameroon, Cape Verde, Central African Republic, Chad, Comoros, Congo, Côte d'Ivoire, Djibouti, Equatorial Guinea, Eritrea, Ethiopia, Gabon, Gambia, Ghana, Guinea, Guinea-Bissau, Kenya, Lesotho, Liberia, Libya, Madagascar, Malawi, Mali, Mauritania, Mauritius, Morocco, Mozambique, Namibia, Niger, Nigeria, Rwanda, Senegal, Seychelles, Sierra Leone, Somalia, South Africa, Sudan, Swaziland, Tanzania, Togo, Tunisia, Uganda, Zaire, Zambia, Zimbabwe.

Sub-Saharan Africa: Angola, Benin, Botswana, Burkina Faso, Burundi, Cameroon, Cape Verde, Central African Republic, Chad, Comoros, Congo, Côte d'Ivoire, Djibouti, Equatorial Guinea, Eritrea, Ethiopia, Gabon, Gambia, Ghana, Guinea, Guinea-Bissau, Kenya, Lesotho, Liberia, Madagascar,

Malawi, Mali, Mauritania, Mauritius, Mozambique, Namibia, Niger, Nigeria, Rwanda, Senegal, Seychelles, Sierra Leone, Somalia, South Africa, Sudan, Swaziland, Tanzania, Togo, Uganda, Zaire, Zambia, Zimbabwe.

Americas: Argentina, Bahamas, Barbados, Belize, Bolivia, Brazil, Canada, Chile, Colombia, Costa Rica, Cuba, Dominica, Dominican Republic, Ecuador, El Salvador, Guatemala, Guyana, Haiti, Honduras, Jamaica, Mexico, Nicaragua, Panama, Paraguay, Peru, St Vincent & the Grenadines, Suriname, Trinidad & Tobago, Uruguay, USA, Venezuela.

North America: Canada, Mexico, USA.

Central America: Barbados, Bahamas, Belize, Costa Rica, Cuba, Dominica, Dominican Republic, Guatemala, Haiti, Honduras, Jamaica, Nicaragua, Panama, El Salvador, St Vincent & the Grenadines, Trinidad & Tobago.

South America: Argentina, Bolivia, Brazil, Chile, Colombia, Ecuador, Guyana, Paraguay, Peru, Suriname, Uruguay, Venezuela.

Asia: Afghanistan, Bangladesh, Bhutan, Brunei, Cambodia, China, India, Indonesia, Japan, Kazakhstan (1992–), North Korea, South Korea, Kyrgyzstan (1992–), Laos, Malaysia, Maldives, Mongolia, Myanmar, Nepal, Pakistan, Philippines, Singapore, Sri Lanka, Taiwan, Tajikistan (1992–), Thailand, Turkmenistan (1992–), Uzbekistan (1992–), Viet Nam.

Europe: Albania, Armenia (1992–), Austria, Azerbaijan (1992–), Belarus (1992–), Belgium, Bosnia and Herzegovina (1992–), Bulgaria, Croatia (1992–), Cyprus, Czechoslovakia (–1992), Czech Republic (1993–), Denmark, Estonia (1991–), Finland, France, Georgia (1992–), Germany, German DR (–1990), Greece, Hungary, Iceland, Ireland, Italy, Latvia (1991–), Liechtenstein, Lithuania (1991–), Luxembourg, Macedonia (1992–), Malta, Moldova (1992–), Monaco, Netherlands, Norway, Poland, Portugal, Romania, Russia (1992–), Slovakia (1993–), Slovenia (1992–), Spain, Sweden, Switzerland, Turkey, UK, Ukraine (1992–), USSR (–1991), Yugoslavia (–1991), Yugoslavia (Serbia and Montenegro) (1992–).

Middle East: Bahrain, Egypt, Iran, Iraq, Israel, Jordan, Kuwait, Lebanon, Oman, Qatar, Saudi Arabia, Syria, United Arab Emirates, North Yemen (–1990), South Yemen (–1990),Yemen (1991–).

Oceania: Australia, Fiji, Kiribati, Marshall Islands, Micronesia, New Zealand, Palau, Papua New Guinea, Samoa, Solomon Islands, Tonga, Tuvalu, Vanuatu.

Association of South-East Asian Nations (ASEAN): Brunei, Indonesia, Malaysia, Philippines, Singapore, Thailand, Viet Nam (1995–)

European Union (EU): Austria (1995–), Belgium, Denmark, Finland (1995–), France, Germany, Greece, Ireland, Italy, Luxembourg, Netherlands, Portugal, Spain, Sweden (1995–), UK.

NATO: Belgium, Canada, Denmark, France, Germany, Greece, Iceland, Italy, Luxembourg, Netherlands, Norway, Portugal, Spain, Turkey, UK, USA.

Organisation for Economic Co-operation and Development (OECD): Australia, Austria, Belgium, Canada, Czech Rep. (1995–), Denmark, Finland, France, Germany, Greece, Hungary (1996–), Iceland, Ireland, Italy, Japan, South Korea (1996–), Luxembourg, Mexico (1994–), Netherlands, New Zealand, Norway, Poland (1996–), Portugal, Spain, Sweden, Switzerland, Turkey, UK, USA.

Organisation of Petroleum Exporting Countries (OPEC): Algeria, Ecuador (–1992), Gabon, Indonesia, Iran, Iraq, Kuwait, Libya, Nigeria, Qatar, Saudi Arabia, United Arab Emirates, Venezuela.

Organization for Security and Co-operation in Europe (OSCE): Albania (1991–), Armenia (1992–), Austria, Azerbaijan (1992–), Belarus (1992–), Belgium, Bosnia and Herzegovina (1992–), Bulgaria, Canada, Croatia (1992–), Cyprus, Czechoslovakia (–1992), Czech Republic (1993–), Denmark, Estonia (1991–), Finland, France, Georgia (1992–), Germany, German DR (–1990), Greece, Hungary, Iceland, Ireland, Italy, Kazakhstan (1992–), Kyrgyzstan (1992–), Latvia (1991–), Liechtenstein, Lithuania (1991–), Luxembourg, Macedonia (1995–), Malta, Moldova (1992–), Monaco, Netherlands, Norway, Poland, Portugal, Romania, Russia (1992–), San Marino, Slovakia (1992–), Slovenia (1992–), Spain, Sweden, Switzerland, Tajikistan (1992–), Turkey, Turkmenistan (1992–), UK, Ukraine (1992–), USA, USSR (–1992), Uzbekistan (1992–), Yugoslavia (–1991), Yugoslavia (Serbia and Montenegro) (1992–).

Appendix 9B. Register of the trade in and licensed production of major conventional weapons, 1996

IAN ANTHONY, GERD HAGMEYER-GAVERUS, PIETER D. WEZEMAN and SIEMON T. WEZEMAN

This register lists major weapons on order or under delivery, or for which the licence was bought and production was under way or completed during 1996. 'Year(s)' of deliveries' includes aggregates of all deliveries and licensed production since the beginning of the contract. Sources and methods for the data collection, and the conventions, abbreviations and acronyms used, are explained in appendix 9C. Entries are alphabetical, by recipient, supplier and licenser.

Recipient/ supplier (S) or licenser (L)	No. ordered	Weapon designation	Weapon description	Year of order/ licence	Year(s) of deliveries	No. delivered/ produced	Comments
Algeria							
L: UK	3	Kebir Class	Patrol craft	(1990)		..	Algerian designation El Yadekh Class
Argentina							
S: France	2	AS-365N Dauphin-2	Helicopter	(1994)	1996	2	For Coast Guard
	4	AS-555UN Fennec	Helicopter	1993	1996	4	For Navy
USA	40	A-4M Skyhawk-2	FGA aircraft	1993	1996	(10)	Ex-US Marine Corps; incl 6 TA-4J trainer version; deal worth $125 m; incl 8 spare engines
	6	P-3B Orion	ASW/MP aircraft	1996		..	Ex-US Navy; for Navy; EDA aid
	(15)	Super King Air-200	Light transport ac	(1993)	1995	(1)	Ex-US Air Force and US Army
	1	AN/SPS-67	Surveillance radar	1994		..	On 1 ex-US Navy Newport Class landing ship
	1	Phalanx	CIWS	1994		..	On 1 ex-US Navy Newport Class landing ship
	1	Newport Class	Landing ship	(1994)		..	Ex-US Navy; 2-year lease worth $1.8 m; status uncertain
Australia							
S: Canada	97	LAV-25	AIFV	1992	1994–96	(97)	Deal worth $88 m; incl 33 Bison APC, 10 ARV, 9 APC/CP, 2 ambulance and 10 surveillance

Recipient/ supplier (S) or licenser (L)	No. ordered	Weapon designation	Weapon description	Year of order/ licence	Year(s) of deliveries	No. delivered/ produced	Comments
							version; Australian designation ASLAV; assembled in Australia
	14	LAV-25	AIFV	1996		..	Australian designation ASLAV
Israel	..	Have Nap	ASM	1996		..	For F-111C fighter/bomber aircraft
Sweden	8	9LV	Fire control radar	(1991)	1996	(1)	For 8 Meko-200ANZ Type (Anzac Class) frigates
	8	Sea Giraffe-150	Surveillance radar	1991	1996	1	For 8 Meko-200ANZ Type (Anzac Class) frigates
UK	12	Hawk-100	FGA/trainer aircraft	1996		..	Deal worth $1.6 b incl 28 licensed production
USA	12	C-130J-30 Hercules	Transport aircraft	1995		..	Deal worth $670 m; option on 24 more
	4	P-3B Orion	ASW/MP aircraft	1994	1995–96	(4)	Ex-US Navy; incl 3 for training and 1 for spares only
	8	127mm/54 Mk-45	Naval gun	(1989)	1994–96	(3)	For 8 Meko-200ANZ Type (Anzac Class) frigates
	8	AN/SPS-49	Surveillance radar	1993	1996	(1)	For 8 Meko-200ANZ Type (Anzac Class) frigates
	8	Seasparrow VLS	ShAM system	(1991)	1996	(1)	For 8 Meko-200ANZ Type (Anzac Class) frigates
	12	RGM-84A Harpoon	ShShM	1995		..	Deal worth $38 m incl 21 training missiles
	(128)	RIM-7M Seasparrow	ShAM	(1991)	1996	(16)	For 8 Meko-200ANZ Type (Anzac Class) frigates
L: Germany	10	Meko-200ANZ Type	Frigate	1989	1996	1	Incl 2 for New Zealand; option on 2 more for New Zealand; Australian designation Anzac Class
Italy	6	Gaeta Class	MCM ship	1994		..	Australian designation Huon Class
Sweden	6	Type-471	Submarine	1987	1996	1	Deal worth $2.8 b; Australian designation Collins Class
UK	28	Hawk-100	FGA/trainer aircraft	1996		..	Deal worth $1.6 b incl 12 delivered direct
Austria							
S: France	22	RAC	Surveillance radar	1995		..	Deal worth $129 m (offsets $344 m) incl 500 Mistral missiles and 76 launchers
	500	Mistral	Portable SAM	1993	1993–96	(500)	Deal worth $129 m (offsets $344 m) incl 22 RAC radars; deal incl also 76 launchers
Germany	87	RJPz-1 Jaguar-1	Tank destroyer (M)	1996		..	Ex-German Army; deal worth $1.4 m
	..	HOT-2	Anti-tank missile	1996		..	For 87 RJPZ-1 tank destroyers
Netherlands	(114)	Leopard-2	Main battle tank	1996		..	Ex-Dutch Army; deal worth $236 m

Supplier (S)	No. ordered	Weapon designation	Weapon description	Year of order	Year(s) of deliveries	No. delivered	Comments
USA	54	M-109A5 155mm	Self-propelled gun		1996	(6)	Austrian designation M-109A5Ö; deal worth $48.6 m
Bahrain							
S: Netherlands	25	AIFV	AIFV	(1995)	1996	(25)	Ex-Dutch Army
USA	14	Bell-209/AH-1E	Combat helicopter	1994	1995–96	(14)	Ex-US Army
	10	Bell-209/AH-1E	Combat helicopter	1995		..	Ex-US Army
	6	Bell-209/AH-1E	Combat helicopter	1995		..	Ex-US Army; refurbished before delivery
	1	AN/SPG-60 STIR	Fire control radar	1995		..	On 1 ex-US Navy FFG-7 Class frigate
	1	AN/SPS-49	Surveillance radar	1995		..	On 1 ex-US Navy FFG-7 Class frigate
	1	AN/SPS-55	Surveillance radar	1995		..	On 1 ex-US Navy FFG-7 Class frigate
	1	I-HAWK SAMS	SAM system	1995		..	Ex-US Army; EDA aid
	1	Phalanx	CIWS	1995		..	On 1 ex-US Navy FFG-7 Class frigate
	1	Standard-1 ShAMS	ShAM system	1995		..	On 1 ex-US Navy FFG-7 Class frigate
	1	WM-28	Fire control radar	1995		..	On 1 ex-US Navy FFG-7 Class frigate
	..	MIM-23B HAWK	SAM	1995		..	Ex-US Army; for 1 I-Hawk SAM system
	60	RIM-66B Standard-1MR	ShAM	1995		..	For 1 FFG-7 Class frigate
	1	FFG-7 Class	Frigate	1995		..	Ex-US Navy; status uncertain
Bangladesh							
S: China	4	T-43 Class	Minesweeper	(1993)	1995–96	2	Bangladeshi designation Sagar Class
Belgium							
S: France	14	LG-1 105mm	Towed gun	1996	1996	(6)	Deal worth $11 m
USA	2	MD Explorer	Helicopter	1996	1996	2	Option on 1 more; for Gendarmerie
	(72)	AIM-120B AMRAAM	Air-to-air missile	1995		..	For F-16A/B-MLU FGA aircraft
Belize							
S: UK	(1)	Firefly-160	Trainer aircraft	1996		..	

Recipient/ supplier (S) or licenser (L)	No. ordered	Weapon designation	Weapon description	Year of order/ licence	Year(s) of deliveries	No. delivered/ produced	Comments
Bosnia-Herzegovina							
S: Egypt	12	D-30 122mm	Towed gun	1996	1996	12	Ex-Egyptian Army; gift
	12	M-46 130mm	Towed gun	1996	1996	12	Ex-Egyptian Army; gift
USA	15	Bell-205/UH-1H	Helicopter	1996	1996	15	Ex-US Army; part of 'Train and equip' aid programme
	80	M-113A2	APC	1996	1996	80	Ex-US Army; part of 'Train and equip' aid programme
	45	M-60A3 Patton-2	Main battle tank	1996	1996	45	Ex-US Army; part of 'Train and equip' aid programme
UAE	36	L-118 105mm	Towed gun	1996	1996	(36)	Ex-UAE Army
Botswana							
S: Canada	13	CF-5A Freedom Fighter	FGA aircraft	1996	1996	(3)	Ex-Canadian Air Force; refurbished before delivery; deal worth $50 m; incl 3 CF-5D trainer version
UK	(12)	L-118 105mm	Towed gun	(1994)	1995–96	(12)	Ex-Belgian Army resold to producer; refurbished before delivery; probably incl some Spartan APCs
	36	Scorpion	Light tank	(1994)	1995–96	(36)	
Brazil							
S: Belgium	61	Leopard-1A1	Main battle tank	1995	1996	61	Ex-Belgian Army
France	20	AS-550L1 Fennec	Helicopter	1992	1993–96	(20)	Deal worth $25 m
	57	Eryx	Anti-tank missile	1995	1996	(57)	
	(100)	Mistral	Portable SAM	1994	1996	(50)	
Germany	4	Grajau Class	Patrol craft	1993	1995–96	4	
	2	Grajau Class	Patrol craft	1996		..	
Italy	6	Albatros Mk-2	ShAM system	1995	1995–96	..	For refit of 6 Niteroi Class frigates; deal worth $160 m incl 13 Orion RTN-30X and 7 RAN-20S radars and Aspide missiles

Supplier/Recipient	No. ordered	Weapon designation	Weapon description	Year of order	Year of delivery	No. delivered	Comments
	13	Orion RTN-30X	Fire control radar	1995		..	For refit of 6 Niteroi Class frigates; deal worth $160 m incl 7 RAN-20S radars, 6 Albatros ShAM systems and Aspide missiles
	7	RAN-20S	Surveillance radar	1995		..	For refit of 6 Niteroi Class frigates; deal worth $160 m incl Orion 13 RTN-30X radars, 6 Albatros ShAM systems and Aspide missiles
	(144)	Aspide	ShAM	1996		..	For 6 refitted Niteroi Class frigates; deal worth $48.5 m
Sweden	5	Erieye	AEW radar	1994		..	Deal worth $125 m; for EMB-120 AEW aircraft
	(2)	Giraffe-40	Surveillance radar	(1994)	1995–96	(2)	For use with ASTROS-2 MLR/coast defence system
	..	RBS-56 Bill	Anti-tank missile	1995	1996	(50)	Deal worth $9.3 m; for Marines
UK	9	Super Lynx	ASW helicopter	1993		..	Deal worth $221 m incl refurbishment of 5 Brazilian Navy Lynx to Super Lynx; for Navy
	1	114mm Mk-8	Naval gun	1994		..	For 1 Improved Inhaúma (Barroso) Class frigate
	(36)	L-118 105mm	Towed gun	1994	1995–96	(36)	Deal worth $60 m incl L-16 81mm mortars
	4	MM-38 ShShMS	ShShM system	1994	1995–96	3	On 4 ex-UK Navy Broadsword Class frigates
	8	Seawolf ShAMS	ShAM system	1994	1995–96	6	On 4 ex-UK Navy Broadsword Class frigates
	8	Type-911	Fire control radar	1994	1995–96	6	On 4 ex-UK Navy Broadsword Class frigates
	4	Type-967/968	Surveillance radar	1994	1995–96	3	On 4 ex-UK Navy Broadsword Class frigates
	..	Seawolf	ShAM	1994	1995–96	(96)	For 4 Broadsword Class frigates
	4	Broadsword Class	Frigate	1994	1995–96	3	Ex-UK Navy; Brazilian designation Greenhalgh Class
USA	13	S-61/SH-3D Sea King	Helicopter	1994	1995–96	13	Ex-US Navy; deal worth $900,000; EDA aid
	14	LVTP-7A1	APC	1995		..	Deal worth $23 m incl 1 ARV and 1 APC/CP version
	91	M-60A3 Patton-2	Main battle tank	1996		..	Ex-US Army; lease
L: Germany	1	SNAC-1	Submarine	1995		..	Brazilian designation Tocantins Class
	3	Type-209/1400	Submarine	1984	1994–96	2	Brazilian designation Tupi Class
Brunei							
S: Indonesia	1	CN-235	Transport aircraft	1995		..	
	3	CN-235MPA	MP aircraft	1995		..	
UK	6	Hawk-100	FGA/trainer aircraft	1996		..	

Recipient/ supplier (S) or licenser (L)	No. ordered	Weapon designation	Weapon description	Year of order/ licence	Year(s) of deliveries	No. delivered/ produced	Comments
USA	4	Hawk-200	FGA aircraft	1996	..	:	Deal worth $948 m
	3	Yarrow-95m Type	Frigate	1995	..	:	
	4	S-70A/UH-60L	Helicopter	1996	..	:	
Bulgaria S: Russia	6	Yak-18T	Light aircraft	1995	1996	6	Ex-Russian Army; gift
	100	BMP-1	AIFV	1995	1996	100	Ex-Russian Army; gift
	100	T-72	Main battle tank	1995	1996	100	Ex-Russian Army; gift
Cambodia S: Czech Republic	6	L-39Z Albatros	Jet trainer aircraft	(1994)	1996	(6)	Ex-Czech Air Force; deal worth $3.6 m incl refurbishment and training in Israel
Canada S: France	1 600	Eryx	Anti-tank missile	1996	1996	1 600	Deal worth $17 m
Netherlands	24	STIR	Fire control radar	(1985)	1992–96	(24)	For 12 Halifax (City) Class frigates
Sweden	12	Sea Giraffe-150	Surveillance radar	(1985)	1992–96	(12)	For 12 Halifax (City) Class frigates
UK	(152)	MSTAR	Battlefield radar	1994	1995–96	(100)	For use on 152 LAV-25 (Coyote) AIFVs
USA	2	C-130/L-100-30	Transport aircraft	1996	..	:	Deal worth $79 m
	12	AN/SPS-49	Surveillance radar	1985	1992–96	(12)	For 12 Halifax (City) Class frigates
	12	RGM-84A ShShMS	ShShM system	1983	1992–96	(12)	For 12 Halifax (City) Class frigates
	12	Seasparrow VLS	ShAM system	1983	1992–96	(12)	Deal worth $75 m incl missiles, for 12 Halifax (City) Class frigates
	(192)	RGM-84A Harpoon	ShShM	1988	1992–96	(192)	For 12 Halifax (City) Class frigates
	(336)	RIM-7H Seasparrow	ShAM	1984	1992–96	(336)	Deal worth $75 m incl 12 Seasparrow VLS ShAM systems; for 12 Halifax (City) Class frigates
L: Switzerland	203	LAV-25	AIFV	1993	1996	(100)	Deal worth $367 m; Canadian designation Coyote
	240	Piranha-3 8x8	APC	1995	..	:	Deal worth $1.49 b incl option on 411 more

Supplier	No. ordered	Weapon designation	Weapon description	Year of order	Year of deliveries	No. delivered	Comments
USA	100	Bell-412	Helicopter	1992	1994–96	(78)	Deal worth $558 m; Canadian designation CH-146 Griffon
Chile							
S: Belgium	20	Mirage-5 MIRSIP	FGA aircraft	1994	1995–96	20	Ex-Belgian Air Force Mirage-5s rebuilt to MIRSIP standard; incl 5 trainer version; deal worth $54 m incl 5 Mirage-5BA FGA aircraft, Chilean designation Elkan
	5	Mirage-5BA	FGA aircraft	1994	1995–96	5	Ex-Belgian Air Force; incl 1 Mirage-5BP trainer version
France	4	AS-532SC Cougar	ASW helicopter	1988	1995–96	(4)	Deal worth $77 m; for Navy
	:	AM-39 Exocet	Air-to-ship missile	1992		:	For 6 Navy AS-532SC helicopters
	:	Mistral	Portable SAM	(1990)	1991–96	(1 200)	
Israel	(4)	Barak ShAMS	ShAM system	1989	1993–95	(2)	For refit of 4 Prat (County) Class destroyers
	4	ELM-2106	Surveillance radar	(1989)	1993–95	(2)	For refit of 4 Prat (County) Class destroyers
	8	ELM-2221	Fire control radar	(1989)	1993–95	(4)	For refit of 4 Prat (County) Class destroyers
	2	Gabriel ShShMS	ShShM system	1996		:	On 2 ex-Israeli Navy Reshef Class FAC(M)s
	2	Orion RTN-10X	Fire control radar	1996		:	On 2 ex-Israeli Navy Reshef Class FAC(M)s
	2	Phalanx	CIWS	1996		:	On 2 ex-Israeli Navy Reshef Class FAC(M)s
	2	THD-1040 Neptune	Surveillance radar	1996		:	On 2 ex-Israeli Navy Reshef Class FAC(M)s
	:	Barak	ShAM	1989	1993–95	(32)	For 4 refitted Prat (County) Class destroyers
	(24)	Gabriel-2	ShShM	1996		:	For 2 ex-Israeli Navy Reshef Class FAC(M)s
	:	Python-3	Air-to-air missile	(1988)	1992–96	(132)	For upgraded Mirage-50 (Pantera) and F-5E (Tigre III) fighters
Sweden	2	Reshef Class	FAC(M)	1996		:	Ex-Israeli Navy; designation uncertain
	1	Alvsborg Class	Minelayer	1996		:	Ex-Swedish Navy; refitted before delivery; deal worth $2.5 m
UK	30	Scorpion	Light tank	1995	1995–96	(30)	Ex-UK Army; for Marines
USA	1	Boeing-737-500	Transport aircraft	1996		:	For VIP transport
L: Switzerland	(120)	Piranha 8x8D	APC	(1991)	1993–96	(82)	
UK	:	Rayo	MRL	1995		:	Status uncertain

Recipient/ supplier (S) or licenser (L)	No. ordered	Weapon designation	Weapon description	Year of order/ licence	Year(s) of deliveries	No. delivered/ produced	Comments
China							
S: France	(5)	DRBV-15 Sea Tiger	Surveillance radar	1986	1987–96	4	For 3 Luhu Class (Type-052) and some Luda-2 Class (Type-051) destroyers
Israel	1	ELM-2075 Phalcon	AEW radar	(1996)		..	Fitted in China on 1 ex-civilian Boeing-707
Russia	24	Su-27 Flanker	Fighter aircraft	1995	1996	24	Deal worth $2.2 b; incl 6 Su-27UB trainer version
	(200)	T-80U	Main battle tank	1993	1996	(200)	
	(4)	SA-10b SAMS	SAM system	1992	1993	(3)	
	(288)	AA-11 Archer	Air-to-air missile	1995	1996	(288)	For 24 Su-27 fighters
	(192)	SA-10 Grumble	SAM	(1992)	1993	(144)	For 4 SA-10b SAM systems
	2	Kilo Class	Submarine	(1994)		..	
UK	(6)	Searchwater	AEW radar	1996		..	Deal worth $62 m; for use on Y-8 AEW aircraft
USSR	(2)	Ka-27 Helix-A	ASW helicopter	(1991)		..	For Navy
Ukraine	(144)	AA-10a Alamo	Air-to-air missile	1995	1996	(144)	For 24 Su-27 Flanker fighters
L: France	(30)	AS-365N Dauphin-2	Helicopter	1988	1992–96	(5)	Chinese designation Z-9A-100 Haitun
	..	SA-321H Super Frelon	Helicopter	(1981)	1985–96	(15)	Chinese designation Z-8
Israel	..	Python-3	ShAM	(1989)	1990–96	(3 840)	Chinese designation PL-8H
	..	Python-3	Air-to-air missile	1990	1990–96	(5 637)	Chinese designation PL-9
Russia	120	Su-27SK Flanker	Fighter aircraft	1996		..	Chinese designation J-11
Colombia							
S: Brazil	..	EE-11 Urutu	APC	(1994)		..	
	..	EE-9 Cascavel	Armoured car	(1994)		..	
Canada	12	Bell-212	Helicopter	(1994)	1994–96	(12)	
Germany	3	Do-328-100	Transport aircraft	1996	1996	2	For military airline SATENA
Russia	10	Mi-17 Hip-H	Helicopter	1996	1996	(2)	For Army; deal worth $49 m
USA	6	S-70/UH-60 Blackhawk	Helicopter	1993	1994–96	6	
	12	S-70/UH-60 Blackhawk	Helicopter	1996		..	

Supplier (S)	No. ordered	Weapon designation	Weapon description	Year of order	Year(s) of deliveries	No. delivered	Comments
Congo							
S: Italy	3	G-222	Transport aircraft				
Croatia							
S: Canada	10	Bell-206B JetRanger-3	Helicopter	1996		..	Deal worth $15 m
Georgia	(10)	Su-25 Frogfoot	Ground attack ac	(1995)		..	Supplier uncertain
Switzerland	(3)	PC-9	Trainer aircraft	(1996)	1996	(3)	
Cyprus							
S: Russia	43	BMP-3	AIFV	1995	1995–96	41	Deal worth $68 m
	41	T-80U	Main battle tank	1996	1996	(41)	Deal worth $82 m
	..	SA-10a SAMS	SAM system	1996		..	
	(344)	AT-10 Bastion	Anti-tank missile	(1995)	1995–96	(344)	For 43 BMP-3 AIFVs
	(246)	AT-11 Sniper	Anti-tank missile	1996	1996	(246)	For 41 T-80U tanks
	..	SA-10 Grumble	SAM	1996		..	
Czech Republic							
S: Poland	11	W-3 Sokol	Helicopter	1995	1996	(8)	Exchanged for 10 ex-Czech Air Force MiG-29 fighters
Denmark							
S: France	8	RAC	Surveillance radar	1996		..	Deal worth $35 m
Germany	14	TRS-3D	Surveillance radar	1990	1993–95	(5)	For 14 Flyvefisken Class (Stanflex-300 Type) patrol craft/MCM ships
Italy	1	RAT-31SL	Surveillance radar	1995		..	
Sweden	(14)	9LV	Fire control radar	(1988)	1989–96	(14)	For 14 Flyvefisken Class (Stanflex-300 Type) patrol craft/MCM ships
USA	8	MLRS 227mm	MRL	1996		..	Deal worth $20 m; option on more; for 4 Flyvefisken Class (Stanflex-300 Type) patrol craft/MCM ships
	4	Seasparrow VLS	ShAM system	1993		..	
	..	AIM-120A AMRAAM	Air-to-air missile	1994		..	For F-16A/B-MLU FGA aircraft

Recipient/ supplier (S) or licenser (L)	No. ordered	Weapon designation	Weapon description	Year of order/ licence	Year(s) of deliveries	No. delivered/ produced	Comments
	840	FIM-92A Stinger	Portable SAM	1991	1994-96	(840)	Deal worth $150 m
	..	RIM-7H Seasparrow	ShAM	(1994)		..	For 4 Flyvefisken Class (Stanflex-300 Type) patrol craft/MCM ships
Ecuador							
S: Argentina	36	M-114A1 155mm	Towed gun	1995		..	Ex-Argentine Army; illegal deal worth $34 m incl 18 M-101A1 guns and small arms
Israel	4	Kfir C-7	FGA aircraft	1995	1996	4	Ex-Israeli Air Force
Egypt							
S: Netherlands	599	AIFV	AIFV	1994	1996	599	Ex-Dutch Army; deal worth $135 m incl 12 M-577 APC/CPs and training; incl 210 AIFV-TOW tank destroyers, 6 AIFV-CP APC/CPs and 79 AIFV-APC APCs
	12	M-577A1	APC/CP	1994	1996	12	Ex-Dutch Army; deal worth $135 m incl 599 AIFVs and training
USA	24	AH-64A Apache	Combat helicopter	1990	1995-96	(24)	Deal worth $488 m incl 492 AGM-114A missiles; aid
	12	AH-64A Apache	Combat helicopter	1995	1996	(6)	Deal worth $518 m incl armament
	46	F-16C Fighting Falcon	FGA aircraft	1991	1994-96	46	'Peace Vector IV' programme worth $1.6 b incl armament; incl 12 F-16D trainer version; from Turkish production line
	21	F-16C Fighting Falcon	FGA aircraft	1996		..	Financed by USA
	2	Gulfstream-4	Transport aircraft	1996		..	Deal worth $80 m; for VIP transport
	2	S-70/UH-60 Blackhawk	Helicopter	1995		..	Deal worth $42 m incl 2 spare engines; for VIP transport
	10	SH-2F Seasprite	ASW helicopter	1994		..	Ex-US Navy; refurbished to SH-2G before delivery
	24	M-109/SP-122 122mm	Self-propelled gun	1996		..	Deal worth $28 m; FMF aid
	130	M-901 ITV	Tank destroyer (M)	1995		..	Ex-US Army
	1	AN/SPG-60 STIR	Fire control radar	1996	1996	(1)	On 1 ex-US Navy FFG-7 Class frigate

No.	Weapon designation	Weapon description	Year of order	Year(s) of deliveries	No. delivered	Comments
2	AN/SPG-60 STIR	Fire control radar	1996		..	On 2 ex-US Navy FFG-7 Class frigates
2	AN/SPS-55	Surveillance radar	1996		..	On 2 ex-US Navy FFG-7 Class frigates
1	AN/SPS-55	Surveillance radar	1996	1996	(1)	On 1 ex-US Navy FFG-7 Class frigate
1	Phalanx	CIWS	1996	1996	(1)	On 1 ex-US Navy FFG-7 Class frigate
2	Phalanx	CIWS	1996		..	On 2 ex-US Navy FFG-7 Class frigates
30	Scout	Surveillance radar	1992	1995–96	(30)	For Coastal Border Surveillance System (CBSS)
1	Standard-1 ShAMS	ShAM system	1996	1996	(1)	On 1 ex-US Navy FFG-7 Class frigate
2	Standard-1 ShAMS	ShAM system	1996		..	On 2 ex-US Navy FFG-7 Class frigates
1	WM-28	Fire control radar	1996	1996	(1)	On 1 ex-US Navy FFG-7 Class frigate
2	WM-28	Fire control radar	1996		..	On 2 ex-US Navy FFG-7 Class frigates
927	AGM-114K Hellfire	Anti-tank missile	1996		..	Deal worth $45 m
271	AIM-7M Sparrow	Air-to-air missile	1996		..	For F-16C fighters; deal worth $80 m
..	BGM-71D TOW-2	Anti-tank missile	1996		..	Deal worth $59 m
(36)	RIM-66B Standard-1MR	ShAM	1996	1996	(36)	For 1 ex-US Navy FFG-7 Class frigate
34	RIM-66B Standard-1MR	ShAM	1996		..	For 1 ex-US Navy FFG-7 Class frigate
40	RIM-66B Standard-1MR	ShAM	1996		..	For 1 ex-US Navy FFG-7 Class frigate
29	UGM-84A Sub Harpoon	SuShM	1990	1992–96	(29)	For 4 refitted Romeo Class submarines; deal worth $69 m
1	FFG-7 Class	Frigate	1996	1996	1	Ex-US Navy; Egyptian designation Sharm el-Sheik Class
1	FFG-7 Class	Frigate	1996		..	Ex-US Navy; aid; Egyptian designation Sharm el-Sheik Class
1	FFG-7 Class	Frigate	1996	1996	..	Ex-US Navy; deal worth $188 m; Egyptian designation Sharm el-Sheik Class
L: USA						
31	M-1A1 Abrams	Main battle tank	1996	1990–96	(3 232)	..
..	AIM-9P Sidewinder	Air-to-air missile	(1988)			
Eritrea						
S: Italy						
6	MB-339FD	Jet trainer aircraft	1996	1996	..	Deal worth $45 m
Estonia						
S: France						
..	Rasit-E	Battlefield radar	1996	1996		

Recipient/ supplier (S) or licenser (L)	No. ordered	Weapon designation	Weapon description	Year of order/ licence	Year(s) of deliveries	No. delivered/ produced	Comments
Israel	(13)	Mapats	Anti-tank missile	(1993)	1994–96	(13)	
Finland							
S: Italy	1	Bell-412EP/AB-412EP	Helicopter	1995	1996	1	For Border Guard
Russia	3	SA-11 SAMS	SAM system	1996	1996	(1)	Deal worth $185 m incl missiles; part of payment of Russian debt
	(288)	SA-11 Gadfly	SAM	1996	1996	(96)	Deal worth $185 m incl 3 SA-11 SAM systems; part of payment of Russian debt
Sweden	4	Giraffe-100	Surveillance radar	1992	1993–96	(4)	Incl assembly from kits in Finland
USA	57	F/A-18C Hornet	FGA aircraft	1992	1993–96	:	
	7	F/A-18D Hornet	FGA/trainer aircraft	1992	1995–96	(7)	
	(250)	AIM-120A AMRAAM	Air-to-air missile	1992	1996	(25)	For 64 F/A-18C/D FGA aircraft
	480	AIM-9S Sidewinder	Air-to-air missile	1992	1996	(50)	For 64 F/A-18C/D FGA aircraft
France							
S: Brazil	80	EMB-312 Tucano	Trainer aircraft	1991	1993–96	(50)	Deal worth $170 m
South Africa	5	Husky	AMV	1996	1996	(3)	Part of 'Chubby' mine-clearing system; for use in Bosnia
	5	Meerkat	AMV	1996	1996	(3)	Part of 'Chubby' mine-clearing system; for use in Bosnia
Spain	7	CN-235	Transport aircraft	1996		:	Deal worth $90 m (offsets 100%, incl Spanish order for 15 AS-552UL helicopters)
USA	4	E-2C Hawkeye	AEW&C aircraft	1995		:	For Navy
	5	KC-135A Stratotanker	Tanker aircraft	1994		:	Ex-US Air Force; deal worth $220 m; refurbished to KC-135R before delivery
Germany							
S: Netherlands	4	LW-08	Surveillance radar	(1989)	1994–96	(4)	For 4 Brandenburg Class (Type-123) frigates

No.	Designation	Description	Year of order	Year(s) of delivery	No. delivered	Comments
5	SMART	Surveillance radar	1989	1994–96	(5)	For 4 Brandenburg Class (Type-123) frigates and 1 shore-based training centre
8	STIR	Fire control radar	1989	1994–96	(8)	For 4 Brandenburg Class (Type-123) frigates
(9)	HARD	Surveillance radar	1995		..	For 3 ASRAD SAM systems
7	Super Lynx	ASW helicopter	1996		..	Deal worth $154 m; UK export designation Lynx Mk-88A; for Navy
4	Seasparrow VLS	ShAM system	1989	1994–96	(4)	For 4 Brandenburg Class (Type-123) frigates
96	AIM-120A AMRAAM	Air-to-air missile	1991	1995	48	For refurbished F-4F FGA aircraft; deal worth $53.6 m; options on 224 more
96	AIM-120B AMRAAM	Air-to-air missile	1995		..	
(64)	RIM-7H Seasparrow	ShAM	1989	1994–96	(64)	For 4 Brandenburg Class (Type-123) frigates
(1 065)	RIM-116A RAM	ShAM	1985	1989–96	(1 065)	For 3 refitted Lütjens (Adams) Class destroyers, 4 Brandenburg (Type-123), 8 Bremen (Type-122) and 3 Type-124 frigates and 10 refitted Gepard (Type-143A) Class FAC(M)s

Sweden

UK

USA

L: USA

Ghana

S: Italy

No.	Designation	Description	Year of order	Year(s) of delivery	No. delivered	Comments
4	Bell-412/AB-412	Helicopter	1995	1996	(1)	

Greece

S: France

No.	Designation	Description	Year of order	Year(s) of delivery	No. delivered	Comments
5	TRS-3050 Triton-G	Surveillance radar	(1986)	1994–96	(2)	For 5 Jason Class landing ships
5	TRS-3220 Pollux	Fire control radar	(1986)	1994–96	(2)	For 5 Jason Class landing ships
4	DA-08	Surveillance radar	(1989)	1992–96	(2)	For 4 Meko-200HN Type (Hydra Class) frigates
4	MW-08	Surveillance radar	(1989)	1992–96	(2)	For 4 Meko-200HN Type (Hydra Class) frigates
8	STIR	Fire control radar	1989	1992–96	(4)	For 4 Meko-200HN Type (Hydra Class) frigates
..	Penguin Mk-2-7	Air-to-ship missile	1996		..	For S-70B/SH-60B helicopters
1	Martello-743D	Surveillance radar	1995		..	
20	AH-64A Apache	Combat helicopter	(1991)	1995–96	(12)	Deal worth $505 m incl 3 spare engines; for Army
9	Bell 209/AH-1P	Combat helicopter	1994		..	Ex-US Army; deal worth $2.4 m
40	F-16C Fighting Falcon	FGA aircraft	1993		..	'Peace Xenia' programme worth $1.8 b incl 10 spare engines and 40 LANTIRN pods; incl 8 F-16D trainer version

Netherlands

Norway

UK

USA

Recipient/ supplier (S) or licenser (L)	No. ordered	Weapon designation	Weapon description	Year of order/ licence	Year(s) of deliveries	No. delivered/ produced	Comments
	(4)	P-3A Orion	ASW/MP aircraft	1994	1995-96	(4)	Ex-US Navy; incl 2 for training and 2 for spares only
	4	P-3B Orion	ASW/MP aircraft	1994	1996	(1)	Ex-US Navy; lease worth $69 m; refurbished before delivery
	5	S-70B/SH-60B Seahawk	ASW helicopter	1991	1994-96	5	Deal worth $161 m; option on 3 more; Greek designation Aegean Hawk
	4	127mm/54 Mk-45	Naval gun	(1989)	1992-96	(2)	For 4 Meko-200HN Type (Hydra Class) frigates
	8	Phalanx	CIWS	1988	1992-96	4	For 4 Meko-200HN Type (Hydra Class) frigates
	4	Phalanx	CIWS	1996		..	Deal worth $46 m; for refit of 4 Kimon (Adams) Class destroyers
	4	RGM-84A ShShMS	ShShM system	1989	1992-96	(2)	For 4 Meko-200HN Type (Hydra Class) frigates
	4	Seasparrow VLS	ShAM system	1988	1992-96	(2)	For 4 Meko-200HN Type (Hydra Class) frigates
	446	AGM-114A Hellfire	Anti-tank missile	1991	1995-96	(300)	For 20 AH-64A helicopters
	52	AGM-88B HARM	Anti-radar missile	1994		..	Deal worth $27 m; for F-16 fighters
	84	AGM-88B HARM	Anti-radar missile	1996		..	Deal worth $90 m incl 50 AIM-120B missiles
	100	AIM-120A AMRAAM	Air-to-air missile	(1995)		..	Deal worth $70 m
	50	AIM-120B AMRAAM	Air-to-air missile	1996		..	For F-16C/D FGA aircraft; deal worth $90 m incl 84 AGM-88B missiles
	40	ATACMS	SSM	1996		..	Deal worth $60 m
	32	RGM-84A Harpoon	ShShM	1993	1995-96	(32)	Part of deal worth $170 m incl torpedoes, ASROC and ammunition for Knox Class frigates
	..	RIM-7H Seasparrow	ShAM	(1988)	1992-96	(32)	For 4 Meko-200HN Type (Hydra Class) frigates
	..	UGM-84A Sub Harpoon	SuShM	(1989)	1993-96	(24)	For 4 Type-209 (Glavkos Class) submarines
L: Austria	267	Steyr 4K-7FA	APC	1987	1990-96	(267)	Greek designation Leonidas-2; incl around 90 for export
Germany	3	Meko-200HN Type	Frigate	1988	1996	1	Deal worth $1.2 b incl 1 delivered direct (offsets $250 m); partly financed by Germany and USA; Greek designation Hydra Class

	No.	Weapon designation	Weapon description	Year of order	Year(s) of deliveries	No. delivered	Comments
Hungary							
S: Belarus	100	T-72	Main battle tank	(1996)	1996	100	Ex-Belarus Army; deal worth $13 m
Russia	97	BTR-80	APC	1995	1996	(97)	For Border Guard
	(68)	BTR-80	APC	1995	1996	(68)	
	(320)	BTR-80	APC	1994	1996	(320)	
India							
S: Italy	(6)	Seaguard TMX	Fire control radar	1993		:	For 3 Improved Godavari Class (Project-16A Type) frigates
Russia	8	MiG-29SE Fulcrum-C	FGA aircraft	1994	1996	8	
	2	MiG-29UB Fulcrum	Fighter/trainer ac	1995	1996	2	
	40	Su-30M Flanker	FGA aircraft	1996		:	Deal worth $1.8 b; incl 12 Su-30MK2 version and 20 other improved version
	12	2S6 Tunguska	AAV(G/M)	1995	1995–96	(12)	
	3	SS-N-2 ShShMS	ShShM system	1993	1993	:	For 3 Improved Godavari Class (Project-16A Type) frigates
	:	AA-11 Archer	Air-to-air missile	1995	1996	(180)	For 10 MiG-29SE/UB FGA aircraft
	(192)	SA-19 Grisom	SAM	1995	1995–96	(192)	For 12 2S6 AAV(G/M)s
	:	SS-N-22 Sunburn	ShShM	1992	1992	:	For 4 Delhi Class (Project-15 Type) destroyers
	:	SS-N-2e Styx	ShShM	1993	1993	:	For 3 Improved Godavari Class (Project-16A Type) frigates
USSR	8	Bass Tilt	Fire control radar	1983	1989–96	(5)	For 8 Khukri Class (Project-25/25A Type) corvettes
	7	Bass Tilt	Fire control radar	(1987)	1991–96	(5)	For 7 Tarantul-1 (Vibhuti) Class FAC(M)s
	8	Cross Dome	Surveillance radar	(1983)	1989–96	(5)	For 8 Khukri Class (Project-25/25A Type) corvettes
	7	Plank Shave	Surveillance radar	(1987)	1991–96	(5)	For 7 Tarantul-1 (Vibhuti) Class FAC(M)s
	8	Plank Shave	Surveillance radar	(1983)	1989–96	(5)	For 8 Khukri Class (Project-25/25A Type) corvettes
	8	SS-N-2 ShShMS	ShShM system	1983	1989–96	(5)	For 8 Khukri Class (Project-25/25A Type) corvettes
	7	SS-N-2 ShShMS	ShShM system	1987	1991–96	(5)	For 7 Tarantul-1 (Vibhuti) Class FAC(M)s
	:	SA-N-5 Grail	ShAM	(1983)	1989–96	(200)	For 8 Khukri Class (Project-25/25A Type) corvettes
	:	SA-N-5 Grail	ShAM	1987	1991–96	(200)	For 7 Tarantul-1 (Vibhuti) Class FAC(M)s
	:	SS-N-2d Styx	ShShM	1983	1989–96	(40)	For 8 Khukri Class (Project-25/25A Type) corvettes
	:	SS-N-2d Styx	ShShM	1987	1991–96	(40)	For 7 Tarantul-1 (Vibhuti) Class FAC(M)s

Recipient/ supplier (S) or licenser (L)	No. ordered	Weapon designation	Weapon description	Year of order/ licence	Year(s) of deliveries	No. delivered/ produced	Comments
L: France	:	PSM-33	Surveillance radar	1988	1990–96	(7)	For Coast Guard
Germany	33	Do-228MP	MP aircraft	1983	1987–96	(33)	For Navy
	(27)	Do-228MP	MP aircraft	(1989)	1991–96	(12)	Option on 1 more
	1	Aditya Class	Support ship	1987	1996	1	
Korea, South	8	Sukanya Class	OPV	1987	1990–96	6	Incl 4 Samar Class for Coast Guard
Netherlands	212	Flycatcher	Fire control radar	(1987)	1988–96	(162)	Indian designation PTW-519
UK	15	Jaguar International	FGA aircraft	1993	1995–96	(10)	Indian designation Shamsher
	2	Magar Class	Landing ship	1985	1994–96	2	
USSR	165	MiG-27L Flogger-J	FGA aircraft	1983	1984–96	(165)	Indian designation Bahadur
	7	Tarantul-1 Class	FAC(M)	1987	1991–96	5	Indian designation Vibhuti Class
Indonesia							
S: Australia	14	N-22B Missionmaster	Transport aircraft	1996		:	Ex-Australian Air Force
	6	N-24A Nomad	Transport aircraft	1996		:	Ex-Australian Army
France	20	LG-1 105mm	Towed gun	1994	1995–96	(20)	Deal worth $17.5 m incl ammunition; for Marines
	18	VBL	Scout car	1996		:	Option on 46 more
	:	Mistral	Portable SAM	1996		:	For Navy
	:	Mistral	Portable SAM	1996		:	
Germany	5	Wiesel	Scout car	1996		:	
	2	Wiesel-2	APC	1996		:	
	16	Muff Cob	Fire control radar	1992	1993–96	16	Former GDR equipment; on 16 Parchim Class corvettes
	30	Strut Curve	Surveillance radar	1992	1993–96	30	Former GDR equipment; on 16 Parchim corvettes, 12 Frosch-1 landing ships and 2 Frosch-2 supply ships
UK	16	Parchim Class	Corvette	1992	1993–96	16	Former GDR ships; refitted before delivery
	14	Hawk-100	FGA/trainer aircraft	1993	1996	(8)	
	10	Hawk-200	FGA aircraft	1993	1996	(8)	
	16	Hawk-200	FGA aircraft	1996		:	
	(30)	Scorpion-90	Light tank	1995	1995–96	(30)	

Supplier	No.	Weapon designation	Weapon description	Year of order	Year(s) of deliveries	No. delivered	Comments
USA	(91)	Stormer	APC			(31)	Incl 2 APC/CPs and some ambulance version
	(14)	AR-325	Surveillance radar	1989	1991–95	(10)	
	2	TA-4J Skyhawk	FGA/trainer aircraft	(1996)	1996	2	Ex-US Navy
L: Germany	4	PB-57 Type	Patrol craft	1993		..	Indonesian designation Singa Class
USA	1	Bell-412	Helicopter	1996		..	Deal worth $4.2 m; for Navy
Iran							
S: China	(10)	ESR-1	Surveillance radar	1992	1994–96	10	On 10 Hudong Class FAC(M)s
	(10)	Rice Lamp	Fire control radar	1992	1994–96	10	On 10 Hudong Class FAC(M)s
	..	C-802	ShShM	1992	1995–96	(80)	For 10 Hudong Class FAC(M)s
	(10)	C-802 ShShMS	ShShM system	1992	1994–96	10	On 10 Hudong Class FAC(M)s
	(10)	Hudong Class	FAC(M)	1992	1994–96	10	On 10 Hudong Class FAC(M)s
Poland	110	T-72M1	Main battle tank	(1993)	1994–96	110	
Russia	1	Kilo Class	Submarine	1993	1996	1	
USSR	(200)	T-72	Main battle tank	1989	1993–94	120	
Ukraine	(16)	SS-N-22 Sunburn	ShShM	(1993)	1995	(12)	For coast defence system
Israel							
S: France	5	AS-565SA Panther	ASW helicopter	1994	1996	2	Ordered through USA; partly financed by USA; Israeli designation Aralef
Germany	22	TB-20 Trinidad	Trainer aircraft	(1994)	1996	22	Israeli designation Paskosh
Germany	2	Dolphin Class	Submarine	1991		..	Deal worth $570 m; financed by Germany
Russia	45	BRDM-2	Scout car	1994	1995	15	Ex-Russian Army; for PLO police; gift
USA	(25)	Bell-209/AH-1E	Combat helicopter	(1995)	1996	(14)	Ex-US Army
	21	F-15I Strike Eagle	Fighter/bomber ac	1994		..	Deal worth $1.76 b (offsets $1 b); financed by USA
	4	F-15I Strike Eagle	Fighter/bomber ac	1995		..	
	42	MLRS 227mm	MRL	1995	1995–96	(12)	Deal worth $108m incl 1500 rockets
	36	M-48 Chaparral	AAV(M)	1996		..	Ex-US Army; EDA aid
	..	FIM-92A Stinger	Portable SAM	(1993)	1993–95	(300)	Ex-US Army; EDA aid
	500	MIM-72C Chaparral	SAM	1996		..	Ex-US Army; EDA aid

Recipient/ supplier (S) or licenser (L)	No. ordered	Weapon designation	Weapon description	Year of order/ licence	Year(s) of deliveries	No. delivered/ produced	Comments
Italy							
S: UK	24	Tornado ADV F-Mk-3	Fighter aircraft	1994	1995-96	(12)	Ex-UK Air Force; 10-year lease worth $360 m incl $200 m for logistical support
	..	Sky Flash	Air-to-air missile	1994	1995	(48)	For 24 Tornado ADV fighters
USA	13	AV-8B Harrier-2 Plus	FGA aircraft	1990	1996	(3)	Deal worth $522 m; assembled in Italy; for Navy
	42	AGM-65G Maverick	ASM	1994	1996	(14)	Deal worth $25 m; for Navy AV-8B+ FGA aircraft
	33	AIM-120A AMRAAM	Air-to-air missile	1994	1996	(12)	Deal worth $23 m; for Navy; for AV-8B+ FGA aircraft
	..	BGM-71D TOW-2	Anti-tank missile	1987	1990-96	(1 560)	For A-129 helicopters
L: France	23 000	Milan-2	Anti-tank missile	1984	1985-96	(19 133)	
Germany	2	Type-212	Submarine	1996		..	Option on 2 more
USA	77	Bell-412SP/AB-412SP	Helicopter	1980	1983-96	(72)	Incl 18 for Army, 34 for Police and 25 for Coast Guard; more produced for export and civil customers; incl Bell-412HP and Bell-412EP versions
Japan							
S: Italy	4	127mm/54	Naval gun	(1988)	1993-96	3	For 4 Kongo Class destroyers
Sweden	2	Saab 340B SAR-200	MP aircraft	1996	1995-96	..	For Coast Guard; for SAR; deal worth $21 m
UK	6	BAe-125-800	Transport aircraft	1992	1995-96	(6)	For SAR; Japanese designation U-125A; HS-X programme
USA	4	BAe-125/RH-800	Transport aircraft	1995		..	For SAR; Japanese designation U-125A; option on 20 more; HS-X programme
	2	Boeing-767/AWACS	AEW&C aircraft	1993		..	Deal worth $840 m
	2	Boeing-767/AWACS	AEW&C aircraft	1994		..	Deal worth $773 m
	1	C-130H Hercules	Transport aircraft	1995	1996	1	Deal worth $43 m
	(9)	Gulfstream-4	Transport aircraft	1994	1996	1	
	..	S-76C	Helicopter	1993	1994	2	For Maritime Safety Agency; for SAR
	36	MLRS 227mm	MRL	1993	1994-96	27	Deal worth $362 m

	No. ordered	Weapon designation	Weapon description	Year of order	Year of deliveries	No. delivered	Comments
	12	AN/SPG-62	Fire control radar	(1988)	1993–95	(6)	For 4 Kongo Class destroyers
	2	AN/SPY-1D	Surveillance radar	1992	1995–96	(2)	Part of Aegis air defence system for 2 Kongo Class destroyers
	1	AN/SPY-1D	Surveillance radar	(1993)		..	Part of Aegis air defence system for 1 Kongo Class destroyer
	6	Phalanx	CIWS	1988	1993–96	(6)	Deal worth $66 m; for 3 Kongo Class destroyers
	2	Phalanx	CIWS	1995		:	Deal worth $7.7 m; for 1 Kongo Class destroyer
	3	RGM-84A ShShMS	ShShM system	1994	1995–96	(2)	For 3 Kongo Class destroyers
	3	Standard VLS	ShAM system	1990	1995–96	(2)	Part of Aegis air defence system for 3 Kongo Class destroyers
	16	AGM-84A Harpoon	Air-to-ship missile	1994	1995	(6)	
	..	RIM-7H Seasparrow	ShAM	1993		:	Deal worth $13.4 m
L: France	..	MO-120-RT-61 120mm	Mortar	1992	1993–96	(212)	
Germany	..	FH-70 155mm	Towed gun	(1982)	1984–96	(430)	
USA	(90)	Bell-209/AH-1S	Combat helicopter	1982	1984–96	(84)	For Army
	(52)	CH-47D Chinook	Helicopter	(1984)	1986–96	(38)	For Army
	(22)	CH-47D Chinook	Helicopter	(1984)	1986–96	(16)	
	3	EP-3C Orion	ELINT aircraft	1992	1995–96	2	For Navy
	..	F-15DJ Eagle	FGA/trainer aircraft	1978	1988–96	(28)	
	..	F-15J Eagle	FGA aircraft	1978	1982–96	(152)	
	..	Hughes-500/OH-6D	Helicopter	1977	1978–95	206	For Army and Navy
	..	P-3C Orion Update -3	ASW/MP aircraft	1988	1991–96	31	For Navy
	(67)	S-70/UH-60J Blackhawk	Helicopter	1988	1991–96	(24)	Incl 18 for Navy and 6 for Army
	(100)	S-70B/SH-60J Seahawk	ASW helicopter	1988	1991–96	(51)	For Navy; incl 21 for SAR
	3	UP-3D Orion	EW aircraft	1994		:	For Navy
	1 330	AIM-7M Sparrow	Air-to-air missile	1990	1990–96	(1 156)	Deal worth $477 m
	..	BGM-71C I-TOW	Anti-tank missile	(1983)	1985–96	(8 454)	
Jordan							
S: USA	4	Bell 209/AH-1P	Combat helicopter	1995		..	Ex-US Army; incl 2 TAH-1P trainer version; EDA aid
	18	Bell-205/UH-1H	Helicopter	1995	1996	18	Ex-US Army; EDA aid

Recipient/ supplier (S) or licenser (L)	No. ordered	Weapon designation	Weapon description	Year of order/ licence	Year(s) of deliveries	No. delivered/ produced	Comments
	1	C-130H Hercules	Transport aircraft	(1996)		..	Ex-US Air Force; aid
	12	F-16A Fighting Falcon	FGA aircraft	1996		..	Ex-US Air Force; lease
	4	F-16B Fighting Falcon	FGA/trainer aircraft	1996		..	Ex-US Air Force; lease
	4	S-70A/UH-60L	Helicopter	1995	1995	2	Ex-US Army; deal worth $67 m incl 2 spare engines
	50	M-60A3 Patton-2	Main battle tank	1995	1996	50	Ex-US Army; EDA aid
	3	AN/TPQ-36	Tracking radar	1995	1996	3	Ex-US Army; EDA aid
	2	AN/TPQ-37	Tracking radar	1995	1996	2	Ex-US Army; EDA aid
Kazakhstan							
S: Russia	..	Su-27 Flanker	Fighter aircraft	(1995)	1996	(4)	Ex-Russian Air Force
	..	BMP-2	AIFV	1995	1996	55	Ex-Russian Army
	..	BTR-80	APC	(1995)	1996	10	Ex-Russian Army
	..	T-72	Main battle tank	1995	1996	63	Ex-Russian Army
Korea, North							
S: USSR	..	Drum Tilt	Fire control radar	(1979)	1981–94	(15)	For 15 Soju Class FAC(M)s
	..	SS-N-2 ShShMS	ShShM system	(1979)	1981–94	(15)	For 15 Soju Class FAC(M)s
	..	Square Tie	Surveillance radar	(1979)	1981–94	(15)	For 15 Soju Class FAC(M)s
L: USSR	..	SA-16	Portable SAM	(1989)	1992–96	(100)	
Korea, South							
S: France	(67)	Crotale NG SAMS	SAM system	(1989)		..	Korean designation Pegasus
	984	Mistral	Portable SAM	1992	1993–96	(800)	Deal worth $180 m incl 130 launchers (offsets 25%)
Italy	3	127mm/54	Naval gun	(1993)		..	For 3 Okpo Class (KDX-2000 Type) frigates
Netherlands	2	Goalkeeper	CIWS	(1991)		..	For 1 Okpo Class (KDX-2000 Type) frigate
	4	Goalkeeper	CIWS	1995		..	For 2 Okpo Class (KDX-2000 Type) frigates
	1	MW-08	Surveillance radar	1994		..	For 1 Okpo Class (KDX-2000 Type) frigate; option on more

Supplier	No.	Weapon designation	Weapon description	Year of order	Year(s) of deliveries	No. delivered/produced	Comments
	2	STIR	Fire control radar	(1992)		..	For 1 Okpo Class (KDX-2000 Type) frigate; option on more
Russia	..	BMP-3	AIFV	1995	1996	(43)	Payment for Russian debt to South Korea
	..	T-80U	Main battle tank	1995	1996	(57)	Payment for Russian debt to South Korea
	(344)	AT-10 Bastion	Anti-tank missile	1995	1996	(240)	For 43 BMP-3 AIFVs
	..	AT-11 Sniper	Anti-tank missile	1995	1996	342	For 57 T-80U tanks
	(45)	AT-7 Saxhorn	Anti-tank missile	1995	1996	(45)	Payment for Russian debt to South Korea; for technical evaluation
	(45)	SA-18	Portable SAM	1995	1996	(45)	Payment for Russian debt to South Korea; for technical evaluation
USA	48	F-16C Fighting Falcon	FGA aircraft	1991	1994–96	(44)	Incl 36 assembled from kits; deal worth $2.52 b incl 72 licensed production, 12 spare engines and 20 LANTIRN pods
	10	RH-800XP	Reconnaissance ac	1996		..	Deal worth $460 m; also used for SIGINT
	(120)	S-70/UH-60 Blackhawk	Helicopter	1990	1993–96	(100)	Ex-US Air Force; lease
	30	T-38 Talon	Jet trainer aircraft	1996	1996	15	
	29	MLRS 227mm	MRL	1996		..	Deal worth $624 m incl 1626 rockets, 1008 practice rounds, 14 M-577A2 APC/CPs, 4 M-88A1 ARVs, 9 simulators and 54 trucks
	14	M-577A2	APC/CP	(1996)		..	Deal worth $624 m incl 29 MLRS MRLs, ammunition, 9 MLRS simulators, 4 M-88A1 ARVs and 54 trucks
	4	M-88A1	ARV	(1996)		..	Deal worth $624 m incl 29 MLRS MRLs, ammunition, 9 MLRS simulators, 14 M-577A2 APC/CPs and 54 trucks
	3	AN/SPS-55	Surveillance radar	1994		..	For 3 Okpo Class (KDX-2000 Type) frigates
	1	RGM-84A ShShMS	ShShM system	(1992)		..	For 1 Okpo Class (KDX-2000 Type) frigate
	2	Seasparrow VLS	ShAM system	(1994)		..	Deal worth $57 m; for 2 Okpo Class (KDX-2000 Type) frigates
	132	AGM-88A HARM	Anti-radar missile	1995		..	For F-16C/D FGA aircraft
	190	AIM-120A AMRAAM	Air-to-air missile	1993	1995–96	(190)	For F-16C/D FGA aircraft
	300	AIM-9S Sidewinder	Air-to-air missile	1994	1994–96	(300)	Deal worth $34 m
	(46)	RGM-84A Harpoon	ShShM	1996		..	

Recipient/ supplier (S) or licenser (L)	No. ordered	Weapon designation	Weapon description	Year of order/ licence	Year(s) of deliveries	No. delivered/ produced	Comments
L: Germany	45	RIM-7H Seasparrow	ShAM	1992		..	For Okpo Class (KDX-2000 Type) frigates; deal worth $19 m
	..	UGM-84A Sub Harpoon	SuShM	(1994)	1995	(3)	For Type-209 submarines
L: USA	3	Type-209/1200	Submarine	1989	1995-96	2	Korean designation Chang Bogo Class
	3	Type-209/1200	Submarine	1994		..	Deal worth $510 m; Korean designation Chang Bogo Class
USA	72	F-16C Fighting Falcon	FGA aircraft	1991			Deal worth $2.52 b incl 48 delivered direct, 12 spare engines and 20 LANTIRN pods
	(526)	M-109A2 155mm	Self-propelled gun	1992	1993-96	(420)	Developed for Korean production; incl 5 prototypes
	(1 092)	K-1 ROKIT	Main battle tank	1981	1984-96	(1 092)	Incl 2 prototypes
	..	K-1A1	Main battle tank	(1994)	1996	(2)	Incl ARV and APC/CP versions
	57	LVTP-7A1	APC	1995		..	
Kuwait							
S: Egypt	2	AN/TPS-63	Surveillance radar	(1993)	1994	1	For 8 P-37BRL Type FAC(M)s
France	8	MRR-3D	Surveillance radar	1995		..	Deal worth $54 m
	1	TRS-22XX	Surveillance radar	1995		..	Deal worth $475 m incl $10 m for training
	8	P-37BRL Type	FAC(M)	1995		..	
Italy	11	Skyguard SAMS	SAM system	(1988)	1989-91	(6)	For use with Amoun air defence system
Russia	(27)	BM-23 300mm Smerch	MRL	1994	1995-96	(18)	
	(76)	BMP-3	AIFV	1994	1995-96	(76)	For 76 BMP-3 AIFVs
UK	(608)	AT-10 Bastion	Anti-tank missile	(1994)	1995-96	(608)	
	254	MCV-80 Desert Warrior	AIFV	1993	1995-96	(166)	Deal worth $740 m (offsets 30%); incl 21 APC/CP, repair and ARV versions
	..	Sea Skua SL	ShShM	1996			For 8 PB-37 BRL Type FAC(M)s
USA	218	M-1A2 Abrams	Main battle tank	1992	1995-96	(166)	Deal worth $4 b including 16 M-113A3 APCs, 30 M-577A3 APC/CPs, 46 M-88A1 ARVs and ammunition

No. ordered	Weapon designation	Weapon description	Year of order	Year(s) of deliveries	No. delivered/ produced	Comments
46	M-88A1	ARV	1992	1995–96	(46)	Deal worth $4 b including 218 M-1A2 tanks, 16 M-113A3 APCs, 30 M-577A3 APC/CPs and ammunition
70	Pandur	APC	1996		..	Incl APC/PC, mortar carrier, ARV, ambulance and armoured car versions; option on 200 more
6	I-HAWK SAMS	SAM system	1992	1995–96	..	
5	Patriot SAMS	SAM system	(1993)	1996	(5)	Deal worth $327 m incl 210 missiles (offsets 30%)
40	AGM-84A Harpoon	Air-to-ship missile	1988	1996	(20)	For F/A-18C/D fighters
(466)	BGM-71C I-TOW	Anti-tank missile	1993	1995–96	(312)	For 233 MCV-80 AIFVs
210	MIM-104 PAC-2	SAM	(1993)	1995–96	(210)	For 5 Patriot SAM systems
342	MIM-23B HAWK	SAM	1992		..	

Lebanon
S: Israel

No. ordered	Weapon designation	Weapon description	Year of order	Year(s) of deliveries	No. delivered/ produced	Comments
20	M-66 160mm SP	Self-propelled mortar	(1994)	1996	20	Ex-Israeli Army; for South Lebanese Army

USA

| 16 | Bell-205/UH-1H | Helicopter | 1996 | 1996 | 16 | Ex-US Army; aid |
| .. | M-113A2 | APC | 1994 | 1995–96 | 335 | Ex-US Army; aid |

Lithuania
S: Poland

5	Mi-2 Hoplite	Helicopter	1996	1996	5	Ex-Polish Air Force; gift
3	P-37 Barlock-A	Surveillance radar	1996	1996	3	Designation uncertain; ex-Polish Air Force
2	P-40 Knife Rest	Surveillance radar	1996	1996	2	Ex-Polish Air Force
2	PRV-11 Side Net	Surveillance radar	1996	1996	2	Designation uncertain; ex-Polish Air Force

Luxembourg
S: USA

| 24 | M-1114 ECV | APC | 1996 | 1996 | 24 | Deal worth $4.2 m |

Macedonia
S: Russia

| 4 | Mi-17 Hip-H | Helicopter | 1995 | 1995–96 | (4) | |

Malaysia
S: France

| 2 | MM-40 ShShMS | ShShM system | 1993 | | .. | For 2 Lekiu Class frigates |
| 16 | MM-40 Exocet | ShShM | 1993 | | .. | For 2 Lekiu Class frigates |

Recipient/ supplier (S) or licenser (L)	No. ordered	Weapon designation	Weapon description	Year of order/ licence	Year(s) of deliveries	No. delivered/ produced	Comments
Indonesia	6	CN-235	Transport aircraft	1995	1996	(6)	Option on more; deal worth $102 m (offsets incl Indonesian order for 20 MD-3-160 trainer aircraft and 500 cars)
Italy	2	Albatros Mk-2	ShAM system	1995		..	On 2 Assad Class corvettes
	2	Albatros Mk-2	ShAM system	1996		..	On 2 Assad Class corvettes
	2	Otomat/Teseo ShShMS	ShShM system	1995		..	On 2 Assad Class corvettes
	2	Otomat/Teseo ShShMS	ShShM system	1996		..	On 2 Assad Class corvettes
	2	RAN-12L/X	Surveillance radar	1995		..	On 2 Assad Class corvettes
	2	RAN-12L/X	Surveillance radar	1996		..	On 2 Assad Class corvettes
	4	RTN-10X	Fire control radar	1995		..	On 2 Assad Class corvettes
	4	RTN-10X	Fire control radar	1996		..	On 2 Assad Class corvettes
	(12)	Aspide	ShAM	1995		..	For 2 Assad Class corvettes
	(12)	Aspide	ShAM	1996		..	For 2 Assad Class corvettes
	(24)	Otomat Mk-2	ShShM	1995		..	For 2 Assad Class corvettes
	(24)	Otomat Mk-2	ShShM	1996		..	For 2 Assad Class corvettes
	2	Assad Class	Corvette	1995		..	Originally built for Iraq but embargoed
	2	Assad Class	Corvette	(1996)		..	Originally built for Iraq; handed over to Iraqi crews but impounded to cover Iraqi debts to producer
Netherlands	2	DA-08	Surveillance radar	1992		..	For 2 Lekiu Class frigates
Sweden	2	Sea Giraffe-150	Surveillance radar	1992		..	For 2 Lekiu Class frigates
UK	4	ST-1802SW	Fire control radar	1992		..	On 2 Lekiu Class frigates
	2	Seawolf VLS	ShAM system	1992		..	On 2 Lekiu Class frigates
	32	Seawolf VL	ShAM	1993		..	For 2 Lekiu Class frigates
	504	Starburst	Portable SAM	1993	1995–96	(250)	
	2	Lekiu Class	Frigate	1992		..	For 2 Lekiu Class frigates
USA	8	F/A-18D Hornet	FGA/trainer aircraft	1993		..	Deal worth $600 m incl training
	2	S-70C	Helicopter	1996		..	Option on 10 more (offsets $250 m) For VIP transport
	30	AGM-65D Maverick	ASM	1993		..	For F/A-18D FGA/trainer aircraft
	25	AGM-84A Harpoon	Air-to-ship missile	1993		..	For F/A-18D FGA/trainer aircraft
	20	AIM-7M Sparrow	Air-to-air missile	1993		..	For F/A-18D FGA/trainer aircraft

Supplier/recipient	No.	Weapon designation	Weapon description	Year of order	Year of deliveries	No. delivered	Comments
Ukraine	40	AIM-9S Sidewinder	Air-to-air missile	1993	1995	..	For F/A-18D FGA/trainer aircraft
	..	AA-10a Alamo	Air-to-air missile	1994		131	For 18 MiG-29SE FGA aircraft
L: Switzerland	20	MD3-160	Trainer aircraft	1993	1995–96	(20)	More built for export and civilian customers
Malta							
S: Netherlands	2	SA-316B Alouette-3	Helicopter	(1996)	1996	2	Ex-Dutch Army; deal worth $300 000
Mauritius							
S: Chile	1	Guardian Class	OPV	1994	1996	1	Deal worth $22 m; Mauritian designation Vigilant Class
Mexico							
S: USA	20	Bell-205/UH-1D	Helicopter	(1996)	1996	(20)	Ex-US Army; EDA aid
	4	S-70/UH-60 Blackhawk	Helicopter	1994		..	Deal worth $14 m
Morocco							
S: France	2	OPV-64	OPV	1993	1995–96	2	Moroccan designation Rais Bargach Class
	2	OPV-64	OPV	1994	1996	1	Moroccan designation Rais Bargach Class
	1	OPV-64	OPV	1996		..	Moroccan designation Rais Bargach Class
USA	14	T-37C	Jet trainer aircraft	(1995)	1996	14	Ex-US Air Force
Myanmar							
S: China	24	A-5C Fantan	FGA aircraft	(1992)	1996	(12)	
	(144)	PL-2B	Air-to-air missile	1992	1996	(72)	For 24 A-5C FGA aircraft
	6	Hainan Class	Patrol craft	1994		..	
Russia	5	Mi-17 Hip-H	Helicopter	1996		..	
Netherlands							
S: Canada	7	CH-47C Chinook	Helicopter	(1993)	1995–96	7	Deal worth $16 m; ex-Canadian Air Force; refurbished to CH-47D in USA before delivery

Recipient/ supplier (S) or licenser (L)	No. ordered	Weapon designation	Weapon description	Year of order/ licence	Year(s) of deliveries	No. delivered/ produced	Comments
France	17	AS-532U2 Cougar	Helicopter	1993	1996	(8)	Deal worth $242 m (offsets 120%)
USA	12	AH-64A Apache	Combat helicopter	1995	1996	12	Ex-US Army; on loan till delivery of AH-64D helicopters; deal worth $12
	30	AH-64D Longbow	Combat helicopter	1995		..	Deal worth $686 m (offsets $873 m)
	6	CH-47D Chinook	Helicopter	1993		..	
	2	Standard VLS	ShAM system	(1996)		..	Deal worth $54 m; for 2 LCF Type frigates
	605	AGM-114K Hellfire	Anti-tank missile	1995	1996	(50)	For AH-64D helicopters; deal worth $127 m
	200	AIM-120A AMRAAM	Air-to-air missile	1995		..	For F-16 A/B-MLU FGA aircraft
New Zealand							
S: Australia	2	Meko-200ANZ Type	Frigate	1989		..	Deal worth $554.7 m; New Zealand designation Te Kaha Class; option on 2 more
France	23	Mistral	Portable SAM	1996		..	Deal worth $32.7 m incl 12 launchers
Sweden	2	9LV	Fire control radar	1991		..	For 2 Meko-200ANZ Type (Te Kaha Class) frigates
	2	Sea Giraffe-150	Surveillance radar	1991		..	For 2 Meko-200ANZ Type (Te Kaha Class) frigates
USA	2	127mm/54 Mk-45	Naval gun	(1989)		..	For 2 Meko-200ANZ Type (Te Kaha Class) frigates
	2	AN/SPS-49	Surveillance radar	(1993)		..	For 2 Meko-200ANZ Type (Te Kaha Class) frigates
	2	Phalanx	CIWS	1994	1995–96	(2)	Deal worth $17.6 m; for refit of 2 Leander Class frigates
	2	Seasparrow VLS	ShAM system	1992		..	For 2 Meko-200ANZ Type (Te Kaha Class) frigates
	..	RIM-7M Seasparrow	ShAM	(1991)		..	For 2 Meko-200ANZ Type (Te Kaha Class) frigates
Nigeria							
L: USA	60	Air Beetle	Trainer aircraft	1992	1993–96	(48)	
Norway							
S: France	7 200	Eryx	Anti-tank missile	1993	1995–96	(2 200)	Deal worth $115 m incl 424 launchers; option on more (offsets incl production of components)

Supplier	No.	Weapon designation	Weapon description	Year of order	Year(s) of deliveries	No. delivered	Comments
Italy	3	RAT-31S	Surveillance radar	1994	1996	..	
Sweden	104	CV-9030	AIFV	1994	1996	4	Deal worth $241 m (offsets $184 m); option on more
UK	2	S-61/Sea King HAR-3	Helicopter	1993	1996	(1)	Deal worth $22.2 m; UK export designation Sea King Mk-43B
USA	12	MLRS 227mm	MRL	1995	1995–96	..	Deal worth $199 m incl 360 rockets
	24	AN/TPQ-36A	Tracking radar	1994	1995–96	(12)	For Norwegian Advanced Surface-to-Air Missile System (NASAMS)
	..	AGM-114A Hellfire	Anti-tank missile	1996	1996	..	For coast defence; deal worth $36.6 m; assembled in Sweden
	148	AIM-120A AMRAAM	SAM	1994	1995–96	(108)	Deal worth $106 m; for Norwegian Advanced Surface-to-Air Missile System (NASAMS)
	500	AIM-120A AMRAAM	Air-to-air missile	1996	1995–96	..	For F-16A/B MLU FGA aircraft; deal worth $150 m
Oman							
S: France	51	VBL	Scout car	1996	1996	..	
	2	Crotale NG Naval	ShAM system	1992	1996	2	For 2 Qahir Class (Muheet Type) corvettes
	2	DRBV-51C	Fire control radar	(1992)	1996	2	For 2 Qahir Class (Muheet Type) corvettes
	2	MM-40 ShShMS	ShShM system	1992	1996	2	For 2 Qahir Class (Muheet Type) corvettes
	(32)	MM-40 Exocet	ShShM	1992	1996	(32)	For 2 Qahir Class (Muheet Type) corvettes
	(16)	VT-1	ShAM	1992	1996	(16)	For Crotale NG ShAM system for 2 Qahir Class (Muheet Type) corvettes
	3	Vigilante-400 Type	Patrol craft	1993	1995–96	3	Omani designation Al Bushra Class; option on 5 more; 'Mawj' programme
Netherlands	2	MW-08	Surveillance radar	1992	1996	2	For 2 Qahir Class (Muheet Type) corvettes
	2	STING	Fire control radar	(1992)	1996	2	For 2 Qahir Class (Muheet Type) corvettes
Pakistan	4	Supporter	Trainer aircraft	1995	1996	4	
Switzerland	5	Skyguard	Fire control radar	1995		..	For use with 10 GDF-005 35mm AA guns
UK	18	Challenger-2	Main battle tank	1993	1995–96	(18)	Deal worth $225 m incl 4 Challenger ARVs, 2 Challenger training tanks and 4 Stormer APC/CPs; option on 18 more
	80	Piranha 8x8	APC	1994	1995–96	(40)	Deal worth $138 m; incl ARV, APC/CP, 81mm mortar carrier and other versions; option on 46 more

Recipient/ supplier (S) or licenser (L)	No. ordered	Weapon designation	Weapon description	Year of order/ licence	Year(s) of deliveries	No. delivered/ produced	Comments
USA	2	Qahir Class	Corvette	1992	1996	2	Deal worth $265 m; 'Muheet' programme
	50	M-60A3 Patton-2	Main battle tank	1995	1996	50	Ex-US Army; gift
	..	BGM-71D TOW-2	Anti-tank missile	(1996)		..	For use on VBL scout cars
Pakistan							
S: Belarus	(1 920)	AT-11 Sniper	Anti-tank missile	1996		..	For 320 T-80UD tanks
China	..	K-8 Karakorum-8	Jet trainer aircraft	1987	1994–96	(30)	Incl some assembled in Pakistan; some components produced in Pakistan; status of planned licensed production uncertain
France	..	T-85-IIAP	Main battle tank	1990	1992–96	(282)	
	3	Atlantique-1	ASW/MP aircraft	1994	1996	3	Ex-French Navy; gift; for spares only
	20	Mirage-3E	Fighter aircraft	1996		..	Ex-French Air Force; refurbished before delivery; deal worth $120 m
	20	Mirage-3E	Fighter aircraft	1996		..	Ex-French Air Force
	..	SM-39 Exocet	SuShM	1994		..	Deal worth $100 m; for 3 Agosta-90B Type submarines
	2	Agosta-90B Type	Submarine	1994		..	Incl 1 assembled in Pakistan; deal worth $750 m incl 1 licensed production
	1	Eridan Class	MCM ship	1992	1996	1	Pakistani designation Munsif Class; prior to licensed production
Netherlands	6	DA-08	Surveillance radar	1994		..	For refit of 6 Tariq (Amazon) Class frigates
Russia	12	Mi-17 Hip-H	Helicopter	1995	1996	12	For Army; deal worth $32 m
Sweden	6	9LV	Fire control radar	1994		..	For refit of 6 Tariq (Amazon) Class frigates
USA	10	Bell-209/AH-1S	Combat helicopter	1990		..	Deal worth $89 m incl spare engines; delivery embargoed between 1992 and 1995
	3	P-3C Orion Update 2.5	ASW/MP aircraft	(1990)	1996	(1)	Deal worth $240 m; delivery embargoed between 1992 and 1995
	24	M-198 155mm	Towed gun	1988	1996	24	Delivery embargoed between 1992 and 1995
	(4)	AN/TPQ-36	Tracking radar	(1990)	1996	(4)	Deal worth $65 m; delivery embargoed between 1992 and 1995

	No.	Weapon designation	Weapon description	Year of order	Year(s) of deliveries	No. delivered	Comments
	4	AN/TPQ-37	Tracking radar	(1985)	1987–96	(4)	Delivery of last embargoed between 1992 and 1995
	28	AGM-84A Harpoon	Air-to-ship missile	1990	1996	(10)	For P-3C ASW/MP aircraft; delivery embargoed between 1992 and 1995
	360	AIM-9L Sidewinder	Air-to-air missile	1988		..	For F-16 fighters; delivery embargoed between 1992 and 1995
Ukraine	(320)	T-80UD	Main battle tank	1996		..	Deal worth $550 m
L: China	..	Anza-2	SAM	(1988)	1989–96	(750)	Deal worth $750 m incl 2 delivered direct
France	1	Agosta-90B Type	Submarine	1994	1996	..	Pakistani designation Munsif Class
	1	Eridan Class	MCM ship	1992		..	
Italy	..	Skyguard	Fire control radar	(1988)	1989–96	(109)	For use with GDF-002 35mm AA guns
Palau							
S: Australia	(1)	ASI-315	Patrol craft	1995	1996	1	Pacific Forum aid programme
Paraguay							
S: Taiwan	2	Bell-205/UH-1H	Helicopter	(1996)	1996	2	Ex-Taiwanese Army; gift
Peru							
S: Belarus	12	MiG-29 Fulcrum	Fighter aircraft	1996	1996	(4)	Ex-Belarus Air Force; incl 2 MiG-29UB trainer version
	(180)	AA-10a Alamo	Air-to-air missile	1996	1996	(72)	For 10 MiG-29 fighter aircraft
	(144)	AA-8 Aphid	Air-to-air missile	1996	1996	(48)	For 12 MiG-29/MiG-29UB fighter aircraft; designation uncertain
Cyprus	3	Mi-26 Halo	Helicopter	(1995)	1996	3	Second-hand
Netherlands	2	Dokkum Class	Minesweeper	1996	1996	2	Ex-Dutch Navy; Peruvian designation Carrasco Class
Russia	(6)	Mi-17 Hip-H	Helicopter	(1995)	1996	(6)	
USA	11	A-37B Dragonfly	Ground attack ac	1996	1996	..	Ex-US Air Force; gift
Ukraine	4	An-32 Cline	Transport aircraft	1994	1996	4	Ex-Ukranian Air Force; option on more
Philippines							
S: Russia	20	Yak-18T	Light aircraft	(1993)	1994–96	(20)	

Recipient/ supplier (S) or licenser (L)	No. ordered	Weapon designation	Weapon description	Year of order/ licence	Year(s) of deliveries	No. delivered/ produced	Comments
L: UK	142	FS-100 Simba	APC	1992	1994–96	133	Deal worth $46 m incl 8 delivered direct; incl 4 assembled from kits
Poland							
S: Czech Republic	10	MiG-29 Fulcrum	Fighter aircraft	1995	1995–96	10	Ex-Czech Air Force; exchanged for 11 W-3 helicopters; incl 1 MiG-29UB trainer version
Germany	18	Mi-24 Hind-D	Combat helicopter	1995	1996	18	Former GDR equipment; gift
Portugal							
S: USA	25	F-16A Fighting Falcon	FGA aircraft	1996	..	..	Ex-US Air Force; deal worth $258 m
Qatar							
S: France	12	Mirage-2000-5	FGA aircraft	1994		..	
	4	Crotale NG Naval	ShAM system	1992	1996	3	For 4 Vita (Barzan) Class FAC(M)
	4	MM-40 ShShMS	ShShM system	1992	1996	3	For 4 Vita (Barzan) Class FAC(M)s
	4	MRR-3D	Surveillance radar	(1992)	1996	3	For 4 Vita (Barzan) Class FAC(M)s
	4	TRS-3051 Triton	Surveillance radar	(1992)	1996	3	For 4 Vita (Barzan) Class FAC(M)s
	..	Apache/MAW	ASM	1994		..	For Mirage-2000-5 FGA aircraft
	..	MICA-EM	Air-to-air missile	1994		..	Deal worth $280 m incl R-550 missiles; for 12 Mirage 2000-5 FGFA aircraft
	(64)	MM-40 Exocet	ShShM	1992	1996	(48)	For 4 Vita (Barzan) Class FAC(M)s
	500	Mistral	Portable SAM	1990	1992–96	(500)	
	..	R-550 Magic-2	Air-to-air missile	1994		..	Deal worth $280 m incl MICA-EM missiles; for 12 Mirage 2000-5 FGA aircraft
Netherlands	4	Goalkeeper	CIWS	1992	1996	3	For 4 Vita (Barzan) Class FAC(M)s
	4	STING	Fire control radar	(1992)	1996	3	For 4 Vita (Barzan) Class FAC(M)s
UK	(15)	Hawk-100	FGA/trainer aircraft	1996		..	
	4	Piranha 8x8	APC	1996		..	
	40	Piranha 8x8 AGV-90	Armoured car	1996		..	Incl 4 APC version
	..	Starburst	Portable SAM	1996		..	

No. ordered	Weapon designation	Weapon description	Year of order	Year of deliveries	No. delivered	Comments
Romania						
S: France						
2	VT-46M Type	Patrol craft	1996	1996	..	Deal worth $155 m
4	Vita Class	FAC(M)	1992	1992	3	Deal worth $200 m; Qatari designation Barzan Class
USA						
(200)	R-550 Magic-2	Air-to-air missile	1996	1996	..	For MiG-21, MiG-23 and MiG-29 fighter aircraft
4	C-130B Hercules	Transport aircraft	1995	1995	2	Ex-US Air Force
5	AN/FPS-117	Surveillance radar	1995	1995	..	Deal worth $82 m
L: France						
..	SA-330 Puma	Helicopter	1977	1978–94	(125)	
USA						
96	Bell-209/AH-1W	Combat helicopter	1995	1995	..	Replacing planned production of Bell-209/AH-1F helicopters
USSR						
..	SA-7 Grail	Portable SAM	(1978)	1978–96	(475)	
Rwanda						
S: South Africa						
..	Mamba Mk-2	APC	1996	1996	(2)	Status uncertain; deal worth $18 m incl small arms
Saudi Arabia						
S: Canada						
1 117	LAV-25	AIFV	1990	1992–96	(1 117)	Deal worth $700 m; incl 111 LAV-TOW tank destroyers, 130 LAV-90mm armoured cars, 73 LAV-120mm mortar carriers and 449 in other versions; for National Guard
France						
..	Piranha 8x8	APC	(1990)	1996	(20)	For SAR
12	AS-532U2 Cougar	Helicopter	1996	..	..	
2	Castor-2J	Fire control radar	1994	..	..	On 2 Improved La Fayette Class (F-3000S Type) frigates
2	Crotale Naval ShAMS	ShAM system	1994	..	..	On 2 Improved La Fayette Class (F-3000S Type) frigates
2	DRBV-15C Sea Tiger-2	Surveillance radar	1994	..	..	On 2 Improved La Fayette Class (F-3000S Type) frigates
2	DRBV-26C	Surveillance radar	1994	..	..	On 2 Improved La Fayette Class (F-3000S Type) frigates
2	MM-40 ShShMS	ShShM system	1994	..	..	On 2 Improved La Fayette Class (F-3000S Type) frigates

Recipient/ supplier (S) or licenser (L)	No. ordered	Weapon designation	Weapon description	Year of order/ licence	Year(s) of deliveries	No. delivered/ produced	Comments
	..	MM-40 Exocet	ShShM	1994		..	For 2 Improved La Fayette Class (F-3000S Type) frigates
	..	VT-1	ShAM	1990		..	For 2 Improved La Fayette Class (F-3000S Type) frigates
	2	La Fayette Class	Frigate	1994		..	Deal worth $3.42 b incl other weapons, construction of a naval base and training (offsets 35%)
Switzerland	(20)	PC-9	Trainer aircraft	1994	1995–96	16	Sold through UK; part of 'Al Yamamah II' deal
	18	Skyguard	Fire control radar	1992	1994–96	(18)	For use with GDF-005 35 mm AA guns
UK	20	Hawk	Jet trainer aircraft	1993	1996	(2)	Part of 'Al Yamamah II' deal
	(60)	Hawk-200	FGA aircraft	1993		..	Part of 'Al Yamamah II' deal; UK export designation Hawk-205
	48	Tornado IDS	FGA aircraft	1993	1996	(4)	Part of 'Al Yamamah II' deal
	73	AMS 120mm	Mortar	1996	1996	(5)	Deal worth $57 m incl ammunition; for 73 LAV-25 APC/mortar carriers delivered from Canada
USA	3	Sandown Class	MCM ship	1988	1991–96	3	Option on 3 more; Saudi designation Al Jawf Class
	8	C-130H Hercules	Transport aircraft	1990	1992	(1)	Deal worth $320 m incl 2 C-130H-30 version
	72	F-15S Strike Eagle	Fighter/bomber ac	1992	1995–96	(8)	Deal worth $9 b incl 24 spare engines, 48 LANTIRN pods and armament
	(8)	S-70/UH-60 Blackhawk	Helicopter	(1992)		..	Deal worth $225 m; for Medevac
	13	Patriot SAMS	SAM system	1992	1995–96	(9)	Deal worth $1.03 b incl 1 SAM system for training and 761 MIM-104 PAC-2 missiles
	900	AGM-65D Maverick	ASM	1992	1995–96	(250)	For 72 F-15S fighter/bomber aircraft; incl AGM-65G version
	300	AIM-7M Sparrow	Air-to-air missile	1992	1995–96	(40)	For 72 F-15S fighter/bomber aircraft
	300	AIM-9S Sidewinder	Air-to-air missile	1992	1995–96	(40)	For 72 F-15S fighter/bomber aircraft
	761	MIM-104 PAC-2	SAM	1992	1995–96	(511)	Deal worth $1.03 b incl 13 operational and 1 training Patriot SAM systems
Singapore **S: Israel**	6	Barak ShAMS	ShAM system	(1992)	1996	1	For 6 Type-62-001 (Victory Class) corvettes

No.	Weapon designation	Weapon description	Year of order	Year(s) of deliveries	No. delivered	Comments
Sweden						
6	EL/M-2221	Fire control radar	1992	1996	1	For 6 Type-62-001 (Victory Class) corvettes
12	EL/M-2228	Fire control radar	(1993)	1996	(3)	For 12 Fearless Class patrol craft/FAC(M)s
(96)	Barak	ShAM	(1992)	1996	(16)	For 6 Type-62-001 (Victory Class) corvettes
1	Sjöormen Class	Submarine	1995	1996	1	Ex-Swedish Navy; refitted before delivery; for training
UK						
18	FV-180 CET	AEV	1995		..	Incl 3 for SAR
USA						
6	CH-47D Chinook	Helicopter	1994	1996	(6)	
8	F-16C Fighting Falcon	FGA aircraft	1994		..	'Peace Carven II' programme worth $890 m incl 10 F-16D trainer version, 50 AIM-7M and 36 AIM-9S missiles
12	F-16C Fighting Falcon	FGA aircraft	1996		..	Lease with option to buy in 1999; to be kept in USA for training
10	F-16D Fighting Falcon	FGA/trainer aircraft	1994		..	'Peace Carven II' programme worth $890 m incl 8 F-16C fighter aircraft, 50 AIM-7M and 36 AIM-9S missiles
4	KC-135A Stratotanker	Tanker aircraft	1996		..	Ex-US Air Force; deal worth $280 m incl refurbishment to KC-135R
24	AGM-84A Harpoon	Air-to-ship missile	1996		..	Deal worth $39 m; for Fokker-50 Maritime Enforcer ASW/MP aircraft
50	AIM-7M Sparrow	Air-to-air missile	1994		..	Deal worth $890 m incl 18 F-16C/D FGA aircraft and 36 AIM-9S missiles
30	AIM-9S Sidewinder	Air-to-air missile	1994		..	Deal worth $890 m incl 18 F-16C/D FGA aircraft and 50 AIM-7M missiles
L: USA						
(2)	LPD Type	Landing ship	1994		..	Designed for production in Singapore; option on 2 more
Slovakia						
S: Russia						
8	MiG-29S Fulcrum-C	FGA aircraft	1995	1995–96	8	Payment for Russian debt to Slovakia
Ukraine						
..	AA-10a Alamo	Air-to-air missile	1995	1995	14	For MiG-29 FGA aircraft
Slovenia						
S: Israel						
..	Model-839 155mm	Towed gun	1996		(2)	Incl assembly in Slovenia

Recipient/ supplier (S) or licenser (L)	No. ordered	Weapon designation	Weapon description	Year of order/ licence	Year(s) of deliveries	No. delivered/ produced	Comments
South Africa							
S: Switzerland	60	PC-7 Turbo Trainer	Trainer aircraft	1993	1994–96	(60)	Deal worth $130 m (offsets 55%); South African designation Astra
USA	2	C-130B Hercules	Transport aircraft	1995			Ex-US Air Force; gift
	3	C-130B Hercules	Transport aircraft	1996	1996	(1)	Ex-US Marines; gift
Spain							
S: France	15	AS-532U2 Cougar	Helicopter	1996		..	Deal worth $205 m (offsets 100%)
	840	Mistral	Portable SAM	1991	1992–96	(750)	Deal worth $154 m incl 200 launchers (offsets 50%)
Germany	108	Leopard-2	Main battle tank	1995	1995–96	108	Ex-German Army; 5-year lease worth $33 m; Spanish designation Leopard-2A4E
Italy	1	RAN-30X	Surveillance radar	(1993)		..	For Meroka CIWS on 1 LPD Type AALS
	2	RAT-31S	Surveillance radar	1992		..	Deal worth $23.4 m (offsets 150%); option on 2 more
Qatar	3	Mirage F-1B	FGA/trainer aircraft	1994	1994	1	Ex-Qatari Air Force; deal worth $132 m incl 10 Mirage F-1C FGA aircraft
	10	Mirage F-1C	FGA aircraft	1994	1994–96	10	Ex-Qatari Air Force; deal worth $132 m incl 3 Mirage F-1B trainer version; Spanish designation C-14
UK	56	L-118 105mm	Towed gun	1995	1996	(18)	Deal worth $63 m incl ammunition
USA	8	AV-8B Harrier-2 Plus	FGA aircraft	1992	1996	5	Deal worth $257 m; for Navy; assembled in Spain
	24	F/A-18A Hornet	FGA aircraft	1995	1995–96	12	Ex-US Navy; option on 6 more; deal worth $288 m; refurbished before delivery; Spanish designation C-15
	6	S-70B/SH-60B Seahawk	ASW helicopter	1991		..	Deal worth $251 m; for Navy
	1	TAV-8B Harrier-2	FGA/trainer aircraft	1992		..	Deal worth $25 m; for Navy
	83	M-110A2 203mm	Self-propelled gun	1991	1993–96	(80)	CFE cascade; ex-US Army
	(31)	M-577A2	APC/CP	1993	1996	(15)	Ex-US Army

No.	Weapon designation	Weapon description	Year of order	Year of deliveries	No. delivered	Comments
4	AN/SPY-1F	Surveillance radar	1996		..	Deal worth $750 m; part of AEGIS air defence system for 4 F-100 Class frigates
2	AN/VPS-2 Modified	Fire control radar	(1993)		..	For 2 Meroka CIWS on 1 LPD Type AALS
L: Germany						
200	Leopard-2A5	Main battle tank	1995	1995	..	Spanish designation Leopard-2A5E
UK 4	Sandown/CME Type	MCM ship	1993	1993	..	Deal worth $381 m
USA (2 000)	BGM-71F TOW-2	Anti-tank missile	1987	1995–96	(245)	Deal also incl 200 launchers
Sri Lanka						
S: China 6	F-7M Airguard	Fighter aircraft	(1995)	(1995)	..	
Israel 3	Kfir C-2	FGA aircraft	(1995)	1996	3	Incl 1 Kfir TC-2 trainer version
Kazakhstan 4	An-24 Coke	Transport aircraft	(1995)	1996	4	Second-hand; lease; flown by Kazakh crew
Ukraine 4	An-32 Cline	Transport aircraft	(1995)	1996	4	
3	Mi-17 Hip-H	Helicopter	(1995)	1996	3	Ex-Ukrainian Air Force
6	Mi-24 Hind-D	Combat helicopter	1995	1995–96	6	Ex-Ukrainian Air Force
Sudan						
S: China (6)	F-7M Airguard	Fighter aircraft	(1995)	1996	(6)	
Sweden						
S: France ..	TRS-2620 Gerfaut	Surveillance radar	1993	1993–96	(50)	Deal worth $17.7 m, for CV-90 AAV(G)s
Germany 350	BMP-1	AIFV	1994	1995	2	Former GDR equipment
120	Leopard-2A5	Main battle tank	1994	1996	(5)	Deal worth $770 m incl 160 ex-GermanArmy Leopard-2 tanks (offsets 100%, incl assembly of 91); option on 90 more; Swedish designation Strv-122
(1 054)	MT-LB	APC	1993	1993–96	(606)	Former GDR equipment; deal worth $10.3 m incl 228 2S1 self-propelled gun chassis for spares; incl 200 for spares only; Swedish designation Pbv-401
Israel 1	ELM-2190	Battlefield radar	1996	1996	1	For mine detection; for use with Swedish forces in Bosnia

Recipient/ supplier (S) or licenser (L)	No. ordered	Weapon designation	Weapon description	Year of order/ licence	Year(s) of deliveries	No. delivered/ produced	Comments
USA	100	AIM-120A AMRAAM	Air-to-air missile	1994		..	Deal worth $190 m (offsets 100%); for JAS-39 FGA aircraft
Switzerland							
S: USA	34	F/A-18C/D Hornet	FGA aircraft	1993	1996	(2)	Deal worth $2.3 b; incl 8 F/A-18D trainer version; incl assembly of 32 in Switzerland
	150	AIM-120A AMRAAM	Air-to-air missile	(1993)	1996	(10)	For 34 F/A-18C/D FGA aircraft
	..	AIM-9L Sidewinder	Air-to-air missile	(1988)	1996	(16)	For 34 F/A-18C/D FGA aircraft
	12 000	BGM-71D TOW-2	Anti-tank missile	(1985)	1988–96	(8 475)	Deal worth $209 m incl 400 launchers and night vision sights; assembled in Switzerland
	3 500	FIM-92A Stinger	Portable SAM	1988	1993–96	(3 500)	Deal worth $315 m (offsets 70%, incl production of components)
Syria							
S: Korea, North	(150)	SS-1 Scud-C	SSM	1989	1991–96	(150)	Part of deal worth $1.6 b; status uncertain
Russia	54	MiG-29S Fulcrum-C	FGA aircraft	1994	..	..	Part of deal worth $1.6 b; status uncertain
	350	T-72	Main battle tank	1994	..	..	Part of deal worth $1.6 b; status uncertain
	..	SA-16 Gimlet	Portable SAM	1994	..	..	Part of deal worth $1.6 b; status uncertain
Taiwan							
S: Canada	30	Bell-206B JetRanger-3	Helicopter	1996	..	..	For training
France	60	Mirage-2000-5	FGA aircraft	1992	1996	(10)	Deal worth $2.6 b (offsets 10%); option on 40 more
	12	Castor-2C	Fire control radar	1995	..	..	On 6 La Fayette (Kang Ding) Class frigates
	6	DRBV-26C	Surveillance radar	1995	1996	2	On 6 La Fayette (Kang Ding) Class frigates
	6	TRS-3051 Triton	Surveillance radar	1995	1996	2	On 6 La Fayette (Kang Ding) Class frigates
	(960)	MICA-EM	Air-to-air missile	(1992)	1996	(120)	Deal worth $1.2 b incl 400 R-550 missiles; for 60 Mirage-2000-5 FGA aircraft
	(400)	R-550 Magic-2	Air-to-air missile	1992	1996	(60)	Deal worth $1.2 b incl 960 MICA-EM missiles; for 60 Mirage-2000-5 FGA aircraft

	No.	Weapon designation	Weapon description	Year of order	Year(s) of deliveries	No. delivered	Comments
USA	6	La Fayette Class	Frigate	1991	1996	2	Deal worth $2.8 b; Taiwanese designation Kang Ding Class
	(12)	C-130H Hercules	Transport aircraft	1993	1993–96	(12)	Deal worth $200 m
	4	C-130H Hercules	Transport aircraft	1996	1996	:	
	150	F-16A Fighting Falcon	FGA aircraft	1992	1996	(60)	Deal worth $5.8 b incl 600 AIM-7M and 900 AIM-9S missiles; incl 30 F-16B trainer version
	1	127mm/54 Mk-45	Naval gun	1994		:	For 1 Tien Tan Class (PFG-2 Type) frigate; deal worth $21 m
	160	M-60A3 Patton-2	Main battle tank	1991	1995–96	(160)	Ex-US Army; deal worth $91 m; refurbished before delivery
	:	AN/FPS-117	Surveillance radar	1992		:	For 7 FFG-7 (Cheng Kung) Class frigates
	7	AN/SPG-60 STIR	Fire control radar	(1989)	1993–96	(4)	For 7 FFG-7 (Cheng Kung) Class frigates
	2	AN/SPS-10	Surveillance radar	1994	1996	2	On 2 ex-US Navy Newport Class landing ships
	7	AN/SPS-49	Surveillance radar	(1989)	1993–96	(4)	For 7 FFG-7 (Cheng Kung) Class frigates
	(3)	Patriot MADS	SAM system	1994		:	Deal worth $1.3 b incl missiles
	7	Phalanx	CIWS	1991	1993–96	(4)	For 7 FFG-7 (Cheng Kung) Class frigates
	2	Phalanx	CIWS	1994	1996	2	On 2 ex-US Navy Newport Class landing ships
	6	Phalanx	CIWS	1995	1996	2	Deal worth $75 m incl 6 Mk-75 76mm guns and ammunition; for 6 La Fayette (Kang Ding) Class frigates
	1	Standard VLS	ShAM system	1993		:	Deal worth $103 m; for 1 Tien Tan Class (PFG-2 Type) frigate
	7	Standard-1 ShAMS	ShAM system	1989	1993–96	(4)	For 7 FFG-7 (Cheng Kung) Class frigates
	7	WM-28	Fire control radar	(1989)	1993–96	(4)	For 7 FFG-7 (Cheng Kung) Class frigates
	600	AIM-7M Sparrow	Air-to-air missile	1992	1996	(240)	Deal worth $5.8 b incl 150 F-16A/B FGA aircraft and 900 AIM-9S missiles
	900	AIM-9S Sidewinder	Air-to-air missile	1992	1996	(360)	Deal worth $5.8 b incl 150 F-16A/B FGA aircraft and 600 AIM-7M missiles
	1 299	FIM-92A Stinger	Portable SAM	1996		:	Deal worth $200 m incl 79 Avenger AAV(M)s, 50 man-portable launchers and training
	200	MIM-104 PAC-2	SAM	1994		:	For 3 Patriot MADS SAM systems
	:	RIM-116A RAM	ShAM	1993		:	For PFG-2 (Tien Tan) Class frigates
	:	RIM-66B Standard-1MR	ShAM	(1995)	1995–96	(63)	For FFG-7 (Cheng Kung) Class frigates

Recipient/ supplier (S) or licenser (L)	No. ordered	Weapon designation	Weapon description	Year of order/ licence	Year(s) of deliveries	No. delivered/ produced	Comments
L: USA	2	Newport Class	Landing ship	1994	1996	(2)	Ex-US Navy; lease
	7	FFG-7 Class	Frigate	1989	1993–96	4	Taiwanese designation Cheng Kung Class
Thailand							
S: Canada	20	Bell-212	Helicopter	1993		:	Deal worth $130 m
China	1	Similan Class	Support ship	1993	1996	1	
Czech Republic	4	L-39Z Albatros	Jet trainer aircraft	1996	1996	(4)	
France	3	AS-332L2 Super Puma	Helicopter	1995		:	For VIP transport
	24	LG-1 105mm	Towed gun	1996	1996	(12)	
	:	Mistral	Portable SAM	1996		:	
Germany	3	Do-228-200MP	MP aircraft	1995	1995–96	3	For Navy
Italy	2	Gaeta Class	MCM ship	1996		:	Deal worth $120 m
Spain	1	CN-235	Transport aircraft	1995	1996	1	For Police
	9	Harrier Mk-50/AV-8A	FGA aircraft	1995		:	Ex-Spanish Navy; incl 2 Harrier Mk-54/TAV-8A trainer version; deal worth $90 m; for Navy
	1	Chakri Naruebet Class	Aircraft-carrier	1992		:	Deal worth $257 m without armament and radars
Sweden	:	Giraffe-40	Surveillance radar	1996	1996	(1)	For Air Force
	15	RBS-70 Mk-2	Portable SAM	1996		:	Deal worth $4 m incl 3 launchers
UK	2	Jetstream-41	Transport aircraft	1995	1995–96	(2)	For Army
USA	17	A-7E Corsair-2	FGA aircraft	1994	1995–96	(17)	Ex-US Navy; incl 3 for spares only; deal worth $81.6 m incl 4 TA-7C trainer version; for Navy
	12	F-16A Fighting Falcon	FGA aircraft	1991	1995–96	(8)	Deal worth $547 m incl 6 F-16B trainer version
	8	F/A-18C/D Hornet	FGA aircraft	1996		:	Incl 4 F/A-18D trainer version
	6	S-70B/SH-60B Seahawk	ASW helicopter	1993	1996	(1)	Deal worth $186 m; for Navy
	6	S-76/H-76 Eagle	Helicopter	1995	1996	(6)	
	2	127mm/54 Mk-42/9	Naval gun	1992	1994	1	On 2 ex-US Navy Knox Class frigates
	12	M-106A3	APC/mortar carrier	1995		:	Deal worth $85 m incl 18 M-901A3 tank destroyers, 21 M-125A3 APC/mortar carriers, 12 M-577A3 APC/CPs and 19 M-113A3 APCs

No.	Weapon designation	Weapon description	Year of order	Year(s) of deliveries	No. produced	Comments
19	M-113A3	APC	1995		..	Deal worth $85 m incl 12 M-577A3 APC/CPs, 18 M-901A3 tank destroyers, 21 M-125A3 and 12 M-106A3 mortar carriers; incl 9 ambulance and 10 ARV versions
21	M-125A3 81mm	APC/mortar carrier	1995		..	Deal worth $85 m incl 18 M-901A3 tank destroyers, 12 M-106A3 APC/mortar carriers, 12 M-577A3 APC/CPs and 19 M-113A3 APCs
12	M-577A3	APC/CP	1995		..	Deal worth $85 m incl 18 M-901A3 tank destroyers, 12 M-106A3 and 21 M-125A3 APC/mortar carriers and 19 M-113A3 APCs
101	M-60A3 Patton-2	Main battle tank	1995	1995–96	(101)	Ex-US Army; deal worth $127 m
18	M-901 ITV	Tank destroyer (M)	1995		..	Deal worth $85 m incl 12 M-577A3 APC/CPs, 21 M-125A3 and 12 M-106A3 mortar carriers and 19 M-113A3 APCs
2	AN/SPG-53	Fire control radar	1992	1994	1	On 2 ex-US Navy Knox Class frigates
2	AN/SPS-10	Surveillance radar	1992	1994	1	On 2 ex-US Navy Knox Class frigates
2	AN/SPS-40B	Surveillance radar	1992	1994	1	On 2 ex-US Navy Knox Class frigates
1	AN/SPS-52C	Surveillance radar	1994		..	For Chakri Naruebet Class aircraft-carrier; ex-US Navy
2	LAADS	Surveillance radar	1993	1995–96	(2)	Deal worth $11.8 m
4	Phalanx	CIWS	1994		..	For 1 Chakri Nareubet Class aircraft-carrier
2	Phalanx	CIWS	1992	1994	1	On 2 ex-US Navy Knox Class frigates
2	RGM-84A ShShMS	ShShM system	1992	1994	1	On 2 ex-US Navy Knox Class frigates
3	W-2100	Surveillance radar	1995		..	Deal worth $180 m incl communication network and training
8	RGM-84A Harpoon	ShShM	(1996)		..	For 1 Phutthayotfa Chulalok (Knox) Class frigate
2	Knox Class	Frigate	1992	1994	1	Ex-US Navy; 5-year lease worth $4.3 m; Thai designation Phutthayotfa Chulalok Class
Tunisia						
S: Czech Republci						
12	L-59	Jet trainer aircraft	1994	1995–96	12	
USA						
(2)	C-130B Hercules	Transport aircraft	1996		..	Ex-US Air Force
4	S-61R Pelican	Helicopter	1994		..	Ex-US Army; deal worth $1.3 m; EDA aid

Recipient/ supplier (S) or licenser (L)	No. ordered	Weapon designation	Weapon description	Year of order/ licence	Year(s) of deliveries	No. delivered/ produced	Comments
Turkey							
S: Canada	10	Bell-206L LongRanger	Helicopter	1993		..	Deal worth $25 m incl licensed production of 14
France	20	AS-532U2 Cougar	Helicopter	1993	1995-96	(20)	Deal worth $253 m (offsets $162 m)
	14	TRS-22XX	Surveillance radar	(1989)	1993-96	14	Deal worth $150 m (offsets $63 m); incl 10 assembled in Turkey
Germany	365	M-52T 155mm turret	Turret	(1994)	1995-96	(365)	For refurbishment of M-52 105mm self-propelled guns to M-52T
	197	RATAC-S	Battlefield radar	1992	1995-96	(60)	Incl assembly in Turkey; Turkish designation Askarad
	1	FPB-57	FAC(M)	1993		..	Turkish designation Yildiz Class
	1	Meko-200 Type	Frigate	1994		..	Deal worth $525 m incl licensed production of 1; Turkish designation Barbaros Class
Israel	150	Popeye-2	ASM	1996		..	For F-4E FGA aircraft
Italy	20	Bell-206B/AB-206B	Helicopter	1994	1995-96	(20)	Deal worth $18.7m; for training
	3	RAT-31SL	Surveillance radar	1995		..	
	4	Seaguard	CIWS	1990	1995-96	(4)	For 2 Meko-200 Type (Barbaros Class) frigates
	4	Seaguard	CIWS	(1994)		..	For 2 Meko-200 Type (Barbaros Class) frigates
	2	Seaguard TMX	Fire control radar	1991	1994-96	(2)	For 2 FPB-57 Type (Yildiz Class) FAC(M)s
	2	Seaguard TMX	Fire control radar	(1990)	1995-96	(2)	For 2 Meko-200 Type (Barbaros Class) frigates
	(48)	Aspide	ShAM	(1990)	1995-96	(48)	For 2 Meko-200 Type (Barbaros Class) frigates
Netherlands	3	MW-08	Surveillance radar	1995		..	For 3 FPB-57 Type (Yildiz Class) FAC(M)s
	3	STING	Fire control radar	1995		..	For 3 FPB-57 Type (Yildiz Class) FAC(M)s
	4	STIR	Fire control radar	(1994)		..	For 2 Meko-200 Type (Barbaros Class) frigates
Russia	19	Mi-17 Hip-H	Helicopter	(1994)	1995-96	(19)	Deal worth $65 m; for Gendarmerie
UK	2	AWS-6	Surveillance radar	(1991)	1994-96	(2)	For 2 FPB-57 Type (Yildiz Class) FAC(M)s
	2	AWS-6	Surveillance radar	(1990)	1995-96	(2)	For 2 Meko-200 Type (Barbaros Class) frigates
	2	AWS-6	Surveillance radar	(1994)		..	For 2 Meko-200 Type (Barbaros Class) frigates
	2	AWS-9	Surveillance radar	(1990)	1995-96	(2)	For 2 Meko-200 Type (Barbaros Class) frigates
	2	AWS-9	Surveillance radar	(1994)		..	For 2 Meko-200 Type (Barbaros Class) frigates
USA	4	CH-47D Chinook	Helicopter	1996		..	For 2 Meko-200 Type (Barbaros Class) frigates

No.	Weapon designation	Weapon description	Year of order	Year(s) of deliveries	No. delivered/ produced	Comments
7	KC-135A Stratotanker	Tanker aircraft	1994		..	Ex-US Air Force; refurbished to KC-135R before delivery
2	127mm/54 Mk-45	Naval gun	(1990)	1995–96	(2)	For 2 Meko-200 Type (Barbaros Class) frigates
2	127mm/54 Mk-45	Naval gun	(1994)		..	For 2 Meko-200 Type (Barbaros Class) frigates
24	MLRS 227mm	MRL	1993		..	Deal worth $289 m incl 1772 rocket pods
2	AN/SPS-49	Surveillance radar	1995		..	On 2 ex-US Navy FFG-7 Class frigates
5	AN/TPQ-36	Tracking radar	1992	1995–96	(4)	Deal worth $28 m
13	Blindfire	Fire control radar	1995	1996	(13)	Ex-US Air Force; EDA aid; for use with Rapier SAM systems
2	Phalanx	CIWS	1995	1995	..	On 2 ex-US Navy FFG-7 Class frigates
2	RGM-84A ShShMS	ShShM system	1990	1995–96	(2)	For 2 Meko-200 Type (Barbaros Class) frigates
2	RGM-84A ShShMS	ShShM system	(1994)		..	For 2 Meko-200 Type (Barbaros Class) frigates
2	RGM-84A ShShMS	ShShM system	(1991)	1994–96	(2)	For 2 FPB-57 Type (Yildiz Class) FAC(M)s
..	RGM-84A ShShMS	ShShM system	1993		..	For 3 FPB-57 Type (Yildiz Class) FAC(M)s
14	Rapier SAMS	SAM system	1995	1996	(14)	Ex-US Air Force; EDA aid
2	Seasparrow ShAMS	ShAM system	1990	1995	1	For 2 Meko-200 Type (Barbaros Class) frigates
2	Seasparrow VLS	ShAM system	1994		..	For 2 Meko-200 Type (Barbaros Class) frigates
80	AIM-120A AMRAAM	Air-to-air missile	1993		..	Deal worth $52 m; for F-16C/D FGA aircraft
200	AIM-9M Sidewinder	Air-to-air missile	(1992)	1996	(100)	Deal worth $23 m
500	AIM-9S Sidewinder	Air-to-air missile	1994		..	Deal worth $55 m incl 30 training missiles
72	ATACMS	SSM	(1996)		..	Deal worth $47.9 m
40	RGM-84A Harpoon	ShShM	1990	1995–96	(40)	Deal worth $62 m
..	RGM-84A Harpoon	ShShM	(1991)	1994–96	(32)	For 2 FPB-57 Type (Yildiz Class) FAC(M)s
16	RGM-84A Harpoon	ShShM	1994		..	Deal worth $15.3 m; for 1 Meko-200 Type (Barbaros Class) frigate
16	RGM-84A Harpoon	ShShM	1995		..	For 3 FPB-57 Type (Yildiz Class) FAC(M)s
..	RGM-84A Harpoon	ShShM	1993		..	For 2 ex-US Navy FFG-7 (Gaziantep) Class frigates
(72)	RIM-66B Standard-1MR	ShAM	1995		..	For 2 Meko-200 Type (Barbaros Class) frigates
..	RIM-7H Seasparrow	ShAM	(1994)		..	For 2 Meko-200 Type (Barbaros Class) frigates
515	Rapier	SAM	1995	1996	(515)	Ex-US Air Force; EDA aid
..	UGM-84A Sub Harpoon	SuShM	(1993)	1994–96	(12)	For 4 Type-209/1400 (Preveze Class) submarines
2	FFG-7 Class	Frigate	1995		..	Ex-US Navy; aid; Turkish designation Gaziantep Class; status uncertain

Recipient/ supplier (S) or licenser (L)	No. ordered	Weapon designation	Weapon description	Year of order/ licence	Year(s) of deliveries	No. delivered/ produced	Comments
L: Canada	1	FFG-7 Class	Frigate	1995		..	Ex-US Navy; Turkish designation Gaziantep Class; status uncertain
Germany	14	Bell-206L LongRanger	Helicopter	1993		..	Deal worth $25 m incl 10 delivered direct
	2	FPB-57 Type	FAC(M)	1991	1994-96	2	Deal worth $143 m; Turkish designation Yildiz Class
	2	FPB-57 Type	FAC(M)	1993		..	Deal worth $250 m incl 1 delivered direct; Turkish designation Yildiz Class
	1	Meko-200 Type	Frigate	1990	1996	1	Deal worth $465 m incl 1 delivered direct; Turkish designation Barbaros Class
	1	Meko-200 Type	Frigate	1994		..	Deal worth $525 m incl 1 delivered direct; Turkish designation Barbaros Class
Spain	4	Type-209/1400	Submarine	1987	1994-96	2	Turkish designation Preveze Class
	50	CN-235M	Transport aircraft	1991	1992-96	(37)	Deal worth $550 m incl 2 delivered direct
UK	..	Shorland S-55	APC	(1990)	1994-96	(30)	For Gendarmerie
USA	40	F-16C Fighting Falcon	FGA aircraft	1992	1996	(2)	Deal worth $2.8 b incl 12 spare engines
	40	F-16C Fighting Falcon	FGA aircraft	1994		..	Deal worth $1.8 b
	650	AIFV	AIFV	1988	1990-96	(350)	Deal worth $1.08 b incl 830 APC, 48 tank destroyer and 170 APC/mortar carrier version (offsets $705 m)
	170	AIFV-AMV	APC/mortar carrier	1988	1993-96	(170)	Deal worth $1.08 b incl 650 AIFV, 830 APC and 48 tank destroyer version (offsets $705 m)
	830	AIFV-APC	APC	1988	1991-96	(750)	Deal worth $1.08 b incl 650 AIFV, 48 tank destroyer and 170 APC/mortar carrier version (offsets $705 m)
UK							
S: Canada	9	Bell-412HP	Helicopter	1996	1996	4	Operated by civilian company for UK armed forces pilot training
France	38	AS-350B Ecureuil	Helicopter	1996	1996	..	Operated by civilian company for UK armed forces pilot training

Supplier	No. ordered	Weapon designation	Weapon description	Year of order	Year of deliveries	No. delivered	Comments
Japan	2	AS-355 Twin Ecureuil	Helicopter	(1995)	1996	2	For Army
South Africa	1	Sea Crusader Class	Cargo ship	1996	1996	1	Leased from civilian owner
	3	Husky	AMV	1996	1996	3	Part of 'Chubby' mine-clearing system; for use with IFOR in Bosnia; ex-South African Army; refurbished before delivery
	3	Meerkat	AMV	1996	1996	3	Part of 'Chubby' mine-clearing system; for use with IFOR in Bosnia; ex-South African Army; refurbished before delivery
USA	25	C-130J-30 Hercules	Transport aircraft	1994	1996	1	Deal worth $1.56 b (offsets 100%); UK designation Hercules C-Mk-4; option on 5 more
	3	CH-47D Chinook	Helicopter	1993	1995-96	(3)	UK designation Chinook HC-Mk-2
	14	CH-47D Chinook	Helicopter	1995		..	Incl 8 MH-47E version; deal worth $365 m; UK designation Chinook HC-Mk-2
	2	Phalanx	CIWS	1994		..	Deal worth $25 m; for 2 support ships
	..	AGM-114 Longbow	Anti-tank missile	1996		..	For AH-64D Longbow helicopters; assembled in UK
	210	AIM-120A AMRAAM	Air-to-air missile	1992	1995-96	(140)	Deal worth $226 m; for Navy Sea Harrier FRS-2 fighters
	65	BGM-109	SLCM	1995		..	Deal worth $142 m; for 1 Swiftsure and 6 Trafalgar Class submarines
L: USA	67	AH-64D Longbow	Combat helicopter	1995		..	Deal worth $3.95 b (offsets 100%)
	..	BGM-71D TOW-2	Anti-tank missile	(1985)	1986-96	(27 577)	For Lynx AH-1 helicopters
USA							
S: Belarus	2	Su-27 Flanker	Fighter aircraft	(1995)	1995-96	(2)	Ex-Belarus Air Force
Canada	135	Bell-206B JetRanger-3	Helicopter	1993	1993-96	(135)	For Army; for training; US designation TH-67A Creek
Israel	17	Piranha 8x8	APC	1995		..	Chassis for LAV-AD AAV(G/M); for Marines
	2	Astra SPX	Transport aircraft	1996		..	Deal worth $20.8 m
	1 725	K-6 120mm	Mortar	1990	1991-96	(1 725)	US designations M-120 and M-121
	50	Have Nap	ASM	1996		..	Deal worth $39 m
South Africa	5	RG-31 Charger	APC	1996	1996	5	For use in peacekeeping operations; option on 5 more

Recipient/ supplier (S) or licenser (L)	No. ordered	Weapon designation	Weapon description	Year of order/ licence	Year(s) of deliveries	No. delivered/ produced	Comments
UK	20	Shorts-330UTT	Transport aircraft	1993	1995-96	(20)	Second-hand; deal worth $100 m; refurbished to C-23B+ Sherpa before delivery
L: Italy	12	Osprey Class	MCM ship	1986	1993-95	4	
Japan	180	Beechjet-400T	Light transport ac	1990	1991-96	(180)	Deal worth $925 m; for training; US designation T-1A Jayhawk; TTTS programme
Switzerland	(711)	PC-9	Trainer aircraft	1995		..	Incl 339 for Navy
UK	199	Hawk	Jet trainer aircraft	1986	1988-96	(68)	For Navy; US designation T-45A Goshawk; VTXTS or T-45TS programme; incl 2 prototypes
	14	Ramadan Class	Patrol craft	1990	1992-96	13	US designation Cyclone Class; option on more
United Arab Emirates							
S: France	7	AS-565SA Panther	ASW helicopter	1995		..	For Abu Dhabi; deal worth $235 m
	390	Leclerc	Main battle tank	1993	1994-96	(80)	Deal worth $4.6 b incl 46 Leclerc ARVs (offsets 60%)
	46	Leclerc ARV	ARV	1993	1996	(2)	Deal worth $4.6 b incl 390 Leclerc tanks (offsets 60%)
	..	AS-15TT	Air-to-ship missile	1995		..	For AS-565SA helicopters
Germany	12	G-115T	Trainer aircraft	1995	1996	(6)	Deal worth $5.5 m; option on 12 more
Netherlands	85	M-109A3 155mm	Self-propelled gun	1995		..	Ex-Dutch Army; refurbished before delivery for $33 m; for Abu Dhabi
	2	Goalkeeper	CIWS	1996		..	For refit of 2 Kortenaer Class frigates
	10	Scout	Surveillance radar	1996		..	For refit of 2 Kortenaer Class Frigates and 8 other ships
	2	Kortenaer Class	Frigate	1996		..	Ex-Dutch Navy; deal worth $320 m incl refit and training
Romania	10	SA-330 Puma	Helicopter	1994		..	Deal worth $37 m; for Abu Dhabi
Russia	6	BM-23 300mm Smerch	MRL	1996		..	
USA	10	AH-64A Apache	Combat helicopter	1994	1996	(6)	Deal worth $150 m; for Abu Dhabi
	360	AGM-114A Hellfire	Anti-tank missile	1994	1996	(216)	For 10 AH-64A helicopters

	No. ordered	Weapon designation	Weapon description	Year of order	Year of delivery	No. delivered	Comments
Venezuela							
S: Poland	636	AGM-114A Hellfire	Anti-tank missile	1996	1996	..	For AH-64A helicopters
	6	M-28 Skytruck	Light transport ac	(1995)	1996	(2)	Option on 12 more; for National Guard
Viet Nam							
S: Russia	2	Bass Tilt	Fire control radar	1995	1996	(1)	On 2 Tarantul-1 Class FAC(M)s
	2	Plank Shave	Surveillance radar	1995	1996	..	On 2 Tarantul-1 Class FAC(M)s
	2	SS-N-2 ShShMS	ShShM system	1995	1996	(1)	On 2 Tarantul-1 Class FAC(M)s
	(80)	SA-N-5 Grail	ShAM	1995	1996	(40)	For 2 Tarantul-1 Class FAC(M)s
	(16)	SS-N-2d Styx	ShShM	1995	1996	(8)	For 2 Tarantul-1 Class FAC(M)s
	2	Tarantul-1 Class	FAC(M)	1994	1996	(1)	For 2 Tarantul-1 Class FAC(M)s
Ukraine	(108)	AA-10a Alamo	Air-to-air missile	(1994)	1995–96	(108)	For 6 Su-27SK/UB fighters; may incl other AA-10 versions
Zimbabwe							
S: France	21	ACMAT APC	APC	1996	1996	21	
USA	2	C-130B Hercules	Transport aircraft	1995		..	Ex-US Air Force; gift

Abbreviations and acronyms

ac	Aircraft
AAV	Anti-aircraft vehicle
AALS	Amphibious assault landing ship
AEV	Armoured engineer vehicle
AEW	Airborne early-warning
AEW&C	Airborne early-warning and control
AIFV	Armoured infantry fighting vehicle
APC	Armoured personnel carrier
APC/CP	Armoured personnel carrier/command post
ARM	Anti-radar missile
ARV	Armoured recovery vehicle
ASM	Air-to-surface missile
ASW	Anti-submarine warfare
CIWS	Close-in weapon system
EDA	Excess Defense Articles
ELINT	Electronic intelligence
EW	Electronic warfare
FAC	Fast attack craft
FGA	Fighter/ground attack
(G)	Gun-armed
IFOR	Implementation Force
incl	Including/includes
(M)	Missile-armed
MCM	Mine countermeasures
Medevac	Medical evaluation

MP	Maritime patrol
MRL	Multiple rocket launcher
OPV	Offshore patrol vessel
SAM	Surface-to-air missile
SAR	Search and rescue
ShAM	Ship-to-air missile
ShShM	Ship-to-ship missile
SIGINT	Signals intelligence
SLCM	Submarine-launched cruise missile
SuShM	Submarine-to-ship missile
VIP	Very important person
VLS	Vertical launch system

Conventions:

. .	Data not available or not applicable
( )	Uncertain data or SIPRI estimate
m	million (10^6)
b	billion (10^9)

Appendix 9C. Sources and methods

I. The SIPRI sources

The sources of the data presented in the arms trade registers are of five general types: newspapers; periodicals and journals; books, monographs and annual reference works; official national documents; and documents issued by international and inter-governmental organizations. The registers are largely compiled from information contained in around 200 publications searched regularly.

Published information cannot provide a comprehensive picture because the arms trade is not fully reported in the open literature. Published reports provide partial information, and substantial disagreement among reports is common. Therefore, the exercise of judgement and the making of estimates are important elements in compiling the SIPRI arms trade data base. Order dates and the delivery dates for arms transactions are continuously revised in the light of new information, but where they are not disclosed the dates are estimated. Exact numbers of weapons ordered and delivered may not always be known and are sometimes estimated—particularly with respect to missiles. It is common for reports of arms deals involving large platforms—ships, aircraft and armoured vehicles—to ignore missile armaments classified as major weapons by SIPRI. Unless there is explicit evidence that platforms were disarmed or altered before delivery, it is assumed that a weapons fit specified in one of the major reference works such as the *Jane's* or *Interavia* series is carried.

II. Selection criteria

SIPRI arms trade data cover five categories of major weapons or systems: aircraft, armour and artillery, guidance and radar systems, missiles, and warships. Statistics presented refer to the value of the trade in these five categories only. The registers and statistics do not include trade in small arms, artillery under 100-mm calibre, ammunition, support items, services and components or component technology, except for specific items. Publicly available information is inadequate to track these items satisfactorily.

There are two criteria for the selection of major weapon transfers for the registers. The first is that of military application. The aircraft category excludes aerobatic aeroplanes and gliders. Transport aircraft and VIP transports are included only if they bear military insignia or are otherwise confirmed as military registered. Micro-light aircraft, remotely piloted vehicles and drones are not included although these systems are increasingly finding military applications.

The armour and artillery category includes all types of tanks, tank destroyers, armoured cars, armoured personnel carriers, armoured support vehicles, infantry combat vehicles as well as multiple rocket launchers, self-propelled and towed guns and howitzers with a calibre equal to or above 100 mm. Military lorries, jeeps and other unarmoured support vehicles are not included.

The category of guidance and radar systems is a residual category for electronic-tracking, target-acquisition, fire-control, launch and guidance systems that are either (*a*) deployed independently of a weapon system listed under another weapon category (e.g., certain ground-based SAM launch systems) or (*b*) shipborne missile-launch or point-defence (CIWS) systems. The values of acquisition, fire-control, launch and guidance systems on aircraft and armoured vehicles are included in the value of the respective aircraft or armoured vehicle. The reason for treating shipborne systems separately is that a given type of ship is often equipped with numerous combinations of different surveillance, acquisition, launch and guidance systems.

The missile category includes only guided missiles. Unguided artillery rockets, man-portable anti-armour rockets and free-fall aerial munitions (e.g., 'iron bombs') are excluded. In the naval sphere, anti-submarine rockets and torpedoes are excluded.

The ship category excludes small patrol craft (with a displacement of less than 100 t), unless they carry cannon with a calibre equal to or above 100 mm; missiles or torpedoes; research vessels; tugs and ice-breakers. Combat support vessels such as fleet replenishment ships are included.

The second criterion for selection of items is the identity of the buyer. Items must be destined for the armed forces, paramilitary forces, intelligence agencies or police of another country. Arms supplied to guerrilla forces pose a problem. For example, if weapons are delivered to the Contra rebels they are listed as imports to Nicaragua with a comment in the arms trade register indicating the local recipient. The entry of any arms transfer is made corresponding to the five weapon categories listed above. This means that missiles and their guidance/launch vehicles are often entered separately under their respective category in the arms trade register.

III. The value of the arms trade

The SIPRI system for arms trade evaluation is designed as a *trend-measuring device*, to permit measurement of changes in the total flow of major weapons and its geographic pattern.[1] Expressing the evaluation in monetary terms reflects both the quantity and quality of the weapons transferred. Aggregate values and shares are based only on *actual deliveries* during the year/years covered in the relevant tables and figures.

The SIPRI valuation system is not comparable to official economic statistics such as gross domestic product, public expenditure and export/import figures. The monetary values chosen do not correspond to the actual prices paid, which vary considerably depending on different pricing methods, the length of production runs and the terms involved in individual transactions. For instance, a deal may or may not cover spare parts, training, support equipment, compensation, offset arrangements for the local industries in the buying country, and so on. Furthermore, to use only actual sales prices—even assuming that the information were available for all deals, which it is not—military aid and grants would be excluded, and the total flow of arms would therefore not be measured.

Production under licence is included in the arms trade statistics in such a way as to reflect the import share embodied in the weapon. In reality, this share is normally high in the beginning, gradually decreasing over time. However, as SIPRI makes a single estimate of the import share for each weapon produced under licence, the value of arms produced under licence agreements may be slightly overstated.

---

[1] Additional information is contained in Brzoska, M., 'The SIPRI price system', *SIPRI Yearbook 1987: World Armaments and Disarmament* (Oxford University Press: Oxford 1987), appendix 7D; Sköns, E., 'Sources and methods', *SIPRI Yearbook 1992: World Armaments and Disarmament* (Oxford University Press: Oxford, 1992), appendix 8D; and SIPRI, *Sources and Methods for SIPRI Research on Military Expenditure, Arms Transfers and Arms Production*, SIPRI Fact Sheet, Stockholm, Jan. 1995.

Part III. Non-proliferation, arms control and disarmament, 1996

10. Multilateral military-related export control measures

IAN ANTHONY, SUSANNA ECKSTEIN and
JEAN PASCAL ZANDERS

I. Introduction

In 1996 changes occurred in the membership or status of three of the multilateral military-related export control regimes discussed in this chapter: the
Australia Group, the Nuclear Suppliers Group (NSG), and the Wassenaar
Arrangement on Export Controls for Conventional Arms and Dual-Use Goods
and Technologies.[1]

The Republic of Korea (South Korea) became a new member of the Australia Group, bringing its membership to 30 states. Brazil, South Korea and
Ukraine joined the NSG, bringing its membership to 34. At the meeting in
1996 where the Wassenaar Arrangement was formally established, Argentina,
Bulgaria, South Korea, Romania and Ukraine participated for the first time in
the discussions which have been held by the group, putting its founder
membership at 33 states. Brazil—which had been accepted as a member of the
Missile Technology Control Regime (MTCR) in 1995—participated in the
1996 MTCR plenary meeting, bringing its membership to 28 states. These
regimes are discussed in sections II–V.

The other regime discussed in this chapter is the European Union (EU) regulation for exports of dual-use technologies (section VI). Table 10.1 lists the
members of six regimes—those mentioned above and the Zangger Committee—and shows that participation is still a highly concentrated activity,
confined to 36 states.

II. The Wassenaar Arrangement

The Wassenaar Arrangement on Export Controls for Conventional Arms and
Dual-Use Goods and Technologies was formally established in Vienna in July
1996. It seeks to prevent destabilizing accumulations of conventional arms and
specific dual-use technologies and thereby contribute to regional and international security and stability. In the framework of the Arrangement, members
exchange information and discuss policy approaches. However, the Arrange-

---

[1] For background information about the structure and terms of reference of 6 multilateral regimes and
for developments up to the end of 1994, see Anthony, I. *et al.*, 'Multilateral weapon-related export con-
trol measures', *SIPRI Yearbook 1995: Armaments, Disarmament and International Security* (Oxford
University Press: Oxford, 1995), pp. 597–633; and for developments in 1995, see Anthony, I. and
Stock, T., 'Multilateral military-related export control measures', *SIPRI Yearbook 1996: Armaments,
Disarmament and International Security* (Oxford University Press: Oxford, 1996), pp. 537–51.

SIPRI Yearbook 1997: Armaments, Disarmament and International Security

Table 10.1. Membership of multilateral military-related export control regimes, as of 1 January 1997

State	Zangger Committee 1974	NSG[a] 1978	Australia Group[b] 1985	MTCR[c] 1987	EU dual-use regulation 1995	Wassenaar Arrangement 1996
Argentina		x	x	x	n.a.	x
Australia	x	x	x	x	n.a.	x
Austria	x	x	x	x	x	x
Belgium	x	x	x[d]	x	x	x
Brazil	x	x[f]		x[f]	n.a.	
Bulgaria	x	x			n.a.	x
Canada	x	x	x	x	n.a.	x
Czech Republic	x	x	x		n.a.	x
Denmark	x	x	x	x	x	x
Finland	x	x	x	x	x	x
France	x	x	x	x	x	x
Germany	x	x	x	x	x	x
Greece	x	x	x	x	x	x
Hungary	x	x	x	x	n.a.	x
Iceland			x[d]	x	n.a.	
Ireland	x	x	x	x	x	x
Italy	x	x	x	x	x	x
Japan	x	x	x	x	n.a.	x
Korea, South[e]		x[f]	x[d,f]		n.a.	x
Luxembourg	x	x	x[d]	x	x	x
Netherlands	x	x	x	x	x	x
New Zealand		x	x	x	n.a.	x
Norway	x	x	x	x	n.a.	x
Poland	x	x	x		n.a.	x
Portugal	x	x	x	x	x	x
Romania	x	x	x		n.a.	x
Russia	x	x		x	n.a.	x
Slovakia	x	x	x		n.a.	x
South Africa	x	x		x	n.a.	
Spain	x	x	x	x	x	x
Sweden	x	x	x	x	x	x
Switzerland	x	x	x	x	n.a.	x
Turkey					n.a.	x
Ukraine		x[f]			n.a.	x
UK	x	x	x	x	x	x
USA	x	x	x[d]	x	n.a.	x

Note: The years in the column headings indicate when the export control regime was formally established, although the groups may have met on an informal basis before then.

[a] The Nuclear Suppliers Group.

[b] The European Commission is represented in the Australia Group as an observer.

[c] The Missile Technology Control Regime.

[d] A member of the Australia Group which had not ratified the Chemical Weapons Convention as of 1 Jan. 1997.

[e] South Korea is an observer to the Zangger Committee.

[f] This state became a member of the regime in 1996.

ment does not have collective decision authority. All decisions are taken by member states independently and are implemented through national procedures.[2]

States participating in the Wassenaar Arrangement are obliged to maintain national controls on transfers of items in the List of Dual-Use Goods and Technologies and the Munitions List developed by experts from the participating states. The participating states agreed to implement the elements of the Arrangement in their national export control systems by 1 November 1996.[3] In the framework of the Arrangement, members have agreed to notify one another both of aggregate transfers to non-participating states and of individual cases where licences to transfer an item have been denied. At least in the first stage, members have not agreed to refuse a licence for a transfer of the same product to the same destination where a partner in the Arrangement has denied a licence application. However, for the dual-use goods subject to control, they have agreed to notify partners in the Arrangement within 60 days if they do grant a licence for such a transfer.[4] In April 1996 Russia initially refused to accept this procedure but modified its position before the establishment of the Arrangement after certain transitional arrangements were agreed, giving Russia time to modify its national regulations.[5]

Neither the Munitions List nor the List of Dual-Use Goods and Technologies was released as part of the so-called Initial Elements of the Wassenaar Arrangement, although individual governments may release the lists unilaterally. However, it is stated that the dual-use list includes a sub-set of items considered to be 'very sensitive' for the purposes of decisions to export.[6]

The participating states have agreed to information exchanges of three types. For conventional arms, information is to be exchanged on a six-monthly basis regarding deliveries of equipment conforming to the categories used in the context of the United Nations Register of Conventional Arms to countries that do not participate in the Wassenaar Arrangement. However, the information is to be provided together with details of the model and type of equipment transferred—which is not required for the UN Register.[7] For dual-use goods there are specific reporting obligations associated with different schedules within the agreed list of goods and technologies. Finally, countries may present any information they consider relevant or raise any issue of concern in the Wassenaar forum. For example, at the December 1996 plenary meeting the

[2] The Wassenaar Arrangement on Export Controls for Conventional Arms and Dual-Use Goods and Technologies: Initial Elements, Press statement, 12 July 1996 (available at the SIPRI Arms Transfers Project Internet address URL <http://www.sipri.se/projects/arms trade/wass_initialelements.html>).

[3] The Wassenaar Arrangement . . . (note 2).

[4] The Wassenaar Arrangement . . . (note 2), Section II, Scope.

[5] 'As export control group starts, US watches Russian actions', *Wireless File (European Edition)*, United States Information Agency, 17 July 1996, URL <gopher://198.80.36.82:70/0R27426453-27432300-range/archives/1996/pdq.96>.

[6] The Wassenaar Arrangement . . . (note 2), Section III, Control Lists.

[7] The Wassenaar Arrangement . . . (note 2), Section VI, Procedures for the Exchange of Information on Arms.

issue of implementation of the 1996 UN embargo on arms transfers to Afghanistan was raised.[8]

Aside from the plenary and other meetings in the framework of the Wassenaar Arrangement, six countries—France, Germany, Italy, Russia, the United Kingdom and the United States—have agreed to meet for 'more intensive consultations and more intrusive information sharing'.[9]

The participating states agreed that the Arrangement would be open in principle to all countries on the condition that they meet certain criteria. The criteria are: (a) whether the country is a producer or exporter of arms or industrial equipment subject to control; and (b) the non-proliferation policies of the country, including adherence to existing multilateral export control regimes, the 1968 Non-Proliferation Treaty (NPT), the 1972 Biological and Toxin Weapons Convention (BTWC) and the 1993 Chemical Weapons Convention (CWC); and (c) the country's maintenance and application of effective national export controls.[10]

The Wassenaar Arrangement is not directed at any state or group of states. However, in the framework of the discussions among the participating states transfers of conventional arms and dual-use items to certain destinations are currently considered to be cause for serious concern. Among these destinations is Iran. The Czech Republic, Hungary, Poland and Russia have given the United States bilateral assurances outside the framework of the Wassenaar Arrangement that they will not conclude further agreements for arms transfers to Iran. However, none of these states is willing to break existing contracts or to deny Iran supplies of spare parts that are essential for the operation of equipment already delivered.[11]

III. The Nuclear Suppliers Group

The NSG is a forum for discussing and coordinating export control policies with a view to preventing the acquisition of nuclear weapons by non-nuclear weapon states.

The main recent additional feature of the NSG Guidelines for Transfers of Nuclear-related Dual-use Equipment, Material and Related Technology is the requirement for an agreement between the International Atomic Energy Agency (IAEA) and the recipient state requiring the application of full-scope safeguards (that is, safeguards on all fissionable materials in its current and

---

[8] The Wassenaar Arrangement on Export Controls for Conventional Arms and Dual-Use Goods and Technologies, Press statement, 13 Dec. 1996 (available at the SIPRI Arms Transfers Project Internet address URL <http://www.sipri.se/projects/armstrade/wass_press9612.html>).

[9] 'The Wassenaar Arrangement', Address by Under-secretary of State for Arms Control and International Security Affairs Lynn E. Davis, Carnegie Endowment for International Peace, 23 Jan. 1996. For the list of parties to the NPT, the BTWC and the CWC as of 1 Jan. 1997, see annexe A in this volume.

[10] The Wassenaar Arrangement . . . (note 2), Appendix 4, Participation.

[11] Sullivan, P., 'Export controls: conventional arms and dual-use technologies', *National Defense University Strategic Forum*, no. 100 (Dec. 1996), URL <http://198.80.36.91/ndu/inss/strforum/forum100.html>. Sullivan is Deputy Director of the US Defense Technology Security Administration.

peaceful activities) before controlled items will be transferred.[12] The NSG Guidelines also require the recipient to establish physical protection against unauthorized use of transferred materials and facilities. The members of the NSG exchange information on nuclear programmes of potential concern from a proliferation perspective. In addition, the Guidelines call for consultations among members before controlled items are transferred to these programmes to reduce the risk that any given transfer will contribute to an increased risk of nuclear-weapon proliferation.

The members of the NSG also require recipients to provide an end-use statement before any transfer of controlled items takes place. This is to reduce the risk that controlled items will be diverted to unsafeguarded facilities or activities. The members are not obliged to use any standard form of end-use document but their national document should require a statement from the recipient country specifying how controlled items will be used, stating that they will not be used for proscribed activities and that the consent of the supplier will be obtained before any item is retransferred.

After the decision on 'Principles and Objectives for Nuclear Non-Proliferation and Disarmament' had been adopted at the NPT Review and Extension Conference in May 1995,[13] the NSG agreed at its 1996 Plenary Meeting to 'promote openness and transparency through further dialogue and cooperation with non-member countries'. A special working group was established to further this objective.[14]

In 1996 two new members joined the NSG, Brazil and South Korea. Brazil joined the Group at the April 1996 Buenos Aires Plenary Meeting after the Brazilian Congress approved national nuclear-related export regulations. Historically, the commitment of Brazil to the international norm against nuclear weapon proliferation has been questioned, and accession to the NSG raised the issue of the criteria for membership—Brazil is still not a party to the NPT.

Brazil began to discuss the issue of modifying its export control laws and regulations in the early 1990s. By 1992 a draft law was submitted by the President to the Brazilian Congress on export controls for sensitive goods and services. This included the measures needed to regulate exports of goods with military applications including conventional arms and items associated with the development of weapons of mass destruction. The Brazilian Congress passed this draft into law in October 1995 as Law 9112. Under the law, exports of sensitive goods require prior permission from several federal agencies under the overall coordination of the Strategic Affairs Secretariat in the administration of the Brazilian President. An inter-ministerial working group was established under the overall coordination of the Strategic Affairs Secretariat to prepare and review more specific regulations.

---

[12] The most recent version of the NSG Guidelines was transmitted to the IAEA as INFCIRC/254/Rev.2/Part2/Mod.1 (Guidelines for Transfers of Nuclear-related Dual-use Equipment, Material and Related Technology), 19 Mar. 1996.

[13] For a discussion of the conference, see Simpson, J., 'The nuclear non-proliferation regime after the NPT Review and Extension Conference', *SIPRI Yearbook 1996* (note 1), pp. 561–89.

[14] Press statement: Nuclear Suppliers Group plenary meeting, Buenos Aires, 25–26 Apr. 1996.

In making these changes to its national procedures the Brazilian Government stated two objectives: (*a*) to create the means by which Brazil can implement and enforce its commitments in the field of disarmament and non-proliferation of weapons of mass destruction; and (*b*) export control regulations were seen as a basic precondition if Brazil was to gain unrestricted access to advanced technology from the major suppliers. The lack of export regulations was seen by Brazil as an obstacle to its strengthening of trade links with countries which have advanced technology and which participate in export control regimes.

In recent years Brazil has taken a series of steps intended to reassure the international community that it has no intention to develop nuclear weapons. The 1991 quadripartite Agreement on the Exclusively Peaceful Utilization of Nuclear Energy between Argentina, Brazil, the IAEA and the Brazilian–Argentine Agency for Accounting and Control of Nuclear Materials (ABACC), which entered into force in 1994, and the entry into force for Brazil of the Tlatelolco Treaty in 1994 were the most important of these. Through these steps Brazil has accepted legal commitments which can be compared with those accepted by parties to the NPT. Under these conditions the members of the NSG decided to admit Brazil to the group in spite of the fact that Brazil has not signed the NPT.[15]

For Ukraine, the basis for nuclear-related export controls is a Presidential Decree of January 1993.[16] Based on this decree a decision by the Ukrainian Cabinet of Ministers of March 1993 introduced a list of nuclear dual-use equipment subject to export control.[17] In March 1995, as a prelude to joining the NSG, the Ukrainian delegation sent a letter to the IAEA stating that Ukraine would conduct its nuclear exports in accordance with the NSG Guidelines specified in IAEA document INFCIRC/254.[18]

In South Korea, the 1993 Public Notice on Export and Import of Strategic Commodities, a regulation under the Foreign Trade Act, was revised in October 1995 to include all the items on the Zangger Committee trigger list and the nuclear dual-use items specified in the NSG Guidelines.[19]

The members of the NSG have also made efforts to secure voluntary adherence to the NSG Guidelines from countries which are not members. Particular attention has been paid to nuclear dual-use exports by Belarus, China, Kazakhstan and Lithuania.

---

[15] Brazil has, however, unilaterally accepted NPT-equivalent undertakings. See Goodby, J. E. *et al.*, 'Nuclear arms control', *SIPRI Yearbook 1995* (note 1), p. 663.

[16] Presidential Decree on Improvement of State Export Control, no. 3, 3 Jan. 1993.

[17] *Nuclear Successor States of the Soviet Union*, Nuclear Weapon and Sensitive Export Status Report, no. 4 (Monterey Institute for International Studies: Monterey, Calif., May 1996).

[18] IAEA Document INFCIRC/254/Rev.2/Part 1 (Guidelines for Nuclear Transfers) and INFCIRC/254/Rev.2/Part 2 (Guidelines for Nuclear-related Dual-Use Transfers), Oct. 1995 .

[19] The Public Notice on Export and Import of Strategic Commodities of 1 July 1993 established an export control system that was compatible with the activities of the Coordinating Committee for Multilateral Export Controls (COCOM), which was dissolved in Mar. 1994. *Korea's New Export Control System*, attachment to INFCIRC/490, IAEA Vienna, 19 Oct. 1995; and Yang Woo Park, 'South Korea', *Worldwide Guide to Export Controls* (Export Control Publications: Chertsey, Surrey, Nov. 1995). For a discussion of the Nuclear Exporters Committee, known as the Zangger Committee, see Anthony *et al.*, *SIPRI Yearbook 1995* (note 1), p. 546; and Anthony and Stock, *SIPRI Yearbook 1996* (note 1), p. 546.

China is the most important supplier of dual-use nuclear equipment outside the NSG because of its status as a nuclear weapon state. On 11 May 1996 China announced that it would not provide further assistance to nuclear facilities which were not subject to full IAEA safeguards. This announcement followed discussions between the USA and China. At the same time, the USA and China also agreed to hold further bilateral consultations on export control policies. US Secretary of State Warren Christopher stated that one of the main issues of concern to the USA was Chinese nuclear and military cooperation with Iran.[20] In November 1996 the US State Department issued a statement that, after discussions with Chinese officials and with the information available, it had concluded that China was 'operating within the assurances they have given' regarding non-proliferation.[21]

IV. The Australia Group

The Australia Group is an informal group whose objective is to limit the transfer of chemical precursors, equipment used in the production of chemical and biological weapons (CBW), and biological warfare agents and organisms. The participating states have agreed to apply decisions taken collectively through their national export control systems. Created in 1985, the original objective of the Australia Group was to prevent CW proliferation while the negotiations to complete the CWC were being undertaken. Subsequently, it has also acted to prevent BW proliferation during the process of developing improved measures to ensure compliance with the BTWC.

Two events in 1995 modified the focus of the group. The first was the discovery of the extent of Iraq's CBW programmes through the work of the UN Special Commission on Iraq (UNSCOM) after the 1991 Persian Gulf War. The second event—the use of Sarin by a group of religious extremists in an attack on passengers on the Tokyo subway[22]—raised serious challenges to the previous approaches to CBW non-proliferation, which focused on state actors rather than also taking into consideration the activities of sub-state groups.

The CWC will introduce a comprehensive verification system and, progressively, a discriminatory regime for the trade with non-states parties in the chemicals listed in Schedules 1–3 of the CWC. The CWC also requires parties to enact legislation penalizing acts prohibited under the convention committed by nationals or by individuals operating on their territory—providing a mechanism for action against terrorism involving chemicals. The BTWC does not contain similar provisions, and the modest proposals for transparency made at the Fourth Review Conference of the BTWC[23] cannot be an effective substitute. Already criticized from various quarters, the chances of introducing veri-

[20] Secretary of State Warren Christopher, 'American interests and the US–China relationship', Address before the Council on Foreign Relations, 17 May 1996, in *US Department of State Dispatch*, 27 May 1996.

[21] Voice of America, 21 Nov. 1996, URL <gopher://gopher.voa.gov:70/00/newswire/thu/U-S-CHINA-IRAN>.

[22] See also chapter 13 in this volume.

[23] For a discussion of the Fourth BTWC Review Conference, see chapter 13 in this volume.

fication mechanisms into the BTWC will depend largely on the success of the CWC regime.

The most recent annual meeting of the Australia Group was held in Paris on 14–17 October 1996. Thirty states attended, including, for the first time, South Korea. The European Commission attended as an observer. No changes were made to the Australia Group's so-called warning lists.[24] At the meeting Hungary announced its intention to ratify the CWC and so become the 65th party—triggering the process towards entry into force of the convention on 29 April 1997.[25]

In this way, the relationship between the work of the Australia Group and the purposes and objectives of the CWC has become a more immediate issue.[26] All the Australia Group members had signed the CWC by the end of 1996. Although all the members had pledged to be among the first 65 states to ratify the Convention,[27] five—Belgium, Iceland, South Korea, Luxembourg and the United States—were not. All the Australia Group participants are parties to the BTWC.[28] The participating states have endorsed measures for strengthening confidence in both treaty regimes but noted that 'the maintenance of effective export controls will remain an essential practical means of fulfilling obligations under the CWC and the BTWC'.[29]

In October 1996 the Australia Group issued a press release on the anticipated entry into force of the CWC, stating that:

Representatives at the Australia Group meeting recalled that all of the participating countries are taking steps at the national level to ensure that relevant national regulations promote the object and purpose of the CWC and are fully consistent with the Convention's provisions when the CWC enters into force for each of these countries. They noted that the practical experience each country had obtained in operating export licensing systems intended to prevent assistance to chemical weapons programmes have been especially valuable in each country's preparations for implementation of key obligations under the CWC. They noted in this context that these national systems are aimed solely at avoiding assistance for activities which are prohibited under the Convention, while ensuring they do not restrict or impede trade and other exchanges facilitated by the CWC.[30]

In essence, this position was unchanged from that of the previous year.[31] The press release reiterated that national export licensing systems are aimed 'at

---

[24] The Australia Group export control lists include: chemical weapon precursors; dual-use chemical manufacturing facilities and equipment, and related technology; biological agents; animal pathogens; dual-use biological equipment; and plant pathogens.

[25] See chapter 13 in this volume.

[26] See Anthony et al., SIPRI Yearbook 1995 (note 1), p. 611, and Anthony and Stock, SIPRI Yearbook 1996 (note 1), pp. 548–49, for discussions of the Australia Group and its relationship to the CWC after entry into force.

[27] Anthony and Stock (note 1), p. 547.

[28] For the full list of states which have signed or ratified the CWC and the BTWC as of 1 Jan. 1997, see annexe A in this volume.

[29] Australia Group meeting, 14–17 October 1996, Press release, Paris, 17 Oct. 1996.

[30] Australia Group Countries welcome prospective entry into force of the Chemical Weapons Convention, Press release, Australian Embassy, Paris, 17 Oct. 1996.

[31] Anthony and Stock (note 1), p. 547.

preventing inadvertent assistance to the production of CBW and [are] administered in a streamlined and effective manner which allows trade and the exchange of technology for peaceful purposes to flourish'.[32]

Taking the United States as an example, US trade statistics indicated that, in 1991, 38 000 export licences were issued for dual-use technologies, with a few hundred applications denied or returned without action. In 1992 less than 3 per cent of the value ($640.5 billion) of all goods exported from the USA was goods subject to specific licensing requirements, of which the value of goods that were denied export licences amounted to less than $2 billion. In 1983–93, the share of US chemical and allied industry investment in the developing world remained steady at around 21 per cent, the major impediments to further investment being national barriers in the developing countries rather than unilateral restrictions imposed by the exporting states.[33]

The Australia Group also announced that a number of the participants will host regional seminars prior to the entry into force of the CWC to inform other states of the relevance of national policies.[34]

These statements and regional initiatives are part of an attempt to depolarize the divergent positions on Article XI of the CWC (Economic and Technological Development), which have cast a shadow over the discussions in the Preparatory Commission (PrepCom) of the Organisation for the Prohibition of Chemical Weapons (OPCW).

After the CWC enters into force the Australia Group will have to balance the implications of Article I (General Obligations) and Article XI of the CWC—which has already placed the Australia Group in diametrical opposition to many developing countries.[35] Their frustration was expressed most forcefully in a statement to the PrepCom by India:

. . . as we enter the final phase of this Commission, I would like to reiterate my Government's expectation that the [Chemical Weapons] Convention, if implemented in the letter and spirit of its provisions will result in enhanced trade in chemicals, equipment and technology for peaceful purposes amongst States Parties. We regret that discussions on Article XI of the Convention have come to a cul-de-sac. Unless countries which are party to export control regimes operating outside the scope of the Convention agree that the provisions of the Convention supersede all existing

[32] Australia Group Meeting (note 29).

[33] Roberts, B., 'Article III: Non-Transfer', eds G. S. Pearson and M. R. Dando, *Strengthening the Biological Weapons Convention: Key Points for the Fourth Review Conference* (Quaker United Nations Office: Geneva, 1996), p. 35.

[34] Seminars on CWC implementation were sponsored by the Provisional Technical Secretariat and hosted by Austria (6–8 Mar. 1996); Iran (23–26 Apr. 1996); and Japan (16–17 Oct. 1996). Another seminar was sponsored and hosted by Romania (21–22 Oct. 1996) for the Central and East European countries and the Commonwealth of Independent States.

[35] Article I of the CWC commits states parties never to assist, encourage or induce, in any way, anyone to engage in any activity prohibited under the convention. Article XI commits states parties not to maintain any barriers restricting or impeding trade for legitimate purposes with other states parties and to review their national regulations in the field of trade in chemicals in order to render them consistent with the object and purpose of the CWC. For the text of the CWC, see *SIPRI Yearbook 1993: World Armaments and Disarmament* (Oxford University Press: Oxford, 1993), appendix 14A, pp. 735–56 (also available at the SIPRI CBW Project Internet address URL <http://www.sipri.se/projects/group-cw/CWCrtf.html>.

arrangements upon entry into force, the provisions of this Article cannot be implemented as intended. Without this benevolent interaction among countries—which can enhance trust and cooperation, especially in today's age of liberalised trade—the Convention may end up with only a selectively regulatory role. Parties to a multilateral Convention of this nature, who have submitted themselves to the verification and fact-finding provisions of the Convention should not be subject to demands by some other States Parties to furnish end-user certificates or be refused the import of chemicals and equipment, as this would only create two classes of States Parties and make the implementation of the Convention contentious.[36]

Several other developing countries have also expressed concern about the possible non-implementation of Article XI.

A key aspect of this debate is whether trade restrictions contained in the CWC apply only to the scheduled chemicals or whether the obligation in Article I not to assist any CW programme also extends to other potentially relevant compounds. The Australia Group warning list for chemicals differs from the set of scheduled chemicals subject to control in the framework of the CWC.[37] Absent the national controls harmonized in the Australia Group, the unlicensed transfer of chemicals which are unscheduled for CWC purposes but which may none the less pose a threat to the CWC regime would be permitted—a logic rejected by states participating in the Australia Group.[38]

V. The Missile Technology Control Regime

The aim of the MTCR is to restrict the proliferation of missiles, unmanned air vehicles and related technology for those systems capable of carrying a 500-kg payload a distance of at least 300 km.[39] The MTCR is a voluntary arrangement in which countries interested in restricting the proliferation of specific goods and technologies exchange information and coordinate their national activities. The MTCR does not act as a decision-making authority; each member is responsible for implementing group decisions through national laws and regulations. However, within the regime the members have developed common approaches to the issue of transfers of a specified list of controlled items.

The MTCR is not intended to interfere with civilian activities—such as meteorology or the peaceful uses of space—that depend on equipment and technologies which have characteristics similar to some missiles.

[36] Preparatory Commission for the Organisation for the Prohibition of Chemical Weapons document PC-XV/10, 16 Dec. 1996, p. 2.
[37] Mathews, R. J., 'A comparison of the Australia Group List of Chemical Weapon Precursors and the CWC Scheduled Chemicals', *Chemical Weapons Convention Bulletin*, no. 21 (Sep. 1993), pp. 1–3.
[38] See, e.g., Australia: National Export Licensing Measures, PrepCom Document PC-XIII/B/WP.9, 26 Mar. 1996.
[39] A fact sheet released by the United States Arms Control and Disarmament Agency uses a slightly wider formulation than that used in the MTCR Guidelines, including the phrase 'missiles, unmanned air vehicles, and related technology for those systems capable of carrying a 500 kilogram payload at least 300 kilometers, as well as systems intended for the delivery of weapons of mass destruction (WMD)'. In addition to missiles, this formulation would cover all systems designed and developed specifically for delivering nuclear, chemical or biological weapons. *The Missile Technology Control Regime* (US Arms Control and Disarmament Agency: Washington, DC, 28 May 1996), URL <http://www.acda.gov/factshee/exptcon/mtcr96.htm>.

Apart from its annual plenary meeting, MTCR members also hold inter-sessional discussions at which government experts can address specific issues. In 1996 inter-sessional meetings addressed regional aspects of missile prolif-eration and the issue of how to regulate the transshipment of missiles and associated technologies, including shipment through countries which are not regime members. Transshipment of equipment and technologies has the poten-tial to undermine the effectiveness of end-user statements. The July 1996 seminar on transshipment issues was held in Washington and included repre-sentatives from 12 MTCR member states and 7 non-member states.[40]

In 1996 one of the main issues for discussion among members of the regime was that of new members. One country, Ukraine, has taken steps to join the MTCR but has not been accepted as a member by the regime, which operates by consensus. Another country, Brazil, completed the national measures required before participation in the regime is possible and in 1996 attended an MTCR plenary meeting for the first time. The relationship between the MTCR and Brazil and Ukraine is examined in the section below.

South Korea has also expressed a wish to join the MTCR. In 1979 the South Korean Government gave the United States an undertaking that it would not develop missiles with a range longer than 180 km. However, in the light of the further development of longer-range missiles by North Korea (including the development of missiles with ranges over 1000 km) South Korea examined the development of missiles for its own use with ranges at least up to the 300-km range contained in the MTCR Equipment and Technology Annex.[41] The United States, which supports South Korean membership in the MTCR in principle, would prefer the existing commitment to remain in place, arguing that it is not necessary for South Korea to match North Korea on a system-by-system basis in order to safeguard its security. According to some reports, an agreement was reached in December 1996 which would make it possible for South Korea to join the regime.[42]

A second issue under discussion was the relationship between the MTCR member states and countries which are outside the regime. There is no multi-lateral arms control treaty or agreement addressing the issue of the use, possession, production or trade in missiles. Efforts to develop such an agree-ment or treaty, proposed by Canada several years ago, have not led to any progress. The issue of the relationship between MTCR members and non-members has several elements. First is the relationship with countries which have significant ballistic missile-production capacities but are not members of the MTCR (China and North Korea are prominent in this group). It has been

---

[40] 'Letter from the President to the Speaker of the House of Representatives and the President of the Senate, 12 Nov. 1996', *Wireless File (Europe)*, 13 Nov. 1996, URL <http://www.usis.usemb.se/wireless/300/eur307.htm>.

[41] 'Restrictions on domestic-produced ROK missiles should be lifted', *Hanguk Ilbo* (Seoul), 26 Sep. 1995, p. 3 (in Korean), in 'Editorial urges US to abolish restriction on ROK missiles', Foreign Broadcast Information Service, *Daily Report–Arms Control and Proliferation Issues (FBIS-TAC)*, FBIS-TAC-95-006, 6 Dec. 1995, p. 22; and *Tong-a-ilbo* (Seoul), 9 Oct. 1995 (in Korean), in 'Government to abrogate missile pact with US to join MTCR', FBIS-TAC-95-006, 6 Dec. 1995, p. 21.

[42] See, e.g., *The Australian*, 4 Dec. 1996, p. 8.

acknowledged by members that in the absence of a multilateral agreement or treaty the regime is strengthened through cooperation with other countries, and China, Israel, Romania and Ukraine (although non-members) have made unilateral statements of their intention to adhere to the MTCR Guidelines.[43] The second element is relations with countries which are developing or buying ballistic missiles with a particular focus on the Persian Gulf and South Asia.[44]

In June 1996 the members of the MTCR held a meeting on regional missile-proliferation issues which focused on South Asia and the Persian Gulf. Information was exhanged between MTCR members about the current status of four missile programmes of concern—in all likelihood these were programmes in India, Iran, Iraq and Pakistan. As noted above, there is no multilateral agreement which focuses on the use, possession, production or trade of missiles. These systems are not limited in the framework of European conventional arms control. Even countries which are among the leading advocates of greater transparency in armaments have serious reservations about revealing their own missile stocks. In most countries outside Europe not only are the size and characteristics of missile arsenals considered secret but also the interest in arms control as a form of conflict management is low. However, assuming that governments could be persuaded to engage in such discussions, the nature of missile technology has usually been considered to make regional approaches to arms control inappropriate.[45] Consequently, MTCR members consider that the regime encourages restraint in missile programmes in these regions while reinforcing the national security of all states.[46]

Criteria for MTCR membership: a comparison of Brazil and Ukraine

In January 1994 the Ukrainian Government took a decision to seek membership of the MTCR.[47] The decision followed two years of internal discussion about the advantages and disadvantages of such a step. While Brazil joined the MTCR in 1995, the membership of Ukraine has not been approved. However, as noted above, Ukraine currently adheres to the MTCR Guidelines without being a member of the regime.

While both Brazil and Ukraine have significant capacities to design, develop and produce ballistic missiles, Ukrainian capabilities are more significant and more highly developed than those of Brazil.[48]

[43] Frieman, W., 'New members of the club: Chinese participation in arms control regimes, 1980–95', *Nonproliferation Review*, vol. 3, no. 3 (spring–summer 1996), p. 20.

[44] 'Control of missile technology', Opening speech of David Davis, Minister of State, Foreign and Commonwealth Office, at the MTCR Plenary Meeting, Edinburgh, 8 Oct. 1996.

[45] The missile attacks by Libya against the Italian island of Lampedusa in 1986 and by Iraq against Israel in 1991 underline the difficulty of defining who should be included in a 'region' for the purposes of discussing missile-related arms control.

[46] Missile Technology Control Regime holds plenary meeting in Edinburgh, UK Foreign and Commonwealth Office Press release, Edinburgh, 10 Oct. 1996.

[47] US–Ukrainian missile export controls agreement, Press release, Office of the Vice-President, Washington, DC, 13 May 1994; and Sharov, Y., 'Ukraine and the MTCR', *The Monitor*, vol. 1, no. 2 (spring 1995). Sharov was then First Secretary in the Ukrainian Ministry of Foreign Affairs.

[48] The largest missile-production facility in the world is the Pivdenmash complex located at Dnepropetrovsk in Ukraine while a Ukrainian design bureau led the development of several Soviet

Both Brazil and Ukraine intend to participate in the development of civilian space activities—a market which is expected to grow significantly in the future. The Brazilian Space Agency (AEB) has prepared a National Policy on the Development of Space Activities (PNDAE) to promote the development of space activities in the national interest.[49] Brazil intends to develop space systems, infrastructure and activities in order to participate in future civilian telecommunications, weather and climate forecasting, inventory and monitoring of natural resources, and navigation and scientific research.

As with dual-use nuclear technologies, Brazil saw integration into the international export control system as removing an obstacle to access to advanced technology from the major suppliers.[50] This became even more important as Russia—a potential source of technology—has progressively joined the international export control system.

Ukraine has based a major element of its programme for converting military production facilities on the development of a civilian space programme. During the Soviet period, space launch vehicles as well as missiles were developed in Ukraine, including the Zenith and Cyclone rockets. However, the programmes for civilian space activity are integrated with those of cooperation partners in Russia and Kazakhstan. Many of the payloads which these rockets are expected to place in space are from Canada, the United States and Western Europe.[51] As Russia has become more fully integrated into the MTCR it has given bilateral assurances to the USA as well as to its new MTCR partners that it will not contribute to civilian programmes which may have the side-effect of stimulating the development of equipment and technology listed in Category 1 of the MTCR Equipment and Technology Annex. As a result, the issues of missile proliferation and civilian space programmes have inevitably become interlinked.[52]

---

ballistic missiles, including the SS-24 intercontinental ballistic missile (ICBM). Ukraine was a major production centre for SS-18 and SS-24 ICBMs. Moreover, the missile industry has significant political influence given that President Leonid Kuchma is a former director of the missile design bureau Yuzhmash. Hoydysh, D., *Ukrainian Export Control: Trip Report*, Unpublished paper for the Lawyers Alliance for World Security, 21 Apr. 1995; Zamyatin, V., 'Kiev promises not to pry too much into other countries' secrets', *Kommersant-Daily*, 20 Sep. 1995 (in Russian), in 'Prospects for Ukraine's military space program viewed', FBIS-TAC-95-006, 6 Dec. 1995, pp. 170–71; and Biletsky, V., Kotova, O. and Potekhin, O., *Conversion in Ukraine: Problems and Prospects,* Analytical Report no. 4 (Friedrich-Ebert-Stiftung: Kiev, Dec. 1994), p. 90.

[49] Brazilian National Policy on the Development of Space Activities (PNDAE), URL <http:/www.brasil.emb.nw.dc.us/es-pndae.htm>, 15 Nov. 1995.

[50] The Brazilian Center for Aerospace Technology has been holding discussions with British Aerospace and the French company SAGEM about joint development of satellite launch vehicles. *Defense News*, 11–17 Mar. 1996, p. 26. In addition, Brazil and Russia have discussed the prospect of cooperation between their civilian space programmes. *World Aerospace and Defense Intelligence*, 9 June 1995, p. 15; and Casado, J., *O Estado de Sao Paulo,* 30 Apr. 1995, p. A4 (in Portuguese), in 'Rocket program, technology gains outlined', FBIS-TAC-95-003, 29 June 1995, pp. 12–14.

[51] The US company Rockwell International Space Systems has agreed to market Ukrainian launch services to potential Western customers. *World Aerospace and Defense Intelligence*, 10 May 1996, p. 5. With Rockwell as a partner, Yuzhmash hopes to be able to compete with such companies as Lockheed Martin, McDonnell Douglas and Arianespace in what is expected to be a growing market for satellite launches.

[52] Zaborsky, V., 'Ukraine's missile industry and national space program: MTCR compliance or proliferation threat?', *The Monitor*, vol. 1, no. 3 (summer 1995).

During the initial phases of the discussions between Ukraine and members of the MTCR, the fact that Ukraine was not a party to the NPT and the lack of a national export control system were cited as obstacles to regime membership.[53] Ukraine has since 1994 been a party to the NPT and has also taken steps to introduce national export controls.

In March 1992 the Ukrainian Cabinet of Ministers established the State Expert and Technical Commission to develop a national export control system. On 3 January 1993 the Ukrainian President issued a Decree on Improving State Export Control and, based on this authority, the Cabinet of Ministers established the State Commission on Export Control as a policy-making body and an Expert–Technical Committee to execute agreed policies.[54]

In March 1993 the Cabinet of Ministers approved a control list which included a section on missile technology and equipment but which was not harmonized with the MTCR Equipment and Technology Annex. However, in July 1995 the Cabinet of Ministers issued a new decision on the export, import and transshipment of missiles which was in line with the annex.[55]

Given that Brazil and Ukraine have similarities in their national policies and capabilities with regard to missile technologies, what is the explanation for their differential treatment as far as MTCR membership is concerned?

The primary difference between the two countries is their attitude towards their domestic missile programmes rather than international missile transfers. Brazil has made it clear that it will not incorporate long-range ballistic missiles into the force structure of the Brazilian armed forces. President Fernando Henrique Cardoso made a statement to this effect on 18 August 1995, declaring that Brazil does not intend to produce, import or export long-range ballistic missiles.[56]

Ukraine, by contrast, continues to see ballistic missiles as an important capability which can enhance its national security. According to Victor Zaborsky, a Ukrainian researcher working in the United States, the position of the Ukrainian Government can be summarized as 'everything which is not prohibited by arms control treaties is allowed'.[57] Under its commitments in the 1987 Treaty on the Elimination of Intermediate-Range and Shorter-Range Nuclear Missiles (INF Treaty) and the 1992 Lisbon Protocol to the 1991 START I Treaty, Ukraine is not allowed to produce or possess missiles with ranges between 500 and 5500 km. However, there are no treaties or agreements which prevent Ukraine from developing, producing and deploying

[53] Interview with the then Minister of Defence and chairman of the Commission on Export Controls in *Narodna Armiya (Kiev)*, 19 Jan. 1995 (in Ukrainian), in Joint Publication Research Studies, *Military Affairs (JPRS-UMA)*, JPRS-UMA-95-003, 11 Jan. 1995.

[54] Tsimbalyuk, V., 'Export controls in Ukraine', *The Monitor*, vol. 1, no. 4 (fall 1995), pp. 1, 3–4. Tsimbalyuk was at that time Chairman of the Expert–Technical Committee.

[55] Statute on the Procedure for Controls on the Export, Import and Transit of Missile Technology as well as Equipment, Materials and Technology that are Used in the Creation of Missile Weaponry, Decree no. 563 of the Cabinet of Ministers, 27 July 1995, *Zibrannya Ostanov Uryadu Ukrayiny*, no. 11 (Nov. 1995), (in Ukrainian), in FBIS-SOV-96-029, 12 Feb. 1996, pp. 52–82.

[56] 'Missile Technology Control Regime', Position Paper on Brazilian Foreign Policy, Brazilian Embassy, Washington, DC, URL <http://www.brasil.emb.nw.dc.us/fppp09mi.htm>, 15 Nov. 1995.

[57] Zaborsky, V., 'US–Ukrainian talks on MTCR: is compromise possible?', *The Monitor*, vol. 2, no. 3 (summer 1996), pp. 1, 5.

ballistic and cruise missiles with ranges of up to 500 km or air- and sea-based cruise missiles with no range limitations.[58]

Ukraine also retains a number of shorter-range Scud-B missiles in its inventory and the United States has suggested that this is inconsistent with MTCR membership. An unnamed US State Department official is quoted as saying, 'one of our national criteria for supporting a country's membership [of MTCR] is that they forgo offensive missiles'.[59]

It is possible that the refusal of MTCR members to admit Ukraine to the regime also reflected some residual concerns about Ukrainian export licensing procedures and technology transfers.[60] Ukrainian export licensing includes the use of general licences which permit multiple shipments of specified items to certain countries without the need for a new authorization from the licensing authority as well as individual licences which require a new authorization for each shipment. General licences were to be used by Ukraine for transactions involving other members of the Commonwealth of Independent States (CIS). As noted above, the Ukrainian civilian space programme is closely integrated with those of Russia and Kazakhstan. To some extent, therefore, the effectiveness of Ukrainian export controls is tied to the development of an overall CIS export control system designed to prevent unauthorized retransfers of controlled items.[61]

VI. The European Union dual-use export controls

The European Union export control system for dual-use goods entered into force on 1 July 1995.[62] In effect, the members of the EU have agreed to recognize one another's national export control systems for specific goods and technologies. This represents the first step towards the establishment of a common

[58] Statement of Yevgeny Sharov, Ukrainian Ministry of Foreign Affairs, to a seminar on export control organized by the Committee on Critical Technologies (Russia) and the Monterey Institute of International Studies (USA), in FBIS-TAC-95-006, 6 Dec. 1995, pp. 148–50.

[59] *Defense News*, 30 Sep.–6 Oct. 1996, p. 46. The Scud-B has a range of *c.* 280 km.

[60] In early 1996 press reports suggested that China may have acquired details of SS-18 intercontinental ballistic missiles from Ukraine. Three Chinese citizens were expelled from Ukraine in Jan. 1996. According to the statement of the Ukrainian Security Service department in Dnepropetrovsk, 'in disregard of the established rules of control over missile technologies, the Chinese acquired a number of blueprints on the development of inter-continental ballistic missile engines'. Interfax (Moscow), 2 Feb. 1996, in 'Ukraine: Chinese Embassy protests expulsion of 3 nationals', Foreign Broadcast Information Service, *Daily Report–Central Eurasia (FBIS-SOV)*, FBIS-SOV-96-024, 5 Feb. 1996. In Dec. 1996 US newspapers quoted intelligence reports that Ukrainian technicians would assist Libya with the maintenance of its inventory of ballistic missiles acquired from the Soviet Union. This was denied by the Ukrainian Foreign Ministry. Markus, U., 'Ukraine denies selling arms to Libya', Open Media Research Institute (OMRI) *OMRI Daily Digest*, no. 237, part II (10 Dec. 1996), URL <http://www.omri.cz> (hereafter, references to the *OMRI Daily Digest* refer to the Internet edition at this URL address); and Markus, U., 'Ukraine concerned over arms sales allegations', *OMRI Daily Digest*, no. 239, part II (12 Dec. 1996); and *Warsaw Voice*, 15 Dec. 1996, p. 8.

[61] In 1996 the members of the CIS took some steps to implement the 1992 Agreement on Joint Measures in the Sphere of Export Controls. On 16 May the Interstate Council of the CIS approved the creation of a single customs space for CIS members including closer cooperation between national authorities in export control. Latypov, U., 'Integration in the CIS and problems of export controls', *The Monitor*, vol. 2, no. 3 (summer 1996).

[62] Council Regulation (EC) 3381/94 of 19 December 1994 setting up a Community regime for the control of exports of dual-use goods. *Official Journal L367/37*, 31 Dec. 1994.

system for the control of exports of dual-use goods in the member states of the EU.[63] While the aim of the EU regulation is to ensure the uniform application of export controls by all the member states towards third countries, the specific decisions and control arrangements—such as the issuing of licences—are left to the members. The objective is to be effective as a non-proliferation instrument while imposing the minimum restrictions on intra-community sales of dual-use items.

The legal basis of the export controls is twofold—a consequence of the division of competence between the EU and its member states. Whereas the export controls on dual-use goods fall within the competence of the EU, the lists defining the goods to be controlled were found to be a matter affecting the national security of member states and therefore subject to the common foreign and security policy (CFSP). Therefore, the provisions of the EU Regulation itself are based on Article 113 of the 1957 Treaty of Rome (Treaty Establishing the European Economic Community), while a separate Council Decision includes five annexes which specify the items to be subject to control and specific destinations.[64] The annexes contain the lists of products subject to export control (Annex I), the countries to which exports of these products are generally authorized (Annex II), guidelines on export policies agreed upon by the member states (Annex III) and highly sensitive goods which are subject to controls even between member states (Annexes IV and V). Changes or amendments to these lists can be made only by the member states and require a consensus.[65] The export control system, as constructed, has been described as a compromise between the EU competence in general trade matters and the national prerogative that member states retain in the areas of foreign, security and defence policy.[66]

The EU regulation provides for different types of export authorization. An individual licence may be required for the export to third countries (that is, countries not specified in Annex II of the regulation) of dual-use goods listed in Annex I.[67] A simplified procedure, in the form of a general licence, is available if the goods are intended for one of the destinations listed in Annex II.[68] The list of 'friendly countries' in Annex II is illustrative, with no requirement to use general licences for trade with these countries. No list of sensitive or

[63] The need for such a system arose in the early 1990s with the implementation of the 1986 Single European Act, the aim of which was to remove intra-community trade barriers and ensure the free movement of goods between member states. Anthony *et al.* (note 1), pp. 616–19.

[64] Council Decision of 19 December 1994 on the joint action adopted by the Council on the basis of Article J.3 of the Treaty on European Union concerning the control of exports of dual-use goods, Decision 94/942/CFSP. *Official Journal L367/37*, 31 Dec. 1994.

[65] To make the decision-making process more efficient, limitations to the consensus rule have been suggested.

[66] Taylor, T. and Cornish, P., 'The Single European Market and Strategic Export Control', Paper presented at the Economic and Scientific Research Council (ESRC) Conference on the Single European Market, Exeter University, 8–11 Sep. 1994, p. 11.

[67] The licensing requirement is described in Article 3 of the Council Regulation (note 62). Annex I corresponds to the dual-use items appearing on the lists of 4 non-proliferation regimes: the Australia Group, the MTCR, the NSG and the Wassenaar Arrangement.

[68] Described in Article 6 of the Council Regulation (note 62) and Article 3 of the Council Decision (note 64).

proscribed destinations exists and it is left to the discretion of each member state to decide whether or not goods listed in Annex I should be exported to a certain destination. There are also cases in which EU member states (notably Germany and the United Kingdom) issue general licences for exports of some dual-use goods to non-EU destinations such as India.

When deciding whether to grant an export authorization, authorities have to take into consideration the guidelines contained in Annex III.[69] An export authorization may be made subject to certain requirements and conditions—such as end-use statements—but this is not a requirement.[70]

The EU regulation also contains a 'catch-all' clause under which unlisted goods may also require an export authorization if the exporter has been informed by the authorities that the goods are, or may be intended, for use in connection with weapons of mass destruction.[71] Conversely, the exporter is obliged to inform the national authorities if he is aware that goods are intended for such purposes.[72]

Once a licence has been issued in one member state, it is automatically valid for exports from any other member state.[73] This is one of the main features of the EU regulation, and to simplify matters even further the European Commission has designed a single form whose use is gaining widespread acceptance throughout the EU. However, EU member states are not obliged to use these forms and some countries continue to use national documents.

During the discussion of the EU regulation, the prospect of exporters established in one state being able to apply for licences from a state operating less stringent controls was raised. To avoid this, exporters must apply for licences in the countries where they are legally established.[74] If the goods to be exported are located in another member state, a consultation between the licensing authorities of the states has to take place before a licence is granted. In extreme cases, where vital national security interests are concerned, a member state can take action to prevent the export of these goods from taking place.

Several members were concerned about intra-EU transfers of what were considered to be the most sensitive dual-use goods—mostly items on the NSG and MTCR equipment lists but also items related to information security. For the latter items, contained in Annex IV, a three-year transitional period was agreed during which they will still be subject to intra-Union controls.[75] It was agreed that after three years a review would consider whether intra-EU con-

[69] Article 8 of the Council Regulation (note 62).
[70] Eavis, P., 'EC regulations', ed. J. Thurlow, *Worldwide Guide to Export Controls* (Export Control Publications: Chertsey, Surrey, 1996). There are differences in national procedures of EU member states regarding both the end-user and end-use documents required for licensing purposes.
[71] Article 4 of the Council Regulation (note 62). This provision was controversial during the negotiation of the regulation and several countries, including Sweden, argued that it was inconsistent with their constitutions. Sweden, however, has made use of this provision on a number of occasions.
[72] Member states may even require notification if the exporter suspects that the goods are intended for such purposes.
[73] Article 6 of the Council Regulation (note 62).
[74] Article 7 of the Council Regulation (note 62). See also Explanatory Note published by the Services of the European Commission.
[75] Article 19 of the Council Regulation (note 62) and Article 5 of the Council Decision (note 64).

trols on these items could also be lifted. Products listed in Annex V are treated as military rather than dual-use products in the national regulations of more than one member state. In these countries, intra-Union transfers of such items are also subject to controls under national arms export regulations.[76]

To ensure an effective export control system at the EU level, direct cooperation and exchange of information between the competent authorities of the member states is encouraged. A coordinating group—consisting of one representative from each member state and chaired by a representative of the European Commission—has been established.[77] The task of this group is to examine questions concerning the application of the regulation and measures which should be taken by member states to inform exporters of their obligations under the regulation. As of June 1996, the group had met five times.[78]

The EU regulation is directly applicable in all the EU member states (according to Article 189 of the Treaty of Rome) and each member is obliged to take appropriate measures to ensure its proper enforcement.[79] Member states must inform the European Commission of the laws, regulations and administrative provisions adopted in order to implement the regulation, and the Commission is responsible for forwarding this information to other member states. Every two years the Commission has to present a report to the European Parliament and the Council on the application of the regulation.[80]

The Commission monitors the implementation of the regulation and may propose amendments to it at any time. Amendments to the annexes are discussed within the Council ad hoc working group on dual-use goods and are focused on updating the lists of dual-use goods so that they correspond to the lists of the four main supplier regimes. In 1996, following the establishment of the Wassenaar Arrangement (which, as noted above, also includes a list of dual-use goods and technologies), Annex I was amended.[81]

Since it entered into force, the EU regulation has encountered a number of problems. The main problem was the mutual recognition of licences by customs officials at the perimeter of the EU. Uncertain about the validity of documents presented, customs officers invoked a consultation procedure which involved two national authorities and the European Commission. The delay (perhaps up to two weeks) while this cross-checking and consultation took place reduced the credibility of the EU export control system in the eyes of industry. Additional guidelines regarding when and how such consultation should take place have been published by the Commission.[82]

---

[76] Article 20 of the Council Regulation (note 62) and Article 6 of the Council Decision (note 64). At the end of the transitional period, a decision will be taken on whether some of the goods are to be included permanently within the scope of the rules on dual-use goods.

[77] Article 16 of the Council Regulation (note 62).

[78] Eavis (note 70).

[79] Article 17 of the Council Regulation (note 62).

[80] Article 18 of the Council Regulation (note 62).

[81] Council Decision 96/613/CFSP of 22 October 1996 amending Decision 94/942/CFSP on the joint action adopted by the Council on the basis of Article J.3 of the Treaty on European Union concerning the control of exports of dual-use goods. *Official Journal L278/39*, 30 Oct. 1996.

[82] Eavis (note 70).

Member states can go further than the existing consultation procedures if they wish, informing each other about potential programmes of concern either through EU mechanisms or in the framework of the Wassenaar Arrangement.

The EU regulation has been criticized as 'the lowest common denominator among export control systems of the EU member states'.[83] In the view of the Commission, the twin-pillar system of a regulation and a decision operating together is cumbersome and should ideally be changed. The dual-use regulation is probably a step towards a more integrated export control system rather than the end-point. However, since the national export control regimes of the member states are not uniform and the implementation and enforcement practices of the licensing and customs authorities differ, it was probably inevitable that the first stage of an export control system would be modest.

If the EU regulation is to meet its underlying objective—to establish a single European market in dual-use goods without the risk of diversion of these goods and technologies to undesirable weapon programmes—it will be necessary to satisfy the member states that it is being applied in a uniform and effective manner.

---

[83] Rudney, R. and Anthony, T. J., 'Beyond COCOM: a comparative study of five national export control systems and their implications for a multilateral nonproliferation regime', *Comparative Strategy*, vol. 15, no. 1 (Jan.–Mar. 1996), p. 52.

11. Nuclear arms control

SHANNON KILE

I. Introduction

In 1996 progress was made in advancing the nuclear arms control agenda. Most notably, the Comprehensive Nuclear Test-Ban Treaty (CTBT) was adopted overwhelmingly in the United Nations General Assembly, a historic achievement that—among other benefits—stands to strengthen the long-term vitality of the global nuclear non-proliferation regime.[1] Earlier in the year international efforts to curb the spread of nuclear weapons received a boost when the African Nuclear-Weapon-Free Zone Treaty was opened for signature in Cairo.[2]

In addition, in the USA and across the former USSR the large-scale dismantlement of strategic nuclear weapons and associated infrastructure proceeded apace within the framework of the 1991 Treaty on the Reduction and Limitation of Strategic Offensive Arms (START I Treaty), with Belarus and Ukraine completing the transfer to Russia of the nuclear warheads based on their territories. The progress made in eliminating nuclear arms in the former Soviet republics was facilitated by the bilateral assistance provided by the USA under its Cooperative Threat Reduction (CTR) programme; this assistance also supported a growing range of activities aimed at enhancing the security of fissile materials in the former Soviet nuclear weapon complex.

However, in 1996 there were clear signs that the momentum behind further nuclear arms control and confidence-building measures was waning. In Geneva, the Conference on Disarmament (CD) had yet to form a committee to negotiate a global convention banning the production of fissile material for nuclear explosives. The political atmosphere between Russia and the USA— the two former cold war adversaries, which together account for more than 95 per cent of the world's operational nuclear weapons—was becoming less conducive to arms control cooperation. The prospects for the Russian Parliament's ratification of the 1993 Treaty on Further Reduction and Limitation of Strategic Offensive Arms (START II Treaty) looked increasingly gloomy, despite the US Senate's endorsement of the accord in January. Furthermore, bilateral talks on a number of important confidence-building and transparency measures, including a nuclear stockpile data exchange agreement and a warhead dismantlement monitoring regime, remained in limbo. Negotiations between Russia and the USA to clarify the scope of the 1972 Anti-Ballistic

---

[1] See chapter 12 in this volume.
[2] The text of the treaty is reprinted in *SIPRI Yearbook 1996: Armaments, Disarmament and International Security* (Oxford University Press: Oxford, 1996), pp. 593–601. The signatories of the treaty are listed in annexe A in this volume.

Missile (ABM) Treaty continued to generate discord, with powerful voices on Capitol Hill in Washington calling for the USA to abandon the ABM Treaty altogether.

This chapter reviews the principal nuclear arms control and non-proliferation developments in 1996. Section II describes the progress made by the parties to START I in eliminating strategic nuclear weapons; it also describes the US Senate's vote to ratify START II and looks at the problems facing that treaty in gaining the Russian Parliament's approval. Section III highlights the principal denuclearization activities under way in the former Soviet republics supported by the CTR and other US-funded assistance programmes. Section IV examines the continuing deadlock in US–Russian negotiations to distinguish between strategic and theatre (i.e., non-strategic) missile defence systems within the framework of the ABM Treaty. Section V reviews the status of negotiations at the CD on a fissile material cut-off treaty. Section VI looks at regional and global initiatives to curb the proliferation of nuclear weapons. It describes the establishment of the African nuclear weapon-free zone and reviews the progress made in implementing the 1994 US–North Korean Agreed Framework. It also summarizes the International Court of Justice ruling on the legality of nuclear weapons. Finally, appendix 11A presents data on the nuclear forces of the five declared nuclear weapon states.

II. The START treaties

The 1991 START I and 1993 START II treaties form the twin pillars of an arms control regime which promises to shape a more stable and transparent strategic environment of shrinking nuclear arsenals.[3] Over the course of 1996 the five parties to START I continued to eliminate strategic nuclear delivery vehicles (SNDVs) and associated launchers well ahead of interim reduction deadlines. In addition, milestones in settling the contentious fate of the former Soviet strategic nuclear arsenal were achieved within the START I framework when Belarus and Ukraine declared that they had completed transferring to Russia the last of the former Soviet strategic nuclear warheads based on their soil. The prospects for implementing the deeper cuts in Russian and US nuclear arsenals mandated by the follow-on START II Treaty were given a major boost in January 1996 when the US Senate voted overwhelmingly to ratify the accord. However, as the year ended the treaty had yet to be brought up for a ratification vote in Russia's Federal Assembly. Against the background of intensifying parliamentary opposition to START II, the possibility loomed that the treaty would never legally enter into force.

[3] For a description of the provisions of the START I Treaty, see Cowen Karp, R., 'The START Treaty and nuclear arms control', *SIPRI Yearbook 1992: World Armaments and Disarmament* (Oxford University Press: Oxford, 1992), pp. 13–26. For a description of the provisions of the START II Treaty, see Lockwood, D., 'Nuclear arms control', *SIPRI Yearbook 1993: World Armaments and Disarmament* (Oxford University Press: Oxford, 1993), pp. 554–59.

Implementation of the START I Treaty

The START I Treaty was signed by the USA and the former USSR on 31 July 1991, following nearly a decade of negotiations. In May 1992 the foreign ministers of the USA, Russia and the three non-Russian former Soviet republics with nuclear weapons based on their territories—Belarus, Kazakhstan and Ukraine—signed the Lisbon Protocol, making all five states parties to the treaty. The three non-Russian former Soviet republics committed themselves in the protocol to meet the USSR's nuclear arms reduction obligations and also pledged to accede to the 1968 Non-Proliferation Treaty (NPT) as non-nuclear weapon states (NNWS) 'in the shortest possible time'.[4]

The entry into force of START I was subsequently blocked by the impasse that arose in late 1993 when Ukraine attached conditions to its ratification that were tantamount to an official repudiation of its commitment to remove all nuclear weapons based on its territory.[5] After a period of intense high-level diplomatic activity the presidents of Russia, Ukraine and the USA signed a trilateral statement in January 1994.[6] The Ukrainian Parliament subsequently removed its reservations regarding the implementation of START I provisions and voted in November 1994 to accede to the NPT as a NNWS. START I entered into force on 5 December 1994, when the Lisbon Protocol signatory states exchanged the instruments of ratification at a Conference on Security and Co-operation in Europe (CSCE) summit meeting in Budapest, Hungary.[7]

Under START I, the USA and the former Soviet republics parties to the treaty committed themselves to making phased reductions in strategic nuclear forces over a seven-year period, with interim ceilings imposed after three and five years (table 11.1). Belarus, Kazakhstan and Ukraine will not retain any warheads or deployed SNDVs. At the end of the implementation period on 5 December 2001, Russia and the USA may deploy no more than 1600 SNDVs and 6000 treaty-accountable warheads each, of which no more than 4900 may be deployed on intercontinental ballistic missiles (ICBMs) and submarine-launched ballistic missiles (SLBMs).

During 1996, the USA and Russia continued to reduce their strategic forces ahead of the START I implementation schedule. As the year began, the USA

---

[4] Excerpts from the text of the Lisbon Protocol are reproduced in *SIPRI Yearbook 1993* (note 3), appendix 11A, pp. 574–75. In May 1992 the leaders of Belarus, Kazakhstan and Ukraine also sent letters to President George Bush committing their respective countries to eliminating all the strategic nuclear weapons on their territory within 7 years of the START I Treaty's entry into force.

[5] Lockwood, D., 'Nuclear arms control', *SIPRI Yearbook 1994* (Oxford University Press: Oxford, 1994), p. 640. The Russian Parliament ratified the START I Treaty in Nov. 1992 with the stipulation that Russia would not deposit the instruments of ratification until the other 3 former Soviet republics had committed themselves to fully implement the treaty's provisions and to accede to the NPT as NNWS.

[6] In return for receiving from Russia and the USA security guarantees, pledges of financial assistance and compensation for nuclear warheads withdrawn to Russia, Ukrainian President Leonid Kravchuk agreed to a timetable for the deactivation and transfer to Russia of a portion of the former Soviet strategic nuclear forces based in Ukraine. He also repeated his pledge that Ukraine would accede to the NPT as a NNWS and would remove all nuclear weapons on its territory, reportedly within 3 years. The Trilateral Statement is reproduced in *SIPRI Yearbook 1994* (note 5), pp. 677–78.

[7] For more detail on the developments clearing the way for the START I Treaty's entry into force, see Goodby, J., Kile, S. and Müller, H., 'Nuclear arms control', *SIPRI Yearbook 1995: Armaments, Disarmament and International Security* (Oxford University Press: Oxford, 1995), pp. 636–39.

Table 11.1. START I ceilings in 1997, 1999 and 2001[a]

Category	5 Dec. 1997	5 Dec. 1999	5 Dec. 2001
Strategic nuclear delivery vehicles (SNDVs)[b]	2 100	1 900	1 600
Total warheads	9 150	7 950	6 000
Warheads attributed to ICBMs and SLBMs	8 050	6 750	4 900

[a] These ceilings applied equally to the USA and the USSR as the signatories of START I. The USSR's obligations were assumed by Russia as its legal successor state and later by Belarus, Kazakhstan and Ukraine. Only Russia will retain SNDVs and nuclear warheads at the end of the implementation period.

[b] Deployed ICBMs and their associated launchers, deployed SLBMs and their associated launchers, and deployed heavy bombers.

Source: START I Treaty.

had already deactivated (by removing the warheads from the launch vehicles) all the land-based missile launchers it plans to eliminate under the treaty, and all the B-52 heavy bombers scheduled for dismantlement had been retired to an elimination facility at Davis-Monthan Air Force Base (AFB), Arizona.[8] By July, the USA had removed from START accountability 392 missile launchers (ICBMs and SLBMs) and 260 B-52 heavy bombers since September 1990.[9] These reductions put the USA below the second START I intermediate ceiling on launchers (1900) that comes into effect in December 1999.

Russia continued to make rapid progress in drawing down its strategic nuclear force levels towards the START I limits. The accelerated pace of reductions in part reflected the fact that older weapons were not being replaced with the more advanced systems envisioned in the Soviet strategic forces modernization plans at the time of the START I Treaty negotiating end-game in the late 1980s.[10] By July 1996, Russia had eliminated 440 ICBM silos (primarily for obsolete types of missile) and 276 SLBM launchers since September 1990; it deployed 6756 treaty-accountable warheads, a number nearing the final START I warhead ceiling.

On 1 June 1996 Ukrainian President Leonid Kuchma announced that the last of the strategic nuclear warheads based in Ukraine had been transferred to Russia for dismantlement, making Ukraine the second of the former Soviet republics to fulfil its pledge to become free of nuclear weapons.[11] With the

[8] Walter B. Slocombe, Undersecretary of Defense for Policy, Prepared remarks before the Senate Armed Services Committee, 17 May 1995. The deactivated weapon systems remain START-accountable, however, until they have been rendered permanently inoperative in accordance with the procedures specified in the START Treaty's Protocol on Conversion or Elimination.

[9] START I Memorandum of Understanding (MOU), 1 Sep. 1990; and START I MOU, 1 July 1996. Following the treaty's entry into force, the parties are required to update every 6 months the START I MOU data on the number, type and location of the strategic nuclear weapons on their territories. The initial START MOU data were valid as of Sep. 1990.

[10] Sokov, N., *Russia's Approach to Deep Reductions of Nuclear Weapons: Opportunities and Problems*, Occasional Paper no. 27 (Henry L. Stimson Center: Washington, DC, June 1996), pp. 18–19.

[11] Statement by the President of Ukraine marking the completion on 1 June 1996 of the process of withdrawing strategic nuclear weapons from the territory of Ukraine, UN document A/51/157, 6 June 1996.

dissolution of the USSR in 1991, Ukraine inherited some 1800 strategic nuclear warheads (most of which were carried on SS-19 and SS-24 ICBMs), although operational control over the weapons remained in the hands of Moscow. Ukraine also inherited some 2500 former Soviet tactical nuclear warheads, which had all been transferred to Russia by May 1992.[12] The denuclearization of Ukraine marked an important step towards settling the vexing Soviet nuclear weapon legacy and provided a boost for global non-proliferation efforts.

Ukraine has pledged to destroy all former Soviet missiles and launch silos in accordance with START elimination procedures. Some Ukrainian government officials and industry representatives have argued in favour of converting the deactivated SS-24s into commercial satellite launch vehicles rather than destroying them (the START Treaty provides that ICBMs may be eliminated by conversion into space launch vehicles); the development of a commercial space industry is an important component of Ukraine's plans to convert its military industries to civilian use.[13] However, its participation in international space projects is hindered by the fact that it has not been accepted as a member in the Missile Technology Control Regime (MTCR).[14]

Russian officials have complained about the slow pace of missile silo elimination in Ukraine.[15] According to the 1 July 1996 START Memorandum of Understanding (MOU), Ukraine had dismantled only 3 of the 130 former Soviet SS-19 silos on its territory and none of the 46 SS-24 silos. In addition, the agreement between the Russian and Ukrainian defence ministries, under which Ukraine will transfer to Russia 25 heavy bombers (10 Tu-160 Blackjack and 15 Tu-95MS Bear aircraft), has been held up by a dispute over compensation arrangements.[16]

Kazakhstan had become the first of the former Soviet republics to fulfil its denuclearization pledge when in April 1995 it transferred to Russia the last of 898 nuclear warheads removed from the 104 SS-18 ICBMs based at two sites

---

[12] On 17 May 1996 Russia and Ukraine settled a long-standing dispute when Russia agreed to grant Ukraine $450 million in compensation for the withdrawn tactical nuclear weapons; the money reportedly will be offset against Ukraine's debts for supplies of Russian gas and oil. Intelnews (Kiev), 19 May 1996, in 'Russia agrees to compensation for tactical N-weapons', Foreign Broadcast Information Service, *Daily Report–Central Eurasia (FBIS–SOV)*, FBIS-SOV-96-098, 20 May 1996, pp. 47–48.

[13] Zaborsky, V., 'Ukraine nuke policy struggle continues over fate of ICBMs', *Defense News*, vol. 11, no. 46 (18–24 Nov. 1996), p. 28; and Zaborsky, V., 'US–Ukrainian talks on MTCR: is compromise possible?', *The Monitor*, vol. 2, no. 3 (summer 1996), pp. 1, 5. Some Ukrainian parliamentarians have urged the government not to destroy all the launch silos, arguing that they are valuable assets which can be used for civilian purposes. Levytskyy, M., 'The explosion near Pervomaysk was not only military in character', *Za Vilnu Ukrayinu* (Lvov), 16 Jan. 1996, pp. 1, 2, in FBIS-SOV-96-016, 24 Jan. 1996, pp. 55–56.

[14] See chapter 10 in this volume.

[15] Obolenskiy, G., 'Russia forced to take responsibility', *Krasnaya Zvezda*, 5 Sep. 1996, p. 3, in FBIS-SOV-96-176, 10 Sep. 1996, p. 5; and Interfax (Moscow), 29 Mar. 1996, in 'Moscow to procure 25 strategic bombers from Ukraine', FBIS-SOV-96-063, 1 Apr. 1996, p. 19. The former Soviet ICBMs based in Ukraine remain treaty-accountable until the associated launch silos are destroyed.

[16] In late Nov. 1996 Russia reportedly agreed to provide Ukraine with *c*. $350 million in compensation for the bombers, to be deducted from Ukraine's energy debt to Russia. Markus, U., 'Ukrainian president on halting Black Sea Fleet division', Open Media Research Institute (OMRI), *OMRI Daily Digest*, no. 231, part II, 2 Dec. 1996. URL <http:www.omri.cz> (hereafter, references to *OMRI Daily Digest* refer to the Internet edition at this URL address).

on its territory.[17] As 1996 began, the series of financial and other disputes between Moscow and Almaty which had slowed the destruction of the SS-18 silos were resolved within the framework of a joint Kazakh–Russian commission, thereby paving the way for the rapid elimination of all SS-18 silos in Kazakhstan. On 29 August Russian Strategic Rocket Forces personnel destroyed the last missile silo in Kazakhstan, which was located at the former Soviet ICBM base in Derzhavinsk.[18]

On 23 November Belarus transferred to Russia the last of the nuclear warheads for the 81 SS-25 ICBMs which had been based at Mozyr and Lida; the transfer of the remaining 16 missiles was completed on 27 November.[19] The withdrawal of the former Soviet nuclear weapons had been suspended in July 1995 by Belarussian leader Alexander Lukashenko in a move reportedly connected with his government's efforts to reduce its debts to Russia. In the autumn of 1996, Lukashenko had threatened to renege on Belarus' pledge to withdraw the missiles unless NATO promised not to deploy nuclear weapons on the territories of new member-states in Central Europe.[20] With the completion of the withdrawal, Russia became the sole nuclear weapon state on the territory of the former Soviet Union.

The START II Treaty

The START II Treaty was signed by US President George Bush and Russian President Boris Yeltsin on 3 January 1993. It bans all land-based strategic ballistic missiles with multiple independently targetable re-entry vehicles (MIRVs), which many experts consider to be the most destabilizing weapons in the US and Russian strategic nuclear arsenals. It commits Russia and the USA to reduce their strategic nuclear forces in two phases: the first runs simultaneously with the START I Treaty's seven-year implementation period, ending on 5 December 2001; the second will end on 1 January 2003, by which date the two parties may not deploy more than 3500 strategic nuclear warheads.[21] This ceiling represents about one-third the size of the US and Soviet strategic nuclear arsenals before the signing of START I in July 1991.[22]

[17] 'US congratulates Kazakhstan for removal of nuclear weapons', *Wireless File* (United States Information Service, US Embassy: Stockholm, 26 May 1995); and Clarke, D. 'Kazakhstan free of nuclear weapons', *OMRI Daily Digest*, vol. 1, no. 82 (26 Apr. 1995). The 40 Bear-H heavy bombers and their associated AS-15 ALCMs inherited by Kazakhstan had been flown back to Russia in early 1994.

[18] Ladin, A., 'Missile base acquires civilian status', *Krasnaya Zvezda*, 12 Sep. 1996, p. 1, in FBIS-SOV-96-179, 13 Sep. 1996, p. 13.

[19] Reuter, 'Russia takes over missiles', *International Herald Tribune*, 28 Nov. 1996, p. 3; and Interfax (Moscow), 23 Nov. 1996, in 'Last Russian nuclear warheads removed from Belarus', FBIS-SOV-96-228, 23 Nov. 1996.

[20] Parrish, S., 'Lukashenko suggests joint opposition to NATO', *OMRI Daily Digest*, no. 221, part I (14 Nov. 1996).

[21] Under the terms of the treaty, the final reductions could be implemented by 31 Dec. 2000 if the USA provides Russia with sufficient assistance in dismantling its strategic offensive arms.

[22] START II does not require nuclear warheads to be dismantled, nor does it limit the number of nuclear warheads held in inactive stockpiles. The US Department of Defense reportedly plans to maintain an additional 2500 nuclear warheads as a hedge against the emergence of new threats. Hitchens, T., 'Study: US underestimates nuclear arsenal numbers, cost', *Defense News*, vol. 10, no. 29 (17–23 July 1995), p. 14.

US ratification of START II

On 26 January 1996 the US Senate ratified the START II Treaty by a vote of 87 to 4. President Bill Clinton hailed the Senate's overwhelming endorsement of the treaty as a historic decision that marked a 'big step back from the nuclear precipice'.[23]

Although there was little organized opposition to START II on Capitol Hill, the Senate's ratification vote came over three years after the treaty had been transmitted to it by President Bush. Ratification hearings had been suspended in August 1993 because of the diplomatic impasse over the future nuclear weapon status of Ukraine that was blocking the entry into force of START I.[24] In April 1995 Senate action on the treaty was stalled again by the legislative log-jam created by the chairman of the Foreign Relations Committee, Senator Jesse Helms, who suspended all activity in the committee in order to compel the Clinton Administration to accept passage of legislation to reorganize parts of the US foreign affairs bureaucracy. It was not until a compromise reorganization bill had been agreed in mid-December 1995 that START II could be brought to the Senate floor for a ratification vote.

The resolution of ratification contained eight binding conditions and 12 declarations, which are non-binding expressions of the Senate's intent.[25] Especially noteworthy is the second attached condition, which stipulates that the Senate's ratification of START II 'changes none of the rights of either party with respect to the provisions of the ABM Treaty, in particular, Articles 13, 14 and 15';[26] this condition anticipates a decision by the Russian Parliament to link its ratification of START II to the conclusion of an ABM Treaty demarcation agreement that would sharply circumscribe US ballistic missile defence options (see section IV below). Other conditions include one on financial arrangements, which specifies that the exchange of the START II instruments of ratification will not be contingent upon the USA providing guarantees to pay for Russia's implementation of treaty provisions. The Senate also attached a condition stipulating that if START II is not ratified by Russia, then the president must consult with the Senate prior to reducing US strategic nuclear forces below START I levels.[27]

---

[23] 'Clinton, Christopher welcome "historic" Senate START II vote', *Wireless File* (United States Information Agency: Washington, DC, 30 Jan. 1996), Internet version current on 2 Feb. 1996, URL <gopher://pubgopher.srce.hr:70/11/usis/casopisi/wf>; and Towell, P., 'Senate approves START II', *Congressional Quarterly*, vol. 54, no. 4 (27 Jan. 1996), p. 226.

[24] The entry into force of the START I Treaty was a precondition for the START II Treaty's entry into force, since all the START I provisions—including the verification regime—apply to START II (except for specific modifications, such as for the heavy bomber counting rules). Lockwood (note 3), pp. 556–59.

[25] For a summary, see Cerniello, C., 'Resolution conditions, declarations highlight Senate concerns', *Arms Control Today*, vol. 26, no. 1 (Feb. 1996), p. 30.

[26] *Congressional Record*, 26 Jan. 1996, p. S461. These articles set out the rights of the parties to undertake to amend the provisions of the treaty or to withdraw from it altogether.

[27] A related declaration on the asymmetry of reductions calls on the president to carry out treaty-mandated cuts in US nuclear forces 'so that the number of accountable warheads under the START I and START II Treaties possessed by the Russian Federation in no case exceeds the comparable number of accountable warheads possessed by the United States'. *Congressional Record*, 26 Jan. 1996, p. S462.

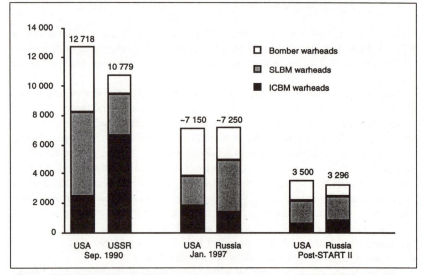

Figure 11.1. US and Soviet/Russian strategic nuclear forces: 1990, 1997 and after implementation of the START II Treaty

Note: Figures for Jan. 1997 do not include strategic nuclear delivery systems which have been deactivated or retired although they remain treaty-accountable according to the START counting rules.

Source: Provided by Robert S. Norris, of the Natural Resources Defense Council (NRDC), and William M. Arkin.

Strategic nuclear forces September 1990

US delivery vehicles
   ICBMs: 450 Minuteman II; 500 Minuteman III; 50 Peacekeeper (MX).
   SLBMs: 192 Poseidon (C-3); 384 Trident I (C-4); 96 Trident II (D-5).
   Bombers: 66 B-52G; 95 B-52H; 97 B-1B.

Russian delivery vehicles
   ICBMs: 326 SS-11; 40 SS-13; 188 SS-17; 308 SS-18; 300 SS-19; 56 SS-24 (silo-based); 33 SS-24 (rail-mobile); 288 SS-25 (road-mobile).
   SLBMs: 192 SS-N-6; 280 SS-N-8; 12 SS-N-17; 224 SS-N-18; 120 SS-N-20; 112 SS-N-23.
   Bombers: 17 Tu-95 Bear A/B; 46 Tu-95 Bear G; 57 Tu-95 Bear-H (equipped to carry 16 nuclear-armed cruise missiles each); 27 Tu-95 Bear-H (equipped to carry six nuclear-armed cruise missiles each); 15 Tu-160 Blackjack.

Current strategic nuclear forces, January 1997

US delivery vehicles
   ICBMs: 525 Minuteman III; 50 Peacekeeper (MX).
   SLBMs: 192 Trident I (C-4); 216 Trident II (D-5).
   Bombers: 71 B-52H; 48 B-1B; 13 B-2.

Russian delivery vehicles
   ICBMs: 180 SS-18; 160 SS-19; 10 SS-24 (silo-based); 36 SS-24 (rail-mobile); 369 SS-25 (road-mobile).
   SLBMs: 208 SS-N-18; 120 SS-N-20; 112 SS-N-23.

Bombers: 56 Tu-95 Bear-H (equipped to carry 16 nuclear-armed cruise missiles each); 32 Tu-95 Bear-H (equipped to carry six nuclear-armed cruise missiles each); 25 Tu-160 Blackjack.

Note: Figures for the Russian bomber force assume that Ukraine has completed the sale/transfer of its former Soviet bombers to Russia. It was announced in Nov. 1995 that not all of these aircraft will return to service and will be used instead to provide spare parts and maintenance support.

Post-START II strategic nuclear forces, projected

US delivery vehicles
ICBMs: 450/500 Minuteman III downloaded to 1 warhead each.
SLBMs: 336 Trident II (D-5) downloaded to 5 warheads each.
Bombers: 32 B-52H (equipped to carry 20 air-launched cruise missiles, ALCMs/advanced cruise missiles, ACMs each); 30 B-52H (equipped to carry 12 ALCMs/ACMs each); 21 B-2.

Russian delivery vehicles
ICBMs: 605 SS-25 (road-mobile); 90 SS-25 (based in converted SS-18 silos); 105 SS-19 downloaded to 1 warhead each.
SLBMs: 176 SS-N-18; 120 SS-N-20 downloaded to 6 warheads each; 112 SS-N-23.
Bombers: 35 Tu-95 Bear-H (equipped to carry 16 nuclear cruise missiles each); 20 Tu-95 Bear-H (equipped to carry six nuclear cruise missiles each); 10 Tu-160 Blackjack.

Note: Assumptions for Russian strategic forces under START I, START II and potentially START III: The assumption that Russia will be able to provide enough resources to its Strategic Rocket Forces to build and deploy up to 700 SS-25s (road-mobile and silo-based) and a road-mobile follow-on is increasingly untenable. At the current production rate of 10 to 20 SS-25/27s per year it is highly unlikely that hundreds more missiles will ever be deployed. To force Russia to build more missiles, submarines and bombers to reach the 3500 warhead ceiling imposed by START II is neither logical nor wise. To leapfrog to a START III level of, say, 2000 warheads would alleviate this problem and result in fewer deployed warheads.

A Russian START III force of 2000 warheads might be composed of, e.g.: 500 ICBM warheads (305 SS-25 mobile, 90 SS-25 silo, 105 SS-19 silo), 1048 SLBM warheads (100 SS-N-20 downloaded to 6 warheads each and 112 SS-N-23), and 440 bomber warheads (5 Tu-160 Blackjack, 20 Tu-95 Bear-H16 and 10 Tu-95 Bear-H6).

Sources: For US forces: START I Treaty Memorandum of Understanding, 1 Sep. 1990; START I Treaty Memorandum of Understanding, 5 Dec. 1994; START I Treaty Memorandum of Understanding, 1 July 1995; START I Treaty Memorandum of Understanding, 1 Jan. 1996; START I Treaty Memorandum of Understanding, 1 July 1996; Senate Committee on Foreign Relations, START II Treaty, Executive Report 104–10, 15 Dec. 1995; William S. Cohen, Secretary of Defense, *Annual Report to the President and the Congress*, Apr. 1997, pp. 207–11; William J. Perry, Secretary of Defense, *Annual Report to the President and the Congress*, Mar. 1996, pp. 213–18; US Air Force Public Affairs, personal communications; *Bulletin of the Atomic Scientists*; Natural Resources Defense Council (NRDC); and authors' estimates.

For Russian forces: Arbatov, A. (ed.), *Implications of the START II Treaty for US–Russian Relations* (Henry L. Stimson Center: Washington, DC, 1993), p. 6; Sorokin, K. E., 'The nuclear strategy debate', *Orbis*, vol. 38, no. 1 (winter 1994), pp. 19–40; Statement of Ted Warner, Senior Defense Analyst, RAND Corporation, before the Senate Foreign Relations Committee, 3 Mar. 1992, as cited in *The START Treaty*, Senate Hearing 102–607, Part 1 (US Government Printing Office: Washington, DC, 1992), pp. 228–29; START I Treaty Memorandum of Understanding, Sep. 1990; Gromov, F., 'Reforming the Russian Navy', *Naval Forces*, vol. 14, no. 4 (1993), p. 10; US Office of Naval Intelligence, Director of Naval Intelligence Posture Statement (June 1994), p. 13; and authors' estimates.

Russian ratification proceedings

Under the provisions of the 1993 Russian Constitution, treaty ratification requires a simple majority vote in both the lower (Duma) and upper (Federation Council) chambers of parliament.[28] Within the Duma, the International Affairs Committee and the Defence Committee are the principal parliamentary bodies responsible for considering START II ratification. The Geopolitics Committee and the Security Committee are also actively involved in the ratification proceedings.

The START II Treaty was clearly in trouble in the Duma as 1996 began. Polls of deputies taken early in the year suggested that a majority were opposed to ratifying the accord.[29] However, the senior military leadership continued to generally favour ratification, with the Strategic Rocket Forces command emerging as one of the treaty's most consistent supporters.[30] The military's opinion on the issue is influential in parliament, and observers consider its support to be essential for the treaty to have any chance of winning the Duma's approval.[31]

The year began with President Yeltsin urging the Duma to move promptly to ratify the treaty in advance of the summit meeting on nuclear safety issues scheduled to be held in Moscow in April. However, deliberations within the Defence Committee in late January reportedly revealed strong opposition to key START II provisions, as did discussions in closed-door hearings held before the International Affairs Committee in March.[32] As campaigning for the June presidential elections got under way, proponents of ratification moved to postpone legislative action on the treaty in order to prevent it from becoming a political lightning rod for opposition to Yeltsin's leadership that might spell its defeat.[33] Parliamentary leaders continued to defer action on the treaty into the autumn in the wake of President Yeltsin's health problems and virtual disappearance from the political scene.

In an effort to tip the balance in favour of START II ratification, US Defense Secretary William Perry addressed the Duma on 17 October. He urged the legislators to approve the treaty as signed, arguing that its provisions were fair for both parties and would yield considerable budget savings for

---

[28] Some observers believe that the Federation Council is likely to defer to the deliberations of the Duma with regard to START II ratification. Lepingwell, J., 'START II and the politics of arms control in Russia', *International Security*, vol. 20, no. 2 (fall 1995), p. 78.

[29] Yuryev, Y., 'Regarding START 2 ratification: Duma pollsters pass their verdict', *Kommersant Daily*, 1 Mar. 1996, p. 4 (in Russian), in Foreign Broadcast Information Service, *Proliferation and Arms Control Issues (FBIS–TAC)*, FBIS-TAC-96-004, 20 Mar. 1996, p. 42; and ITAR-TASS, 29 Feb. 1996, in 'Duma committee chairman views START II', FBIS-SOV-96-042, 1 Mar. 1996, p. 13.

[30] Litovkin, V., 'Ratification of START II Treaty is Russian politicians' strategic weapon', *Izvestiya*, 31 Jan. 1996, p. 1, in FBIS-SOV-96-022, 1 Feb. 1996, p. 16; and Yurkin, A., 'Rocket commander on readiness, future prospects', ITAR-TASS, 16 Dec. 1996, in FBIS-SOV-96-243, 16 Dec. 1996.

[31] Sokov (note 10), p. 25.

[32] ITAR-TASS, 2 Feb. 1996, in 'No Duma committee consensus on START II Treaty, FBIS-SOV-96-023, 2 Feb. 1996, p. 8; and Gornostayev, D., 'Chances for ratification of the START II Treaty diminish more and more', *Nezavisimaya Gazeta*, 6 Mar. 1996, p. 2, in FBIS-SOV-96-045, 6 Mar. 1996, p. 9.

[33] Yerastov, A., 'How not to bring down the "ceiling"', *Trud*, 6 Feb. 1996, p. 4, in FBIS-SOV-96-025, 6 Feb. 1996, p. 17; and Hitchens, T. and Zhigulsky, A., 'Russia may fail to ratify START II by April deadline', *Defense News*, vol. 11, no. 5 (5–11 Feb. 1996), p. 16.

Russia as well as the USA.[34] However, despite his assurances of the USA's willingness to help finance the costs of Russia's implementation of treaty-mandated cuts, Perry's remarks were viewed by sceptical Duma deputies as having done little to boost the prospects for a favourable ratification vote. The year ended with prospects for START II ratification appearing bleak, especially in the absence of a vigorous push for its approval from an ailing Yeltsin.

START II and Russian security policy concerns

Support in Russia for START II has been undermined by the treaty's linkage to wider security policy controversies that are fuelling tensions in Russia's relations with the USA and fostering an atmosphere of mistrust that is not conducive to the arms control process. Within the Duma, the highly contentious issue of NATO enlargement moved to the fore of the START II ratification debate in 1996. Some deputies have come to view their vote on the treaty as an instrument of leverage in halting or modifying Western plans to enlarge NATO's membership to include former Warsaw Pact member states in Central Europe.[35] A growing number of lawmakers, including the chairmen of the Duma's Security and Defence Committees, have urged the Duma to reject START II in the light of these plans.[36] The nationalist backlash generated by the issue of NATO enlargement is also contributing to a hardening of Russian attitudes towards other nuclear arms control arrangements and is stimulating a renewed emphasis on tactical nuclear weapons in Russian military doctrine.

Support for START II has been further eroded by concerns about the USA's seemingly equivocal attitude towards the 1972 ABM Treaty, which is widely defended in Russia as being the cornerstone of a stable strategic nuclear balance. Russian defence officials and parliamentarians have expressed particular concern about moves in the Republican-controlled US Congress to abandon the treaty and to mandate the construction of a nationwide ballistic missile defence system to protect the population of the USA—moves they interpret as being directed against Russia. Throughout the year they continued to insist that a favourable START II ratification vote would be possible only if the USA pledged not to abrogate the ABM Treaty.[37] The Russian legislature has also linked approval of the treaty to a satisfactory conclusion of the stalled

---

[34] Perry stated that the USA would save 'almost $5 billion over the next seven years by avoiding the costs of maintaining and operating systems that would be dismantled under START II'; it would cost c. $600 million to dismantle weapons under the treaty. Remarks of US Secretary of Defense William Perry to the Duma Parliament, 17 Oct. 1996, *Wireless File* (United States Information Service, US Embassy: Stockholm, 18 Oct. 1996).

[35] Erlich, J., 'Russia may link NATO expansion to START II follow-on', *Defense News*, vol. 11, no. 41 (14–20 Oct. 1996), p. 66; and Fedorov, Y., 'What is behind the bargaining over START II?', *Moskovskie Novosti*, no. 42 (25 June–2 July 1995), p. 14, in FBIS-SOV-95-145-S, 28 July 1995, pp. 1–2.

[36] Interfax (Moscow), 7 Jan. 1997, in 'Duma committee chief opposes ratification of START-2 Treaty', FBIS-SOV-97-005, 7 Jan. 1997; and Clarke, D., 'Rokhlin against START II ratification', *OMRI Daily Digest*, no. 185, part I (24 Sep. 1996).

[37] Vladimir Lukin, Chairman of the International Affairs Committee, warned that 'ratifying [START II] will be absolutely unrealistic if the United States unilaterally pulls out of the ABM Treaty'. Quoted in 'US Senate ratifies START II as Congress loiters on ABM brink', *Disarmament Diplomacy*, no. 2 (Feb. 1996), p. 36.

talks in Geneva on a US proposal to clarify the scope of the ABM Treaty to permit the development and deployment of a new generation of advanced-capability theatre missile defence systems (see section IV below).

Russian objections to START II provisions

Critics of START II in Russia have raised several technical and budgetary concerns about the fairness of the treaty. Although the Duma's final decision about the fate of START II is likely to be made primarily on the basis of pre-vailing political sentiments, these concerns have figured prominently in the ratification debate. They have led to a growing chorus of calls from parlia-mentarians and defence experts who support the treaty in principle to incorporate amendments to it as binding ratification conditions.

One of the most frequently voiced complaints is that START II will have an inequitable impact on the two signatories' respective strategic forces.[38] Russian critics point out that the treaty's ban on MIRVed ICBMs—the most powerful and important component of Russia's strategic nuclear forces—means that Russia must comprehensively restructure its strategic forces; more-over, this must be carried out rapidly during a period of acute national econo-mic distress. By contrast, the USA can preserve the present structure of its strategic forces 'triad' and can keep (albeit in smaller numbers) the air- and sea-based weapons in which it enjoys a comparative technological advantage. In addition, critics point out that Russia will have to build a large number of expensive new single-warhead missiles in order to make up for what they con-sider will be a shortfall in the land-based missile force created by the elimina-tion of MIRVed ICBMs.[39]

A related objection to START II is that Russia cannot afford to meet the treaty's implementation timetable given its present economic disarray. One proposal gaining favour among defence officials and parliamentarians involves extending the schedule for completing the final START II force reductions. Supporters of an extension point out that the deadline date for the reductions specified in the treaty—1 January 2003—was predicated on the assumption that START II would enter into force in the year of its signature (1993) and is now unrealistic for Russia.[40] They argue that pushing back this date approximately three to five years would make it easier to obtain approval for the treaty. First, Russia could spread the substantial expenditures needed to

[38] Another major Russian complaint is that the START II 'downloading' provision leaves the USA in a better position than Russia to rapidly reconstitute its strategic forces and stage a 'break-out' from the treaty regime. For more detail about this and other Russian criticisms of START II, see Kile, S. and Arnett, E., 'Nuclear arms control', *SIPRI Yearbook 1996* (note 2), pp. 632–39.

[39] Otherwise, the proportion of bomber- and submarine-delivered weapons in the mix of strategic forces is set to become greater than that which Russian force planners deem satisfactory for technical and operational reasons. Some Russian opponents of START II argue that deploying a new generation of MIRVed ICBMs would be much more cost-effective than deploying single-warhead ICBMs, particularly in response to a US decision to build a nationwide missile defence system. See, e.g., Surikov, A., 'START II ratification is inadvisable: Russia needs new missile instead of treaty', *Segodnya*, 5 Apr. 1996, p. 5, in FBIS-SOV-96-068, 8 Apr. 1996, pp. 15–17.

[40] Arbatov, A., 'Eurasian letter: a Russian-US security agenda', *Foreign Policy*, no. 104 (fall 1996), p. 109.

safely dismantle the large numbers of SNDVs to be eliminated under START II. Second, the decommissioning of many existing MIRVed ICBMs would then more or less coincide with the end of their useful service lives. Third, Russia would have more time to manufacture and deploy the approximately 500 new single-warhead SS-27 (an SS-25 follow-on missile, designated Topol M in Russia) ICBMs needed to maintain numerical parity with the USA's strategic forces under the START II ceiling.[41] One prominent Russian member of parliament and defence specialist cautions that the political importance of this last consideration should not be underestimated: nuclear equality with the USA is the sole remaining legacy of Russia's superpower status and is seen as guaranteeing that the USA will treat Russia with respect.[42]

US defence officials have discouraged discussion of proposals to amend the START II reduction schedule. Their reticence in part reflects concern that the US Senate, which must approve any substantive amendments to the treaty, will be reluctant to grant Russia extra time to build more nuclear weapons. More specifically, Pentagon officials in Washington are not convinced that Russian claims of a need to extend the implementation period are well justified, given the rapid progress that Russia has already made in eliminating strategic offensive arms under START I.[43] Indeed, the USA has offered Russia financial assistance to accelerate the START II elimination schedule, as provided for under the terms of the treaty. Independent analysts have also pointed out that since Russia lacks the resources to increase the low production rates of its SS-25 and SS-27 ICBMs, extending the START II implementation schedule by three to five years would not necessarily permit Russia to deploy a significantly larger number of new single-warhead ICBMs.[44]

Towards deeper nuclear arms reductions

Senior Russian military officers and defence officials, including Defence Minister Igor Rodionov, have continued to express interest in a follow-on START III treaty that would further reduce Russian and US strategic nuclear forces.[45] The idea of making deeper cuts, beyond those required by START II, has been an appealing one in Moscow because it goes a considerable way

[41] Arbatov (note 40); Gornostayev (note 32); and Dudnik, V., 'What meets Russia's interests', *Rossiyskaya Gazeta,* 17 Feb. 1996, p. 7, in FBIS-TAC-96-004, 20 Mar. 1996, pp. 39–40.

[42] Arbatov (note 40), p. 110.

[43] A senior Pentagon official rejected suggestions that the START II implementation schedule should be extended, arguing that Russia was already 'so far ahead of the START drawdown curve' that it could meet the 2003 deadline without undue difficulty. News briefing, Office of the Assistant Secretary of Defense (Public Affairs), 16 Oct. 1996.

[44] Mendelsohn, J., 'START II and beyond', *Arms Control Today,* vol. 26, no. 8 (Oct. 1996), p. 7. The development and procurement of the single-warhead Topol-M ICBM has been delayed by severe funding shortfalls. Yudin, P., 'Moscow's budget squeeze may stall new nuke missile', *Defense News,* vol. 11, no. 33 (19–25 Aug. 1996), pp. 1, 18.

[45] Hoffman, D., 'Appeal for START 2 Treaty', *International Herald Tribune,* 17 Oct. 1996, p. 3. In a Sep. 1994 speech before the UN General Assembly, President Yeltsin had proposed a 'treaty on nuclear security and strategic stability' among the nuclear weapon states aimed at reducing the number of warheads and delivery vehicles in their arsenals. UN document A/48/PV.5, 26 Sep. 1994.

towards solving Russian force structure problems arising from the severe constraints on defence resources—in particular, the costly challenge of modernizing its strategic forces in order to maintain numerical parity with those of the USA. For this reason, Russian proponents of START II ratification have argued that it would be easier to win the Duma's approval of the treaty if the framework of a successor agreement were already in place. In October, Russian Security Council Secretary Ivan Rybkin suggested negotiating a follow-on START III treaty that would address Russian concerns about START II before the Duma voted on the latter accord.[46] However, 1996 ended with the political momentum towards deeper cuts ebbing against the background of continuing US–Russian disagreements over the issues of ballistic missile defences and NATO enlargement.[47]

The Clinton Administration has declared its willingness to open talks with Moscow about a START III treaty that would further reduce US and Russian strategic force levels; however, negotiations cannot begin until the Duma has ratified START II. While no specific limits have been proposed for a follow-on treaty, a ceiling of 2000–2500 deployed warheads has been widely discussed. In his October address to the Duma, US Defense Secretary Perry noted that the prompt conclusion of a START III agreement with a lower warhead ceiling would obviate Russia's need for an expensive interim build-up of single-warhead missiles. He pledged that the USA would begin talks on further nuclear arms cuts once the Russian Parliament had ratified START II. Perry stressed, however, that in the absence of START II ratification the USA would not discuss a follow-on treaty framework and would not reduce its nuclear forces below the START I levels.[48]

This position has come under increasing fire from some arms control advocates, who worry that the Clinton Administration's concern with the sequence of negotiations may thwart efforts to rescue the process; this concern has been echoed by some of the USA's European allies, who have urged the Clinton Administration to move ahead with talks on a START III treaty.[49] There is growing sentiment in the US arms control community that START II urgently needs a political push forward to overcome opposition in the Duma. It has been suggested that Clinton commence informal talks with Yeltsin aimed at producing a joint presidential-level 'statement of principles' committing the two countries to negotiate deeper cuts in their respective strategic nuclear forces; such an agreement, which has a precedent in the June 1992 Joint Understanding that preceded START II, could ease Russian force restructur-

---

[46] Parrish, S., 'Duma still dissatisfied with START II', *OMRI Daily Digest*, no. 205, part I (22 Oct. 1996).

[47] Mann, P., 'Little progress on START 3', *Aviation Week & Space Technology*, vol. 145, no. 23 (2 Dec. 1996), pp. 72–73.

[48] Perry (note 34). The possibility that the Duma might reject START II outright or ratify it with unacceptable conditions has already prompted the Clinton Administration to reassess US nuclear stockpile requirements after the turn of the century. Hitchens, T., 'US weighs nuke budget rise amid START fears', *Defense News*, vol. 11, no. 17 (29 Apr.–5 May 1996), pp. 1, 32.

[49] Bykov, O. and Mendelsohn, J., *START III Negotiations: How Far and How Fast?* Consultation Paper, Atlantic Council of the United States, Oct. 1996; and Drozdiak, W., 'NATO aims to sweeten deal on ties with Russia', *International Herald Tribune*, 16 Jan. 1997, pp. 1, 6.

ing concerns as well as address other perceived shortcomings in the START II Treaty. As 1997 began, the Clinton Administration reportedly was studying the possibility of seeking an agreement with Russia on the outlines of a follow-on START III treaty.[50]

III. Cooperative threat reduction

The Nunn–Lugar programme

The Cooperative Threat Reduction (CTR) programme (often called the Nunn–Lugar programme after the two senators who co-sponsored the original authorizing legislation in 1991) has played the central, albeit often controversial, role in the US Government's efforts to reduce the nuclear weapon-related dangers that accompanied the dissolution of the Soviet Union.[51] The CTR programme began in 1991 under the auspices of the Department of Defense (DOD). Its immediate aim was to provide bilateral US financial and other assistance to Belarus, Kazakhstan, Russia and Ukraine for consolidating the former Soviet nuclear arsenal and ensuring its custodial safety. The programme has since evolved to encompass a wide range of nuclear non-proliferation and demilitarization activities; several important Nunn–Lugar initiatives in the former Soviet republics are now run by the US Departments of Energy and State. By the end of 1996, the USA had committed over $1.5 billion to the support of CTR activities. Table 11.2 summarizes the allocation of Nunn–Lugar funding to Belarus, Kazakhstan, Russia and Ukraine.

Cooperative threat reduction projects fall into three general categories of activity: weapon destruction and dismantlement; chain of custody (that is, ensuring proper control and safeguards over nuclear weapons and fissile material); and demilitarization and defence conversion. Through fiscal year (FY) 1996, approximately one-half of Nunn–Lugar funding was earmarked for projects to facilitate the dismantlement and destruction of strategic nuclear weapons in the former Soviet Union.[52] Supporters of the CTR programme argue that its technological and financial assistance in this area was instrumental in creating incentives for Ukraine to become a non-nuclear weapon state; it has also helped the former Soviet republics to overcome obstacles in meeting their disarmament obligations.

Despite its accomplishments, advocates of the programme have expressed growing frustration that the political commitment in Washington and Moscow to CTR and related activities undertaken by the US Department of Energy (DOE) is not commensurate with the urgency of the dangers posed by 'loose

---

[50] Smith, R. J., 'Clinton weighs further nuclear weapons agreement with Moscow', *International Herald Tribune*, 24 Jan. 1997, p. 5.

[51] For more detail about the CTR programme, see Kile and Arnett (note 38), pp. 640–42.

[52] The programme also provides financial and technical support for the destruction of chemical weapons. The FY 1997 DOD request for CTR funding for the first time includes money to eliminate former Soviet biological weapon research facilities. See also chapter 13 in this volume.

Table 11.2. The US Cooperative Threat Reduction programme: allocation of notified assistance to the former Soviet republics as of 30 September 1996[a]

Figures are in US $m. Figures in italics are percentages.

Country	Notified assistance	Share of funding
Belarus	119.0	*8.3*
Kazakhstan	172.5	*12.0*
Russia	753.8	*52.3*
Ukraine	395.3	*27.4*
Total	**1 440.5**	*100.0*

[a] Does not include administration costs/other assessments.

Source: US Department of Defense.

nukes'.[53] They complain about bureaucratic delays in Washington and the US Congress' lack of follow-through in supporting promising initiatives. They also point with concern to the fact that the programme has been hampered by growing suspicion and hesitation within Russia's powerful Ministry of Atomic Energy (Minatom) about involving the USA so intimately in the activities of its once highly secret nuclear installation. Many of these problems were highlighted in 1996 by a prolonged bureaucratic wrangle between the USA and Russia over removing a cache of 4.3 kg of highly enriched uranium (HEU) stored at a poorly guarded site in Georgia.[54]

In 1996 Nunn–Lugar disarmament assistance to Russia again became the source of controversy in Washington. A US newspaper disclosed the existence of a huge secret underground military complex under construction at Yamanatau in the southern Ural Mountains.[55] The disclosure was seized upon by critics in Congress, who pointed out that Nunn–Lugar assistance can be disbursed only if the president certifies, among other conditions, that Russian military programmes do not exceed 'legitimate defence requirements'; work on the complex, which US officials believe to be a strategic nuclear forces command bunker, appeared to involve considerable expenditure at a time when Russia was claiming financial hardship in meeting its START obligations. The Clinton Administration conceded that the construction of the underground complex seemed inappropriate given Russia's economic crisis but claimed that it did not constitute excessive military modernization.[56]

[53] See, e.g., Allison, G., *et al.*, *Avoiding Nuclear Anarchy: Containing the Threat of Loose Russian Nuclear Weapons and Fissile Material*, Center for Science and International Affairs (CSIA), Kennedy School of Government, Harvard University, CSIA Studies in International Security no. 12 (MIT Press: Cambridge, Mass., 1996).

[54] Gordon, M., 'US concern mounts over "loose nukes"', *International Herald Tribune*, 6 Jan. 1997, pp. 1, 9.

[55] Gordon, M., 'Russia builds secret military site in Urals', *New York Times*, 16 Apr. 1996, pp. A1, 16.

[56] Parrish, S., 'US officials say Urals project is defensive', *OMRI Daily Digest*, no. 76, part I (17 Apr. 1996).

Another CTR-related controversy arose again in 1996 as Republicans in Congress sought to cut US funding for nuclear threat-reduction programmes, alleging that Russia was violating the Biological and Toxic Weapons Convention as well as the bilateral Chemical Weapons Data Exchange and Destruction Agreements.[57] While acknowledging that there were grounds for concern about Russia's compliance record, the Clinton Administration nevertheless certified that Russia remained committed to meeting all the conditions for receiving assistance set out in the Nunn–Lugar legislation, including complying with relevant arms control agreements. The White House recommended continuing CTR programme assistance to Russia, which at the end of the year totalled $753 million in notified funds.

Enhancing security of nuclear weapon-usable materials

In 1996 Nunn–Lugar funds were earmarked for a wide array of activities aimed at enhancing nuclear material security, export control regulations, and weapon transport and storage security. During the January meeting of the US–Russian Joint Commission on Technological Cooperation (the Gore–Chernomyrdin Commission),[58] US Secretary of Energy Hazel O'Leary and Russian Minister of Atomic Energy Viktor Mikhailov signed a statement on the construction of a long-delayed facility at the Mayak nuclear complex intended for storage of fissile material, in particular the plutonium pits from dismantled warheads.[59] The total cost of the storage facility, which reportedly will hold up to 40 per cent of Russia's weapon plutonium, is estimated to be $330 million; the cost is to be shared by Russia and the USA.[60] During the meeting of the Gore–Chernomyrdin Commission in July, O'Leary and Mikhailov signed an agreement on measures to enhance the security and protection of fissile material being transported from one site to another during the warhead dismantlement process.[61]

One of the Nunn–Lugar programme's highest priorities in 1996 continued to be to create an effective fissile material physical control and accounting (MPC&A) regime for fissile material in Russia and elsewhere in the former USSR. The serious security shortcomings identified at many nuclear facilities (such as research reactors, fuel fabrication facilities, uranium enrichment plants, nuclear storage sites and nuclear weapon production facilities) have

[57] Woolf, A. F., *Nunn-Lugar Cooperative Threat Reduction Programs: Issues for Congress*, Congressional Research Service Report CRS 96-804F, 30 Sep. 1996.

[58] The Gore–Chernomyrdin Commission, which was established in 1993 as a joint initiative of US Vice-President Al Gore and Russian Prime Minister Viktor Chernomyrdin, meets regularly to promote cooperation on a wide range of issues related to energy, environmental protection, science and technology, health, space exploration and defence conversion. Fact Sheet: Gore–Chernomyrdin Commission, US Department of State, Bureau of Public Affairs, Washington, DC, 21 Sep. 1994.

[59] Medeiros, E., 'US, Russia enhance nuclear security cooperation during Washington talks', *Arms Control Today*, vol. 26, no. 1 (Feb. 1996), p. 23.

[60] ITAR-TASS, 15 May 1996, in 'Deputy premier reports US allocation for plutonium store', FBIS-SOV-96-096, 16 May 1996; and 'Plans proceeding for new Russian plutonium storage site', *Disarmament Diplomacy*, no. 5 (May 1996), p. 44.

[61] Medeiros, E., 'Gore–Chernomyrdin Commission expands nuclear safety cooperation', *Arms Control Today*, vol. 26, no. 5 (July 1996), pp. 25, 29.

spurred increased US funding of a variety of measures aimed at preventing the unauthorized diversion of HEU, plutonium and other weapon-usable nuclear material.

Over the course of the year, cooperation between the DOE and Minatom and its government counterparts in other former Soviet republics led to announcements of a spate of new agreements to initiate or extend MPC&A assistance projects;[62] however, virtually all these projects were uncompleted at the end of the year. Some encouraging progress was made within the framework of the DOE-sponsored laboratory-to-laboratory programme. This promising programme began in early 1995 as a trial effort to bring together US and Russian laboratory personnel to collaborate on improving fissile material control and accounting at five nuclear research centres in Russia.[63] In 1996 new MPC&A projects were initiated at a number of Minatom nuclear weapon design and production facilities in Russia, including Tomsk-7, Chelyabinsk-70 and Arzamas-16, as well as at facilities in several other former Soviet republics.[64] By August, the DOE had begun cooperative projects at 44 sites in Belarus, Georgia, Kazakhstan, Latvia, Lithuania, Russia and Uzbekistan. For FY 1997, the DOE requested $95 million for MPC&A activities (both for laboratory-to-laboratory and for government-to-government programmes) as part of a projected $400 million in spending for improving fissile material security over the next five years.[65]

The US–Russian HEU Agreement

In 1996 there was progress in implementing the 1993 HEU Agreement,[66] which has been hailed as a significant step in reducing the risk of diversion or theft of weapon-grade uranium recovered from dismantled warheads.[67] Under the terms of the HEU deal, the United States Enrichment Corporation (USEC), a quasi-governmental agency privatized at the end of 1996, will purchase from Russia over 20 years up to 500 tonnes of HEU extracted from nuclear warheads for use as civilian reactor fuel. The agreement specifies that Russia will blend down the recovered HEU with low-enriched uranium (LEU) to make LEU enriched to approximately 4.4 per cent; not less than 10 tonnes of

---

[62] Beginning in 1996, the DOE assumed managerial and funding responsibilities for most US-supported activities to enhance fissile material security in Russia and elsewhere in the former USSR.

[63] This 'bottom-up' strategy has been cited as a cost-effective and generally successful approach to combating the nuclear leakage problem, not least because DOE rules (unlike those of the DOD) allow US funds to be spent on Russian goods and services in developing a locally designed and produced MPC&A system. Johnson, K., *US–FSU Threat Reduction Programs: Effectiveness of Current Efforts and Prospects for Future Cooperation*, Center for International Security Affairs, Los Alamos National Laboratory, Los Alamos, N. Mex., Aug. 1995, pp. 20–29.

[64] United States General Accounting Office (GAO), *Nuclear Nonproliferation: Status of US Efforts to Improve Nuclear Material Controls in Newly Independent States*, GAO/NSIAD/RCED-96-89 (GAO: Gaithersburg, Md., Mar. 1996), pp. 37–38. Discussions with the Russian Navy were also initiated concerning the security of the HEU fuel used in naval propulsion reactors.

[65] Ellis, J., 'Nunn-Lugar's mid-life crisis', *Survival*, vol. 39, no. 1 (spring 1997), p. 90.

[66] For the text of the HEU Agreement, see *SIPRI Yearbook 1994* (note 5), pp. 673–75.

[67] For a comprehensive discussion of the agreement, see Falkenrath, R., 'The HEU deal', Allison, *et al* (note 53), appendix C, pp. 229–93.

blended-down HEU per year will be purchased in the first five years and not less than 30 tonnes per year thereafter. The total deal is valued at nearly $12 billion, although prices are to be negotiated each year to reflect international uranium market conditions.

A series of disputes between Russia and the USA over price and compensation arrangements were largely resolved in 1995, thereby paving the way for shipments to the USA of blended-down Russian HEU extracted from dismantled nuclear warheads. In 1996, Russia was to send LEU containing the equivalent of 12 tonnes of HEU to the USA. A new contract signed in November specifies that USEC will purchase the LEU equivalent of 18 tonnes in 1997, 24 tonnes in 1998 and 30 tonnes per year in 1999–2000.[68]

A second dispute involving the HEU agreement was resolved in principle when presidents Clinton and Yeltsin settled the outstanding differences that had stymied implementation of transparency annexes to the deal worked out in 1995. At the end of their summit meeting in Moscow on 21 April, the two leaders issued a joint statement announcing that they had reached agreement on measures to verify that diluted HEU purchased by the USA had in fact been extracted from newly dismantled Russian nuclear warheads rather than from stockpiles not previously used in weapons or from other sources.[69] The agreed transparency measures provide US monitors with 'direct access' to the blending down of Russian HEU, which takes place at the Ural Electro-mechanical Plant (Yekaterinburg-45).[70] In return, Russia has reciprocal monitoring rights at the USEC plant where arriving shipments of LEU are processed, as well as at a number of commercial fuel fabrication facilities, in order to verify that the material is not re-enriched for use in nuclear weapons. However, at the end of the year negotiations on implementing the transparency and inspection measures had yet to be finalized despite the presidential agreement in principle.

Fissile material stockpile agreements

In 1996 there was no resumption of the negotiations between Russia and the USA on a comprehensive set of measures to increase the transparency of their respective fissile material stockpiles. The negotiations had been given a boost by a joint declaration issued by presidents Clinton and Yeltsin at their May 1995 summit meeting in Moscow calling for the conclusion of agreements for a regular exchange of detailed information on aggregate stockpiles of nuclear weapons and fissile material. The declaration also called for the reciprocal

[68] Parrish, S., 'Russia, US agree to accelerate uranium deal', *OMRI Daily Digest*, no. 228, part I (25 Nov. 1996).
[69] The Clinton Administration had faced mounting criticism in the USA for its inability to verify that the diluted HEU purchased from Russia had indeed been extracted from dismantled nuclear weapons. Broad, W., 'Clinton scrambling to show A-arms pacts are verified', *International Herald Tribune*, 30 Jan. 1996, p. 5.
[70] Cerniello, C., 'Clinton–Yeltsin summit in Moscow yields gain on arms control issues', *Arms Control Today*, vol. 26, no. 3 (Apr. 1996), p. 20; and Bolsunovsky, A., 'How to utilize fissile materials after dismantling Russian warheads', *The Monitor*, vol. 2, no. 4 (fall 1996), p. 1.

monitoring at storage facilities of US and Russian fissile material removed from nuclear warheads and declared to be 'excess to national security requirements'.[71]

Bilateral talks on the stockpile transparency measures got under way in the Joint Working Group on Safeguards, Transparency and Irreversibility (ST&I), a forum created under the auspices of the Gore–Chernomyrdin Commission. One of the measures under discussion was a US proposal for reciprocal inspections of nuclear warhead storage and dismantlement sites to verify the rate at which warheads are being dismantled. Another measure proposed by the USA was a demonstration of techniques for verifying the presence of plutonium pits (the designs of which are highly classified) and other nuclear weapon components stored in sealed containers.[72] After a promising beginning, the talks have remained effectively suspended since late 1995. The key stumbling-block is the inability of the two sides to reach an intergovernmental cooperation agreement on the exchange of classified stockpile data, which is a legal requirement for moving forward on the transparency and irreversibility measures.[73] Russia withdrew from negotiations on the cooperation agreement without explanation in October 1995 and has shown little interest in resuming them. US negotiators expressed concern that the talks had become an increasing political liability in Russia, with officials there unwilling to share sensitive nuclear weapon information against the background of growing nationalist opposition to arms control cooperation with the USA.[74]

IV. The ABM Treaty and ballistic missile defence

During 1996 the debate over ballistic missile defences and the future of the 1972 ABM Treaty continued to strain relations between Russia and the USA as well as generate partisan controversy on Capitol Hill.[75] The talks under way between Russia and the USA in the Standing Consultative Commission (SCC) over a US proposal to clarify the scope of the ABM Treaty remained dead-

[71] Joint Statement on the Transparency and Irreversibility of the Process of Reducing Nuclear Weapons, 10 May 1995, *Wireless File* (United States Information Service, US Embassy: Stockholm, 10 May 1995), pp. 16–17.

[72] Cochran, T., 'Progress in US–Russian transparency and fissile material disposition', Paper presented at the Fifth ISODARCO Beijing Seminar on Arms Control, Chengdu, China, Nov. 1996, p. 2.

[73] Carnegie Endowment for International Peace and the Monterey Institute of International Studies, *The Nuclear Successor States of the Soviet Union: Nuclear Weapon and Sensitive Exports Status Report*, no. 4 (May 1996), p. 24.

[74] Parrish, S., 'Russia blocks progress on nuclear agreements', *OMRI Daily Digest*, vol. 2, no. 15 (22 Jan. 1996); and Hitchens, T., 'US fears Russia vote may stymie nuke talks', *Defense News*, vol. 11, no. 8 (26 Feb.–3 Mar. 1996), p. 4.

[75] The ABM Treaty was signed by the United States and the Soviet Union on 26 May 1972 and entered into force in Oct. of that year. Amended in a Protocol in 1974, the treaty obligates the parties not to undertake to build a nationwide defence system against strategic ballistic missile attack and limits the development and deployment of missile defences. Among other provisions, it prohibits the parties from giving air defence missiles, radars or launchers the technical ability to counter strategic ballistic missiles or from testing them in a strategic ABM mode.

locked;[76] a partial demarcation agreement reached at mid-year offered little progress towards resolving the impasse. In the Republican-controlled US Congress, there were renewed efforts to pass legislation requiring the Pentagon to develop and deploy a multi-site nationwide defence system designed to protect the territory of the United States against ballistic missile attack. These moves were resisted by the Clinton Administration, which has refused to abandon outright the ABM Treaty.

The ABM Treaty demarcation talks

In November 1993 the USA initiated discussions with Russia in the SCC to clarify the scope of the ABM Treaty to permit the testing and deployment of a planned family of US advanced-capability theatre missile defence (TMD) systems. The Clinton Administration argues that the new TMD systems are needed to protect US troops and allies in future conflicts from an increasing number of putative adversaries armed with ballistic missiles. However, its attempts to move ahead with developing the new systems while at the same time remaining in compliance with the ABM Treaty have elicited strong criticism from Russia for overstepping what is permitted by the treaty and strong criticism from lawmakers in Congress for being unduly constrained by the treaty.

While some Russian officials and analysts agree in principle that missile defences are needed as a hedge against the proliferation of ballistic missiles, Moscow has approached the SCC negotiations primarily from the perspective of Russia's strategic nuclear posture *vis-à-vis* that of the USA. It vigorously opposes US efforts to exclude the new advanced-capability TMD systems from the constraints of the ABM Treaty, arguing that doing so would open the door to the deployment of US missile defence systems with considerable 'inherent capabilities' against Russian strategic nuclear forces and thereby undermine the stabilizing logic of mutual assured destruction codified in the treaty. Russian officials have also been anxious to halt or severely curtail planned US TMD programmes in order to forestall an expensive new defensive arms race.

The negotiations in the SCC between Russia and the USA have revolved around a series of proposals and counter-proposals put forward to establish a technical line of demarcation between theatre missile defence systems, which are not limited by the ABM Treaty, and strategic missile defence systems, which are limited.[77] As 1996 began, little headway had been made towards reaching a demarcation agreement, despite a joint statement on missile defences issued by presidents Clinton and Yeltsin at their May 1995 summit

---

[76] The SCC is the body established in the ABM Treaty to address implementation questions. In June 1996 Russia and the USA reached preliminary agreement with Belarus, Kazakhstan and Ukraine on the procedures for allowing them to succeed to the rights and obligations of the USSR under the treaty.

[77] TMD systems occupy a 'grey zone' and are not formally subject to the restrictions imposed by the ABM Treaty, which limits only strategic ABM systems. However, the line of demarcation between strategic and theatre ballistic missiles is not clearly defined and the technical characteristics of defences against them overlap considerably.

meeting which outlined a broader political approach to resolving the issue.[78] However, by mid-year the talks in the SCC had moved forward considerably in the wake of a decision by Clinton and Yeltsin during their April summit meeting in Moscow to complete by the end of June an initial demarcation agreement on lower-velocity TMD systems, to be followed by an agreement covering higher-velocity systems by October.[79]

The completion of the first stage of a demarcation agreement was announced in New York on 23 September by US Secretary of State Warren Christopher and Russian Foreign Minister Yevgeniy Primakov, confirming a tentative deal reached in the SCC in June; negotiations aimed at concluding the second stage of an agreement, covering higher-velocity missile defence systems, were to follow in the October session of the SCC.[80] The initial agreement permitted the testing and deployment of systems with interceptor speeds of 3 km/s or less, provided that the systems were not tested against ballistic targets with speeds above 5 km/s (corresponding to missiles with ranges exceeding 3500 km); it also included a number of confidence-building measures related to missile interceptor flight-testing. Within these constraints the USA would be able to develop its planned 'lower-tier' TMD systems, such as the Patriot Advanced Capability-3 (PAC-3) and the Navy's Area Defense system as well as the more capable Theater High-Altitude Area Defense (THAAD) system, which would not be restricted by the ABM Treaty; Russia would be able to develop its new S-400 air defence system.[81]

The agreement on lower-velocity missile defences did little to bridge the gulf between the US and Russian positions on higher-velocity anti-missile systems, which lay at the centre of the impasse in the SCC demarcation talks. These differences had been highlighted by a letter sent by Primakov to Christopher in June which was subsequently leaked to a US newspaper. The Primakov letter listed Russia's guidelines for the second phase of demarcation talks in the SCC. Among other elements, the guidelines included: a ban on space-based tracking and guidance sensors; a ban on space-based systems 'which make use of other physical principles' (such as lasers); and a ban on testing interceptor systems against both multiple re-entry vehicles carried by ballistic missiles and any re-entry vehicle carried by strategic ballistic missiles.[82] It also proposed 'setting limits on the number and geography for deployment of

---

[78] According to the criteria set out in the joint statement, missile defence systems must not 'pose a realistic threat to the strategic forces of the other side' and must not 'be tested to give such systems that capability' in order to be permitted under the ABM Treaty. 'Text of the Clinton–Yeltsin joint statement on theatre missile defence systems', 10 May 1995, *Wireless File* (note 71), p. 14.

[79] Cerniello, C., 'US, Russia near agreement on lower-velocity TMD systems', *Arms Control Today*, vol. 26, no. 5 (July 1996), pp. 19, 27.

[80] 'US–Russian Joint Statement on Missile Defence', 23 Sept. 1996, *Disarmament Diplomacy*, no. 8 (Sep. 1996), pp. 27–28; and Erlanger, S., 'US and Russia agree on missile defenses', *International Herald Tribune*, 25 Sep. 1996, p. 2.

[81] Cerniello (note 70).

[82] A ban on space-based tracking and guidance sensors would prohibit US plans to use targeting information (called 'cueing data') from satellite-based sensors to significantly enhance the effectiveness of missile interceptor systems. A ban on lasers would preclude development of the USAF's Airborne Laser Project, which is intended to intercept missiles in the ascent phase of their trajectories.

high-velocity non-strategic ABM systems'.[83] The guidelines set out in the letter, which drew sharp criticism in the USA from proponents of a robust ballistic missile defence programme, underscored Russia's long-standing opposition to permitting the development and deployment of advanced-capability theatre missile defence systems it saw as potentially jeopardizing its strategic nuclear deterrent.

The extent of the unresolved differences between Russia and the USA over missile defences became even more apparent in late October, when the two sides unexpectedly cancelled the signing of the agreement on lower-velocity TMD systems announced the previous month. Russian officials rejected the US position that the agreement would have immediate effect and allow flight-testing to commence as soon as it was signed; they argued that the more problematic second phase of negotiations, covering higher-velocity systems, must be completed before any testing could begin.[84] They also continued to insist that no unilateral decisions should be made regarding the compliance of higher-velocity TMD systems under the ABM Treaty.[85] At the end of the year, the two sides remained 'kilometers apart' in the words of one arms control advocate, and there were few signs that a resolution of the dispute was imminent.[86]

V. A ban on the production of fissile material for nuclear explosives

The Conference on Disarmament, the United Nations arms control negotiating forum, had only two formal mandates in 1996. The first mandate was for a comprehensive test-ban treaty, which was adopted by the UN General Assembly in September after its adoption had been blocked in the CD. The second mandate was for a worldwide ban on the production of fissile material for use in nuclear weapons.

The idea of a global convention to halt the production of HEU and separated plutonium for nuclear explosives gained momentum after it had been raised by President Clinton in a speech before the UN General Assembly in September

---

[83] Excerpts from the letter are reproduced in Institute for Defense and Disarmament Studies (IDDS), *Arms Control Reporter* (IDDS: Brookline, Mass.), sheet 603.B.278, July 1996. Primakov's letter also referred to assurances offered by the Clinton Administration that the USA would not conduct flight-tests of high-velocity TMD systems for the next 3 years; Administration officials denied that any such assurances had been given. Cerniello (note 70), p. 19.

[84] Reuter, 'Russia reneges on missile defenses deal', 30 Oct. 1996; and Associated Press, 'US–Russia test accord founders', *International Herald Tribune*, 31 Oct. 1996, p. 6.

[85] The Clinton Administration has certified unilaterally that the planned Navy Theatrewide (upper tier) system, which uses an interceptor missile having a speed of up to 4.5 km/s, is in compliance with the ABM Treaty. Prepared remarks by Paul G. Kaminski, Undersecretary of Defense for Acquisition and Technology, to the Military Research and Development and Military Procurement subcommittees, House National Security Committee, 27 Sep. 1996.

[86] Mendelsohn, J., 'Kilometers apart on missile defense', *Arms Control Today*, vol. 26, no. 5 (July 1996), p. 2.

1993.[87] In December that body signalled the broad international support for such an agreement when it adopted by consensus a resolution endorsing Fissile Material Cut-Off Treaty (FMCT) negotiations.[88] The CD agreed in March 1995 to establish an Ad Hoc Committee with a mandate to 'negotiate a non-discriminatory, multilateral and internationally and effectively verifiable treaty banning the production of fissile material for nuclear weapons or other nuclear explosive devices'.[89]

However, by the end of 1996 negotiations for a fissile material production ban still had not been opened because members of the CD, which operates by consensus, were unable to agree on how to proceed; the large differences between them which had produced a weak negotiating mandate persisted. A number of non-aligned states continue to insist on including existing stock-piles of fissile material in the negotiating mandate, with these stockpiles to be placed under international safeguards. This proposal has generated strong opposition from the five permanent members of the UN Security Council (that is, the five declared nuclear weapon states) and, among others, India. They insist that the mandate should apply only to the future production of fissile material.[90] Negotiations on a production cut-off were further hindered in 1996 by the attempts of India and several CD member states to link the talks to the start of new negotiations on a global treaty aimed at eliminating nuclear weapons completely.

VI. Other nuclear non-proliferation and disarmament developments

US–North Korean Agreed Framework

The US–North Korean Agreed Framework was signed on 21 October 1994.[91] It was the product of intense high-level diplomatic bargaining between the USA and North Korea to resolve the crisis arising from North Korea's non-compliance with its NPT obligations to allow International Atomic Energy Agency (IAEA) inspection of its nuclear programme.[92] Under the terms of the agreement, North Korea has halted the operation of the 5-megawatt (MW) research reactor and plutonium reprocessing plant at Yongbyon and has frozen construction work on two large reactors (a 50-MW reactor at Yongbyon and a

---

[87] Although the Clinton proposal urged a worldwide ban, its immediate aim was to defuse an incipient nuclear arms race in South Asia by halting the build-up of nuclear weapon-usable material in India and Pakistan. Goodby, Kile and Müller (note 7), pp. 657–58.

[88] UN General Assembly Resolution 48/75L, 16 Dec. 1993.

[89] Conference on Disarmament document CD/1299, 24 Mar. 1995.

[90] None of the P5 states is believed to be producing plutonium or HEU currently for weapon purposes.

[91] Agreed Framework of 21 October 1994 between the United States of America and the Democratic People's Republic of Korea, IAEA document INFCIRC/457, 2 Nov. 1994.

[92] For more detail about the genesis of the Agreed Framework, see Goodby, Kile and Müller (note 7), pp. 653–54. North Korea's non-compliant behaviour had raised international suspicions, particularly in the USA, that it was diverting separated plutonium from a research reactor at Yongbyon for use in nuclear explosives.

200-MW reactor at Taechon).[93] In return, the USA has organized in cooperation with Japan and South Korea an international consortium, the Korean Peninsula Energy Development Organization (KEDO), which has begun to underwrite the costs of compensatory oil supplies (500 000 tonnes of heavy fuel oil per annum) to North Korea.[94] KEDO is also responsible for providing North Korea with two 1000-MW light water reactors (LWRs), to be built on North Korea's east coast in cooperation with South Korea's Electric Power Corporation.[95]

Despite rising political tensions on the Korean Peninsula, there was some progress in 1996 in implementing the Agreed Framework. Preliminary construction work on the two LWRs, the total cost of which is estimated to be approximately $5.5 billion, got under way in the autumn of 1996 following the conclusion of five implementing protocols between North Korea and KEDO establishing the legal foundations for the work.[96] However, the diplomatic imbroglio over the incursion of a North Korean submarine into South Korean waters in September led to KEDO suspending contacts with Pyongyang. North Korea's subsequent statement of regret for the incident in December paved the way for work on the reactors to resume in the spring of 1997. Construction is to be halted in several years' time pending the satisfactory conclusion of an IAEA special inspection to clarify how North Korea disposed of its spent reactor fuel. The work on the reactors will then resume, and North Korea will proceed with a phased dismantling of its nuclear plants and related facilities.

According to US officials, the North Korean nuclear programme remains frozen and under close IAEA supervision.[97] However, in September the IAEA Director-General, Hans Blix, reported incomplete progress in the IAEA's attempts to verify the full scope of the North Korea's suspended nuclear programme. He also stated that North Korea was still not in full compliance with its IAEA safeguards agreement.[98]

[93] The 5-MW reactor is thought to be capable of producing c. 7 kg of plutonium per year; the 2 reactors under construction were expected to yield another 200 kg of plutonium annually. United States General Accounting Office, Nuclear Nonproliferation: Implications of the US/North Korean Agreement on Nuclear Issues, GAO/RCED/NSIAD-97-8 (GAO: Gaithersburg, Md., Oct. 1996), p. 3.

[94] KEDO is responsible for verifying that the fuel oil is used only to generate heat and electricity, as specified in the 1994 Agreed Framework.

[95] An LWR is much less likely to be used to clandestinely manufacture nuclear weapons than the graphite-moderated reactor at Yongbyon.

[96] 'US-North Korea accord: precarious progress maintained', Disarmament Diplomacy, no. 9 (Sep. 1996), p. 53. These protocols spell out what KEDO will provide to North Korea and specify the conditions under which the consortium and its contractors will work.

[97] Lynn E. Davis, Undersecretary of State for Arms Control and International Security Affairs, Address to the American Bar Association, Washington, DC, 24 Apr. 1996, US State Department, Dispatch, vol. 7, no. 18 (29 Apr. 1996), p. 212.

[98] Disarmament Diplomacy (note 96). To allay US nuclear proliferation concerns, the Agreed Framework mandated the IAEA to verify North Korean statements on past fissionable material production.

Nuclear weapon-free zones

Treaty of Pelindaba

The African Nuclear-Weapon-Free Zone Treaty (the Treaty of Pelindaba), was signed by 43 African nations at a ceremony in Cairo on 11 April 1996.[99] The opening for signature of the treaty marked the culmination of over 30 years of activity within the Organization of African Unity (OAU) to create a nuclear weapon-free zone across the continent of Africa. Following South Africa's accession to the NPT as a non-nuclear weapon state, an OAU Group of Experts was convened in 1993 to initiate the process of drafting a treaty. The final treaty text was adopted by an OAU summit meeting in June 1995 after it overcame the objections of some North African states, which insisted that the zone be linked to a similar one covering the Middle East.[100]

The treaty covers the territory of the continent of Africa, island states which are members of the OAU and island territories considered by the OAU to be part of Africa. It prohibits the parties from undertaking to research, develop, manufacture, stockpile, test or acquire nuclear explosives; it also prohibits the stationing of nuclear explosives on the territory of the parties. The treaty affirms the right of each party to permit visits by foreign ships and aircraft and does not affect passage rights through territorial waters guaranteed by international law.[101] All parties must apply full-scope IAEA safeguards to their civilian nuclear activities.

There are three protocols to the treaty. At the Cairo ceremony China, France, the UK and the USA signed Protocols 1 and 2, under which the declared nuclear weapon states agree not to use or threaten to use nuclear weapons against any states parties to the treaty and agree not to test or assist the testing of nuclear weapons within the African zone.[102] The third protocol may be signed by France and Spain, as the two states with dependent territories in the zone, and obligates them to observe certain treaty provisions with respect to these territories.[103]

The Treaty of Rarotonga

The Treaty of Rarotonga prohibits the manufacture, acquisition, possession, stationing and testing of nuclear explosive devices in the South Pacific Nuclear Weapon-Free Zone. The treaty was opened for signature by the

---

[99] The Cairo Declaration, Adopted on the occasion of the Signature of the African Nuclear Weapon-Free Zone Treaty (the Treaty of Pelindaba), Cairo, Egypt, 11 Apr. 1996, Conference on Disarmament document CD/1390, 16 Apr. 1996.

[100] Goodby, Kile and Müller (note 7), pp. 661–62.

[101] See annexe A in this volume.

[102] Britain qualified its signature with a statement that the Treaty zone of application did not include Diego Garcia Island, a British territory in the Indian Ocean. Russia signed the protocols on 11 May, qualifying its signature with a statement that it did not accept the inclusion of the Chagos Archipelago islands within the Treaty zone of application.

[103] France has signed and ratified this protocol, as well as the other two; Spain had not signed it as of 1 Jan. 1997. See annexe A in this volume.

members of the South Pacific Forum in August 1985. At the end of 1996, 12 states were parties to the treaty.[104]

On 25 March 1996, France, the UK and the USA signed three protocols to the treaty;[105] the other two declared nuclear weapon states, China and Russia, had already signed and ratified Protocols II and III (Protocol I did not apply to them), which prohibit the testing of nuclear weapons within the zone as well as the use or threat to use nuclear weapons against any treaty party.[106] France had previously refused to sign the protocols because of the location of its nuclear test site in the South Pacific. For its part, the USA had been reluctant to encourage the anti-nuclear policies of some states in the zone, particularly those of New Zealand.

International Court of Justice ruling on nuclear weapons

In a highly-publicized case watched by government officials and nuclear disarmament activists alike, the International Court of Justice (ICJ) in The Hague, also known as the World Court, issued on 8 July 1996 an advisory opinion on the legality of nuclear weapons. The ICJ ruling came in response to a 1994 request from the UN General Assembly for its opinion on whether the use of, or threat to use, nuclear weapons is 'in any circumstances' permitted under international law.[107] In the autumn of 1995 the ICJ had heard arguments from 22 UN member states, with four of the five nuclear weapon states (all except China) urging the court not to issue an opinion on the matter.

The ICJ's ruling concluded that the use of nuclear weapons might be legal only *in extremis*. The justices ruled—on the deciding vote of the Court President, with the other 14 judges split evenly—that 'in view of the current state of international law . . . the Court cannot conclude definitively whether the threat or use of nuclear weapons would be lawful or unlawful in an extreme circumstance of self-defence, in which the very survival of a State would be at stake'. However, they also ruled—again by a split vote—that 'the threat or use of nuclear weapons would be generally contrary to the rules of international law applicable in armed conflict, and in particular the principles and rules of humanitarian law'.[108]

The ambiguous nature of the ICJ opinion disappointed those disarmament advocates who had hoped for a more categorical judgement against nuclear weapons. However, some activists were encouraged by the fact that seven

---

[104] *Fact Sheet: South Pacific Nuclear Free Zone Treaty* (White House, Office of the Press Secretary: Washington, DC, 22 Mar. 1996). The members of the South Pacific Forum are listed in the Glossary.

[105] Joint Statement by the Governments of France, the United Kingdom and the United States on the Signing of the Protocols to the South Pacific Nuclear Free Zone Treaty, 22 Mar. 1996, reproduced in *Disarmament Diplomacy*, no. 3 (Mar. 1996), p. 22; and Press release, Embassy of France in Fiji, 23 Mar. 1996. France and the UK attached reservations to Article 1 (dealing with so-called 'negative security assurances') of Protocol II.

[106] Under Protocol I, France, the UK and the USA committed themselves to apply the basic provisions of the Treaty to their respective territories in the zone of application.

[107] UN General Assembly Resolution 49/75K, 15 Dec. 1994.

[108] International Court of Justice, Advisory Opinion on the Legality of the Threat or Use of Nuclear Weapons, 8 July 1996, *International Legal Materials*, 35 I.L.M. 809 (1996).

judges had believed that the use of, or threat to use, nuclear weapons in general violated international law and by the fact that three of the judges believed that it was always illegal.[109] In addition, some observers maintained that the most important long-term aspect of the Court's ruling was its unanimous decision that 'there exists an obligation to pursue in good faith and bring to a conclusion leading to nuclear disarmament in all its aspects'; by in effect declaring that Article VI of the NPT—from which its language was drawn—had become part of customary international law, the Court added a new dimension to arguments in favour of nuclear disarmament.[110]

The Canberra Commission

With the end of the cold war, the abolition of nuclear weapons has become the subject of discussion in several working groups of prominent experts around the globe.[111] The Canberra Commission on the Elimination of Nuclear Weapons was set up in 1995 by the Australian Government as an independent body to consider 'practical steps towards a nuclear weapon-free world including the related problem of maintaining stability and security during the transitional period and after the goal is accomplished'.[112] The commission's Final Report, which was published in August 1996, offered a pragmatic step-by-step approach to reducing the size and spread of nuclear arsenals in the near term and eventually to eliminating them altogether.[113] Although the commission did not reach a consensus on what should be the time-frame for nuclear disarmament, its work attests to the fact that the legitimacy of nuclear weapons in post-cold war international politics is coming under increasing critical scrutiny.

VII. Conclusions

The year 1996 witnessed several developments that advanced the nuclear arms control agenda. The large-scale deactivation of strategic nuclear weapons proceeded ahead of the deadlines set out in the START I Treaty. Within the START I framework, Belarus and Ukraine transferred to Russia the last

---

[109] Carnahan, B., 'World Court delivers opinion on legality of nuclear weapon use', *Arms Control Today*, vol. 26, no. 5 (July 1996), p. 24; and 'Inconclusive World Court ruling on nuclear weapons', *Disarmament Diplomacy*, no. 7 (July/Aug. 1996), pp. 44–45.

[110] Carnahan (note 109).

[111] See, e.g., *An Evolving US Nuclear Posture: Second Report of the Steering Committee Project on Eliminating Weapons of Mass Destruction*, Report no. 19 (Henry L. Stimson Center: Washington, DC, Dec. 1996).

In a widely-noted Dec. 1996 letter, a group of 61 retired generals and admirals from 17 countries, including the former commander of the US strategic nuclear forces, issued a manifesto addressing 'a challenge of the highest possible historic importance: the creation of a nuclear weapons-free world'. State of the World Forum, 'Statement on nuclear weapons by international generals and admirals', 5 Dec. 1996.

[112] Statement by the Prime Minister, the Hon. J. Keating, Australian Initiative for a Nuclear Weapon-Free World, Canberra, 26 Nov. 1995.

[113] Canberra Commission, *Report of the Canberra Commission on the Elimination of Nuclear Weapons*, Canberra, Australia, Aug. 1996.

nuclear warheads based on their territories, thereby helping to settle the fate of the former Soviet nuclear arsenal. In addition, the overwhelming support of the UN General Assembly for the CTBT, the establishment of a nuclear weapon-free zone in Africa and the widespread attention given to an ICJ ruling on the legality of nuclear weapons reflected the growing disapprobation attached by the international community to the acquisition, possession or use of nuclear weapons.

Despite these achievements, the nuclear arms control agenda is by no means complete. International efforts to negotiate a legally binding global convention to ban the production of fissile material for nuclear explosives have stalled in the CD. Furthermore, the momentum behind the considerable post-cold war nuclear arms control progress made by Russia and the USA is waning. The START II Treaty faces an uncertain fate in the Russian Parliament. US–Russian negotiations to clarify the scope of the ABM Treaty remain stymied amidst growing calls on Capitol Hill for the USA to abandon the treaty altogether. The two countries have also been unable to reach agreement on a series of transparency and irreversibility measures intended to 'lock in' and make permanent their achievements in eliminating nuclear weapons.

In addition, greater attention must be given to one of the most important issues that has emerged on the post-cold war nuclear arms control agenda: namely, how to enhance the security and safely dispose of the vast quantity of fissile material left over from the former Soviet nuclear weapon complex. The USA and Russia made some progress in addressing this challenge in 1996, but much remains to be done.

Perhaps the most hopeful sign for nuclear arms control in 1996 was that it is now possible for scholars and statesmen to begin 'thinking the unthinkable' and to give serious attention to formulating a long-term strategy not only for reducing the size and spread of nuclear arsenals but, eventually, also for eliminating them completely. While it is clear that the abolition of nuclear weapons is not a realistic short-term goal, there are many concrete steps which can be taken by the international community to reduce the risks and dangers arising from these uniquely destructive weapons.

Appendix 11A. Tables of nuclear forces

ROBERT S. NORRIS and WILLIAM M. ARKIN

After significant reductions over the past six years the nuclear arsenals of the five declared nuclear weapon powers have stabilized. Tables 11A.1 and 11A.2 provide a breakdown of US and Russian operational strategic arsenals with notes about developments in 1996. For the USA and Russia the number of warheads has decreased by one-third and the number of platforms by one-half from the peak of the late 1980s.

The arsenals of the second-tier powers, Britain, France and China—depicted in tables 11A.3, 11A.4 and 11A.5—are in the 260–450 warhead range, many orders of magnitude less than those of the USA and Russia. Plans for British and French forces are well known while the size and composition of China's future arsenal is unknown.

Table 11A.1. US strategic nuclear forces, January 1997

Type	Designation	No. deployed	Year first deployed	Range (km)[a]	Warheads x yield	Warheads in stockpile
Bombers						
B-52H[b]	Stratofortress	71/44	1961	16 000	ALCM 5–150 kt	400
					ACM 5–150 kt	400
B-1B[c]	Lancer	95/48	1986	19 000⎫	Bombs, various	1 000
B-2[d]	Spirit	13/10	1994	11 000⎭		
Total		**179/102**				**1 800**
ICBMs						
LGM-30G[e]	Minuteman III			13 000		
	Mk-12	200	1970		3 x 170 kt	600
	Mk-12A	325	1979		3 x 335 kt	975
LGM-118A	MX/Peacekeeper	50	1986	11 000	10 x 300 kt	500
Total		**575**				**2 075**
SLBMs						
UGM-96A[f]	Trident I C4	192	1979	7 400	8 x 100 kt	1 536
UGM-133A[g]	Trident II D5	216		7 400		1 728
	Mk-4	..	1992		8 x 100 kt	1 344
	Mk-5	..	1990		8 x 475 kt	384
Total		**408**				**3 264**

[a] Range for aircraft indicates combat radius, without in-flight refuelling.

[b] B-52Hs can carry up to 20 air-launched cruise missiles (ALCMs)/advanced cruise missiles (ACMs) each. Because of a shrinking bomber force only about 400 ALCMs and 400 ACMs are deployed, with several hundred other ALCMs in reserve. The Nuclear Posture Review (NPR) released on 22 Sep. 1994 recommended retaining 66 B-52Hs. The Air Force has since recommended retaining 71. The B-52Hs have been consolidated at two bases, the 2nd Bomb Wing at Barksdale Air Force Base (AFB), Louisiana, and the 5th Bomb Wing at Minot AFB, North Dakota. The first figure in the No. deployed column is the total number of B-52Hs in the inventory, including those for training, test and backup. The second figure is the operational number available for nuclear and conventional missions.

c The B-1B can carry up to 24 B61 and/or B83 bombs. Four have crashed and 1 is used as a ground trainer at Ellsworth AFB, South Dakota, and is not considered operational. The USA has almost completed the reorientation of its B-1Bs to non-nuclear missions. By the end of 1997 the B-1B will be out of the SIOP (Single Integrated Operational Plan [for strategic nuclear weapons]) mission altogether. With the fleet in transition, 10 B-1Bs currently serve with the Air National Guard at McConnell AFB, Kansas. Ten others serve with the 366th Composite Wing at Mountain Home AFB, Idaho, 41 are at Dyess AFB, Texas, 25 are at Ellsworth AFB, and 2 test planes are at Edwards AFB, California. The aircraft will count towards START I Treaty limits, but not towards START II Treaty limits. The first figure in the No. deployed column is the total number of B-1Bs in the inventory, including those for training, test and backup. The second figure is the operational number available for nuclear and conventional missions.

d The first B-2 bomber was delivered to the 509th Bombardment Wing at Whiteman AFB, Missouri, on 17 Dec. 1993. Four more were delivered in 1994, 3 in 1995, and 5 in 1996 bringing the total to 13. At the direction of Congress all 6 (instead of 5) aircraft originally in the test programme will be modified to achieve operational capability. The cost of upgrading the 6th aircraft will be $493 million. Initially, the first 16 B-2s will be capable of carrying only the B83 nuclear bomb. Eventually, all 21 operational B-2s will be capable of carrying the B61 and B83 bombs. The 509th Bomb Wing will have two squadrons, the 393rd and the 715th, each with 8 aircraft. The first figure in the No. deployed column is the total number of B-2s delivered to Whiteman. The 2nd figure is an approximate number of those available for nuclear and conventional missions.

e The 500 Minuteman III intercontinental ballistic missiles (ICBMs) are being consolidated from 4 to 3 bases. Minuteman III missiles are being transferred from Grand Forks AFB, North Dakota to Malmstrom AFB, Montana at a rate of about 1 missile per week, with the transfer due to be completed by the autumn of 1998. When completed there will be 200 Minuteman IIIs at Malmstrom, and 150 each at Minot AFB, North Dakota and F. E. Warren AFB, Wyoming. In downloading the 3-warhead missiles to a single warhead (to comply with the START II Treaty's ban on multiple-warhead ICBMs), it was decided to replace the higher-yield W78 and the lower-yield W62 with single W87 warheads taken from the 50 MX missiles that will be retired. A $5.2 billion programme is under way to extend the operational life of the Minuteman III missiles and improve their capability to the year 2020. There are 3 major parts to the programme: a now completed upgrade of the consoles at launch control centres, the purchase of improved guidance systems, and the 'repouring' of new solid propellant in 2 of the missile's 3 stages.

After removal of 450 Minuteman IIs from their silos at Ellsworth, Malmstrom and Whiteman, a programme of silo destruction commenced. On 13 Sep. 1996 the 149th Minuteman II silo was blown up at Ellsworth. The 150th silo (and one launch control centre) may become a museum.

f The W76 warheads from the Trident I missiles are being fitted on Trident II submarines home-ported at Kings Bay, Georgia, and are supplemented by 400 W88 warheads, the number built before production was halted in 1990.

g One new Ohio Class Trident submarine, the *USS Wyoming* (SSBN-742), the 17th of the class, joined the fleet in a commissioning ceremony on 13 July 1996. The 18th, and last, Trident submarine (*USS Louisiana*) will be delivered in Aug. 1997. In the NPR there were two major decisions about nuclear-powered ballistic-missile submarines (SSBNs). The 1st specified that if the START II Treaty is implemented the number of SSBNs would be reduced to 14, either by retiring 4 SSBNs based in Bangor, Maine, or by converting them to special-purpose submarines. The 2nd is to purchase additional Trident II D-5 submarine-launched ballistic missiles (SLBMs) to retrofit the 4 submarines that now carry the Trident I. The expanded programme now calls for the purchase of 462 missiles at a cost of $27.7 billion. If START II is implemented the number of warheads per missile is planned to be reduced from 8 to 5.

Table 11A.1 *Notes, contd*

Sources: William S. Cohen, Secretary of Defense, *Annual Report to the President and the Congress*, April 1997, pp. 207–11; William J. Perry, Secretary of Defense, *Annual Report to the President and the Congress*, Mar. 1996, pp. 213–18; START I Treaty Memorandum of Understanding, 1 Sep. 1990; START I Treaty Memorandum of Understanding, 5 Dec. 1994; START I Treaty Memorandum of Understanding, 1 July 1995; START I Treaty Memorandum of Understanding, 1 Jan. 1996; START I Treaty Memorandum of Understanding, 1 July 1996; Senate Committee on Foreign Relations, START II Treaty, Executive Report 104–10, 15 Dec. 1995; US Air Force Public Affairs, personal communications; *Bulletin of the Atomic Scientists*; and Natural Resources Defense Council (NRDC).

Table 11A.2. Russian strategic nuclear forces, January 1997

Type	NATO designation	No. deployed	Year first deployed	Range (km)^a	Warheads x yield	Warheads in stockpile
Bombers						
Tu-95M^b	Bear-H6	32	1984	12 800	6 x AS-15A ALCMs, bombs	192
Tu-95M^b	Bear-H16	56	1984	12 800	16 x AS-15A ALCMs, bombs	896
Tu-160^c	Blackjack	25	1987	11 000	12 x AS-15B ALCMs or AS-16 SRAMs, bombs	300
Total		**113**				**1 388**
ICBMs^d						
SS-18^e	Satan	180	1979	11 000	10 x 550/750 kt	1 800
SS-19^f	Stiletto	160	1980	10 000	6 x 550 kt	960
SS-24 M1/M2^g	Scalpel	36/10	1987	10 000	10 x 550 kt	460
SS-25^h	Sickle	369	1985	10 500	1 x 550 kt	389
Total		**755**				**3 589**
SLBMs^i						
SS-N-18 M1	Stingray	208	1978	6 500	3 x 500 kt	624
SS-N-20^j	Sturgeon	120	1983	8 300	10 x 200 kt	1 200
SS-N-23	Skiff	112	1986	9 000	4 x 100 kt	448
Total		**440**				**2 272**

^{a} Range for aircraft indicates combat radius, without in-flight refuelling.

^{b} According to the 1 July 1996 START I MOU, the Bear bombers are deployed as follows: Bear-H16s—19 at Mozdok (Russia), 16 at Ukrainka (Russia) and 21 at Uzin (Ukraine); and Bear-H6s—2 at Mozdok, 26 at Ukrainka and 4 at Uzin. The 40 Bear-H bombers (27 Bear-H6s and 13 Bear-H16s) that were based in Kazakhstan were withdrawn to Russia, including some 370 AS-15 ALCM warheads. The 25 Bear bombers in Ukraine are poorly maintained and not fully operational.

^{c} Nineteen Blackjacks are based in Ukraine at Priluki; the remaining 6 are in Russia at Engels AFB near Saratov. The Blackjacks at Priluki are poorly maintained and not fully operational. An agreement announced on 24 Nov. 1995 calls for Ukraine to eventually return the 19 Blackjacks, 25 Bears and more than 300 cruise missiles to Russia. The precise timing of the transfer and the amount of money to be paid were not made public. It is likely that most of the aircraft will be used for spare parts to support the bombers in Russia, with only a very few, if any at all, returning to service.

d Deactivation and retirement of ICBMs and their launchers proceeds through at least 4 stages. In stage 1, an ICBM is removed from alert status by electrical and mechanical procedures. Next, warheads are removed from the missile. In stage 3 the missile is withdrawn from the silo. Finally, to comply with START I elimination provisions the silo is blown up and eventually filled in with concrete. The number of missiles and warheads will vary depending upon which stage the analyst chooses to feature.

e In the Sep. 1990 START I Treaty MOU, the USSR declared 104 SS-18s in Kazakhstan (at Derzhavinsk and Zhangiz-Tobe) and 204 in Russia (30 at Aleysk, 64 at Dombárosvki, 46 at Kartaly and 64 at Uzhur). All of the SS-18s in Kazakhstan and 24 in Russia are considered to be non-operational, leaving 180 in Russia. On 29 Aug. the last SS-18 silo in Kazakhstan was blown up. Under the START I Treaty Russia is permitted to retain 154 SS-18s. If the START II Treaty is fully implemented, all SS-18 missiles will be destroyed, but Russia may convert up to 90 SS-18 silos for deployment of single-warhead ICBMs.

f In the original START I Treaty MOU, the USSR declared 130 SS-19s in Ukraine and 170 in Russia. The Nov. 1995 agreement (see note *c*) included the sale of 32 SS-19s, once deployed in Ukraine, back to Russia. Some SS-19s in Russia are being withdrawn from service. Under START II Russia may keep up to 105 SS-19s downloaded to 1 warhead each.

g Of the original 56 silo-based SS-24 M2s, 46 were in Ukraine at Pervomaysk and 10 in Russia at Tatishchevo. By the end of 1996 only the 10 in Russia were considered operational. All 36 rail-based SS-24 M1s are in Russia—at Bershet, Kostroma and Krasnoyarsk.

h By 27 Nov. 1996 the last of the former Soviet SS-25 missiles based in Belarus and their warheads were shipped back to Russia. The new variant of the SS-25 is called the Topal M by the Russians and designated the SS-27 by the US Government. It is assembled at Votkinsk in Russia and is the only Russian strategic weapon system still in production. Flight testing began on 20 Dec. 1994 and has continued during 1995 and 1996. The first few SS-25/27s may become operational in 1997, but at a production rate of 10–20 missiles per year it will take some time for significant numbers of them to be fielded.

i Approximately one-half of the SSBN fleet has been withdrawn from operational service. The table assumes that all the Yankee Is, Delta Is and Delta IIs and 1 Delta III have been withdrawn from operational service, leaving 26 SSBNs of 3 classes (13 Delta IIIs, 7 Delta IVs and 6 Typhoons). All of these SSBNs are based on the Kola Peninsula (at Nerpichya, Olenya and Yagelnaya) except for 9 Delta IIIs, which are based at Rybachi (15 km south-west of Petropavlovsk) on the Kamchatka Peninsula. No additional SSBN production is expected before the year 2000.

j A follow-on to the SS-N-20, called the SS-NX-26, is in development and is expected to be flight-tested soon and deployed during this decade. A second new SLBM, for a new class of SSBN that might replace the Typhoon and Delta IV, is also under development.

Sources: START I Treaty Memorandum of Understanding, 1 Sep. 1990; START I Treaty Memorandum of Understanding, 5 Dec. 1994; START I Treaty Memorandum of Understanding, 1 July 1995; START I Treaty Memorandum of Understanding, 1 Jan. 1996; START I Treaty Memorandum of Understanding, 1 July 1996; 'Nuclear notebook', *Bulletin of the Atomic Scientists,* May/June 1997; International Institute for Strategic Studies (IISS), *The Military Balance 1996–1997* (Oxford University Press: Oxford, 1996), p. 113; and Natural Resources Defense Council (NRDC).

Table 11A.3. British nuclear forces, January 1997

Type	Designation	No. deployed	Year first deployed	Range (km)[a]	Warheads x yield	Warheads in stockpile
Aircraft						
GR.1/1A	Tornado	96[b]	1982	1 300	1–2 x 200–400 kt	100[c]
SSBNs/SLBMs[d]						
D-5	Trident II	32	1994	7 400	4–6 x 100 kt	160[e]

[a] Range for aircraft indicates combat radius, without in-flight refuelling.

[b] The Royal Air Force (RAF) operates 8 squadrons of dual-capable Tornado GR.1/1A aircraft. These include 4 squadrons at RAF Bruggen, Germany (Nos 9, 14, 17 and 31); 2 squadrons previously at RAF Marham were redeployed to RAF Lossiemouth in 1994 (they replaced the Buccaneer S2B in the maritime strike role and were redesignated Nos 12 and 617); and 2 reconnaissance squadrons at RAF Marham (Nos 2 and 13). Each squadron has 12 aircraft. It is likely that a less than full complement of nuclear bombs is assigned to Tornadoes with maritime strike and reconnaissance roles.

[c] The total stockpile of WE-177 tactical nuclear gravity bombs was estimated to have been about 200, of which 175 were versions A and B. The C version of the WE-177 was assigned to selected Royal Navy (RN) Sea Harrier FRS.1 aircraft and anti-submarine warfare (ASW) helicopters. The 1992 White Paper stated that 'As part of the cut in NATO's stockpile we will also reduce the number of British free-fall nuclear bombs by more than half'. A number of British nuclear bombs were returned to the UK from bases in Germany. The 1993 White Paper stated that the WE-177 'is currently expected to remain in service until well into the next century'. On 4 Apr. 1995 the government announced that the remaining WE-177s would be withdrawn by the end of 1998. On 1 May 1996 Defence Secretary Michael Portillo announced that RAF Bruggen would close in 2002. The Tornadoes (4 years after becoming non-nuclear) will be reassigned to bases in the UK.

[d] The UK built and deployed 4 Resolution Class SSBNs, commonly called Polaris submarines after the missiles they carried. The 1st boat (*HMS Resolution*) went on patrol in mid-June 1968, the 4th (*HMS Revenge*) in Sep. 1970. The total number of patrols for the 4 boats over the 28-year period was 229. *Revenge* was retired on 25 May 1992 after 56 patrols. *Resolution* was decommissioned on 22 Oct. 1994 after 61 patrols. *HMS Renown* was decommissioned on 24 Feb. 1996 after 52 patrols, and *HMS Repulse* was withdrawn from service on 28 Aug. 1996 after 60 patrols. The Chevaline warheads are being dismantled.

The 1st submarine of the new class, *HMS Vanguard*, went on its first patrol in Dec. 1994. The 2nd, *HMS Victorious*, entered service in Dec. 1995. The 3rd, *HMS Vigilant*, was launched in Oct. 1995 and will enter service in the summer or autumn of 1998. The 4th and final boat of the class, *HMS Vengeance*, is under construction. Its estimated launch date is 1998 with service entry in late 2000 or early 2001. The current estimated cost of the programme is $18.8 billion.

Each Vanguard Class SSBN carries 16 US-produced Trident II D-5 SLBMs. It has never been publicly stated exactly how many missiles the UK is purchasing from the USA. We estimate the number to be 70, but it should be noted that there are no specifically US or British Trident II missiles. There is a pool of SLBMs at Strategic Weapons Facility Atlantic at the Kings Bay Submarine Base, Georgia. The UK has title to a certain number of SLBMs but does not actually own them. A missile that is deployed on a US SSBN may at a later date deploy on a British one, or vice versa.

[e] It is assumed that the UK will only produce enough warheads for 3 boatloads of missiles, a practice followed with Polaris. Thus, it is estimated that 240 warheads for 48 missiles (assuming 5 warheads per missile) will be produced, plus another 10% for spares and maintenance.

This would mean a future British nuclear stockpile in the 275-warhead range of only one type. The Ministry of Defence has announced that, 'each submarine will deploy with no more than 96 warheads [i.e., multiple independently targetable re-entry vehicles, MIRV x 6], and may carry significantly fewer'. The number will certainly be lower as the 'sub-strategic' mission for Trident is fully implemented. A MOD official described this mission as follows: 'A sub-strategic strike would be the limited and highly selective use of nuclear weapons in a manner that fell demonstrably short of a strategic strike, but with a sufficient level of violence to convince an aggressor who had already miscalculated our resolve and attacked us that he should halt his aggression and withdraw or face the prospect of a devastating strategic strike.'

The sub-strategic mission has begun with *Victorious* and 'will become fully robust when *Vigilant* enters service', according to the 1996 White Paper. The plan is to put a single warhead on some Trident II SLBMs and have them assigned to targets once covered by WE-177 gravity bombs. For example, a submarine could be armed with 10, 12 or 14 of its SLBMs carrying an average of 5 warheads per missile, and the other 2, 4 or 6 missiles armed with just one. There is some flexibility in the choice of yield of the Trident warhead. (Choosing to detonate only the unboosted primary could produce a yield of 1 kt or less. Choosing to detonate the boosted primary could produce a yield of a few kilotons.) With the sub-strategic mission the submarine would have approximately 56–72 warheads on board during its patrol. Following this logic we conclude that a more accurate future operational stockpile for the SSBN fleet is about 200 warheads. The number on patrol at any given time would be two SSBNs with about 120–130 warheads. A 3rd SSBN could put to sea fairly rapidly while the 4th is undergoing overhaul and maintenance.

Sources: Norris, R. S., Burrows, A. S. and Fieldhouse, R. W., *Nuclear Weapons Databook Vol. V: British, French, and Chinese Nuclear Weapons* (Westview: Boulder, Colo., 1994), p. 9; Secretary of State for Defence, *Statement on the Defence Estimates 1996*, Cmnd 3223 (Her Majesty's Stationery Office: London, May 1996): and 'Nuclear notebook', *Bulletin of the Atomic Scientists*, Nov./Dec. 1996, pp. 64–67.

Table 11A.4. French nuclear forces, January 1997[a]

Type	No. deployed	Year first deployed	Range (km)[b]	Warheads x yield	Warheads in stockpile
Land-based aircraft[c]					
Mirage 2000N/ASMP	45	1988	2 750	1 x 300 kt ASMP	45
Carrier-based aircraft					
Super Étendard[d]	24	1978	650	1 x 300 kt ASMP	20
SLBMs[e]					
M4A/B	48	1985	6 000	6 x 150 kt	288
M45	16	1996	6 000	6 x 100 kt	96

[a] On 22 and 23 Feb. 1996 President Jacques Chirac announced several reforms for the French armed forces in 1997–2002. The decisions in the nuclear area were a combination of the withdrawal of several obsolete systems and a commitment to modernize those that remain.

After officials considered numerous plans to replace the silo-based S3D intermediate-range ballistic missile (IRBM) during President François Mitterrand's tenure, President Chirac announced that the missile would be retired and there would be no replacement. On 16 Sep. 1996 all 18 missiles on the Plateau d'Albion were deactivated. It will take 2 years and cost $77.5 million to fully dismantle the silos and complex.

In July 1996, after 32 years of service, the Mirage IVP relinquished its nuclear role and was retired. Five Mirage IVPs will be retained for reconnaissance missions at Istres. The other planes will be put into storage at Châteaudun.

Table 11A.4 *Notes, contd*

b Range for aircraft indicates combat radius, without in-flight refuelling, and does not include the 90- to 350-km range of the Air-Sol Moyenne Portée (ASMP) air-to-surface missile.

c The 3 squadrons of Mirage 2000Ns have now assumed the 'strategic' role, in addition to their 'pre-strategic' one. A 4th Mirage 2000N squadron at Nancy—now assigned a conventional role—is scheduled to be replaced with Mirage 2000Ds. Those aircraft may be modified to carry the ASMP and distributed to the 3 2000N squadrons at Luxeuil and Istres, along with the Mirage IVP's ASMP missiles. In his Feb. speech Chirac said that a longer-range ASMP (500 km *vs* 300 km, sometimes called the 'ASMP Plus') will be developed for service entry in about a decade.

The Rafale is planned to be the multi-purpose Navy and Air Force fighter/bomber for the 21st century. Its roles include conventional ground attack, air defence, air superiority and nuclear delivery of the ASMP and/or ASMP Plus. The carrier-based Navy version will be introduced first, with the Air Force Rafale D attaining a nuclear-strike role in approximately 2005.

d France built 2 aircraft-carriers, 1 of which entered service in 1961 (*Clemenceau*) and the other in 1963 (*Foch*). Both were modified to handle the AN 52 nuclear gravity bomb carried by Super Étendard aircraft. The *Clemenceau* was modified in 1979 and the *Foch* in 1981. The AN 52 was retired in July 1991. Only the *Foch* was modified to 'handle and store' the replacement ASMP, and approximately 20 were allocated for 2 squadrons—*c*. 24 Super Étendard aircraft. The *Clemenceau* was never modified to 'handle and store' the ASMP; the 32 780 ton aircraft-carrier will be decommissioned in Sep. 1997. The new aircraft-carrier *Charles de Gaulle* is scheduled to enter service in Dec. 1999, 3 years behind schedule. At that time the *Foch* will be laid up. The *Charles de Gaulle* will have a single squadron of Super Étendard aircraft (with presumably about 10 ASMPs) until the Rafale M is introduced in 2002. At about that time a 2nd carrier may be ordered. The Navy plans to purchase a total of 60 Rafale-M aircraft, of which the 1st 16 will perform an air-to-air role. Missions for subsequent aircraft may include the ASMP and/or ASMP Plus.

e The lead SSBN, *Le Triomphant*, was rolled out from its construction shed in Cherbourg on 13 July 1993. It was scheduled to depart on its 1st patrol by the end of 1996 armed with the M45 SLBM and new TN 75 warheads. The 2nd SSBN, *Le Téméraire*, is under construction and will not be ready until 1999. The schedule for the 3rd, *Le Vigilant*, has slipped and it will not be ready until 2001. The service date for the 4th SSBN is *c*. 2005. The authors estimate that eventually there will be 288 warheads for the fleet of 4 new Triomphant Class SSBNs, because only enough missiles and warheads will be purchased for 3 boats. This loading is the case today with 5 submarines in the fleet—only 4 sets of M4 SLBMs were procured. President Chirac announced on 23 Feb. 1996 that the 4th submarine would be built and that a new SLBM, known as the M51, will replace the M45 and be ready for service in the period 2010–2015.

Sources: Norris, R. S., Burrows, A. S. and Fieldhouse, R. W., *Nuclear Weapons Databook Vol. V: British, French, and Chinese Nuclear Weapons* (Westview: Boulder, Colo., 1994), p. 10; *Air Actualités: Le Magazine de l'Armée de l'Air*; and Address by M. Jacques Chirac, President of the Republic, at the École Militaire, Paris, 23 Feb. 1996.

Table 11A.5. Chinese nuclear forces, January 1997

Type	NATO designation	No. deployed	Year first deployed	Range (km)[a]	Warheads x yield	Warheads in stockpile
Aircraft[a]						
H-6	B-6	120	1965	3 100	1–3 bombs	120
Q-5	A-5	30	1970	400	1 x bomb	30
Land-based missiles[b]						
DF-3A	CSS-2	50	1971	2 800	1 x 3.3 Mt	50
DF-4	CSS-3	20	1980	4 750	1 x 3.3 Mt	20
DF-5A	CSS-4	7	1981	13 000+	1 x 4–5 Mt	7
DF-21A	CSS-5	36	1985–86	1 800	1 x 200–300 kt	36
SLBMs[c]						
Julang-1	CSS-N-3	12	1986	1 700	1 x 200–300 kt	12
Tactical weapons						
Artillery/ADMs,[d] Short-range missiles					low kt	120

[a] All figures for bomber aircraft are for nuclear-configured versions only. Hundreds of aircraft are also deployed in non-nuclear versions. The Hong-5 has been retired and the Hong-7 will not have a nuclear role. Aircraft range is equivalent to combat radius. Assumes 150 nuclear gravity bombs for the force, with estimated yields of between 10 kt and 3 Mt.

[b] The Chinese define missile ranges as follows: short-range, < 1000 km; medium-range, 1000–3000 km; long-range, 3000–8000 km; intercontinental range, > 8000 km. The nuclear delivery capability of the medium-range M-9 is unconfirmed and not included. China is also developing 2 other ICBMs. The DF-31, with a range of 8000 km and carrying one 200- to 300-kt warhead, was deployed in 1997; the 1200-km range DF-41 is scheduled for deployment around 2010 and may be MIRVed if China develops that capability.

[c] The 8000-km range Julang-2 (NATO designation CSS-N-4), to carry one 200- to 300-kt warhead, will be available in the late 1990s.

[d] ADM = atomic demolition mine

Sources: Norris, R. S., Burrows, A. S. and Fieldhouse, R. W., *Nuclear Weapons Databook Vol. V: British, French, and Chinese Nuclear Weapons* (Westview: Boulder, Colo., 1994), p. 11; Lewis, J. W. and Hua Di, 'China's ballistic missile programs: technologies, strategies, goals', *International Security*, vol. 17, no. 2 (fall 1992), pp. 5–40; Allen, K. W., Krumel, G. and Pollack, J. D., *China's Air Force Enters the 21st Century* (RAND: Santa Monica, Calif., 1995); International Institute for Strategic Studies (IISS), *The Military Balance 1996–1997* (Oxford Univerity Press: Oxford, 1996), p. 179; and 'Nuclear notebook', *Bulletin of the Atomic Scientists*, Nov./Dec. 1996, pp. 64–67.

12. The Comprehensive Nuclear Test-Ban Treaty

ERIC ARNETT

I. Introduction

The Comprehensive Nuclear Test-Ban Treaty (CTBT) was completed and opened for signature in September 1996. Among other things, this historic event was made possible by a watershed in Chinese security policy making, the military's recommendation for continued testing having been overruled at the highest level. By the end of the year, the majority of states had signed the treaty and only one—India—had declared unconditionally that it would not. India's refusal to sign the CTBT could prevent the treaty from achieving its full legal force, although the international norm against testing which it embodies is universally accepted.

Section II reviews the year's developments, including India's position and other controversies that could carry over into the treaty regime. Section III assesses the implications of the treaty for nuclear norms and modernization. The chapter concludes with a discussion of the treaty's long-term prospects in section IV. The text of the CTBT is reproduced in appendix 12A, and a report on nuclear testing in 1996 is included in appendix 12B.

II. Developments in 1996

On 10 September 1996, the UN General Assembly voted overwhelmingly to adopt the CTBT as negotiated at the Conference on Disarmament (CD). The vote was 158 : 3 with five abstentions.[1] The three states that voted against the resolution were Bhutan, India and Libya. Two weeks later, on 24 September, the first 71 states signed the treaty at a ceremony in New York. On 10 October Fiji became the first state to ratify the CTBT. On 20 November a Preparatory Commission of the then 134 signatories met to discuss implementation of the treaty prior to its entry into force. By the end of the year 137 states had signed the treaty.[2]

The failure of the CD to reach consensus

The 1996 session of the CD's Ad Hoc Committee on the Nuclear Test Ban resolved a number of difficult issues and produced a draft treaty that nearly

[1] UN General Assembly Resolution 245, 10 Sep. 1996.
[2] See annexe A for a list of signatories to the CTBT.

gained consensus. In the end, this process was stymied by only one of India's many reservations, but at least four other issues reviewed in this section may have an effect on the treaty's long-term viability, if not its entry into force: peaceful nuclear explosions (PNEs), inspections, the use of data acquired through national technical means (NTM) of verification in decision making, and the composition of regional groups.[3]

India

After more than a year of constructive work in the Ad Hoc Committee, India reversed course and began to play a blatantly obstructive role in the negotiations. The Indian delegation began tabling new proposals for treaty language months after other CD members had agreed not to open new issues so that the disagreements already identified could be resolved. In November 1995 the efforts of the Indian Defence Ministry and Department of Atomic Energy and sympathetic editorial writers to portray the CTBT as a threat to India's nuclear option finally resulted in a policy crisis.[4] Although the proposition that India cannot maintain the option without testing and would not be free to withdraw from the treaty in a crisis is hard to credit, the Congress (I) Government of Prime Minister P. V. Narasimha Rao was under pressure from the stridently pro-nuclear Bharatiya Janata Party (BJP) during a national election campaign. Although many observers believe that Narasimha Rao himself supported the CTBT, he bowed to political necessity. In any case the Congress Party lost the election.

After its reversal of policy India staked out a radical new position, putting forward new proposals on the treaty's scope and verification procedures that undid compromises made by China, Indonesia and others.[5] India also argued that the CTBT should include a commitment to negotiate complete nuclear disarmament by a certain date. Ultimately, Ambassador Arundhata Ghose signalled a willingness to stand aside as long as India was not required to sign it, a proposal that was unacceptable to at least four other CD members—China, Pakistan, Russia and the UK—which insisted that all 44 states operating nuclear reactors must sign.

---

[3] These issues have been reviewed in earlier SIPRI publications: Arnett, E., 'The comprehensive nuclear test ban', *SIPRI Yearbook 1995: Armaments, Disarmament and International Security* (Oxford University Press: Oxford, 1995); and Arnett, E. (ed.), SIPRI, *Implementing the Comprehensive Test Ban: New Aspects of Definition, Organization and Verification* (Oxford University Press: Oxford, 1995).

[4] The claim that India's nuclear establishment would collapse without the option of testing had been noted as early as the spring of 1994. Deshingkar, G., 'India', ed. E. Arnett, *Nuclear Weapons After the Comprehensive Test Ban: Implications for Modernization and Proliferation*, SIPRI Research Report No. 8 (Oxford University Press: Oxford, 1996). Deshingkar's paper was drafted for a June 1994 workshop.

[5] Indeed, India would probably have objected to these provisions on other grounds if they had been accepted. The proposal on the scope of the treaty, for example, would have entailed intrusive inspections that India (and others) would have found difficult to accept.

The list of 44[6]

The requirement that India sign and ratify the treaty for it to enter into force is rooted in the perception that the treaty must capture the nuclear programmes of a certain minimum set of states to be effective. The United States and other states opposed this logic on the grounds that the CTBT would be sufficiently effective with only the nuclear weapon states, although the participation of others was certainly desirable. Observers differ as to whether the four that insisted on all 44 countries intended mainly to ensure the treaty's non-proliferation benefits or were cynically attempting to prevent its entry into force. Indeed, opinions vary as to which of the states were most insistent, some saying China and Russia, others Pakistan and still others blaming the UK.

In any event, India refused to allow a consensus on the treaty at the CD on the grounds that it violated its sovereignty. Most of the other 44 states appear not to have that concern: only North Korea and Pakistan have not yet signed, Pakistan on the grounds that it can only do so when India does.

China

At the beginning of 1996, China's positions on many issues were so far from the emergent consensus that observers began to wonder whether the Chinese delegation in Geneva was simply buying time for its test programme. In fact, once the decision to stop testing was announced in June, China quickly made a number of important compromises. Some of these apparently are still contested by critics of the CTBT in China and could be grist for debate before ratification.

China relaxed its demand that PNEs be permitted in exchange for the assurance that such explosions could be reviewed at periodic review conferences, although Chinese officials acknowledged that such reviews were unlikely to lead to revisions of the prohibition. China's nuclear establishment continues to express interest in PNEs and is still discussing their potential contribution to economic development with Russian colleagues. However, it has not proved possible to secure funding from the Chinese Government.[7]

The primary means for verifying compliance with the CTBT will be an International Monitoring System (IMS) of seismic, atmospheric radionuclide monitoring, hydroacoustic and infrasound stations feeding data to national and international data centres. This infrastructure and the CTBT Organization (CTBTO) are expected to cost $80 million a year to maintain. The relatively low cost is not an accident but a strict design requirement that pervaded the negotiations. This low-cost approach was opposed by China (as well as India and others) on the grounds that, unless a much more robust IMS were created,

---

[6] The 44 countries are indicated in the list of signatories in annexe A.

[7] Personal communication with a Ministry of Defence official, 12 Nov. 1996. Russian influence on Chinese thinking about and interest in PNEs is evident in He Zuoxiu, 'Peaceful nuclear explosions are widely useful', *Chinese Science News*, 27 Dec. 1995; and 'Sino-Russian symposium on peaceful nuclear explosions held in Beijing', *Chinese Science News*, 27 Dec. 1995.

some decisions on inspections would have to be made on the basis of information from other sources, including the NTM of the most technologically advanced states.[8]

Finally, the Chinese military is uneasy about allowing inspections to verify that tests have not taken place. This concern is aggravated by the risk that the controversies over permitted activities and inspections will lead to requests for inspections of sensitive laboratories.[9] Even in a society as open as that of the USA, it may not be possible to fully reassure all treaty partners that sub-critical tests are not hydronuclear experiments or even low-yield tests.[10] The difficulties in states with more secretive nuclear establishments, such as China, Israel and Russia, will be all the greater. Other states parties will then have to decide whether to request inspections in spite of the specific assertions of China and Israel in the negotiating record that such activities were not grounds for inspection.[11]

Israel and its region

A final concern arose regarding the distribution of states in geographic regions for the purpose of selecting members of the Executive Council. Reflecting both historical animosities in the region and the deterioration of the Middle East peace process,[12] a number of states in the region objected to Israel's being grouped with them. Although ultimately even Iran (the last hold-out on the issue) stood aside in the negotiations, a number of predominantly Muslim states have yet to sign the treaty. Libya, which had waived its right to block consensus in the CD but opposed the treaty at the UN General Assembly, specifically cited the grouping of Israel in the Middle East as its reason. Iraq and Syria also expressed reservations.[13]

---

[8] China has been concerned about the political use of US NTM since the US Navy harassed a Chinese freighter, the *Yinhe*, because of suspicions (later proved erroneous) that it was carrying chemical weapon precursors to Iran, a transfer that would not contravene international law in any case. US NTM for monitoring compliance with the CTBT are expected to improve in the coming years as the costs of stations now funded mainly by the USA are shifted to the IMS, for which the USA will pay only roughly 25%. The 75% savings will be ploughed back into NTM for monitoring compliance with the CTBT.

[9] Nuclear tests would most likely be conducted far from settled areas, whereas permitted activities like sub-critical tests could in principle be undertaken in laboratories.

[10] Sub-critical tests are experiments permitted under the CTBT in which some atoms undergo fission but no chain reaction is sustained. In a hydronuclear experiment, which is not permitted under the 'true zero' scope of the CTBT, a chain reaction is briefly sustained. In a nuclear test, a prolonged chain reaction is sustained. The DOE has developed some voluntary transparency and confidence-building measures for its programme of sub-critical tests. Other suggestions are presented in von Hippel, F. and Jones, S., 'Take a hard look at subcritical tests', *Bulletin of the Atomic Scientists*, no. 52, vol. 6 (Nov./Dec. 1996), p. 47; Jones, S., 'Subcritical experiments and the CTBT' (Princeton University Program on Nuclear Policy Alternatives: Princeton, N.J., 1996); and von Hippel, F., Li Bin and Jones, S., 'Verification that underground subcritical tests are indeed subcritical' (Princeton University Program on Nuclear Policy Alternatives: Princeton, N.J., 1996).

[11] For Israel's position, see Conference on Disarmament document CD/NTB/WP.114, 17 June 1994, p. 1. This document is excerpted in Arnett, 'The comprehensive nuclear test ban' (note 3), p. 713.

[12] See chapter 3 in this volume.

[13] The predominantly Muslim states of the Middle East that had not signed as of 15 Apr. 1997 were Iraq, Lebanon, Libya, Saudi Arabia, Sudan and Syria. Notably, Egypt, Iran, Turkey, and most of the Maghrebi and pro-Western Persian Gulf states had signed.

The treaty completed and opened for signature

Of the controversies discussed above, only India's inclusion in the list of 44 ultimately prevented consensus on the treaty text. Despite India's objections, the text was presented to the UN General Assembly, adopted and opened for signature on the same timetable as it would have been if consensus had been achieved, although it had to be presented by Australia on behalf of the 'Friends of the Treaty' rather than forwarded by the CD.

Some observers suggested that the CD had shown its inability to complete even a simple treaty that had been in the works for 40 years before receiving its CD negotiating mandate in August 1993. In addition to the disconcerting precedent of one state blocking consensus on a treaty apparently supported by all the others,[14] the CD's long-term viability was subject to question for other reasons, including its size, composition and agenda. After three years of wrangling over the admission of Iraq and Israel, the CD was expanded to 61 members in 1996 and action is already foreseen on the admission of 16 more. Although the new members have waived their right to block consensus for their first two years of membership, they will have that right by the time the CD has concluded another treaty. Many of these new members have little interest in key items that are or might be on the CD agenda and therefore might link them to concerns that are more important to them.

Despite these difficulties, the CD is regularly recognized as the only appropriate forum for negotiating global disarmament measures and efforts to negotiate significant agreements elsewhere are likely to be viewed with suspicion. Furthermore, the adoption of the CTBT in 1996 demonstrated that there exist alternatives to consensus at the CD for treaties that have reached what is generally accepted to be a mature stage of negotiation.

III. Implications for the nuclear regime

The importance of the CTBT has become the subject of debate on both sides. Assorted critics have dismissed it as worse than useless. Those who think the CTBT goes too far and prevents needed modernization say it will not stop other states cheating or proliferating. Those who think it does not go far enough say it cannot stop modernization and does not contribute to disarmament but serves only as a distraction. The debate over the list of 44 has added an additional element of uncertainty about the treaty's status. Nevertheless, the treaty's advocates point out that the norm against testing is now universally accepted regardless of legal technicalities. Although modernization of nuclear delivery systems has become more important than modernization of warheads, the CTBT does have an important effect on both established arsenals and proliferation. It may also have an enabling effect on

---

[14] 'Apparently' because several members of the CD did not vote for the CTB in the UN General Assembly and have not yet signed it, suggesting that they were simply allowing India to take the heat. Members of the CD that had not signed by 15 Apr. 1997 were Cameroon, Cuba, India, Iraq, Libya, Nigeria, North Korea, Pakistan, Syria and Zimbabwe.

further disarmament measures (although Russian ratification of START II will be more important in this regard).[15] This section considers the status of the CTBT if it does not enter into force promptly and its effect on the nuclear weapon states.

The status of the CTBT

Once China stopped testing, the norm of not testing had been effectively accepted by every state in the international system. This universal acceptance of the norm is unprecedented in the nuclear age and could only be strengthened by the completion of the CTBT and its signature by the majority of states. Even non-signatory states have said that they will not test for the foreseeable future and the norm can be seen as having the power of customary law. There remain two items of unfinished business, however: securing the ratifications of the 44 key signatories and completing the other conditions for the treaty to enter into force. While it is desirable that both these items be accomplished, it is not clear that failure to do so will necessarily lead to the unravelling of the test ban.

By 31 December 1996 only one signatory had ratified the CTBT: Fiji. Doubts linger about the willingness of key states to ratify, especially since ratification cannot be used as a means of gaining entry into force and thereby encouraging more ratifications, as in the case of the Chemical Weapons Convention (CWC).[16] The strengthening of the Republican majority in the 1996 US Senate elections—particularly the re-election of Foreign Relations Committee chairman Jesse Helms—was a blow to the CTBT's chances for ratification, despite support for the treaty in the Clinton Administration.[17] Helms is one of the most deeply anti-arms control members of the legislature and the Republican campaign platform condemned the CTBT.[18]

The CTBT is also the object of legislative derision in Russia, where— unlike START II—it has no real supporters to balance strong opposition from the Ministry of Atomic Energy (Minatom). Some members of the Chinese National People's Congress have reportedly criticized the treaty too, although they are likely to ratify it after a waiting period if Russia and the USA do so.[19] Israel stands by its position of insisting on widespread acceptance of the treaty

---

[15] See chapter 11 in this volume.

[16] The CWC simply required 65 ratifications in order for it to enter into force. After the 65th ratification the remaining signatories had a fixed period in which to ratify if they wished to participate in decision-making bodies. Signatories therefore had an incentive to help achieve the quota of 65 and then to ratify in time to participate. In the case of the CTBT, states cannot accelerate entry into force and their ratification only counts if they are one of the 44. See also chapter 13 in this volume.

[17] The US nuclear establishment has also accepted the CTBT. Realizing that testing is no longer politically feasible in the USA, it is seeking to secure a similar constraint on other states while guaranteeing a high level of funding. They are expected to testify to the Senate in favour of the CTBT.

[18] The most outspoken opponent of the CTBT has been House National Security Committee chairman Floyd Spence, who would like to abolish the Department of Energy and resume testing under the aegis of the Pentagon. Spence, F. D., *The Clinton Administration and Nuclear Stockpile Stewardship: Erosion by Design* (National Security Committee: Washington, DC, 1996).

[19] Grounds for criticism include the ban on PNEs, fear of inspections and the permitted use of NTM. Personal communication from a Chinese defence official, 12 Nov. 1996.

in the Middle East. Foreign Minister David Levy specifically put this in the context of ratification while in New York for the signing: 'When we get down to ratifying the treaty we will also take into consideration the attitude of other countries in the area'.[20] As noted above, key Arab states have still not signed the treaty.

For the treaty to enter into force, not only must the 41 signatories with nuclear reactors ratify it, but India, North Korea and Pakistan must sign and ratify it, too. Several US officials have expressed the hope that India would respond positively to friendly persuasion and perhaps gentle pressure and sign as soon as 1998, the earliest date at which the treaty could enter into force in any event. For example, the senior director for defence policy and arms control at the National Security Council, Robert Bell, stated: 'It is our hope that India will come to accept that it's in its own national security interest to sign this treaty'.[21] Persuading India to sign is seen as less difficult than convincing China, Pakistan, Russia and the UK—the four states that insisted on the list of 44—to amend the treaty to allow entry into force without India.

Even if it is not possible to bring the treaty into force for the time being, many of its essential features will be in place.[22] The treaty-mandated IMS and International Data Centre will be fully operational by September 1998 and, combined with information available from national and independent monitoring means, should be able to detect any illegal tests, which are unlikely in any case.[23] If an ambiguous event were detected, a conference of signatories could be convened and might reasonably expect to be invited to inspect the relevant site. In any case, the ultimate authority for assessing the response to noncompliant behaviour or unresolved suspicions will be the same with or without entry into force: the UN Security Council.[24]

The effects of the CTBT[25]

The norm embodied in the CTBT has already had an effect beyond its political significance for non-proliferation. All five nuclear establishments in the nuclear weapon states parties to the 1968 Non-Proliferation Treaty (NPT)

---

[20] Agence France-Presse, 'Israel signs global nuclear test ban treaty', 25 Sep. 1996.

[21] Cerniello, C., 'CTB treaty opened for signature after approval by the United Nations', *Arms Control Today*, Sep. 1996, p. 23. In the same vein, Assistant Secretary of State Thomas McNamara has stated: 'Internal and international pressures will build on India to change its position'. Reuter, 'US ponders next step with India on test ban', 25 Sep. 1996.

[22] US President Bill Clinton recognized this at the signing ceremony, saying the signed treaty was tantamount to a legal ban 'even before the treaty formally enters into force'. Clinton further commented that the ban 'will help to prevent the nuclear powers from developing more advanced and more dangerous weapons'. *Remarks by the President in Address to the 51st General Assembly of the United Nations* (White House: Washington, DC, 24 Sep. 1996).

[23] Arnett, E., 'The complementary roles of national, private and multinational means of verification', ed. Arnett (note 4).

[24] See the section on 'Goals of inspections' in Arnett, E., 'The proscription on preparing to test: consequences for verification', ed. Arnett (note 4), pp. 56–63.

[25] This section is developed from Arnett, E.; 'Implications of the comprehensive test ban for nuclear weapon programmes and decision making', ed. Arnett (note 3). See also chapters 7 and 11 in this volume.

have at one time or another in the past five years recommended more tests, but they have been overruled at the highest level or had their testing plans curtailed. In some cases, these tests would have allowed modernization based on new warhead designs. In others, they would simply have facilitated adaptation of existing warheads to new delivery systems or tinkering with measures relating to reliability, safety and security. In all five cases, however, modernization is linked to potentially provocative and possibly destabilizing changes in nuclear doctrine, whether by active officials or critics in opposition who might one day serve as officials. By preventing these tests, the CTBT is having an effect that is practically independent of whether it enters into force.

China

Despite the technical success of China's two final tests in 1996, the Ministry of National Defence (MND) informed the government that more nuclear tests were required. A countervailing recommendation from the Ministry of Foreign Affairs was accepted, however, and China ceased testing and signed the CTBT as a greater contribution to its security in the current international environment.[26] China will move forward with its intercontinental ballistic missile (ICBM) modernization programme and its troubled submarine-launched ballistic missile (SLBM) programme, but is not expected to increase the total number of warheads in its arsenal.[27] Indeed, the diminished relevance of tactical nuclear weapons to China's security, apparent reductions in the bomber force and cancellation of a new intermediate-range ballistic missile (IRBM) suggest that the size of the arsenal may be decreasing,[28] despite speculation about a move in the direction of a more provocative nuclear doctrine.[29]

France

In 1993, conservatives in the French legislature suggested that 10–20 tests were necessary despite then President François Mitterrand's moratorium on

[26] Personal communication with an MND official, 12 Nov. 1996. An anonymous 'senior Chinese disarmament negotiator' told Reuter: 'Our plan has been shortened and cut for the sake of the treaty'. Macartney, J., 'China hopes test treaty can be concluded this year', Reuter, 15 July 1996. For the view that China's previous behaviour in the negotiations demonstrated cynical free-riding in arms control (and, implicitly, that China's decision to limit its nuclear capability by stopping its test programme marks a decisive change in favour of a foreign policy based on cooperative engagement) see Johnston, A. I., 'Learning versus adaptation: explaining change in Chinese arms control policy in the 1980s and 1990s', *China Journal*, no. 35 (Jan. 1996), p. 57. See also Mathews, J., 'Extra! a "second" China does the right thing', *International Herald Tribune*, 12 Dec. 1996.

[27] Personal communication with an MND official, 12 Nov. 1996.

[28] The Japan Defense Agency's *Defense of Japan* annual suggests that the strategic bomber force was deactivated in 1984, about the time that Deng Xiaoping concluded that China would not face the risk of global or nuclear war for several decades. See also Litai Xue, 'China's military modernization and security policy', *Korean Journal of International Studies*, vol. 24, no. 4 (1993), p. 497. On the cancellation of the DF-25 IRBM, see Arnett, E., 'Chinese blow cold on East Wind missile plan', *Jane's Defence Weekly*, 4 Dec. 1996.

[29] For a controversial survey, see Johnston, A. I., 'China's new "old thinking": the concept of limited deterrence', *International Security*, vol. 20, no. 3 (winter 1995/96), pp. 5–42.

testing. The conservatives said that the tests should be used to develop a new variable-yield warhead and that there should be a programme of simulations to maintain the stockpile under the CTBT.[30] The variable-yield warhead would have been part of a modernization plan for two new SLBMs and a new air-launched cruise missile (ALCM) in the context of a doctrine in which nuclear weapons may have been seen as more usable.[31] When a conservative president, Jacques Chirac, was elected in 1995, the test programme was curtailed to eight and then six tests, none of which was for the variable-yield warhead. After the June 1996 Defence Review, a more modest course of modernization will be taken and there is some question as to whether the full stewardship programme will be funded.[32] (Stewardship is the term for activities related to maintaining safe and reliable nuclear weapons without violating the CTBT.)

Russia

Less is known about Russia's plans for nuclear warhead modernization, although most strategic systems are being improved and 'Russianized' (i.e., made and fitted with Russian components only) and Minatom remains enthusiastic about PNEs.[33] Viktor Mikhailov, the Minister of Atomic Energy, has speculated that Russia could field low-yield nuclear weapons without testing simply by draining tritium from existing warheads and that this might be an appropriate response to NATO enlargement.[34] Russian military officers have expressed interest in low-yield weapons for regional contingencies.[35] The CTBT prevents the yields of these weapons from being certified and thereby limits the confidence of the military in their advantages over higher-yield weapons. Development, weaponization and certification of new warhead types and PNE devices are also prevented.

---

[30] Galy-Dejean, R. *et al.*, *La Simulation des Essais Nucléaires*, Rapport d'Information 847 (Commission de la Défense, Assemblée Nationale: Paris, 1993). See also Garwin, R., *et al.*, *A Report on Discussions Regarding the Need for Nuclear Test Explosions to Maintain French Nuclear Weapons under a Comprehensive Test Ban* (Federation of American Scientists and Natural Resources Defense Council: Washington, DC, 1995).

[31] For a debate on the nature of proposed doctrinal changes, see Yost, D. S., 'Nuclear debates in France', *Survival*, vol. 36, no. 4 (winter 1994–95); and ensuing correspondence.

[32] As seen in chapter 7, the new SLBM and ALCM will now be derivatives of existing models. The French stewardship programme, PALEN (Préparation à la Limitation des Essais Nucléaires), may not be funded to the full $2 billion required and the opposition socialists would like to kill it in favour of sharing expertise with the USA. Arnett, E., 'Nuclear club gets clubbier', *Bulletin of the Atomic Scientists*, vol. 52, no. 3 (May/June 1996).

[33] See chapter 7 in this volume.

[34] Mikhailov, V., Andryushin, I. and Chernyshov, A., 'NATO's expansion and Russia's security', *Vek*, 20 Sep. 1996, cited in Paine, C. E., 'The CTBT in the Context of Nuclear Disarmament Obligations, Nuclear Deterrent Strategies, and Nonproliferation Objectives' (Natural Resources Defense Council: Washington, DC, 1996).

[35] 'Interview with Army General Pavel Grachev, Minister of Defence', *Nezavisimaya Gazeta*, 9 June 1994; and Baychursin, I., 'Russia's nuclear missiles are not targeted anywhere, but the Strategic Missile Forces are on combat duty', *Nezavisimaya Gazeta*, 15 Dec. 1994, cited in Kristensen, H. M. and Handler, J., *Changing Targets: Nuclear Doctrine from the Cold War to the Third World* (Greenpeace International: Washington, DC, 1995), p. 28.

The UK

The UK had three tests scheduled to be conducted at the US Nevada test site when the US Congress unilaterally legislated the US test moratorium in 1992. Since then the UK has been ambivalent about the CTBT,[36] decisively de-emphasizing nuclear modernization in favour of its conventional weapon technology base.[37] With nuclear modernization a lower priority and less latitude for preparing a hedge or breakout programme, the UK may well see the most pronounced decline in its nuclear weapon establishment,[38] despite having one of the most conservative governments among the NPT nuclear weapon states.

The USA

Requests by the US Department of Energy (DOE) to resume testing in 1992 and 1993 were based on a perceived need for safety improvements, not modernization. Since then, the DOE has accepted that it is unlikely to conduct another nuclear test and is reconfiguring its technology base in favour of an ambitious stewardship programme. This has not meant the end of US nuclear modernization, however. In 1996, it was revealed that the USA is developing an earth-penetrating variant of its B-61 bomb. The B-61 warhead can be repackaged without testing because of previous work done on earth penetrators during the 1980s, including tests in 1988 and 1989.[39] Similarly, guidance upgrades for the Minuteman III ICBM are possible without testing. On the other hand, a ban on testing does prevent the certification (testing to confirm performance) of low-yield weapons that some commentators have called for the USA to deploy for regional contingencies. The very purpose of these weapons—their hypothetical 'usability' because of lower collateral damage—is undermined if their yield cannot be predicted precisely in the role for which they are developed or adapted, despite US work on low-yield weapons dating back to the 1970s. The US Arms Control and Disarmament Agency concludes: 'A "no testing" regime will mean low confidence in any new design, making new types of nuclear weapons very unlikely. For cautious military planners, including the USA, it means that new types of nuclear weapons will be virtually out of the question.'[40]

[36] Lewis, P., 'The United Kingdom', ed. Arnett (note 3).

[37] See chapter 7 in this volume.

[38] Lewis (note 36).

[39] Harold Smith, the Deputy Assistant Secretary of Defense for Nuclear Programs, revealed that the new B-61 would be operational in 1996. Erlich, J., 'Bunker-busting bomb prompts US discord', *Defense News*, 24 Feb. 1997, pp. 1, 18; and Mello, G., *B61-11 Concerns and Background* (Los Alamos Study Group: Santa Fe, N. Mex., 1997).

[40] Arms Control and Disarmament Agency, *Threat Control through Arms Control: Annual Report to the Congress 1995* (ACDA: Washington, DC, 1996), p. 11.

IV. Conclusions

Although the norm of not testing is now universally accepted, and can only be strengthened by more signatures and ratifications of the CTBT, it is still possible that the regime could be undermined by a state resuming its nuclear test programme. This could come about as the result of either of two developments, both of which are quite different from the traditional concern with large-scale covert testing that complicated the debate during the cold war.

The first concern is that the political situation could change either within a state or at the international level so that a government would reverse its decision not to test. This could come about as the result of greater influence on the part of the nuclear weapon establishment that still saw a requirement for testing, or if a state saw its security situation deteriorating.[41]

The second concern is that weapons already in the arsenal cannot be maintained reliably and safely without testing. Spokesmen for the US DOE say that its $4-billion-a-year stewardship programme is technologically risky and could fail.[42] This possibility has already been seized upon by opponents of the treaty.[43] In effect the DOE has grounds for an open-ended demand for funds and might still fail to certify the reliability, safety and security of the arsenal after its annual review some years from now, even if its budget is maintained in the face of declining spending for most other military and scientific activities. The other nuclear weapon states face tighter budget constraints and perhaps less political opposition to nuclear weapons and testing.

---

[41] This is seen as the only situation in which India would need to test and exercise its nuclear option. Balachandran, G., 'CTBT and Indian security', *Times of India*, 3 Sep. 1996. Such a deterioration might be the result of another state deploying missile defences.

[42] 'Statement of Harold P. Smith' in US Congress, Committee on National Security, *Hearings on National Defense Authorization Act for Fiscal Year 1996: Title I—Procurement* (US Government Printing Office: Washington, DC, 1996), p. 820; and Arnett (note 32), p. 12. The plan and the sturdiness of its funding level are reviewed in Lawler, A., 'Big projects could threaten weapons labs' research base', *Science*, 24 May 1996, pp. 1092–93.

[43] Spence (note 18), pp. 4–6.

Appendix 12A. The Comprehensive Nuclear Test-Ban Treaty

COMPREHENSIVE NUCLEAR TEST-BAN TREATY

10 September 1996

Preamble

The States Parties to this Treaty (hereinafter referred to as 'the States Parties'),

Welcoming the international agreements and other positive measures of recent years in the field of nuclear disarmament, including reductions in arsenals of nuclear weapons, as well as in the field of the prevention of nuclear proliferation in all its aspects,

Underlining the importance of the full and prompt implementation of such agreements and measures,

Convinced that the present international situation provides an opportunity to take further effective measures towards nuclear disarmament and against the proliferation of nuclear weapons in all its aspects, and *declaring* their intention to take such measures,

Stressing therefore the need for continued systematic and progressive efforts to reduce nuclear weapons globally, with the ultimate goal of eliminating those weapons, and of general and complete disarmament under strict and effective international control,

Recognizing that the cessation of all nuclear weapon test explosions and all other nuclear explosions, by constraining the development and qualitative improvement of nuclear weapons and ending the development of advanced new types of nuclear weapons, constitutes an effective measure of nuclear disarmament and non-proliferation in all its aspects,

Further recognizing that an end to all such nuclear explosions will thus constitute a meaningful step in the realization of a systematic process to achieve nuclear disarmament,

Convinced that the most effective way to achieve an end to nuclear testing is through the conclusion of a universal and internationally and effectively verifiable comprehensive nuclear test-ban treaty, which has long been one of the highest priority objectives of the international community in the field of disarmament and non-proliferation,

Noting the aspirations expressed by the Parties to the 1963 Treaty Banning Nuclear Weapon Tests in the Atmosphere, in Outer Space and Under Water to seek to achieve the discontinuance of all test explosions of nuclear weapons for all time,

Noting also the views expressed that this Treaty could contribute to the protection of the environment,

Affirming the purpose of attracting the adherence of all States to this Treaty and its objective to contribute effectively to the prevention of the proliferation of nuclear weapons in all its aspects, to the process of nuclear disarmament and therefore to the enhancement of international peace and security,

Have agreed as follows:

Article I. Basic Obligations

1. Each State Party undertakes not to carry out any nuclear weapon test explosion or any other nuclear explosion, and to prohibit and prevent any such nuclear explosion at any place under its jurisdiction or control.

2. Each State Party undertakes, furthermore, to refrain from causing, encouraging, or in any way participating in the carrying out of any nuclear weapon test explosion or any other nuclear explosion.

Article II. The Organization

A. General Provisions

1. The States Parties hereby establish the Comprehensive Nuclear Test-Ban Treaty Organization (hereinafter referred to as 'the Organization') to achieve the object and purpose of this Treaty, to ensure the implementation of its provisions, including those for international verification of compliance with it, and to provide a forum for consultation and cooperation among States Parties.

2. All States Parties shall be members of the Organization. A State Party shall not be deprived of its membership in the Organization.

3. The seat of the Organization shall be Vienna, Republic of Austria.

4. There are hereby established as organs of the Organization: the Conference of the States Parties, the Executive Council and the

Technical Secretariat, which shall include the International Data Centre.

5. Each State Party shall cooperate with the Organization in the exercise of its functions in accordance with this Treaty. States Parties shall consult, directly among themselves, or through the Organization or other appropriate international procedures, including procedures within the framework of the United Nations and in accordance with its Charter, on any matter which may be raised relating to the object and purpose, or the implementation of the provisions, of this Treaty.

6. The Organization shall conduct its verification activities provided for under this Treaty in the least intrusive manner possible consistent with the timely and efficient accomplishment of their objectives. It shall request only the information and data necessary to fulfil its responsibilities under this Treaty. It shall take every precaution to protect the confidentiality of information on civil and military activities and facilities coming to its knowledge in the implementation of this Treaty and, in particular, shall abide by the confidentiality provisions set forth in this Treaty.

7. Each State Party shall treat as confidential and afford special handling to information and data that it receives in confidence from the Organization in connection with the implementation of this Treaty. It shall treat such information and data exclusively in connection with its rights and obligations under this Treaty.

8. The Organization, as an independent body, shall seek to utilize existing expertise and facilities, as appropriate, and to maximize cost efficiencies, through cooperative arrangements with other international organizations such as the International Atomic Energy Agency. Such arrangements, excluding those of a minor and normal commercial and contractual nature, shall be set out in agreements to be submitted to the Conference of the States Parties for approval.

9. The costs of the activities of the Organization shall be met annually by the States Parties in accordance with the United Nations scale of assessments adjusted to take into account differences in membership between the United Nations and the Organization.

10. Financial contributions of States Parties to the Preparatory Commission shall be deducted in an appropriate way from their contributions to the regular budget.

11. A member of the Organization which is in arrears in the payment of its assessed contribution to the Organization shall have no vote in the Organization if the amount of its arrears equals or exceeds the amount of the contribution due from it for the preceding two full years. The Conference of the States Parties may, nevertheless, permit such a member to vote if it is satisfied that the failure to pay is due to conditions beyond the control of the member.

B. The Conference of the States Parties

Composition, Procedures and Decision-making

12. The Conference of the States Parties (hereinafter referred to as 'the Conference') shall be composed of all States Parties. Each State Party shall have one representative in the Conference, who may be accompanied by alternates and advisers.

13. The initial session of the Conference shall be convened by the Depositary no later than 30 days after the entry into force of this Treaty.

14. The Conference shall meet in regular sessions, which shall be held annually, unless it decides otherwise.

15. A special session of the Conference shall be convened:
(*a*) When decided by the Conference;
(*b*) When requested by the Executive Council; or
(*c*) When requested by any State Party and supported by a majority of the States Parties.

The special session shall be convened no later than 30 days after the decision of the Conference, the request of the Executive Council, or the attainment of the necessary support, unless specified otherwise in the decision or request.

16. The Conference may also be convened in the form of an Amendment Conference, in accordance with Article VII.

17. The Conference may also be convened in the form of a Review Conference in accordance with Article VIII.

18. Sessions shall take place at the seat of the Organization unless the Conference decides otherwise.

19. The Conference shall adopt its rules of procedure. At the beginning of each session, it shall elect its President and such other officers as may be required. They shall hold office until a new President and other officers are elected at the next session.

20. A majority of the States Parties shall constitute a quorum.

21. Each State Party shall have one vote.

22. The Conference shall take decisions on matters of procedure by a majority of members present and voting. Decisions on matters of substance shall be taken as far as possible by consensus. If consensus is not attainable when an issue comes up for decision, the President of the Conference shall defer any vote for 24 hours and during this period of deferment shall make every effort to facilitate achievement of consensus, and shall report to the Conference before the end of this period. If consensus is not possible at the end of 24 hours, the Conference shall take a decision by a two-thirds majority of members present and voting unless specified otherwise in this Treaty. When the issue arises as to whether the question is one of substance or not, that question shall be treated as a matter of substance unless otherwise decided by the majority required for decisions on matters of substance.

23. When exercising its function under paragraph 26 (*k*), the Conference shall take a decision to add any State to the list of States contained in Annex 1 to this Treaty in accordance with the procedure for decisions on matters of substance set out in paragraph 22. Notwithstanding paragraph 22, the Conference shall take decisions on any other change to Annex 1 to this Treaty by consensus.

Powers and Functions

24. The Conference shall be the principal organ of the Organization. It shall consider any questions, matters or issues within the scope of this Treaty, including those relating to the powers and functions of the Executive Council and the Technical Secretariat, in accordance with this Treaty. It may make recommendations and take decisions on any questions, matters or issues within the scope of this Treaty raised by a State Party or brought to its attention by the Executive Council.

25. The Conference shall oversee the implementation of, and review compliance with, this Treaty and act in order to promote its object and purpose. It shall also oversee the activities of the Executive Council and the Technical Secretariat and may issue guidelines to either of them for the exercise of their functions.

26. The Conference shall:

(*a*) Consider and adopt the report of the Organization on the implementation of this Treaty and the annual programme and budget of the Organization, submitted by the Executive Council, as well as consider other reports;

(*b*) Decide on the scale of financial contributions to be paid by States Parties in accordance with paragraph 9;

(*c*) Elect the members of the Executive Council;

(*d*) Appoint the Director-General of the Technical Secretariat (hereinafter referred to as 'the Director-General');

(*e*) Consider and approve the rules of procedure of the Executive Council submitted by the latter;

(*f*) Consider and review scientific and technological developments that could affect the operation of this Treaty. In this context, the Conference may direct the Director-General to establish a Scientific Advisory Board to enable him or her, in the performance of his or her functions, to render specialized advice in areas of science and technology relevant to this Treaty to the Conference, to the Executive Council or to States Parties. In that case, the Scientific Advisory Board shall be composed of independent experts serving in their individual capacity and appointed, in accordance with terms of reference adopted by the Conference, on the basis of their expertise and experience in the particular scientific fields relevant to the implementation of this Treaty;

(*g*) Take the necessary measures to ensure compliance with this Treaty and to redress and remedy any situation that contravenes the provisions of this Treaty, in accordance with Article V;

(*h*) Consider and approve at its initial session any draft agreements, arrangements, provisions, procedures, operational manuals, guidelines and any other documents developed and recommended by the Preparatory Commission;

(*i*) Consider and approve agreements or arrangements negotiated by the Technical Secretariat with States Parties, other States and international organizations to be concluded by the Executive Council on behalf of the Organization in accordance with paragraph 38 (*h*);

(*j*) Establish such subsidiary organs as it finds necessary for the exercise of its functions in accordance with this Treaty; and

(*k*) Update Annex 1 to this Treaty, as appropriate, in accordance with paragraph 23.

C. The Executive Council

Composition, Procedures and Decision-making

27. The Executive Council shall consist of 51 members. Each State Party shall have the

right, in accordance with the provisions of this Article, to serve on the Executive Council.

28. Taking into account the need for equitable geographical distribution the Executive Council shall comprise:

(*a*) Ten States Parties from Africa;

(*b*) Seven States Parties from Eastern Europe;

(*c*) Nine States Parties from Latin America and the Caribbean;

(*d*) Seven States Parties from the Middle East and South Asia;

(*e*) Ten States Parties from North America and Western Europe; and

(*f*) Eight States Parties from South-East Asia, the Pacific and the Far East.

All States in each of the above geographical regions are listed in Annex 1 to this Treaty. Annex 1 to this Treaty shall be updated, as appropriate, by the Conference in accordance with paragraphs 23 and 26 (*k*). It shall not be subject to amendments or changes under the procedures contained in Article VII.

29. The members of the Executive Council shall be elected by the Conference. In this connection, each geographical region shall designate States Parties from that region for election as members of the Executive Council as follows:

(*a*) At least one-third of the seats allocated to each geographical region shall be filled, taking into account political and security interests by States Parties in that region designated on the basis of the nuclear capabilities relevant to the Treaty as determined by international data as well as all or any of the following indicative criteria in the order of priority determined by each region:

(i) Number of monitoring facilities of the International Monitoring System;

(ii) Expertise and experience in monitoring technology; and

(iii) Contribution to the annual budget of the Organization;

(*b*) One of the seats allocated to each geographical region shall be filled on a rotational basis by the State Party that is first in the English alphabetical order among the States Parties in that region that have not served as members of the Executive Council for the longest period of time since becoming States Parties or since their last term, whichever is shorter. A State Party designated on this basis may decide to forgo its seat. In that case, such a State Party shall submit a letter of renunciation to the Director-General, and the seat shall be filled by the State Party following next-in-order according to this sub-paragraph; and

(*c*) The remaining seats allocated to each geographical region shall be filled by States Parties designated from among all the States Parties in that region by rotation or elections.

30. Each member of the Executive Council shall have one representative on the Executive Council, who may be accompanied by alternates and advisers.

31. Each member of the Executive Council shall hold office from the end of the session of the Conference at which that member is elected until the end of the second regular annual session of the Conference thereafter, except that for the first election of the Executive Council, 26 members shall be elected to hold office until the end of the third regular annual session of the Conference, due regard being paid to the established numerical proportions as described in paragraph 28.

32. The Executive Council shall elaborate its rules of procedure and submit them to the Conference for approval.

33. The Executive Council shall elect its Chairman from among its members.

34. The Executive Council shall meet for regular sessions. Between regular sessions it shall meet as may be required for the fulfilment of its powers and functions.

35. Each member of the Executive Council shall have one vote.

36. The Executive Council shall take decisions on matters of procedure by a majority of all its members. The Executive Council shall take decisions on matters of substance by a two-thirds majority of all its members unless specified otherwise in this Treaty. When the issue arises as to whether the question is one of substance or not, that question shall be treated as a matter of substance unless otherwise decided by the majority required for decisions on matters of substance.

Powers and Functions

37. The Executive Council shall be the executive organ of the Organization. It shall be responsible to the Conference. It shall carry out the powers and functions entrusted to it in accordance with this Treaty. In so doing, it shall act in conformity with the recommendations, decisions and guidelines of the Conference and ensure their continuous and proper implementation.

38. The Executive Council shall:

(*a*) Promote effective implementation of,

and compliance with, this Treaty;

(b) Supervise the activities of the Technical Secretariat;

(c) Make recommendations as necessary to the Conference for consideration of further proposals for promoting the object and purpose of this Treaty;

(d) Cooperate with the National Authority of each State Party;

(e) Consider and submit to the Conference the draft annual programme and budget of the Organization, the draft report of the Organization on the implementation of this Treaty, the report on the performance of its own activities and such other reports as it deems necessary or that the Conference may request;

(f) Make arrangements for the sessions of the Conference, including the preparation of the draft agenda;

(g) Examine proposals for changes, on matters of an administrative or technical nature, to the Protocol or the Annexes thereto, pursuant to Article VII, and make recommendations to the States Parties regarding their adoption;

(h) Conclude, subject to prior approval of the Conference, agreements or arrangements with States Parties, other States and international organizations on behalf of the Organization and supervise their implementation, with the exception of agreements or arrangements referred to in sub-paragraph (i);

(i) Approve and supervise the operation of agreements or arrangements relating to the implementation of verification activities with States Parties and other States; and

(j) Approve any new operational manuals and any changes to the existing operational manuals that may be proposed by the Technical Secretariat.

39. The Executive Council may request a special session of the Conference.

40. The Executive Council shall:

(a) Facilitate cooperation among States Parties, and between States Parties and the Technical Secretariat, relating to the implementation of this Treaty through information exchanges;

(b) Facilitate consultation and clarification among States Parties in accordance with Article IV; and

(c) Receive, consider and take action on requests for, and reports on, on-site inspections in accordance with Article IV.

41. The Executive Council shall consider any concern raised by a State Party about possible non-compliance with this Treaty and abuse of the rights established by this Treaty.

In doing so, the Executive Council shall consult with the States Parties involved and, as appropriate, request a State Party to take measures to redress the situation within a specified time. To the extent that the Executive Council considers further action to be necessary, it shall take, *inter alia*, one or more of the following measures:

(a) Notify all States Parties of the issue or matter;

(b) Bring the issue or matter to the attention of the Conference;

(c) Make recommendations to the Conference or take action, as appropriate, regarding measures to redress the situation and to ensure compliance in accordance with Article V.

D. The Technical Secretariat

42. The Technical Secretariat shall assist States Parties in the implementation of this Treaty. The Technical Secretariat shall assist the Conference and the Executive Council in the performance of their functions. The Technical Secretariat shall carry out the verification and other functions entrusted to it by this Treaty, as well as those functions delegated to it by the Conference or the Executive Council in accordance with this Treaty. The Technical Secretariat shall include, as an integral part, the International Data Centre.

43. The functions of the Technical Secretariat with regard to verification of compliance with this Treaty shall, in accordance with Article IV and the Protocol, include *inter alia*:

(a) Being responsible for supervising and coordinating the operation of the International Monitoring System;

(b) Operating the International Data Centre;

(c) Routinely receiving, processing, analysing and reporting on International Monitoring System data;

(d) Providing technical assistance in, and support for, the installation and operation of monitoring stations;

(e) Assisting the Executive Council in facilitating consultation and clarification among States Parties;

(f) Receiving requests for on-site inspections and processing them, facilitating Executive Council consideration of such requests, carrying out the preparations for, and providing technical support during, the conduct of on-site inspections, and reporting to the Executive Council;

(*g*) Negotiating agreements or arrangements with States Parties, other States and international organizations and concluding, subject to prior approval by the Executive Council, any such agreements or arrangements relating to verification activities with States Parties or other States; and

(*h*) Assisting the States Parties through their National Authorities on other issues of verification under this Treaty.

44. The Technical Secretariat shall develop and maintain, subject to approval by the Executive Council, operational manuals to guide the operation of the various components of the verification regime, in accordance with Article IV and the Protocol. These manuals shall not constitute integral parts of this Treaty or the Protocol and may be changed by the Technical Secretariat subject to approval by the Executive Council. The Technical Secretariat shall promptly inform the States Parties of any changes in the operational manuals.

45. The functions of the Technical Secretariat with respect to administrative matters shall include:

(*a*) Preparing and submitting to the Executive Council the draft programme and budget of the Organization;

(*b*) Preparing and submitting to the Executive Council the draft report of the Organization on the implementation of this Treaty and such other reports as the Conference or the Executive Council may request;

(*c*) Providing administrative and technical support to the Conference, the Executive Council and other subsidiary organs;

(*d*) Addressing and receiving communications on behalf of the Organization relating to the implementation of this Treaty; and

(*e*) Carrying out the administrative responsibilities related to any agreements between the Organization and other international organizations.

46. All requests and notifications by States Parties to the Organization shall be transmitted through their National Authorities to the Director-General. Requests and notifications shall be in one of the official languages of this Treaty. In response the Director-General shall use the language of the transmitted request or notification.

47. With respect to the responsibilities of the Technical Secretariat for preparing and submitting to the Executive Council the draft programme and budget of the Organization, the Technical Secretariat shall determine and maintain a clear accounting of all costs for each facility established as part of the International Monitoring System. Similar treatment in the draft programme and budget shall be accorded to all other activities of the Organization.

48. The Technical Secretariat shall promptly inform the Executive Council of any problems that have arisen with regard to the discharge of its functions that have come to its notice in the performance of its activities and that it has been unable to resolve through consultations with the State Party concerned.

49. The Technical Secretariat shall comprise a Director-General, who shall be its head and chief administrative officer, and such scientific, technical and other personnel as may be required. The Director-General shall be appointed by the Conference upon the recommendation of the Executive Council for a term of four years, renewable for one further term, but not thereafter. The first Director-General shall be appointed by the Conference at its initial session upon the recommendation of the Preparatory Commission.

50. The Director-General shall be responsible to the Conference and the Executive Council for the appointment of the staff and for the organization and functioning of the Technical Secretariat. The paramount consideration in the employment of the staff and in the determination of the conditions of service shall be the necessity of securing the highest standards of professional expertise, experience, efficiency, competence and integrity. Only citizens of States Parties shall serve as the Director-General, as inspectors or as members of the professional and clerical staff. Due regard shall be paid to the importance of recruiting the staff on as wide a geographical basis as possible. Recruitment shall be guided by the principle that the staff shall be kept to the minimum necessary for the proper discharge of the responsibilities of the Technical Secretariat.

51. The Director-General may, as appropriate, after consultation with the Executive Council, establish temporary working groups of scientific experts to provide recommendations on specific issues.

52. In the performance of their duties, the Director-General, the inspectors, the inspection assistants and the members of the staff shall not seek or receive instructions from any Government or from any other source external to the Organization. They shall refrain from any action that might reflect

adversely on their positions as international officers responsible only to the Organization. The Director-General shall assume responsibility for the activities of an inspection team.

53. Each State Party shall respect the exclusively international character of the responsibilities of the Director-General, the inspectors, the inspection assistants and the members of the staff and shall not seek to influence them in the discharge of their responsibilities.

E. Privileges and Immunities

54. The Organization shall enjoy on the territory and in any other place under the jurisdiction or control of a State Party such legal capacity and such privileges and immunities as are necessary for the exercise of its functions.

55. Delegates of States Parties, together with their alternates and advisers, representatives of members elected to the Executive Council, together with their alternates and advisers, the Director-General, the inspectors, the inspection assistants and the members of the staff of the Organization shall enjoy such privileges and immunities as are necessary in the independent exercise of their functions in connection with the Organization.

56. The legal capacity, privileges and immunities referred to in this Article shall be defined in agreements between the Organization and the State Parties as well as in an agreement between the Organization and the State in which the Organization is seated. Such agreements shall be considered and approved in accordance with paragraph 26 (*h*) and (*i*).

57. Notwithstanding paragraphs 54 and 55, the privileges and immunities enjoyed by the Director-General, the inspectors, the inspection assistants and the members of the staff of the Technical Secretariat during the conduct of verification activities shall be those set forth in the Protocol.

Article III. National Implementation Measures

1. Each State Party shall, in accordance with its constitutional processes, take any necessary measures to implement its obligations under this Treaty. In particular, it shall take any necessary measures:

(*a*) To prohibit natural and legal persons anywhere on its territory or in any other place under its jurisdiction as recognized by international law from undertaking any activity prohibited to a State Party under this Treaty;

(*b*) To prohibit natural and legal persons from undertaking any such activity anywhere under its control; and

(*c*) To prohibit, in conformity with international law, natural persons possessing its nationality from undertaking any such activity anywhere.

2. Each State Party shall cooperate with other States Parties and afford the appropriate form of legal assistance to facilitate the implementation of the obligations under paragraph 1.

3. Each State Party shall inform the Organization of the measures taken pursuant to this Article.

4. In order to fulfil its obligations under the Treaty, each State Party shall designate or set up a National Authority and shall so inform the Organization upon entry into force of the Treaty for it. The National Authority shall serve as the national focal point for liaison with the Organization and with other States Parties.

Article IV. Verification

A. General Provisions

1. In order to verify compliance with this Treaty, a verification regime shall be established consisting of the following elements:

(*a*) An International Monitoring System;

(*b*) Consultation and clarification;

(*c*) On-site inspections; and

(*d*) Confidence-building measures.

At entry into force of this Treaty, the verification regime shall be capable of meeting the verification requirements of this Treaty.

2. Verification activities shall be based on objective information, shall be limited to the subject matter of this Treaty, and shall be carried out on the basis of full respect for the sovereignty of States Parties and in the least intrusive manner possible consistent with the effective and timely accomplishment of their objectives. Each State Party shall refrain from any abuse of the right of verification.

3. Each State Party undertakes in accordance with this Treaty to cooperate through its National Authority established pursuant to Article III, paragraph 4, with the Organization and with other States Parties to facilitate the verification of compliance with this Treaty by *inter alia*:

(*a*) Establishing the necessary facilities to participate in these verification measures and establishing the necessary communication;

(*b*) Providing data obtained from national stations that are part of the International Monitoring System;

(c) Participating, as appropriate, in a consultation and clarification process;

(d) Permitting the conduct of on-site inspections; and

(e) Participating, as appropriate, in confidence-building measures.

4. All States Parties, irrespective of their technical and financial capabilities, shall enjoy the equal right of verification and assume the equal obligation to accept verification.

5. For the purposes of this Treaty, no State Party shall be precluded from using information obtained by national technical means of verification in a manner consistent with generally recognized principles of international law, including that of respect for the sovereignty of States.

6. Without prejudice to the right of States Parties to protect sensitive installations, activities or locations not related to this Treaty, States Parties shall not interfere with elements of the verification regime of this Treaty or with national technical means of verification operating in accordance with paragraph 5.

7. Each State Party shall have the right to take measures to protect sensitive installations and to prevent disclosure of confidential information and data not related to this Treaty.

8. Moreover, all necessary measures shall be taken to protect the confidentiality of any information related to civil and military activities and facilities obtained during verification activities.

9. Subject to paragraph 8, information obtained by the Organization through the verification regime established by this Treaty shall be made available to all States Parties in accordance with the relevant provisions of this Treaty and the Protocol.

10. The provisions of this Treaty shall not be interpreted as restricting the international exchange of data for scientific purposes.

11. Each State Party undertakes to cooperate with the Organization and with other States Parties in the improvement of the verification regime, and in the examination of the verification potential of additional monitoring technologies such as electromagnetic pulse monitoring or satellite monitoring, with a view to developing, when appropriate, specific measures to enhance the efficient and cost-effective verification of this Treaty. Such measures shall, when agreed, be incorporated in existing provisions in this Treaty, the Protocol or as additional sections of the Protocol,

in accordance with Article VII, or, if appropriate, be reflected in the operational manuals in accordance with Article II, paragraph 44.

12. The States Parties undertake to promote cooperation among themselves to facilitate and participate in the fullest possible exchange relating to technologies used in the verification of this Treaty in order to enable all States Parties to strengthen their national implementation of verification measures and to benefit from the application of such technologies for peaceful purposes.

13. The provisions of this Treaty shall be implemented in a manner which avoids hampering the economic and technological development of the States Parties for further development of the application of atomic energy for peaceful purposes.

Verification Responsibilities of the Technical Secretariat

14. In discharging its responsibilities in the area of verification specified in this Treaty and the Protocol, in cooperation with the State Parties the Technical Secretariat shall, for the purpose of this Treaty:

(a) Make arrangements to receive and distribute data and reporting products relevant to the verification of this Treaty in accordance with its provisions, and to maintain a global communications infrastructure appropriate to this task;

(b) Routinely through its International Data Centre, which shall in principle be the focal point within the Technical Secretariat for data storage and data processing:

(i) Receive and initiate requests for data from the International Monitoring System;

(ii) Receive data, as appropriate, resulting from the process of consultation and clarification, from on-site inspections, and from confidence-building measures; and

(iii) Receive other relevant data from States Parties and international organizations in accordance with this Treaty and the Protocol;

(c) Supervise, coordinate and ensure the operation of the International Monitoring System and its component elements, and of the International Data Centre, in accordance with the relevant operational manuals;

(d) Routinely process, analyse and report on International Monitoring System data according to agreed procedures so as to permit the effective international verification of this Treaty and to contribute to the early resolution of compliance concerns;

(e) Make available all data, both raw and

processed, and any reporting products, to all States Parties, each State Party taking responsibility for the use of International Monitoring System data in accordance with Article II, paragraph 7, and with paragraphs 8 and 13 of this Article;

(f) Provide to all States Parties equal, open, convenient and timely access to all stored data;

(g) Store all data, both raw and processed, and reporting products;

(h) Coordinate and facilitate requests for additional data from the International Monitoring System;

(i) Coordinate requests for additional data from one State Party to another State Party;

(j) Provide technical assistance in, and support for, the installation and operation of monitoring facilities and respective communication means, where such assistance and support are required by the State concerned;

(k) Make available to any State Party, on its request, techniques utilized by the Technical Secretariat and its International Data Centre in compiling, storing, processing, analysing and reporting on data from the verification regime; and

(l) Monitor, assess and report on the overall performance of the International Monitoring System and of the International Data Centre.

15. The agreed procedures to be used by the Technical Secretariat in discharging the verification responsibilities referred to in paragraph 14 and detailed in the Protocol shall be elaborated in the relevant operational manuals.

B. The International Monitoring System

16. The International Monitoring System shall comprise facilities for seismological monitoring, radionuclide monitoring including certified laboratories, hydroacoustic monitoring, infrasound monitoring, and respective means of communication, and shall be supported by the International Data Centre of the Technical Secretariat.

17. The International Monitoring System shall be placed under the authority of the Technical Secretariat. All monitoring facilities of the International Monitoring System shall be owned and operated by the States hosting or otherwise taking responsibility for them in accordance with the Protocol.

18. Each State Party shall have the right to participate in the international exchange of data and to have access to all data made available to the International Data Centre.

Each State Party shall cooperate with the International Data Centre through its National Authority.

Funding the International Monitoring System

19. For facilities incorporated into the International Monitoring System and specified in Tables 1-A, 2-A, 3 and 4 of Annex 1 to the Protocol, and for their functioning, to the extent that such facilities are agreed by the relevant State and the Organization to provide data to the International Data Centre in accordance with the technical requirements of the Protocol and relevant operational manuals, the Organization, as specified in agreements or arrangements pursuant to Part I, paragraph 4 of the Protocol, shall meet the costs of:

(a) Establishing any new facilities and upgrading existing facilities unless the State responsible for such facilities meets these costs itself;

(b) Operating and maintaining International Monitoring System facilities, including facility physical security if appropriate, and application of agreed data authentication procedures;

(c) Transmitting International Monitoring System data (raw or processed) to the International Data Centre by the most direct and cost-effective means available, including, if necessary, via appropriate communications nodes, from monitoring stations, laboratories, analytical facilities or from national data centres; or such data (including samples where appropriate) to laboratory and analytical facilities from monitoring stations; and

(d) Analysing samples on behalf of the Organization.

20. For auxiliary network seismic stations specified in Table 1-B of Annex 1 to the Protocol the Organization, as specified in agreements or arrangements pursuant to Part I, paragraph 4 of the Protocol, shall meet the costs only of:

(a) Transmitting data to the International Data Centre;

(b) Authenticating data from such stations;

(c) Upgrading stations to the required technical standard, unless the State responsible for such facilities meets these costs itself;

(d) If necessary, establishing new stations for the purposes of this Treaty where no appropriate facilities currently exist, unless the State responsible for such facilities meets these costs itself; and

(e) Any other costs related to the provision of data required by the Organization as specified in the relevant operational manuals.

21. The Organization shall also meet the cost of provision to each State Party of its requested selection from the standard range of International Data Centre reporting products and services, as specified in Part I, Section F of the Protocol. The cost of preparation and transmission of any additional data or products shall be met by the requesting State Party.

22. The agreements or, if appropriate, arrangements concluded with States Parties or States hosting or otherwise taking responsibility for facilities of the International Monitoring System shall contain provisions for meeting these costs. Such provisions may include modalities whereby a State Party meets any of the costs referred to in paragraphs 19 (*a*) and 20 (*c*) and (*d*) for facilities which it hosts or for which it is responsible, and is compensated by an appropriate reduction in its assessed financial contribution to the Organization. Such a reduction shall not exceed 50 per cent of the annual assessed financial contribution of a State Party, but may be spread over successive years. A State Party may share such a reduction with another State Party by agreement or arrangement between themselves and with the concurrence of the Executive Council. The agreements or arrangements referred to in this paragraph shall be approved in accordance with Article II, paragraphs 26 (*h*) and 38 (*i*).

Changes to the International Monitoring System

23. Any measures referred to in paragraph 11 affecting the International Monitoring System by means of addition or deletion of a monitoring technology shall, when agreed, be incorporated into this Treaty and the Protocol pursuant to Article VII, paragraphs 1 to 6.

24. The following changes to the International Monitoring System, subject to the agreement of those States directly affected, shall be regarded as matters of an administrative or technical nature pursuant to Article VII, paragraphs 7 and 8:

(*a*) Changes to the number of facilities specified in the Protocol for a given monitoring technology; and

(*b*) Changes to other details for particular facilities as reflected in the Tables of Annex 1 to the Protocol (including, *inter alia*, State responsible for the facility; location; name of facility; type of facility; and attribution of a facility between the primary and auxiliary

seismic networks).

If the Executive Council recommends, pursuant to Article VII, paragraph 8 (*d*), that such changes be adopted, it shall as a rule also recommend pursuant to Article VII, paragraph 8 (*g*), that such changes enter into force upon notification by the Director-General of their approval.

25. The Director-General, in submitting to the Executive Council and States Parties information and evaluation in accordance with Article VII, paragraph 8 (*b*), shall include in the case of any proposal made pursuant to paragraph 24:

(*a*) A technical evaluation of the proposal;

(*b*) A statement on the administrative and financial impact of the proposal; and

(*c*) A report on consultations with States directly affected by the proposal, including indication of their agreement.

Temporary Arrangements

26. In cases of significant or irretrievable breakdown of a monitoring facility specified in the Tables of Annex 1 to the Protocol, or in order to cover other temporary reductions of monitoring coverage, the Director-General shall, in consultation and agreement with those States directly affected, and with the approval of the Executive Council, initiate temporary arrangements of no more than one year's duration, renewable if necessary by agreement of the Executive Council and of the States directly affected for another year. Such arrangements shall not cause the number of operational facilities of the International Monitoring System to exceed the number specified for the relevant network; shall meet as far as possible the technical and operational requirements specified in the operational manual for the relevant network; and shall be conducted within the budget of the Organization. The Director-General shall furthermore take steps to rectify the situation and make proposals for its permanent resolution. The Director-General shall notify all States Parties of any decision taken pursuant to this paragraph.

Cooperating National Facilities

27. States Parties may also separately establish cooperative arrangements with the Organization, in order to make available to the International Data Centre supplementary data from national monitoring stations that are not formally part of the International Monitoring System.

28. Such cooperative arrangements may be established as follows:

(a) Upon request by a State Party, and at the expense of that State, the Technical Secretariat shall take the steps required to certify that a given monitoring facility meets the technical and operational requirements specified in the relevant operational manuals for an International Monitoring System facility, and make arrangements for the authentication of its data. Subject to the agreement of the Executive Council, the Technical Secretariat shall then formally designate such a facility as a cooperating national facility. The Technical Secretariat shall take the steps required to revalidate its certification as appropriate;

(b) The Technical Secretariat shall maintain a current list of cooperating national facilities and shall distribute it to all States Parties and;

(c) The International Data Centre shall call upon data from cooperating national facilities, if so requested by a State Party, for the purposes of facilitating consultation and clarification and the consideration of on-site inspection requests, data transmission costs being borne by that State Party. The conditions under which supplementary data from such facilities are made available, and under which the International Data Centre may request further or expedited reporting, or clarifications, shall be elaborated in the operational manual for the respective monitoring network.

C. Consultation and Clarification

29. Without prejudice to the right of any State Party to request an on-site inspection, States Parties should, whenever possible, first make every effort to clarify and resolve, among themselves or with or through the Organization, any matter which may cause concern about possible non-compliance with the basic obligations of this Treaty.

30. A State Party that receives a request pursuant to paragraph 29 directly from another State Party shall provide the clarification to the requesting State Party as soon as possible, but in any case no later than 48 hours after the request. The requesting and requested States Parties may keep the Executive Council and the Director-General informed of the request and the response.

31. A State Party shall have the right to request the Director-General to assist in clarifying any matter which may cause concern about possible non-compliance with the basic obligations of this Treaty. The Director-General shall provide appropriate information in the possession of the Technical Secretariat

relevant to such a concern. The Director-General shall inform the Executive Council of the request and of the information provided in response, if so requested by the requesting State Party.

32. A State Party shall have the right to request the Executive Council to obtain clarification from another State Party on any matter which may cause concern about possible non-compliance with the basic obligations of this Treaty. In such a case, the following shall apply:

(a) The Executive Council shall forward the request for clarification to the requested State Party through the Director-General no later than 24 hours after its receipt;

(b) The requested State Party shall provide the clarification to the Executive Council as soon as possible, but in any case no later than 48 hour after receipt of the request;

(c) The Executive Council shall take note of the clarification and forward it to the requesting State Party no later than 24 hours after its receipt;

(d) If the requesting State Party deems the clarification to be inadequate, it shall have the right to request the Executive Council to obtain further clarification from the requested State Party. The Executive Council shall inform without delay all other States Parties about any request for clarification pursuant to this paragraph as well as any response provided by the requested State Party.

33. If the requesting State Party considers the clarification obtained under paragraph 32 (d) to be unsatisfactory, it shall have the right to request a meeting of the Executive Council in which States Parties involved that are not members of the Executive Council shall be entitled to take part. At such a meeting, the Executive Council shall consider the matter and may recommend any measure in accordance with Article V.

D. On-Site Inspections

Request for an On-Site Inspection

34. Each State Party has the right to request an on-site inspection in accordance with the provisions of this Article and Part II of the Protocol in the territory or in any other place under the jurisdiction or control of any State Party, or in any area beyond the jurisdiction or control of any State.

35. The sole purpose of an on-site inspection shall be to clarify whether a nuclear weapon test explosion or any other nuclear explosion has been carried out in violation of Article I and, to the extent possible, to gather

any facts which might assist in identifying any possible violator.

36. The requesting State Party shall be under the obligation to keep the on-site inspection request within the scope of this Treaty and to provide in the request information in accordance with paragraph 37. The requesting State Party shall refrain from unfounded or abusive inspection requests.

37. The on-site inspection request shall be based on information collected by the International Monitoring System, on any relevant technical information obtained by national technical means of verification in a manner consistent with generally recognized principles of international law, or on a combination thereof. The request shall contain information pursuant to Part II, paragraph 41 of the Protocol.

38. The requesting State Party shall present the on-site inspection request to the Executive Council and at the same time to the Director-General for the latter to begin immediate processing.

Follow-up After Submission of an On-Site Inspection Request

39. The Executive Council shall begin its consideration immediately upon receipt of the on-site inspection request.

40. The Director-General, after receiving the on-site inspection request, shall acknowledge receipt of the request to the requesting State Party within two hours and communicate the request to the State Party sought to be inspected within six hours. The Director-General shall ascertain that the request meets the requirements specified in Part II, paragraph 41 of the Protocol, and, if necessary, shall assist the requesting State Party in filing the request accordingly, and shall communicate the request to the Executive Council and to all other States Parties within 24 hours.

41. When the on-site inspection request fulfils the requirements, the Technical Secretariat shall begin preparations for the on-site inspection without delay.

42. The Director-General, upon receipt of an on-site inspection request referring to an inspection area under the jurisdiction or control of a State Party, shall immediately seek clarification from the State Party sought to be inspected in order to clarify and resolve the concern raised in the request.

43. A State Party that receives a request for clarification pursuant to paragraph 42 shall provide the Director-General with explanations and with other relevant information

available as soon as possible, but no later than 72 hours after receipt of the request for clarification.

44. The Director-General, before the Executive Council takes a decision on the on-site inspection request, shall transmit immediately to the Executive Council any additional information available from the International Monitoring System or provided by any State Party on the event specified in the request, including any clarification provided pursuant to paragraphs 42 and 43, as well as any other information from within the Technical Secretariat that the Director-General deems relevant or that is requested by the Executive Council.

45. Unless the requesting State Party considers the concern raised in the on-site inspection request to be resolved and withdraws the request, the Executive Council shall take a decision on the request in accordance with paragraph 46.

Executive Council Decisions

46. The Executive Council shall take a decision on the on-site inspection request no later than 96 hours after receipt of the request from the requesting State Party. The decision to approve the on-site inspection shall be made by at least 30 affirmative votes of members of the Executive Council. If the Executive Council does not approve the inspection, preparations shall be stopped and no further action on the request shall be taken.

47. No later than 25 days after the approval of the on-site inspection in accordance with paragraph 46, the inspection team shall transmit to the Executive Council, through the Director-General, a progress inspection report. The continuation of the inspection shall be considered approved unless the Executive Council, no later than 72 hours after receipt of the progress inspection report, decides by a majority of all its members not to continue the inspection. If the Executive Council decides not to continue the inspection, the inspection shall be terminated, and the inspection team shall leave the inspection area and the territory of the inspected State Party as soon as possible in accordance with Part II, paragraphs 109 and 110 of the Protocol.

48. In the course of the on-site inspection, the inspection team may submit to the Executive Council, through the Director-General, a proposal to conduct drilling. The Executive Council shall take a decision on

such a proposal no later than 72 hours after receipt of the proposal. The decision to approve drilling shall be made by a majority of all members of the Executive Council.

49. The inspection team may request the Executive Council, through the Director-General, to extend the inspection duration by a maximum of 70 days beyond the 60-day time-frame specified in Part II, paragraph 4 of the Protocol, if the inspection team considers such an extension essential to enable it to fulfil its mandate. The inspection team shall indicate in its request which of the activities and techniques listed in Part II, paragraph 69 of the Protocol it intends to carry out during the extension period. The Executive Council shall take a decision on the extension request no later than 72 hours after receipt of the request. The decision to approve an extension of the inspection duration shall be made by a majority of all members of the Executive Council.

50. Any time following the approval of the continuation of the on-site inspection in accordance with paragraph 47, the inspection team may submit to the Executive Council, through the Director-General, a recommendation to terminate the inspection. Such a recommendation shall be considered approved unless the Executive Council, no later than 72 hours after receipt of the recommendation, decides by a two-thirds majority of all its members not to approve the termination of the inspection. In case of termination of the inspection, the inspection team shall leave the inspection area and the territory of the inspected State Party as soon as possible in accordance with Part II, paragraphs 109 and 110 of the Protocol.

51. The requesting State Party and the State Party sought to be inspected may participate in the deliberations of the Executive Council on the on-site inspection request without voting. The requesting State Party and the inspected State Party may also participate without voting in any subsequent deliberations of the Executive Council related to the inspection.

52. The Director-General shall notify all States Parties within 24 hours about any decision by and reports, proposals, requests and recommendations to the Executive Council pursuant to paragraphs 46 to 50.

Follow-up after Executive Council Approval of an On-Site Inspection

53. An on-site inspection approved by the Executive Council shall be conducted without delay by an inspection team designated by the Director-General and in accordance with the provisions of this Treaty and the Protocol. The inspection team shall arrive at the point of entry no later than six days following the receipt by the Executive Council of the on-site inspection request from the requesting State Party.

54. The Director-General shall issue an inspection mandate for the conduct of the on-site inspection. The inspection mandate shall contain the information specified in Part II, paragraph 42 of the Protocol.

55. The Director-General shall notify the inspected State Party of the inspection no less than 24 hours before the planned arrival of the inspection team at the point of entry, in accordance with Part II, paragraph 43 of the Protocol.

The Conduct of an On-Site Inspection

56. Each State Party shall permit the Organization to conduct an on-site inspection on its territory or at places under its jurisdiction or control in accordance with the provisions of this Treaty and the Protocol. However, no State Party shall have to accept simultaneous on-site inspections on its territory or at places under its jurisdiction or control.

57. In accordance with the provisions of this Treaty and the Protocol, the inspected State Party shall have:

(*a*) The right and the obligation to make every reasonable effort to demonstrate its compliance with this Treaty and, to this end, to enable the inspection team to fulfil its mandate;

(*b*) The right to take measures it deems necessary to protect national security interests and to prevent disclosure of confidential information not related to the purpose of the inspection;

(*c*) The obligation to provide access within the inspection area for the sole purpose of determining facts relevant to the purpose of the inspection, taking into account sub-paragraph (*b*) and any constitutional obligations it may have with regard to proprietary rights or searches and seizures;

(*d*) The obligation not to invoke this paragraph or Part II, paragraph 88 of the Protocol to conceal any violation of its obligations under Article I; and

(*e*) The obligation not to impede the ability of the inspection team to move within the inspection area and to carry out inspection activities in accordance with this Treaty and the Protocol. Access, in the context of an on-site inspection, means both the physical access of the inspection team and the inspection equipment to, and the conduct of inspection activities within, the inspection area.

58. The on-site inspection shall be conducted in the least intrusive manner possible, consistent with the efficient and timely accomplishment of the inspection mandate, and in accordance with the procedures set forth in the Protocol. Wherever possible, the inspection team shall begin with the least intrusive procedures and then proceed to more intrusive procedures only as it deems necessary to collect sufficient information to clarify the concern about possible non-compliance with this Treaty. The inspectors shall seek only the information and data necessary for the purpose of the inspection and shall seek to minimize interference with normal operations of the inspected State Party.

59. The inspected State Party shall assist the inspection team throughout the on-site inspection and facilitate its task.

60. If the inspected State Party, acting in accordance with Part II, paragraphs 86 to 96 of the Protocol, restricts access within the inspection area, it shall make every reasonable effort in consultations with the inspection team to demonstrate through alternative means its compliance with this Treaty.

Observer

61. With regard to an observer, the following shall apply:

(*a*) The requesting State Party, subject to the agreement of the inspected State Party, may send a representative, who shall be a national either of the requesting State Party or of a third State Party, to observe the conduct of the on-site inspection;

(*b*) The inspected State Party shall notify its acceptance or non-acceptance of the proposed observer to the Director-General within 12 hours after approval of the on-site inspection by the Executive Council;

(*c*) In case of acceptance, the inspected State Party shall grant access to the observer in accordance with the Protocol;

(*d*) The inspected State Party shall, as a rule, accept the proposed observer, but if the inspected State Party exercises a refusal, that fact shall be recorded in the inspection report. There shall be no more than three observers from an aggregate of requesting States Parties.

Reports of an On-Site Inspection

62. Inspection reports shall contain:

(*a*) A description of the activities conducted by the inspection team;

(*b*) The factual findings of the inspection team relevant to the purpose of the inspection,

(*c*) An account of the cooperation granted during the on-site inspection;

(*d*) A factual description of the extent of the access granted, including the alternative means provided to the team, during the on-site inspection; and

(*e*) Any other details relevant to the purpose of the inspection. Differing observations made by inspectors may be attached to the report.

63. The Director-General shall make draft inspection reports available to the inspected State Party. The inspected State Party shall have the right to provide the Director-General within 48 hours with its comments and explanations, and to identify any information and data which, in its view, are not related to the purpose of the inspection and should not be circulated outside the Technical Secretariat. The Director-General shall consider the proposals for changes to the draft inspection report made by the inspected State Party and shall wherever possible incorporate them. The Director-General shall also annex the comments and explanations provided by the inspected State Party to the inspection report.

64. The Director-General shall promptly transmit the inspection report to the requesting State Party, the inspected State Party, the Executive Council and to all other States Parties. The Director-General shall further transmit promptly to the Executive Council and to all other States Parties any results of sample analysis in designated laboratories in accordance with Part II, paragraph 104 of the Protocol, relevant data from the International Monitoring System, the assessments of the requesting and inspected States Parties, as well as any other information that the Director-General deems relevant. In the case of the progress inspection report referred to in paragraph 47, the Director-General shall transmit the report to the Executive Council within the time-frame specified in that paragraph.

65. The Executive Council, in accordance with its powers and functions, shall review the inspection report and any material provided pursuant to paragraph 64, and shall address any concerns as to:

(*a*) Whether any non-compliance with this

Treaty has occurred; and

(b) Whether the right to request an on-site inspection has been abused.

66. If the Executive Council reaches the conclusion, in keeping with its powers and functions, that further action may be necessary with regard to paragraph 65, it shall take the appropriate measures in accordance with Article V.

Frivolous or Abusive On-Site Inspection Requests

67. If the Executive Council does not approve the on-site inspection on the basis that the on-site inspection request is frivolous or abusive, or if the inspection is terminated for the same reasons, the Executive Council shall consider and decide on whether to implement appropriate measures to redress the situation, including the following:

(a) Requiring the requesting State Party to pay for the cost of any preparations made by the Technical Secretariat;

(b) Suspending the right of the requesting State Party to request an on-site inspection for a period of time, as determined by the Executive Council; and

(c) Suspending the right of the requesting State Party to serve on the Executive Council for a period of time.

E. Confidence-building Measures

68. In order to: (a) contribute to the timely resolution of any compliance concerns arising from possible misinterpretation of verification data relating to chemical explosions; and (b) assist in the calibration of the stations that are part of the component networks of the International Monitoring System, each State Party undertakes to cooperate with the Organization and with other States Parties in implementing relevant measures as set out in Part III of the Protocol.

Article V. Measures to Redress a Situation and to Ensure Compliance, Including Sanctions

1. The Conference, taking into account, *inter alia*, the recommendations of the Executive Council, shall take the necessary measures, as set forth in paragraphs 2 and 3, to ensure compliance with this Treaty and to redress and remedy any situation which contravenes the provisions of this Treaty.

2. In cases where a State Party has been requested by the Conference or the Executive Council to redress a situation raising problems with regard to its compliance and fails to fulfil the request within the specified time, the Conference may, *inter alia*, decide to restrict or suspend the State Party from the exercise of its rights and privileges under this Treaty until the Conference decides otherwise.

3. In cases where damage to the object and purpose of this Treaty may result from non-compliance with the basic obligations of this Treaty, the Conference may recommend to States Parties collective measures which are in conformity with international law.

4. The Conference, or alternatively, if the case is urgent, the Executive Council, may bring the issue, including relevant information and conclusions to the attention of the United Nations.

Article VI. Settlement of Disputes

1. Disputes that may arise concerning the application or the interpretation of this Treaty shall be settled in accordance with the relevant provisions of this Treaty and in conformity with the provisions of the Charter of the United Nations.

2. When a dispute arises between two or more States Parties, or between one or more States Parties and the Organization, relating to the application or interpretation of this Treaty, the parties concerned shall consult together with a view to the expeditious settlement of the dispute by negotiation or by other peaceful means of the parties' choice, including recourse to appropriate organs of this Treaty and, by mutual consent, referral to the International Court of Justice in conformity with the Statute of the Court. The parties involved shall keep the Executive Council informed of actions being taken.

3. The Executive Council may contribute to the settlement of a dispute that may arise concerning the application or interpretation of this Treaty by whatever means it deems appropriate, including offering its good offices, calling upon the States Parties to a dispute to seek a settlement through a process of their own choice, bringing the matter to the attention of the Conference and recommending a time-limit for any agreed procedure.

4. The Conference shall consider questions related to disputes raised by States Parties or brought to its attention by the Executive Council. The Conference shall, as it finds necessary, establish or entrust organs with tasks related to the settlement of these disputes in conformity with Article II, paragraph 26 (j).

5. The Conference and the Executive

Council are separately empowered, subject to authorization from the General Assembly of the United Nations, to request the International Court of Justice to give an advisory opinion on any legal question arising within the scope of the activities of the Organization. An agreement between the Organization and the United Nations shall be concluded for this purpose in accordance with Article II, paragraph 38 (h).

6. This Article is without prejudice to Articles IV and V.

Article VII. Amendments

1. At any time after the entry into force of this Treaty, any State Party may propose amendments to this Treaty, the Protocol, or the Annexes to the Protocol. Any State Party may also propose changes, in accordance with paragraph 7, to the Protocol or the Annexes thereto. Proposals for amendment shall be subject to the procedures in paragraphs 2 to 6. Proposals for changes, in accordance with paragraph 7, shall be subject to the procedures in paragraph 8.

2. The proposed amendment shall be considered and adopted only by an Amendment Conference.

3. Any proposal for an amendment shall be communicated to the Director-General, who shall circulate it to all States Parties and the Depositary and seek the views of the States Parties on whether an Amendment Conference should be convened to consider the proposal. If a majority of the States Parties notify the Director-General no later than 30 days after its circulation that they support further consideration of the proposal, the Director-General shall convene an Amendment Conference to which all States Parties shall be invited.

4. The Amendment Conference shall be held immediately following a regular session of the Conference unless all States Parties that support the convening of an Amendment Conference request that it be held earlier. In no case shall an Amendment Conference be held less than 60 days after the circulation of the proposed amendment.

5. Amendments shall be adopted by the Amendment Conference by a positive vote of a majority of the States Parties with no State Party casting a negative vote.

6. Amendments shall enter into force for all States Parties 30 days after deposit of the instruments of ratification or acceptance by all those States Parties casting a positive vote at the Amendment Conference.

7. In order to ensure the viability and effectiveness of this Treaty, Parts I and III of the Protocol and Annexes 1 and 2 to the Protocol shall be subject to changes in accordance with paragraph 8, if the proposed changes are related only to matters of an administrative or technical nature. All other provisions of the Protocol and the Annexes thereto shall not be subject to changes in accordance with paragraph 8.

8. Proposed changes referred to in paragraph 7 shall be made in accordance with the following procedures:

(a) The text of the proposed changes shall be transmitted together with the necessary information to the Director-General. Additional information for the evaluation of the proposal may be provided by any State Party and the Director-General. The Director-General shall promptly communicate any such proposals and information to all States Parties, the Executive Council and the Depositary;

(b) No later than 60 days after its receipt, the Director-General shall evaluate the proposal to determine all its possible consequences for the provisions of this Treaty and its implementation and shall communicate any such information to all States Parties and the Executive Council;

(c) The Executive Council shall examine the proposal in the light of all information available to it, including whether the proposal fulfils the requirements of paragraph 7. No later than 90 days after its receipt, the Executive Council shall notify its recommendation, with appropriate explanations, to all States Parties for consideration. States Parties shall acknowledge receipt within 10 days;

(d) If the Executive Council recommends to all States Parties that the proposal be adopted, it shall be considered approved if no State Party objects to it within 90 days after receipt of the recommendation. If the Executive Council recommends that the proposal be rejected, it shall be considered rejected if no State Party objects to the rejection within 90 days after receipt of the recommendation;

(e) If a recommendation of the Executive Council does not meet with the acceptance required under sub-paragraph (d), a decision on the proposal, including whether it fulfils the requirements of paragraph 7, shall be taken as a matter of substance by the Conference at its next session;

(f) The Director-General shall notify all States Parties and the Depositary of any decision under this paragraph;

(g) Changes approved under this procedure shall enter into force for all States Parties 180 days after the date of notification by the Director-General of their approval unless another time period is recommended by the Executive Council or decided by the Conference.

Article VIII. Review of the Treaty

1. Unless otherwise decided by a majority of the States Parties, ten years after the entry into force of this Treaty a Conference of the States Parties shall be held to review the operation and effectiveness of this Treaty, with a view to assuring itself that the objectives and purposes in the Preamble and the provisions of the Treaty are being realized. Such review shall take into account any new scientific and technological developments relevant to this Treaty. On the basis of a request by any State Party, the Review Conference shall consider the possibility of permitting the conduct of underground nuclear explosions for peaceful purposes. If the Review Conference decides by consensus that such nuclear explosions may be permitted, it shall commence work without delay, with a view to recommending to States Parties an appropriate amendment to this Treaty that shall preclude any military benefits of such nuclear explosions. Any such proposed amendment shall be communicated to the Director-General by any State Party and shall be dealt with in accordance with the provisions of Article VII.

2. At intervals of ten years thereafter, further Review Conferences may be convened with the same objective, if the Conference so decides as a matter of procedure in the preceding year. Such Conferences may be convened after an interval of less than ten years if so decided by the Conference as a matter of substance.

3. Normally, any Review Conference shall be held immediately following the regular annual session of the Conference provided for in Article II.

Article IX. Duration and Withdrawal

1. This Treaty shall be of unlimited duration.

2. Each State Party shall, in exercising its national sovereignty, have the right to withdraw from this Treaty if it decides that extraordinary events related to the subject matter of this Treaty have jeopardized its supreme interests. Withdrawal shall be effected by giving notice six months in advance to all other States Parties, the Executive Council, the Depositary and the United Nations Security Council. Notice of withdrawal shall include a statement of the extraordinary event or events which a State Party regards as jeopardizing its supreme interests.

Article X. Status of the Protocol and the Annexes

The Annexes to this Treaty, the Protocol, and the Annexes to the Protocol form an integral part of the Treaty. Any reference to this Treaty, includes the Annexes to this Treaty, the Protocol and the Annexes to the Protocol.

Article XI. Signature

This Treaty shall be open to all States for signature before its entry into force.

Article XII. Ratification

This Treaty shall be subject to ratification by States Signatories according to their respective constitutional processes.

Article XIII. Accession

Any State which does not sign this Treaty before its entry into force may accede to it at any time thereafter.

Article XIV. Entry into Force

1. This Treaty shall enter into force 180 days after the date of deposit of the instruments of ratification by all States listed in Annex 2 to this Treaty, but in no case earlier than two years after its opening for signature.

2. If this Treaty has not entered into force three years after the date of the anniversary of its opening for signature, the Depositary shall convene a Conference of the States that have already deposited their instruments of ratification on the request of a majority of those States. That Conference shall examine the extent to which the requirement set out in paragraph 1 has been met and shall consider and decide by consensus what measures consistent with international law may be undertaken to accelerate the ratification process in order to facilitate the early entry into force of this Treaty.

3. Unless otherwise decided by the Conference referred to in paragraph 2 or other such conferences, this process shall be repeated at subsequent anniversaries of the opening for signature of this Treaty, until its entry into force.

4. All States Signatories shall be invited to attend the Conference referred to in para-

graph 2 and any subsequent conferences as referred to in paragraph 3, as observers.

5. For States whose instruments of ratification or accession are deposited subsequent to the entry into force of this Treaty, it shall enter into force on the 30th day following the date of deposit of their instruments of ratification or accession.

Article XV. Reservations

The Articles of and the Annexes to this Treaty shall not be subject to reservations. The provisions of the Protocol to this Treaty and the Annexes to the Protocol shall not be subject to reservations incompatible with the object and purpose of this Treaty.

Article XVI. Depositary

1. The Secretary-General of the United Nations shall be the Depositary of this Treaty and shall receive signatures, instruments of ratification and instruments of accession.

2. The Depositary shall promptly inform all States Signatories and acceding States of the date of each signature, the date of deposit of each instrument of ratification or accession, the date of the entry into force of this Treaty and of any amendments and changes thereto, and the receipt of other notices.

3. The Depositary shall send duly certified copies of this Treaty to the Governments of the States Signatories and acceding States.

4. This Treaty shall be registered by the Depositary pursuant to Article 102 of the Charter of the United Nations.

Article XVII. Authentic Texts

This Treaty, of which the Arabic, Chinese, English, French, Russian and Spanish texts are equally authentic, shall be deposited with the Secretary-General of the United Nations.

Source: UN General Assembly document A/50/1027, 26 Aug. 1996, annex.

Appendix 12B. Nuclear explosions, 1945–96

RAGNHILD FERM

I. Introduction

In 1996 three nuclear tests[1] were conducted: one by France and two by China. Russia, the United States and the United Kingdom observed unilateral moratoria on nuclear tests throughout the year. No state has conducted a nuclear explosion since the Comprehensive Nuclear Test-Ban Treaty (CTBT) was opened for signature on 24 September 1996.[2]

II. The United States and the United Kingdom

The last US test was carried out on 23 September 1992 and the last British test on 26 November 1991. President George Bush announced a nine-month test moratorium in October 1992 and President Bill Clinton extended it twice (in July 1993 and January 1995). As a result of the US moratorium, the UK had to abandon its nuclear weapon testing as it could not use the Nevada test site, where all British tests had been conducted since 1962.

The US Department of Defense announced in 1995 that six subcritical high-explosive experiments involving nuclear materials would be conducted at the Nevada test site—two in 1996 and four in 1997—to ensure the safety and reliability of the US nuclear arsenal.[3] However, this programme was postponed and no such experiments were conducted in 1996.[4]

III. Russia

The last Soviet test was carried out on 24 October 1990. In January 1991 the Soviet Council of Ministers announced a moratorium which was extended by President Mikhail Gorbachev in October 1991 and, after the dissolution of the Soviet Union, by President Boris Yeltsin in October 1992. In October 1993 the Russian Government declared that it intended to continue to observe the moratorium. Accordingly, although Russia inherited the Soviet nuclear programme it has not conducted a nuclear explosion. When Kazakhstan became an independent state in 1991 it closed the former Soviet test site at Semipalatinsk. The other former Soviet test site, on Novaya Zemlya, in Russia, has not been closed but no nuclear explosions have been conducted there for over six years.

---

[1] The term nuclear 'test' denotes explosions conducted in nuclear weapon test programmes. The tables in this appendix list all nuclear explosions, including so-called peaceful nuclear explosions (PNEs), the atomic bombs dropped on Hiroshima and Nagasaki in 1945 and (for the USA, the Soviet Union/Russia and France) tests for safety purposes irrespective of the yields and irrespective of whether they have caused a nuclear explosion or not.

[2] See also chapter 12 and appendix 12A in this volume.

[3] 'New contractor announced for Nevada Test Site; secretary outlines plans for site', *DOE News*, US Department of Energy press release, 27 Oct. 1995.

[4] Subcritical experiments are designed not to reach nuclear criticality, i.e., there is no nuclear explosion and no energy release. Subcritical experiments are not included in the SIPRI statistics.

A detailed history of the Soviet nuclear testing programme was made known in the USA in October 1996 through reports in the media.[5] The 2000-page study, written by about 200 Russian nuclear weapon scientists under contract to the US Defense Special Weapons Agency, reveals new facts and details of the Soviet nuclear programme. The study, which is not publicly available, was carried out for nearly four years and had the approval and participation of the Russian Minister of Atomic Energy. Of special interest to experts in the West is the new information concerning the early years of the Soviet nuclear weapon testing programme. A list of all 715 Soviet nuclear explosions, including information on dates, purpose, yield and location, was released by the Russian scientists in mid-1996.[6] Some of the test data were previously known by the Natural Resources Defense Council (NRDC) and were included in the tables of nuclear explosions in the *SIPRI Yearbook 1996*.

IV. France

Two days after its test on 27 January 1996 French President Jacques Chirac announced that France had concluded its nuclear testing programme. France is the first nuclear testing state to start the process of closing its test site. The cost of the dismantlement is estimated at 235 million francs in 1997 and 68 million francs in 1998.[7] In 1966–96, 193 tests were conducted in French Polynesia—46 in the atmosphere and 147 under ground.

At the request of the French Foreign Minister, the International Atomic Energy Agency (IAEA) is conducting a study of the overall radiological situation at the Mururoa and Fangataufa atolls where French nuclear testing took place for almost 30 years.[8] Starting in early July 1996, an international team of scientists collected terrestrial and marine samples at the atolls for about one month. The samples were then forwarded to several laboratories for analysis. In addition, the team is evaluating the long-term radiological situation in the area. The full report of the study will be published in early 1998.

V. China

Unlike the other declared nuclear weapon states, China has never implemented a test moratorium, as it has claimed that it had conducted only about 2 per cent of the total number of nuclear explosions and needed to conduct more tests to finalize its nuclear weapon programme. Only after having conducted its second test of 1996, on 29 July (approximately two months before it signed the CTBT) did China pledge to forgo nuclear testing.[9]

---

[5] 'Russians wrote atomic history for Pentagon', *Washington Post*, 27 Oct. 1996.

[6] Ministry of the Russian Federation for Atomic Energy and Ministry of Defense of the Russian Federation, USSR *Nuclear Weapons Tests and Peaceful Nuclear Explosions, 1949 through 1990* (Russian Federal Nuclear Center–All-Russian Research Institute of Experimental Physics (VNIIEF): Sarov, 1996).

[7] Assemblée Nationale, *Rapport fait au nom de la Commission des Finances, de l'Économie Générale et du Plan sur le projet de loi de finances pour 1997*, Document no. 3030 (Assemblée Nationale: Paris, 5 Nov. 1996), Annexe no. 40, p. 27.

[8] International Atomic Energy Agency (IAEA) press release PR 96/16, 6 Aug. 1996. Similar studies were previously conducted by the IAEA at the former Soviet test site in Semipalatinsk, Kazakhstan, and on the Bikini Atoll in the South Pacific, where over 20 US tests were carried out in the period 1946–58.

[9] Conference on Disarmament document CD/1410, 29 July 1996.

Table 12B.1. Registered nuclear explosions in 1996

Date	Origin time (GMT)	Latitude (deg)	Longitude (deg)	Region	Body wave magnitude[a]
France					
27 Jan.	212959.5	22.27 S	138.78.W	Fangataufa	5.3
China					
8 June	025559.4	41.65 N	88.76 E	Lop Nor	6.3
29 July	014859.1	41.69 N	88.35 E	Lop Nor	5.3

[a] Body wave magnitude (m_b) indicates the size of the event. In order to be able to give a reasonably correct estimate of the yield it is necessary to have detailed information, for example, on the geological conditions of the area where the test is conducted. Giving the m_b figure is therefore an unambiguous way of listing the size of an explosion. m_b data for the French test were provided by the Australian Seismological Centre, Australian Geological Survey Organisation, Canberra and data for the Chinese tests by the Hagfors observatory of the Swedish National Defence Research Establishment (FOA).

Table 12B.2. Estimated number of nuclear explosions, 1945–1996

a = atmospheric (or in a few cases under water); u = underground

Year	USA[a] a	USA[a] u	USSR/Russia a	USSR/Russia u	UK[a] a	UK[a] u	France a	France u	China a	China u	India a	India u	Total
1945	3	–	–	–	–	–	–	–	–	–	–	–	3
1946	2[b]	–	–	–	–	–	–	–	–	–	–	–	2
1947	–	–	–	–	–	–	–	–	–	–	–	–	–
1948	3	–	–	–	–	–	–	–	–	–	–	–	3
1949	–	–	1	–	–	–	–	–	–	–	–	–	1
1950	–	–	–	–	–	–	–	–	–	–	–	–	–
1951	15	1	2	–	–	–	–	–	–	–	–	–	18
1952	10	–	–	–	1	–	–	–	–	–	–	–	11
1953	11	–	5	–	2	–	–	–	–	–	–	–	18
1954	6	–	10	–	–	–	–	–	–	–	–	–	16
1955	17[b]	1	6[b]	–	–	–	–	–	–	–	–	–	24
1956	18	–	9	–	6	–	–	–	–	–	–	–	33
1957	27	5	16[b]	–	7	–	–	–	–	–	–	–	55
1958	62[c]	15	34	–	5	–	–	–	–	–	–	–	116
1959	–	–	–	–	–	–	–	–	–	–	–	–	–[d]
1960	–	–	–	–	–	–	3	–	–	–	–	–	3[d]
1961	–	10	58[b]	1	–	–	1	1	–	–	–	–	71[d]
1962	39[b]	57	78	1	–	2	–	1	–	–	–	–	178
1963[e]	4	43	–	–	–	–	–	3	–	–	–	–	50
1964	–	45	–	9	–	2	–	3	1	–	–	–	60
1965	–	38	–	14	–	1	–	4	1	–	–	–	58
1966	–	48	–	18	–	–	6	1	3	–	–	–	76
1967	–	42	–	17	–	–	3	–	2	–	–	–	64
1968	–	56	–	17	–	–	5	–	1	–	–	–	79
1969	–	46	–	19	–	–	–	–	1	1	–	–	67
1970	–	39	–	16	–	–	8	–	1	–	–	–	64

Year	USA[a] a	USA[a] u	USSR/Russia a	USSR/Russia u	UK[a] a	UK[a] u	France a	France u	China a	China u	India a	India u	Total
1971	–	24	–	23	–	–	5	–	1	–	–	–	53
1972	–	27	–	24	–	–	4	–	2	–	–	–	57
1973	–	24	–	17	–	–	6	–	1	–	–	–	48
1974	–	22	–	21	–	1	9	–	1	–	–	1	55
1975	–	22	–	19	–	–	–	2	–	1	–	–	44
1976	–	20	–	21	–	1	–	5	3	1	–	–	51
1977	–	20	–	24	–	–	–	9	1	–	–	–	54
1978	–	19	–	31	–	2	–	11	2	1	–	–	66
1979	–	15	–	31	–	1	–	10	1	–	–	–	58
1980	–	14	–	24	–	3	–	12	1	–	–	–	54
1981	–	16	–	21	–	1	–	12	–	–	–	–	50
1982	–	18	–	19	–	1	–	10	–	1	–	–	49
1983	–	18	–	25	–	1	–	9	–	2	–	–	55
1984	–	18	–	27	–	2	–	8	–	2	–	–	57
1985	–	17	–	10	–	1	–	8	–	–	–	–	36[f]
1986	–	14	–	–	–	1	–	8	–	–	–	–	23[f]
1987	–	14	–	23	–	1	–	8	–	1	–	–	47[f]
1988	–	15	–	16	–	–	–	8	–	1	–	–	40
1989	–	11	–	7	–	1	–	9	–	–	–	–	28
1990	–	8	–	1	–	1	–	6	–	2	–	–	18
1991	–	7	–	–	–	1	–	6	–	–	–	–	14
1992	–	6	–	–	–	–	–	–	–	2	–	–	8[g]
1993	–	–	–	–	–	–	–	–	–	1	–	–	1[g]
1994	–	–	–	–	–	–	–	–	–	2	–	–	2[g]
1995	–	–	–	–	–	–	–	5	–	2	–	–	7[g]
1996	–	–	–	–	–	–	–	1	–	2	–	–	3
Subtotal[h]	217	815	219	496	21	24	50	160	23	22	–	1	2 048
Total[h]	**1 032**		**715**		**45**		**210**		**45**		**1**		**2 048**

[a] All British tests from 1962 were conducted jointly with the USA at the Nevada Test Site, so the number of US tests is actually higher than indicated here. The British Labour Government observed a unilateral moratorium on testing in 1965–74.

[b] One of these tests was carried out under water.

[c] Two of these tests were carried out under water.

[d] The UK, the USA and the USSR observed a moratorium on testing in the period Nov. 1958–Sep. 1961.

[e] On 5 Aug. 1963 the USA, the USSR and the UK signed the Partial Test Ban Treaty (PTBT), prohibiting nuclear explosions in the atmosphere, in outer space and under water.

[f] The USSR observed a unilateral moratorium on testing in the period Aug. 1985–Feb. 1987.

[g] The USSR observed a moratorium on testing from Jan. 1991 and the USA from Oct. 1992; France observed a moratorium in the period Apr. 1992–Sep. 1995.

[h] The totals include US, Soviet and French tests (not British tests) for safety purposes irrespective of the yields and irrespective of whether or not they caused a nuclear explosion. Twenty per cent of the Soviet and 6% of the US tests were so-called salvo experiments which had multiple explosives (or salvos); each of these experiments is counted as 1 explosion.

Sources for tables 12B.1–12B.2

Swedish National Defence Research Establishment (FOA), various estimates, including information from the International Data Center of the CD Ad Hoc Group of Scientific Experts Third Technical Test, GSETT-3; Reports from the Australian Seismological Centre, Australian Geological Survey Organisation, Canberra; US Department of Energy (DOE), *Summary List of Previously Unannounced Tests* (DOE: Washington, DC, 1993); US Department of Energy (DOE), *Nuclear Detonations Redefined as Nuclear Tests* (DOE: Washington, DC, 1994); Norris, R. S., Burrows, A. S. and Fieldhouse, R. W., 'British, French and Chinese nuclear weapons', *Nuclear Weapons Databook, Vol. V* (Natural Resources Defense Council [NRDC]: Washington, DC, 1994); 'Assessment of French nuclear testing' (Direction des centres d'experimentations nucléaires [DIRCEN] and Commissariat à l'Energie Atomique [CEA]); 'Known nuclear tests worldwide, 1945–1995', *Bulletin of the Atomic Scientists*, vol. 52, no. 3 (May/June 1996), pp. 61–63; and Ministry of the Russian Federation for Atomic Energy and Ministry of Defense of the Russian Federation, *USSR Nuclear Weapons Tests and Peaceful Nuclear Explosions, 1949 through 1990* (Russian Federal Nuclear Center–All-Russian Research Institute of Experimental Physics (VNIIEF): Sarov, 1996).

13. Chemical and biological weapon developments and arms control

JEAN PASCAL ZANDERS, SUSANNA ECKSTEIN and JOHN HART

I. Introduction

The development of the treaty regimes banning chemical weapons (CW) and biological weapons (BW) made 1996 an important year as regards chemical and biological warfare (CBW). The 1993 Chemical Weapons Convention (CWC) received the required number of ratifications and will enter into force on 29 April 1997. The Fourth Review Conference of the 1972 Biological and Toxin Weapons Convention (BTWC) was held in November–December. It endorsed the efforts by the Ad Hoc Group in 1995 and 1996 to negotiate a verification protocol for the BTWC.

Throughout 1996 CBW-related topics drew global attention. Although Russia and the United States failed to ratify the CWC in 1996, both made some progress towards destroying their respective CW stocks. The United Nations Special Commission on Iraq (UNSCOM) continued to investigate whether Iraq's CW and BW programmes have been completely eliminated. New information regarding possible exposure of coalition troops to chemical warfare agents during the 1991 Persian Gulf War was released in the United Kingdom and the United States, although experts still advance different opinions about the causes of the so-called Gulf War Syndrome. The trials against the Aum Shinrikyo sect revealed the scope of its preparations for chemical and even biological terrorism.

Part II deals with the institutional and procedural preparations for the entry into force of the CWC. Part III focuses on issues relating to the destruction of the Russian and US CW stockpiles as well as on old and abandoned chemical weapons. Part IV discusses the efforts to strengthen the BTWC disarmament regime. Part V deals with CBW proliferation concerns and Part VI with other CBW-related issues such as Gulf War Syndrome and the Aum Shinrikyo trials in Tokyo.

II. Implementation of the CWC

The CWC prohibits the development, production, stockpiling, transfer and use of chemical weapons. It also provides for the total destruction of chemical weapons and CW production facilities in all states parties under international supervision and within specific time-frames.[1]

The deposit of the 65th instrument of ratification of the CWC by Hungary on 31 October 1996 triggered the 180-day countdown to entry into force. Nineteen other states also deposited ratifications in 1996, bringing the total number to 67 by the end of the year.[2] There was optimism that the number of states parties would increase considerably before entry into force. Imminent deposits by Benin, Bolivia, Gabon, Ghana, Kenya, Mali, Nigeria, Togo and the United Arab Emirates were expected.[3] Belgium completed its ratification process in 1996 but still had to deposit its instrument. Luxembourg introduced the ratification bill into parliament on 11 October. It remained committed to be a state party before entry into force, and parliamentary action was expected in early 1997.[4] It thus appeared that, in accordance with their pledges, all European Union members will be original states parties.[5] China approved the CWC on 30 December but did not deposit its instrument of ratification in 1996.[6]

The two largest CW possessors, Russia and the USA, failed to be among the first 65 ratifiers, despite public pledges to do so. In the first half of 1996 opposition against the CWC in the USA became more vocal and concerted, leading to the Clinton Administration's request on 12 September to postpone the ratification debate. Two letters addressed to Senate Majority Leader Trent Lott had broken the sense of widespread industrial and bipartisan political support. Both the National Federation of Independent Business and senior military officers and high-ranking members of the Reagan and Bush administrations expressed serious doubts about the CWC.[7] After Republican presidential candidate Bob Dole withdrew his support, Republican senators Jon Kyl and Trent Lott drafted a resolution providing that the USA would only comply with the CWC if all other states ratified it and if the Central Intelligence Agency (CIA) certified that it could be confident of catching any 'cheaters'.[8] Adoption would

---

[1] The Convention on the Prohibition of the Development, Production, Stockpiling, and Use of Chemical Weapons and on their Destruction was signed at Paris on 13 Jan. 1993. It is reproduced in *SIPRI Yearbook 1993: World Armaments and Disarmament* (Oxford University Press: Oxford, 1993), appendix 14A, pp. 735–56.

[2] For a complete list of the states which have signed or ratified the CWC see Annexe A in this volume.

[3] *Chemical Weapons Convention Bulletin*, no. 33 (Sep. 1996), p. 33.

[4] Private communication with Luxembourg Foreign Ministry, 15 Jan. 1997.

[5] Statement made by the representative of Ireland on behalf of the European Union at the fourteenth session of the Preparatory Commission for the Organisation for the Prohibition of Chemical Weapons, Preparatory Commission (PrepCom) document PC-XIV/11, 22 July 1996.

[6] Xinhua (Beijing), 1042 GMT 30 Dec. 1996 (in English), in 'China: decisions of 23d session of NPC Standing Committee cited', Foreign Broadcast Information Service, *Daily Report–China (FBIS-CHI)*, FBIS-CHI-96-251, 31 Dec. 1996.

[7] Letter from D. Danner, Vice President, Federal Government Relations, National Federation of Independent Business to Trent Lott, 9 Sep. 1996, *Congressional Record*, 9 Sep. 1996, p. S10070, Congressional Record On-line via GPO Access, URL <wais.access.gpo.gov>; letter from W. P. Clark *et al.* to Trent Lott, 9 Sep. 1996, *Congressional Record*, 9 Sep. 1996, pp. S10070–71. Among the signatories were W. P. Clark, former national security adviser, C. Weinberger and R. B. Cheney, former secretaries of defense, J. J. Kirkpatrick, former ambassador to the UN, and E. Meese III, former attorney-general.

[8] Towell, P., 'Chemical weapons ban delayed as Dole joins objectors', *Congressional Quarterly*, vol. 54, no. 37 (14 Sep. 1996), p. 2608.

have imposed impossible standards.[9] The November elections returned a reinforced Republican majority to Congress, so that success in the ratification of the CWC in President Bill Clinton's second term seemed far from ensured.

In Russia the CWC had not been scheduled for consideration in the Duma by the end of 1996. In December the Russian representative told the Preparatory Commission (PrepCom) of the Organisation for the Prohibition of Chemical Weapons (OPCW) that the procedural documents needed to submit the CWC to the Federal Assembly had been completed and were being considered by the Russian Government. The main problem delaying ratification appeared to be the high cost of the chemical demilitarization programme, for which Russia expects 'concrete contribution[s]' from other states.[10]

The participation of some countries is of particular interest to international security. Iran is gradually moving towards ratification[11] whereas Egypt, Iraq, Libya, Syria[12] as well as North Korea are still among the 33 non-signatory states.[13] At the end of 1996 the number of signatory states was 160.

The Preparatory Commission for the OPCW and the Provisional Technical Secretariat

On entry into force of the convention the OPCW, the monitoring and verification organization of the CWC, will be set up in The Hague. The PrepCom, which began meeting in February 1993, established the infrastructure to enable the OPCW to carry out its tasks and developed procedures for the implementation of the CWC.[14] The Provisional Technical Secretariat (PTS), established at the first plenary session, assists the PrepCom in building up the future OPCW and its Technical Secretariat. It is also responsible for the international preparations necessary for implementation of the CWC.[15]

---

[9] *Congressional Record*, 12 Sep. 1996, pp. S10420-S10421.

[10] Statement by the delegation of the Russian Federation at the fifteenth session of the Preparatory Commission for the Organisation for the Prohibition of Chemical Weapons, PrepCom document PC-XV/15, 18 Dec. 1996, pp. 1–2.

[11] Institute for Defense and Disarmament Studies, 'Statement by Sergey Batsanov, Director of External Relations OPCW', *Arms Control Reporter* (IDDS: Brookline, Mass.), sheet 704.B.603, Feb. 1996.

[12] In Cairo, Arab League officials stated in a report to be submitted to a meeting of League foreign ministers on 14 Sep. that a League commission would urge member states not to sign the CWC until Israel joins the Non-Proliferation Treaty. *Chemical Weapons Convention Bulletin* (note 3), p. 35.

[13] As of 31 Dec. 1996 the non-signatory states were: Angola, Andorra, Antigua and Barbuda, Barbados, Belize, Bhutan, Bosnia and Herzegovina, Botswana, Grenada, Egypt, Eritrea, Iraq, Jamaica, Jordan, Kiribati, Korea (North), Lebanon, Libya, Macedonia (Former Yugoslav Republic of), Mozambique, Niue (for whose security and foreign relations New Zealand is responsible), Palau, Sao Tome and Principe, Solomon Islands, Somalia, Sudan, Suriname, Syria, Taiwan (not officially recognized as an independent state by the UN), Tonga, Trinidad and Tobago, Tuvalu and Vanuatu. *Chemical Weapons Convention Bulletin*, no. 34 (Dec. 1996), p. 8.

[14] Resolution establishing the Preparatory Commission for the Organisation for the Prohibition of Chemical Weapons (the Paris Resolution), adopted in Paris, 13 Jan. 1993. The PrepCom is composed of all signatory states and conducts its work in plenary sessions, working groups and expert groups. All PrepCom decisions are taken by consensus. Provisional Technical Secretariat of the Preparatory Commission for the Organisation for the Prohibition of Chemical Weapons, Information Series 2, Rev. 5, Sep. 1996, p. 1.

[15] Provisional Technical Secretariat of the Preparatory Commission for the Organisation for the Prohibition of Chemical Weapons (note 14), p. 2.

With the deposit of the 65th ratification, phase II of the preparations for entry into force began and the PrepCom shifted its attention to the most pressing technical, financial and administrative issues.[16] During this phase operational costs will increase significantly. Some of the immediate costs will include recruitment of additional staff, inspector training, procurement of equipment and renting of interim facilities. In order to ensure that funds were available for phase II, signatory states were asked to pay their contributions to a separate account to which access was blocked until 'trigger point'.[17] Concern was none the less expressed as to whether preparations could be completed in time for the First Conference of States Parties in May 1997.[18]

In 1996 the PrepCom held three plenary sessions.[19] Towards the middle of the year the concern that neither Russia nor the USA would be original states parties began to dominate discussions.[20] The elimination of their large CW stockpiles and related facilities had been a major goal of the CWC negotiations.[21] The PrepCom counted on their being states parties because of their technical expertise in CW-related matters and their major financial contributions towards treaty implementation.[22] Although neither country has ratified the 1990 Bilateral Destruction Agreement (BDA),[23] the PrepCom none the less hoped that the BDA would be in effect before entry into force of the CWC.[24] The PrepCom considered three scenarios. If Russia and the USA are original states parties and the BDA is in effect, the number of inspectors

[16] The PrepCom budget is in 2 parts. Part I covers the 'steady-state' expenses for continued PTS staffing and the activities of the PrepCom from commencement of the PrepCom process until entry into force. Part II of the budget covers the build-up of staff and activities in the 6-month period immediately before entry into force. The calculated contribution of each signatory state is based on the UN Scale of Financial Assessments.

[17] Report of the Commission, PrepCom document PC-XIV/29, 27 July 1996.

[18] Institute for Defense and Disarmament Studies (note 11).

[19] The 13th session, on 18–22 Mar., was attended by 87 states; the 14th session, on 22–26 July, by 88 states; and the 15th session, on 16–20 Dec., by 90 states. PrepCom documents PC-XIII/CRP.3, 21 Mar. 1996; PC-XIV/29, 27 July 1996; and PC-XV/25, 21 Dec. 1996.

[20] See, e.g., the statements of Bulgaria, PrepCom document PC-XIV/15, 22 July 1996; Latin American and Caribbean Group, PrepCom document PC-XIV/19, 22 July 1996; New Zealand, PrepCom document PC-XIV/21, 24 July 1996; Pakistan, PrepCom document PC-XIV/23, 24 July 1996; and Chile, PrepCom document PC-XIV/27, 24 July 1996.

[21] Concerns have been raised that non-participation by Russia and the USA would turn the disarmament treaty into a non-proliferation compromise. The consequences of an entry into force without the United States of America and the Russian Federation: a proposal by the Islamic Republic of Iran, PrepCom document PC-XIV/12, 22 July 1996.

[22] The contributions of states are assessed in accordance with the UN Scale of Financial Assessments under which a state pays an amount based on the size of its GDP. In addition, the OPCW draft budget for 1997 was prepared on the assumption that 80 states will have ratified the CWC at entry into force, among them Russia and the USA, whose combined contribution to the OPCW budget based on the UN Scale of Financial Assessments will be approximately 30%. PrepCom document PC-XV/A/WP.3, 11 Sep. 1996.

[23] The US–Soviet/Russian Agreement [between the United States of America and the Union of Soviet Socialist Republics] on Destruction and Non-Production of Chemical Weapons and on the Measures to Facilitate the Multilateral Convention on Banning Chemical Weapons (BDA) was agreed by the Soviet Union and the USA on 1 June 1990. The full text is reproduced in *SIPRI Yearbook 1991: World Armaments and Disarmament* (Oxford University Press: Oxford, 1991), appendix 14A, pp. 536–39.

[24] The Executive Council may limit OPCW verification to measures complementary to those under other bilateral or multilateral agreements only if it considers that the verification provisions of such an agreement are consistent with those mentioned in Article IV, para. 13 of the CWC and Part IV(A) of the Verification Annex. The states parties to such an agreement must keep the OPCW fully informed.

required shortly after the CWC's entry into force will be 140 according to the original assumptions for the OPCW budget. If the BDA is not in place, then 210 inspectors will be required shortly after entry into force of the CWC. In both scenarios an additional 71 inspectors will be required six months after entry into force to provide adequate resources for the conduct of industry inspections. If Russia and the USA are not original states parties, the number of required inspectors shortly after entry into force will be 88, with an additional 62 inspectors needed six months later.[25] At one point Iran proposed to convene a high-level meeting before entry into force to consider the consequences and options if neither Russia nor the USA had become states parties,[26] but other countries dismissed the idea.

The need to plan and prepare for inspector training was another important issue. For most of 1996 uncertainty regarding the trigger point caused considerable concern as to whether the CWC time-lines for inspector training could be met.[27] In addition, the OPCW cannot employ citizens from states which are not parties to the CWC. This affects the recruitment of both inspectors and phase II staff.

The inspector recruitment process progressed as follows.[28] The selection of candidates for training group A, the majority of whom will conduct the initial inspections of declared CW-related facilities, was completed. The 150 selected trainees from 56 signatory states were scheduled to attend courses between 17 January and 30 May 1997.[29] The selection of candidates for training group B was not completed in 1996. As of 4 December 1996, 57 candidates from 26 signatory states had been provisionally selected.[30] This second group will not start its training programme until after entry into force. From both training groups, only those participants who are nationals from states parties and have successfully completed the course will be offered employment.[31]

The general training scheme[32] for the candidates is divided into three 'modules': a basic course (Module 1), a specialist course (Module 2) and an on-site trial inspection training (Module 3). These modules will take approximately

[25] Expert Group on Programme of Work and Budget, Secretariat Discussion Paper, Verification resources requirements: variations on a theme, PrepCom document EG PoWB, 9–24 Oct. 1996, PoWB paper no. 12, 3 Oct. 1996.

[26] The consequences of an entry into force without the United States of America and the Russian Federation: a proposal by the Islamic Republic of Iran (note 21).

[27] Note by the Executive Secretary, issues for consideration in the light of the current situation regarding ratification, PrepCom document PC-XIV/5, 4 July 1996.

[28] The elaborate verification regime provided for under the CWC involves systematic on-site inspections of declared CW-related military facilities. Routine verification will also be applied to chemical industry facilities which produce chemicals listed in 1 of the 3 schedules of the CWC. In addition, any facility on the territory of any state party can be subject to a challenge inspection. The training and recruitment process of the future inspectors of the OPCW has been designed to correspond to the initial inspection requirements immediately after entry into force. Provisional Technical Secretariat of the Preparatory Commission for the Organisation for the Prohibition of Chemical Weapons (note 14).

[29] The training will take place in China, the Czech Republic, Finland, France, Germany, India, Italy, Japan, the Netherlands, Romania, Russia, the Slovak Republic, Switzerland, the UK and the USA. PrepCom document, press release no. 127, 17 Jan. 1997.

[30] Report of the Executive Secretary, PrepCom document PC-XV/5, 12 Dec. 1996. pp. 13–14.

[31] PrepCom document, press release no. 127 (note 29).

[32] A definitive outline of the general training scheme was provided in a note by the Executive Secretary, PrepCom document PC-XV/B/10, 6 Nov. 1996.

five months to complete. A draft inspection manual, to be used during training, has been completed and was distributed to the training centres.[33]

Preparations for the First Session of the Conference of the States Parties in The Hague on 6 May 1997, which will mark the start of the OPCW, have begun.[34] The Executive Council and the Director-General of the Technical Secretariat will be elected, and draft agreements, provisions and guidelines prepared by the PrepCom will be considered and approved. A special body, the Committee on Preparations for the First Conference of States Parties, has been established to make the necessary administrative and logistical arrangements for the First Conference of States Parties, develop the rules of procedure and prepare the final report of the PrepCom.[35]

As in recent years, Article XI on economic and technological development received considerable attention in 1996.[36] The 'full and proper implementation' of the article was advocated by several delegations, who expressed the view that export controls are incompatible with the CWC, impede legitimate economic development and must be abandoned immediately after entry into force.[37] Opposing views were also expressed. Australia and several other signatory states argued that national export licensing measures which are applied on a non-discriminatory basis are consistent with Article XI and necessary to ensure compliance with the basic obligations in Article I not to assist any state or individual in any activity prohibited under the CWC.[38]

On 11 September the OPCW Laboratory and Equipment Store was officially opened in Rijswijk, the Netherlands. It will be fully operational by entry into force.

Working Group A[39]

The Expert Group on the Programme of Work and Budget prepared the 1997 budget of the PrepCom, which was later approved.[40] Part I of the budget (13 214 800 Dutch guilders) covers ongoing activities of the current staff and is complemented by the 1996 part II budget (30 403 600 guilders) which covers additional activities such as inspector training, procurement of equipment

---

[33] Report of the Executive Secretary (note 30).

[34] Report of the Executive Secretary (note 30). According to Article VIII of the CWC, the 1st session of the conference must be convened not later than 30 days after entry into force.

[35] The Committee on Preparations for the First Session of the States Parties, PrepCom document PC-XIV/29, 27 July 1996.

[36] Article XI aims at the fullest possible exchange among states parties of chemicals, equipment and scientific and technological information relating to the development and application of chemistry for purposes not prohibited by the CWC. States parties have undertaken to review their national regulations in this field in order to render them consistent with the object and purpose of the CWC.

[37] See, e.g., the Indian statement in PrepCom document PC-XIII/B/WP.7, 23 Feb. 1996.

[38] PrepCom document PC-XIII/B/WP.9, 26 Mar. 1996. Most Western states argue that Article I takes precedence over Article XI.

[39] Working Group A deals primarily with organizational issues, such as rules of procedure, staff and finance matters. The expert groups prepare recommendations on specific issues, which are then put forward to the working groups and the plenary sessions for approval. Provisional Technical Secretariat of the Preparatory Commission for the Organisation for the Prohibition of Chemical Weapons (note 14).

[40] Report of the Commission, PrepCom document PC-XV/25, 21 Dec. 1996.

and staff increases from the trigger point to entry into force.[41] The first draft of the 1997 OPCW budget, which will be the basis for discussions by signatory states, has been prepared and work on the preliminary draft has begun.[42] The draft OPCW financial regulations were finalized by the Finance Group and have now been approved.[43]

The Expert Group on the OPCW Headquarters and other Agreements continued to work on the draft OPCW headquarters agreement, which has also been provisionally approved.[44] Already during phase II more office space will be required to accommodate the increased number of personnel. As the OPCW building is not expected to be completed before mid-1998, a consequence of unanticipated problems, additional temporary office space will have to be found.

Working Group B[45]

In 1996 the expert groups under Working Group B developed detailed inspection procedures for verification activities at industrial sites and CW storage and destruction facilities. It was originally anticipated that the expert groups would develop agreed procedures well in advance of the trigger point, which would then be considered and approved by the First Conference of States Parties. By the end of 1996, however, some aspects still required full agreement.

The Expert Group on Chemical Industry Issues made progress on the draft model agreements for schedule 1 and 2 facilities.[46] Work on a draft Declaration Handbook is close to completion.[47] Sections A (general introduction), B (industrial declarations) and C (declarations required under Part VI[48] of the Verification Annex) of the handbook progressed the furthest.[49] However, a number of issues relevant to the submission of declarations remained unresolved. These include the method of reporting aggregate national data for chemicals listed on schedules 2 and 3 of the CWC, the definition of discrete organic chemicals and agreement on scheduled chemicals in low concentrations.[50] Unless such issues are resolved by entry into force, states parties may

[41] Prorated 1997 Part I Programme of Work and Budget of the Commission, PrepCom document PC-XV/A/WP.2/Rev.1, 12 Nov. 1996; and Eleventh Report of the Expert Group on Programme of Work and Budget, PrepCom document PC-XI/A/WP.5, 16 June 1995.

[42] Report of the Executive Secretary (note 30).

[43] Draft report of the Commission, PrepCom document PC-XIII/CRP.3, 21 Mar. 1996.

[44] This approval will become final if no objections from any delegation are received by 10 Jan. 1997. Report of the Executive Secretary (note 30).

[45] Working Group B is responsible for the development of detailed procedures for verification and technical cooperation and assistance. Provisional Technical Secretariat of the Preparatory Commission for the Organisation for the Prohibition of Chemical Weapons (note 14).

[46] Report of the Executive Secretary (note 30).

[47] The Declaration Handbook contains the forms to be used for the initial declarations to be submitted to the OPCW not later than 30 days after entry into force. Report of the Executive Secretary (note 30).

[48] Part VI addresses 'Activities not prohibited under this Convention in accordance with article VI, regime for Schedule 1 chemicals and facilities related to such chemicals'.

[49] Report of the Executive Secretary (note 30).

[50] Report of the Executive Secretary (note 30); and Report of the Commission (note 40).

have to decide on a national basis how to handle them when submitting their initial declarations.[51]

The Expert Group on Chemical Weapons Issues was split into two groups in 1996.[52] Group 1 concentrated on the development of model facility agreements for CW storage, production and destruction facilities. Group 2 focused on developing inspection procedures for verification of destruction of CW stockpiles and former CW production facilities. Criteria for toxicity, corrosiveness and other technical factors remain unresolved.

There was limited progress on the draft model facility agreement for CW destruction facilities.[53] The issue of installation of continuous monitoring instruments is still being considered.[54] Group II discussed the criteria to determine the acceptability of a converted CW production facility for the production of highly toxic chemicals and the quantification of the destruction endpoint for chemical weapons.[55] Some progress was achieved on the issue of 'levelling out'.[56]

The Expert Group on Old and Abandoned CW continued to work on the development of guidelines for determining the usability of chemical weapons produced between 1925 and 1946 and on other old and abandoned CW issues, including costs associated with verification of their destruction.[57]

The first draft of a handbook on chemicals was distributed to signatory states for comment. This handbook will become an appendix to the Declaration Handbook. It notes the most common chemical substances covered under the three schedules of the CWC. The draft lists 400 chemicals. Its aim is to assist states parties in identifying declarable activities.[58]

The Expert Group on Confidentiality considered issues related to the exercise of jurisdiction and compensation for losses caused by breaches of confidentiality as well as practical steps to implement the draft OPCW confidentiality policy.[59]

Revised model legislation for national implementation of the CWC was published by the PrepCom on 31 May.[60] A report of the Executive Secretary on 12 December stated that the PTS was aware of the fact that there had been little progress in drafting national implementation legislation in a number of

[51] Report of the Executive Secretary (note 30).
[52] PrepCom document PC-XIV/29 (note 17).
[53] Report of the Executive Secretary (note 30).
[54] Report of the Executive Secretary (note 30).
[55] Report of the Executive Secretary (note 30).
[56] Levelling out refers to the concept of agreed levels of destruction of CW (para. 15, Part IV(A) of the Verification Annex) or chemical weapon production facilities (para. 28, Part V of the Verification Annex) within time periods specified by the convention. The order of destruction of CW is also based on the principle of levelling out. This means that when several states parties possess CW at entry into force, the state(s) possessing larger amounts are required to destroy them at a faster pace than the state(s) possessing less. Verification Annex, Part IV(A) para. 15. The same principle applies to CW production facilities. Verification Annex, Part V, para. 28.
[57] Report of the Executive Secretary (note 30).
[58] Note by the Secretariat, Handbook on Chemicals, Appendix 2 of the OPCW Declaration Handbook, PrepCom document, 28 Aug. 1996.
[59] Report of the Executive Secretary (note 30).
[60] Note by the Executive Secretary, model national implementing legislation, PrepCom document PC-XI/7/Rev.1, 31 May 1996.

states.[61] Governments were reminded that, according to Article VII, each state party is required to adopt the measures necessary to implement its obligations under the CWC.

III. Other arms control and disarmament activities

CW destruction

The Russian Federation

The Russian Federation ratified neither the BDA nor the CWC in 1996. On 27 December the State Duma passed a comprehensive CW destruction act on its third reading by a vote of 345–0 with one abstention.[62] It is based on a revised Russian CW destruction programme entitled 'Special federal programme, destruction of CW stockpiles in the Russian Federation'[63] (decree no. 305, see table 13.1). Decree 305, introduced on 21 March 1996, calls for on-site CW destruction to begin in 1998. It also envisages conversion of CW agents.[64] There have been at least two previous draft destruction plans for Russia's chemical weapon stockpile, issued in 1992 and 1994, respectively.[65] Russia has a declared stockpile of approximately 40 000 agent tonnes. Destruction operations were not begun in 1996.

[61] Report of the Executive Secretary (note 30).

[62] Parrish, S., 'Duma passes law on chemical weapons destruction', Open Media Research Institute (OMRI), *OMRI Daily Digest*, 2 Jan. 1997, URL <http://search.omri.cz>; Interfax, 27 Dec. 1996, 'Russian Duma passes law on destruction of chemical weapons'. Version current on 14 Jan. 1996, URL <http://www.maximov.com/News/recent.cgi?ref=1337>. The act was introduced in the Duma in Dec. 1995. Stock, T., Haug, M. and Radler, P., 'Chemical and biological weapon developments and arms control', *SIPRI Yearbook 1996: Armaments, Disarmament and International Security* (Oxford University Press: Oxford, 1996), chapter 15, p. 667. On 23 Jan. 1997, however, the Federation Council, the legislative upper house, rejected the bill. From the *Segodnya* newscast presented by announcer Andrey, NTV (Moscow), 0900 GMT 23 Jan. 1997 (in Russian), in 'Russia: Council rejects law on chemical weapons disposal', Foreign Broadcast Information Service, *Daily Report–Soviet Union (FBIS-SOV)*, FBIS-SOV-97-015, 24 Jan. 1997. The bill can be considered by a joint committee. Alternatively, the bill could be passed by 2/3 of the Duma in a 2nd vote. Article 105 of the Constitution of the Russian Federation.

[63] Russian Federation, Special federal programme, destruction of chemical weapons stockpiles in the Russian Federation, PrepCom document PC-XIV/B/WP.7, 25 June 1996; and 'Federalnaya tselevaya programma' [Special federal program], *Rossiyskaya Gazeta*, 2 Apr. 1996, pp. 5–6. Russian CW are stored at Kambarka, Udmurtia Republic; Gorny, Saratov oblast; Kizner, Udmurtia Republic; Maradikovsky, Kirov oblast; Pochep, Bryansk oblast; Leonidovka, Penza oblast; and Shchuchye, Kurgan oblast.

[64] Major-General Victor Kholstov, commander of Russia's Chemical, Radiological and Bacteriological Troops, has been quoted as saying that conversion of blister agents will occur. Yurkin, A., ITAR-TASS (Moscow), 1712 GMT 23 Jan. 1996 (in English), in 'Russian army commander: Russia willing to scrap chemical weapons', FBIS-SOV-96-016, 24 Jan. 1996. Additional details of decree 305 are provided in Stock, Haug and Radler (note 62)

[65] Russian Federation, Comprehensive program for the Multistage Destruction of Chemical Weapons in the Russian Federation (draft), 1992. Russian Federation, Conception: Destruction of Chemical Armament (draft), 1994. Stockpile estimates between the 1994 and 1996 draft destruction plans differ in 2 respects. The 1994 plan stated that 2% of Russia's CW mustard–lewisite mixture was weaponized (i.e., prepared to be delivered as weapons). In the 1996 plan the number is 40%. The 1994 plan also stated that 10% of Russia's lewisite was weaponized. The number given in the 1996 plan is 2%. In general, the 1996 plan is more concise than previous plans.

Table 13.1. Breakdown of expenditures and financing of Russian chemical weapon stockpile destruction

Figures are in b. roubles at 1995 prices. Figures in brackets are inconsistent with totals but appear so in the Russian-language original.

Breakdown of expenditures	Duration of financing (years)	1995[a]	1996	1997	1998	1999	2000–2005	2006–2009	Total financing
Safety measures	15	2.7	6.4	60.9	38.3	37.3	145.8	9.0	**300.4**
Scientific/experimental testing	6	28.5	20.1	210.3	108.4	78.2	35.4	..	**480.9**
Establishment of CWDFs and solid waste storage areas (total)	..	..	..	..	..	..	..	..	**2 876.6**
Construction of CWDFs	15	27.0	40.6	609.4	765.0	638.1	277.0	180.0[b]	**[2 561.6]**
Construction of solid waste storage areas	12	..	..	..	15.0	70.0	230.0	24.5[b]	**[315.0]**
Operation of CWDFs and solid waste storage areas (including closure)	12	..	..	..	23.5	73.6	2 655.9	328.4	**3 081.4**
Implementation of federal destruction laws	13	..	..	298.6	314.3	394.3	1 535.6	457.2	**[3 300.0[c]]**
Ensuring readiness of CWSFs and CWDFs for international inspection[d]	10	..	0.1	7.8	5.0	5.9	32.0	..	**50.8**
Other expenditures	15	11.2	76.9	908.7	543.9	646.5	3 750.6	614.1	**6 551.9**
Total		69.4	144.1	2 095.7	1 813.4	1 943.9	8 662.3	1 613.2	**[16 642.0]**

CWDF = chemical weapon destruction facility, CWSF = chemical weapon storage facility.

[a] Figures for each year or period of years represent total financing for the year or period.
[b] The indicated amount will be spent on completion of infrastructure elements at CWDFs and solid waste storage areas.
[c] 300 b. roubles are provided for possible one-time compensation for damage to health or property in the event of an accident.
[d] Russia will appropriate necessary funding to guarantee that national and international inspections are conducted according to the provisions of the CWC.

Source: 'Federalnaya tselevaya programma' [Special federal programme], *Rossiyskaya Gazeta*, 2 Apr. 1996, pp. 5–6; and Russian Federation, 'Special federal programme, destruction of chemical weapons stockpiles in the Russian Federation', PrepCom document PC-XIV/B/WP.7, 25 June 1996, pp 19–20.

Chemical weapon destruction efforts were hindered by a lack of funding, including a failure to allocate funds earmarked for CW destruction, and by local and federal opposition to the draft destruction plan and the manner in which it has been implemented.[66] Hearings on CW destruction held by the Duma Committee on the Environment on 21 May also demonstrated that a number of fundamental aspects of destruction, including choice of destruction technologies, were either unfamiliar or objectionable to a significant number of those who spoke during the hearings.[67]

Russian officials continued to emphasize the need for foreign financial assistance to be able to carry out destruction,[68] which they estimated as amounting to at least 35–50 per cent of the total destruction cost.[69] The total cost of destruction was estimated at between $3.3 billion[70] and $5 billion.[71] Foreign assistance for destruction of Russian chemical weapons will probably depend in part, however, on whether Russia ratifies the CWC.[72]

Germany continued to assist with the destruction of lewisite at Gorny. It provided 'mobile and stationary laboratories' as well as equipment to ensure the safe transfer of lewisite from its storage containers and for decontamination. By the end of 1996 an estimated 25 million Deutschmarks (DM) had been spent since 1993, when the programme began.[73] The *Netherlands* officially announced it will offer assistance for the destruction of the lewisite stockpiled at Kambarka.[74] An agreement of intent was signed between the Netherlands and Russia.[75] The total amount spent will be approximately 5 mil-

[66] Primarily because of perceived inadequate participation by groups and individuals outside the Russian military establishment in the Russian CW destruction process.

[67] Green Cross, Russia, organized a 2nd on-site hearing in Izhevsk on 14–16 May 1996. Green Cross, Russia, 'Final document, the second public hearing on the problem of the chemical weapons destruction in the area of the town of Kambarka', Izhevsk, Russia, 14–16 May 1996; and Government of Udmurtia Republic and the National Organization of International Green Cross, Russia, 'Vtoriye publichnyie slushaniya po probleme unitchtozheniya khimicheskogo oruzhiya' [Second public hearings on the problem of chemical weapon destruction], Izhevsk, Russia, 14–16 May 1996. The Moscow Center for Policy Studies in Russia (PIR Center) published interviews with leading officials and experts on Russian CW destruction. *Khimicheskoe oruzhiye i problemy ego unichtozheniya* [Chemical weapons and problems of their destruction], no. 1 (PIR Center: Moscow, spring 1996); and 'Interviu mesyatsa' [Interview of the month] with Col.-Gen. S. Petrov, *Yadernii kontrol*, no. 13 (PIR Center: Moscow, Jan. 1996), pp. 2–6.

[68] Parrish, S., 'Deputy: Russia needs foreign assistance to destroy chemical weapons', *OMRI Daily Digest*, no. 141, part I (23 July 1996). Statement by the delegation of the Russian Federation at the fifteenth session of the Preparatory Commission for the Organisation for the Prohibition of Chemical Weapons (note 10).

[69] US General Accounting Office (GAO), *Weapons of Mass Destruction: Reducing the Threat from the Former Soviet Union*, appendix II, 'Destruction and dismantlement projects, CTR: an update', GAO/NSIAD-95-165 (US General Accounting Office: Washington, DC, 9 June 1995), p. 17.

[70] Parrish (note 68).

[71] 'West to help in safe but costly disposal of Russia's CW stocks', *Jane's Defence Weekly*, vol. 26, no. 6 (7 Aug. 1996), p. 15.

[72] 'West to help in safe but costly disposal of Russia's CW stocks' (note 71).

[73] Striedl, E., Office for Military Sciences, Munich, Germany, Private communication on 'German assistance for the destruction of chemical weapons in Russia', 4 Dec. 1996.

[74] 'West to help in safe but costly disposal of Russia's CW stocks' (note 71).

[75] Yurkin, A., ITAR-TASS (Moscow), 1222 GMT 11 Nov. 1996 (in English), in 'Russia: general says financial aid needed to eliminate chemical arms', FBIS-SOV-96-219, 13 Nov. 1996. Dutch assistance will focus on 4 projects: (*a*) soil remediation, (*b*) assistance with treatment of people who come in contact with lewisite, (*c*) provision of a mobile analytical laboratory to assess the environmental impact of destruction operations, and (*d*) development of the means to transfer lewisite into smaller containers. The initial emphasis will be on soil remediation, which is scheduled to begin in 1997 or 1998. The

lion guilders per year for five years. The *Swedish* National Defence Research Establishment (FOA) continued the second phase of its assistance programme for the Kambarka facility, worth 2.6 million Swedish crowns.[76] FOA is offering to examine ways to reduce the risk of accidents during storage or destruction operations. It will also investigate ways of minimizing the consequences of an accident.[77] *Finland* was reportedly considering destruction assistance to Russia within the framework of the Dutch programme. *Italy* was also reported to be considering destruction assistance.[78]

US assistance for Russian CW destruction is allocated within the framework of the Cooperative Threat Reduction (CTR) programme, also known as the Nunn–Lugar programme.[79] The CTR programme is scheduled to end in 2001. Between 1992 and 5 August 1996, 5 per cent of both the total amount of CTR funds obligated ($1 040 790 810) and the total amount disbursed ($571 064 508) were spent on the CW component. Sixty million dollars out of a total of $73 million allocated for Russian CW destruction for fiscal year (FY) 1996 were removed, however, when President Clinton did not certify to Congress that Russia was in compliance with international obligations related to biological weapons.[80] In 1996 US assistance focused on the construction of a pilot CW destruction facility at Shchuchye[81] and the establishment of a central CW destruction analytical laboratory in Moscow.[82] In late autumn the United States awarded a $600 million contract for the construction of a pilot CW destruction facility at Shchuchye.[83] It also awarded a $5.7 million contract

remaining 3 projects are still in the early planning stages. Their future may depend on how the soil-remediation project progresses. Private communication with TNO Prins Maurits Laboratory (Netherlands Organisation for Applied Scientific Research), 24 May 1996.

[76] Könberg, M., 'Swedish–Russian cooperation project concerning the lewisite storage facility in Kambarka', Paper presented at the Conference on Dismantlement and Destruction of Nuclear, Chemical and Conventional Weapons, Bonn, Germany, 19–21 May 1996, p. 5.

[77] Könberg (note 76), p. 2. A risk analysis was produced during the 1st phase worth 1 million Swedish crowns (approximately $125 000).

[78] Unattributed report: 'Finland and the Netherlands to clear up weapons in Russia', *NRC Handelsblad* (Rotterdam) 23 Feb. 1996, p. 7 (in Dutch), in 'Netherlands, Finland to participate in Russian CW cleanup project', Foreign Broadcast Information Service, *Daily Report–Arms Control & Proliferation Issues (FBIS-TAC)*, FBIS-TAC-96-004, 20 Mar 1996; and 'West to help in safe but costly disposal of Russia's CW stocks' (note 71).

[79] See also chapter 11 in this volume. Senators Sam Nunn and Richard Lugar co-sponsored the original authorizing legislation in 1991.

[80] US GAO, *Weapons of Mass Destruction: Status of the Cooperative Threat Reduction Program*, GAO/NSIAD-96-222 (US General Accounting Office: Washington, DC, Sep. 1996), pp. 19, 21, 28–29. A total of $68 million was allocated for Russian CW destruction in 1992–96. Funding for the elimination of former Soviet BW research facilities was included for the first time in the FY 1997 Department of Defense request for funding.

[81] *Specifications for Engineering Management Support (EMS) for a Russian Chemical Weapons Destruction Facility*, CTR document, request for proposal, DACA87-96-R-0031 (Engineering and Support Center, Huntsville, Ala., 16 Aug. 1996).

[82] Lajoie, R. (Maj.-Gen.), 'US support to the Russian CW destruction program', Paper presented at Conference on Dismantlement and Destruction of Nuclear, Chemical and Conventional Weapons, Bonn, Germany, 19–21 May 1996, pp. 1, 5. See also decree no. 1447 of 7 Dec. 1996, 'O sozdanii tsentralnoi laboratorii po chimiko-analiticheskomu kontroliu za rabotami v oblasti khimicheskoro razaruzheniu' [On the establishment of a central chemical analytical laboratory for work in the area of chemical disarmament], *Rossiyskaya Gazeta*, 19 Dec. 1996.

[83] US GAO (note 80), p. 21; *Specifications for Engineering Management Support (EMS) for a Russian Chemical Weapons Destruction Facility* (note 81); 'Russian demil plant', *Military Engineer*,

on 18 October 1996 for design and renovation of the central analytical laboratory in Moscow.[84]

US chemical weapon destruction assistance to Russia is closely associated with a continuing joint evaluation of Russia's nerve agent destruction technology. The Russian–US Joint Evaluation Program on the Russian two-stage nerve agent destruction process, which is being conducted within the framework of the BDA and a 1994 Plan of Work addendum to the agreement, was initiated in part because the USA wished to learn more about a technology with which it was unfamiliar before allocating money to support it.[85] The exercise was also viewed as useful in promoting closer cooperation between the two countries. A technical report was issued in March 1996 following a review of test results by a six-member Peer Review Committee composed of three Americans and three Russians.[86] Further activities related to the optimization of the technology for scaled-up destruction at Shchuchye were continued in 1996. The criteria for successful evaluation of the technology were to demonstrate the effectiveness of the technology in irreversibly destroying both Russian and US nerve agents,[87] the safety of the technology and the 'scientific credibility of the technology'.[88] All criteria were met or exceeded. A destruction efficiency of 99.999 per cent or higher, for example, was achieved.[89] Another result of the joint evaluation was the provision by the USA of approximately $4.7 million worth of analytical equipment.[90]

CW destruction in the United States

The US chemical weapon stockpile is stored at nine locations (see table 13.2). In January 1996 the USA declassified additional information about its stock-

vol. 88, no. 579 (Aug./Sep. 1996), p. 12; and 'Parsons selected for Russian chemical weapons destruction facility', *San Marino Tribune* (California), 19 Dec. 1996.

[84] US Army, 'Corps awards contracts for projects in Russia, Egypt', *Contract Announcement*, no. 96-17 (21 Oct. 1996), pp. 1–2.

[85] US GAO (note 69), p. 5.

[86] The technology for destruction of G-agents (sarin and soman) consists of, first, mixing them with monoethanolamine and water. Second, the reaction products are combined with calcium hydroxide and bitumen. For V agents, the first step is to treat the agent with a mixture known as RD-4. Bitumen is then added to the initial reaction products. The bitumenized final product has a level IV toxicity (the lowest level) on the Russian toxicity scale. Bechtel National, Inc. and US Army Program Manager for Cooperative Threat Reduction (PM-CTR), *Joint Evaluation of the Russian Two-Stage Chemical Agent Destruction Process, Final Technical Report: Phases 1 & 2* (Bechtel National, Inc. and US Army Program Manager for Cooperative Threat Reduction, July 1996 revision).

[87] The CWC requires that each destruction technology be 'essentially irreversible', para. 12, Part IV (A) of the Verification Annex. A single-stage chemical reaction would not meet this requirement because, in principle, such reactions are reversible. Using a 2-stage process helps to address this requirement.

[88] Bechtel National, Inc. and US Army Program Manager for Cooperative Threat Reduction (note 86), p. xiv.

[89] One of the original criteria was to achieve a destruction efficiency of 99.99%. The CWC does not provide a quantitative standard of destruction efficiency. Bechtel National, Inc. and US Army Program Manager for Cooperative Threat Reduction (note 86), p. 77. The Expert Group on Chemical Weapon Destruction Facilities was unable to reach agreement on the issue of completeness of destruction. Expert Group on Chemical Weapons Destruction Facilities, Interim Report, PrepCom document PC-V/B/WP.17, 3 Dec. 1993, para. 13, p. 8.

[90] Lajoie (note 82), p. 5.

Table 13.2. The US chemical weapon stockpile

Facility	Type of munition	Total (tonnes)
JACADS	H, HD (C,P), sarin (P), VX (P, M, TC)	1 001
Edgewood, Maryland	HD (TC)	1 624
Anniston, Alabama	HD (C, P, TC), GB (C, P, R) VX (P, R, M)	2 254
Blue Grass, Kentucky	H, HD (P), GB (P, R), VX (P, R)	523
Newport, Indiana	VX (TC)	1 269
Pine Bluff, Arkansas	HD (TC), GB (R), VX (R, M)	3 850
Pueblo, Colorado	HT and HD (C, P)	2 611
Tooele, Utah	H, HT, and HD (C, P, TC), GB (C, P, R, B, TC), VX (P, R, M, ST, TC)	13 616
Umatilla, Oregon	HD (TC), GB (P, R, B), VX (P, R, M, ST)	3 717

C = projectiles, B = bombs, GB = sarin, H = form of undistilled mustard, HD = distilled sulphur mustard, HT = runcol mustard (mixture of (bis-(2-chloroethylthioethyl) and bis-(2-chloroethyl) sulphide), M = mine, R = rocket, ST = spray tank, TC = ton container and P = projectile.

Source: Lajoie, R. (Maj.-Gen.), 'US support to the Russian CW destruction program', Paper presented at Conference on Dismantlement and Destruction of Nuclear, Chemical and Conventional Weapons, Bonn, Germany, 19–21 May 1996.

pile. The amount of unitary CW agents is 30 599.55 tonnes; binary components 680.19 tonnes; research, development, test and evaluation inventory 4 363.88 kilograms (kg); and recovered munitions and similar 'non-stockpile' items 6 133.55 kg.[91]

Large-scale destruction operations were begun at Tooele, Utah, on 22 August 1996. A federal judge overruled a request for an injunction against destruction operations and allowed the facility to start work.[92] As of 13 January 1997, the facility had destroyed 53 997.75 kg of GB (sarin) agent and 11 472 M55 GB rockets.[93] Destruction of all mustard agent stored in ton containers, sarin stored in rockets, bombs and ton containers, and VX stored in rockets was completed at the Johnston Atoll Chemical Agent Disposal System (JACADS), located south-west of Hawaii.[94] As of 5 November 1996,

[91] Private communication (telefacsimile) with US delegation to the CWC PrepCom, 6 Feb. 1996. See also 'US chemical weapon stockpile declaration', *Trust & Verify*, no. 65 (Apr. 1996), p. 2.

[92] Associated Press, 'US to destroy toxic weapons', 21 Aug. 1996, URL: <http://www.boston.com/globe/cgi-bin/waisgate.cgi?/WAICdocID=0570828876+1+0+0&WAISaction=retrieve>.

[93] Program Manager for Chemical Demilitarization, 'Tooele processed munition total'. Version current on 15 Jan. 1997, URL <http://www-pmcd.apgea.army.mil/TOTAL/tocdf.html>.

[94] Lajoie (note 82).

99 8604.41 kg and 180 796 munitions had been destroyed.[95] A total of $672 250 were allocated for CW destruction for FY 1996.[96] The total cost of destroying the US stockpile is estimated at $12.4 billion.[97]

While incineration continues to be the US Army's 'baseline' destruction technology, the process of choosing possible alternative destruction technologies continued in accordance with Public Law 102-484, which requires the army to consider alternative destruction technologies for destruction of bulk agent.[98]

All but three of an original 23 external proposals were eliminated by the army. Prior industrial application of the proposed destruction technology was one of the key considerations, as was the requirement that the destruction technology be sufficiently developed to allow destruction of the stockpiles in Aberdeen (Maryland) and Newport (Indiana) to be completed no later than 31 December 2004.[99] The three proposals, plus two developed by the army, were then evaluated by the National Academy of Sciences.[100] The five technologies are: stand-alone neutralization, neutralization followed by biodegradation, molten metal catalytic extraction process, high-temperature gas phase reduction and Silver II electrochemical oxidation.[101]

Both the army and the National Research Council recommend that the technology for neutralization followed by the biodegradation of reaction products, which was developed by the army, be used to destroy the mustard stored in bulk at Aberdeen.[102] They also recommend use of the technology for neutralization followed by mineralization of resulting hydrolysates to destroy the VX stored in bulk at the Newport Chemical Depot.[103]

[95] Program Manager for Chemical Demilitarization, 'Processed munitions totals at Johnston Island'. Version current on 15 Jan. 1997, URL <http://www-pmcd.apgea.army.mil/TOTAL/jitotal.html>.

[96] 'Defense spending', Congressional Quarterly, vol. 54, no. 27 (6 July 1996), p. 1928.

[97] US GAO, Chemical Weapons and Materiel, Key Factors Affecting Disposal Costs and Schedule, GAO/NSIAD9718 (US General Accounting Office: Washington, DC, Feb. 1997), p. 4.

[98] Technical and Economic Analysis Comparing Alternative Chemical Demilitarization Technologies to the Baseline: US Army Material Systems Analysis Activity, Summary Report, special publication no. 75, vol. 1 (US Army: Aberdeen Proving Ground, Md., July 1996), p. 1.

[99] Technical and Economic Analysis Comparing Alternative Chemical Demilitarization Technologies to the Baseline: US Army Material Systems Analysis Activity (note 98), pp. 2, 5.

[100] Panel on Review and Evaluation of Alternative Chemical Disposal Technologies, Board on Army Science and Technology, Commission on Engineering and Technical Systems, and National Research Council, Review and Evaluation of Alternative Chemical Disposal Technologies (National Research Council: Washington, DC, 1996).

[101] 'Alternative technologies identified for further review', Chemical Demilitarization Update, vol. 4, issue 1 (Mar. 1996), p. 3.

[102] US Army Chemical Stockpile Disposal Program, 'Neutralization/biodegradation of mustard agent HD', information sheet. Version current on 15 Jan. 1997, URL <http://www-pmcd.apgea.army.mil/alttech/neutbio.html>.

[103] US Army Chemical Stockpile Disposal Program, 'Neutralization/mineralization of nerve agent VX', information sheet. Version current on 15 Jan. 1997, URL <http://www-pmcd.apgea.army.mil/alttech/neutmin.html>.

Old and abandoned chemical weapons[104]

The *Soviet Union* has reportedly dumped 'small quantities' of chemical weapons into the Black Sea.[105] Ukraine said that dumping of CW by the Soviet Navy during or just after World War II caused $20 billion worth of damage to the environment. Ukraine's Ministry of Defence asked the Russian Government to investigate the matter.[106]

On 14 May–3 June, a Japanese delegation conducted its sixth fact-finding mission to China to investigate CW abandoned there by Japan after World War II. The delegation, which included representatives from the Ministry for Foreign Affairs and the Defence Agency, as well as non-governmental experts, visited the Haerbaling district in Tongyu, Jilin Province.[107] Evidence of the presence of 770 000 chemical munitions was found.[108] This is less than a previous Chinese estimate of 1.8–2 million.[109] Approximately 90 per cent of the weapons are said to be located in the Haerbaling area.[110] Japan is apparently prepared to construct one or more destruction facilities to eliminate these weapons, and destruction could begin in 1998.[111] The multi-billion dollar project will run for 10–15 years.[112] In Japan, government sources described a plan to build an offshore chemical demilitarization facility in Japanese territorial waters close to a port in north-eastern China which will reportedly cost approximately $5.5 billion.[113] On 17 December 1996 officials from the Chinese and Japanese ministries for foreign affairs met in Beijing for a fourth

---

[104] The CWC defines 'abandoned chemical weapons' as 'chemical weapons, including old chemical weapons, abandoned by a State after 1 Jan. 1925 on the territory of another State without the consent of the latter'(art. II, para. 6). It defines 'old chemical weapons' as '(a) chemical weapons which were produced before 1925, or (b) chemical weapons produced in the period between 1925 and 1946 that have deteriorated to such an extent that they can no longer be used as chemical weapons' (art. II, para. 5). An abandoning state party has an obligation to destroy chemical weapons it abandoned on the territory of another state party (art. I, para. 3). Each state party is also obliged to destroy CW which are located in any place under its jurisdiction (art. I, para. 2). The regime for destruction of old and/or abandoned CW is in Part IV(B) of the Verification Annex of the CWC.

[105] 'Russian admiral objects to US presence in Black Sea', *OMRI Daily Digest*, vol. 2, no. 161 (20 Aug. 1996).

[106] 'Soviet chemical dumping', *Jane's Defence Weekly*, vol. 25, no. 6 (17 Apr. 1996), p. 6.

[107] 'Japan sets chemical-arms hunt', *International Herald Tribune*, 9 May 1996, p. 4.

[108] 'China arms dump is surveyed', *International Herald Tribune*, 4 June 1996, p. 4; and Karniol, R., 'Japan set to clean up its chemical hangover', *Jane's Defence Weekly*, vol. 26, no. 9 (28 Aug. 1996), p. 17.

[109] 'Some information on discovered chemical weapons abandoned in China by a foreign state', Conference on Disarmament document CD/1127, CD/CW/WP.384, 18 Feb. 1992; 'China arms dump is surveyed' (note 108); and Stock, Haug and Radler (note 62), p. 665.

[110] Kyodo (Tokyo), 0840 GMT 14 Dec. 1996 (in English), in 'Japan, China: Japan to propose disposal of chemical weapons in China', Foreign Broadcast Information Service, *Daily Report–East Asia (FBIS-EAS)*, FBIS-EAS-96-242, 17 Dec. 1996.

[111] 'Yaponiya izbavit Kitai ot svoego khimoruzhiya' (Japan will free China of chemical weapons), *Krasnaya Zvezda*, 4 Jan. 1996, p. 3; and Karniol (note 108). For information on choice of destruction technologies, see 'M4's molten metal process selected by Japanese firm for chemical weapons cleanup, M4 limited partnership', *Press Release*. Version current on 15 Jan. 1997, URL: <http://m4web.m4lp.com:80/newsris/MITSUBIS.html>.

[112] 'Yaponiya izbavit Kitai ot svoego khimoruzhiya' (note 111).

[113] '17–28 September', *Chemical Weapons Convention Bulletin*, no. 34 (Dec. 1996), pp. 23–24.

round of intergovernmental talks.[114] The Japanese delegation reportedly planned to request China to allow construction of a CW destruction facility approximately 1000 km north-east of Beijing.[115] While Japan prefers to construct a CW destruction facility on Chinese territory, citing the risk of moving chemical weapons in dangerously poor condition, China reportedly prefers that Japan construct a destruction facility outside Chinese territory.[116]

IV. Biological weapon control

In 1996 there was intensive diplomatic activity in the area of biological weapon disarmament. Work was continued in the Ad Hoc Group, which was established by a Special Conference of States Parties in September 1994. The Fourth Review Conference of the parties to the BTWC was held in Geneva on 25 November–6 December 1996 and endorsed further intensification of the discussions in the Ad Hoc Group.

Work of the Ad Hoc Group

The Ad Hoc Group established by the 1994 Special Conference has a mandate to consider verification measures and other proposals to strengthen the BTWC treaty regime to be included in a legally binding instrument. In order to facilitate the negotiations four Friends of the Chair (FoC) were appointed to preside over each of the mandated topics.[117] The Ad Hoc Group held three sessions in 1995 and two in 1996.[118] The group completed its fifth session on 27 September without finalizing its mandated work. Believing that it none the less had made substantial progress, it submitted its report to the Fourth Review Conference for further consideration and endorsement.[119]

In the FoC group dealing with measures to promote compliance, some ideas on declaration of biological defence facilities or programmes, investigations to address a non-compliance concern and on-site investigatory measures appeared to be moving to the centre of a future regime. Another, but less developed, section of the FoC report deals with other mandatory non-challenge visits to facilities to strengthen confidence in the accuracy of declarations and to deter non-compliance. The section on declarations contains a preliminary list of types of biological defence and other relevant facilities, although their definitions will be the subject of future negotiations. In particu-

[114] Kyodo (Tokyo), 0737GMT 13 Dec. 1996 (in English), in 'Japan: talks with PRC over chemical arms disposal set for 17 Dec.', FBIS-EAS-96-241; and Kyodo (note 110).

[115] United Press International (UPI), 'Japan wary of moving WWII China weapons', 14 Dec. 1996, URL <http://biz.yahoo.com/upi/96/12/14/international_news/japanchina_1.html>.

[116] The principle of on-site destruction may have been agreed to following the Dec. bilateral discussions. Platkovskii, A., 'Khimarsenali unitchtozhat na meste' [Chemical arsenals to be destroyed on-site], *Izvestiya*, 20 Dec. 1996, p. 3.

[117] Stock, Haug and Radler (note 62), pp. 688–89.

[118] United Nations Information Service, 'Working group on strengthening of Biological Weapons Convention completes session without finalising work', DC/2561 (27 Sep. 1996), extracted in *Disarmament Diplomacy*, no. 9 (Oct. 1996), pp. 42–43.

[119] BWC/AD HOC GROUP/32, 27 Sep. 1996, p. 3.

lar, the bracketing of parts of the text in the Procedural Report of the fifth session indicates that the negotiators have begun to suggest language for a legally binding document.[120] Broad agreement exists that on-site verification provisions are the key to strengthening the BTWC treaty regime. Some caution has been voiced regarding the modelling of the challenge and non-challenge on-site visits on the CWC without giving due regard to the fundamentally different nature of biological weapons.[121]

By the end of the September session the FoC group on terms and definitions had set up several lists of terms and criteria that require further defining. The first list consists of terms with elements that might need to be discussed in considering the definitions. The second list contains definitions of terms and commentaries that were dealt with in informal consultations and which require further consultation. Other lists itemize human, animal and plant pathogens considered relevant to the development of a list of BW agents. Criteria for each of these groups were also discussed. The FoC group also held preliminary discussions on the potential role of threshold quantities for specific measures to strengthen the BTWC.[122] Much work remains, but agreement 'that it would be useful to have certain terms defined to assist the work of the Compliance Measures Group'[123] demonstrated that at least these two FoCs moved towards consolidating their work into proposals for a legally binding framework.[124]

The FoC group on confidence and transparency measures considered propositions that 'would be voluntary and non-mandatory, and . . . could be included, as appropriate, into a legally binding instrument'.[125] Several lists of measures were proposed: surveillance of publications, surveillance of legislation, and collection of data on transfers and transfer requests and on production, multilateral information sharing, exchange visits and confidence-building visits.[126] This group proceeded with little controversy partly because uncertainty still exists regarding the final application of the confidence-building measures (CBMs) and partly because of the agreement that, even if they were incorporated into a future protocol, they would not—with one possible exception—be mandatory.

The FoC group on Article X, which encourages international cooperation for peaceful purposes, produced a set of elements for structured discussions, comprising 'Scope and content of possible scientific and technical exchanges', 'Greater multilateral cooperation in international public health and disease control', 'Scientific areas which could be promising for cooperation under Article X', 'Institutional, legal and financial arrangements', 'Modalities, safe-

[120] BWC/AD HOC GROUP/32, 27 Sep. 1996, pp. 7–18.

[121] Pearson, G. S., 'Addendum to agenda item 12: consideration of the work of the Ad Hoc Group established by the Special Conference in 1994', eds G. S. Pearson and M. R. Dando, *Strengthening the Biological Weapons Convention: Key Points for the Fourth Review Conference, Addendum to Agenda Item 12* (Quaker United Nations Office: Geneva, 1996), p. 5.

[122] BWC/AD HOC GROUP/32, 27 Sep. 1996, pp. 9–38.

[123] BWC/AD HOC GROUP/32, 27 Sep. 1996, p. 19.

[124] Pearson (note 121), p. 3.

[125] BWC/AD HOC GROUP/32, 27 Sep. 1996, p. 39.

[126] BWC/AD HOC GROUP/32, 27 Sep. 1996, pp. 39–52.

guards and limitations', 'Reporting, administrative and review procedures' and 'Role of Article X within a compliance assurance regime'.[127] As noted in the introductory part of several sections, the range of views is still wide, and the text does not necessarily represent agreement among delegations. The section also contains an annexe, in which *inter alia* some highly contentious issues are discussed such as the relationship between Article X and the other BTWC provisions and the relevance of export control measures to the implementation of Article X. On the whole, it was assessed that:

the FoC on Article X measures has shown a move . . . towards focusing on potential measures relevant to the BTWC and away from measures which could duplicate unnecessarily measures being undertaken by other fora such as Agenda 21 and the Convention on Biological Diversity. There appears to be promise in measures that will implement Article X of the BTWC whilst at the same time improving transparency and building confidence.[128]

Despite the progress to date, questions remain as to whether the Ad Hoc Group will be able to complete its work by 1998.[129] It must be kept in mind that all the papers prepared by the FoC group state that they are without prejudice to the positions of the delegations on the issues under consideration in the Ad Hoc Group and that they do not imply agreement on the scope or content of the papers.[130] The target date of 1998 has also met with opposition, and at the Fourth Review Conference delegates agreed that the enforcement protocol should be ready before the next review conference, in 2001.[131] However, one useful outcome of the Ad Hoc Group meeting in September 1996 was agreement to intensify the work of the Ad Hoc Group in 1997.[132] This decision was supported by the Fourth Review Conference, which encouraged the Ad Hoc Group to review its method of work and to move towards a negotiating format.[133] There is hope that substantial progress will be made towards the development of a verification protocol to the BTWC in 1997.

The Fourth Review Conference

The endorsement of the work of the Ad Hoc Group may be one of the most significant outcomes of the Fourth Review Conference. Although the importance of confidence-building measures was reaffirmed, the Final Document noted that participation in the CBMs since the Third Review Conference in September 1991 has not been universal and that not all responses have been

[127] BWC/AD HOC GROUP/32, 27 Sep. 1996, pp. 51–60.
[128] Pearson (note 121), p. 6. Agenda 21 comprises a series of aspirations relating to the environment and development.
[129] This objective was proposed, among others, by the USA. 'Remarks by the President in address to the 51st General Assembly of the United Nations', White House Press Release, 24 Sep. 1996, White House Virtual Library, URL <http://library.whitehouse.gov/>.
[130] BCW/AD HOC GROUP/32, 27 Sep. 1996, p. 5.
[131] Final Declaration of the Fourth Review Conference BWC/CONF.IV/9, Part II, p. 29.
[132] Meetings are scheduled for 3–21 Mar., 14 July–1 Aug. and 15 Sep.–3 Oct. 1997. BCW/AD HOC GROUP/32, 27 Sep. 1996, p. 4.
[133] Final Declaration of the Fourth Review Conference (note 131).

prompt or complete. In addition, it recognized that some states parties experienced difficulties regarding the preparation of CBM responses.[134] However, the Final Document contained no modifications to the modalities of the existing CBMs or clarifications of the existing CBMs to address these issues.[135] In view of the potential of BW terrorist threats the delegates included language in the Final Document that under Article III, which bans the transfer of items covered under the BTWC for prohibited purposes, states parties should ensure that individuals or subnational groups should be prevented from acquiring biological and toxin weapons.[136] The conference emphasized the increasing importance of Article X in view of recent scientific and technological developments and also stressed that the measures to implement this article had to be consistent with the objectives and purposes of the BTWC.[137] It also reiterated that the provisions of Article III should not be used to impose restrictions or limitations on the transfer for permitted purposes of scientific knowledge, technology, equipment and materials under Article X.[138]

On the opening day of the review conference Iran submitted an unannounced proposal to amend the BTWC by inserting the word 'use' both in the title and in Article I of the convention.[139] The Iranian representative argued that the BTWC, as it stands, relies on the 1925 Geneva Protocol to cover the prohibition of use. The latter agreement, however, is subject to reservations by some contracting parties so that instead of a complete ban on use it only prohibits first use. In addition, Article VIII of the BTWC rejects an interpretation of the convention that may detract from the commitments of states parties under the Geneva Protocol, so that states with reservations to it may consider the use of BW to be legitimate under certain circumstances.[140] Second, Iran doubted the assumption that the prohibition of development, production and stockpiling precludes the use of BW under all circumstances. Several neutral and non-aligned countries supported the request for amendment.

South Africa, referring to preambular paragraphs 9 and 10 of the BTWC, stated that prevention of use was the ultimate goal of the convention. It proposed language for the final declaration of the Fourth Review Conference that the use of microbial or other biological agents or toxins for other than peaceful purposes would constitute a violation of Article I of the BTWC.[141] France and the Netherlands, on the other hand, submitted language for Article VIII acknowledging that by prohibiting bacteriological methods of warfare the Geneva Protocol forms an essential complement to the BTWC and calling for

---

[134] Final Declaration of the Fourth Review Conference (note 131), p. 19.

[135] These issues are discussed in Pearson, G. S., 'Article V: consultation and cooperation', eds Pearson and Dando (note 121), pp. 59–75; and Hunger, I., 'Article V: confidence-building measures', Pearson and Dando (note 121), pp. 77–92.

[136] Final Declaration of the Fourth Review Conference (note 131), p. 17.

[137] Final Declaration of the Fourth Review Conference (note 131), pp. 23–24.

[138] Final Declaration of the Fourth Review Conference (note 131), p. 17.

[139] BWC/CONF.IV/CRP.1, 25 Nov. 1996; and BWC/CONF.IV/COW/WP.2, 28 Nov. 1996.

[140] For parties to the Geneva Protocol (including indication of states with reservations) see Annexe A in this volume.

[141] 'The use of BTW: a violation of Article I of the BTWC, Working Paper by South Africa', BWC/CONF.IV/COW/WP.1, 27 Nov. 1996.

the withdrawal of all reservations to the Geneva Protocol.[142] All states parties universally condemned the use of BW in war.[143]

According to Article XI of the BTWC any state can submit an amendment. The article had not been invoked before. The amendment can enter into force upon its acceptance by a majority of states parties and thereafter for each remaining state party on the date of acceptance by it. At the Third Review Conference it was agreed that 'the provisions of Article XI should in principle be implemented in such a way as not to affect the universality of the Convention'.[144] Under Article 40 of the 1969 Vienna Convention on the Law of Treaties any proposal to amend a multilateral treaty must be notified to all the contracting states. The Fourth Review Conference therefore requested the states parties to convey their views to the depository states (Russia, the UK and the USA), which will take any measures requested—including the convening of a special conference to consider the Iranian proposal at the earliest possible date, if a majority of states parties so decides.[145] Several delegates, however, expressed the fear that adoption of this amendment might lead to other proposals, which may ultimately weaken the BTWC regime, and that, in view of the required ratification procedures by states parties, states that do not accept the amendment would appear to condone BW use.[146]

At the Fourth Review Conference delegates also welcomed the lifting of reservations to the Geneva Protocol by France and South Africa. During the plenary session on 29 November, the Belgian ambassador also announced that Belgium was close to withdrawing its reservations.[147]

V. CBW proliferation concerns

UNSCOM: chemical and biological weapon-related activities

In 1996 the Iraqi Government was again unable to convince UNSCOM that it had dismantled all its programmes for developing ballistic missiles and weapons of mass destruction. It also remained unclear when sanctions would be lifted. In March, however, UNSCOM chairman Rolf Ekéus suggested that the UN's ongoing monitoring and verification programme may have to be continued for up to 15–20 years.[148] Approximately 115 facilities were being monitored for possible CW-related activities and 86 sites for BW-related activities.[149] Later, in July, Ekéus also said that 6–16 long-range missiles capable of carrying chemical or biological warheads remained unaccounted for.[150] On 20 May the UN Security Council and the Iraqi Government signed

[142] BWC/CONF.IV/COW/WP.3, 28 Nov. 1996.

[143] Report of the Committee of the Whole, BWC/CONF.IV/9, Part III, p. 39.

[144] Final Declaration of the Third Review Conference, BWC/CONF.III/23.

[145] Final Declaration. of the Fourth Review Conference (note 131), p. 27.

[146] Report of the Committee of the Whole, BWC/CONF.IV/9, Part III, p. 39.

[147] Zanders, J. P., participating for SIPRI in the Fourth Review Conference, 29 Nov. 1996.

[148] Black, I., 'UN monitor says Iraqi checks will continue', *The Guardian*, 13 Mar. 1996, p. 7.

[149] UN Security Council document S/1996/848, 11 Oct. 1996, pp. 21, 23.

[150] 'UN arms envoy is provoking trouble, Iraq asserts', *International Herald Tribune*, 28 Aug. 1996, p. 8. In all, up to 85 missiles with ranges above the 150-km range limit set by the UN Security Council

an agreement allowing UN-supervised sale of oil with proceeds to go towards war reparations and the purchase of humanitarian supplies for Iraq.[151]

Iraq continued to hinder or prevent UNSCOM inspections (table 13.3 lists inspections in 1996).[152] On 12 June the UN Security Council adopted Resolution 1060 which stated that the Iraqi refusal to allow unimpeded inspections was unacceptable and called upon the Iraqi Government to stop hindering inspections.[153] Ten days later Iraqi Deputy Foreign Minister Tariq Aziz signed an agreement confirming the right of UN inspectors to visit any area suspected of containing information or materials which would indicate a violation of UN resolutions.[154] On 19 July, however, an UNSCOM team was withdrawn after being denied the use of roads leading to inspection sites.[155] Following high-level talks on 26–28 August 1996, subsequent inspections were conducted in September without incident.[156]

Destruction of a biological weapon research and production facility at Al Hakam, approximately 60–80 km south-west of Baghdad, as well as BW-related equipment from two BW facilities at Al Manal and Al Safah, was completed in June 1996.[157] Although UNSCOM believed that it has destroyed the major part of Iraq's BW-related facilities, it said that significant gaps of information on Iraq's BW programme remained.[158] Iraq reportedly weaponized (prepared the agents to be delivered as weapons) at least 25 missile warheads and 166 air bombs with BW agents.[159] Before the Persian Gulf War, Iraq reportedly produced 2500 litres of aflatoxin, 8500 litres of anthrax and 19 000 litres of botulinum.[160]

may still be unaccounted for. Associated Press, 'UN inspector: Iraq may still be holding long-range missiles', 21 Oct. 1996, URL <http://www1.trib.com/NEWS/HEAD/un18.html>.

[151] Bruce, J., 'USA to keep close watch on Iraqi oil money', Jane's Defence Weekly, vol. 25, no. 23 (5 June 1996), p. 16.

[152] In Mar. 1996, e.g., an UNSCOM team was delayed for several hours before being allowed to enter a total of 5 sites. On 11–12 June another inspection team was denied access to sites at Abu Ghurib. 'UN demands access to Iraqi sites', International Herald Tribune, 20 Mar. 1996, p. 1; UN Security Council document S/1996/258, 11 Apr. 1996, pp. 6–7; and 'Iraq: some relief but renewed tensions', Disarmament Diplomacy, no. 6 (June 1996), pp. 52–53. For a chronology of events see UN Security Council document S/1996/182, 12 Mar. 1996. See also UN Security Council document S/PRST/1996/11, 19 Mar. 1996.

[153] UN Security Council document S/RES/1060, 12 June 1996.

[154] UN Security Council document S/1996/463, 24 June 1996.

[155] Medeiros, E., 'Iraq denies UNSCOM access to suspect sites despite pledge', Arms Control Today, vol. 26, no. 5 (July 1996), p. 21.

[156] '13–20 September', Chemical Weapons Convention Bulletin, no. 34 (Dec. 1996), p. 23.

[157] UN Security Council document S/1996/848, 11 Oct. 1996, p. 7; and Bruce, J., 'Iraqi BW plant levelled, but UN mission goes on', Jane's Defence Weekly, vol. 25, no. 25 (19 June 1996), pp. 28–29. In 1995 Iraq admitted that it had an offensive BW programme. Ekéus, R., 'Iraq's biological weapons programme', Memorandum from Executive Chairman of the United Nations Special Commission to the 4th BTWC Review Conference, 20 Nov. 1996, p. 4. Further information on the programme was provided by Saddam Hussein's son-in-law, Hussein Kamel al-Majid, who defected in Aug. 1995. Bruce (see above in this note). Kamel al-Majid was Iraq's Industry Minister and head of the Military Industrialization Corporation at the time of his defection. 'Beware Iraq's biowar legacy', Jane's International Defence Review, vol. 29 (June 1996), p. 104. In Feb. Kamel al-Majid was killed after returning to Baghdad. Rathmell, A., 'Oil sales bring respite for Saddam', Jane's Intelligence Review, vol. 8, no. 6 (June 1996), p. 259.

[158] UN Security Council document S/1996/848, 11 Oct. 1996, p. 7.

[159] 'Iraq, just saying no', The Economist, vol. 339, no. 7971 (22 June 1996), p. 48.

[160] Finnegan, P. 'Limited US action may boost Iraqi biological threat', Defense News, vol. 11, no. 38 (1996), pp. 3, 42.

In February 1996 Iraq submitted a draft full, final and complete disclosure (FFCD) of its CW development programme.[161] Yet questions concerning the accounting for VX precursors, which Iraq said it unilaterally destroyed, for example, were not answered to the satisfaction of UNSCOM officials. On 22 June Iraq provided its third FFCD of its chemical and its sixth FFCD of its biological programmes.[162]

In January 1996 Jordanian authorities confiscated Russian-made missile guidance components sent to Iraq in violation of UN sanctions.[163] UNSCOM officials also believed that Iraq took delivery of components for missiles with ranges of 'over thousands of kilometres'.[164] UNSCOM confirmed the delivery of missile components to Iraq in July 1995.[165] The United Nations also continued efforts to remove 130 missile motors for analysis in the USA in order to determine, in part, whether Iraq had upgraded them with domestically produced components.[166] On 27 March 1996 the UN Security Council adopted Resolution 1051, providing for the monitoring of exports and imports of materials and technologies by Iraq.[167] The UN export/import monitoring system for Iraq entered into effect on 10 October 1996.

Other proliferation allegations

Iran has allegedly received and is producing chemical weapons. A report on the US Department of Defense GulfLINK web site on Gulf War Syndrome stated that chemical and biological weapons as well as nuclear material had been transported on lorries from Iraq to Iran during the Gulf War.[168] The documents were removed when US intelligence officials expressed concern that they revealed internal methods and sources. Certain parts were also said to be classified. Access to the disputed section was restored after the documents had been reviewed and changed.[169] Written responses by the CIA to questions by the Senate Select Committee on Intelligence stated that Iran has 'several

---

[161] UN Security Council document S/1996/258, 11 Apr. 1996, p. 16.

[162] UN Security Council document S/1996/848, 11 Oct. 1996, pp. 11, 19, 22.

[163] 'Jordan seizes missile parts bound for Iraq', *Defense and Disarmament Review*, Feb. 1996, p. 297. The equipment was part of a shipment consisting of 10 crates which arrived at an Amman airport from Moscow on 10 Nov. and included 115 gyroscopes. Bruce, J., 'Jordan confirms parts were Iraq-bound', *Jane's Defence Weekly*, vol. 25, no. 1 (3 Jan. 1996), p. 3.

[164] UN Security Council document S/1996/258, 11 Apr. 1996, p. 13.

[165] UN Security Council document S/1996/258, 11 Apr. 1996, p. 14.

[166] Blanche, E., 'Iraq says missile dig will prove it has no "Scuds"', *Jane's Defence Weekly*, vol. 27, no. 3 (22 Jan. 1997), p. 5.

[167] UN Security Council document S/RES/1051, 27 Mar. 1996. The resolution states in part that information on imports of sensitive items should be provided to the joint UNSCOM–International Atomic Energy Agency unit. It remained unclear when Iraq would begin taking steps to implement national legislation to conform to the resolution's reporting requirements. The verification mechanism cannot take effect without the enactment of such legislation. UN Security Council document S/1996/258, 11 Apr. 1996, p. 5. For a compendium of terms to the Handbook for Notification of Exports to Iraq, Security Council Resolution 1051 (1996), see UN Security Council document S/1996/303, 18 Apr. 1996.

[168] The GulfLINK URL is <http://www.dtic.dla.mil/gulflink>.

[169] Associated Press, Rothberg, D., 'Iraq said to have secreted chemical, biological weapons in Iran', 3 Nov. 1996, URL <http://www1.trib.com/NEWS/HEAD/iraqchemical1.html>.

Table 13.3. UNSCOM inspections, 1 January–16 December 1996 (country dates)[a]

Type of inspection/date	Team
Chemical	
16 Aug. 1995–15 Jan.	CG 4
15 Jan.–15 Apr.	CG 5
24 Feb.–12 Mar.	CW 26/UNSCOM 129B
2 Apr.–30 June	CG 6
13–22 May	CW 28/UNSCOM 138
1 July–18 Dec.	CG 7
3–13 Aug.	CW 29/UNSCOM 140
18–22 Sep.	CW 30/UNSCOM 161
29 Nov.–11 Dec.	CW 27/UNSCOM 135
2–6 Dec.	CW 33/UNSCOM 170
18 Dec.–[into 1997]	CG 8
Biological	
2 Nov. 1995–27 Jan.	BG 3
12–18 Jan.	BW 30/UNSCOM 133
23–30 Jan.	BW 32/UNSCOM 136
28 Jan.–3 Apr.	BG 4
24 Feb.–1 Mar.	BW 33/UNSCOM 139
3 Apr.–30 June	BG 5
30 Apr.–7 May	BW 34/UNSCOM 142
11–20 May	BW 35/UNSCOM 145
19 May–30 June	BW 31/UNSCOM 134
11–13 June	BW 37/UNSCOM 151
1–8 July	BW 36/UNSCOM 146
1 July–28 Sep.	BG 6
25 July–3 Aug.	BW 38/UNSCOM 152
29 July–7 Aug.	BW 39/UNSCOM 154
13–20 Sep.	BW 40/UNSCOM 157
29 Sep.–7 Jan. 1997	BG 7
14–23 Oct.	BW 41/UNSCOM 159
11–18 Nov.	BW 43/UNSCOM 163
2–8 Dec.	BW 42/NSCOM 160
12–17 Dec.	BW 44/UNSCOM 167
Ballistic missile	
16 Nov. 1995–13 Feb.	MG 6
14–18 Jan.	BM 35/UNSCOM 120
1–5 Feb.	FFCD/M 1 Mission
14 Feb.–11 Mar.	MG 7
5–7 Mar.	Expert Mission
8–17 Mar.	BM 39/UNSCOM 143
10 Mar.–15 May	MG 8
20–23 Mar.	FFCD/M 2 Mission
25 Mar.– 2 Apr.	BM 37/UNSCOM 137
2–6 Apr.	BM 40/UNSCOM 144
22–27 Apr.	BM 38A/UNSCOM 141
5–10 May	Special Mission 1
15 May–9 Aug.	MG 9
28 May–1 June	FFCD/M 3 Mission
10–16 June	BM 41/UNSCOM 150
15–19 July	BM-42/UNSCOM 155
19–22 July	Special Mission 2
20 July–3 Aug.	BM 38B/UNSCOM 141B
3–7 Aug.	MG 9A

Type of inspection/date	Team
9 Aug.–22 Nov.	MG 10
13–17 Aug.	Special Mission 3
19 Aug.–4 Sep.	BM 38C/UNSCOM 141C
20–24 Sep.	BM 43/UNSCOM 162
21–28 Oct.	BM 45/UNSCOM 161
4–6 Nov.	BM 47/UNSCOM 168
6–16 Nov.	BM 44/UNSCOM 158
11–16 Nov.	MG 10/B
18–30 Nov.	BM 38D/UNSCOM 141D
22 Nov.–[into 1997]	MG 11
27 Nov.–2 Dec.	MG 11A
Nuclear	
12 Dec. 1995–4 Jan.	NMG 95-19
4–27 Jan.	NMG 96-01
27 Jan.–12 Feb.	NMG 96-02
12 Feb.–5 Mar.	NMG 96-03
5–25 Mar.	NMG 96-04
26 Mar.–15 Apr.	NMG 96-05
15 Apr.–6 May	NMG 96-06
6–27 May	NMG 96-07
13–19 May	IAEA 30/UNSCOM 147
27 May–17 June	NMG 96-08
17 June–8 July	NMG 96-09
8–30 July	NMG 96-10
30 July–20 Aug.	NMG 96-11
20 Aug.–15 Sept.	NMG 96-12
10 Sep.–1 Oct.	NMG 96-13
1–22 Oct.	NMG 96-14
22 Oct.–12 Nov.	NMG 96-15
12 Nov.–3 Dec.	NMG 96-16
3–19 Dec.	NMG 96-17
19 Dec. 1996–9 Jan. 1997	NMG 96-18
Export/import missions	
30 Apr.–9 May	UNSCOM 128 (EXIM-2)
20–22 May	Special Mission
20 May–2 Aug.	EG-1
3 Aug.–20 Nov.	EG-2
14–25 Nov.	UNSCOM 165 (EXIM-3)
21 Nov.–8 Jan. 1997	EG-3
Technical support missions	
11–20 May	OST 9B
6–26 June	PM2-96
5–28 Aug.	OST 8J
30 Sep.–22 Oct.	OST 9C

a In addition, special missions were conducted on 7–10 Mar., 18–19 Apr., 19–22 June, 26–28 Aug., 19–21 Oct., 21–25 Nov. and 6–11 Dec.

BM = ballistic missiles, BW = biological weapons, CG = Chemical Monitoring Group, CW = chemical weapons, IAEA = International Atomic Energy Agency, MG = Missile Monitoring Group, NMG = Nuclear Monitoring Group.

Source: Information provided by UNSCOM spokesman.

thousand tons' of chemical warfare agents, including cyanide, phosgene and sulphur mustard. The CIA alleged that Iran has an annual CW production capacity of 1000 tonnes and is currently pursuing a nerve agent production capability.[170] US intelligence also said that Chinese and Indian companies were supplying Iran with complete pesticide production facilities, including glass-lined vessels and air filtration units, which US officials were concerned could also be used for the production of chemical weapons.[171] Iranian officials denied that Iran was developing chemical weapons and that technology or materials for their manufacture were shipped through Italy.[172]

During a visit to Cairo in April US Secretary of Defense William Perry stated that Libya was constructing an underground CW production facility at Tarhunah, approximately 65 km south-east of Tripoli.[173] Work reportedly began in 1990.[174] Perry said that the USA would take the steps necessary to prevent the facility from becoming operational.[175] Libyan leader Colonel Muammar Qadhafi responded by saying that the facility is part of the Great Man-Made River Project, an irrigation scheme to divert water from aquifers in the south of the country to the Mediterranean coast.[176] Partly in an attempt to forestall possible US military action and with the agreement of Qadhafi, Egyptian President Hosni Mubarak sent investigators to visit Tarhunah. The team reported seeing tunnels but no equipment. At a press interview Mubarak expressed his belief that US officials also realized that 'no activity' was currently taking place inside the tunnels.[177] During the same period French President Jacques Chirac was quoted as saying that he was unable to confirm US allegations.[178] The US Department of State responded by reaffirming the US claim.[179] German intelligence reportedly possesses blueprints of the site.[180] The CIA estimated that the facility could become operational in 1997 or

[170] Starr, B., 'Iran has vast stockpiles of CW agents, says CIA', *Jane's Defence Weekly*, vol. 26, no. 7 (14 Aug. 1996), p. 3.
[171] Smith, R. J., 'Chinese exports fuel Iran effort on poison gas', *International Herald Tribune*, 9–10 Mar. 1996; and 'India helping to make poison gas', *Asian Recorder*, 29 July–4 Aug. 1996, p. 25796.
[172] IRNA (Tehran), 1021 GMT 12 Nov. 1995 (in English), in 'Foreign ministry denies PRC chemical warfare aid', Foreign Broadcast Information Service, *Daily Report–Near East and South Asia (FBIS-NES)*, FBIS-NES-95-218, 13 Nov. 1995; and Unattributed report: 'Iran: victims of chemical weapons', *Il Giorno* (Milan) 11 Oct. 1995, p. 6 (in Italian), in 'Officials deny chemical weapons allegations', FBIS-TAC-95-006, 6 Dec. 1995.
[173] 'Cairo and Paris want proof against Libya', *International Herald Tribune*, 8 Apr. 1996, p. 7; and 'Libya–US chemical weapons dispute', *Disarmament Diplomacy*, no. 4 (Apr. 1996), p. 44.
[174] Rosenthal, A., 'America to Gaddafi: stop poison gas plant or face an attack', *International Herald Tribune*, 20–21 Apr. 1996, p. 6.
[175] 'Cairo and Paris want proof against Libya' (note 173).
[176] 'Gaddafi tunnels into trouble both within and without', *Jane's Defence Weekly*, vol. 26, no. 11 (11 Sep. 1996), p. 24.
[177] Lancaster, J., 'Libyan arms factory a myth, Mubarak says', *International Herald Tribune*, 31 May 1996, p. 2.
[178] 'Cairo and Paris want proof against Libya' (note 173).
[179] 'USA stands by Libya CW claim', *Jane's Defence Weekly*, vol. 25, no. 23 (5 June 1996), p. 16.
[180] 'Huge chemical arms plant near completion in Libya, US says', *New York Times* News Service, 24 Feb. 1996.

1998.[181] However, work at Tarhunah apparently stopped after the US accusations.[182]

Allegations of German involvement in the construction of the Tarhunah facility in early 1996 became more credible when, on 9 August 1996, two German businessmen, suspected of supplying Libya with equipment for the production of chemical weapons from 1990 to 1993, were arrested in Germany.[183] Prosecutors in Mönchengladbach alleged that they had purchased chemical process control equipment from Siemens and adapted it for nerve-agent production before exporting it to Libya via Antwerp through a Belgian front company owned by Berge Balanian. It was later revealed that Balanian, who is originally from Lebanon, had previously worked as an informant for the German intelligence service.[184] The total value of the computerized equipment was estimated at 3.2 million DM. The equipment may have been supplied by two German companies.[185] Other German companies are reported to have sold equipment for drilling Tarhunah's system of tunnels.[186]

South Africa's Office for Serious Economic Offences (OSEO) continued to investigate apparent financial irregularities connected with Project Coast (also known as Project B, or Jota[187]), the code-name for that country's secret CBW research programme started in 1980 by the South African Defence Force (SADF).[188] In the autumn of 1994 the OSEO delivered a report to South Africa's Justice Minister Dullah Omar which suggested that when Roodeplaat Research Laboratories (RRL)[189] and Delta G. Scientific,[190] companies involved in the project, were privatized before the 1994 general elections company

---

[181] 'US claims huge Libya chemical weapons plant', *Disarmament Diplomacy*, no. 3 (Mar. 1996), p. 50.

[182] Podlich, M., 'Pentagon says Libya has stopped construction at suspected CW plant', *Arms Control Today*, vol. 26, no. 4 (May/June 1996), p. 26.

[183] Ulfkotte, U., 'Hilft Deutschland beim Bau einer Libyschen Giftgasfabrik?' [Did Germany help with the construction of a Libyan poison gas factory?], *Frankfurter Allgemeine Zeitung*, 28 Feb. 1996, p. 4; and AP/AFP, 'Affäre um Giftgas-Technologie für Libyen weitet sich aus' [Affair about poison gas technology for Libya broadens], *Süddeutsche Zeitung*, 26 Aug. 1996, p. 2.

[184] 'BND räumt Kontakt zu Hauptverdächtigem der Giftgas-Affäre ein' [BND ends contacts with main suspect of poison-gas affair], *Süddeutsche Zeitung*, 21 Aug. 1996; 'Brüssel weist Bericht über Exporterlaubnis zurück' [Brussels denies report about export permission], *Frankfurter Rundschau*, 15 Oct. 1996; 'Lebanon nabs man suspected of smuggling weapons material to Libya', *Compass*, 15 Oct. 1996, URL <http://www.compass-news.com/bin/sharchst.cgi?File=10151225.18&Country=Libya>; and DPA/AFP, 'Justiz bittet um Auslieferung in der Giftgas-Affäre' [Justice department requests extradition in poison-gas affair], *Frankfurter Rundschau*, 16 Oct. 1996.

[185] 'German firms' continued involvement in Libya's plans', *The Independent*, 20 Aug. 1996, p. 11; and 'Germany cracks nerve gas case', *International Herald Tribune*, 20 Aug. 1996, p. 1.

[186] Bonner, R., 'Germany charges 3 in sales to Libya: equipment allegedly intended for manufacture of nerve gas', *International Herald Tribune*, 22 Aug. 1996, pp. 1, 6.

[187] Sole, S. and Seery, B., 'Top team to reopen probe into arms project's missing millions', *Sunday Independent* (South Africa), 19 May 1996.

[188] 'South African CW investigation', *Jane's Defence Weekly*, vol. 25, no. 25 (19 June 1996), p. 29; and Brümmer, S., 'Secret chemical war remains secret', *Weekly Mail & Guardian*, 23 Aug. 1996, URL <http://wn.apc.org/wmail/issues/960823/NEWS35.html>. Project Coast was apparently terminated in 1993. 'SANDF asked to explain irregularities', *Star* (South Africa), 18 Aug. 1996.

[189] RRL has since been liquidated. Sole, S. and Seery, B., 'SA's chemical warfare project to be exposed', *Sunday Independent* (South Africa), 5 Dec. 1996. The laboratory was said to have succeeded in developing an infertility shot for use against blacks. Sole, S. and Seery, B., 'SADF wanted to make blacks infertile', *Sunday Independent* (South Africa), 18 Aug. 1996.

[190] Delta G. Scientific was sold to Sentrachem in 1993. Sole, S. and Seery, B., 'SA's chemical warfare project to be exposed' (note 189).

directors may have received up to 18 million Rand. Numerous questions have been raised about the role of personal relationships between company executives and former or current high-ranking government officials, including members of the SADF and the Ministry of Finance, at the time the companies were liquidated.[191] On 3 April 1996 the South African cabinet lifted security measures on the project but, apparently, only in so far as was necessary to allow the OSEO to complete its investigation into possible financial mismanagement.[192] The OSEO investigation may take an additional two years to complete.[193]

On 8 April police in Japan arrested Li Chong Chun, a Kobe resident of Korean ancestry, for having purchased 50 kg of sodium fluoride and 50 kg of hydrofluoric acid. Chun, acting for a Pyongyang trading company, shipped the sodium fluoride on 24 January and the hydrofluoric acid on 15 February on *North Korean* cargo ships loaded with rice provided by a Japanese food aid programme.[194] A report based on information from defectors stated that North Korea produced over 20 different chemical agents, including adamsite, chloroacetophenone, chlorobenzylidene malonitrile, hydrogen cyanide, mustard, phosgene, sarin, soman, tabun, VM and VX. North Korea is also said to have weaponized chemical multiple rocket-launcher munitions ranging in size from 80 mm to 240 mm.[195] While acknowledging the difficulties in making accurate estimates, the report suggested that the country has a peacetime production capacity of 4500 tonnes per year which could be expanded to 12 000 tonnes per year in time of war. North Korea is currently believed to have 1000–5000 tonnes of chemical weapons.[196]

During the period of the Dayton peace talks on Bosnia and Herzegovina the Granada television company retained three researchers from the Swedish National Defence Research Establishment (FOA) to examine samples taken from an alleged former *Yugoslav* chemical weapon production facility in Mostar. When these samples (e.g., earth and gas mask filters) were tested, isopropyl methylphosphonic acid and methylphosphonic acid were detected. The researchers concluded that sarin had probably been produced at the facility.[197] It has been suggested that Bosnian Serbs removed equipment from the Mostar

---

[191] Sole and Seery (note 187), 19 May 1996; and Sole, S. and Seery, B., 'General faces second grilling on R50m giveaway', *Sunday Independent* (South Africa), 18 Aug. 1996.

[192] A letter by Deputy President Thabo Mbeki to the legislative committee investigating the affair supported head of the SADF, General Georg Meiring, when he refused to provided testimony concerning Project Coast in an open hearing. Le May, J., 'Chemical weapons details under wraps', *Argus* (South Africa), 25 Aug. 1996; and Seery, B., 'South Africa "exported chemical weapons technology to Middle East"', *Sunday Independent* (South Africa), 25 Aug. 1996.

[193] Brümmer, S., 'Millions missing from chemical weapons project', *Mail & Guardian*, 16 May 1996, URL <http://www.mg.co.za/mg/news/96may/16may-chemical.html>.

[194] 'Korean resident arrested for sarin chemical export', *Daily Yomiuri*, 9 Apr. 1996, URL <http://www.yomiuri.co.jp/index-e.htm>.

[195] Bermudez, J., 'Inside North Korea's CW infrastructure', *Jane's Intelligence Review*, vol. 8, no. 8 (Aug. 1996), p. 380.

[196] Bermudez (note 195), p. 382.

[197] 'Foa-analys avslöjar, spår av nervgas i f.d. Jugoslavien' [FOA analysis reveals traces of nerve gas in the former Yugoslavia], *FOA Tidningen*, vol. 33, no. 5/6 (Dec. 1995), p. 48 (in Swedish); and Bartholomew, R., 'Will Serbia sign and ratify the CWC????, the Balkans and CW: is it avoidable?', *ASA Newsletter*, 14 June 1996.

facility to Lucani in 1992.[198] In addition to allegations concerning the manufacture of sarin, there continued to be claims that Bosnian Serb forces used BZ, a hallucinogenic agent, against Bosnian Government forces defending Srebrenica in July 1995.[199]

Syria is alleged to be constructing a chemical weapon production facility in Aleppo. The USA reportedly gave Germany copies of satellite surveillance photographs of the plant, which apparently has a design similar to that of Libya's Tarhunah facility. The German Government is investigating the possible involvement of German companies.[200]

In 1996 the continuation of several illicit BW armament programmes was alleged. The USA continued to voice concern in 1996 that *Russia* is not in compliance with the BTWC and may be retaining an offensive BW capability, despite President Boris Yeltsin's April 1992 decree to ban all activities contravening the convention.[201] Russia persistently denied the allegations.[202] During 1996 the United States also claimed that *Egypt, Iran, Iraq, Libya* and *Syria* possibly maintained BW programmes. The Defense Intelligence Agency, in particular, alleged that Russian expertise was flowing to these countries.[203]

VI. Other CBW-related issues

Gulf War Syndrome

Gulf War Syndrome is a collective name given to a variety of ailments and disorders suffered by especially US and British veterans of the Persian Gulf War. No single, coherent explanation for the phenomena has yet been provided. Extreme stress in war and its direct physiological effects on health were advanced in November by the Presidential Advisory Committee on Gulf War Veterans' Illnesses as another, but more plausible, potential cause.[204]

However, no such complaints from veterans appear to have emanated from France or some other allies in the theatre of operations. This seems to confirm the view that CBW pre-treatments, perhaps in combination with insect repellents and insecticides or with the smoke from burning oil wells, may have

---

[198] Bartholomew (note 197).

[199] Moore, P., 'Did Serbs use poison gas at Srebrenica?', *OMRI Daily Digest*, no. 16, part II (23 Jan. 1996).

[200] Lambrecht, R. and Müller, L., 'Giftgas gegen Israel' [Poison gas against Israel], *Stern*, no. 25 (5 June 1996), pp. 16–21.

[201] Office of the Secretary of Defense, *Proliferation: Threat and Response* (US Government Printing Office: Washington, DC, Apr. 1996), p. 32; and Waller, J. M., 'Natan Sharansky urges West to work with Lebed; ACDA finds Moscow violating arms treaties and manufacturing germ weapons', *Russia Reform Monitor*, no. 172 (American Foreign Policy Council: Washington, DC, 8 Aug. 1996), via International Relations and Security Network <ISN@CC1.KULEUVEN.AC.BE>.

[202] At the Fourth Review Conference of the BTWC it declared formally that the Russian Federation has never produced nor stockpiled such weapons and abides by all provisions of the BTWC. Zanders, J. P., participating for SIPRI in the Fourth Review Conference, 27 Nov. 1996.

[203] Starr (note 170); and Starr, B., 'Egypt and Syria are BW capable, says agency', *Jane's Defence Weekly*, vol. 26, no. 8 (21 Aug. 1996), p. 15.

[204] Ember, L., 'Stress may be cause of Gulf War Syndrome ailments', *Chemical and Engineering News*, vol. 74, no. 48 (25 Nov. 1996), p. 38.

been a factor.[205] It also questions whether Gulf War Syndrome may have been primarily caused by psychological factors or the stress of war.

The political debate surrounding Gulf War Syndrome intensified in the latter half of 1996 with the release of new data. Late in June the US Department of Defense admitted that hundreds of soldiers—a figure that eventually rose to over 20 000—may have been exposed to CW agents after US troops blew up a munition depot at Khamisiyah, north-west of Basra, in March 1991.[206] Throughout the autumn new data on the possible exposure of US troops to harmful agents emerged, while the CIA experienced great difficulty to model the nerve-agent cloud drift.[207] It was also reported in early December that military logs prepared for General Norman Schwarzkopf in March 1991 showed an unexplained eight-day gap.[208]

Also in December 1996 British Armed Forces Minister Nicholas Soames apologized for misinforming Parliament of the extent to which British troops had been exposed to organophosphate pesticides.[209] Two months earlier the government had admitted for the first time that soldiers had been exposed to the chemicals.[210] Soames announced a plan to conduct health checks on 18 000 troops, of whom half will be Gulf War veterans. Twenty per cent of the Czech veterans of the war suffer similar symptoms, and in view of the new US information the Czech Defence Ministry ordered fresh medical tests of all veterans to determine the cause of the continuing medical problems.[211]

In its final report, published on 6 January 1997, the Presidential Advisory Committee acknowledged the presumption of exposure to CW agents but denied the implication of a presumption of long-term health effects.[212] The next day the results of another major investigation were published which strongly suggested that the veterans suffered from nervous damage resulting from the synergistic effects of exposure to several chemical compounds, such as pesticides, insect repellents and possibly CW agents.[213]

[205] See also Stock, Haug and Radler (note 62), p. 705.

[206] Graham, B. and Brown, D., 'US troops were near toxic gas blast in Gulf', *Washington Post* (22 June 1996), p. A01; and Central Intelligence Agency, *CIA Report on Intelligence Related to Gulf War Illnesses* (2 Aug. 1996). Version current on 11 Dec. 1996, URL <http://www.dtic.dla.mil/gulflink/cia_report/102496_war.html#1>.

[207] Aldinger, C., 'Pentagon delays CIA data on Gulf War ills', *Washington Post* (11 Oct. 1996), p. A10.

[208] Shenon, P., 'Records on chemical arms in Gulf War are incomplete, Pentagon admits', *International Herald Tribune*, 6 Dec. 1996, p. 3; and 'Transcript: Pentagon spokesman's Thursday briefing Dec. 5', *Wireless File* (United States Information Service, US Embassy: Stockholm, 6 Dec. 1996), URL <http://www.usis.usemb.se/wireless/500/eur502.htm>.

[209] Butcher, T, 'Soames apology for misleading MPs about war', *Electronic Telegraph*, 11 Dec. 1996, URL <http://www.telegraph.co.uk/et/access?ac=156216619733&pg=//96/12/11/ngulf11.html>.

[210] Butcher, T, 'Gulf troops did face dangerous gases, says MOD', *Electronic Telegraph*, 5 Oct. 199), URL <http://www.telegraph.co.uk/et/access?ac=156216619733&pg=//96/10/5/ngulf05.html>.

[211] Rybavora, N., 'Czechs to re-examine health of Persian War veterans', *Boston Globe*, 26 Oct. 1996, URL <http://www.boston.com/globe/ap/cgi-bin/retrieve.cgl?%2Fapwir%2Fworld%2F300%2F037>.

[212] Brown, D., 'Panel on Gulf War veterans' illnesses affirms most US efforts', *Washington Post*, 7 Jan. 1997, p. A11.

[213] Brown, D., 'New studies indicate 6 patterns of Gulf "Syndrome"', *Washington Post*, 9 Jan. 1997, p. A01.

Tokyo nerve gas attack trials

The trials against Aum Shinrikyo members for the 1995 nerve agent attack in the Tokyo underground revealed the extent of the religious sect's preparations to engage in chemical and biological terrorism. By April 1996, 177 cult members had been indicted[214] and 26 convicted.[215] The trial of sect leader Shoko Asahara began on 24 April 1996.[216] Although Asahara refused to plead guilty or not guilty,[217] a number of cult members testified against him. Prosecutors have gathered over 15 000 pieces of evidence against Asahara, whose trial could take up to 10 years to complete. If convicted, he could be executed. The cult was also accused of manufacturing illegal guns and developing biological agents and laser weapons.[218]

During 1996 scattered incidents attributed to the cult continued to occur. On 7 April unidentified fumes in the Tokyo underground, possibly tear gas, resulted in 13 or 14 commuters being taken to hospital.[219] On 11 December the police discovered a container with 30–40 ml of VX on the bank of the Tamagawa Aqueduct in Kodaira, a western suburb of Tokyo.[220] The nerve agent had been produced by an Aum Shinrikyo chemist.[221] In 1996 two victims of the Tokyo sarin attack remained in coma.[222] Other victims continue to suffer from various ailments including chronic headaches, amnesia and psychological disorders.[223]

VII. Conclusions

The creation of a global, verifiable CW disarmament regime is firmly on course. The strength and relevance of that regime, however, will depend on how some outstanding issues are resolved in the near future. The domestic political, economic and other factors influencing a decision by Russia and the USA on ratification of the CWC are complex, and predictions of when or even whether the two countries will deposit their instruments of ratification cannot be made with any degree of certainty. Restrictions on chemical trade and

---

[214] 'Japan, Asahara and O.J.', *The Economist*, vol. 339, no. 7964 (4 May 1996), pp. 58–59.

[215] Guest, R., 'Cult leader refuses to enter gas deaths plea', *Electronic Telegraph*, 25 Apr. 1996, URL <http://www.telegraph.co.uk>.

[216] Rafferty, K., 'Doomsday cult trial grips Japan', *Guardian Weekly*, vol. 154, no. 18 (5 May 1996), p. 4. Shoko Asahara's original name was Chizuo Matsumoto.

[217] Ernsberger, R. and Takayama, H., 'The guru goes to court', *Newsweek*, 6 May 1996, p. 23.

[218] Reuter, 'Japan cult guru evicted from subway gas trial', 7 Nov. 1996, URL <http://www.excite.com/NEWS/961107/17.INTERNATIONAL_SUBWAY.html>.

[219] 'Tokyo subway fumes sicken 14', *International Herald Tribune*, 8 Apr. 1996, p. 4; and 'Fumes sicken 14 in Japan subway', *Times of India*, vol. 159, no. 83 (8 Apr. 1996), p. 1.

[220] 'Bottle of VX gas found in Tokyo suburb', *Japan Times* 12 Dec. 1996, URL <http://www.japantimes.co.jp/news/news12-96/news12-12html#story6>; and 'Cult member leads Japan police to nerve gas', CNN Interactive, 12 Dec. 1996, URL <http://www.cnn.com/WORLD/9612/12/japan.subway.reut/index.html>.

[221] 'VX gas found buried in Tokyo', *Asahi News*, 13 Dec. 1996, URL <http://www.asahi.com/english/enews/enews.html#enews_5034>.

[222] Garran, R., 'TV station suppressed cult story, MPs told', *The Australian*, 20 Mar. 1996, p. 6.

[223] Garran (note 222); and Parry, R., 'Cult gas attack haunts sole UK victim', *The Independent*, 20 Mar. 1996, p. 8.

effective implementation of the CWC may, however, play the key role in convincing both countries to ratify. Although it is difficult to predict the content of national declarations to the OPCW, entry into force of the CWC will almost certainly serve as a catalyst to initiate new destruction programmes for chemical weapons and old and abandoned CW and to stimulate the destruction efforts of existing programmes. Finally, as the quantity of chemical weapons is reduced the threat of terrorism and export control and national development issues will probably receive further increased attention.

Implementation of the CWC should also provide insight into how a verification regime under the BTWC could be structured. Although the problems remain formidable, some encouraging signs emerged in 1996 that the BTWC might become a verifiable disarmament treaty early in the next century.

14. Conventional arms control

ZDZISLAW LACHOWSKI

I. Introduction

In 1996 European interest was reawakened in arms control and its role within the concept of comprehensive and cooperative security of the Organization for Security and Co-operation in Europe (OSCE). Alongside the process of completing and amending the implementation of the 1990 Treaty on Conventional Armed Forces in Europe (the CFE Treaty),[1] a subregional arms control negotiation was concluded in the former Yugoslavia and an arms reduction process got off to a new although somewhat faltering start. Within the OSCE, the first steps were taken towards adapting the CFE Treaty to the new and future security circumstances, on the one hand, and towards giving some coherence and structure to participating states' arms control endeavours, on the other. Once more the entry into force of the 1992 Open Skies Treaty was blocked by the failure of Belarus, Russia and Ukraine to ratify it,[2] and its future as a legally binding regime is at risk. Outside Europe, while lip-service was paid to its role in reducing tensions and promoting political *détente*, conventional arms control has made little headway and is even faltering in some parts of the world. Some progress was made towards achieving a ban on anti-personnel land-mines.

This chapter covers the major issues and developments relating to conventional arms control in 1996, especially the negotiation and implementation of revisions to the European regional and subregional arms control agreements, security cooperation, with emphasis on a new framework for arms control efforts in the OSCE area and on developments concerning anti-personnel land-mines. Appendix 14A reviews developments in the field of confidence- and security-building measures (CSBMs) and the implementation of those agreed in the Vienna Document 1994.[3] Some key documents on conventional arms control from 1996 are reproduced in appendix 14B.

---

[1] The CFE Treaty and Protocols are reproduced in Koulik, S. and Kokoski, R., SIPRI, *Conventional Arms Control: Perspectives on Verification* (Oxford University Press: Oxford, 1994), pp. 211–76.

[2] The Ukrainian Parliament rejected ratification of the treaty on 16 Sep. 1996. Nevertheless, both Belarus and Ukraine have declared their readiness to ratify it provided Russia does so. The Open Skies Treaty must be seen in the context of Russia's relations with the West (the NATO enlargement dispute), the potential financial risks of its implementation and the adequacy of the national technical means of verification (NTM) of Russia and the USA. Institute for Defense and Disarmament Studies, *Arms Control Reporter* (IDDS: Brookline, Mass.), sheet 409.B.51, 1996.

[3] The Vienna Document 1994 is reproduced in *SIPRI Yearbook 1995: Armaments, Disarmament and International Security* (Oxford University Press: Oxford, 1995), pp. 779–820.

SIPRI Yearbook 1997: Armaments, Disarmament and International Security

Table 14.1. CFE ceilings, liabilities, reductions and holdings, as of 1 January 1997

State[a]	Tanks				ACVs				Artillery				Aircraft				Helicopters			
	Ceil.	Liab.	Red.	Hold.	Ceil.	Liab.	Red.	Hold.	Ceil.	Liab.	Red.	Hold.	Ceil.	Liab.	Red.	Hold.	Ceil.	Liab.	Red.	Hold.
Armenia	220	0	0	102	220	65	18	218	285	0	0	225	100	0	0	6	50	0	0	7
Azerbaijan[b]	220	0	13	270	220	0	71	557	285	0	42	301	100	0	0	48	50	0	0	15
Belarus	1 800	1 773	1 773	1 778	2 600	1 341	1 341	2 518	1 615	3	3	1 533	294	130	130	286	80	0	0	71
Belgium	334	28	28	334	1 099	284	284	678	320	58	58	312	232	0	0	166	46	0	0	46
Bulgaria	1 475	794	794	1 475	2 000	332	332	1 985	1 750	404	410	1 750	235	100	100	235	67	0	0	43
Canada	77	0	0	0	277	0	0	0	38	0	0	0	90	0	0	0	0	0	0	0
Czech Republic	957	1 123	1 123	952	1 367	1 217	1 217	1 367	767	1 409	1 409	767	230	51	57	143	50	0	0	36
Denmark	353	146	146	343	316	0	0	286	553	149	149	503	106	0	1	74	12	0	0	12
France	1 306	39	39	1 156	3 820	570	570	3 574	1 292	0	0	1 192	800	0	0	650	396	66	66	326
Georgia	220	0	0	79	220	0	0	102	285	0	0	92	100	0	0	6	50	0	0	3
Germany	4 166	2 566	2 566	3 248	3 446	4 257	4 257	2 537	2 705	1 623	1 623	2 058	900	140	140	560	306	0	0	205
Greece	1 735	1 013	1 099	1 735	2 534	0	449	2 325	1 878	505	517	1 878	650	0	79	486	30	0	0	20
Hungary	835	510	510	797	1 700	65	531	1 300	840	207	207	840	180	0	31	141	108	0	0	59
Italy	1 348	300	324	1 283	3 339	537	537	3 031	1 955	205	205	1 932	650	0	0	516	139	56	71	132
Moldova	210	0	0	210	210	0	59	209	250	0	0	155	50	0	0	27	50	0	0	0
Netherlands	743	0	0	722	1 080	261	261	610	607	59	59	448	230	0	0	181	50	22	91	12
Norway	170	127	127	170	225	57	57	199	527	17	17	246	100	0	0	74	0	0	0	0
Poland	1 730	120	130	1 729	2 150	301	900	1 442	1 610	741	770	1 581	460	61	94	384	130	0	0	94
Portugal	300	0	0	186	430	0	0	346	450	0	0	320	160	0	3	105	26	0	0	0
Romania	1 375	1 591	1 591	1 375	2 100	973	973	2 091	1 475	2 423	2 423	1 466	430	78	78	372	120	0	0	16
Russia[c]	6 400	3 187	3 188	5 541	11 480	5 416	5 419	10 198	6 415	658	660	6 011	3 416	1 002	1 029	2 891	890	99	99	812
Slovakia	478	578	578	478	683	443	443	683	383	679	679	383	115	30	30	113	25	0	0	19
Spain	794	371	481	725	1 588	0	0	1 194	1 310	87	88	1 230	310	0	0	200	90	0	0	28
Turkey	2 795	1 060	1 060	2 563	3 120	0	0	2 424	3 523	122	122	2 843	750	0	115	362	103	0	0	25
UK	1 015	183	183	521	3 176	30	30	2 411	636	0	0	436	900	0	0	624	384	5	5	289
Ukraine[c]	4 080	1 974	1 974	4 063	5 050	1 545	1 551	4 847	4 040	0	5	3 764	1 090	550	550	940	330	0	0	294
USA	4 006	192	639	1 115	5 372	0	5	1 849	2 492	0	5	612	784	0	0	220	431	0	0	126
For. WTO	20 000	12 650	12 764	18 639	30 000	11 698	12 855	27 517	20 000	6 524	6 574	18 868	6 800	2 002	2 099	5 592	2 000	99	99	1 469
NATO	19 142	6 025	6 692	14 101	29 825	5 996	6 450	21 464	18 286	2 825	2 843	14 010	6 662	140	338	4 218	2 026	149	233	1 221
Total	39 142	18 675	19 456	32 740	59 825	17 694	19 305	48 981	38 286	9 349	9 417	32 878	13 462	2 142	2 437	9 810	4 026	248	332	2 690

[a] Iceland, Kazakhstan and Luxembourg have no weapon limits in the application zone.   [b] Reduction continues.   [c] TLE belonging to the Black Sea Fleet is not included.

Source: Consolidated matrix on the basis of data available as of 1 January 1997, Joint Consultative Group, 18 Mar. 1997.

Table 14.2. Total TLE liabilities and reductions, as of 1 January 1997

State[a]	Reductions Total liability	Reduction	% of total	State[a]	Reductions Total liability	Reduction	% of total
Armenia	65	18	0.04	Netherlands	342	411	0.85
Azerbaijan	..	126	0.26	Norway	201	201	0.42
Belarus	3 247	3 247	6.75	Poland	2 223	2 855	5.93
Belgium	370	370	0.77	Portugal	0	3	0.01
Bulgaria	1 630	1 636	3.40	Romania	5 065	5065	10.53
Canada	0	0	0.00	Russia[c]	10 362	10 395	21.61
Czech Rep.	3 800	3 806	7.91	Slovakia	1 730	1 730	3.60
Denmark	146	147	0.31	Spain	458	569	1.18
France	824	824	1.71	Turkey	1 182	1 302	2.71
Georgia	0	0	0.00	UK	218	218	0.45
Germany	8 586	8 586	17.85	Ukraine[c]	4 069	4 075	8.47
Greece	1 518	2 144	4.46	USA	192	644	1.34
Hungary	782	1 379	2.87	**Former WTO**	**32 973**	**34 391**	**71.49**
Italy	1 098	1 137	2.36	**NATO**	**15 135**	**16 556**	**34.41**
Moldova	0	59	0.12	**Total**	**48 108**	**50 947**	**105.90**

[a] Iceland, Kazakhstan and Luxembourg have no weapon limits in the application zone.
[b] Reduction continues.
[c] TLE belonging to the Black Sea Fleet is not included.

Source: Consolidated matrix on the basis of data available as of 1 January 1997, Joint Consultative Group, 18 Mar. 1997.

II. Conventional arms control in Europe: the CFE Treaty

The CFE Treaty set equal ceilings within its Atlantic-to-the-Urals (ATTU) application zone on military equipment of the groups of states parties, originally the NATO and the Warsaw Treaty Organization (WTO) states (now 30 states parties[4]), which would be essential for launching surprise attack and initiating large-scale offensive operations. The reduction of excess treaty-limited equipment (TLE) was carried out in three phases by 16 November 1995. By mid-1996 more than 58 000 pieces of conventional armaments and equipment had been destroyed or converted for non-military purposes, including more than 50 000 TLE items reduced in the ATTU zone. Tables 14.1 and 14.2 provide data on the situation in the application zone as of 1 January 1997. This process was accompanied by extensive verification which encompassed almost 2600 inspections (table 14.3). Under the politically binding 1992 Concluding Act of the Negotiation on Personnel Strength of Conventional Armed Forces in Europe (the CFE-1A Agreement[5]), and in the cooperative political climate, some 1.2 million persons left the ranks of the European conventional armed forces.

---

[4] A list of states parties to the CFE Treaty is given in annexe A in this volume.
[5] The text of the CFE-1A Agreement is reproduced in *SIPRI Yearbook 1993: World Armaments and Disarmament* (Oxford University Press: Oxford, 1993), pp. 683–89.

Table 14.3. CFE inspections hosted and conducted by states parties by the end of the residual level validation period, March 1996

State	Hosted	% of total	Con-ducted	% of total	State	Hosted	% of total	Con-ducted	% of total
Armenia	10	0.39	4	0.15	Moldova	7	0.27	0	0.00
Azerbaijan	26	1.01	0	0.00	Netherlands	37	1.43	89	3.44
Belarus	99	3.83	14	0.54	Norway	11	0.04	40	1.55
Belgium	26	1.01	65	2.51	Poland	119	4.61	116	4.49
Bulgaria	108	4.18	91	3.52	Portugal	2	0.01	14	0.54
Canada	0	0.00	22	0.85	Romania	195	7.55	97	3.75
Czech Rep.	230	8.90	110	4.25	Russia	425	16.45	415	16.05
Denmark	16	0.62	39	1.51	Slovakia	91	3.52	37	1.43
France	88	3.41	165	6.38	Spain	47	1.82	83	3.21
Georgia	5	0.20	0	0.00	Turkey	72	2.79	57	2.20
Germany	330	12.78	309	11.95	UK	54	2.09	265	10.25
Greece	68	2.63	32	1.24	Ukraine	310	12.00	63	2.44
Hungary	96	3.72	102	3.94	USA	66	2.56	275	10.63
Italy	41	1.56	71	2.75					
Luxembourg	2	0.08	11	0.43	**Total**	**2 581**	**100.00**	**2 586**	**100.00**

Source: Selected data on the implementation of the CFE Treaty obligations, Permanent Mission of the Slovak Republic to the OSCE, 4 June 1996.

The major questions on the agenda of or related to CFE Treaty implementation in 1997 discussed here are: (*a*) reduction and non-compliance issues; (*b*) the flank issue; and (*c*) the future of the treaty.

Reduction and non-compliance problems

To comply with the CFE Treaty ceilings excess TLE items were to be destroyed or disabled as provided for in the Protocol on Reductions. Each state party was to have eliminated totally its reduction liability in each of the five categories of conventional armaments and equipment limited by the treaty—battle tanks, armoured combat vehicles (ACVs), heavy artillery, combat aircraft and attack helicopters—by the end of the third reduction phase.[6]

By the 16 November 1995 deadline, several states parties had still not fulfilled some treaty commitments and these remained unfulfilled in 1996. Although it had met the overall reduction goals, Russia still had the greatest number of liabilities. At the end of the reduction process it had regional shortfalls in the destruction of conventional armaments and equipment beyond the Urals (some 9000 items), having destroyed only one-third of its liabilities, and in naval infantry and coastal defence equipment (owing to the still unresolved dispute with Ukraine over the Black Sea Fleet division and the status of the Sevastopol base). Russia also failed to meet the flank ceilings (as discussed below). Following the Western insistence regarding the liabilities beyond the

[6] The CFE Treaty (note 1), Article VIII, para. 4(C).

Table 14.4. Destruction or conversion of conventional armaments and equipment beyond the Urals to civilian equipment, valid as of March 1997

Area	Tanks	%	ACVs	%	Artillery	%	Total	%
Liability								
Beyond the Urals	6 000		1 500		7 000		14 500	
Naval infantry/ coastal defence	331		488		436		1 255	
Reductions								
Beyond the Urals	2 733	*45.6*	1 837	*122.5*	4 289	*61.3*	8 859	*61.1*
Naval infantry/ coastal defence	331	*100.0*	488	*100.0*	436	*100.0*	1 255	*100.0*

Source: Joint Consultative Group, Group on Treaty Operation and Implementation, JCG.REF (G10I)/61/97, 18 Mar. 1997.

Urals (not subject to verification) the Russian representative stated at the First CFE Treaty Review Conference in Vienna (15–31 May 1996) that, under the politically binding Soviet statement of 14 June 1991,[7] Russia would demonstrate that holdings on its territory had been destroyed or rendered militarily unusable by applying several methods, including the provision of physical and documentary evidence, exposure of tanks and ACVs to 'the influence of atmospheric factors', visits and examination by experts, and notifications of transfers of armaments and equipment to other parties within the ATTU zone. Russia pledged to pursue the reduction goal together with Kazakhstan and Uzbekistan with the aim of completion by the year 2000. If, however, the quota of 6000 battle tanks subject to reduction were not fully met, Russia would cover a shortfall of up to 2300 tanks by eliminating an equal number of ACVs in excess of the quota of 1500. The shortfall in tank destruction would be eliminated subsequently, and the process of elimination would depend on the tanks' operational and service life and on the resources available.[8] Subsequent visits to destruction sites beyond the Urals allowed Western teams to verify that Russia had been abiding by the terms of its pledge, having destroyed almost two-thirds of its liabilities (table 14.4).

Russia's attempts to use its Caucasian neighbours' CFE quotas were not fully successful, which contributed to its reporting difficulties.

---

[7] Statement of the Representative of the Union of Soviet Socialist Republics in the Joint Consultative Group, Vienna, 14 June 1991. In the run-up to the signing of the CFE Treaty during 1989–90, the USSR withdrew some 57 300 pieces of conventional armaments and equipment beyond the Urals. This move eroded trust and was seen as an attempt to evade an obligation to destroy excess TLE in the ATTU zone. In the June statement the USSR pledged to destroy or convert 14 500 items, to use some to replace or repair old equipment, and to store the rest.

[8] CFE, Final Document of the First Conference to Review the Operation of the Treaty on Conventional Armed Forces in Europe and the Concluding Act of the Negotiation on Personnel Strength. Vienna, 15–31 May 1996, CFE-TRC/DG.2 Rev.5, 31 May 1996, Annex E: Statement of the representative of the Russian Federation to the Review Conference of the Treaty on Conventional Armed Forces in Europe. For excerpts from the text of the Final Document and the annexes see appendix 14B in this volume.

Table 14.5. Reductions of TLE belonging to naval infantry and coastal defence forces required by the legally binding Soviet pledge of 14 June 1991

Numbers in parentheses indicate the percentage of liabilities reduced.

State/Area	Tanks	ACVs	Artillery	Total
Liabilities of				
Russia				
Outside ATTU zone	331	488	436	1 255
Inside ATTU zone	331	488	436	1 255
Ukraine	271	749	208	1 228
Sub-total in ATTU zone	602	1 237	644	2 483
Total	**933**	**1 725**	**1 080**	**3 738**
Reductions by				
Russia				
Outside ATTU zone	331	488	436	1 255
Inside ATTU zone	331	488	436	1 255
Ukraine[a]	0	0	0	0
Sub-total in ATTU zone	331 *(55.0)*	488 *(39.5)*	436 *(67.7)*	1 255 *(50.5)*
Total	**662** *(71.0)*	**976** *(56.6)*	**872** *(80.7)*	**2 510** *(67.2)*

[a] Reduction incomplete because of the unwillingness of the Russian Federation to resolve the status of the naval infantry and coastal defence holdings located in Ukraine.

Source: Consolidated matrix on the basis of data available as of 1 January 1997, Joint Consultative Group, 18 Mar. 1997.

Belarus failed to reach both the November 1995 deadline and the second, 26 April 1996, deadline agreed by the CFE Joint Consultative Group (JCG). The Belarus Government had promised to get rid of the remaining 104 ACVs and some 130 tanks by the First CFE Treaty Review Conference[9] but failed to make good their commitment. They had transferred some excess equipment to Bulgaria and Hungary. Belarus failed to submit data at the annual exchange at the end of 1996 but was declared to have completed its reductions as of 1 January 1997.

The three Caucasian states, entangled in a web of civil wars, ethnic conflicts and domestic crises, have come under criticism for failing to resolve the problem of their 'unaccounted for and uncontrolled' TLE. Armenia and Azerbaijan had long failed to declare their equipment holdings and accept any formal destruction liability. At the end of the reduction process, Armenia had surplus ACVs and Azerbaijan claimed that it could not account for some 700 TLE items lost to rebel forces in Nagorno-Karabakh. Georgia had also been declared as not in compliance with the treaty because of its inability to report its holdings on time because of the civil war. Another sensitive problem was that of the Russian holdings deployed in Armenia, Georgia and Moldova,

[9] Open Media Research Institute (OMRI), *OMRI Daily Digest,* no. 85 (30 Apr. 1996), URL <http://www.omri.cz>; and Interfax (Moscow), 28 Mar. 1996, in 'Belarus: Minsk destroys combat aircraft under CFE Treaty', Foreign Broadcast Information service, *Daily Report–Central Eurasia (FBIS-SOV),* FBIS-SOV-96-062, 29 Mar. 1996, p. 60.

partly to avoid reduction. Russia has approached the three governments on that problem, but with no conclusive result.[10]

Ukraine was reported to have had excess equipment in active-duty units, including that assigned to the Black Sea Fleet, over which it is in dispute with Russia.

Finally, Hungary, Poland, Romania and Slovakia[11] were claimed to have designated some equipment for export instead of destroying it.[12]

All these and other questions were discussed and recommendations were made both in the JCG and at the First CFE Treaty Review Conference.[13] At the OSCE Lisbon Summit in December the JCG was urged to intensify efforts to resolve the implementation issues in parallel with the process of future work on the CFE Treaty, negotiations on which were to be started in 1997.[14]

Cascading

Under the CFE Treaty (Article VIII, para. 8) states may 'cascade' or transfer excess TLE to other states in the same group (NATO or the former WTO), thereby reducing their own reduction liabilities. The recipients must assume responsibility for any necessary reductions. Cascading excess weapons, which was used extensively by NATO members, seemed to be impossible for the former WTO states after the breakup of the Eastern bloc: but cascading among this group of states intensified from late spring 1995 as the CFE Treaty reduction deadline drew near. Transfers of heavy weapons, especially by Russia, are also motivated by the need to repay debts and bolster economic ties and exports among former allies. By August 1996 Bulgaria had received the third and last delivery of military equipment from Russia free of charge; the whole package included 100 T-72 tanks, 100 BMP-1P armoured infantry fighting vehicles (AIFVs) and 12 Mi-24 attack helicopters.[15] In April 1996 Hungary

[10] In early 1996, Russian holdings in these 3 countries were *c.* 360 tanks, 750 ACVs and 430 artillery pieces. The 1995 Russian–Georgian agreement (still unratified) on stationing Russian troops and weapons is still strongly opposed by the opposition in Georgia. According to Georgian estimates, Russia stations some 200 tanks, up to 570 ACVs and 220 artillery pieces in 4 military bases in Georgia. Aladashvili, I., 'Divided quotas and lost levers', DGHE (Tbilisi), 5–15 Feb. 1996 (in Georgian), in 'Georgia: article analyses transfer of CFE quotas to Russia', FBIS-SOV-96-039, 27 Feb. 1996, p. 59. For figures for the individual north Caucasian countries, see Lachowski, Z., 'Conventional arms control and security cooperation in Europe', *SIPRI Yearbook 1996: Armaments, Disarmament and International Security* (Oxford University Press: Oxford, 1996), footnote 24, pp. 713–14.

[11] In Aug. 1996 Slovakia announced that under its armed forces' reorganization plans it intends to seek renegotiation of its CFE limits and increase its holdings of attack helicopters from 19 to 40 (its limit is 25); on the other hand its air force inventory would drop to 72 aircraft (the limit is 115 aircraft). *OMRI Daily Digest*, no. 163 (22 Aug. 1996); and *Jane's Defence Weekly*, 15 Nov. 1996, p. 3.

[12] Dean, J., 'Future of the CFE Treaty', *BASIC Paper,* no. 17 (6 May 1996). Version current on 6 May 1996, URL <http://www.igc.apc.org/basic/bpaper17.html>.

[13] CFE (note 8). Annex D to the Final Document enumerates the topics that were discussed during the First CFE Treaty Review Conference.

[14] OSCE, Lisbon Document, DOC.S/1/96, 3 Dec. 1996. The appended Document adopted by the states parties to the Treaty on Conventional Armed Forces in Europe on the scope and parameters of the process commissioned in Paragraph 19 of the Final Document of the First CFE Treaty Review Conference is reproduced in appendix 5A in this volume.

[15] 'Russia to give Bulgaria tanks, armored vehicles', Interfax (Moscow), 30 Jan. 1996, in Foreign Broadcast Information Service, *Arms Control and Proliferation Issues (FBIS-TAC)*, FBIS-TAC-96-003, 5 Mar. 1996, p. 43. A Bulgarian newspaper reported that Bulgaria refused to accept the Mi-24 heli-

Table 14.6. Russian and Ukrainian entitlements in the former flank zone and in the redefined flank zone, under the Final Document of the First CFE Treaty Review Conference

	Tanks	ACVs	Artillery
Russia			
Temporary deployments within former flank zone, until 31 May 1999	1 897	4 397	2 422
Limits within former flank zone after 31 May 1999	1 800	3 700[a]	2 400
Redefined flank zone entitlements	700	780	1 280
plus those in storage	(600)	(800)	(400)
Ukraine			
Odessa *oblast*	400	400	350
Redefined flank zone entitlements (former Odessa MD minus Odessa *oblast*)	280	350	500
plus those in storage	(400)	(–)	(500)

[a] No more than 552 located within the Astrakhan and Volgograd *oblasts* (regions) respectively; no more than 310 within the eastern part of the Rostov *oblast*; and no more than 600 within the Pskov *oblast*.

Source: Final Document of the First Conference to Review the Operation of the Treaty on Conventional Armed Forces in Europe and the Concluding Act of the Negotiation on Personnel Strength, Vienna, 15–31 May 1996, Annex A, Document agreed among the states parties to the Treaty on Conventional Armed Forces in Europe of 19 November 1990.

announced the purchase of 100 T-72 tanks from Belarus at a reduced price to replace its old T-55 tanks; it also imported 435 out of a total of 555 BTR-80 armoured personnel carriers (APCs) to be delivered from Russia in 1996–97. Slovakia will receive 8 MiG-29s from Russia as partial payment of the latter's $1.2 million debt.[16]

The flank issue and the First CFE Treaty Review Conference solution

The long-standing flank question remained the most vexed and contentious issue after the November 1995 deadline. In the run-up to the First CFE Treaty Review Conference in May 1996 NATO and Russia moved closer to resolving the dispute: the Western governments agreed to negotiate the flank issue further on the basis of 'redrawing' the CFE zone map. The NATO states most concerned with this issue, Norway and Turkey (the latter very reluctantly), consented to areas where Russian troops would be acceptable in return for further Russian concessions concerning transparency and Russia's announce-

copters because of their low technical grade and envisaged high costs for repair and maintenance. *OMRI Daily Digest*, no. 42 (28 Feb. 1996).

[16] *Defense News*, 19–25 Feb. 1996; *Arms Control Reporter*, sheets 407.B.536–37, 1996; *Segodnya*, 18 Sep. 1996, p. 2; and Information on Plans for the Deployment of Major Weapons and Equipment Systems in 1996 in CPC Survey on CSBM Information Exchanged in Preparation of the Annual Implementation Assessment Meeting 1997, OSCE document REF.SEC/24/97, 20 Jan. 1997.

ment of a timetable for partial military withdrawal from Chechnya. The US and Russian presidents' declarations at the Group of Seven (G7) summit meeting on 19–20 April 1996 hinted at the flexibility accorded by the USA in allowing Russia to temporarily adjust its deployments in the flank zone.

The First CFE Treaty Review Conference was virtually dominated by the flank question. The initial positions were similar to those of former follow-up gatherings of the Conference on Security and Co-operation in Europe (CSCE), with Russia wanting to discuss new solutions and changes ('modernization') and the USA insisting on reviewing compliance and implementation. However, the similarity ended there and the conference was otherwise characterized by a cooperative search for a compromise solution.

The Final Document retained a special regime for the former flank zone while introducing a number of changes. It scaled down the size of the flank zone—defined in Article V, paragraph 1(A)—by reallocating several *oblasts* to the CFE rear (extended) zone (Russia) and expanded central (outer) zone (Ukraine).[17] These are the Pskov *oblast* in north-western Russia; the Volgograd *oblast*; the Astrakhan *oblast*; the part of the Rostov *oblast* east of a line extending from Kushchevskaya to Volgodonsk to the Volgograd *oblast* border, including Volgodonsk, the Kushchevskaya storage site and repair facility, and a narrow corridor in Krasnodar *kray* leading to Kushchevskaya, in southern Russia; and the Odessa *oblast* in western Ukraine. The weapon limits for the redefined flank zone were not changed, while the Russian area of the former flank zone received new, higher limits and Ukraine received new limits for the Odessa *oblast*. Russia agreed to freeze its holdings of battle tanks, ACVs and artillery at the levels current at the time of the agreement until the new limits come into effect on 31 May 1999; by this time it will have complied with the numerical limitations set by the Final Document and reduced its holdings by some 100 tanks, 700 ACVs and 22 artillery pieces (table 14.6). Before 31 May 1999 the states parties will also decide whether to allow the three TLE categories in designated permanent storage sites (DPSS), including those subject to regional numerical limitations, to be located with active units.

Russia also obtained confirmation of its rights to temporarily deploy the three categories of weapons within and outside its territory and to reallocate the current quotas of these armaments under the 1992 Tashkent Agreement 'by means of free negotiations and with full respect for the sovereignty of the states parties involved'.[18]

In return for these changes, Russia will provide additional, more frequent information on its part of the former flank zone, and Ukraine will notify more on its holdings in the Odessa *oblast*. Both states are to accept additional

---

[17] CFE (note 8), Annex A.

[18] This enabled the removal of Azerbaijan's strong objections to the flank compromise at the First CFE Review Conference. The Statement by the Chairman of the Review Conference affirmed that temporary deployments and reallocation of quotas will not be applicable to Azerbaijan. For the text of the Agreement on the Principles and Procedures for Implementing the Treaty on Conventional Armed Forces in Europe, the Tashkent Document, see *SIPRI Yearbook 1993* (note 5), pp. 671–77.

Figure 14.1. Redefinition of the CFE flank zone

declared site inspections within the *oblasts* now excluded. Russia also agreed to sub-ceilings on ACVs deployed in each of the regions removed from the flank zone.

The Final Document was to enter into force upon confirmation of its approval by all states parties, or by 15 December 1996. However, because only a dozen states had ratified or otherwise approved the flank deal by that date, the OSCE Lisbon Summit agreed to extend the deadline for approval until

15 May 1997. In the meantime, several of the most concerned states (chiefly Azerbaijan, Georgia, Moldova and Ukraine) strongly criticized the agreement as being too favourable to Russia and detrimental to their own national interests. A re-emergence of the flank issue within the CFE adaptation process cannot be ruled out.

Criticism from the Baltic states

The flank agreement raised concern among the Baltic states. Their autumn 1991 decision to dissociate themselves from the CFE regime meant that they had no influence over the agreement to increase Russia's ceiling for ACVs (from 180 to 600) in the adjacent Pskov *oblast*. The Baltic states were apparently not consulted beforehand, and Estonia and Latvia in particular were taken by surprise by the Vienna compromise, and particularly by the US consent to it. The Baltic states deplored the fact that a reduction agreement permitted an increased military presence near their borders, decreasing their sub-regional security.[19]

The future of the CFE Treaty

The new situation in Europe, the disappearance of the Eastern bloc and the prospect of NATO enlargement have challenged many of the cold war premises that upheld the treaty (e.g., the group structure, the focus on arms concentrations in Central Europe, the zonal system, including the flank zone, and the limited treaty adherence). NATO enlargement will have a profound effect on the evolution of the post-cold war conventional arms control regime, and, even though NATO and Russia officially denied any linkage between the two issues throughout 1996, potential NATO enlargement impinged decisively on the direction and scope of proposed adaptations to the treaty.

Adapting the CFE Treaty regime to the qualitatively new situation of an eastward enlargement of the Alliance has brought various issues to the fore, notably whether new members' entitlements should be counted against those of the former WTO or those of the NATO group. The former solution seems out of the question as it would create a series of problems with regard to the entitlements of the new members and the Central Zone allotments and inspections. In the latter case, since NATO has not made use of all its entitlements, it was proposed that each new 'group of states parties' would reduce its entitlements by the available headroom, to prevent Russia from increasing its holdings excessively, or Central European national entitlements would be accommodated within NATO headroom (excess of entitlements over holdings).[20]

---

[19] 'The issue is more about the preservation of the agreement [i.e., the CFE Treaty] than about the Baltic states. The Baltics are to some extent sacrificed for the benefit of general interests', stated Latvian Foreign Minister Valdis Birkavs on 3 June, continuing: 'The agreement is very fragile . . . and if it is not extended our situation will be worse'. *Baltic Times*, no. 12 (6–12 June 1996), pp. 1, 8.

[20] For a discussion of various scenarios see Mendelsohn, J., 'The CFE Treaty: in retrospect and under review', *Arms Control Today*, vol. 26, no. 3 (Apr. 1996), pp. 10–11. See also Schmidt, H.-J., 'NATO and arms control: alliance enlargement and the CFE Treaty', *PRIF Reports*, no. 42 (Peace Research Institute Frankfurt: Frankfurt, July 1996).

Table 14.7. National TLE headroom after completion of the reduction process, as of 1 January 1997

State[a]	Tanks	ACVs	Artillery	Aircraft	Helicopters	Total
Armenia	118	2	60	94	43	317
Azerbaijan	− 50	− 237	− 16	52	35	− 216
Belarus	22	82	82	8	9	203
Belgium	0	421	8	66	0	495
Bulgaria	0	15	0	0	24	39
Canada	77	277	38	90	0	482
Czech Republic	5	0	0	87	14	106
Denmark	10	30	50	32	0	122
France	150	246	100	150	70	716
Georgia	141	118	193	94	47	593
Germany	918	909	647	340	101	2 915
Greece	0	209	0	164	10	383
Hungary	38	400	0	39	49	526
Italy	65	308	23	134	7	537
Moldova	210	1	95	23	50	379
Netherlands	21	470	159	49	38	737
Norway	0	26	281	26	0	333
Poland	1	708	29	76	36	850
Portugal	114	84	130	55	26	409
Romania	0	9	9	58	104	180
Russia	859	1 282	404	525	78	3 148
Slovakia	0	0	0	2	6	8
Spain	69	394	80	110	62	715
Turkey	232	696	680	388	78	2 074
UK	494	765	200	276	95	1 830
Ukraine	17	203	276	150	36	682
USA	2 891	3 523	1 880	564	305	9 163
Total former WTO	**1 361**	**2 583**	**1 132**	**1 208**	**531**	**6 815**
Total NATO	**5 041**	**8 358**	**4 276**	**2 444**	**792**	**20 911**

[a] Iceland, Luxembourg and Kazakhstan have no weapon limits in the application zone.

Source: Based on table 14.1.

As the issue of NATO enlargement evolved during the year, Russia kept emphasizing its opposition and, in indirect reference to the CFE Treaty context, stressed the alternatives: renegotiation/modernization or abrogation of the treaty. In turn, the Western states had to address the implications of NATO enlargement for the treaty.

Russian withdrawal from the CFE Treaty would clearly harm rather than improve Russia's strategic position and, notwithstanding its military's bellicose rhetoric, Moscow seems well aware of this. Apart from destroying the basic premises of security and stability in Europe, such a move could seriously impair or completely ruin the chances of negotiating a new agreement better tailored to the new security needs. However, Russian analysts and negotiators have long pointed out that the ratio of Russian to NATO forces has changed in

NATO's favour since the end of the cold war and claim that NATO enlargement would exacerbate this imbalance. The new multipolar environment
clearly requires a new approach to security on all sides. NATO must present
new arrangements to assure Russia that enlargement would enhance rather
than diminish Russian security (such as a NATO–Russian charter); and Russia
must come to see its own security in new, non-adversarial terms. A careful
'modernization' of the CFE Treaty should be accompanied by other militarily
significant steps, such as additional CSBMs, joint NATO/non-NATO
manoeuvres, and assurances that NATO will not deploy nuclear weapons on
the territories of new members in Central Europe in peacetime. This would
make the treaty more relevant to the new situation, cap national holdings
(hopefully all over Europe), lower the still excessive levels of armaments, and
enhance confidence and stability.

As the May 1996 review conference approached and preparations continued
towards NATO enlargement, Russia intensified its efforts to focus the conference's attention on treaty 'modernization'—rather than renegotiation, as it
had demanded in 1995.

In bilateral and multilateral (JCG) talks with other states parties, Russia suggested a far-reaching 'modernization' of the treaty in the light of the changed
security situation in Europe. Despite the long-standing NATO stance that it
would consider changes in the CFE regime only if Russia first complied with
the existing provisions, some Western states had modified their position in the
run-up to the review conference. Apparently concerned about Russia, still
wary of Germany and with an eye to its interests *vis-à-vis* the USA and
NATO, France strongly advocated eliminating the overall group limits
through formal amendment of the treaty to safeguard the CFE Treaty regime.[21]
The USA also stated that 'it is prepared, provided the flank issue is resolved,
to initiate a process at the review conference which will lead ultimately toward
the modernization of the treaty to reflect changed realities' and 'to establish
the viability of this regime for the indefinite future'.[22] Some Central European
states expressed a readiness to start discussing 'modernization' of the treaty
after the OSCE Lisbon Summit, but a number of governments were reluctant
to rush into full negotiations too soon.[23] The move from a bloc-to-bloc
approach to a multipolar, national-based regime, especially before the scope
and character of NATO enlargement are decided, was seen as a complex step.

The review conference could not seriously discuss the substance of adapting
the CFE Treaty, since only the Russian proposal was on the table at that time,
and NATO and the Visegrad countries had not yet prepared their positions.
The task of the conference was to give the JCG the go-ahead to work on the
mandate of the negotiation on adaptation. The participants declared their

---

[21] Dean (note 12).

[22] See interview with US Ambassador Thomas Graham, Jr, chief US delegate to the Vienna First CFE
Treaty Review Conference: 'The CFE treaty review conference: strengthening the "cornerstone" of
European security', *Arms Control Today*, vol. 26, no. 3 (Apr. 1996), p. 5.

[23] Fournier, S. and Kokkinides, T., 'East–West differences may impede progress at CFE', *BASIC
Reports*, no. 52 (13 May 1996), p. 3.

willingness to start an immediate process aimed at improving the operation of the treaty, defining the 'scope and parameters' of the process and considering 'measures and adaptations' to this effect. A progress report on the intermediate results and recommendations on the way ahead was to be considered during the OSCE summit meeting.

In line with the Vienna pledge, the issue of adapting the CFE Treaty was addressed in the JCG.

CFE Treaty modernization proposals

The proposals submitted in 1996 showed the sides to be heading towards compromise. Russia proposed a broad agenda for the conventional arms control regime to address not only the CFE Treaty but also other premises of military stability in Europe. Central European participants stressed in particular the readjustment aspects of adaptation, chiefly in relation to NATO enlargement. NATO, the least keen on modernization and careful to maintain a wide margin of manoeuvre in post-Lisbon Summit negotiations, opted for a limited but considerate approach.

Russia

In the proposal on 'modernization' submitted to the JCG before the review conference,[24] and in that presented jointly with Belarus on 29 October,[25] Russia was careful not to create any explicit linkage between changes in the CFE Treaty and NATO enlargement, and evidently sought to make the latter more difficult. Its idea of a 'supplementary agreement', called for in the spring of 1996, was dropped, and Russia demanded specific measures to 'adapt' the treaty: (*a*) revision of the group structure with a system specifying national levels and a mechanism to modify them; (*b*) numerical limitations and adjustment of the sufficiency levels for one state; (*c*) regulation of the status of conventional armed forces stationed on foreign territory; (*d*) revision of regional limitations; (*e*) revision of TLE storage provisions (towards higher ceilings on temporarily deployed equipment and lower levels of equipment in DPSS); (*f*) 'applicability' of the treaty in crisis and conflict situations; (*g*) enabling the use of armed forces for peacekeeping purposes; (*h*) possible accession by other OSCE states; (*i*) inclusion of additional categories of weapons and equipment (especially concerning aviation); and (*j*) strengthening verification and the exchange of information. Russia also called for freezing the holdings of each state/group of states at the levels of 17 November 1995, refraining from stationing troops and weapons on foreign territory and freezing the numbers of such forces at the levels at the end of the reduction process.

---

[24] Statement by V. N. Kulebyakin, Head of the Delegation of the Russian Federation to the Joint Consultative Group, Vienna, 23 Apr. 1996.

[25] Proposal by Belarus and Russia to the JCG, 'Document of the states parties to the Treaty on Conventional Armed Forces in Europe on the direction to be taken in further work aimed at adapting the Treaty in a changing environment', Vienna, 29 Oct. 1996.

The 'Group of Four'

In September 1996 the Visegrad Group presented to the JCG its 'first thoughts'[26] on the scope and parameters of the adaptation. The group paper covered: (*a*) principles (preservation of the treaty's integrity, non-interference with its ongoing operation, avoiding detriment to states' security interests, the right of each state to freely choose or change its security arrangements or guarantees, limiting adaptation to ensure the proper functioning of the CFE regime); (*b*) aims and objectives (emphasizing the elimination of local force concentrations); (*c*) ways and means for the adaptation (including a separate document, non-interference with CFE implementation, making the JCG a negotiating forum); and (*d*) a preliminary list of methods for discussion. These questions included: revision of the group structure with a possibility of national levels; permanent stationing of TLE on the territories of CFE parties; geographical differentiation; aggregate overall ceilings; redefinition of the rules for changing national ceilings; national quotas for inspections; strengthening of cooperative elements in the regime; review of TLE categories; provisions on stored equipment; readjustment of counting rules for TLE; possible opening up of the treaty for others; and the applicability of the treaty in crisis situations. The Visegrad Group proposal had a considerable bearing on the NATO suggestions that were soon to follow.

NATO

On 8 October NATO announced its readiness to enter negotiations in 1997 on the balance of conventional weapons,[27] suggesting 'measures and adaptations' rather than a wider-ranging 'modernization' of the conventional arms control regime. The NATO document demonstrated a cautious approach, wrapped in general terms, to possible changes in the CFE Treaty, reflecting not only an attempt to respond to Russia's demands and further sound out its intentions but also an apparent continued lack of consensus among its members on priorities.[28] The Allies were not able to decide which option to prioritize in addressing the future system of limitation to replace the group structure and were clearly unable to choose between a national and a regional approach. NATO's emphasis was on the integrity of the treaty, selectivity (as against renegotiation), enhanced security, compatibility with other security arrangements (the freedom of each state to choose its security arrangements or guarantees) and non-interference with the ongoing implementation of the treaty as the principles guiding the adaptation process. The list of issues to be addressed included a review of the group structure, preserving the zonal principle, the promotion of verification and exchange of information and,

[26] A non-paper presented by the 'Group of Four' (the Czech Republic, Hungary, Poland and Slovakia) to the JCG, 24 Sep. 1996.

[27] NATO proposal on 'Scope and parameters of the process for improving the operation of the CFE Treaty', Vienna, 8 Oct. 1996, submitted by the Delegation of Greece to the JCG.

[28] Kokkinides, T., 'NATO proceeds cautiously on CFE adaptation', *BASIC Reports*, no. 54 (28 Oct. 1996), pp. 1–2.

possibly, consideration of voluntary accession by other states. At the same time, NATO advocated maintaining all existing categories and types of TLE and opposed any increase in current limits or decrease in area of application; it also excluded the possibility of the adaptation process dealing with questions outside the scope of the CFE Treaty.

The Lisbon Summit CFE agenda

In December 1996 the OSCE Lisbon Summit agreed on a document setting the terms of reference for the future work on the CFE Treaty as commissioned at the First CFE Treaty Review Conference.[29] The convergence of the positions of the main actors and the West's willingness to accommodate Russia's desire to adapt the treaty allowed the participating states to agree on the scope and parameters of the 1997 talks: their general aims and objectives, principles, scope, timetable, modalities and other matters. The document covered all the NATO proposals and some of those put forward by Russia (and Belarus).

In defining the scope of the negotiations it was agreed to retain all categories of TLE (without increasing their total numbers in the application area), the information and verification regimes and the area of application. The states parties will consider the evolution of the group structure; the functioning of the treaty limitations (including maximum levels on holdings, a possible system of national TLE limits, the development of redistribution mechanisms, and provisions on zonal and aggregate numbers preserving the principles of zonal limitations and avoiding destabilizing accumulations of forces); stationing of forces; and provisions on verification, notification, information exchange and stored equipment. They will also address the possibility of other states acceding to the treaty and the means to ensure its functioning during cases of crisis and conflict, provisions for involvement in UN or OCSE peace-keeping operations, extending the treaty's coverage to include new or expanded categories of conventional armaments or equipment and permitting temporary deployments.

The negotiations started in the JCG on 21 January 1997. The states parties are to report on the results to the OSCE Copenhagen ministerial meeting by the end of the year; in the meantime, they are to inform OSCE participating states not party to the CFE Treaty of their work and progress, exchange views and consider the OSCE states' views on their own security. During the period of negotiations, the states parties are committed to show restraint in relation to the current postures and capabilities of their conventional forces, in particular with respect to force levels and deployments, in order not to diminish the security of any state party.[30]

---

[29] OSCE (note 14).

[30] The restraint clause was originally conceived by Russia as a freeze on the current deployment pattern of forces, to preclude future NATO deployments resulting from Alliance enlargement. Negotiated by Russia and the USA, it was presented in Lisbon as a confidence-building measure. After difficult US–Russian–Visegrad (Polish) negotiations, it was included in a milder and more general version in the Document adopted by the states parties to the Treaty on Conventional Armed Forces in Europe . . . (note 14), Article VI.

III. Subregional arms control in Europe

In the first half of 1996, the Dayton Agreement subregional arms control negotiations on numerical limits on the heavy weapons of the former combatants in the former Yugoslavia, as mandated by the Annex 1-B Agreement on Regional Stabilization (Article IV)[31] and carried out under OSCE auspices, encountered a number of obstacles, stalling tactics and delays. The problems concerned data gathering, breaches in weapon rules, verification, information exchanges and the status of the Republika Srpska (or the Bosnian Serbs) at the negotiating table. To discuss and settle these issues, a Bosnian Joint Consultative Commission was set up at the end of February. On 14 March, the small-arms embargo on Bosnia and Herzegovina was lifted by the UN Security Council, in accordance with the provisions of the Dayton Agreement. The next day the Bosnian 'train-and-equip' conference opened in Ankara, Turkey, under US and Turkish sponsorship, with the aim of re-arming the Federation of Bosnia and Herzegovina. Disagreement arose between the European Union (EU) and the USA concerning a commitment to earmark some $800 million to re-arm the Federation's troops and establish a military balance. The EU saw this as risking an arms race rather than reducing the possibility of military confrontation in the subregion.

The OSCE assisted the parties in their negotiations on armaments and manpower agreements as well as in their information exchanges and verification (including verification of declared holdings), although this assistance was not welcomed equally by all the parties.

The Florence Agreement

After six months of negotiations the Agreement on Sub-Regional Arms Control (the Florence Agreement) was signed at the ministerial meeting of the Peace Implementation Council in Florence on 14 June 1996 (eight days later than set out in the Dayton Agreement) by Bosnia and Herzegovina and its two entities (the Muslim–Croat Federation of Bosnia and Herzegovina and the Bosnian Serb Republika Srpska), Croatia and Yugoslavia (Serbia and Montenegro).[32] The agreement includes six protocols (on reduction, aircraft reclassification, information exchange, existing types of armaments, inspections and the Sub-Regional Consultative Commission—SRCC). The agreement entered into force upon signature on 14 June 1996. It is of unlimited duration but must remain in effect at least 42 months before any party decides to withdraw.

---

[31] Excerpts from the 1995 General Framework Agreement for Peace in Bosnia and Herzegovina (the Dayton Agreement), including Annex 1-B, are reproduced in *SIPRI Yearbook 1996* (note 10), pp. 235–50.

[32] The text of the Florence Agreement is reproduced in appendix 14B.

Table 14.8. Limitations on holdings and manpower and maximum agreed numbers for armoured infantry fighting vehicles of the five parties to the Florence Agreement

Party	Tanks	ACVs[a]	AIFV[b]	Artillery	Aircraft	Heli-copters	Man-power[c]
FR Yugoslavia	1 025	850	152	3 750	155	53	124 339
Croatia	410	340	76	1 500	62	21	65 000
Bosnia and Herzegovina	410	340	76	1 500	62	21	60 000
Federation of Bosnia and Herzegovina	273	227	38	1 000	41	14	55 000
Republika Srpska	137	113	38	500	21	7	56 000

[a] Armoured combat vehicles.

[b] Armoured infantry fighting vehicles are not limited by the agreement. AIFVs assigned to peacetime internal security forces, however, in excess of the maximum agreed numbers, shall constitute a portion of the permitted levels for ACVs (Article XI of the Florence Agreement).

[c] Manpower limits are as declared by the parties.

Limitations and reductions

The agreement was modelled on the CFE Treaty and set numerical limits on five categories of armaments—battle tanks, ACVs, artillery pieces of 75 mm and above, combat aircraft and attack helicopters—of the ex-combatants in a ratio of 5:2:2 for Yugoslavia (Serbia and Montenegro), Bosnia and Herzegovina, and Croatia, respectively, and a ratio of 2:1 for Bosnia's two 'entities'. AIFVs assigned to peacetime internal security forces, not capable of ground combat against an external enemy, are not formally limited by the agreement, but the parties agreed on maximum numbers for AIFVs to avoid circumvention of the provisions of the agreement. In separate political statements each party declared limitations on its military manpower as of 1 September 1996. Reciprocal mistrust and reluctance to reintegrate military forces are reflected in the fact that the manpower limits declared by the Federation of Bosnia and Herzegovina and the Republika Srpska do not add up to those declared by Bosnia and Herzegovina (table 14.8).

The agreement envisages specific methods for arms reductions: destruction (the predominant method), conversion to non-military purposes, use for static display or ground instructional purposes, use as ground targets, reclassification and export (table 14.9).

Reductions were to be effected in two phases and completed within 16 months, by 1 November 1997. By 1 January 1997 (the end of Phase I) each party was to have reduced 40 per cent of its total liabilities for artillery, aircraft and helicopters and 20 per cent of its total liabilities for tanks and ACVs. By the end of Phase II each party was to have reduced all agreement-limited equipment (ALE) in each of the five categories. It is estimated that some 6000 weapon items will have been destroyed by the end of the reduction period.

Table 14.9. Methods of disposal of equipment limited under the Florence Agreement

Disposal method[a]	Battle tanks	ACVs	Artillery	Combat aircraft	Attack helicopters
Destruction	0	0	0	0	0
Accident (1)	0	0	0	0	0
Conversion (2)	0	0	x	x	x
Static display (3)	0	0	0	0	0
Ground targets (4)	0	0	0[b]	x	x
Instruction (5)	x	x	x	0	0
Reclassification (6)	x	x	x	0[c]	x
Export (7)	0	0	0	0	0
Decommissioning (8)	0	0	0	0	0

0 = Permitted; x = Not permitted

[a] The following limits apply to the different disposal methods: (1) no more than 1.5% of holdings; (2) for tanks—5.7% or 150 pieces, whichever is greater; for ACVs—15% or 150 pieces; (3) no more than 8 items of each category; (4) no more than 2.5% of the ceiling for tanks and ACVs, and no more than 50 pieces of self-propelled artillery; (5) no more than 5% of each; (6) no more than 50 specified aircraft; (7) no more than 25% of total reduction liability during a single reduction phase; and (8) 1% or 100 pieces, whichever is greater, of which no more than 75 tanks, ACVs and artillery pieces and no more than 25 attack helicopters and combat aircraft.

[b] Only self-propelled artillery.

[c] Only specific models or versions of combat-capable trainer aircraft (G-4 Galeb; MiG-21U; NJ-22; J-21).

Verification

The limits on holdings are subject to a verification regime similar to that of the CFE Treaty. It provides for on-site monitoring of the reduction schedule and of exports of armaments limited by the agreement, extensive information exchange and notifications, intrusive inspections and an impartial international role—played by the Personal Representative of the OSCE Chairman-in-Office or his/her designated agent(s)—to assist the parties in the implementation of the agreement and to ensure that it is implemented in good faith.

Implementation

The Sub-Regional Consultative Commission was established to handle compliance issues and differences that might arise during implementation, to revise and draw up additional measures to enhance its workability, and to take appropriate steps in the event of dispute. The commission is to meet at least once every three months. It has the power to amend the agreement, but its decisions would require consensus. The chairmanship of the commission was to rotate among the parties after 1996; in the meantime, the Personal Representative agreed to act as chairman.[33]

[33] The London Peace Implementation Conference recommended that OSCE Personal Representative Ambassador Robert H. Frowick remain as Chairman until the end of 1997. Bosnia and Herzegovina 1997: Making Peace Work, Peace Implementation Conference, London, 4–5 Dec. 1996, p. 9.

Information exchanged by the parties on their holdings, effective as of 1 July 1996, was the basis for the four-month baseline validation period for inspections (to 31 October). The reduction period began on 1 November (parties could start reductions earlier). A four-month residual level validation period to enable the calculation of inspection quotas would follow (1 November 1997–1 March 1998).

The status of implementation

The agreement is being implemented in an environment scarred by recent war and lacking in stability. The parties were pressured to agree on arms control and confidence-building measures (CBMs) by external powers, and the fact that three of the five parties comprise one state and two entities compounds the difficulties. On 18 June, the United Nations formally ended the embargo on heavy-weapon transfers to the former Yugoslavia. At that time it was esti-mated that the Yugoslav Army would have to scrap a quarter of its holdings; the Republika Srpska would have to make the largest reductions and destroy some 400 tanks and more than 1000 pieces of heavy artillery. Other parties could increase their holdings in some of the categories.

The withdrawal of all foreign forces and the alleged termination of intelli-gence and other military cooperation with Iran,[34] as well as the integration of Muslim and Croat forces under a new defence law, made it possible to put the US-led and largely Muslim-financed rearmament programme for the Federa-tion into effect. On 9 July the Office of the US President outlined the US train-and-equip programme, envisaging the shipment of $100 million in defence articles and services, including: 45 M-60 tanks, 80 M-113 APCs, 15 utility (not attack) helicopters, 46 100 M-16 rifles, 1000 machine-guns and 840 light anti-tank weapons. All the equipment will be fully mission-capable and will include related ammunition, spares and support equipment. The train-and-equip programme, criticized by Western Europe during the year, was to serve multiple, reinforcing purposes, including the establishment of a single Federation defence ministry and joint command; orienting Federation forces on a Western model; integrating donated equipment into the Federation force structure; reducing destabilizing foreign influences in the Federation; provid-ing leverage for continued compliance with the Dayton Agreement; and enab-ling the withdrawal of the Implementation Force (IFOR), and its successor the Stabilization Force (SFOR), on a timely basis.[35]

---

[34] However, allegations that Iran was supplying weapons to Bosnia and Herzegovina through Croatia persisted in the autumn of 1996. *Defense News*, 4–10 Nov. 1996, p. 16. For several weeks in Oct./Nov. the USA therefore delayed the unloading in Ploce harbour of the weapons it furnished to Bosnia.

[35] Fact Sheet: White House outlines Train and Equip program, *Wireless File* (US Information Service: US Embassy: Stockholm), 9 July 1996. Version current on 9 July 1996. URL <gopher://198.80.36.82:70/0R25983932-25986913-range/archives/1996/pdq.96>. In addition to the arms, a private US firm under contract to the Federation will train Bosnian troops, orienting the forces on a Western model. The programme, and the purchase of additional military equipment, will be funded from $140 million pledged by Brunei, Kuwait, Malaysia, Saudi Arabia and the United Arab Emirates. Poland declined the US invitation to join the train-and-equip programme by supplying 45 T-72 tanks to Bosnia and Herzegovina, and by choosing to remain neutral and not to arm any side. *International Herald Tribune*, 4 Sep. 1996, p. 5.

In August, inspection teams started to make reciprocal visits. The results were not made public, but discrepancies and refusals to accept inspections of declared and undeclared sites were reported.[36] Non-compliance with the terms of the Florence Agreement was made public in October. Western intelligence data revealed blatant discrepancies between declared reduction liabilities and actual stocks of heavy weapons. While NATO documents on specific numbers are classified, the Republika Srpska had to admit possessing more heavy weapons than initially declared.[37] It had tried to avoid its obligation to destroy excess tanks and artillery pieces by allocating them for export or research and development (R&D) under Article III. NATO inspectors asserted that many of the tanks so earmarked were actually too old to be sold. The Republika Srpska was also accused of having some 2500 artillery pieces, about twice as many as the number declared. As a result of this the reduction liability for the Republika Srpska was disproportionately low. Charges of cheating or abusing Article III exceptions were not only directed at the Serbs; Croatia was said to possess some 500 more artillery pieces than reported, and the Federation of Bosnia and Herzegovina was found to have one and a half times the 2000 artillery pieces it claimed to have.[38]

During the first six months implementation of the agreement varied from party to party, with the Republika Srpska being the most frequently upbraided, and neither inspections nor reductions were fully implemented by the end of 1996. The international community, IFOR in particular, had to repeatedly demonstrate a determination to see that the parties fulfilled their arms control commitments, sometimes using various methods of persuasion and dissuasion. The Peace Implementation Conference in London in December welcomed the progress made but deplored the continued delays on baseline validation inspections and Phase I reductions. The parties therefore agreed, among other things, to submit precise and comprehensive data on their holdings by 16 December 1996; to adjust their reduction liabilities to bring them into line with this data exchange, with a proviso that Article III exemptions will account for no more than 5 per cent of the total holdings; to submit complete reduction plans for 1996 if they had not completed Phase I reductions; and to complete Phase I reductions by 31 December 1996.[39]

---

[36] Lazanski, M., 'Brothers by virtue of Dayton', NIN (Belgrade), 27 Sep. 1996 (in Serbo-Croat), in 'FRY: inspections, visits by former enemy armies viewed', Foreign Broadcast Information Service, *Daily Reports–East Europe (FBIS–EEU)*, FBIS-EEU-96-206, 24 Oct. 1996; and SRNA (Belgrade), 22 Oct. 1996 (in Serbo-Croat), in 'B-H: Federation army refuses RS, FRY inspection teams', FBIS-EEU-96-206, 22 Oct. 1996.

[37] HINA (Zagreb), 29 Nov. 1996 (in English), in 'B-H: Federation army starts reduction of arms', FBIS-EEU-96-236-A, 9 Dec. 1996.

[38] NATO countries' intelligence estimates of the Bosnian Serbs' artillery holdings varied from 1374 to 2584, and even more. *International Herald Tribune*, 11 Oct. 1996, p. 5, and 19–20 Oct. 1996, p. 2. Brig.-Gen. Ramiz Drekovic of the Bosnian Federation Army admitted that the Federation still has to destroy 1940 pieces of artillery. 'Limits for army arsenals', *Dnevni Avaz*, 15 Nov. 1996 (in Serbo-Croat), in 'B-H: General views arms control agreement; inspections started', FBIS-EEU-96-226, 22 Nov. 1996.

[39] London Peace Implementation Conference (note 33), pp. 8–10.

Table 14.10. Implementation of the Sub-Regional Arms Control Agreement in 1996—Phase I[a]

Equipment	Yugoslavia	Croatia	Bosnia and Herzegovina	Federation of Bosnia and Herzegovina	Republika Srpska	Total
Tanks						
Holdings	1 562	284	–	130	531	
Exceptions	–	–	–	– (24)	338 (344)	
Ceilings	1 025	410	410	273	137	
Reduction liabilities	537	–	–	–	394	
Phase I liabilities	107	–	–	–	79	186
Phase I reduction	**239**	–	–	–	**13**	**252**
ACVs						
Holdings	1 099	161	–	85	257	
Exceptions	152	17	–	4 (24)	136 (141)	
Ceilings	850	340	340	227	113	
Reduction liabilities	97	–	–	–	144	
Phase I liabilities	39	–	–	–	21	60
Phase I reduction	**15**	–	–	–	**2**	**17**
Artillery						
Holdings	4 998	2 184	–	2 940	1 355	
Exceptions	170	–	–	– (377[b])	776 (880)	
Ceilings	3 750	1 500	1 500	1 000	500	
Reduction liabilities	1 248	684	–	1 940	855	
Phase I liabilities	449	274	–	776	342	1 841
Phase I reduction	**390**	**297**	–	**746**	**30**	**1 463**
Aircraft						
Holdings	230	27	–	–	18	
Exceptions	–	–	–	–	–	
Ceilings	155	62	62	41	21	
Reduction liabilities	75	–	–	–	–	
Phase I liabilities	30	–	–	–	–	30
Phase I reduction	**18**	–	–	–	–	**18**
Helicopters						
Holdings	56	4	–	–	7	
Exceptions	–	–	–	–	–	
Ceilings	53	21	21	14	7	
Reduction liabilities	3	–	–	–	–	
Phase I liabilities	1	–	–	–	–	1
Phase I reduction	–	–	–	–	–	
Total Phase I liabilities	626	274	–	776	442	2 118
Total Phase I reduction	662	297	–	746	45	1 750

[a] Figures in parentheses are new or revised declared exceptions as of 16–17 Dec. 1996.

[b] The Croatian part declared separately an exception of 197 artillery pieces.

Sources: Estimates based on Institute for Defense and Disarmament Studies, *Arms Control Reporter* (IDDS: Brookline, Mass.), sheets 402.B.347 and 402.B.355–6, 1996.

At the end of Phase I, 1750 heavy weapon items had been reduced. Only Croatia had fully met its reduction liabilities. The Federal Republic of Yugoslavia had reduced significantly more tanks than required. The Federation of Bosnia and Herzegovina, which began to destroy its surplus weapons only in early December, was reported to have almost completely met its Phase I liability (with German and Italian assistance); however, the issue of dividing the Bosnian and Croatian reduction liability had still not been resolved (they report separately). The Republika Srpska 'met' its reduction liability by scrapping the small amounts of weapons it had notified. The January 1997 SRCC meeting arrived at a common interpretation of the application of Article III counting rules; the parties were to recalculate their liabilities and provide corrected data. This was especially aimed at having the Republika Srpska authorities provide appropriate corrections.[40] It was decided that the residual liabilities from Phase I should be transferred to Phase II.

An unequivocal link has been established between the mandate for the negotiations on a regional balance in and around the former Yugoslavia, under Article V of the Agreement on Regional Stabilization annexed to the Dayton Agreement, and the implementation of subregional arms control under Article IV. The mandate is dependent on the implementation of the Florence Agreement.

IV. The OSCE Forum for Security Co-operation: the new agenda

The OSCE Forum for Security Co-operation (FSC) continued to work in two working groups in 1996, its focus shifting steadily towards the future framework for arms control (Working Group B). Its results were highly criticized at the end of the year—in the two years since the 1994 CSCE Budapest Summit Meeting it had not agreed on a single document. Various reasons were given: the rapid evolution of the security situation in the OSCE area; uncertainties about the new Euro-Atlantic strategic environment; and the parallel debate on a future security model for Europe.[41] Since neither the Helsinki Programme for Immediate Action of the Helsinki Document 1992[42] nor the further tasks set out in Chapter V of the 1994 Budapest Summit Declaration[43] turned out to be fully adequate to the new requirements and challenges, the participating states decided at the Lisbon Summit that the FSC should revise its priorities and focus on a new agenda. Section III of the Lisbon Document, on a framework for arms control, and section IV, on the development of the agenda for

---

[40] A Report on Implementation of the Agreement on Sub-Regional Arms Control by Ambassador Vigleik Eide, Personal Representative of the OSCE Chairman-in-Office, Permanent Council, OSCE document REF.PC/77/97, 13 Feb. 1997; and *Arms Control Reporter*, sheet 402.B.355–6, 1997.

[41] OSCE Review Meeting 1996, Report of the Chairman-in-Office to the Lisbon Meeting, Vienna, 22 Nov. 1996, p. 8.

[42] For excerpts from the Annex on the Programme for Immediate Action, see the text of the Helsinki Summit Declaration in *SIPRI Yearbook 1993* (note 5), pp. 205–206.

[43] For the text of the 1994 Budapest Summit Declaration see *SIPRI Yearbook 1995* (note 3), pp. 309–311.

the FSC, aim to restore and strengthen the role of arms control in enhancing stability and security, and to coordinate and harmonize it with other instruments such as preventive diplomacy and post-conflict rehabilitation across the OSCE area through a variety of ways and means.[44]

The aims and scope of both agendas notwithstanding, the prospect for their success must be seen in connection with the current focus on reshaping the CFE Treaty regime. The outcome will determine the overall debate and concept of post-cold war arms control in Europe.

The agenda for the FSC

The Lisbon Summit agreed that the FSC should:[45]

1. Pursue full *implementation of all agreed arms control agreements, obligations and commitments,* with an emphasis on the Code of Conduct on politico-military aspects of security, including consideration of a follow-up conference on the latter;

2. Address *regional measures,* where implementation had so far been less than satisfactory and an agreed conceptual framework was still far off;

3. *Develop a web of arms control agreements* through the OSCE framework for arms control (see below) to support cooperative approaches and address security concerns; develop the security dialogue function of the FSC to ensure regular information exchange on progress in separate arms control negotiations and allow the FSC views to be taken into consideration; and

4. *Strengthen agreed measures and develop new ones* to promote CSBM regimes, increase transparency and predictability and examine how to use them in preventive diplomacy, crisis management and post-conflict rehabilitation; and develop Norm- and Standard-Setting Measures (NSSMs), such as the Code of Conduct, the Guidelines Governing Conventional Arms Transfers and the Principles Governing Non-Proliferation.[46]

The participants also committed themselves to increase the efficiency of the working methods of the FSC, achieve greater cohesion between the FSC and the Permanent Council in complementary fields of activity, extend the experience of the FSC to partner Mediterranean states and consider measures to complement the international efforts to solve the anti-personnel land-mines problem and fight terrorism.

---

[44] OSCE, Lisbon Document 1996 (note 14), section III, A Framework for Arms Control, FSC.DEC/8/96 (reproduced in appendix 5A in this volume), and section IV, Development of the Agenda of the Forum for Security Co-operation, FSC.DEC/9/96.

[45] OSCE, Lisbon Document 1996 (note 44), section IV.

[46] A list of non-consensual suggestions regarding new measures was presented in OSCE, Lisbon Document 1996 (note 44), section IV.

A framework for arms control

The framework for arms control adopted by the Lisbon Summit[47] in accordance with the 1994 Budapest Review Conference decision will serve as a guide for future arms control negotiations and as a basis for the establishment of a flexible agenda for future work on arms control. It will complement ongoing work in the OSCE on the Security Model for Europe for the 21st Century.[48]

In order to help promote responses to the *challenges and risks* that may be dealt with through arms control measures, the following issues are to be addressed: military imbalances; inter-state tensions and conflicts; major internal disputes; enhancing transparency and predictability regarding military intentions; helping democratic political control over military, paramilitary and security forces; ensuring compatibility of multinational military and political organizations with the OSCE's concept of security; ensuring that no state strengthens its security at the expense of the security of others or regards any part of the OSCE area as a particular sphere of interest; ensuring the international legal status of the foreign troops on a state's territory; ensuring full implementation of arms control agreements at all times; ensuring the adequacy of arms control agreements to security needs; and ensuring full cooperation in combating terrorism.

The underlying *principles* for negotiation are listed as sufficiency, transparency through information exchange, verification and limitations on forces. The *goals and methods* for arms control measures include: strengthening the concept of the indivisibility of security; improving existing OSCE-wide measures; reducing regional instability and military imbalances among states; stabilizing specific crisis situations; examining the issue of limitations on armed forces and constraints on their activities; respect for the legitimate security interests of each state; transparency, consultation and cooperation in the evolution or establishment of alliances and other organizations, recognizing the right of each state to choose or change its own security arrangements; ensuring transparency by providing information on the implementation of regional or other agreements not binding on all OSCE states; and improving existing verification provisions and developing new ones.

V. Conventional arms control endeavours outside Europe

Despite a growing awareness that conventional arms control is one of the major instruments needed to reverse arms races, reduce tensions and promote political *détente*, non-OSCE regions have continued to lag far behind Europe in this respect. One reason is that these processes began or started gaining momentum after the end of the cold war. Their slow advancement reflects both their short history and a variety of political, military and economic factors in various regions. Some regions regard arms control as a Western

---

[47] OSCE Lisbon Document 1996 (note 44), section III.
[48] OSCE Lisbon Document 1996 (note 44), section III, para I (3).

concept with less relevance to their own security dilemmas; others, such as South-East Asia, seem to perceive their security in terms of arms build-ups rather than arms control. With few exceptions, they are not yet able to go beyond political declarations and gestures.[49]

In the context of the former Sino-Soviet border, talks on border demarcation in Shanghai between China, Kazakhstan, Kyrgyzstan, Russia and Tajikistan led to an agreement on confidence-building in the military sphere on 26 April 1996. The agreement renounced the use or threat of force, unilateral military superiority, and the use of troops stationed in the border area for an attack on another side. It also included some CBMs within a 100 km-wide zone on both sides of the approximately 8000 km-long border China shares with the four other countries, including the provision of information on temporary entry of troops and weapons, limiting the number and geographical scope of border-area field exercises and movements, inviting observers, taking measures to prevent hazardous military activities, and enhancing friendly contacts between military forces and border troops. The parties also stated their intention to intensify talks on agreeing mutual cuts in armed forces along the border.[50] In early 1997 it was announced that an agreement on mutual reductions would be signed in April 1997 by the five heads of state.[51]

The CBMs agreed on 29 November by the foreign ministers of China and India included a restriction on exercises above division size without prior notification and restrictions on combat aircraft flights near the Line of Actual Control (LAC) in north-eastern India, to facilitate demarcation of their 4000 km-long border. The agreement committed the two states to refrain from engaging in military activities that threaten the other side or undermine stability along the Sino-Indian border and mutually agreed unspecified reductions in their respective armed forces along the LAC. Communication links between Chinese and Indian sector headquarters have also been installed.[52]

The slowly evolving Latin American dialogue on conventional arms control and CBMs was crowned with the Organization of American States (OAS) Declaration of Santiago on CSBMs of 10 November 1995 and the Central American Democratic Security Treaty of 15 December 1995 envisaging limitations on armed forces and a series of CSBMs. Both agreements were adopted at high-level meetings, but the ensuing dialogue has not yet produced militarily significant effects. The lack of progress is generally blamed on the continuing weakness of civilian governments *vis-à-vis* their military establishments in Latin America.[53]

---

[49] For a review of the record of arms control endeavours in different parts of the world see 'Special issue: regional security, arms control and disarmament, *Defense Analysis*, vol. 12, no. 1 (Apr. 1996).

[50] United Nations, Agreement between the Russian Federation, the Republic of Kazakhstan, the Kyrgyz Republic, the Republic of Tajikistan and the People's Republic of China on confidence building in the military field in the border area, UN document A/51/137, 17 May 1996.

[51] Kazakh Television First Programme (Almaty), 2 Jan. 1997 (in Russian), in FBIS-SOV-97-005, 2 Jan. 1997.

[52] *Arms Control Reporter*, sheet 454.B.231, 1996; and *Jane's Defence Weekly*, 20 Nov. 1996, p. 15.

[53] *Arms Control Reporter*, sheets 840.B.25–27, 1996; Mowle, T. S. and Balmaseda, G., 'Controlling weapons in Latin America: a treaty proposal', and Aravena, F. R., 'Confidence-building measures: help-

In South-East Asia, the CBM Working Group (co-chaired by Indonesia and Japan) of the Association of South-East Asian Nations (ASEAN) Regional Forum, established in 1994, is working on proposals aimed at lowering the probability of armed conflict by reducing suspicion and increasing dialogue (e.g., on security concepts, voluntary submissions of defence policy statements, high-level contacts and exchanges between military academies and participation in the UN Register of Conventional Arms[54]). While some CBMs have been adopted by South-East Asian states (e.g., the establishment of joint border committees), prospects for the adoption of conventional arms control measures are poor in the face of the region's ongoing arms build-up and procurement plans.[55]

In the Middle East, the regional arms control and security talks associated with the peace process have been in abeyance since 1995. Despite the optimism expressed in previous years, the arms control talks will probably not be revived until the final stage of the peace process.[56]

VI. Anti-personnel land-mines

There was a significant shift in attitudes towards the elimination of anti-personnel land-mines in 1996.[57] Further progress was recorded in the wake of the 1995 Review Conference of the Convention on Prohibitions or Restrictions on the Use of Certain Conventional Weapons Which May be Deemed to Be Excessively Injurious or to Have Indiscriminate Effects (the CCW Convention), often referred to as the 'Inhumane Weapons Convention'. The Review Conference highlighted the extent of the problem, gained widespread support for a ban and at its concluding session adopted an amended Protocol II on prohibitions or restrictions on the use of mines, booby-traps and other devices, including further restrictions on the use, production and transfer of anti-personnel land-mines.

The pursuit of a total ban on these inhumane weapons, which pose a great threat to civilians, is a matter of growing international, public and governmental concern. Land-mines kill or maim some 26 000 people each year (90 per cent of whom are civilians). It is estimated that there are 85–110 million anti-personnel land-mines in 68 countries (Afghanistan, Angola, Cambodia, Mozambique and the former Yugoslavia being most affected), and every year some 2 million new mines are laid. Thanks mainly to the efforts of non-governmental organizations (NGOs), which built a wave of international public opinion against land-mines and pressured governments into negotia-

ing to ensure the security of the Western Hemisphere', both in *Disarmament* (UN: New York), vol. 19, no. 2 (1996), pp. 69–85 and 86–97, respectively.

[54] See chapter 9 in this volume.

[55] Thayer, C., 'Arms control in South-East Asia', *Defense Analysis*, vol. 12, no. 1 (Apr. 1996), pp. 82–83.

[56] See chapter 3 in this volume.

[57] For discussion of the developments in this field in 1995 see Goldblat, J., 'Land-mines and blinding laser weapons: the Inhumane Weapons Convention Review Conference', *SIPRI Yearbook 1996* (note 10), pp. 753–64.

tions, the cause of land-mine prohibition made considerable headway. In 1996, 30 additional states called for a total ban, bringing the number of states supporting a ban to 53. The United Nations and the participants of the Ottawa International Strategy Conference have been instrumental, although competitive, in promoting the goal.

Amended Protocol II

Between the Review Conference session on 15–19 January 1996 and the spring session (24 April–3 May) several additional countries took unilateral action towards eliminating or limiting the use of anti-personnel land-mines. Hungary and Turkey adopted moratoria on the transfer of land-mines; Australia banned military use of land-mines; and Germany renounced their use and announced destruction of its existing stocks. In April the UK stated that it would back an international prohibition on land-mines and, in the interim, destroy nearly half of its existing stocks of non-self-destructing mines (all British land-mines are currently non-self-destructing). It also pledged to pursue early international agreement on the elimination of all non-self-destructing land-mines. The UK will use such mines solely in exceptional circumstances, strictly in accordance with the laws of armed conflict and the amended Protocol II to the CCW Convention. In addition the UK announced that it would seek alternatives to its remaining land-mines and, if such an alternative were found, it would cease to use and would destroy its stockpiles.[58]

The amended Protocol II, adopted by 55 countries, is legally binding, replaces the original protocol and will enter into force six months after 20 states have ratified it. The most important amendments include:[59]

1. The scope of the international rules governing the use of anti-personnel land-mines was expanded to include *internal* armed conflicts as well as conflicts between states. The amended protocol applies to all non-international armed conflict except 'disturbances', and its provisions must be observed at all times, both in peacetime and in conflict.

2. All undetectable anti-personnel mines are banned. All mines of this type produced after 1 January 1997 must include devices or materials, equivalent to an 8-gram piece of iron, that would make them detectable. Mines produced before that date must also be made detectable, but states parties may defer compliance for up to nine years after entry into force of the amended protocol.

3. Strict detectability for all land-mines and stricter rules on marking, monitoring and clearing non-self-destructing mines are required. All anti-personnel land-mines must either be kept within marked and protected mine-

---

[58] 'UK policy statement on landmines, 22 April 1996', *BASIC Reports*, no. 51 (30 Apr. 1996), p. 3.
[59] Protocol on Prohibitions or Restrictions on the Use of Mines, Booby-traps and Other Devices as Amended on 3 May (Protocol II of the Convention on Prohibitions or Restrictions on the Use of Certain Conventional Weapons Which May be Deemed to Be Excessively Injurious or to Have Indiscriminate Effects), Geneva, 3 May 1996. See *Disarmament*, vol. 19, no. 2 (1996), pp. 105–22.

fields or be equipped with self-destruction and self-deactivation mechanisms to ensure that they will not pose a long-term threat to the civilian population. Remotely delivered anti-personnel mines are banned unless information is recorded on their estimated location, the number and type of mines laid, and the date and time of emplacement.

4. Responsibility for the maintenance or clearance of land-mines rests with the party that laid them.

5. A ban on the transfer of prohibited mines and several other restrictions were imposed. Transfer of all anti-personnel mines to states not parties to Protocol II (unless they agree to abide by it) is also banned. Serious violations will be punishable by legal action.

6. Annual meetings will be held to discuss the implementation of the protocol, and the next Review Conference will convene not later than 2001.

The protocol has met with criticism, mainly from NGOs united in the International Campaign to Ban Landmines (ICBL) and the International Committee of the Red Cross (ICRC). The USA and other Western countries were reproached for promoting the continued use of mines and being guided mainly by military and economic considerations.[60] The ICBL and the ICRC pointed to some of the protocol's major deficiencies: (a) countries can continue to produce, export and use long-lasting mines as long as they pledge to follow certain rules for deployment; (b) the definition of an anti-personnel mine ('primarily designed to explode') was changed, which may lead to circumvention and the use of anti-tank mines with anti-handling devices, hybrid versions (combining the features of anti-personnel and anti-tank mines) and other types of mine; and (c) the absence of verification provisions and the nine-year transition period weaken the agreement further—new restrictions on the use of non-self-destructing mines are liable to include a wide range of exceptions.

Towards a global ban

The amended Protocol II led to a series of steps and initiatives, and the land-mine ban process gained momentum in the latter half of the year. President Bill Clinton declared on 16 May that the USA would cease to use non-self-destructing land-mines and destroy its existing stocks by the end of 1999, with one exception (the Korean Peninsula). He also pledged aid for land-mine clearance.[61] Denmark announced a ban on its military forces' use of anti-

[60] Goose, S. D., 'CCW states fail to stem crisis; US policy now an obstacle', *Arms Control Today*, vol. 26, no. 5 (July 1996), pp. 9, 14–17.

[61] *Arms Control Reporter*, sheets 860.3.12–18, 1996. The USA promised to spend c. $50 million to clear land-mines (c. $32 million for demining programmes in 14 countries in Africa, Asia and Latin America; an initial $8.5 million for a Mine Action Center in Sarajevo coordinating mine information, education and demining activities; and about $7 million for R&D on technology for the needs of humanitarian demining operations. 'U.S. efforts to address problem of landmines', White House fact sheet, 16 May 1996. Version current on 24 June 1996, created: 16 May 1996, URL <gopher://198.80.36.82:70/0R16255631-16258663-range/archives/1996/pdq.96>. On 15 Aug. 1996 the USA announced its intention to spend $50 million to clear mines from Bosnia ($15 million) and other battlefields. *Defense News*, 19–25 Aug. 1996, p. 2. In 1997 the USA will invest another $47 million in demining activities, including $14 million devoted to R&D. 'Banning, clearing deadly landmines top

personnel land-mines.[62] Several countries and international bodies criticized weaknesses in the protocol and the European Parliament passed a resolution pointing to its deficiencies.

At its 26th General Assembly meeting in early June 1996 the OAS called for a moratorium on the production, use and transfer of land-mines in the Americas. Its resolution also provided for the opening of a register at the OAS General Secretariat to record the existing stocks of land-mines and the status of mine clearance.[63] In September Central American foreign ministers signed an agreement prohibiting the production, use and possession of or trade in anti-personnel land-mines, and in December the OAS Permanent Council approved a report recommending that the Organization aim to conclude its mine-clearing operations in Central America by 2000.[64] On 18 July Germany presented a seven-point programme on land-mines envisaging: (a) an international ban; (b) help with mine clearance (education and training); (c) a contribution by German armed forces; (d) requests for NATO and EU participation; (e) speedy application of the amended Protocol II; (f) use of financial and technological cooperation as an instrument to encourage the affected countries to become more involved; and (g) support of international efforts, particularly from the UN, to cope with the problem.[65]

The subject of mine clearance and peacekeeping was taken up at the UN Security Council in August.[66] On 26 September Italian Foreign Minister Lamberto Dini announced Italy's intention to abandon the production and export of anti-personnel land-mines. Also in September, the 96th Inter-Parliamentary Union Conference in Beijing renewed its earlier call for the pursuit of a comprehensive ban on anti-personnel land-mines and of mine clearance efforts (with reservations by China,[67] Cuba, Libya and Viet Nam).

On 3–5 October Canada hosted the International Strategy Conference in Ottawa to further a complete ban on land-mines. It was attended by 71 states (47 full participants—known as the 'Ottawa Group'—and 24 observer states plus dozens of NGOs). China did not attend. The Ottawa Declaration 'Towards a global ban on anti-personnel (AP) mines', signed by 50 states (the Ottawa Group plus Bolivia, Colombia and Iran), called for the enhancement of the ban and elimination of land-mines; (b) universal adherence to the amended Protocol II; (c) a stop to all new deployments; (d) provision of greater resources to mine awareness, mine clearance and victim assistance pro-

U.S.–U.N. priority'. *Wireless File* (US Information Service: US Embassy: Stockholm, 6 Dec. 1996). Version current on 29 Apr. 1997, URL<gopher://198.80.36.82:70/0R51774891-51784869-range/archives/1996/pdq.96>.

[62] *Arms Control Reporter*, sheet 860.3.19, 1996.

[63] *Arms Control Reporter,* sheet 860.3.19–20, 1996.

[64] 'OAS seeks to end demining in Central America by 2000', OAS press release, 17 Dec. 1996. Version current on 17 Dec. 1996, URL <gopher://198.80.36.82:70/0R54393843-54395613-range/archives/1996/pdq.96>.

[65] UN General Assembly/Security Council document A951/266, S/1996/621, 5 Aug. 1996.

[66] For summaries of presentations see *Disarmament Diplomacy*, July/Aug. 1996, pp. 37–44.

[67] A senior Chinese official argued that 'the efforts to solve the problem of landmines should take into account consideration of humanitarian concerns and the justifiable military need for self-defence in sovereign states... [Landmines are] a justifiable means for self-defence in many countries, particularly in those with long land boundaries'. *Disarmament Diplomacy*, Oct. 1996, p. 55.

grammes; (e) support for an envisaged UN General Assembly resolution in 1996 calling *inter alia* for implementing national moratoria, bans and other restrictions on the operational use and transfer of land-mines, and for regional and subregional activities in support of a global ban; and (f) a follow-on conference in Belgium in June 1997.[68]

Several statements were made by participants. Canada announced a plan to destroy a minimum of two-thirds of its land-mine stockpiles and to make an additional contribution (2 million Canadian dollars) to global mine-removal programmes. France stated in a letter to the UN Secretary-General that it 'proposes to arrive at a legally-binding and verifiable international agreement on a total and general prohibition of anti-personnel mines' and will refrain from the use of anti-personnel land-mines 'except where such use is absolutely necessary to protect its forces'. France was also reported to have decided to destroy half its stockpile of land-mines by the end of 1997.[69] Russia, by contrast, was less enthusiastic; a Russian observer proposed that a total ban be achieved gradually.[70]

On 4 November the USA[71] and 84 co-sponsors submitted a draft resolution to the United Nations to 'pursue vigorously an effective, legally-binding' ban on the use, stockpiling, production and transfer of anti-personnel land-mines, calling on all states to accede to the CCW Convention and its amended Protocol II, to comply to the fullest extent possible with the applicable rules of the protocol, and to declare and implement various moratoria, bans and other restrictions already announced by other states on land-mines. The draft resolution also requested the UN Secretary-General to prepare a report for the 52nd session of the UN General Assembly on the steps taken to complete such an agreement and on other steps taken by states to implement such moratoria, bans and other restrictions. The resolution was approved in the First Committee on 13 November, by a vote of 141 to 0, with 10 abstentions, including Russia and China.[72] On 10 December the UN General Assembly voted 155:0 in favour of the resolution (with 10 abstentions).[73]

---

[68] Declaration of the Ottawa Conference: towards a global ban on anti-personnel (AP) mines, International Strategy Conference, Ottawa, 3–5 Oct. 1996. Version current on 27 Apr. 1997, URL <http://www.icrc.org/icrcnews/42f7a.htm>.

[69] Letter of 4 Oct. 1996 to the UN Secretary-General, UN document A/C.1/51/7, 10 Oct. 1996, *Disarmament Diplomacy*, Oct. 1996, p. 43; and *Arms Control Reporter*, sheet 860.3.21–22, 1996.

[70] *Disarmament Diplomacy*, Oct. 1996, p. 55. Russian Foreign Ministry spokesman Gennadiy Tarasov stated: 'We believe it is necessary to advance gradually to a complete ban on such mines, introducing bans and restrictions one after another'. ITAR-TASS (Moscow), 15 Oct. 1996, in 'Russia: Moscow supports initiatives against antipersonnel mines', FBIS-SOV-96-201, 17 Oct. 1996.

[71] In a letter to the US Senate, released on 8 Jan. 1997, President Clinton urged ratification of the Protocols to the CCW Convention and Protocol II in particular. 'Clinton letter to Senate on landmines protocol', *Wireless File* (US Information Service: US Embassy: Stockholm, 8 Jan. 1997). Version current on 8 Jan. 1997, URL <gopher://198.80.36.82:70/0R509889-517351-range/archives/1997/pdq.97>.

[72] Belarus, China, Cuba, Israel, North Korea, South Korea, Russia, Pakistan, Syria and Turkey abstained. A Russian representative stated that solidarity with victims of land-mines should be expressed through intensification of mine-clearing efforts and a ban on export rather than on their use and production; China criticized the vote as a 'beauty and popularity contest' and said that the right to self-defence must be taken into account in disarmament endeavours. Other countries offered similar justifications for their abstentions. *Jane's Defence Weekly*, 4 Dec. 1996, p. 4.

[73] UN General Assembly Resolution A/51/45S, 10 Dec. 1996.

On 13 December the Austrian Parliament banned totally and for an unlimited period the production, procurement, sale mediation, import, export, transit, use and possession of land-mines. It also announced legislation to prevent the transformation of anti-tank mines into anti-personnel mines.[74]

On 17 January 1997, the USA decided to seek to initiate negotiations on a worldwide ban in the 61-member Conference on Disarmament (CD), which includes all the major producers and exporters, rather than pursue it within the Ottawa process, a step criticized as a potential brake on progress towards a ban.[75] The USA also announced that it will permanently ban the export and transfer of anti-personnel land-mines and that its land-mine stockpile will be maintained at the current level.[76]

By early 1997 four different positions on a land-mine ban were represented by: (*a*) the Ottawa Group backed by many European countries, South Africa and developing countries such as Nicaragua, Panama and the Philippines; (*b*) a group of countries that believes the CD to be the best forum, but that sees the Ottawa process as helpful in applying further pressure on other states (Australia, Britain, France, Italy and the USA); (*c*) countries that reject any talks outside the CD (China, India, Iran, Libya, Pakistan, Russia and Syria); and (*d*) some nations, such as Cuba, South Korea and Sri Lanka, which claim that because they are located in areas of continuing conflict they cannot abandon land-mines.

VII. Conclusions

The post-cold war phase of the implementation of conventional arms control in Europe came to an end in 1996, and a new period of negotiation and conceptualization was opened up. Key issues were the need to adapt the CFE Treaty to the new security conditions arising from the breakup of the bloc system on the continent, and the prospective enlargement of NATO. A time of intensive debate will follow on the ambitious agenda set out at the OSCE Lisbon Summit. The adaptation of the CFE Treaty stands a good chance of being achieved in a relatively short period of time unless it falls victim to the political battles being waged around NATO enlargement. The latter half of 1997, after the Atlantic Alliance has decided on its membership, will be a test for the negotiations.

The place of arms control in the European security debate has also been re-evaluated in the light of post-cold war failures and successes in handling conflicts and crises and the need to complete pan-European arms control. The

---

[74] Letter dated 29 Jan. 1997 addressed to the Secretary-General of the Conference from the Permanent Representative of Austria transmitting the 'Federal law on the Ban of Anti-Personnel Mines', Adopted by the Austrian Parliament, Conference on Disarmament document CD/1444, 4 Feb. 1997.

[75] It is feared that Russia and China, CD members outside the Ottawa Group, will thwart progress in this UN body.

[76] Letter dated 21 January 1997 addressed to the Secretary-General of the Conference on Disarmament from the Permanent Representative of the United States of America to the Conference on Disarmament transmitting a Statement by the Press Secretary of the White House and a Fact Sheet on United States Initiatives on Anti-Personnel Landmines, CD document CD/1442, 22 Jan. 1997.

international community, equipped with guidelines for security cooperation and an agenda for current and future arms control, will be able to deal more effectively with the challenges and risks facing it in the foreseeable future. It remains to be seen whether the new framework and approach will be adequate to deal with present and future threats and uncertainties.

Effective handling of subregional problems will be critical for the overall success of arms control and peace efforts in the OSCE area. The Florence Agreement is working towards a military balance among former warring parties, with the help and support of the international community. With the conclusion of the subregional arms reduction and verification process in the spring of 1998, the international community will face the challenge of accommodating the Balkan subregional arms control endeavours to those of the states parties to the CFE Treaty, a goal so far strongly resisted by neighbours of the former Yugoslavia. Until the former belligerents formulate their ultimate political goals, the implementation of the military security aspects of the Dayton Agreement will be hard to achieve.

Outside Europe, conventional arms control is little more than a dialogue or a trudge through first-generation CBM agreements. Although progress is not very impressive, there is a general awareness that this kind of instrument is needed to build security and confidence among regional actors.

In the global context, the problem of land-mines has acquired a special importance as the toll of civilian casualties rises. The success of efforts to achieve a global ban will depend largely on the stance taken by the main producers and exporters. The United States has taken some significant steps towards a ban, but its decision (supported by France and the UK) to side-step the Ottawa Group in favour of the CD has reduced the chances of rapid progress. The focus seems to have shifted towards a phased approach, with a ban on exports being seen as the first step. Russia has shown some interest in considering such a step-by-step approach but China still appears reluctant to follow this course. All this diminishes the chance of signing a total ban in December 1997, as proposed by Canada at the 1996 International Strategy Conference in Ottawa.

Appendix 14A. Confidence- and security-building measures in Europe

ZDZISLAW LACHOWSKI

I. Introduction

Confidence- and security-building measures (CSBMs) are currently implemented, agreed or under discussion on three planes in Europe: (*a*) across the area of the Organization for Security and Co-operation in Europe (OSCE), under the Vienna Document 1994; (*b*) subregional (in Bosnia and Herzegovina); and (*c*) local (bilateral agreements). Several amendments to the Vienna Document have been proposed and introduced, and the debate on streamlining and updating CSBMs has continued. A number of questions remain about the relevance of CSBMs, particularly their applicability in conflict areas or times of crisis. These and other issues were addressed at the 1996 Annual Implementation Assessment Meeting (AIAM), in the working groups of the OSCE Forum for Security Co-operation (FSC) and at the OSCE Review Meeting in Vienna.

II. Assessment of the implementation of the Vienna Document

The sixth Annual Implementation Assessment Meeting, held on 4–6 March 1996 in the framework of the OSCE Forum for Security Co-operation, reviewed the implementation of the Vienna Document 1994 of the Negotiations on Confidence- and Security-Building Measures and discussed suggestions aimed at improving and adapting the Document to current security requirements.

The meeting focused on the difficulties in implementing the document, identifying methods by which to achieve full implementation and setting the course for the future tasks of the FSC. The meeting broke off into six working groups and the topics addressed included:

1. *Annual exchange of information.* Proposals were made on simultaneous presentation of military information; presentation of the annual exchange and the Global Exchange of Military Information in a single document, preferably on a given date or within one month (December); and how to avoid and report non-compliance (the role of the Conflict Prevention Centre, CPC, in sending reminders of impending obligations, indicating shortcomings, providing support, etc.).

2. *Defence planning.* Proposals were made to extend the deadline for defence planning submissions from two to three months; to exchange documents on a fixed date; to exchange complete information every third year (unless major changes occur); and to review the time-limit for clarification (to be lengthened or abolished).

3. *Military activities.* Participants considered how to ensure implementation in crisis situations and whether the document needs to be adapted to 'foul-weather' conditions. Despite the obvious difficulties it was recommended that observations be carried out in crisis or conflict situations and that notification be effected. Peacekeeping activities should be considered in this context. It was proposed that the Vienna Document should cover the military operations of paramilitary forces.

4. *Annual calendars and constraining provisions.* The main proposal was to extend the time-frame for an activity involving 40 000 troops or 900 tanks or (additionally) 2000 ACVs from two to three years.

5. *Compliance and verification.* A series of changes were proposed to develop and improve verification and to further implementation: a review of annual quotas for evaluation visits and inspections; an increase in the number and size of inspection teams and their national/multinational composition; combining quotas for inspections and evaluation visits and their distribution over the year; establishing an OSCE arms control agency; and perhaps creating a role for the CPC regarding coordination issues.

6. *Risk reduction.* It was proposed that the three existing measures (regarding unusual activities and hazardous incidents and dispelling concerns about activities) be combined. New (unspecified) provisions were also called for to reflect the new realities in Europe.

7. *Contacts.* A new requirement for every state to host one air base visit within a five-year period and the extension of air base provisions to ground units/military facilities were proposed. There was a discussion on notifying contacts (obligatorily or voluntarily).

8. *Communications.* The following topics were addressed: the role of the CPC as a nodal point for relaying messages to states not yet connected to the Communications Network; closer coordination between political and technical representatives of states regarding implementation, software applications and the operation of the network; ensuring a standardized technical review and interoperability of existing systems through establishment of a Configuration Control Board—a technical sub-group within the Communications Group (CG); and increasing the decision-making capability of the CG on matters with financial implications and other matters.

9. *Implications of implementation.* Possible forms of assessing the implementation of the Code of Conduct on Politico-Military Aspects of Security were discussed: a special assessment procedure for the code; its further development in the context of the Security Model for Europe for the 21st Century; the AIAM as the appropriate forum in which to discuss the code in future, and so on. Moreover, development of new stabilizing measures was addressed (more operationality, verification etc.).[1]

III. Improving the Vienna Document 1994

In 1995–96 the FSC discussed and agreed several amendments to the Vienna Document 1994. In the autumn of 1995 two decisions were taken by the FSC to be annexed to the document:

1. With regard to the observation of certain military activities and notifiable military activities conducted without advance notice to the troops involved, invitations will be extended together with the notification given in accordance with paragraph 39.1 (at the time the troops commence the activities) and replies will be given not later than three days after the invitation is issued.[2]

---

[1] For a fuller review of suggestions and proposals see OSCE, Annual Implementation Assessment Meeting 1996, Survey of Suggestions, OSCE document REF.SEC/156/96 (Conflict Prevention Centre, Vienna, 25 Mar. 1996).

[2] FSC, 126th Plenary Meeting, FSC.DEC/18/95, *Journal*, no. 130 (18 Oct. 1995).

2. Under annual exchange of information on defence planning (para. 15) (*a*) the states will notify the date of approval of the military budget for the forthcoming fiscal year by the national authorities concerned; (*b*) negative information (NIL) on force planning should be stated where applicable (15.2); (*c*) information on the preceding fiscal year will refer to the most recent fiscal year for which figures are available, in order to enable states to provide their annual information in one package (15.3); and (*d*) the word 'available' under information on budgets (15.4) refers to relevant and releasable facts, figures and/or estimates under consideration in the national procedures for defence planning (15.1.2).[3]

The FSC agreed that five decisions of the sixth AIAM be annexed to the Vienna Document:

1. A new common schedule of five-year periods for participating states to arrange air base visits (para. 20) would begin on 1 January 1997.[4]
2. The CPC would forward messages received over the OSCE Communications Network to those participating states not connected to it, and states hooked up to the network will include the CPC as a nodal point for messages that should be forwarded to states not connected.[5]
3. Under defence planning (para. 15), the time-frame for states to submit their defence planning documents would be extended to three months.[6]
4. Participating states with no armed forces will inform all other states of this (para. 15) in order to facilitate the monitoring of implementation.[7]
5. Under constraining provisions, ACVs were included and the time-frame between significant military activities was extended to three years.[8]

The implementation record

The Vienna Document was also reviewed during the OSCE Review Meeting in Vienna in November 1996.[9] In spite of the generally positive assessment of the implementation of CSBMs, some shortcomings were identified. The number of states providing military information has increased over the years. However, 11 countries have still not provided information on defence planning and another 8 have provided it only once in the three-year period; only 26 of 50 states with a military establishment have participated in such events as visits to air bases, military facilities or demonstrations of weapons and equipment systems, contacts and other cooperative mechanisms; and the communications network does not yet link the capitals of all participating states—the list of cases of non-implementation or non-compliance is longer. The Vienna Document provisions are believed to have an 'all-weather' applicability, but there was no consensus on how to apply these measures or devise new ones in times of crisis. Some delegations believed that the Vienna Document provisions were insufficiently applied, for example, the risk reduction mechanisms or stabilizing measures have scarcely been used to date. It was also felt that regional

[3] FSC, 132nd Plenary Meeting, FSC.DEC/19/95, *Journal*, no. 136 (29 Nov. 1995).
[4] FSC, 146th Plenary Meeting, FSC.DEC/2/96, *Journal*, no. 151 (24 Apr. 1996).
[5] FSC, 147th Plenary Meeting, FSC.DEC/3/96, *Journal*, no. 152 (8 May 1996).
[6] FSC, 152nd Plenary Meeting, FSC.DEC/4/96, *Journal*, no. 157 (19 June 1996).
[7] FSC, 160th Plenary Meeting, FSC.DEC/6/96, *Journal*, no. 165 (9 Oct. 1996).
[8] FSC, 160th Plenary Meeting, FSC.DEC/7/96, *Journal*, no. 170 (13 Nov. 1996).
[9] OSCE, Review Meeting 1996, Report of the Chairman-in-Office to the Lisbon Summit, Vienna, 22 Nov. 1996.

aspects have so far been neglected, although experts and diplomats were unable to be more specific.

In this light, proposals to improve implementation ranged from selective, limited measures (most of which had been discussed and proposed at the AIAM in March) to more substantial reform. Nevertheless the international community remains rather helpless in the face of new challenges and risks, seeking either to streamline the existing measures and supplement them with new, even more detailed provisions or to add new sets of measures, such as those on naval operations and paramilitary and domestic security forces (still awaiting consensus), on the one hand, and those on subregional contingencies, on the other. Some states would like to see a new generation of CSBMs, and perhaps a new document, while others advise full compliance with existing provisions in the first instance. The range of proposals indicates a continuing state of confusion and lack of consensus among participating states.

Aside from general declarations in its proposed framework for arms control and agenda for the FSC,[10] the OSCE Lisbon Summit only managed to produce, at the insistence of a number of concerned states, a list of non-consensual suggestions advanced by one or more participating states. These suggestions included: extension of CSBMs to naval activities; exchange of information on internal security forces; measures concerning the stationing of armed forces; cooperation in defence conversion; measures concerning the deployment of armed forces on foreign territories, including their border movements; regular seminars on military doctrine, preferably at a high military level; an 'OSCE White Paper' on defence issues, based on existing OSCE information and drawing on national experiences; studying the possibility of creating nuclear weapon-free zones in Europe; voluntary participation, on a national basis, in information exchange and verification of regional regimes; transparency with regard to structural, qualitative and operational aspects of armed forces; and unilateral declarations of weapon ceilings.[11]

The overall stalemate in the field of CSBMs is compounded by expectations of the CFE Treaty adaptation talks in Vienna that started on 21 January 1997. The outcome of this negotiation will also have a decisive impact on the future adjustment/revision of the Vienna Document.

Of the planned notifiable activities for 1996,[12] only three exercises were carried out: the Finnish 'Kymi 96' exercise and two NATO 'Dynamic Mix 96' manoeuvres: the command post exercise and field/staff training exercise. The planned 'Atlantic Resolve' exercise was cancelled in July 1996. There were six prior notifications in 1996. The CPC was notified of the deployment of British, French, Italian and US contingents in the NATO Implementation Force (IFOR) and of two non-notifiable exercises: one was voluntary and one was 'in the spirit of para. 136'. Of the four observations in the year, two concerned IFOR (US contingents in Bosnia and Herzegovina and Hungary), and two field training exercises in Poland (the British brigade 'Ulan Eagle 96' exercise and 'Orion 96').

SIPRI has information on four manoeuvres (all to be carried out by NATO) subject to notification planned for 1997. These are listed in table 14A.1.

[10] See chapter 14 in this volume.
[11] OSCE, Lisbon Document 1996, DOC.S/1/96, 3 Dec. 1996, section III, A Framework for Arms Control, FSC.DEC/8/96 (reproduced in appendix 5A in this volume), and section IV, Development of the Agenda of the Forum for Security Cooperation, FSC.DEC/9/96.
[12] Lachowski, Z., 'The Vienna CSBMs in 1995', *SIPRI Yearbook 1996: Armaments, Disarmament and International Security* (Oxford University Press: Oxford, 1996), appendix 16A, table 16A.3.

Table 14A.1. Calendar of planned notifiable military activities in 1997, exchanged by 15 November 1996

States/Location	Dates/Start window	Type/Name of activity	Area	Level of command	No. of troops	Type of forces or equipment	No. and type of divisions	Comments
1. Belgium, Denmark, Germany, Italy, Luxembourg, Netherlands, Norway, Portugal, USA in Norway	27 Feb.–13 Mar.	FTX Adventure Express 97	Storholmen–Storfjellet–Snotind–Salvass-kardfjellet–Vassdalsfjellet–Skaidivarri–Kvalvikfjellet–Kvitfjellet	Div. level, responsibility of Norway COMJTF-NON	16 500[a]	Amphibious, ground and air forces	1 light mech. div. and 1 light mech. brig.	Exercise forces in deployment operations, practise cooperation and interoperability between Norway and allied formations
2. France, Greece, Italy, Netherlands, Spain, UK, USA in Spain	7–20 Apr.	CPX Destined Glory 97	Southern Spain	COMSTRIK-FORSOUTH	> 3 000	Amphibious units and maritime forces	..	Training of HQ staffs, amphibious units and maritime forces in development of combined amphibious forces Mediterranean concept
3. Canada, Denmark, Germany, France, Greece, Italy, Netherlands, Spain, Turkey, UK, USA	5–19 May	Linked Seas 97	Eastern Atlantic, Iberian Penninsula	CINCIBER-LANT	> 3 000	Maritime forces	..	Peacekeeping operations of a multinational maritime force; deployment into a crisis area
4. Germany, Greece, France, Italy, Netherlands, Spain, Turkey, UK, USA	2–21 Nov.	Dynamic Mix 97	Central/eastern Mediterranean	CINC-SOUTH	>3 000	Marine forces	..	Fleet operations to improve readiness, implement strategy in NATO southern region

[a] Belgium 2, Denmark 50, Germany 1740, Italy 580, Luxembourg 132, Netherlands 700, Norway 11248, Portugal 48, UK 1400 and USA 600.

Note: brig = brigade; CINCIBERLANT = Commander-in-Chief Iberian Atlantic Area; CINCSOUTH = Commander-in-Chief Allied Forces Southern Europe; COMJTFNON = Commander Joint Task Force Northern Norway; COMSTRIKFORSOUTH = Commander Naval Striking and Support Forces Southern Europe; CPX = command post exercise; div. = division; FTX = field training exercise; mech. = mechanized.

That 23 inspections were requested and conducted in 1996 is an encouraging sign. The number of evaluation visits has increased: 72 of the 81 visits requested were paid (including 4 under non-Vienna bilateral CSBM arrangements) to active formations/ units of ground and air forces; but reports were sent to the CPC on only 66 of these. Four visits were paid to air bases during the year; while seven states with air combat forces had not hosted visits before the new five-year cycle began on 1 January 1997.

IV. Subregional CSBMs

The Agreement on Confidence- and Security-building Measures in Bosnia and Herzegovina of 26 January 1996 (known as the Article II Agreement[13]) was basically modelled on the Vienna Document 1994; but some of its parts, particularly those concerning data exchange and inspections, also derived from the Treaty on Conventional Armed Forces in Europe (the CFE Treaty). The implementation of the CSBM agreement, assisted by the Personal Representative of the OSCE Chairman-in-Office, got off to a difficult start. It was put into effect immediately after the end of the year-long bloody war, in 'foul-weather' conditions, by the three parties: the state of Bosnia and Herzegovina and its two component entities, the Republika Srpska and the Federation of Bosnia and Herzegovina, whose armed forces were divided by strong mutual mistrust and, in the case of the Federation, by internal differences. Moreover they negotiated and are implementing the agreement under considerable pressure and the control of the international community (the OSCE, IFOR/the Stabilization Force (SFOR) and the Contact Group). Establishing a minimum degree of confidence is bound to be a difficult and time-consuming process. Moreover, the CSBM process operates alongside arms control in the region, the latter affecting the former's pace of implementation. Subregional confidence building is a unique challenge on all these counts, and its success or failure will determine further international efforts in dealing with other local crisis and conflict situations.

In March two (German- and French-led) teams conducted the first set of dual inspections in Bosnia and Herzegovina (in the Federation and in the Republika Srpska) to demonstrate the problems inspectors would have to deal with. From 18 April regular inspections were carried out to verify baseline data, submitted and exchanged by the parties on 15 February, on military formations and units as well as armaments. During these on-site inspections, inspectors from OSCE participating states offered their assistance in training the parties in the mechanics of conducting CSBM inspections. OSCE countries led the inspection teams, furnished half the inspectors and equipment, and covered the costs of the inspectors and the technical support. The Office for Regional Stabilization of the OSCE Mission to Bosnia and Herzegovina was responsible for assisting in the implementation of the CSBM agreement and played a key role in organizing the initial inspections. Afterwards, the inspections continued on a weekly basis until the end of a 120-day period. Another important CSBM, the start of work of individual military liaison missions to the headquarters, as envisaged by Annex 7 to the agreement, was delayed until June 1996. On 19 June the second official military information exchange took place

---

[13] Established according to the General Framework Agreement for Peace in Bosnia and Herzegovina (the Dayton Agreement), Annex 1-B, Agreement on Regional Stabilization, Article II, Confidence- and Security-Building Measures in Bosnia and Herzegovina. The Agreement on Confidence- and Security-building Measures in Bosnia and Herzegovina, version current on 29 Apr. 1997, URL <http:// www.fsk.ethz.ch/osce/docs/bosaq.htm>.

Table 14A.2. Regional and subregional CSBM notification and observation thresholds for and constraints on military activities, 1996

Document	Notification	Observation	Constraints
Vienna Document 1994 (including the amendments of 20 Nov. 1996)	9000 troops or 250 battle tanks or 500 ACVs or 250 self-propelled and towed artillery pieces, mortars and multiple-rocket launchers (100 mm calibre and above); 3000 in amphibious landing, heliborne landing or parachute drop (obligatory, 42 days in advance; area: Europe plus the Central Asian republics). Air force included in notification if at least 200 aircraft sorties, excluding helicopters, are flown	13 000 troops or 300 tanks or 500 ACVs or 250 artillery pieces, mortars and multiple-rocket launchers (100 mm and above); 3500 in airborne landing, heliborne landing or parachute drop	No more than 1 activity involving more than 40 000 troops or 900 tanks or 2000 ACVs within 3 calendar years; No more than 6 activities involving 13 000–40 000 troops or 300–900 tanks or 500–2000 ACVs within 1 calendar year; Of these, only three activities are allowed involving more than 25 000 troops or 200 tanks. No more than three simultaneous activities each involving more than 13 000 troops or 300 tanks. Communication of activities involving more than 40 000 or 900 tanks planned to carry out in second subsequent calendar year; no activities involving more than 40 000 or 900 tanks unless communicated as above and unless included in the annual calendar by 15 Nov. each year.
Agreement on CSBMs in Bosnia and Herzegovina (1996)	1500 troops or 25 battle tanks or 40 ACVs or 40 artillery pieces (75 mm and above) or 3 combat aircraft or 5 combat helicopters (obligatory, 42 days in advance; area: Bosnia and Herzegovina). Air force included if at least 60 aircraft and/or helicopter sorties are flown	Observers to be invited to the notifiable military activities	Only 1 activity allowed in 1996–97 involving more than 4000 troops including support or 80 tanks or 100 ACVs or 100 artillery pieces (75 mm and above) or 15 aircraft or 20 helicopters. Thereafter, within 2 years only 1 activity involving more than 16 000 troops incl. support or 80 tanks or 100 ACVs or 100 artillery pieces or 25 aircraft or 30 helicopters. Within a year no more than 3 activities, to be carried out separately, involving more than 7000 troops incl. support or 75 tanks or 100 artillery pieces or 15 aircraft or 20 helicopters. Each activity to be communicated by 15 Mar. 1996 and 15 Nov. each year.

pursuant to the Article II Agreement. In June it was reported that a hotline cable was being laid by the Republika Srpska in the area of the Inter-Entity Boundary Line near Lukavica. It would facilitate direct telephone contact between the military forces headquarters and the OSCE Office for Regional Stabilization.[14]

Political developments in and around Bosnia and Herzegovina have had a remarkable effect on confidence and security building. The Personal Representative of the OSCE Chairman-in-Office repeatedly had to diffuse crises during the year and quash the parties' attempts to score political gains at the expense of the agreement. Some political and military leaders in the entities still do not rule out military force as a viable means of pursuing security. The first year of implementation was found to have been satisfactory, but it is too soon to estimate definitely the effectiveness of the agreement as an instrument of promoting and enhancing confidence and security. Incorporating CSBMs into the implementation of the Dayton Agreement is seen as an essential step in the promotion of peace in the region.[15]

Bilateral CSBMs in the Balkans

The 1990s have witnessed the search to enhance confidence beyond the Vienna provisions on a bilateral footing in the Balkan region. A Hungarian–Romanian open skies agreement (11 May 1992) was signed. Bulgaria reached agreements with Turkey (the so-called Sofia and Edirne documents of 1 January 1992 and 12 November 1992, respectively) and Greece (the agreement of 3 December 1992 and the Athens Document of 1993), which envisage the advanced application of CBMs in border areas (notifications and inviting observers to exercises at lower thresholds and exchanges of information).[16] The Vienna Document encouraged participating states to undertake additional measures bilaterally, multilaterally or at the regional level to increase transparency and confidence (para. 136). In 1995 Turkey. was reported to have signed Edirne-like documents with Albania and Macedonia.

On 19 December 1995, Bulgaria and Romania signed a bilateral CSBM document.[17] It provides for notification 42 days in advance of military activities (involving at least 6000 troops or 100 battle tanks or 200 ACVs or 100 artillery pieces) and invitation of observers to the notified exercises (at least 7500 troops or 150 tanks or 300 ACVs or 100 artillery pieces) within a specified border zone; a commitment not to conduct military exercises above the battalion level within the 15-km zone on both sides of the shared border; annual inspections, evaluation visits and visits to military units in the zone of application, in addition to those under the Vienna Document; development of military contacts; and an annual assessment of implementation.

---

[14] *OSCE Newsletter*, vol. 3, nos 3 (Mar. 1996) and 6 (June 1996); see also Schmidt, H.-J., 'Konventionelle Rüstungskontrolle—Instrument zur Stabilisierung des Friedensprozesses im ehemaligen Jugoslawien?' [Conventional arms control—an instrument to stabilize the peace process in the former Yugoslavia], HSFK-Report, no. 10 (Hessische Stiftung Friedens- und Konfliktforschung: Frankfurt, 1996). After relocation of the Bosnian Serbian forces' General Staff to Bijeljina (some 200 km northeast of Sarajevo) direct communication became impossible for technical reasons.

[15] OSCE (note 9), pp. 6–7, and an overview of the implementation of the CSBM agreement by Ambassador Márton Krasznai, Personal Representative of the Chairman-in-Office. OSCE document REF.FSC/9/97, 22 Jan. 1997.

[16] Lachowski, Z., 'The Vienna confidence- and security-building measures in 1992', *SIPRI Yearbook 1993: World Armaments and Disarmament* (Oxford University Press: Oxford, 1993), p. 626.

[17] Document on mutually complementary confidence- and security-building measures and military contacts between the Republic of Bulgaria and Romania, *Bulgarian Military Review*, no. 1 (1996), pp. 69–73.

On 6 September 1996, Hungary and Romania signed in Arad, Romania, an agreement to expand the scope of military information and enhance confidence and security between the two countries.[18] It also builds upon the Vienna Document 1994. Both states undertake to notify each other 42 days in advance of troop movements and invite up to 5 observers to military activities involving at least 6000 troops or 100 battle tanks or 150 ACVs or 75 100-mm artillery pieces or 50 aircraft sorties including helicopters within the 80-km zones adjacent to the common border. In addition, each party will invite up to 5 observers from the other party to a military exercise carried out at the level of (mechanized or tank) battalion. Only military activities at the battalion level will be permitted within a 30-km zone adjacent to the common border. The agreement provides for the annual conduct, on a mutual basis, of 1–2 subunit-level joint training and exercise. The parties undertook to receive two more evaluation visits (Hungary decided to accept five visits altogether instead of one) and two more inspections and one more visit to a military base per year in addition to those of the Vienna Document 1994. Annual implementation assessment meetings will be held alternately in Hungary and Romania.

Regional measures

While the OSCE Review Meeting and Lisbon Summit reiterated acknowledgement of the value of the regional approach, the OSCE participants failed to agree on a conceptual framework. Discrepancies and disputes over problems such as those of definition of the region, the character of measures, the balance between the regional approach and the general framework continued to thwart efforts to reach agreement. The Lisbon Document 1996 encourages states to address regional challenges both in the FSC and on an informal and open-ended basis, and recommends a more effective use of 'stabilizing measures for localized crisis situations', as agreed in 1993. Such initiatives may address and undertake measures tailored to the region and complementary to OSCE-wide efforts with the aim of consolidating or increasing transparency and predictability, promoting good-neighbourly relations in the military field or reducing tension. The Bosnian experience will be of major importance in this regard. Bilateral solutions also give some inspiration regarding how to make better use of existing mechanisms and measures in a sub-regional context.

V. Conclusions

The improvements and progress made in 1996 bear witness to the commitment of OSCE participating states to further the operation of the CSBM regime in Europe, both on regional and sub-regional levels. The implementation record is improving slowly but surely, and new solutions are painstakingly sought, both within the Vienna Document itself and in new measures to adapt CSBMs to current realities, particularly to conflict prevention and crisis management tasks. As with other arms control arrangements, much will depend on the political situation on the continent in the years to come, particularly in the context of NATO enlargement and the adaptation of the European conventional arms control regime.

---

[18] Agreement on confidence- and security-building measures complementing the OSCE Vienna Document 1994 and on the development of military relations between the Government of the Republic of Hungary and the Government of Romania, 6 Sep. 1996.

Appendix 14B. Documents on conventional arms control

FINAL DOCUMENT OF THE FIRST CONFERENCE TO REVIEW THE OPERATION OF THE TREATY ON CONVENTIONAL ARMED FORCES IN EUROPE AND THE CONCLUDING ACT OF THE NEGOTIATION ON PERSONNEL STRENGTH

Vienna, 31 May 1996

The Republic of Armenia, the Azerbaijan Republic, the Republic of Belarus, the Kingdom of Belgium, the Republic of Bulgaria, Canada, the Czech Republic, the Kingdom of Denmark, the French Republic, Georgia, the Federal Republic of Germany, the Hellenic Republic, the Republic of Hungary, the Republic of Iceland, the Italian Republic, the Republic of Kazakstan, the Grand Duchy of Luxembourg, the Republic of Moldova, the Kingdom of the Netherlands, the Kingdom of Norway, the Republic of Poland, the Portuguese Republic, Romania, the Russian Federation, the Slovak Republic, the Kingdom of Spain, the Republic of Turkey, Ukraine, the United Kingdom of Great Britain and Northern Ireland and the United States of America, which are the States Parties to the Treaty on Conventional Armed Forces in Europe of 19 November 1990, hereinafter referred to as the States Parties,

Fulfilling the obligation set forth in Article XXI, paragraph 1, of the Treaty on Conventional Armed Forces in Europe, hereinafter referred to as the Treaty, to conduct a review of the operation of the Treaty, and thereby taking into account the Final Documents of the Extraordinary Conferences of the States Parties of 10 July 1992 in Helsinki and 13 November 1992 in Vienna,

Acting in accordance with the provision of Section VII, paragraph 3, of the Concluding Act of the Negotiation on Personnel Strength of Conventional Armed Forces in Europe of 10 July 1992, hereinafter referred to as the Concluding Act,

Recalling the results of the Extraordinary Conferences held thus far,

Reaffirming all the decisions of the Joint Consultative Group made thus far,

Having met at the First Review Conference, chaired by the Kingdom of the Netherlands, from 15 to 31 May 1996 in Vienna,

Have adopted the following:

I. Introduction

1. The States Parties reaffirm the fundamental role of the Treaty as a cornerstone of European security and their adherence to its goals and objectives. It is their common interest to preserve the integrity of the Treaty and the Concluding Act as well as the predictability and transparency they have created. The States Parties reaffirm their determination to fulfil in good faith all obligations and commitments arising from the Treaty and its associated documents. Bearing that in mind, they commit themselves to enhance the viability and effectiveness of the Treaty.

2. The negotiation, conclusion and implementation of the Treaty and the Concluding Act, as well as the ratification of the Treaty, took place in times of change during which the European security environment evolved significantly. The Warsaw Treaty Organization has ceased to exist. New states have emerged and become States Parties to the Treaty. At the same time, new risks and challenges to security have come to the fore. As a result of common efforts of the States Parties, the Treaty and the Concluding Act have remained vital stabilizing factors in this period of transition and contributed to its peaceful unfolding.

3. The States Parties stress that security and stability in Europe are vitally underpinned by the continuation and enhancement of robust arms control measures. Recognizing the evolution of the European political and security environment, the States Parties are resolved to continue the conventional arms control process, including through the enhancement of the viability and effectiveness of the Treaty. They see this as a common responsibility.

4. The States Parties recognize that the Treaty and the Concluding Act are essential contributions to the achievement of the goals and purposes of the Organization for Security and Co-operation in Europe (OSCE), in particular, the promotion of confidence, stability and security in an undivided Europe. In that context, they stress the importance of the

development of a common and comprehensive security model for Europe for the twenty-first century and the ongoing security dialogue and negotiations in the Forum for Security Co-operation,

II. Review of the operation of the Treaty and the Concluding Act

5. The States Parties note with satisfaction that more than 58,000 pieces of conventional armaments and equipment have been reduced, and that the overall holdings of conventional armaments and equipment within the area of application are substantially lower than the limits set in the Treaty.

More than 2,500 inspections have taken place. A permanent system for regular and routine exchange of Treaty notifications and other information has been developed. The Joint Consultative Group has been firmly established and has demonstrated its utility and importance as the ongoing Treaty forum.

With regard to the Concluding Act, the States Parties note with satisfaction that the personnel strength of conventional armed forces in the area of application was reduced by 1.2 million persons.

(. . .)

III. Future work on the Treaty

19. In view of Sections 1 and II of this Final Document, the States Parties instruct their delegations to the Joint Consultative Group to expand upon their work in accordance with Article XVI of the Treaty. Taking fresh impetus from this Review Conference, they will immediately start a thorough process aimed at improving the operation of the Treaty in a changing environment and, through that, the security of each State Party, irrespective of whether it belongs to a politico-military alliance. As part of this process, the States Parties will consider measures and adaptations with the aim of promoting the objectives of the Treaty and of enhancing its viability and effectiveness, including but not limited to the consideration of proposals already made to that effect. The character of this process should be such as to permit the Treaty to sustain its key role in the European security architecture. Its scope and parameters should be defined as a matter of priority.

20. Until the entry into force of such measures and adaptations, the States Parties will observe all provisions of the Treaty and its associated documents.

21. The States Parties will consider a progress report on the intermediate results of this process at the time of the OSCE Lisbon Summit. This report will, *inter alia*, include recommendations on the way ahead.

***

In accordance with Article XXI, paragraph 1, the States Parties look forward to gathering again in five years time to conduct the second Review of the Operation of the Treaty on Conventional Armed Forces in Europe.

This Final Document together with its Annexes A, B, C, D and E, which are integral to it, having been drawn up in all the official languages of the Organization for Security and Co-operation in Europe, shall be deposited with the Government of the Kingdom of the Netherlands as the designated Depositary for the Treaty, which shall circulate copies of this Final Document to all States Parties.

_____

Annex A. DOCUMENT AGREED AMONG THE STATES PARTIES TO THE TREATY ON CONVENTIONAL ARMED FORCES IN EUROPE OF 19 NOVEMBER 1990

The 30 States Parties to the Treaty on Conventional Armed Forces in Europe of 19 November 1990, hereinafter referred to as the Treaty,

Have agreed as follows:

I

1. Each State Party shall, taking into account the clarification set forth in this Document relating to the area described in Article V, subparagraph 1(A), of the Treaty and taking into account the understandings on flexibility set forth in this Document, comply fully with the numerical limitations set forth in the Treaty, including Article V thereof, no later than 31 May 1999.

2. Paragraph 1 of this Section shall be understood as not giving any State Party, which was in compliance with the numerical limitations set forth in the Treaty, including Article V thereof, as of 1 January 1996, the right to exceed any of the numerical limitations set forth in the Treaty.

3. Pursuant to the Decision of the Joint Consultative Group of 17 November 1995, the States Parties shall co-operate to the maximum extent possible to ensure the full

implementation of the provisions of this Document.

II

1. Within the area described in Article V, subparagraph 1(A), of the Treaty, as understood by the Union of Soviet Socialist Republics at the time the Treaty was signed, the Russian Federation shall limit its battle tanks, armoured combat vehicles, and artillery so that no later than 31 May 1999 and thereafter, the aggregate numbers do not exceed:

(A) 1,800 battle tanks;

(B) 3,700 armoured combat vehicles, of which no more than 552 shall be located within the Astrakhan oblast; no more than 552 shall be located within the Volgograd oblast; no more than 310 shall be located within the eastern part of the Rostov oblast described in Section III, paragraph 1, of this Document; and no more than 600 shall be located within the Pskov oblast; and

(C) 2,400 pieces of artillery.

2. Within the Odessa oblast, Ukraine shall limit its battle tanks, armoured combat vehicles, and artillery so that, upon provisional application of this Document and thereafter, the aggregate numbers do not exceed:

(A) 400 battle tanks;

(B) 400 armoured combat vehicles; and

(C) 350 pieces of artillery.

3. Upon provisional application of this Document and until 31 May 1999, the Russian Federation shall limit its battle tanks, armoured combat vehicles, and artillery, within the area described in Article V, subparagraph 1(A) , of the Treaty, as understood by the Union of Soviet Socialist Republics at the time the Treaty was signed, so that the aggregate numbers do not exceed:

(A) 1,897 battle tanks;

(B) 4,397 armoured combat vehicles; and

(C) 2,422 pieces of artillery.

III

1. For the purposes of this Document and the Treaty, the following territory, as constituted on 1 January 1996, of the Russian Federation shall be deemed to be located in the area described in Article IV, paragraph 2, of the Treaty rather than in the area described in Article V, subparagraph 1(A) of the Treaty: the Pskov oblast; the Volgograd oblast; the Astrakhan oblast; that part of the Rostov oblast east of the line extending from Kushchevskaya to Volgodonsk to the Volgograd

oblast border, including Volgodonsk; and Kushchevskaya and a narrow corridor in Krasnodar kray leading to Kushchevskaya.

2. For the purposes of this Document and the Treaty, the territory of the Odessa oblast, as constituted on 1 January 1996, of Ukraine shall be deemed to be located in the area described in Article IV, paragraph 3, of the Treaty rather than in the area described in Article V, subparagraph 1(A), of the Treaty.

IV

1. The States Parties shall, during the period before 31 May 1999, examine the Treaty provisions on designated permanent storage sites so as to allow all battle tanks, armoured combat vehicles, and artillery in designated permanent storage sites, including those subject to regional numerical limitations, to be located with active units.

2. The Russian Federation shall have the right to utilize to the maximum extent possible the provisions of the Treaty on temporary deployment of battle tanks, armoured combat vehicles, and artillery within its territory and outside its territory. Such temporary deployments on the territory of other States Parties shall be achieved by means of free negotiations and with full respect for the sovereignty of the States Parties involved.

3. The Russian Federation shall have the right to utilize to the maximum extent possible reallocation, in accordance with existing agreements, of the current quotas for battle tanks, armoured combat vehicles and artillery established by the Agreement on the Principles and Procedures for the Implementation of the Treaty on Conventional Armed Forces in Europe, done at Tashkent, on 15 May 1992. Such reallocations shall be achieved by means of free negotiations and with full respect for the sovereignty of the States Parties involved.

4. The Russian Federation shall count against the numerical limitations established in the Treaty and paragraph 1 of Section II of this Document any armoured combat vehicles listed as 'to be removed' in its information exchange of 1 January 1996 that are not so removed by 31 May 1999.

V

1. In addition to the annual information exchange provided pursuant to Section VII, subparagraph 1(C), of the Protocol on Notification and Exchange of Information, the Russian Federation shall provide information equal to that reported in the annual informa-

tion exchange on the area described in Article V, subparagraph 1(A), of the Treaty, as understood by the Union of Soviet Socialist Republics at the time the Treaty was signed, upon provisional application of this Document and every six months after the annual information exchange. In the case of Kushchevskaya the Russian Federation shall provide such additional information every three months after the annual information exchange.

2. Upon provisional application of this Document, Ukraine shall provide 'F21' notifications for its holdings within the Odessa oblast on the basis of changes of five, rather than ten, per cent or more in assigned holdings.

3. Subject to paragraphs 5 and 6 of this Section, the Russian Federation shall, upon provisional application of this Document, accept each year, in addition to its passive declared site inspection quota established pursuant to Section II, subparagraph 10(D), of the Protocol on Inspection, up to a total of 10 supplementary declared site inspections, conducted in accordance with the Protocol on Inspection, at objects of verification:

(A) located within the Pskov oblast; the Volgograd oblast; the Astrakhan oblast; that part of the Rostov oblast east of the line extending from Kushchevskaya to Volgodonsk to the Volgograd oblast border, including Volgodonsk; and Kushchevskaya and a narrow corridor in Krasnodar kray leading to Kushchevskaya;

(B) containing conventional armaments and equipment limited by the Treaty designated by the Russian Federation in its annual information exchange of 1 January 1996 as 'to be removed,' until such time that a declared site inspection confirms that such equipment has been removed.

4. Subject to paragraphs 5 and 6 of this Section, Ukraine shall, upon provisional application of this Document, accept each year, in addition to its passive declared site inspection quota established pursuant to Section II, subparagraph 10(D), of the Protocol on Inspection, up to a total of one supplementary declared site inspection, conducted in accordance with the Protocol on Inspection, at objects of verification located within the Odessa oblast.

5. The number of supplementary declared site inspections conducted at objects of verification pursuant to paragraph 3 or 4 of this Section shall not exceed the number of declared site passive quota inspections, estab-

lished in accordance with Section II, subparagraph 10(D) of the Protocol on Inspection, conducted at those objects of verification in the course of the same year.

6. All supplementary declared site inspections conducted pursuant to paragraph 3 or 4 of this Section:

(A) shall be carried out at the cost of the inspecting State Party, consistent with prevailing commercial rates; and

(B) at the discretion of the inspecting State Party, shall be conducted either as a sequential inspection or as a separate inspection.

VI

1. This Document shall enter into force upon receipt by the Depositary of notification of confirmation of approval by all States Parties. Paragraphs 2 and 3 of Section II, Section IV, and Section V of this Document are hereby provisionally applied as of 31 May 1996 through 15 December 1996. If this Document does not enter into force by 15 December 1996, then it shall be reviewed by the States Parties.

2. This Document, in all six official languages of the Treaty, shall be deposited with the Government of the Kingdom of the Netherlands, as the designated Depositary for the Treaty, which shall circulate copies of this Document to all States Parties.

Annex B. Understandings and agreed interpretations with regard to implementation and ways and means to improve the viability and effectiveness of the Treaty

1. The States Parties stress the need to ensure that relevant Government authorities charged with Treaty implementation fulfil all the obligations of the Decision of the Joint Consultative Group on the cost of inspections dated 23 May 1995.

2. The States Parties agree that pursuant to the Protocol on Inspection, Section VII, paragraph 1,

(a) in case an inspected State Party or the State Party exercising the rights and obligations of the inspected State Party delays an inspection on grounds of force majeure, it shall, in written form, explain the reasons for this delay in detail;

This should take place as follows:

– if force majeure is declared prior to the arrival of the inspection team, through the answer to the relevant notifications;

– if force majeure is declared after the arrival of the inspection team at the point of entry, the explanation should be presented as soon as possible, through diplomatic channels or other official channels.

(b) in case of such a delay due to force majeure, the provisions of Section XI, paragraph 2 of the Protocol on Inspection shall apply.

3. Each State Party shall provide to all other States Parties annually, but not later than 15 December, the complete updated list of inspectors and transport crew members. In case of additions to the list of inspectors and transport crew members, the State Party shall provide the complete updated list highlighting the additions.

4. Each State Party with territory in the area of application shall provide to all other States Parties during the annual exchange of information the standing diplomatic clearance numbers for their aviation transportation means for the subsequent calendar year.

5. Each State Party shall provide to all other States Parties during the annual exchange of information the list of its officially recognized holidays for the subsequent calendar year.

6. The State Party whose inspection team intends to transit the territory of another State Party prior to conducting the inspection should inform the transited State(s) Party (Parties) about the estimated time of transit, cross-border points and transportation means to be used by the inspection team, as well as a list of inspectors and drivers with passport numbers.

7. States Parties agree that a specified area may contain declared sites of their own and stationed forces, but all declared sites within a specified area are excluded from an inspection of the specified area (inspections in accordance with Section VIII of the Protocol on Inspection) as they can be inspected only in accordance with Section VII of the Protocol on Inspection.

8. States Parties agree to send the notification of the intent to inspect simultaneously to the host and the stationing States Parties, if the inspecting State intends to conduct a sequential inspection which involves stationed forces.

9. Where appropriate and with the agreement of the State Party on whose territory an inspection is to be carried out in respect of conventional armaments and equipment limited by the Treaty of a stationing State Party, the stationing State Party shall assist the host nation in the provision of security protection to both the inspection team and the escort

team for the duration of the inspection.

10. Notifications of changes of 10 per cent of holdings:

– The States Parties agree that, pursuant to Section VIII, paragraph 1, subparagraph (B) of the Protocol on Notification and Exchange of Information, the most recent update of information on holdings will always constitute the basis for any subsequent change to be notified under this paragraph.

– The notification of any change of 10 per cent or more shall be given no later than five days after such change occurs. The time period of five days is understood as being five working days.

11. States Parties agree to notify:

– Any changes in the designation of formations or units pursuant to Section I, III and V of the Protocol on Notification and the Exchange of Information at least 42 days in advance;

– Any closures of objects of verification within the last month pursuant to Section V, on the fifteenth of each month;

– Any creation or move to another location of an object of verification, at least 42 days in advance.

12. The States Parties agree that, in addition to the requirements for the submission of information and notifications as prescribed in Article XVII of the Treaty and in paragraph 1 of the Annex on the Format for the Exchange of Information to the Protocol on Notification and Exchange of Information, they will endeavour to supplement the annual exchange of information pursuant to the aforementioned Protocol in written form by an electronic data version on diskette in the agreed format; the written form remaining the official version.

13. Each State Party should notify to all other States Parties its passive declared site inspection quota coincident with each annual exchange of information provided pursuant to the Protocol on Notification and Exchange of Information, Section VII, paragraph 1(C).

(...)

Annex E. Statement of the representative of the Russian Federation to the Review Conference of the Treaty on Conventional Armed Forces in Europe

To promote the implementation of the Statement of the Representative of the Union of Soviet Socialist Republics to the Joint Consultative Group of 14 June 1991 (the Statement of the Soviet Representative), I have been instructed by the Government of the Russian Federation to state the following.

1. It is understood that conventional armaments and equipment in the three Treaty limited categories referred to in paragraph 1 of the Statement of the Soviet Representative (battle tanks, armoured combat vehicles, artillery) will be deemed destroyed or rendered militarily unusable, in accordance with that Statement, upon the application of any of the following methods:

(A) Destruction or conversion of conventional armaments and equipment under procedures that provide sufficient visible evidence, which confirms that they have been destroyed or rendered militarily unusable;

(B) Provision of satisfactory documentary evidence as meeting requirements of sufficient visible evidence, only in case of such armaments and equipment destroyed prior to promulgation of this Statement. The Russian Federation intends to provide such documentary evidence with regard to armaments and equipment destroyed in the area of application of the Treaty after 17 November 1995;

(C) Segregation of battle tanks and armoured combat vehicles exposed to the influence of atmospheric factors, with hatches and covers of engine compartments opened, with the invitation of a group of experts to conduct—at its own expense—an examination of a random sample representative of those conventional armaments and equipment, prior to their removal from a display site for final disposal (scrapping), and notification of such removal;

(D) Visit of group of experts, at its own expense and upon invitation, to count already derelict conventional armaments and equipment;

(E) Notification preceding or accompanying each transfer of conventional armaments and equipment to other States Parties within the area of application of the Treaty, with equivalent relevant notification from the recipient State Party. Such transfers will be done in line with Treaty provisions and will be compatible with the objectives and terms of the Statement of the Soviet Representative.

2. Continuing its efforts aimed at the implementation of the Statement of the Soviet Representative, the Russian Federation will apply methods referred to in paragraph 1 of this Statement to conventional armaments and equipment located on its territory. It will co-operate with the Republic of Kazakstan

and the Republic of Uzbekistan in applying those methods to conventional armaments and equipment located on their territories. The Russian Federation will negotiate the necessary arrangements with those States for the purpose of completing by joint efforts the process referred to in paragraph 1 of Statement of the Soviet Representative by the year 2000.

3. If, despite good faith efforts, the quota of 6,000 battle tanks subject to elimination is not fully met, the shortfall of not more than 2,300 battle tanks will be covered by applying methods referred to in paragraph 1 of this Statement to an equal number of armoured combat vehicles in excess of the quota of 1,500 pieces; and thus the overall process referred to in paragraph 1 of the Statement of the Soviet Representative will be in general deemed completed. Notwithstanding that, a number of battle tanks equal to the above-mentioned shortfall will be subsequently eliminated. The envisaged date for the completion of the process of their elimination will depend on the duration of their operational and service life and on the availability of financial resources. That elimination will be carried out in line with paragraph 1 of this Statement.

4. Upon completion of initial visits referred to in paragraph 1 of this Statement, the Russian Federation will be ready to discuss in the JCG their results and in the light of these to make arrangements, as necessary, for further visits, as well as to discuss possible modalities for further visits. In general, relevant practices established in the process of Treaty implementation will be followed as much as applicable in the organization and conduct of the visits.

Statements of the Chairman of the First Conference to Review the Operation of the Treaty on Conventional Armed Forces in Europe and the Concluding Act of the Negotiation on Personnel Strength of Conventional Armed Forces in Europe:

Notwithstanding the rights of each State as stated in Article XIV of the Treaty, each State Party should attempt to avoid conducting inspections during the officially recognized holidays of the other State Party.

With regard to the phrase 'on the availability of financial resources' in the Statement of the Representative of the Russian Federation as contained in Annex E of the Final Document of the Review Conference of the Treaty on Conventional Armed Forces in Europe, it is understood that this phrase is without prejudice to other arms control obligations.

Temporary deployment and reallocation of quotas referred to in Section IV, paragraphs 2 and 3, of the Document will not be used in the context of the Azerbaijan Republic.

Source: CFE document CFE-TRC/DG.2, Rev.5, 31 May 1996.

AGREEMENT ON SUB-REGIONAL ARMS CONTROL

Florence, 14 June 1996

Guided by the General Framework Agreement for Peace in Bosnia and Herzegovina, Annex 1-B, Agreement on Regional Stabilisation, Article IV, signed in Paris on 14 December 1995, and having engaged in negotiations under the auspices of the Organisation for Security and Co-operation in Europe (hereinafter 'the OSCE') in Vienna from 4 January 1996,

Bosnia and Herzegovina, the Republic of Croatia, the Federal Republic of Yugoslavia, the Federation of Bosnia and Herzegovina and the Republika Srpska, hereinafter, for the purposes of this Agreement, referred to as the 'Parties',

Recalling the agreement of the Parties, as set forth in Article I, Annex 1-B, Agreement on Regional Stabilisation, that establishment of measures for regional stability and arms control is essential to creating a stable peace in the region,

Committed to the objective of establishing new forms of co-operation in the field of security aimed at building transparency and confidence and achieving balanced and stable defence force levels at the lowest numbers consistent with the Parties' respective security and the need to avoid an arms race in the region,

Conscious of the common responsibility of the Parties for seeking to achieve greater stability and security in the region,

Have agreed as follows :

ARTICLE I

1. Each Party shall carry out the obligations in accordance with provisions set forth in this Agreement relating to the armaments limited by the Agreement: battle tanks, armoured combat vehicles, artillery, combat aircraft and attack helicopters.

2. Each Party also shall carry out the other obligations set forth in this Agreement.

3. The Parties affirm that nothing contained in this Agreement or its Protocols shall be interpreted or understood to alter, change, amend, or otherwise modify any of the conditions, provisions, commitments, responsibilities, or obligations of the Parties contained in the General Framework Agreement for Peace in Bosnia and Herzegovina.

4. This Agreement incorporates the Protocol on Reduction; the Protocol on Procedures Governing the Reclassification of Specific Models or Versions of Combat-Capable Trainer Aircraft Into Unarmed Trainer Aircraft, hereinafter referred to as the Protocol on Aircraft Reclassification; the Protocol on Exchange of Information and Notifications, hereinafter referred to as the Protocol on Information Exchange; the Protocol on Existing Types of Armaments, hereinafter referred to as the Protocol on Existing Types; the Protocol on Inspection; the Protocol on The Sub-Regional Consultative Commission. Each of these documents constitutes an integral part of this Agreement.

ARTICLE II

For the purposes of this Agreement:

1. The term 'area of application' means the entire land territory of the Parties within Bosnia and Herzegovina, the Republic of Croatia and the Federal Republic of Yugoslavia.

2. The term 'armaments limited by the Agreement' means battle tanks, armoured combat vehicles, artillery, combat aircraft and attack helicopters subject to the numerical limitations set forth in Article IV of this Agreement.

3. The term 'battle tank' means a self-propelled armoured fighting vehicle, capable of heavy firepower, primarily of a high muzzle velocity direct fire main gun necessary to engage armoured and other targets, with high cross-country mobility, with a high level of self-protection, and which is not designed and equipped primarily to transport combat troops. Such armoured vehicles serve as the principal weapon system of ground-force tank and other armoured formations. Battle tanks are tracked armoured fighting vehicles which weigh at least 16.5 metric tonnes unladen weight and which are armed with a 360-degree traverse gun of at least

75 millimetres calibre. In addition, any wheeled armoured fighting vehicles entering into service which meet all the other criteria stated above shall also be deemed battle tanks.

4. The term 'armoured combat vehicle' means a self-propelled vehicle with armoured protection and cross-country capability. Armoured combat vehicles include armoured personnel carriers, armoured infantry fighting vehicles and heavy armament combat vehicles.

The term 'armoured personnel carrier' means an armoured combat vehicle which is designed and equipped to transport a combat infantry squad and which, as a rule, is armed with an integral or organic weapon of less than 20 millimetres calibre.

The term 'armoured infantry fighting vehicle' means an armoured combat vehicle which is designed and equipped primarily to transport a combat infantry squad, which normally provides the capability for the troops to deliver fire from inside the vehicle under armoured protection, and which is armed with an integral or organic cannon of at least 20 millimetres calibre and sometimes an antitank missile launcher. Armoured infantry fighting vehicles serve as the principal weapon system of armoured infantry or mechanised infantry or motorised infantry formations and units of forces.

The term 'heavy armament combat vehicles' means an armoured combat vehicle with an integral or organic direct fire gun of at least 75 millimetres calibre, weighing at least 6.0 metric tonnes unladen weight, which does not fall within the definitions of an armoured personnel carrier, or an armoured infantry fighting vehicle or a battle tank.

5. The term 'unladen weight' means the weight of a vehicle excluding the weight of ammunition; fuel, oil and lubricants; removable reactive armour; spare parts, tools and accessories; removable snorkelling equipment; and crew and their personal kit.

6. The terms 'armoured personnel carrier look-alike' and 'armoured infantry fighting vehicle look-alike' mean an armoured vehicle based on the same chassis as, and externally similar to, an armoured personnel carrier or armoured infantry fighting vehicle, respectively, which does not have a cannon or gun of 20 millimetres calibre or greater and which has been constructed or modified in such a way as not to permit the transportation of a combat infantry squad. Taking into account the provisions of the Geneva Convention 'For the Amelioration of the Conditions of the Wounded and Sick in Armed Forces in the Field' of 12 August 1949 that confer a special status on ambulances, armoured personnel carrier ambulances shall not be deemed armoured combat vehicles or armoured personnel carrier look-alikes.

7. The term 'artillery' means large calibre systems capable of engaging ground targets by delivering primarily indirect fire. Such artillery systems provide the essential indirect fire support to combined arms formations. Large calibre artillery systems are guns, howitzers, artillery pieces combining the characteristics of guns and howitzers, mortars and multiple launch rocket systems with a calibre of 100 millimetres and above. In addition, any future large calibre direct fire system which has a secondary effective indirect fire capability shall be counted against the artillery ceilings. For the purposes of this Agreement, 'artillery' shall also include those systems with a calibre less than 100 millimetres but greater than 75 millimetres listed in Section I, paragraph 3 of the Protocol on Existing Types.

8. The term 'combat aircraft' means a fixed-wing or variable-geometry wing aircraft armed and equipped to engage targets by employing guided missiles, unguided rockets, bombs, guns, cannons, or other weapons of destruction, as well as any model or version of such an aircraft which performs other military functions such as reconnaissance or electronic warfare. The term 'combat aircraft' does not include primary trainer aircraft.

9. The term 'combat helicopter' means a rotary wing aircraft armed and equipped to engage targets or equipped to perform other military functions. The term 'combat helicopter' comprises attack helicopters and combat support helicopters. The term 'combat helicopter' does not include unarmed transport helicopters.

10. The term 'attack helicopter' means a combat helicopter equipped to employ antiarmour, air-to-ground, or air-to-air guided weapons and equipped with an integrated fire control and aiming system for these weapons. The term 'attack helicopter' comprises specialised attack helicopters and multi-purpose attack helicopters.

11. The term 'specialised attack helicopter' means an attack helicopter that is designed primarily to employ guided weapons.

12. The term 'multi-purpose attack helicopter' means an attack helicopter designed to perform multiple military functions and

equipped to employ guided weapons.

13. The term 'combat support helicopter' means a combat helicopter which does not fulfil the requirements to qualify as an attack helicopter and which may be equipped with a variety of self-defence and area suppression weapons, such as guns, cannons and unguided rockets, bombs or cluster bombs, or which may be equipped to perform other military functions.

14. The term 'reduction site' means a clearly designated location where the reduction of armaments limited by the Agreement will take place.

15. The term 'reduction liability' means the number in each category of armaments limited by the Agreement that a Party commits itself to reduce during the period of 16 months following 1 July 1996 in order to ensure compliance with Article IV.

16. The term 'Personal Representative' means the Personal Representative of the Chairman-in-Office of the OSCE or his/her designated agent(s), who is designated by the Chairman-in-Office in consultation with the Parties in order to assist the Parties in the implementation of this Agreement.

17. The term 'armed forces' means all organisations which possess armaments limited by the Agreement other than those designed and structured to perform peacetime internal security functions.

18. The term 'export site' means a designated location at which armaments are prepared for export and from which they are shipped to a location outside the territory of the exporting Party.

ARTICLE III

1. For the purposes of this Agreement, the Parties shall apply the following counting rules:

All battle tanks, armoured combat vehicles, artillery, combat aircraft and attack helicopters, as defined in Article II and either in the possession of or belonging to the Parties, within the area of application shall be subject to the numerical limitations and other provisions set forth in Article IV with the exception of those which in a manner consistent with a Party's normal practices:

a. are in the process of manufacture, including manufacturing related testing;

b. are used exclusively for the purposes of research and development;

c. belong to historical collections;

d. are awaiting disposal, having been decommissioned from service in accordance with the provisions of Article VII;

e. are awaiting, or are being refurbished for, export or re-export and are temporarily retained within the area of application. Such battle tanks, armoured combat vehicles, artillery, combat aircraft and attack helicopters shall be located elsewhere than at sites declared under the terms of Section III of the Protocol on Information Exchange or at no more than 10 such declared sites which shall have been notified in the previous year s annual information exchange. In the latter case, they shall be separately distinguishable from armaments limited by the Agreement;

f. are, in the case of armoured personnel carriers, armoured infantry fighting vehicles, heavy armament combat vehicles or multi-purpose attack helicopters, held by organisations designed and structured to perform in peacetime internal security functions; or

g. are in transit through the area of application from a location outside the area of application to a final destination outside the area of application, and are in the area of application for no longer than a total of seven days.

2. If, in respect of any such battle tanks, armoured combat vehicles, artillery, combat aircraft or attack helicopters, the notification of which is required under Section IV of the Protocol on Information Exchange, a Party notifies an unusually high number in more than two successive annual information exchanges, it shall explain the reasons in the Sub-Regional Consultative Commission, if so requested.

ARTICLE IV

SECTION I. LIMITATIONS ON ARMAMENTS

1. In recognition of the importance of achieving balanced and stable defence force levels at the lowest numbers consistent with the respective Parties' security, the Parties agree that the establishment of a stable military balance based on the lowest level of armaments will be an essential element in the establishment of peace and security and the building of confidence.

2. All battle tanks, armoured combat vehicles, artillery, combat aircraft and attack helicopters, as defined in Article II, within the area of application and in the possession of or belonging to the Parties shall be subject to the numerical limitations and other provisions of this Article, except as provided for in Articles III, VII and XI.

3. Within the area of application, as defined in Article II, each Party shall limit and, as necessary, reduce its battle tanks, armoured combat vehicles, artillery, combat aircraft and attack helicopters, so that 16 months from 1 July 1996 and thereafter, the armament holdings of any individual Party do not exceed the following ceilings:

The Federal Republic of Yugoslavia:
(1) 1025 battle tanks;
(2) 850 armoured combat vehicles;
(3) 3750 pieces of artillery;
(4) 155 combat aircraft; and
(5) 53 attack helicopters.

The Republic of Croatia:
(1) 410 battle tanks;
(2) 340 armoured combat vehicles;
(3) 1500 pieces of artillery;
(4) 62 combat aircraft; and
(5) 21 attack helicopters.

Bosnia and Herzegovina:
(1) 410 battle tanks;
(2) 340 armoured combat vehicles;
(3) 1500 pieces of artillery;
(4) 62 combat aircraft; and
(5) 21 attack helicopters.

of which:

The Federation of Bosnia and Herzegovina:
(1) 273 battle tanks;
(2) 227 armoured combat vehicles;
(3) 1000 pieces of artillery;
(4) 41 combat aircraft; and
(5) 14 attack helicopters.

The Republika Srpska:
(1) 137 battle tanks;
(2) 113 armoured combat vehicles;
(3) 500 pieces of artillery;
(4) 21 combat aircraft; and
(5) 7 attack helicopters.

ARTICLE V

1. The numerical limits on armaments limited by the Agreement as set forth in Article IV of this Agreement shall be achieved only by means of reduction in accordance with the Protocol on Reduction, the Protocol on Aircraft Reclassification, or by export in accordance with Article VI of this Agreement. The Parties shall have the right to implement all the procedures of the reduction of armaments limited by the Agreement in accordance with the Protocol on Reduction or the Protocol on Procedures Governing the Reduction of Conventional Armaments and Equipment Limited by the Treaty on Conventional Armed Forces in Europe.

2. The categories of armaments limited by the Agreement subject to reduction are battle tanks, armoured combat vehicles, artillery, combat aircraft and attack helicopters. The specific types are listed in the Protocol on Existing Types.

a. Battle tanks and armoured combat vehicles shall be reduced by destruction, export, conversion for non-military purposes, placement on static display, or use as ground targets.

b. Artillery shall be reduced by destruction, export or placement on static display, or, in the case of self-propelled artillery, by use as ground targets.

c. Combat aircraft shall be reduced by destruction, export, placement on static display, use for ground instructional purposes, or, in the case of specific models or versions of combat-capable trainer aircraft, reclassification into unarmed trainer aircraft.

d. Attack helicopters shall be reduced by destruction, export, placement on static display, or use for ground instructional purposes.

3. Armaments limited by the Agreement shall be deemed to be reduced upon execution of the procedures and satisfaction of the criteria established in the Protocol on Reduction or in the Protocol on Procedures Governing the Reduction of Conventional Armaments and Equipment Limited by the Treaty on Conventional Armed Forces in Europe, and upon notification as required by this Agreement. Armaments so reduced shall no longer be counted against the numerical limitations set forth in Article IV of this Agreement.

4. Reductions shall be effected in two phases and completed no later than 16 months after 1 July 1996. The Parties undertake to start the process of reduction as soon as possible after that date, so that:

a. by the end of the first reduction phase, that is, no later than 6 months after 1 July 1996, each Party shall have ensured that at least the following portions of its total reduction liability for each of the categories of armaments limited by the Agreement have been reduced:

(1) 40 percent of its total reduction liability for artillery;

(2) 40 percent of its total reduction liability for combat aircraft;

(3) 40 percent of its total reduction liability for attack helicopters;

(4) 20 percent of its total reduction liability for tanks; and

(5) 20 percent of its total reduction liability

for armoured combat vehicles.

b. by the end of the second reduction phase, that is, no later than 16 months after 1 July 1996, each Party shall have reduced its total reduction liability in each of the categories of armaments limited by the Agreement. Parties carrying out conversion for non-military purposes shall have ensured that the conversion of all battle tanks and armoured combat vehicles in accordance with Section VIII of the Protocol on Reduction shall have been completed by the end of the second reduction phase.

5. Armaments limited by the Agreement to be reduced shall have been declared in the 21 June 1996 exchange of information.

6. No later than 30 days after signature of this Agreement, each Party shall provide notification to all other Parties and to the Personal Representative of its reduction liability. Reduction liability is the difference between a Party's holdings notified in the 21 June 1996 exchange of information and its ceilings for holdings specified in Article IV of this Agreement.

7. Within two months after signature of this Agreement, each Party shall notify the other Parties and the Personal Representative of the locations of its reduction sites where reduction of armaments limited by the Agreement will be carried out.

8. Reduction of armaments limited by the Agreement shall be carried out at reduction sites unless otherwise specified in the Protocol on Reduction.

9. The reduction process shall be subject to inspection without right of refusal, in accordance with the Protocol on Inspection.

ARTICLE VI

1. The numerical limits on armaments limited by the Agreement as set forth in Article IV of this Agreement shall be achieved only by the procedures governing reduction in accordance with the Protocol on Reduction, the Protocol on Aircraft Reclassification, or by export in accordance with this Article. No more than 25 percent of any Party's total reduction liability during a single reduction phase may be achieved by export.

2. In the notification of its reduction liability, in accordance with Article V of this Agreement, each Party shall indicate the approximate amount, if any, by which it plans to decrease its reduction liability through the export of armaments limited by the Agreement in accordance with this Article.

3. Armaments limited by the Agreement exported and counted against a Party's reduction liability shall have been notified as being held by that Party in the 21 June 1996 exchange of information.

4. Armaments limited by the Agreement must be exported outside of the territory of the Party no later than 15 months after 1 July 1996 in order to count against the reduction liability notified in accordance with Article V of this Agreement. Armaments limited by the Agreement which are not exported must be reduced in accordance with the Protocol on Reduction by the end of the reduction period.

5. Each Party shall have the right to inspect, without right of refusal, armaments limited by the Agreement to be exported, in accordance with this Article, at the export site. Inspections of armaments to be exported in accordance with this Article shall be conducted in accordance with the provisions in Sections I, II, III, IV, V, VI, X and XI of the Protocol on Inspection and the following:

a. Inspections of armaments to be exported under this Article shall not count against the quotas established in Section II of the Protocol on Inspection. Inspection teams conducting such inspections shall be composed of inspectors of the Parties to this Agreement. The inspected party shall not be obliged to accept more than two inspections at a time at each export site.

b. Inspections of armaments to be exported shall not interfere with the on-going activities at the export site or unnecessarily hamper, delay or complicate the export process.

c. In addition to the notification of approximate amounts of armaments to be exported in accordance with paragraph 2 of this Article, each Party will notify the other Parties and the Personal Representative no later than the 15th of each month the numbers of armaments to be exported the next calendar month. Such notifications shall include:

(1) the date(s) of export;

(2) the export site(s);

(3) the dates the armaments to be exported will be present for inspection;

(4) the number(s) and type(s) of armaments that will be exported;

(5) The object of inspection(s) from which the armaments have been withdrawn.

d. For the purposes of inspection, such armaments shall be present at the export site for a minimum of three days during the calendar month they are to be exported. The inspection team shall have the right to arrive or depart at any time during these three days, or the day prior to the first day. Throughout the period that the inspection team remains at the export site, it shall have the right to observe the armaments to be exported.

e. In accordance with the provisions set forth in this Article, the inspection team shall have the right to freely record factory serial numbers from the armaments to be exported.

f. At each export site, the inspection team shall be provided with shipping invoice document numbers, shipping vessel name or railroad schedule information, and country of destination of the armaments to be exported.

ARTICLE VII

1. Other than removal from service in accordance with the provisions of Articles V and VI, battle tanks, armoured combat vehicles, artillery, combat aircraft and attack helicopters within the area of application shall be removed from service only by decommissioning, provided that:

a. such armaments limited by the Agreement are decommissioned and awaiting disposal at no more than eight sites which shall be notified as declared sites in accordance with the Protocol on Information Exchange and shall be identified in such notifications as holding areas for decommissioned armaments limited by the Agreement. If sites containing armaments limited by the Agreement decommissioned from service also contain any other armaments, the decommissioned armaments limited by the Agreement shall be separately distinguishable; and

b. the numbers of such decommissioned armaments limited by the Agreement do not exceed, in the case of any individual Party, one percent of its ceilings for holdings of armaments limited by the Agreement pursuant to Article IV, or a total of 100, whichever is greater, of which no more than 75 shall be battle tanks, armoured combat vehicles and pieces of artillery, and no more than 25 shall be attack helicopters and combat aircraft.

2. Notification of decommissioning shall include the number and type of armaments limited by the Agreement decommissioned and the location of decommissioning and shall be provided to all other Parties in accordance with Section III of the Protocol on Information Exchange.

ARTICLE VIII

1. For the purpose of ensuring verification of compliance with the provisions of this Agreement, each Party shall provide notifications and exchange information pertaining to its personnel and armaments in accordance with the Protocol on Exchange of Information and Notifications.

2. Such notifications and exchange of information shall be transmitted in written form through diplomatic or other official channels as may be agreed by the Parties.

3. Each Party shall be responsible for its own information; receipt of such information and of notifications shall not imply validation or acceptance of the information provided.

4. Information shall be exchanged annually by 15 December each year and shall be valid as of 01 January for the next year and one additional exchange of information at the end of the reduction period valid as of the date of the end of the reduction period. In addition, for 1996 information shall be exchanged by 21 June valid as of 01 July.

ARTICLE IX

1. For the purposes of ensuring verification of compliance with the provisions of this Agreement, each Party shall have the right to conduct, and the obligation to accept, within the area of application, inspections in accordance with the Protocol on Inspection.

2. The purpose of such inspections shall be:

a. to verify, on the basis of the information pursuant to the Protocol on Exchange of Information and Notifications, the compliance of the Parties with the numerical limitations set forth in Article IV of this Agreement;

b. to monitor the process of reduction of armaments limited by the Agreement carried out at reduction sites in accordance with Article V of this Agreement and the Protocol on Reduction;

c. to monitor the export of armaments limited by the Agreement used to decrease a reduction liability in accordance with Articles V and VI of this Agreement; and

d. to monitor the certification of reclassified combat-capable trainer aircraft carried out in accordance with the Protocol on Aircraft Reclassification.

3. Verification shall be the responsibility of the Parties. The Personal Representative shall assist the Parties in the implementation.

ARTICLE X

1. The Parties shall create a Sub-Regional Consultative Commission. The Sub-Regional Consultative Commission shall be composed of one high-level representative of each Party. The Personal Representative shall be present for the meetings of the Sub-Regional

Consultative Commission.

2. Chairmanship of the Sub-Regional Consultative Commission shall rotate alphabetically among the Parties, beginning with Bosnia and Herzegovina, changing after every meeting, unless otherwise decided by the Parties.

3. Decisions of the Sub-Regional Consultative Commission shall be taken by consensus. Consensus shall be understood to mean the absence of any objection by any representative of a Party to the taking of a decision or the making of a recommendation.

4. Detailed procedures for the functioning of the Sub-Regional Consultative Commission are set out in the Protocol on the Sub-Regional Consultative Commission.

ARTICLE XI

1. Armoured infantry fighting vehicles held by organisations of a Party designed and structured to perform in peacetime internal security functions, which are not structured and organised for ground combat against an external enemy, are not limited by this Agreement. The foregoing notwithstanding, in order to enhance the implementation of this Agreement and to provide assurance that the number of such armaments held by such organisations shall not be used to circumvent the provisions of this Agreement, armoured infantry fighting vehicles assigned by a Party to organisations designed and structured to perform in peacetime internal security functions in excess of the aggregate number held by such organisations at the time of signature of the Agreement, as notified pursuant to Article VIII, shall constitute a portion of the permitted levels specified in Article IV. If the number of such armoured infantry fighting vehicles reported was less than the maximum agreed number for such armoured infantry fighting vehicles, each Party shall have the right to increase its holdings of such armoured infantry fighting vehicles up to the maximum agreed number. Maximum agreed numbers for such armoured infantry fighting vehicles shall be:

Federal Republic of Yugoslavia	152
Republic of Croatia	76
Bosnia and Herzegovina	76
of which	
Federation of Bosnia and Herzegovina	38
Republika Srpska	38

2. A Party that intends to reassign battle tanks, armoured infantry fighting vehicles, artillery, combat aircraft and attack helicopters in service with its armed forces to any organisation of that Party not a part of its armed forces shall notify all other Parties no later than the date such reassignment takes effect. Such notification shall specify the effective date of the reassignment, the date such armaments are physically transferred, as well as the numbers, by type of the armaments limited by the Agreement being reassigned.

ARTICLE XII

1. This Agreement shall be of unlimited duration. It may be supplemented by a further Agreement by the Parties within the framework of the Review Conference pursuant to Article XIV of this Agreement.

2. The Parties hereby specifically agree not to withdraw from this Agreement during the first 42 months after entry into force of the Agreement. Following the first 42 months after entry into force of the Agreement, each Party shall have the right to withdraw from this Agreement if it determines that extraordinary events related to the subject matter of this Agreement have jeopardized its interests. A Party intending to withdraw shall give notice of its decision to do so to each Party and to the Personal Representative at least 150 days prior to the intended withdrawal from this Agreement. This notice shall be in writing and shall include a statement of the extraordinary events that the Party intending to withdraw regards as having jeopardized its interests.

ARTICLE XIII

Any Party may propose amendments to this Agreement. In 1996 and 1997 the text of a proposed amendment shall be submitted to the Chairman of the Sub-Regional Consultative Commission who shall circulate it to each Party. The Chairman shall convene a meeting of the Sub-Regional Consultative Commission to discuss the proposed amendment. If an amendment is approved by all the Parties it shall enter into force in accordance with the procedures governing the entry into force of this Agreement.

ARTICLE XIV

The Chairman of the Sub-Regional Consultative Commission shall convene a Review Conference on June 11, 1998. After that the Parties shall decide to hold Review Conferences regularly, at least once every second year.

ARTICLE XV

The original of this Agreement, of which the English text is authentic, shall be deposited by each Party. Duly certified copies of this Agreement in Bosnian, Croatian and Serbian shall be transmitted by the Personal Representative to all the Parties.

Source: OSCE document INF/98/96, 18 June 1996.

Annexes

Annexe A. Arms control and disarmament agreements

Annexe B. Chronology 1996

Annexe A. Arms control and disarmament agreements

RAGNHILD FERM

I. Summaries and status of the major multilateral arms control agreements, as of 1 January 1997

Notes

1. The agreements are listed below in the order of the date on which they were signed or adopted; the date on which they entered into force is also given. Where confirmed information on new parties became available in early 1997, this is given in notes.

2. The main source of information is the lists provided by the depositaries of the treaties.

3. For a few major treaties, the substantive parts of the most important reservations and/or declarations are given in footnotes below the list of parties.

4. The Russian Federation, constituted in 1991 as an independent sovereign state, has confirmed the continuity of international obligations assumed by the Soviet Union. The other former Soviet republics which were constituted in 1991 as independent sovereign states have subsequently signed, ratified, acceded or succeeded to agreements in order to become signatories/parties.

5. The Federal Republic of Germany and the German Democratic Republic merged into one state in 1990. All agreements to which the Federal Republic of Germany (West Germany) was a party are in force for the united Germany.

6. The Yemen Arab Republic and the People's Democratic Republic of Yemen merged into one state in 1990. According to a statement by the united Yemen state, all agreements which either state has entered into are in force for Yemen.

7. Czechoslovakia split into two states, the Czech Republic and Slovakia, in 1993. Both states have succeeded to all agreements to which Czechoslovakia was a party.

8. The Federal Republic of Yugoslavia split into several separate states in 1991–92. The international legal status of what remains of the former Yugoslavia—Yugoslavia (Serbia and Montenegro)—is ambiguous, but since it considers that it is the same entity the name 'Yugoslavia' remains in these lists. (The former Yugoslav republics of Bosnia and Herzegovina, Croatia, Macedonia and Slovenia have succeeded, as independent states, to several agreements.)

9. Taiwan, while not recognized as a sovereign state by some nations, is listed as a party to those agreements which it has signed and ratified.

10. Unless otherwise stated, the treaties in this annexe are open to all states for signature, ratification, accession or succession.

11. A complete list of UN member states and year of membership appears in the glossary at the front of this volume. Not all the parties listed in this annexe are UN member states.

Protocol for the prohibition of the use in war of asphyxiating, poisonous or other gases, and of bacteriological methods of warfare (Geneva Protocol)

Signed at Geneva on 17 June 1925; entered into force on 8 February 1928.

The protocol declares that the parties agree to be bound by the prohibition, which should be universally accepted as part of international law.

Parties (132): Afghanistan, Albania, Algeria, Angola,[1] Antigua and Barbuda, Argentina, Australia, Austria, Bahrain,[1] Bangladesh,[1] Barbados, Belarus, Belgium,[1] Benin, Bhutan, Bolivia, Brazil, Bulgaria, Burkina Faso, Cambodia, Cameroon, Canada,[1] Cape Verde, Central African Republic, Chile, China,[1] Côte d'Ivoire, Cuba, Cyprus, Czech Republic, Denmark, Dominican Republic, Ecuador, Egypt, Equatorial Guinea, Estonia, Ethiopia, Fiji,[1] Finland, France, Gambia, Germany, Ghana, Greece, Grenada, Guatemala, Guinea-Bissau, Holy See, Hungary, Iceland, India, Indonesia, Iran, Iraq,[1] Ireland, Israel,[2] Italy, Jamaica, Japan, Jordan,[3] Kenya, Korea (North),[1] Korea (South),[1] Kuwait,[1] Laos, Latvia, Lebanon, Lesotho, Liberia, Libya,[1] Liechtenstein, Lithuania, Luxembourg, Madagascar, Malawi, Malaysia, Maldives, Malta, Mauritius, Mexico, Monaco, Mongolia, Morocco, Nepal, Netherlands,[4] New Zealand, Nicaragua, Niger, Nigeria,[1] Norway, Pakistan, Panama, Papua New Guinea,[1] Paraguay, Peru, Philippines, Poland, Portugal,[1] Qatar, Romania, Russia,[4] Rwanda, Saint Kitts (Christopher) and Nevis, Saint Lucia, Saudi Arabia, Senegal, Sierra Leone, Slovakia, Solomon Islands, South Africa, Spain, Sri Lanka, Sudan, Swaziland, Sweden, Switzerland, Syria, Tanzania, Thailand, Togo, Tonga, Trinidad and Tobago, Tunisia, Turkey, Uganda, UK, Uruguay, USA,[4] Venezuela, Viet Nam,[1] Yemen, Yugoslavia

[1] The protocol is binding on this state only as regards states which have signed and ratified or acceded to it. The protocol will cease to be binding on this state in regard to any enemy state whose armed forces or whose allies fail to respect the prohibitions laid down in it.

[2] The protocol is binding on Israel only as regards states which have signed and ratified or acceded to it. The protocol shall cease to be binding on Israel in regard to any enemy state whose armed forces, or the armed forces of whose allies, or the regular or irregular forces, or groups or individuals operating from its territory, fail to respect the prohibitions which are the object of the protocol.

[3] Jordan undertakes to respect the obligations contained in the protocol with regard to states which have undertaken similar commitments. It is not bound by the protocol as regards states whose armed forces, regular or irregular, do not respect the provisions of the protocol.

[4] The protocol shall cease to be binding on this state with respect to use in war of asphyxiating, poisonous or other gases, and of all analogous liquids, materials or devices, in regard to any enemy state if such state or any of its allies fail to respect the prohibitions laid down in the protocol.

Signed but not ratified: El Salvador

Treaty for collaboration in economic social and cultural matters and for collective self-defence (Brussels Treaty)

Signed at Brussels on 17 March 1948; entered into force on 25 August 1948.

The treaty provides for close cooperation of the parties in the military, economic and political fields.

Original parties (5): Belgium, France, Luxembourg, Netherlands, UK

Accessions (2): Germany, Italy

See also the Protocols of 1954.

Convention on the prevention and punishment of the crime of genocide (Genocide Convention)

Adopted at Paris by the UN General Assembly on 9 December 1948; entered into force on 12 January 1951.

Under the convention any commission of acts intended to destroy, in whole or in part, a national, ethnic, racial or religious group as such is declared to be a crime punishable under international law.

Parties (123): Afghanistan, Albania,* Algeria,* Antigua and Barbuda, Argentina,* Armenia, Australia, Austria, Azerbaijan, Bahamas, Bahrain,* Barbados, Belarus,* Belgium, Bosnia and Herzegovina, Brazil, Bulgaria,* Burkina Faso, Cambodia, Canada, Chile, China,* Colombia, Costa Rica, Côte d'Ivoire, Croatia, Cuba, Cyprus, Czech Republic, Denmark, Ecuador, Egypt, El Salvador, Estonia, Ethiopia, Fiji, Finland,* France, Gabon, Gambia, Georgia, Germany, Ghana, Greece, Guatemala, Haiti, Honduras, Hungary,* Iceland, India,* Iran, Iraq, Ireland, Israel, Italy, Jamaica, Jordan, Korea (North), Korea (South), Kuwait, Laos, Latvia, Lebanon, Lesotho, Liberia, Libya, Liechtenstein, Lithuania, Luxembourg, Macedonia (Former Yugoslav Republic of), Malaysia,* Maldives, Mali, Mexico, Moldova, Monaco, Mongolia,* Morocco,* Mozambique, Myanmar (Burma), Namibia,* Nepal, Netherlands, New Zealand, Nicaragua, Norway, Pakistan, Panama, Papua New Guinea, Peru, Philippines,* Poland,* Romania,* Russia,* Rwanda,* Saint Vincent and the Grenadines, Saudi Arabia, Senegal, Seychelles, Singapore,* Slovakia, Slovenia, Spain,* Sri Lanka, Sweden, Syria, Taiwan, Tanzania, Togo, Tonga, Tunisia, Turkey, Uganda, UK, Ukraine,* Uruguay, USA,* Venezuela,* Viet Nam,* Yemen,* Yugoslavia, Zaire, Zimbabwe

Note: Burundi acceded on 6 January 1997.

*With reservation and/or declaration upon ratification, accession or succession.

Signed but not ratified: Bolivia, Dominican Republic, Paraguay

Geneva Convention (IV) relative to the protection of civilian persons in time of war

Signed at Geneva on 12 August 1949; entered into force on 21 October 1950.

The convention establishes rules for the protection of civilians in areas covered by war and on occupied territories.

Parties (188): Afghanistan, Albania,* Algeria, Andorra, Angola,* Antigua and Barbuda, Argentina, Armenia, Australia,* Austria, Azerbaijan, Bahamas, Bahrain, Bangladesh, Barbados,* Belarus,* Belgium, Belize, Benin, Bhutan, Bolivia, Bosnia and Herzegovina, Botswana, Brazil, Brunei, Bulgaria,* Burkina Faso, Burundi, Cambodia, Cameroon, Canada, Cape Verde, Central African Republic, Chad, Chile, China,* Colombia, Comoros, Congo, Costa Rica, Côte d'Ivoire, Croatia, Cuba, Cyprus, Czech Republic,* Denmark, Djibouti, Dominica, Dominican Republic, Ecuador, Egypt, El Salvador, Equatorial Guinea, Estonia, Ethiopia, Fiji, Finland, France, Gabon, Gambia, Georgia, Germany,* Ghana, Greece, Grenada, Guatemala, Guinea, Guinea-Bissau,* Guyana, Haiti, Holy See, Honduras, Hungary,* Iceland, India, Indonesia, Iran,* Iraq, Ireland, Israel,* Italy, Jamaica, Japan, Jordan, Kazakhstan, Kenya, Kiribati, Korea (North),* Korea (South),* Kuwait,* Kyrgyzstan, Laos, Latvia, Lebanon, Lesotho, Liberia, Libya, Liechtenstein, Lithuania, Luxembourg, Macedonia (Former Yugoslav Republic of),* Madagascar, Malawi, Malaysia, Maldives, Mali, Malta, Mauritania, Mauritius, Mexico, Micronesia, Moldova, Monaco, Mongolia, Morocco, Mozambique, Myanmar (Burma), Namibia, Nepal, Netherlands, New Zealand, Nicaragua, Niger, Nigeria, Norway, Oman, Pakistan,* Palau, Panama, Papua New Guinea, Paraguay, Peru, Philippines, Poland,* Portugal,* Qatar, Romania,* Russia,* Rwanda, Saint Kitts (Christopher) and Nevis, Saint Lucia, Saint

Vincent and the Grenadines, Samoa (Western), San Marino, Sao Tome and Principe, Saudi Arabia, Senegal, Seychelles, Sierra Leone, Singapore,* Slovakia,* Slovenia, Solomon Islands, Somalia, South Africa, Spain, Sri Lanka, Sudan, Suriname,* Swaziland, Sweden, Switzerland, Syria, Tajikistan, Tanzania, Thailand, Togo, Tonga, Trinidad and Tobago, Tunisia, Turkey, Turkmenistan, Tuvalu, Uganda, UK, Ukraine,* United Arab Emirates, Uruguay,* USA,* Uzbekistan, Vanuatu, Venezuela, Viet Nam,* Yemen,* Yugoslavia,* Zaire, Zambia, Zimbabwe

* With reservation and/or declaration upon ratification, accession or succession.

Protocols to the 1948 Brussels Treaty (Paris Agreements on the Western European Union)

Signed at Paris on 23 October 1954; entered into force on 6 May 1955.

The protocols modify the 1948 Brussels Treaty, allowing the Federal Republic of Germany and Italy to become parties in return for controls over German armaments and force levels (annulled, except for weapons of mass destruction, in 1984). The Protocols to the Brussels Treaty are regarded as having created the Western European Union (WEU). Members of the WEU: Belgium, France, Germany, Greece, Italy, Luxembourg, Netherlands Portugal, Spain, UK.

Antarctic Treaty

Signed at Washington, DC, on 1 December 1959; entered into force on 23 June 1961.

Declares the Antarctic an area to be used exclusively for peaceful purposes. Prohibits any measure of a military nature in the Antarctic, such as the establishment of military bases and fortifications, and the carrying out of military manoeuvres or the testing of any type of weapon. The treaty bans any nuclear explosion as well as the disposal of radioactive waste material in Antarctica, subject to possible future international agreements on these subjects.

In accordance with Article IX, consultative meetings are convened at regular intervals to exchange information and hold consultations on matters pertaining to Antarctica, as well as to recommend to the governments measures in furtherance of the principles and objectives of the treaty.

The treaty is subject to ratification by the signatories and is open for accession by UN members or by other states invited to accede with the consent of all the contracting parties whose representatives are entitled to participate in the consultative meetings provided for in Article IX.

Parties (43): Argentina,† Australia,† Austria, Belgium,† Brazil,† Bulgaria, Canada, Chile,† China,† Colombia, Cuba, Czech Republic, Denmark, Ecuador,† Finland,† France,† Germany,† Greece, Guatemala, Hungary, India,† Italy,† Japan,† Korea (North), Korea (South),† Netherlands,† New Zealand,† Norway,† Papua New Guinea, Peru,† Poland,† Romania,* Russia,† Slovakia, South Africa,† Spain,† Sweden,† Switzerland, Turkey, UK,† Ukraine, Uruguay,*† USA†

* With reservation and/or declaration upon ratification, accession or succession.
† Party entitled to participate in the consultative meetings.

The Protocol on Environmental Protection to the Antarctic Treaty (Madrid Protocol) was signed in 1991. Not in force as of 1 January 1997.

Treaty banning nuclear weapon tests in the atmosphere, in outer space and under water (Partial Test Ban Treaty, PTBT)

Signed at Moscow on 5 August 1963; entered into force on 10 October 1963.

Prohibits the carrying out of any nuclear weapon test explosion or any other nuclear explosion: (*a*) in the atmosphere, beyond its limits, including outer space, or under water, including territorial waters or high seas; and (*b*) in any other environment if such explosion causes radioactive debris to be present outside the territorial limits of the state under whose jurisdiction or control the explosion is conducted.

Parties (124): Afghanistan, Antigua and Barbuda, Argentina, Armenia, Australia, Austria, Bahamas, Bangladesh, Belarus, Belgium, Benin, Bhutan, Bolivia, Botswana, Brazil, Bulgaria, Canada, Cape Verde, Central African Republic, Chad, Chile, Colombia, Costa Rica, Côte d'Ivoire, Croatia, Cyprus, Czech Republic, Denmark, Dominican Republic, Ecuador, Egypt, El Salvador, Equatorial Guinea, Fiji, Finland, Gabon, Gambia, Germany, Ghana, Greece, Guatemala, Guinea-Bissau, Honduras, Hungary, Iceland, India, Indonesia, Iran, Iraq, Ireland, Israel, Italy, Jamaica, Japan, Jordan, Kenya, Korea (South), Kuwait, Laos, Lebanon, Liberia, Libya, Luxembourg, Madagascar, Malawi, Malaysia, Malta, Mauritania, Mauritius, Mexico, Mongolia, Morocco, Myanmar (Burma), Nepal, Netherlands, New Zealand, Nicaragua, Niger, Nigeria, Norway, Pakistan, Panama, Papua New Guinea, Peru, Philippines, Poland, Romania, Russia, Rwanda, Samoa (Western), San Marino, Senegal, Seychelles, Sierra Leone, Singapore, Slovakia, Slovenia, South Africa, Spain, Sri Lanka, Sudan, Suriname, Swaziland, Sweden, Switzerland, Syria, Taiwan, Tanzania, Thailand, Togo, Tonga, Trinidad and Tobago, Tunisia, Turkey, Uganda, UK, Ukraine, Uruguay, USA, Venezuela, Yemen, Yugoslavia, Zaire, Zambia

Signed but not ratified: Algeria, Burkina Faso, Burundi, Cameroon, Ethiopia, Haiti, Mali, Paraguay, Portugal, Somalia

Treaty on principles governing the activities of states in the exploration and use of outer space, including the moon and other celestial bodies (Outer Space Treaty)

Signed at London, Moscow and Washington, DC, on 27 January 1967; entered into force on 10 October 1967.

Prohibits the placing into orbit around the earth of any objects carrying nuclear weapons or any other kinds of weapons of mass destruction, the installation of such weapons on celestial bodies, or the stationing of them in outer space in any other manner. The establishment of military bases, installations and fortifications, the testing of any type of weapons and the conduct of military manoeuvres on celestial bodies are also forbidden.

Parties (95): Afghanistan, Algeria, Antigua and Barbuda, Argentina, Australia, Austria, Bahamas, Bangladesh, Barbados, Belarus, Belgium, Benin, Brazil,* Bulgaria, Burkina Faso, Canada, Chile, China, Cuba, Cyprus, Czech Republic, Denmark, Dominican Republic, Ecuador, Egypt, El Salvador, Equatorial Guinea, Fiji, Finland, France, Germany, Greece, Guinea-Bissau, Hungary, Iceland, India, Iraq, Ireland, Israel, Italy, Jamaica, Japan, Kenya, Korea (South), Kuwait, Laos, Lebanon, Libya, Madagascar,* Mali, Mauritius, Mexico, Mongolia, Morocco, Myanmar (Burma), Nepal, Netherlands, New Zealand, Niger, Nigeria, Norway, Pakistan, Papua New Guinea, Peru, Poland, Portugal, Romania, Russia, San Marino, Saudi Arabia, Seychelles, Sierra Leone, Singapore, Slovakia, South Africa, Spain, Sri Lanka, Sweden, Switzerland, Syria, Taiwan, Thailand, Togo, Tonga, Tunisia, Turkey, Uganda, UK, Ukraine, Uruguay, USA, Venezuela, Viet Nam, Yemen, Zambia

* With reservation and/or declaration upon ratification, accession or succession.

Signed but not ratified: Bolivia, Botswana, Burundi, Cameroon, Central African Republic, Colombia, Ethiopia, Gambia, Ghana, Guyana, Haiti, Holy See, Honduras, Indonesia, Iran, Jordan, Lesotho, Luxembourg, Malaysia, Nicaragua, Panama, Philippines, Rwanda, Somalia, Trinidad and Tobago, Yugoslavia, Zaire

Treaty for the prohibition of nuclear weapons in Latin America and the Caribbean (Treaty of Tlatelolco)

Signed at Mexico, Distrito Federal, on 14 February 1967; entered into force on 22 April 1968. The treaty was amended in 1990, 1991 and 1992.

Prohibits the testing, use, manufacture, production or acquisition by any means, as well as the receipt, storage, installation, deployment and any form of possession of any nuclear weapons by Latin American and Caribbean countries.

The parties should conclude agreements with the IAEA for the application of safeguards to their nuclear activities. The IAEA has the exclusive power to carry out special inspections.

The treaty is open for signature by all the independent states of the region.

Under *Additional Protocol I* states with territories within the zone established by the treaty (France, the Netherlands, the UK and the USA) undertake to apply the statute of military denuclearization, as defined in the treaty, to these territories.

Under *Additional Protocol II* the nuclear weapon states—China, France, Russia (at the time of signing, the USSR), the UK and the USA—undertake to respect the statute of military denuclearization of Latin America, as defined and delimited in the treaty, and not to contribute to acts involving a violation of the treaty, nor to use or threaten to use nuclear weapons against the parties to the treaty.

Parties to the original treaty (31): Antigua and Barbuda,[1†] Argentina, Bahamas,[1] Barbados,[1†] Belize,[1] Bolivia,[1] Brazil,[1] Chile,[1†] Colombia,[1†] Costa Rica,[1†] Dominica, Dominican Republic,[1†] Ecuador,[1†] El Salvador,[1†] Grenada,[1†] Guatemala,[1†] Guyana,[1] Haiti,[1] Honduras,[1†] Jamaica,[1†] Mexico,[1†] Nicaragua,[1†] Panama,[1†] Paraguay,[1†] Peru,[1†] Saint Lucia,[†] Saint Vincent and the Grenadines, Suriname,[1†] Trinidad and Tobago,[1†] Uruguay,[†] Venezuela[1†]

Parties to Additional Protocol I: France,[2] Netherlands,[†] UK,[3] USA[4†]

Parties to Additional Protocol II: China,[5] France,[6] Russia,[7] UK,[3] USA[8]

[†] Parties with safeguards agreements in force with the International Atomic Energy Agency (IAEA).

Ratified but not in force as of 1 January 1997: Saint Kitts (Christopher) and Nevis (entered into force 14 February 1997)

Signed but not ratified: Cuba

The amended treaty is fully in force for Argentina, Barbados, Brazil, Chile, Guyana, Jamaica, Mexico, Paraguay, Peru, Suriname, Uruguay and Venezuela.

[1] The treaty is in force for this country in accordance with Article 28 (of the original treaty), which waived the requirements for the entry into force of the treaty, specified in that article.

[2] France declared that Protocol I shall not apply to transit across French territories situated within the zone of the treaty, and destined for other French territories. The protocol shall not limit the participation of the populations of the French territories in the activities mentioned in Article 1 of the treaty, and in efforts connected with the national defence of France. France does not consider the zone described in the treaty as established in accordance with international law; it cannot, therefore, agree that the treaty should apply to that zone.

[3] When signing and ratifying Protocols I and II, the UK made the following declarations of understanding: The signing and ratification by the UK could not be regarded as affecting in any way the legal status of any territory for the international relations of which the UK is responsible, lying within the

limits of the geographical zone established by the treaty. Should any party to the treaty carry out any act of aggression with the support of a nuclear weapon state, the UK would be free to reconsider the extent to which it could be regarded as bound by the provisions of Protocol II.

[4] The USA ratified Protocol I with the following understandings: The provisions of the treaty do not affect the exclusive power and legal competence under international law of a state adhering to this Protocol to grant or deny transit and transport privileges to its own or any other vessels or aircraft irrespective of cargo or armaments; the provisions do not affect rights under international law of a state adhering to this protocol regarding the exercise of the freedom of the seas, or regarding passage through or over waters subject to the sovereignty of a state. The declarations attached by the USA to its ratification of Protocol II apply also to Protocol I.

[5] China declared that it will never send its means of transportation and delivery carrying nuclear weapons to cross the territory, territorial sea or airspace of Latin American countries.

[6] France stated that it interprets the undertaking contained in Article 3 of Protocol II to mean that it presents no obstacle to the full exercise of the right of self-defence enshrined in Article 51 of the UN Charter; it takes note of the interpretation by the Preparatory Commission for the Denuclearization of Latin America according to which the treaty does not apply to transit, the granting or denying of which lies within the exclusive competence of each state party in accordance with international law. In 1974, France made a supplementary statement to the effect that it was prepared to consider its obligations under Protocol II as applying not only to the signatories of the treaty, but also to the territories for which the statute of denuclearization was in force in conformity with Protocol I.

[7] The USSR signed and ratified Protocol II with the following statement:

The USSR proceeds from the assumption that the effect of Article 1 of the treaty extends to any nuclear explosive device and that, accordingly, the carrying out by any party of nuclear explosions for peaceful purposes would be a violation of its obligations under Article 1 and would be incompatible with its non-nuclear weapon status. For states parties to the treaty, a solution to the problem of peaceful nuclear explosions can be found in accordance with the provisions of Article V of the NPT and within the framework of the international procedures of the IAEA. The USSR declares that authorizing the transit of nuclear weapons in any form would be contrary to the objectives of the treaty.

Any actions undertaken by a state or states parties to the treaty which are not compatible with their non-nuclear weapon status, and also the commission by one or more states parties to the treaty of an act of aggression with the support of a state which is in possession of nuclear weapons or together with such a state, will be regarded by the USSR as incompatible with the obligations of those countries under the treaty. In such cases the USSR reserves the right to reconsider its obligations under Protocol II. It further reserves the right to reconsider its attitude to this protocol in the event of any actions on the part of other states possessing nuclear weapons which are incompatible with their obligations under the said protocol.

[8] The USA signed and ratified Protocol II with the following declarations and understandings: Each of the parties retains exclusive power and legal competence, to grant or deny non-parties transit and transport privileges. As regards the undertaking not to use or threaten to use nuclear weapons against the parties, the USA would consider that an armed attack by a party, in which it was assisted by a nuclear weapon state, would be incompatible with the treaty.

Treaty on the non-proliferation of nuclear weapons (Non-Proliferation Treaty, NPT)

Signed at London, Moscow and Washington, DC, on 1 July 1968; entered into force on 5 March 1970.

Prohibits the transfer by nuclear weapon states, to any recipient whatsoever, of nuclear weapons or other nuclear explosive devices or of control over them, as well as the assistance, encouragement or inducement of any non-nuclear weapon state to manufacture or otherwise acquire such weapons or devices. Prohibits the receipt by non-nuclear weapon states from any transferor whatsoever, as well as the manufacture or other acquisition by those states, of nuclear weapons or other nuclear explosive devices.

Non-nuclear weapon states undertake to conclude safeguard agreements with the International Atomic Energy Agency (IAEA) with a view to preventing diversion of nuclear energy from peaceful uses to nuclear weapons or other nuclear explosive devices.

The parties undertake to facilitate the exchange of equipment, materials and scientific and technological information for the peaceful uses of nuclear energy and to ensure that potential benefits from peaceful applications of nuclear explosions will be made available to non-nuclear weapon parties to the treaty. They also undertake to pursue negotiations in good faith on effective measures relating to cessation of the nuclear arms race at an early date and to nuclear disarmament, and on a treaty on general and complete disarmament.

In 1995, 25 years after the entry into force of the treaty, in accordance with Article X, a conference was convened to decide whether the treaty would continue in force indefinitely or would be extended for an additional fixed period or periods. It was decided that the treaty should remain in force indefinitely.

Parties (186): Afghanistan,[†] Albania, Algeria, Antigua and Barbuda,[†] Andorra, Angola, Argentina, Armenia,[†] Australia,[†] Austria,[†] Azerbaijan, Bahamas, Bahrain, Bangladesh,[†] Barbados,[†] Belarus,[†] Belgium,[†] Belize, Benin, Bhutan,[†] Bolivia,[†] Bosnia and Herzegovina, Botswana, Brunei,[†] Bulgaria,[†] Burkina Faso, Burundi, Cambodia, Cameroon, Canada,[†] Cape Verde, Central African Republic, Chad, Chile, China,[1] Colombia, Comoros, Congo, Costa Rica,[†] Côte d'Ivoire,[†] Croatia,[†] Cyprus,[†] Czech Republic,[†] Denmark,[†] Djibouti, Dominica,[†] Dominican Republic,[†] Ecuador,[†] Egypt,[†2] El Salvador,[†] Equatorial Guinea, Eritrea, Estonia, Ethiopia,[†] Fiji,[†] Finland,[†] France,[†3] Gabon, Gambia,[†] Georgia, Germany,[†] Ghana,[†] Greece,[†] Grenada,[†] Guatemala,[†] Guinea, Guinea-Bissau, Guyana, Haiti, Holy See,[†] Honduras,[†] Hungary,[†] Iceland,[†] Indonesia,[†] Iran,[†] Iraq,[†] Ireland,[†] Italy,[†] Jamaica,[†] Japan,[†] Jordan,[†] Kazakhstan,[†] Kenya, Kiribati,[†] Korea (North),[†] Korea (South),[†] Kuwait, Kyrgyzstan, Laos, Latvia,[†] Lebanon,[†] Lesotho,[†] Liberia, Libya,[†] Liechtenstein,[†4] Lithuania,[†] Luxembourg,[†] Macedonia (Former Yugoslav Republic of), Madagascar,[†] Malawi,[†] Malaysia,[†] Maldives,[†] Mali, Malta,[†] Marshall Islands, Mauritania, Mauritius,[†] Mexico,[†5] Micronesia, Moldova, Monaco,[†] Mongolia,[†] Morocco,[†] Mozambique, Myanmar (Burma),[†] Namibia, Nauru,[†] Nepal,[†] Netherlands,[†] New Zealand,[†] Nicaragua,[†] Niger, Nigeria,[†] Norway,[†] Palau, Panama, Papua New Guinea,[†] Paraguay,[†] Peru,[†] Philippines,[†] Poland,[†] Portugal,[†] Qatar, Romania,[†] Russia,[†] Rwanda, Saint Kitts (Christopher) and Nevis,[†] Saint Lucia,[†] Saint Vincent and the Grenadines,[†] Samoa (Western),[†] San Marino, Sao Tome and Principe, Saudi Arabia, Senegal,[†] Seychelles, Sierra Leone, Singapore,[†] Slovakia,[†] Slovenia, Solomon Islands,[†] Somalia, South Africa,[†] Spain,[†] Sri Lanka,[†] Sudan,[†] Suriname,[†] Swaziland,[†] Sweden,[†] Switzerland,[†4] Syria,[†] Taiwan, Tajikistan, Tanzania, Thailand,[†] Togo, Tonga,[†] Trinidad and Tobago,[†] Tunisia,[†] Turkey,[†] Turkmenistan, Tuvalu,[†] Uganda, UK,[†] Ukraine,[†] United Arab Emirates, Uruguay,[†] USA,[†] Uzbekistan, Vanuatu, Venezuela,[†] Viet Nam,[†] Yemen, Yugoslavia,[†] Zaire,[†] Zambia,[†] Zimbabwe[†]

Note: Oman acceded on 23 January 1997.

[†] Safeguards agreements in force with the International Atomic Energy Agency (IAEA), as required by the treaty, or concluded by a nuclear weapon state on a voluntary basis. For Russia (at the time of signing the USSR), the UK and the USA, the IAEA safeguards provide only for non-military nuclear installations.

[1] China stated that the nuclear weapon states should undertake: (*a*) not to be the first to use nuclear weapons at any time and under any circumstances; (*b*) not to use or threaten to use nuclear weapons against non-nuclear weapon countries or nuclear-free zones; and (*c*) to support the establishment of nuclear weapon-free zones, respect the status of such zones and assume corresponding obligations. All states that have nuclear weapons deployed outside of their boundaries should withdraw all those weapons back to their own territories.

[2] Egypt called upon nuclear weapon states to promote research and development of peaceful applications of nuclear explosions in order to overcome all the difficulties at present involved therein.

[3] An agreement between France, the European Atomic Energy Community (Euratom) and the IAEA for the application of safeguards in France had entered into force in 1981. The agreement covers nuclear material and facilities notified to the IAEA by France.

[4] Liechtenstein and Switzerland define the term 'source or special fissionable material' in Article III of the treaty as being in accordance with Article XX of the IAEA Statute, and a modification of this interpretation requires their formal consent; they will accept only such interpretations and definitions of the terms 'equipment or material especially designed or prepared for the processing, use or production of special fissionable material', as mentioned in Article III of the treaty, that they will expressly approve.

[5] On signing the treaty, Mexico stated, *inter alia*, that none of the provisions of the treaty shall be interpreted as affecting in any way whatsoever the rights and obligations of Mexico as a state party to the treaty of Tlatelolco. It is the understanding of Mexico that 'at the present time' any nuclear explosive device is capable of being used as a nuclear weapon and that there is no indication that 'in the near future' it will be possible to manufacture nuclear explosive devices that are not potentially nuclear weapons. However, if technological advances modify this situation, it will be necessary to amend the relevant provisions of the treaty in accordance with the procedure established therein.

Treaty on the prohibition of the emplacement of nuclear weapons and other weapons of mass destruction on the seabed and the ocean floor and in the subsoil thereof (Seabed Treaty)

Signed at London, Moscow and Washington, DC, on 11 February 1971; entered into force on 18 May 1972.

Prohibits implanting or emplacing on the seabed and the ocean floor and in the subsoil thereof beyond the outer limit of a 12-mile seabed zone any nuclear weapons or any other types of weapons of mass destruction as well as structures, launching installations or any other facilities specifically designed for storing, testing or using such weapons.

Parties (93): Afghanistan, Algeria, Antigua and Barbuda, Argentina,[1] Australia, Austria, Bahamas, Belarus, Belgium, Benin, Botswana, Brazil,[2] Bulgaria, Canada,[3] Cape Verde, Central African Republic, China,[4] Congo, Côte d'Ivoire, Croatia, Cuba, Cyprus, Czech Republic, Denmark, Dominican Republic, Equatorial Guinea, Ethiopia, Finland, Germany, Ghana, Greece, Guatemala, Guinea-Bissau, Hungary, Iceland, India,[5] Iran, Iraq, Ireland, Italy,[6] Jamaica, Japan, Jordan, Korea (South), Laos, Latvia, Lesotho, Libya, Liechtenstein, Luxembourg, Malaysia, Malta, Mauritius, Mexico,[7] Mongolia, Morocco, Nepal, Netherlands, New Zealand, Nicaragua, Niger, Norway, Panama, Philippines, Poland, Portugal, Qatar, Romania, Russia, Rwanda, Sao Tome and Principe, Saudi Arabia, Seychelles, Singapore, Slovakia, Slovenia, Solomon Islands, South Africa, Spain, Swaziland, Sweden, Switzerland, Taiwan, Togo, Tunisia, Turkey, UK, Ukraine, USA, Viet Nam,[8] Yemen, Yugoslavia,[9] Zambia

Signed but not ratified: Bolivia, Burundi, Cambodia, Cameroon, Colombia, Costa Rica, Gambia, Guinea, Honduras, Lebanon, Liberia, Madagascar, Mali, Myanmar (Burma), Paraguay, Senegal, Sierra Leone, Sudan, Tanzania, Uruguay

[1] Argentina stated that it interprets the references to the freedom of the high seas as in no way implying a pronouncement of judgement on the different positions relating to questions connected with international maritime law. It understands that the reference to the rights of exploration and exploitation by coastal states over their continental shelves was included solely because those could be the rights most frequently affected by verification procedures. Argentina precludes any possibility of strengthening, through this treaty, certain positions concerning continental shelves to the detriment of others based on different criteria.

[2] Brazil stated that nothing in the treaty shall be interpreted as prejudicing in any way the sovereign rights of Brazil in the area of the sea, the seabed and the subsoil thereof adjacent to its coasts. It is the understanding of Brazil that the word 'observation', as it appears in para. 1 of Article III of the treaty, refers only to observation that is incidental to the normal course of navigation in accordance with international law.

[3] Canada declared that Article I, para. 1, cannot be interpreted as indicating that any state has a right to implant or emplace any weapons not prohibited under Article I, para. 1, on the seabed and ocean floor, and in the subsoil thereof, beyond the limits of national jurisdiction, or as constituting any limitation on the principle that this area of the seabed and ocean floor and the subsoil thereof shall be reserved for exclusively peaceful purposes. Articles I, II and III cannot be interpreted as indicating that any state but

the coastal state has any right to implant or emplace any weapon not prohibited under Article I, para. 1 on the continental shelf, or the subsoil thereof, appertaining to that coastal state, beyond the outer limit of the seabed zone referred to in Article I and defined in Article II. Article III cannot be interpreted as indicating any restrictions or limitation upon the rights of the coastal state, consistent with its exclusive sovereign rights with respect to the continental shelf, to verify, inspect or effect the removal of any weapon, structure, installation, facility or device implanted or emplaced on the continental shelf, or the subsoil thereof, appertaining to that coastal state, beyond the outer limit of the seabed zone referred to in Article I and defined in Article II.

[4] China reaffirmed that nothing in this treaty shall be interpreted as prejudicing in any way the sovereign rights and the other rights of the People's Republic of China over its territorial sea, as well as the sea area, the seabed and subsoil thereof adjacent to its territorial sea.

[5] The accession by India is based on its position that it has full and exclusive rights over the continental shelf adjoining its territory and beyond its territorial waters and the subsoil thereof. There cannot, therefore, be any restriction on, or limitation of, the sovereign right of India as a coastal state to verify, inspect, remove or destroy any weapon, device, structure, installation or facility, which might be implanted or emplaced on or beneath its continental shelf by any other country, or to take such other steps as may be considered necessary to safeguard its security.

[6] Italy stated, inter alia, that in the case of agreements on further measures in the field of disarmament to prevent an arms race on the seabed and ocean floor and in their subsoil, the question of the delimitation of the area within which these measures would find application shall have to be examined and solved in each instance in accordance with the nature of the measures to be adopted.

[7] Mexico declared the treaty cannot be interpreted to mean that a state has the right to emplace weapons of mass destruction, or arms or military equipment of any type, on the continental shelf of Mexico. It reserves the right to verify, inspect, remove or destroy any weapon, structure, installation, device or equipment placed on its continental shelf, including nuclear weapons or other weapons of mass destruction.

[8] Viet Nam stated that no provision of the treaty should be interpreted in a way that would contradict the rights of the coastal states with regard to their continental shelf, including the right to take measures to ensure their security.

[9] In 1974, the Ambassador of Yugoslavia transmitted to the US Secretary of State a note stating that in the view of the Yugoslav Government, Article III, para. 1, of the treaty should be interpreted in such a way that a state exercising its right under this article shall be obliged to notify in advance the coastal state, in so far as its observations are to be carried out 'within the stretch of the sea extending above the continental shelf of the said state'.

Convention on the prohibition of the development, production and stockpiling of bacteriological (biological) and toxin weapons and on their destruction (Biological and Toxin Weapons Convention, BTWC)

Signed at London, Moscow and Washington, DC, on 10 April 1972; entered into force on 26 March 1975.

Prohibits the development, production, stockpiling or acquisition by other means or retention of microbial or other biological agents, or toxins whatever their origin or method of production, of types and in quantities that have no justification of prophylactic, protective or other peaceful purposes, as well as weapons, equipment or means of delivery designed to use such agents or toxins for hostile purposes or in armed conflict. The destruction of the agents, toxins, weapons, equipment and means of delivery in the possession of the parties, or their diversion to peaceful purposes, should be effected not later than nine months after the entry into force of the convention.

Parties (140): Afghanistan, Albania, Argentina, Armenia, Australia, Austria, Bahamas, Bahrain, Bangladesh, Barbados, Belarus, Belgium, Belize, Benin, Bhutan, Bolivia, Bosnia and Herzegovina, Botswana, Brazil, Brunei, Bulgaria, Burkina Faso, Cambodia, Canada, Cape Verde, Chile, China, Colombia, Congo, Costa Rica, Croatia, Cuba, Cyprus, Czech Republic, Denmark, Dominica, Dominican Republic, Ecuador, El Salvador, Equatorial Guinea, Estonia, Ethiopia, Fiji, Finland, France, Gambia, Georgia, Germany,* Ghana, Greece, Grenada, Guatemala, Guinea-Bissau, Honduras, Hungary, Iceland, India,* Indonesia, Iran,

Iraq, Ireland,* Italy, Jamaica, Japan, Jordan, Kenya, Korea (North), Korea (South), Kuwait, Laos, Lebanon, Lesotho, Libya, Liechtenstein, Luxembourg, Macedonia (Former Yugoslav Republic of), Malaysia, Maldives, Malta, Mauritius, Mexico,* Mongolia, Netherlands, New Zealand, Nicaragua, Niger, Nigeria, Norway, Oman, Pakistan, Panama, Papua New Guinea, Paraguay, Peru, Philippines, Poland, Portugal, Qatar, Romania, Russia, Rwanda, Saint Kitts (Christopher) and Nevis, Saint Lucia, San Marino, Sao Tome and Principe, Saudi Arabia, Senegal, Seychelles, Sierra Leone, Singapore, Slovakia, Slovenia, Solomon Islands, South Africa, Spain, Sri Lanka, Suriname, Swaziland, Sweden, Switzerland,* Taiwan, Thailand, Togo, Tonga, Tunisia, Turkey, Turkmenistan, Uganda, UK, Ukraine, Uruguay, USA, Uzbekistan, Vanuatu, Venezuela, Viet Nam, Yemen, Yugoslavia, Zaire, Zimbabwe

* With reservation and/or declaration upon ratification, accession or succession.

Signed but not ratified: Burundi, Central African Republic, Côte d'Ivoire, Egypt, Gabon, Guyana, Haiti, Liberia, Madagascar, Malawi, Mali, Morocco, Myanmar (Burma), Nepal, Somalia, Syria, Tanzania, United Arab Emirates

Convention on the prohibition of military or any other hostile use of environmental modification techniques (Enmod Convention)

Signed at Geneva on 18 May 1977; entered into force on 5 October 1978.

Prohibits military or any other hostile use of environmental modification techniques having widespread, long-lasting or severe effects as the means of destruction, damage or injury to states party to the convention. The term 'environmental modification techniques' refers to any technique for changing—through the deliberate manipulation of natural processes—the dynamics, composition or structure of the Earth, including its biota, lithosphere, hydrosphere and atmosphere, or of outer space. The understandings reached during the negotiations, but not written into the convention, define the terms 'widespread', 'long-lasting' and 'severe'.

Parties (64): Afghanistan, Algeria, Antigua and Barbuda, Argentina, Australia, Austria, Bangladesh, Belarus, Belgium, Benin, Brazil, Bulgaria, Canada, Cape Verde, Chile, Costa Rica, Cuba, Cyprus, Czech Republic, Denmark, Dominica, Egypt, Finland, Germany, Ghana, Greece, Guatemala, Hungary, India, Ireland, Italy, Japan, Korea (North), Korea (South),* Kuwait, Laos, Malawi, Mauritius, Mongolia, Netherlands,* New Zealand, Niger, Norway, Pakistan, Papua New Guinea, Poland, Romania, Russia, Saint Lucia, Sao Tome and Principe, Slovakia, Solomon Islands, Spain, Sri Lanka, Sweden, Switzerland, Tunisia, UK, Ukraine, Uruguay, USA, Uzbekistan, Viet Nam, Yemen

* With reservation and/or declaration upon ratification, accession or succession.

Signed but not ratified: Bolivia, Ethiopia, Holy See, Iceland, Iran, Iraq, Lebanon, Liberia, Luxembourg, Morocco, Nicaragua, Portugal, Sierra Leone, Syria, Turkey, Uganda, Zaire

Protocol (I) additional to the 1949 Geneva Conventions, and relating to the protection of victims of international armed conflict

Signed at Bern on 12 December 1977; entered into force on 7 December 1978.

The protocol confirms that the right of the parties to an international armed conflict to choose methods or means of warfare is not unlimited and that it is prohibited to use weapons or means of warfare which cause superfluous injury or unnecessary suffering.

Parties (146): Albania, Algeria,* Angola,* Antigua and Barbuda, Argentina,* Armenia, Australia,* Austria,* Bahamas, Bahrain, Bangladesh, Barbados, Belarus, Belgium,* Belize, Benin, Bolivia, Bosnia and Herzegovina, Botswana, Brazil, Brunei, Bulgaria, Burkina Faso, Burundi, Cameroon, Canada,* Cape Verde, Central African Republic, Chile, China,* Colombia, Comoros, Congo, Costa Rica, Côte d'Ivoire, Croatia, Cuba, Cyprus, Czech Republic, Denmark,* Djibouti, Dominica, Dominican Republic, Ecuador, Egypt,* El Salvador, Equatorial Guinea, Estonia, Ethiopia, Finland,* Gabon, Gambia, Georgia, Germany,* Ghana, Greece, Guatemala, Guinea, Guinea-Bissau, Guyana, Holy See,* Honduras, Hungary, Iceland,* Italy,* Jamaica, Jordan, Kazakhstan, Korea (North), Korea (South),* Kuwait, Kyrgyzstan, Laos, Latvia, Lesotho, Liberia, Libya, Liechtenstein,* Luxembourg, Macedonia (Former Yugoslav Republic of), Madagascar, Malawi, Maldives, Mali, Malta,* Mauritania, Mauritius, Mexico, Micronesia, Moldova, Mongolia, Mozambique, Namibia, Netherlands,* New Zealand,* Niger, Nigeria, Norway, Oman,* Palau, Panama, Paraguay, Peru, Poland, Portugal, Qatar,* Romania, Russia,* Rwanda, Saint Kitts (Christopher) and Nevis, Saint Lucia, Saint Vincent and the Grenadines, Samoa (Western), San Marino, Sao Tome and Principe,[1] Saudi Arabia,* Senegal, Seychelles, Sierra Leone, Slovakia, Slovenia, Solomon Islands, South Africa, Spain,* Suriname, Swaziland, Sweden,* Switzerland,* Syria,* Tajikistan, Tanzania, Togo, Tunisia, Turkmenistan, Uganda, Ukraine, United Arab Emirates,* Uruguay, Uzbekistan, Vanuatu, Viet Nam, Yemen, Yugoslavia,* Zaire, Zambia, Zimbabwe

* With reservation and/or declaration upon ratification, accession or succession.

[1] In accordance with the provisions of Article 95.2, the protocol enters into force for a party six months after the deposit of its instrument of ratification or accession. This state ratified or acceded to the protocol in the second half of 1996 and the protocol entered into force for that state in 1997.

Convention on the physical protection of nuclear material

Signed at Vienna and New York on 3 March 1980; entered into force on 8 February 1987.

The convention obliges the parties to protect nuclear material for peaceful purposes during transport across their territory or on ships or aircraft under their jurisdiction.

Parties (57): Antigua and Barbuda, Argentina,* Armenia, Australia, Austria, Belarus, Belgium,† Brazil, Bulgaria, Canada, Chile, China,* Croatia, Czech Republic, Denmark,† Ecuador, Estonia, Euratom,*† Finland, France,*† Germany,† Greece,† Guatemala, Hungary, Indonesia,* Ireland,† Italy,*† Japan, Korea (South),* Liechtenstein, Lithuania, Luxembourg,† Macedonia (Former Yugoslav Republic of), Mexico, Monaco, Mongolia,* Netherlands,*† Norway, Paraguay, Peru,* Philippines, Poland,* Portugal, Romania, Russia,* Slovakia, Slovenia, Spain,*† Sweden, Switzerland, Tajikistan, Tunisia, Turkey,* UK,† Ukraine, USA, Yugoslavia

* With reservation and/or declaration upon ratification, accession or succession.

† Belgium, Denmark, France, Germany, Greece, Ireland, Italy, Luxembourg, Netherlands, Spain and the UK signed as Euratom member states.

Signed but not ratified: Dominican Republic, Haiti, Israel, Morocco, Niger, Panama, South Africa

Convention on prohibitions or restrictions on the use of certain conventional weapons which may be deemed to be excessively injurious or to have indiscriminate effects (CCW Convention, or 'Inhumane Weapons' Convention)

Signed at New York on 10 April 1981; entered into force on 2 December 1983.

The convention is an 'umbrella treaty', under which specific agreements can be concluded in the form of protocols.

Protocol I prohibits the use of weapons intended to injure by fragments which are not detectable in the human body by X-rays.

Protocol II prohibits or restricts the use of mines, booby-traps and other devices; amended in 1996; amendments adopted on 3 May 1997. Not in force.

Protocol III restricts the use of incendiary weapons.

Protocol IV, adopted in Vienna on 12 October 1995, prohibits the employment of laser weapons specifically designed to cause permanent blindness to unenhanced vision. Not in force.

The amended Protocol II and Protocol IV will enter into force six months after the date of the deposit of the 20th instrument of ratification, acceptance, approval or accession.

Parties (63): Argentina, Australia, Austria, Belarus, Belgium, Benin, Bosnia and Herzegovina, Brazil, Bulgaria, Canada, China, Croatia, Cuba, Cyprus,* Czech Republic, Denmark, Djibouti,[1] Ecuador, Finland, France,* Georgia, Germany, Greece, Guatemala, Hungary, India, Ireland, Israel, Italy, Japan, Jordan, Laos, Latvia, Liechtenstein, Luxembourg, Macedonia (Former Yugoslav Republic of), Malta, Mauritius, Mexico, Mongolia, Netherlands,* New Zealand, Niger, Norway, Pakistan, Philippines,[1] Poland, Romania, Russia, Slovakia, Slovenia, South Africa, Spain, Sweden, Switzerland, Togo, Tunisia, Uganda, UK, Ukraine, Uruguay, USA, Yugoslavia

Note: Benin is party only to Protocols I and III and France only to Protocols I and II.

* With reservation and/or declaration upon ratification, accession or succession.

[1] In accordance with Article 5.2, the convention enters into force for a state six months after the deposit of the instrument of ratification or accession. This state deposited its instruments of ratification or accession in the second half of 1996 and the convention entered into force for this state in 1997.

Signed but not ratified: Afghanistan, Egypt, Iceland, Morocco, Nicaragua, Nigeria, Portugal, Sierra Leone, Sudan, Turkey, Viet Nam

South Pacific nuclear free zone treaty (Treaty of Rarotonga)

Signed at Rarotonga, Cook Islands, on 6 August 1985; entered into force on 11 December 1986.

Prohibits the manufacture or acquisition by other means of any nuclear explosive device, as well as possession or control over such device by the parties anywhere inside or outside the zone area described in an annex. The parties also undertake not to supply nuclear material or equipment, unless subject to IAEA safeguards, and to prevent in their territories the stationing as well as the testing of any nuclear explosive device and undertake not to dump, and to prevent the dumping of, radioactive wastes and other radioactive matter at sea anywhere within the zone. Each party remains free to allow visits, as well as transit, by foreign ships and aircraft.

The treaty is open for signature by members of the South Pacific Forum.

Under *Protocol 1*, France, the UK and the USA undertake to apply the treaty prohibitions relating to the manufacture, stationing and testing of nuclear explosive devices in the territories situated within the zone, for which they are internationally responsible.

Under *Protocol 2*, China, France, Russia (at the time of signing, the USSR), the UK and the USA undertake not to use or threaten to use a nuclear explosive device against the parties to the treaty or against any territory within the zone for which a party to Protocol 1 is internationally responsible.

Under *Protocol 3*, China, France, the UK, the USA and Russia (at the time of signing, the USSR) undertake not to test any nuclear explosive device anywhere within the zone.

Parties (12): Australia, Cook Islands, Fiji, Kiribati, Nauru, New Zealand, Niue, Papua New Guinea, Samoa (Western), Solomon Islands, Tuvalu, Vanuatu

Signed but not ratified: Tonga

Party to Protocol 1: France; **signed but not ratified:** UK, USA
Parties to Protocol 2: China, France,[1] Russia; **signed but not ratified:** UK,[2] USA
Parties to Protocol 3: China, France, Russia; **signed but not ratified:** UK, USA

[1] France declared that the negative security guarantees set out in Protocol 2 are the same as the CD declaration of 6 April 1995 which were referred to in the UN Security Council Resolution 984 of 11 April 1995.

[2] The UK declared that it will not be bound by the undertakings in Protocol 2 in case of an invasion or any other attack on the UK, its territories, its armed forces or its allies, carried out or sustained by a party to the treaty in association or alliance with a nuclear weapon state or if a party violates its non-proliferation obligations under the treaty.

Treaty on conventional armed forces in Europe (CFE Treaty)

Signed at Vienna on 19 November 1990; entered into force on 9 November 1992.

The treaty sets ceilings on five categories of military equipment (battle tanks, armoured combat vehicles, artillery pieces, combat aircraft and attack helicopters) in an area stretching from the Atlantic Ocean to the Ural Mountains (the Atlantic-to-the-Urals, ATTU, zone).

The treaty was negotiated and signed by the member states of the Warsaw Treaty Organization (WTO) and NATO within the framework of the CSCE (from 1 January 1995 the OSCE).

The **Tashkent Document**, signed by former Soviet republics with territories within the ATTU zone (except the Baltic states) at Tashkent on 15 May 1992, includes the Agreement on the Principles and Procedures for Implementing the CFE Treaty (**Tashkent Agreement**), establishing maximum levels for holdings of armaments and equipment for implementation of the treaty and a number of certain types of helicopters not subject to CFE Treaty limits. The Document also includes a Declaration by which the states recognize how to implement the CFE Treaty after the breakup of the USSR.

All the CFE Treaty parties signed, at Oslo, on 5 June 1992, the Final Document of the Extraordinary Conference of the States Parties to the CFE Treaty (**Oslo Document**), introducing modifications, necessary because of the emergence of new states as a consequence of the breakup of the USSR.

In January 1997 negotiations started to adapt the treaty to the new security environment in Europe.

Parties (30): Armenia, Azerbaijan, Belarus, Belgium, Bulgaria, Canada, Czech Republic, Denmark, France, Georgia, Germany, Greece, Hungary, Iceland, Italy, Kazakhstan, Luxembourg, Moldova, Netherlands, Norway, Poland, Portugal, Romania, Russia, Slovakia, Spain, Turkey, UK, Ukraine, USA

The concluding act of the negotiation on personnel strength of conventional armed forces in Europe (CFE-1A Agreement)

Signed by the parties to the CFE Treaty at Helsinki on 10 July 1992; entered into force simultaneously with the CFE Treaty.

The agreement limits the personnel of the conventional land-based armed forces within the ATTU zone.

Vienna Documents 1990, 1992 and 1994 on confidence- and security-building measures

The Vienna Documents were adopted by all the CSCE states. The Vienna Document 1994 was adopted at Vienna on 28 November 1994.

The **Vienna Document 1990** on Confidence- and Security-Building Measures (CSBMs) repeats many of the provisions in the 1986 Stockholm Document on CSBMs and Disarmament in Europe and expands several others. It establishes a communications network and a risk reduction mechanism. The **Vienna Document 1992** on CSBMs builds on the Vienna Document 1990 and supplements its provisions with new mechanisms and constraining provisions. **The Vienna Document 1994** on CSBMs amends and expands the previous Vienna Documents.

The Vienna Documents were signed by all members of the Conference on Security and Co-operation in Europe (from 1 January 1995 the OSCE).

Treaty on open skies

Signed at Helsinki on 24 March 1992; not in force as of 1 January 1997.

The treaty obliges the parties to submit their territories to short-notice unarmed surveillance flights. The area of application stretches from Vancouver, Canada, eastwards to Vladivostok, Russia.

The Open Skies Treaty was negotiated between the member states of the Warsaw Treaty Organization (WTO) and NATO. It is also open for signature by the former Soviet republics. For six months after entry into force of the treaty, any other OSCE member state may apply for accession. The treaty will enter into force when 20 states have ratified it, including all parties with more than eight 'passive quotas' (Belarus, Canada, France, Germany, Italy, Russia, Turkey, UK, Ukraine, USA).

22 ratifications deposited: Belgium, Bulgaria, Canada, Czech Republic, Denmark, France, Germany, Greece, Hungary, Iceland, Italy, Luxembourg, Netherlands, Norway, Poland, Portugal, Romania, Slovakia, Spain, Turkey, UK, USA

Signed but not ratified: Belarus, Georgia, Kyrgyzstan, Russia, Ukraine

Convention on the prohibition of the development, production, stockpiling and use of chemical weapons and on their destruction (Chemical Weapons Convention, CWC)

Opened for signature at Paris on 13 January 1993; entered into force on 29 April 1997.

The convention prohibits not only the use of chemical weapons (prohibited by the 1925 Geneva Protocol) but also the development, production, acquisition, transfer and stockpiling of chemical weapons. Each party undertakes to destroy its chemical weapons and production facilities.

67 ratifications deposited (as of 1 January 1997): Albania, Algeria, Argentina, Armenia, Australia, Austria, Belarus, Brazil, Bulgaria, Cameroon, Canada, Chile, Cook Islands, Costa Rica, Côte d'Ivoire, Croatia, Czech Republic, Denmark, Ecuador, El Salvador, Ethiopia, Fiji, Finland, France, Georgia, Germany, Greece, Hungary, India, Ireland, Italy, Japan, Latvia, Lesotho, Maldives, Mauritius, Mexico, Moldova, Monaco, Mongolia, Morocco, Namibia, Netherlands, New Zealand, Norway, Oman, Papua New Guinea, Paraguay, Peru, Philippines, Poland, Portugal, Romania, Saudi Arabia, Seychelles, Slovakia, South Africa, Spain, Sri Lanka, Swaziland, Sweden, Switzerland, Tajikistan, Turkmenistan, UK, Uruguay, Uzbekistan

Signed but not ratified (as of 1 January 1997): Afghanistan, Azerbaijan, Bahamas, Bahrain, Bangladesh, Belgium, Benin, Bolivia, Brunei, Burkina Faso, Burundi, Cambodia, Cape Verde, Central African Republic, Chad, China, Colombia, Comoros, Congo, Cuba, Cyprus, Djibouti, Dominica, Dominican Republic, Equatorial Guinea, Estonia, Gabon, Gambia, Ghana, Guatemala, Guinea, Guinea Bissau, Guyana, Haiti, Holy See, Honduras, Iceland, Indonesia, Iran, Israel, Kazakhstan, Kenya, Korea (South), Kuwait, Kyrgyzstan, Laos, Liberia, Liechtenstein, Lithuania, Luxembourg, Madagascar, Malawi, Malaysia, Mali, Malta, Marshall Islands, Mauritania, Micronesia, Myanmar (formerly Burma), Nauru, Nepal, Nicaragua, Niger, Nigeria, Pakistan, Panama, Qatar, Russia, Rwanda, Saint Kitts and Nevis, Saint Lucia, Saint Vincent and the Grenadines, Samoa (Western), San Marino, Senegal, Sierra Leone, Singapore, Slovenia, Tanzania, Thailand, Togo, Tunisia, Turkey, Uganda, Ukraine, United Arab Emirates, USA, Venezuela, Viet Nam, Yemen, Zaire, Zambia, Zimbabwe

Note: By the time the CWC entered into force, additional states had signed and ratified the convention.

Treaty on the Southeast Asia nuclear weapon-free zone (Treaty of Bangkok)

Opened for signature at Bangkok on 15 December 1995; not in force as of 1 January 1997.

Prohibits the development, manufacture, acquisition or testing of nuclear weapons inside or outside the zone area as well as the stationing and transport of nuclear weapons in or through the zone. Each state party may decide for itself whether to allow visits and transit by foreign ships and aircraft. The parties undertake not to dump at sea or discharge into the atmosphere anywhere within the zone any radio-active material or wastes or dispose of radioactive material on land. The parties should conclude an agreement with the IAEA for the application of full-scope safeguards to their peaceful nuclear activities.

The zone includes not only the territories but also the continental shelves and exclusive economic zones of the states parties.

The treaty is open for signature by all states in South-East Asia: Brunei, Cambodia, Indonesia, Laos, Malaysia, Myanmar (Burma), the Philippines, Singapore, Thailand and Viet Nam.

Under a *Protocol* to the treaty China, France, Russia, the UK and the USA are to undertake not to use or threaten to use nuclear weapons against any state party to the treaty or within the Southeast Asia nuclear weapon-free zone.

The treaty will enter into force on the date of the deposit of the 7th instrument of ratification. The protocol will enter into force for each state party on the date of its deposit of the instrument of ratification.

5 ratifications deposited: Brunei, Laos, Malaysia, Myanmar (Burma), Viet Nam

Signed but not ratified: Cambodia, Indonesia, Philippines, Singapore, Thailand

Protocol: no signatures, no ratifications

African nuclear-weapon-free zone treaty (Treaty of Pelindaba)

Opened for signature at Cairo on 11 April 1996; not in force as of 1 January 1997.

Prohibits the research, development, manufacture and acquisition of nuclear explosive devices and the testing or stationing of any nuclear explosive device. Each party remains free to allow visits, as well as transit by foreign ships and aircraft. The treaty also prohibits any attack against nuclear installations. The parties undertake not to dump or permit the dumping of radioactive wastes and other radioactive matter anywhere within the zone. The parties should conclude an agreement with the IAEA for the application of comprehensive safeguards to their peaceful nuclear activities.

'African nuclear-weapon-free zone' means the territory of the continent of Africa, islands states member of the OAU and all islands considered by the OAU to be part of Africa.

The treaty is open for signature by all the states of Africa.

Under *Protocol I* China, France, Russia, the UK and the USA are to undertake not to use or threaten to use a nuclear explosive device against the parties to the Treaty.

Under *Protocol II* China, France, Russia, the UK and the USA are to undertake not to test nuclear explosive devices anywhere within the zone.

Under *Protocol III* states with territories within the zone for which they are internationally responsible, are to undertake to observe certain provisions of the treaty with respect to these territories. This protocol is open for signature by France and Spain.

The treaty will enter into force upon the 28th ratification. The protocols will enter into force at that time for those protocol signatories that have deposited their instruments of ratification.

2 ratifications deposited: Gambia, Mauritius

Signed but not ratified: Algeria, Angola, Benin, Burkina Faso, Burundi, Cameroon, Cape Verde, Central African Republic, Chad, Comoros, Côte d'Ivoire, Djibouti, Egypt, Eritrea, Ethiopia, Gabon, Ghana, Guinea, Guinea-Bissau, Kenya, Lesotho, Liberia, Libya, Malawi, Mali, Mauritania, Morocco, Mozambique, Namibia, Niger, Nigeria, Rwanda, Sao Tome and Principe, Senegal, Seychelles, Sierra Leone, South Africa, Sudan, Swaziland, Tanzania, Togo, Tunisia, Uganda, Zaire, Zambia, Zimbabwe

Protocol I ratification: France;[1] **signed but not ratified:** China, Russia,[2] UK,[3] USA

Protocol II ratification: France; **signed but not ratified:** China, Russia,[2] UK,[3] USA

Protocol III ratification: France

[1] When signing Protocol I France stated that the commitment expressed in Article I of the Protocol is equivalent to the negative security guarantee that France has given to non nuclear states parties to the Non-proliferation treaty, confirmed in a CD statement of 6 April 1995 and in the UN Security Council Resolution 984 of 11 April 1995.

[2] The Russian Government declared that as long as a military base is located on the Chagos archipelago islands it cannot meet the requirements put forward by the treaty for the nuclear weapon-free territories and it considers itself to be bound by the obligations in respect of these territories. As regards Article 1 of Protocol I Russia interprets it as it will not use nuclear weapons against a state which is a party to the treaty excluding in cases of invasion or any other armed attack on Russia.

[3] The British Government declared that it does not accept the inclusion of the British Indian Ocean Territory within the African nuclear weapon-free zone without its consent and it does not accept any legal obligation in respect of that territory by its adherence to Protocols I and II. The UK will not be bound by Protocol I in case of an invasion or any other attack on the UK, its dependent territories, its armed forces or its allies or carried out or sustained by a party to the treaty in association or in alliance with a nuclear weapon state.

Comprehensive nuclear test-ban treaty (CTBT)

Opened for signature at New York on 24 September 1996; not in force as of 1 January 1997.

Prohibits the carrying out of any nuclear weapon test explosion or any other nuclear explosion, and urges each party to prevent any such nuclear explosion at any place under its jurisdiction or control and refrain from causing, encouraging, or in any way participating in the carrying out of any nuclear weapon test explosion or any other nuclear explosion. A Comprehensive Nuclear Test-Ban Treaty Organization is to ensure treaty implementation.

The treaty will enter into force 180 days after the date of the deposit of the instrument of ratification of the 44 states listed in an annexe to the treaty, but in no case earlier than two years after its opening for signature. All the 44 states possess nuclear power reactors and/or nuclear research reactors.

1 ratification deposited: Fiji

Signed but not ratified: Albania, Algeria,[†] Andorra, Angola, Argentina,[†] Armenia, Australia,[†] Austria,[†] Bahrain, Bangladesh,[†] Belarus, Belgium,[†] Benin, Bolivia, Bosnia and Herzegovina, Brazil,[†] Bulgaria,[†] Burkina Faso, Burundi, Cambodia, Canada,[†] Cape Verde, Chad, Chile,[†] China,[†] Colombia,[†] Comoros, Costa Rica, Côte d'Ivoire, Croatia, Cyprus, Czech Republic, Denmark, Djibouti, Dominican Republic, Ecuador, Egypt,[†] El Salvador, Equatorial Guinea, Estonia, Ethiopia, Finland,[†] France,[†] Gabon, Georgia, Germany,[†] Ghana, Greece, Grenada, Guinea, Haiti, Holy See, Honduras, Hungary,[†] Iceland, Indonesia,[†] Iran,[†] Ireland, Israel,[†] Italy,[†] Jamaica, Japan,[†] Jordan, Kazakhstan, Kenya, Korea (South),[†] Kuwait, Kyrgyzstan, Latvia, Lesotho, Liberia, Liechtenstein, Lithuania, Luxembourg, Madagascar, Malawi, Malta, Marshall Islands, Mauritania, Mexico,[†] Micronesia, Monaco, Mongolia, Morocco, Mozambique, Myanmar (Burma), Namibia, Nepal, Netherlands,[†] New Zealand, Nicaragua, Niger, Norway,[†] Panama, Papua New Guinea, Paraguay, Peru,[†] Philippines, Poland,[†] Portugal, Qatar, Romania,[†] Russia,[†] Saint Lucia, Samoa (Western), San Marino, San Tome and Principe, Senegal, Seychelles, Slovakia,[†] Slovenia, Solomon Islands, South Africa,[†] Spain,[†] Sri Lanka, Swaziland, Sweden,[†] Switzerland,[†] Tajikistan, Thailand, Togo, Tunisia, Turkey,[†] Turkmenistan, Uganda, Ukraine,[†] United Arab Emirates, UK,[†] USA,[†] Uruguay, Uzbekistan, Vanuatu, Venezuela, Viet Nam,[†] Yemen, Zaire,[†] Zambia

Note: Suriname signed on 14 January 1997, Brunei on 22 January 1997.

[†] One of the 44 countries whose ratification is required for entry into force.

II. Summaries and status of the major US–Soviet/Russian agreements, as of 1 January 1997

Treaty on the limitation of anti-ballistic missile systems (ABM Treaty)

Signed by the USA and the USSR at Moscow on 26 May 1972; entered into force on 3 October 1972.

The treaty obligates the parties not to undertake to build a nation-wide defence system against strategic ballistic missile attack and limits the development and deployment of permitted missile defences.

A protocol to the ABM Treaty, introducing further numerical restrictions on permitted ballistic missile defences, was signed in 1974.

Treaty on the limitation of underground nuclear weapon tests (Threshold Test Ban Treaty, TTBT)

Signed by the USA and the USSR at Moscow on 3 July 1974; entered into force on 11 December 1990.

The parties undertake not to carry out any individual underground nuclear weapon test having a yield exceeding 150 kilotons.

Treaty on underground nuclear explosions for peaceful purposes (Peaceful Nuclear Explosions Treaty, PNET)

Signed by the USA and the USSR at Moscow and Washington, DC, on 28 May 1976; entered into force on 11 December 1990.

The parties undertake not to carry out any underground nuclear explosion for peaceful purposes having a yield exceeding 150 kilotons or any group explosion having an aggregate yield exceeding 150 kilotons.

Treaty on the elimination of intermediate-range and shorter-range missiles (INF Treaty)

Signed by the USA and the USSR at Washington, DC, on 8 December 1987; entered into force on 1 June 1988.

The treaty obliges the parties to destroy all land-based missiles with a range of 500–5500 km (intermediate-range, 1000–5500 km; and shorter-range, 500–1000 km) and their launchers by 1 June 1991. The INF Treaty was implemented before this date.

Treaty on the reduction and limitation of strategic offensive arms (START I Treaty)[1]

Signed by the USA and the USSR at Moscow on 31 July 1991; entered into force on 5 December 1994.

The treaty requires the USA and Russia to make phased reductions in their offensive strategic nuclear forces over a seven-year period. It sets numerical limits on deployed strategic nuclear delivery vehicles (SNDVs)—ICBMs, SLBMs and heavy bombers—and the nuclear warheads they carry. In the May 1992 Protocol to Facilitate the Implementation of the START Treaty (Lisbon Protocol), Belarus, Kazakhstan and Ukraine also assumed the obligations of the former USSR under the treaty. They pledged to eliminate all the former Soviet strategic weapons on their territories within the seven-year reduction period and to join the NPT as non-nuclear weapon states in the shortest possible time.

Treaty on further reduction and limitation of strategic offensive arms (START II Treaty)

Signed by the USA and Russia at Moscow on 3 January 1993; not in force as of 1 January 1997.

The treaty requires the USA and Russia to eliminate their MIRVed ICBMs and sharply reduce the number of their deployed strategic nuclear warheads to no more than 3000–3500 each (of which no more than 1750 may be deployed on SLBMs) by 1 January 2003 or no later than 31 December 2000 if the USA and Russia reach a formal agreement committing the USA to help finance the elimination of strategic nuclear weapons in Russia.

---

[1] Since Belarus, Kazakhstan and Ukraine have pledged to abide by the START I Treaty, it is generally regarded as a multilateral treaty. However, because of its origin and the fact that the USA and Russia are in the process of finalizing implementation of the treaty provisions, it is listed in this section, with the follow-on US–Russian START II Treaty.

Annexe B. Chronology 1996

RAGNHILD FERM

For the convenience of the reader, key words are indicated in the right-hand column, opposite each entry. They refer to the subject-areas covered in the entry. Definitions of the acronyms can be found on page xiv.

22 Jan.	The USA discloses the exact amount and location of its 31 000 tonnes of chemical weapon agents. In his State of the Union Address (23 Jan.), President Clinton urges the US Senate to ratify the 1993 Chemical Weapons Convention (CWC).	CW; USA
26 Jan.	The US Senate ratifies the 1993 START II Treaty by a vote of 87 to 4.	START; USA
26 Jan.	Representatives of Bosnia and Herzegovina, the Bosnian–Croat Federation and the Bosnian Serbs sign an agreement on confidence- and security-building measures (CSBMs) largely based on the Vienna Document 1994 on Confidence- and Security-Building Measures and adapted to subregional conditions.	Former Yugoslavia
29 Jan.	French President Chirac announces the end of France's nuclear tests.	Nuclear tests; France
9 Feb.	The Irish Republican Army (IRA) explodes a large device in London's Docklands area, ending its 17-month cease-fire.	IRA; UK
22 Feb.	French President Chirac announces that all short-range Hadès missiles will be dismantled, the Plateau d'Albion missile site be closed and the 18 S3D medium-range ballistic missiles based there dismantled. The military uranium enrichment facility in southern France will be closed and no further weapon-grade uranium produced.	France; Nuclear weapons
29 Feb.	A group of states led by Denmark urges the UN Secretary-General to form a Multinational UN Stand-by Forces High Readiness Brigade (SHIRBRIG) for deployment in peace-keeping operations for a maximum of six months until replaced by a regular UN peacekeeping force.	UN; Denmark; Peacekeeping
13 Mar.	Following the withdrawal of the Bosnian Serb forces from the zones of separation, the embargo on deliveries of weapons and military equipment to the republics of the former Yugoslavia, imposed in 1991 by UN Security Council Resolution 713, is terminated, except for deliveries of heavy weapons.	Former Yugoslavia

15 Mar.	The UN Secretary-General launches a 10-year, $25 billion UN System-wide Special Initiative on Africa to support development and peace processes in the continent.	UN; Africa
25 Mar.	France, the UK and the USA sign the three protocols to the 1985 South Pacific Nuclear Free Zone Treaty (Treaty of Rarotonga), in Suva, Fiji, pledging not to station or test nuclear weapons in the area and not to use or threaten to use nuclear weapons against the parties to the treaty.	France, UK, USA/Treaty of Rarotonga; NWFZ
29 Mar.	The European Union (EU) Intergovernmental Conference (IGC) opens in Turin, Italy. The EU heads of government entrust the conference with the task of implementing a common foreign and security policy, including the eventual framing of a common defence policy, which might in time lead to a common defence.	EU
2 Apr.	Russian President Yeltsin and Belarussian President Lukashenko, meeting in Moscow, sign a treaty establishing the foundation for deepening political, economic and military cooperation between the two states.	Russia/Belarus
11 Apr.	The African Nuclear-Weapon-Free Zone Treaty, the Treaty of Pelindaba, is signed in Cairo by 43 African states. The USA, the UK, France and China sign Protocols I and II, pledging not to attack parties to the treaty with nuclear weapons and renouncing the stationing or testing of nuclear weapons in the region. (Russia signs the two protocols on 11 May.) France signs Protocol III, undertaking to apply the provisions of the treaty with respect to its territories in the region.	Treaty of Pelindaba
17 Apr.	US President Clinton, visiting Japan, and Japanese Prime Minister Hashimoto sign a joint declaration committing the USA and Japan to strengthen their security ties. It is confirmed that the USA will station 100 000 troops indefinitely in East Asia, 47 000 of whom will be based in Japan. However, a commitment is made to reduce the US military presence in Okinawa.	USA/Japan
19–20 Apr.	A summit meeting of the G7 states, Russia and Ukraine on nuclear safety and security issues is held in Moscow. A declaration is adopted which includes a statement on the safe storage and disposal of fissile material removed from dismantled nuclear weapons.	G7; Fissile material
25 Apr.	Russian President Yeltsin and Chinese President Jiang Zemin, meeting in Beijing, issue a joint statement on a Russian–Chinese strategic partnership. As a symbol, a telephone 'hot line' will be established between Beijing and Moscow.	Russia/China

26 Apr.	The heads of state and government of China, Russia, Kazakhstan, Kyrgyzstan and Tajikistan sign an agreement in Shanghai, China, on confidence building in the military field in border areas.	CBM; China/ Russia/ Kazakhstan/ Kyrgyzstan/ Tajikistan
3 May	An amended Protocol II on prohibitions or restrictions on the use of mines, booby-traps and other devices, including further restrictions on the use, production and transfer of anti-personnel land-mines, is adopted in Geneva by the Review Conference on the Convention on Certain Conventional Weapons (CCW Convention).	CCW; Land-mines.
7 May	The foreign and defence ministers of the Western European Union (WEU), meeting in Birmingham, UK, declare that the WEU will establish closer links with the EU, to implement EU decisions and actions which have defence implications, and with NATO, to be able to use NATO assets and capabilities, in particular through Combined Joint Task Forces (CJTF), for European operations in the framework of the Petersberg tasks (agreed in 1992).	WEU
13 May	In announcing its proposal for the six-year defence programme, the French Government states that the French nuclear arsenal will be reduced and will require less than 20% of the defence budget by 2002. All land-based nuclear weapons will be eliminated (see *22 Feb.*).	France; Nuclear weapons
15–31 May	The first Review Conference of the 1990 Treaty on Conventional Armed Forces in Europe (CFE Treaty) is held in Vienna. The parties agree on a numerical and geographical reorganization of the flank areas, including a contraction of the areas, which allows Russia and Ukraine to deploy more treaty-limited equipment (TLE) along their respective borders.	CFE
1 June	Ukrainian President Kuchma announces that the last of the strategic nuclear warheads based on Ukraine's territory have been transferred to Russia for dismantlement.	START; Ukraine
3 June	NATO foreign ministers, meeting in Berlin, declare that NATO will build up a European Security and Defence Identity (ESDI) and a Combined Joint Task Forces (CJTF) concept.	NATO
10 June	Russian Nationalities Minister Mikhailov and Chechen Chief of Staff Maskhadov sign in Nazran (the capital of the neighbouring Ingush republic) two protocols: one on Russian troop withdrawal by the end of August and the second on the release of all hostages and prisoners of war.	Russia/ Chechnya

14 June	An Agreement on Subregional Arms Control, negotiated under the mandate of the 1995 Dayton Agreement and under the auspices of the OSCE, is signed at Florence, Italy, at the Ministerial Meeting of the Peace Implementation Council by Croatia, Bosnia and Herzegovina and its two entities—the Muslim-Croat Federation of Bosnia and Herzegovina and the Bosnian-Serb Republika Srpska—and Yugoslavia (Serbia and Montenegro).	Former Yugoslavia; OSCE
16 June	The first democratic presidential elections are held in Russia. No candidate receives the necessary '50 per cent plus one' margin. At a second round, on 3 July, President Yeltsin receives 53.82 per cent of the vote.	Russia
17 June	The Conference on Disarmament (CD) formally admits 23 new member states.	CD
18 June	With the signing of the Agreement on Subregional Arms Control (see *14 June*) the UN Security Council votes to formally end the heavy-arms embargo against the states of the former Yugoslavia.	Former Yugoslavia; UN
21–23 June	A summit meeting of the Arab states (Iraq is not invited) is held in Cairo. The leaders state that for the peace process to continue Israel must withdraw from all occupied Palestinian territories, including Arab Jerusalem, the Syrian Golan heights, and southern Lebanon and its Western Bekaa to enable the Palestinian people to establish an independent state with Arab Jerusalem as its capital.	Middle East
24 June	Israeli Prime Minister Netanyahu states that the Arab summit meeting statement (see above) is unacceptable since Israel will not agree to withdraw from land taken in 1967 as a precondition for peace.	Middle East
8 July	Replying to a request made by the UN General Assembly in Dec. 1994 to rule on the legality of nuclear weapons, the International Court of Justice (ICJ) hands down an advisory opinion, stating that while the use or threat to use nuclear weapons might be legal in an extreme circumstance of self-defence, this would 'generally be contrary to the rules of international law applicable in armed conflict and in particular the principles and rules of humanitarian law'.	ICJ; Nuclear weapons
12 July	Thirty states, meeting in Vienna, agree on the initial elements of the Wassenaar Arrangement on Export Controls for Conventional Arms and Dual-use Goods and Technologies.	Export control
16 July	The Belarussian Parliament puts forth an initiative to create a nuclear weapon-free zone from Ukraine to the Nordic countries.	Belarus; NWFZ

21 July	A peace agreement, mediated by the UN, is signed in Ashkhabad by the Tajik Government and opposition parties. (*See also 23 Dec.*)	Tajikistan
29 July	After having conducted its second nuclear test in 1996, China declares that it will abide by a moratorium on nuclear testing, effective from 30 July.	Nuclear tests; China
14 Aug.	The Canberra Commission on the Elimination of Nuclear Weapons, established in 1995, issues a report, identifying a series of steps and practical measures to bring about a nuclear weapon-free world.	Nuclear weapons
22 Aug.	At a facility in Utah, USA, large-scale chemical weapon destruction operations begin.	CW
23 Aug.	Croatia and Yugoslavia (Serbia and Montenegro) sign an Agreement on Normalization of the Relations between the two states.	Croatia/ Yugoslavia
29 Aug.	The Baltic Action Plan is presented by the US Assistant Secretary of State to the ambassadors of the Baltic states in Washington as a US proposal for bilateral and multilateral cooperation between the USA and the three Baltic states. It includes US aid for integration into Western security institutions; stresses the importance of good relations with the Baltic neighbours, especially Russia; and provides for the signing of individual cooperation charters in 1997 between the USA and Baltic states on aspects of economic, political and security cooperation.	USA/Baltic states
30 Aug.	Following cease-fire agreements of 27 May and 22 Aug. and an agreement on troop withdrawal of 27 Aug., Secretary of the Russian Security Council Lebed and Chechen Chief of Staff Maskhadov sign a peace agreement in Khasaviurt, Dagestan, that finally ends the war in Chechnya. Definition of Chechnya's future political status is postponed until 31 Dec. 2001.	Russia/ Chechnya
2 Sep.	The Philippine Government and the Moro National Liberation Front (MNLF), the largest Muslim opposition faction, sign a peace agreement, ending 24 years of conflict between the two sides on the southern island of Mindanao.	Philippines
10 Sep.	By a vote of 158 to 3, with 5 abstentions, the UN General Assembly adopts the Comprehensive Nuclear Test-Ban Treaty (CTBT) as negotiated at the CD.	UN; CTBT
17 Sep.	The US Secretary of Energy, the Minister of Atomic Energy of the Russian Federation and the Director General of the IAEA meet in Vienna to consider practical measures concerning the application of IAEA verification of weapon-origin fissile materials.	IAEA; USA; Russia

24 Sep.	The Comprehensive Nuclear Test-Ban Treaty (CTBT) is opened for signature at UN Headquarters, New York. The 5 nuclear states together with 66 other states sign the treaty on the first day.	CTBT
1 Oct.	The UN Security Council unanimously adopts Resolution 1074, terminating all sanctions imposed on the Federal Republic of Yugoslavia (Serbia and Montenegro).	UN; Yugoslavia
3–5 Oct.	An international conference on land-mines is held in Ottawa. The states represented at the conference agree to enhance cooperation and coordinate efforts to ensure an international ban on anti-personnel land-mines at the earliest possible date and to secure reductions in new deployments of anti-personnel land-mines.	Land-mines; CCW
8 Oct.	NATO proposes to the Joint Consultative Committee (JCC) to start negotiations in 1997 on adapting the CFE Treaty to the new military situation in Europe.	NATO; CFE
31 Oct.	Hungary ratifies the 1993 Chemical Weapons Convention as the 65th state. In accordance with Article XXI of the convention, it will enter into force 180 days after the 65th state has ratified it (i.e., on 29 Apr. 1997).	CWC
4 Nov.	On behalf of 84 states, the USA introduces a UN resolution to pursue vigorously an effective, legally binding ban on the use, stockpiling, production and transfer of anti-personnel land-mines. (The resolution is adopted by the General Assembly on 10 Dec.)	Land-mines; CCW
4–22 Nov.	The OSCE Review Conference is held in Vienna. Various subjects are discussed including the Vienna Document 1994, global exchange of military information, principles governing conventional arms transfers and a document on stabilizing measures for localized crisis situations.	OSCE
9 Nov.	France, Italy, Portugal and Spain create, in Florence, a European multinational force, which will have the task of acting in peacekeeping missions within the WEU, NATO and the UN.	France, Italy, Portugal, Spain
25 Nov.–6 Dec.	The Fourth Review Conference of the Parties to the Convention on the Prohibition of the Development and Stockpiling of Bacteriological (Biological) and Toxin Weapons and on their Destruction (BTWC) is held in Geneva. Verification measures to strengthen the convention are discussed.	BTWC
27 Nov.	Belarus announces that the last Soviet nuclear missiles based on its territory have been withdrawn to Russia. (On 23 Nov. the associated nuclear warheads had been transferred to Russia for dismantlement, fulfilling Belarus' pledge to become a non-nuclear weapon state.)	START; Belarus;

30 Nov.	A peace agreement is signed in Abidjan, Côte d'Ivoire, by the President of Sierra Leone and the Revolutionary United Front (RUF).	Sierra Leone
2 Dec.	The OSCE heads of state and government, meeting in Lisbon, approve the Lisbon Declaration on a Common and Comprehensive Security Model for Europe for the Twenty-first Century. The participants also give the OSCE the mandate to begin negotiations to adapt the CFE Treaty to the new security environment in Europe.	OSCE; CFE
10 Dec.	The NATO foreign ministers, meeting in Brussels, recommend that the NATO summit meeting scheduled for 8–9 July 1997 invite one or more of the countries that have expressed interest in joining the Alliance to begin accession negotiations. The ministers confirm that 'NATO countries have no intention, no plan and no reason to deploy nuclear weapons on the territory of new members' nor any need to change any aspect of their nuclear policy. They agree to establish a new Atlantic Partnership Council (APC), merging the activities of the North Atlantic Cooperation Council (NACC) and the Partnership for Peace (PFP). They also approve the operational plan for the Stabilization Force (SFOR) which will replace IFOR in Bosnia and be led by NATO for 18 months.	NATO
10 Dec.	The UN General Assembly adopts over 40 resolutions on arms control and disarmament, calling for *inter alia* a complete ban on anti-personnel land-mines, a UN special session devoted to disarmament in 1999, the reduction of nuclear weapons with the ultimate goal of eliminating them, and cooperation between the OSCE and the UN.	UN
20 Dec.	The new NATO-led multinational Stabilization Force (SFOR) takes over from IFOR in the former Yugoslavia.	Former Yugoslavia; NATO
23 Dec.	The Tajik President and the United Tajik Opposition leader sign an agreement in Moscow which goes further than providing for the cessation of hostilities.	Tajikistan
29 Dec.	A peace agreement is signed in Guatemala City by the commanders of the Guatemalan National Revolutionary Unity (URNG) Guerrillas and the President of Guatemala, formally ending 36 years of civil wars.	Guatemala
31 Dec.	The last Russian combat troops leave Grozny, Chechnya.	Russia/ Chechnya

About the contributors

Dr Ramses Amer (Sweden) is a Research Assistant at the Department of Peace and Conflict Research, Uppsala University. His recent publications include *The United Nations and Foreign Military Interventions: A Comparative Study of the Application of the Charter*, 2nd edn (1994), *Peace-keeping in a Peace Process: The Case of Cambodia* (1995) and *The Cambodian Conflict 1979–1991: From Intervention to Resolution* (1996) which he has co-authored with Johan Saravanamuttu and Peter Wallensteen. He has also contributed to articles in international journals, written reports on issues of Asian security and contributed to the *SIPRI Yearbook* since 1995.

Dr Ian Anthony (United Kingdom) is Leader of the SIPRI Arms Transfers Project. He is editor of the SIPRI volume *Arms Export Regulations* (1991), the SIPRI Research Report *The Future of Defence Industries in Central and Eastern Europe* (1994) and author of *The Naval Arms Trade* (SIPRI, 1990) and *The Arms Trade and Medium Powers: Case Studies of India and Pakistan 1947–90* (1991). He has written or co-authored chapters for the *SIPRI Yearbook* since 1988.

William M. Arkin (United States) is an independent expert on defence matters and a consultant to the Natural Resources Defense Council (NRDC). He has previously been Director of the National Security Program of the Institute for Policy Studies (1981–89) and of Military Research at Greenpeace International (1989–94), both in Washington, DC. He is co-editor of the NRDC's *Nuclear Weapons Databook* series and co-author of several of the volumes in the same series. He is also co-author of the *Encyclopedia of the US Military* (1990). His recent publications are *The US Military Online: A Directory for Online Access to the Department of Defense* (1997) and (with Robert Norris) *The Internet and the Bomb: A Research Guide to Policy and Information about Nuclear Weapons* (1997). He has contributed to the *SIPRI Yearbook* since 1985 and is a co-columnist (with Robert S. Norris) for *The Bulletin of the Atomic Scientists*.

Dr Eric Arnett (United States), an engineer, is Leader of the SIPRI Military Technology and International Security Project. In 1988–92 he was Senior Programme Associate in the Program on Science and International Security and Director of the Project on Advanced Weaponry in the Developing World at the American Association for the Advancement of Science. He is the editor of the SIPRI volumes *Nuclear Weapons After the Comprehensive Test Ban: Implications for Modernization and Proliferation* (1996) and *Military Capacity and the Risk of War: China, India, Pakistan and Iran* (1997) and has contributed to the *SIPRI Yearbook* since 1993.

Dr Vladimir Baranovsky (Russia) is Leader of the SIPRI Project on Russia's Security Agenda. He holds the position of Senior Researcher at the Institute of World Economy and International Relations in Moscow where he was Head of the International Security Section (1986–88) and Head of the European Studies Department (1988–92). He is the author of several monographs in Russian including *Zapadnaya Evropa: voenno-politicheskaya integratsiya* [Western Europe: military and political integration] (1988) and *In from the Cold: Germany, Russia and the Future of Europe*

(1992). He is editor of the SIPRI volume *Russia and Europe: The Emerging Security Agenda* (1997) and has contributed to a number of journals and books including the *SIPRI Yearbook* since 1993.

Renaud Bellais (France) is a Ph.D. student in Economics at the Université du Littoral in Dunkerque. In the autumn of 1996 he was an intern on the SIPRI Arms Production Project and was involved in a project on strategies of arms production firms in Western Europe in the 1990s.

Dr Julian Cooper (United Kingdom) is Director of the Centre for Russian and East European Studies and Professor of Russian Economic Studies at the University of Birmingham. His previous research includes projects on science policy, technology and the engineering industry in the former USSR and studies for the European Commission, the International Labour Organization, NATO, the OECD and other international organizations. His recent publications include *The Soviet Defence Industry: Conversion and Reform* (1991), *Science, Technology and Innovation Policies: Federation of Russia* (1994), and articles on the conversion of the defence industry and industrial restructuring. He is also a contributor to *The Post-Soviet Military Industrial Complex* (1994) and to the *SIPRI Yearbook 1995*.

Agnès Courades Allebeck (France) is a Research Assistant on the SIPRI Military Expenditure Project. Within the project she is responsible for the regions of NATO and Africa. She was previously Research Assistant on the SIPRI Arms Trade Project. She is the author of chapters in the SIPRI volumes *Arms Export Regulations* (1991) and *Arms Industry Limited* (1993) and has contributed to the *SIPRI Yearbooks* 1989–94.

Susanna Eckstein (Germany) is a Research Assistant on the SIPRI Chemical and Biological Warfare Project, where she is working among other things on national implementation of the commitments under the Chemical Weapons Convention, and export and import controls. She has co-authored a SIPRI Fact Sheet on the Chemical Weapons Convention (1997).

Ragnhild Ferm (Sweden) is Leader of the SIPRI Arms Control and Disarmament Documentary Survey Project. She has published chapters on nuclear explosions, the comprehensive test ban and arms control agreements, and the annual chronologies of arms control and political events in the *SIPRI Yearbook* since 1982. She is the author of fact sheets on SIPRI research topics in Swedish.

Dr Trevor Findlay (Australia) is Leader of the SIPRI Peacekeeping and Regional Security Project. He is a former Australian diplomat, specializing in arms control, and was Senior Research Fellow at and Acting Head of the Peace Research Centre, Australian National University, Canberra. He is author of *Nuclear Dynamite: The Peaceful Nuclear Explosions Fiasco* (1990), *Peace Through Chemistry: The New Chemical Weapons Convention* (1993), the SIPRI Research Report *Cambodia: The Legacy and Lessons of UNTAC* (1995) and editor of the SIPRI Research Report *Challenges for the New Peacekeepers* (1996). His most recent publication for SIPRI is *Fighting for Peace: The Use of Force in Peace Operations* (forthcoming, 1997). He has contributed to the *SIPRI Yearbook* since 1994.

Paul George (Canada) is Leader of the SIPRI Military Expenditure Project. He was previously an international security consultant in Ottawa, Canada, working on projects with a number of agencies and institutes. He has served as Visiting Professor and Chair of Military and Strategic Studies at Acadia University in Nova Scotia and as a Lecturer in Political Geography and International Relations at Carleton University in Ottawa. His recent publications include research reports on good governance, democratic development, military expenditure and regional security issues for the Canadian International Development Agency and a chapter in *Säkerhet och Utveckling i Afrika* [Security and development in Africa] (1996), published by the Swedish Ministry for Foreign Affairs. He has contributed to the *SIPRI Yearbook* since 1995.

Gerd Hagmeyer-Gaverus (Germany) is Researcher on the SIPRI Arms Transfers Project and Information Technology Manager. He was formerly a Researcher at the Centre for Social Science Research at the Free University of Berlin, where he co-authored several research reports. He has contributed to chapters on military expenditure and arms trade in the *SIPRI Yearbook* since 1985. In 1996 he published two articles on systems designs for international relations databases and in 1997 he co-authored an article on the European arms trade.

Olga Hardardóttir (Iceland) is a Research Assistant on the SIPRI Peacekeeping and Regional Security Project. She was previously employed at SIPRI as a librarian and contributed to the *SIPRI Yearbook 1996*.

John Hart (United States) is a Research Assistant on the SIPRI Chemical and Biological Warfare Project. He is currently involved in the running of a cooperative project with the Bonn International Center for Conversion on Russian chemical weapon destruction. He has co-authored a SIPRI Fact Sheet on the Chemical Weapons Convention (1997) and is co-editor of the forthcoming SIPRI volume *Chemical Weapons Destruction in Russia: Political, Legal and Technical Aspects*.

Birger Heldt (Sweden) is a Research Fellow and was previously responsible for the Armed Conflicts Data Project at the Department of Peace and Conflict Research, Uppsala University. He is the author of *Public Dissatisfaction and the Conflict Behavior of States* (1996), editor of *States in Armed Conflict 1990–91* (1992) and contributor to *States in Armed Conflict* in 1989 and 1992–94. He has also contributed to the *SIPRI Yearbook* in 1991–95.

Ann-Sofi Jakobsson (Sweden) is a Ph.D. student at the Department of Peace and Conflict Research, Uppsala University. She has contributed to the *SIPRI Yearbook* since 1995.

Dr Peter Jones (Canada) is Leader of the SIPRI Middle East Security and Arms Control Project. Prior to joining SIPRI in 1995, he worked for the Canadian Department of Foreign Affairs and International Trade for seven years, focusing on security and arms control issues. He is the author of several articles on Middle East arms control, maritime security, peacekeeping, verification and Open Skies. He was a contributor to the *SIPRI Yearbook 1996*.

Shannon Kile (United States) is a Research Assistant on the SIPRI Project on Russia's Security Agenda. He contributed to the *SIPRI Yearbook* in 1993, 1995 and 1996 and is the author of a chapter in the SIPRI Research Report *The Future of the Defence Industries in Central and Eastern Europe* (1994).

Dr Zdzislaw Lachowski (Poland) is Researcher on the SIPRI Project on Building a Cooperative Security System in and for Europe. He was previously Researcher at the Polish Institute of International Affairs, where he examined problems of European security and the CSCE process in particular and issues concerning West European political integration. He has published extensively on these subjects. He is co-editor of *Wizje Europy* [Visions of Europe] (1989, in Polish) and has contributed to the *SIPRI Yearbook* since 1992.

Evamaria Loose-Weintraub (Germany) is a Research Assistant on the SIPRI Military Expenditure Project. Within the project she is responsible for the regions: Other Europe, Central and South America, the Caribbean and Oceania. She was previously Research Assistant on the SIPRI Arms Trade Project. She is author of a chapter in the SIPRI volume *Arms Export Regulations* (1991) and the SIPRI Research Report *The Future of the Defence Industries in Central and Eastern Europe* (1994) and has contributed to the *SIPRI Yearbook* in 1984–88 and 1992–96.

Dr Robert S. Norris (United States) is Senior Staff Analyst with the Natural Resources Defense Council and Director of the Nuclear Weapons Databook Project in Washington, DC. His principal areas of expertise include writing and research in the areas of nuclear weapon research and production, arms control and nuclear weapon testing. He is co-editor of the NRDC's *Nuclear Weapons Databook* series and co-author of several of the volumes in the series. He has contributed to the *SIPRI Yearbook* since 1985, he is a co-columnist (with William Arkin) for *The Bulletin of the Atomic Scientists* and co-authored the article on nuclear weapons for *The New Encyclopedia Britannica* (1990). One of his recent works (with William Arkin) is *The Internet and the Bomb: A Research Guide to Policy and Information about Nuclear Weapons* (1997).

Dr Adam Daniel Rotfeld (Poland) is Director of SIPRI and Leader of the SIPRI Project on Building a Cooperative Security System in and for Europe. He was head of the European Security Department in the Polish Institute of International Affairs, Warsaw, in 1978–89. He was a member of the Polish Delegation to the Conference on Security and Co-operation in Europe (CSCE) and Personal Representative of the CSCE Chairman-in-Office to examine the settlement of the conflict in the Trans-Dniester region (1992–93). He is the author or editor of over 20 books and more than 200 articles on the legal and political aspects of relations between Germany and the Central and East European states after World War II (recognition of borders, the Munich Agreement and the right of self-determination), human rights, CSBMs, European security and the CSCE process. He is co-editor of the SIPRI volume *Germany and Europe in Transition* (1991) and *Europejski System bezpieczenstwa* in statu nascendi [European security system in statu nascendi] (1990, in Polish). He has written chapters for the *SIPRI Yearbook* since 1991.

Elisabeth Sköns (Sweden) is Leader of the SIPRI Arms Production Project. She has contributed to most editions of the *SIPRI Yearbook* since 1983. Her most recent publications include chapters on the internationalization of the arms industry in the SIPRI volume *Arms Industry Limited* (1993) and in the *Annals of the American Academy of Political and Social Science* (1994); *Weapon Supplies to Trouble Spots*, a background report for the UNDP *Human Development Report 1994* (1994); and a chapter on Sweden's defence industrial policy in *The Arms Production Dilemma* (1994).

Margareta Sollenberg (Sweden) is a Research Assistant on the Armed Conflicts Data Project at the Department of Peace and Conflict Research, Uppsala University. She is editor of *States in Armed Conflict 1994* (1995) and has contributed to the *SIPRI Yearbook* since 1995.

Professor Peter Wallensteen (Sweden) has held the Dag Hammarskjöld Chair in Peace and Conflict Research since 1985 and is Head of the Department of Peace and Conflict Research, Uppsala University. He has recently published studies of the operation and reforms of the UN Security Council and is author of *From War to Peace: On Conflict Resolution in the Global System* (1994). He has co-authored chapters in the *SIPRI Yearbook* since 1988.

Pieter D. Wezeman (Netherlands) is a Research Assistant on the SIPRI Arms Transfers Project. He has contributed to the *SIPRI Yearbook* since 1995.

Siemon T. Wezeman (Netherlands) is a Research Assistant on the SIPRI Arms Transfers Project. He is the co-author (with Edward J. Laurance and Herbert Wulf) of the SIPRI Research Report *Arms Watch: SIPRI Report on the First year of the UN Register of Conventional Arms* (1993), (with Bates Gill and J. N. Mak) of *ASEAN Arms Acquisitions: Developing Transparency* (1995) and (with John Sislin) of *1994 Arms Transfers: A Register of Deliveries From Public Sources*, a SIPRI/MIIS (Monterey Institute of International Relations) study (1995). He has contributed to the SIPRI Research Report *Arms, Transparency and Security in South-East Asia* (1997) and to the *SIPRI Yearbook* since 1993.

Dr Jean Pascal Zanders (Belgium) is Leader of the SIPRI Chemical and Biological Warfare Project. He was previously Research Associate at the Centre for Peace Research at the Free University of Brussels. He has published extensively on chemical and biological weapon issues in English, Dutch and French since 1986. He is author of the Pole-Papers *A New Security (Dis)Order for the Gulf* (1994) and *The Chemical Threat in Iraq's Motives for the Kuwait Invasion* (1995), has contributed to the SIPRI volume *The Challenge of Old Chemical Munitions and Toxic Armament Wastes* (forthcoming, 1997) and has co-authored a SIPRI Fact Sheet on the Chemical Weapons Convention (1997).

Carl Johan Åsberg (Sweden) is a PhD student at the Department of Peace and Conflict Research, Uppsala University. He has contributed to *States in Armed Conflict 1993, 1994* and *1995* and to the *SIPRI Yearbook* since 1994.

SIPRI Yearbook 1997: Armaments, Disarmament and International Security

Oxford University Press, Oxford, 1997, 585 pp.
(Stockholm International Peace Research Institute)
ISBN 0-19-829312-7

ABSTRACTS

ROTFELD, A. D., 'Introduction: The emerging international security agenda', in *SIPRI Yearbook 1997*, pp. 1–14.

The situation during the cold war was marked by high stability and high military threat, while the current state of world affairs is characterized by low military threat and a low level of stability. The essential characteristics of the present strategic environment are often identified as uncertainty and change. A process of shaping a new security system which is adapted to present requirements is taking place on many planes. If the regime of global and international security that is emerging as a result of trial-and-error processes and new experiences is to adhere to declared democratic values it cannot be based on the hegemony of one or several powers. Such a system should give expression to the interdependence of states, where mutual relations are governed by generally accepted principles of international law.

SOLLENBERG, M. and WALLENSTEEN, P., 'Major armed conflicts', in *SIPRI Yearbook 1997*, pp. 17–30.

In 1996, 27 major armed conflicts were waged in 24 locations around the world, compared with 30 major conflicts and 25 conflict locations in 1995. The decline in numbers represents a downward trend for the period of investigation, 1989–96. However, few comprehensive peace agreements were reached and those which were often ran into troubles regarding their implementation. More significantly, the decline in numbers was mainly due to the conflicts becoming inactive rather than the incompatibility being resolved. This also explains why conflicts tended to reoccur after a time of absence. One reoccurring conflict in 1996 was the interstate conflict between India and Pakistan. All other conflicts were internal and this was the first time an interstate conflict was recorded since 1992.

FINDLAY, T., 'Armed conflict prevention, management and resolution', in *SIPRI Yearbook 1997*, pp. 31–67.

The promise of peace initiatives of previous years in Angola, Liberia, the Middle East, Northern Ireland and Bosnia and Herzegovina remained unfulfilled in 1996. Yet breakthroughs occurred in ending lesser known armed conflicts in Sierra Leone, the southern Philippines and Guatemala. Armed conflict in Chechnya ended through negotiations and then Russian withdrawal. United Nations peacekeeping continued to contract. A major non-UN operation in Bosnia managed to keep the peace while proving frustratingly slow at peace building. A multinational force for Zaire was close to deployment before being overtaken by events. Efforts continued to help build African capacities for conflict prevention, management and resolution, but the task is long term.

JONES, P., 'The Middle East', in *SIPRI Yearbook 1997*, pp. 83–101.

Despite four years of peacemaking, a resolution to the Arab–Israeli conflict remained elusive in 1996. The new Israeli Government seemed intent on reviewing what many regarded as the basic understandings of the process on both the Palestinian and the Syrian tracks. This caused many Arab states to review their participation in the process and to halt the normalization of relations with Israel. The Jewish state, meanwhile, accused its interlocutors of failing to live up to their commitments, notably to restrain terrorist attacks against Israel. Violent incidents occurred throughout the year on both sides, with tragic consequences for hundreds of people. As the year ended there were concerns that the fragile process might not be able to take many more of the stresses and strains of the kind imposed on it in 1996. Although the process has been accompanied by bloodshed, much more violence is likely should it collapse completely.

BARANOVSKY, V., 'Conflicts in and around Russia', in *SIPRI Yearbook 1997*, pp. 103–26.

The 1996 presidential election signified an important step towards the consolidation of Russia's political system and enabled the governing élite to solidify its grasp on power. Yet Boris Yeltsin's victory by no means put an end to an intense struggle for power across Russia's political spectrum and between the federal and provincial administrations. 1996 witnessed the cessation of hostilities in Chechnya, although the settlement of the major outstanding issue—the rebellious enclave's political status—has been postponed until 2001. Although Moscow has cultivated closer ties with Belarus, the debate continues to rage over the scope and pace of the integration within the CIS. Russia's active mediation has fostered political dialogue between the conflicting parties in the Trans-Dniester region, Tajikistan and South Ossetia, although the conflicts in Nagorno-Karabakh and Abkhazia remain gridlocked.

GEORGE, P., COURADES ALLEBECK, A. and LOOSE-WEINTRAUB, E., 'Military expenditure', in *SIPRI Yearbook 1997*, pp. 163–84.

Military spending by NATO continued to decline in 1996, led by a reduction of almost 5 per cent in the USA over 1995. A lack of reliable information makes it impossible to derive comparative data for Russia and the CIS countries. The Middle East and South-East Asia continued to increase their military spending. Aggregate expenditure in South Asia remained stable in real terms. However, military expenditure, fuelled by the separatist conflict, grew by 28 per cent in Sri Lanka in the same period. A lack of data makes it difficult to provide comparisons of trends in other regions.

ROTFELD, A. D., 'Europe: in search of cooperative security', in *SIPRI Yearbook 1997*, pp. 127–49.

Three basic issues remained on the European security agenda in 1996: the transformation and eastward enlargement of NATO and the EU; the transatlantic partnership, including the role of the USA in the security system taking shape in Europe and the European pillar of NATO; and establishing the conceptual framework of the OSCE model for European security for the 21st century. Some headway was made on these issues but no definitive agreements were reached. No single organization—whether NATO, the EU, the OSCE or the Council of Europe—can handle the whole European security process. Although the need for a new type of pan-European system is repeatedly acknowledged in official documents, priority has, in practice, been given to the US concept of a new Atlantic community and to the enlargement of NATO and the EU. Instead of focusing on their structures and procedures, security-related organizations and institutions should therefore be striving for greater cooperation.

ARNETT, E., 'Military research and development', in *SIPRI Yearbook 1997*, pp. 211–38.

Global military research and development (R&D) expenditure continues to decline. Total expenditure has decreased to a level of about $49 billion, of which $43 billion is accounted for by NATO. Most is going to combat aircraft and missile defences. Japan and South Korea continue to increase their military R&D activities steadily. Their build-ups are only explicable if the development of an independent arms industry is desirable as an end in itself. Among the five declared nuclear weapon states, the USA and the UK are shifting strongly towards research on conventional weapons, China and Russia are retaining a nuclear emphasis without neglecting conventional systems entirely, and France occupies a position somewhere between.

SKÖNS, E., 'Arms production', in *SIPRI Yearbook 1997*, pp. 239–60.

The decline in the volume of arms production during most of the 1990s is currently levelling out in spite of the still substantial excess capacity in the main arms-producing countries. Instead, dominant developments in the global arms industry now include profound structural changes, commercialization and increased export efforts. The pace of consolidation in the US arms industry has been extremely rapid during 1996 and early 1997. In Russia, a determined defence industrial policy is resulting in new corporate structures and a strong concentration in fewer and larger companies. In Europe, the restructuring process continues at a slower rate.

ANTHONY, I., WEZEMAN, P. D. and WEZEMAN, S. T., 'The trade in major conventional weapons', in *SIPRI Yearbook 1997*, pp. 267–91.

The SIPRI global trend-indicator value of international transfers of major conventional weapons in 1996 was approximately $23 billion in constant (1990) US dollars. This means that the volume of major conventional weapons delivered was unchanged from 1995. The USA remained the dominant exporter while, among importers, the most prominent trend is the growing share of deliveries to North-East Asia. A survey of the potential arms procurement programmes of Central and East European countries suggests that there is little evidence that this subregion will emerge as an important market for major conventional weapons even if some regional countries become members of NATO. Similarly, a survey of Ukraine suggests that the country has limited opportunities to establish itself as a major arms exporter. In 1997 a group of government experts will evaluate the UN Register of Conventional Arms. A major issue will be how to include standardized reporting of equipment holdings and procurement through national production in the Register.

ANTHONY, I., ZANDERS, J. P. and ECKSTEIN, S., 'Multilateral military-related export control measures', in *SIPRI Yearbook 1997*, pp. 345–63.

In 1997 the multilateral regimes concerned with controlling exports of certain goods with potential military significance—the Australia Group, the Missile Technology Control Regime (MTCR), the Nuclear Suppliers Group (NSG) and the Wassenaar Arrangement—continued to increase their membership. The process of integrating former Warsaw Treaty Organization countries as well as some former developing countries into these regimes continued. The European Union dual-use export control system is different from the other multilateral arrangements under discussion because the actions taken in the EU and by its agencies are grounded in law. The activities of the Australia Group continued to be influenced by the existence of international disarmament treaties—the Chemical Weapons Convention and the Biological Weapons Convention—and the activities of the NSG continued to be influenced by a treaty banning the transfer of nuclear weapons.

KILE, S., 'Nuclear arms control', in *SIPRI Yearbook 1997*, pp. 365–93.

The implementation of the START I Treaty proceeded ahead of schedule, with Belarus and Ukraine fulfilling their pledges to withdraw to Russia the former Soviet nuclear warheads based on their territories. However, there were clear signs that the momentum behind further nuclear arms control measures was waning. The Russian Parliament appeared increasingly disinclined to ratify START II, despite the US Senate's approval of the treaty. US–Russian negotiations to clarify the application of the ABM Treaty to theatre missile defence systems continued to spark controversy, and bilateral talks on nuclear confidence-building and transparency measures remained in limbo. At the CD no progress was made towards negotiating a global convention banning the production of fissile material for military purposes.

ARNETT, E., 'The Comprehensive Nuclear Test-Ban Treaty', in *SIPRI Yearbook 1997*, pp. 403–13

The Comprehensive Nuclear Test-Ban Treaty (CTBT) was completed and opened for signature in 1996. China's acceptance of the treaty marked a watershed in its arms-control policy. By the end of the year the majority of states had signed and only one—India—had declared unconditionally that it would not. India's refusal to sign the CTBT could prevent the treaty from achieving its full legal force, although the international norm against testing is universally accepted. Although modernization of delivery systems has become more important than modernization of warheads, the CTBT has an important effect on both established arsenals and proliferation.

FERM, R., 'Nuclear explosions, 1945–96', in *SIPRI Yearbook 1997*, pp. 432–36.

In 1996 three nuclear explosions were conducted; one by France and two by China. France finalized its last series of nuclear tests and after its second test of the year China announced a moratorium on nuclear testing, effective from 30 July. The USA, Russia and the UK abided by their unilateral test moratoria. On 26 September all five nuclear states signed the Comprehensive Nuclear Test-Ban Treaty. In October 1996 a study on Soviet nuclear testing written by Russian nuclear weapon scientists under contract to the US Defense Special Weapons Agency was made known through the mass media. The report, which is not yet publicly available, reveals new facts and details of the Soviet nuclear programme and includes a list of all 715 Soviet nuclear explosions with information on dates, purpose, yield and location of the explosions.

ZANDERS, J. P., ECKSTEIN, S. and HART, J., 'Chemical and biological weapon developments and arms control', in *SIPRI Yearbook 1997*, pp. 437–68.

The Chemical Weapons Convention will enter into force on 29 April 1997. However, some important issues still need resolving. Domestic political, economic and other factors have prevented ratification by the Russian Federation and the USA. Verified destruction of chemical stockpiles and production facilities as well as of old and abandoned chemical weapons will become one of the major political and technological challenges in the next few years. Chemical weapon proliferation and the threat that they may be used by terrorist or criminal organizations may be expected to remain a top security issue for many governments. The Fourth Review Conference of the 1972 Biological and Toxin Weapons Convention (BTWC) endorsed efforts to establish a supplementary Verification Protocol. Although the problems remain formidable, some encouraging signs emerged that the BTWC might become a verifiable disarmament treaty.

LACHOWSKI, Z., 'Conventional arms control', in *SIPRI Yearbook 1997*, pp. 469–510.

Along with the amendment of the CFE Treaty, steps were taken towards adapting the treaty to the future security environment and giving some coherence to arms control endeavours. Efforts are also being made in Europe to adapt CSBMs to new challenges. Conventional arms control and CSBM negotiations on the former Yugoslavia were concluded and reduction processes started. Outside Europe conventional arms control is at an early stage. The problem of land-mines has acquired a special importance because of the toll of civilian casualties. The success of efforts to achieve a global land-mine ban will depend largely on the stance taken by the main producers and exporters. Differing positions on the means of achieving a global ban, including the US decision (supported by France and the UK) to side-step the Ottawa Group and start negotiations in the Conference on Disarmament, have lessened the chances for rapid progress.

Errata

SIPRI Yearbook 1996: Armaments, Disarmament and International Security

Table 8A.1, page 366, the figures for the military expenditure of Switzerland, in US $m., at 1990 prices (CPI-deflated) and exchange rates, should read:

1986, 3 863; 1987, 3 759; 1988, 3 878; 1989, 4 120; 1990, 4 356; 1991, 4 220; 1992, 4 086; 1993, 3 639; 1994, 3 718; and 1995, 3 661.

Page 384, footnote 6, should read:

'Compare with the global estimate of $85–100 billion in 1986 according to Tullberg, R. and Hagmeyer-Gaverus, G., 'World military expenditure', *SIPRI Yearbook 1987: World Armaments and Disarmament* (Oxford University Press: Oxford, 1997), p. 153. In real terms, this represents a 50–55% reduction after inflation.'

Page 403, table 9.9, in the column for Sweden, the second entry should read:

'In office since: 1994'. (The Swedish Government is not a coalition.)

Page 612, footnote 2, line 4 should read:

'from the others are not counted, the CIS total falls to 5875'.

Page 720, first full paragraph, line 4 should read.

'obligations (an 'exclusive zone' like that in south-eastern Turkey). Alongside'.

Page 722, figure 16.1, 'Changes proposed for the CFE Treaty flank zone map realignment':

On the map, the Vologograd *oblast* should be shaded so that it is shown as part of both the NATO and the Russian proposal (i.e., it should be shaded the same way as the Pskov region).

Index, page 815, second column, 'Geneva Protocol (1925) 77' Should read:

'Geneva Protocol (1925) 770'.

INDEX